The Green Book of Language Revitalization in Practice

The Green Book
of Language Revitalization in Practice

Edited by

Leanne Hinton

University of California, Berkeley
Berkeley, California

and

Ken Hale

Massachusetts Institute of Technology
Cambridge, Massachusetts

BRILL

LEIDEN · BOSTON
2013

Originally published by Academic Press, San Diego, California, USA, in 2001 under ISBN 0-12349354-4.

Library of Congress Control Number: 2013941739

ISBN 978-90-04-25449-7 (paperback)

To the brave people who work against all odds to help their endangered heritage languages survive

Contents

About the Title

The title of this volume is an answer to another publication, the UNESCO *Red Book on Endangered Languages*. The *Red Book* is an electronic databank originally compiled in 1993. Parts of this databank are available at *http://www.tooyoo.L .u-tokyo.ac.jp/ichel.html#Redbook* and parts at *http://www.helsinki.fi/~tasalmin/endangered.html*. This project is now being implemented at the International Clearing House for Endangered Languages established at the Department of Asian and Pacific Linguistics, Institute of Cross-Cultural Studies, Faculty of Letters, University of Tokyo.

We hope this *Green Book* will be of use to everyone who wants it to be no longer necessary for their language to be listed in the *Red Book*.

Acknowledgments

Language revitalization is always a group effort, involving the dedication and know-how of numerous people. In writing this book we have been inspired and assisted by dozens of people doing language revitalization or documentation. The contributors to this volume are the first we want to thank, for inspiring us now and over the years. The table of contents may be read as a list of acknowledgements. Besides the authors, we also want to thank the following people, who have either directly or indirectly been of help to us in the writing of this book: Mary Bates Abbott, Danny Ammon, Brian Bielenberg, Elena Benedicto, Loren Bommelyn, Gordon Bussell, James Crawford, Richard and Nora Dauenhauer, Lily Wong Fillmore, Darlene Franco, Victor Golla, Tjeerd de Graaf, Thomas Green, Colette Grinevald, Eloise Jelinek, Michael Krauss, Margaret Langdon, Mary Laughren, Carole Lewis, Martha Macri, Malcolm Margolin, Pam Munro, David Nash, Norvin Richards, Suzanne Romaine, Mary Eunice Romero, Danilo Salamanca, Tapani Salminen, Jane Simpson, Nancy Steele, and Agnes and Matt Vera. We thank our editors, Mark Zadrozny, Amy Pollick, and Elaine Sanders for their helpful encouragement, their appreciation of our topic, and their hard work in making this book happen. Special thanks are due to Ken Hale's assistant, Marilyn Goodrich, who has gone beyond the call of duty to assist in the various inquiries and questions that have come up in the development of this book, even to the extent of postponing a well-earned vacation in the latter stages of typesetting in order to proofread galleys and deal with last-minute problems. And to Ken's wife, Sally, and Leanne's husband, Gary, our constant gratitude, for in the stressful times of book writing and all other times as well, their support and love keep us going.

Contributors

Numbers in parentheses indicate the pages on which the authors' contribution begins.

Robert D. Arnold (45) 1217 Eskridge Blvd. SE, Olympia, Washington 98501-3558

Marie Arviso (203) Crownpoint Community School, P.O. Box 709, Crownpoint, New Mexico 87313

Anna Ash (19) School of Languages, Cultures & Linguistics, University of New England, Armidale, NSW, Australia 2351

Rebecca Blum-Martinez (75) College of Education, Education Administration 109, University of New Mexico, Albuquerque, New Mexico 87131-1231

Pamela Bunte (255) Departments of Anthropology and Linguistics, F03 310, California State University, Long Beach, 1250 Bellflower Blvd., Long Beach, California 90840

Laura Buszard-Welcher (331) Department of Linguistics, University of California at Berkeley, Berkeley, California 94720-2650

Colleen Cotter (301) Department of Linguistics, 480 Intercultural Center, Georgetown University, Washington, D.C. 20057-1051

jessie little doe fermino (19) Wôpanâak Language Reclamation Project, P.O. Box 2221, Mashpee, Massachusetts 02649

Robert Franklin (255) Department of Anthropology, California State University, Dominguez Hills, Carson, California (Deceased)

Stephen Greymorning (287) Department of Anthropology, Social Science Bldg., University of Montana, Missoula, Montana 59812-1001

Ken Hale (19, 83, 115, 199, 227, 251, 273, 277, 283, 299, 313, 351, 385) Department of Linguistics and Philosophy, Massachusetts Institute of Technology, Room E39-320, 77 Massachusetts Ave., Cambridge, Massachusetts 02139

Leanne Hinton (3, 39, 51, 61, 101, 103, 129, 179, 191, 217, 239, 251, 265, 349, 367, 413, 419, 425) Department of Linguistics, 1203 Dwinelle Hall, University of California, Berkeley, California 94720-2650

Wayne Holm (203) Department of Language, Culture, and Community Services, Navajo Department of Education, Division of Diné Education, Window Rock, Arizona 86515

Alana Johns (355) Department of Linguistics, 130 St. George Street, University of Toronto, Toronto, Ontario, Canada M5S 1A1

Kauanoe Kamanā (147) Ka Haka 'Ula O Ke'elikōlani College of Hawaiian Language, 200 W. Kawili St., University of Hawai'i, Hilo, Hawai'i 96720-4091

Jeanette King (119) Māori Department, Private Bag 4800, University of Canterbury, Christchurch, New Zealand

Paul V. Kroskrity (317) Department of Anthropology, University of California, Los Angeles, 3211 Hershey Hall, Box 951553, Los Angeles, California 90095-1553

Irene Mazurkewich (355) Department of Linguistics, Memorial University of Newfoundland, St. John's, Newfoundland, Canada A1B 3X9

Teresa L. McCarty (371) Department of Language, Reading and Culture, 1430 E. 2nd Street, University of Arizona, Tucson, Arizona 85721-0069

Gerald Morgan (107) Rhiwlas, Cliff Terrace, Aberystwyth SY23 2DN UK

Sam L. No'eau Warner (133) Department of Hawaiian, Indo-Pacific Languages, and Literatures, 2540 Mai Le

Way, Room 255, University of Hawai'i at Mānoa, Honolulu, Hawai'i 96822

Regis Pecos (75) Governor of Cochiti, Pueblo, P.O. Box 70, Cochiti Pueblo, Cochiti, New Mexico 87072

Paul R. Platero (87) P.O. Box 3969, Cañoncito, New Mexico 87026

Jennifer F. Reynolds (317) 1242 Harvard Street #6, Santa Monica, California 90404

Christine P. Sims (63) Department of Education and Linguistics, Division of LLSS-Hokona #231, University of New Mexico, Albuquerque, New Mexico 87131

Clay Slate (389) 2020 Summit Drive, Farmington, New Mexico 87401

Sarah E. Supahan (195) Director, Indian Education Program and Native Languages, Klamath-Trinity Joint Unified School District, Hoopa, California 95546

Terry Supahan (195) PO Box 389, Orleans, California 95556

Lucille J. Watahomigie (371) Peach Springs School District No. 8, PO Box 360, Peach Springs, Arizona 86434-0360

William H. Wilson (147) Ka Haka 'Ula O Ke'elikōlani College of Hawaiian Language, University of Hawai'i, 200 W. Kawili St., Hilo, Hawai'i 96720-4091

Akira Y. Yamamoto (371) Department of Anthropology, University of Kansas, Lawrence, Kansas 66045-2110

Linda Yamane (429) 1195-B Rousch Ave., Seaside, California 93955

Ofelia Zepeda (371) Department of Linguistics and American Indian Studies, Douglass Building, Room 200E, University of Arizona, Tucson, Arizona 85712

Jeanerette Jacups-Johnny and Elaina Supahan, speaking, teaching, learning, reviving Karuk. (Photograph Copyright © 2001 Dugan Aguilar)

PART I

INTRODUCTION

1

Language Revitalization: An Overview

LEANNE HINTON

Department of Linguistics
University of California at Berkeley
Berkeley, California

In a world of around 250 nations, there are over 6,000 languages. This means that there are very few languages with a country of their own. A language that is not a language of government, nor a language of education, nor a language of commerce or of wider communication is a language whose very existence is threatened in the modern world. Michael Krauss (1992) estimates that at the rate things are going, over half of the languages of the world could be extinct within a hundred years. These imperiled tongues have come to be known as "endangered languages."

THE PLIGHT OF INDIGENOUS LANGUAGES

Indigenous languages—those that can trace a long existence in the locale in which they are used today—are the languages with which this book is concerned. When an indigenous group is a minority in a country governed by speakers of a different language, the language of the indigenous group is potentially in danger of diminishing in use and perhaps eventually becoming extinct. Immigrant minorities are also very likely to undergo language shift, either voluntarily or involuntarily (Hinton, 2000, in press), as part of their assimilation to their new country. It must be noted that in the turmoil of today's world, some languages may be spoken primarily by immigrants who are refugees from genocide, and their languages may be endangered or even extinct in their original homelands. But there is one important difference between most immigrant languages and indigenous languages: in most cases, the immigrants' heritage languages are still strong in the old country. In fact, many people of immigrant

descent who do not know their language of heritage manage to learn that language through classes or during visits to the homeland. But as for indigenous minorities, their languages are endemic to small areas and have no national status anywhere, nor is there anywhere to go to learn their ancestral tongue. When an indigenous group stops speaking its language, the language disappears from the face of the earth.

The languages of indigenous groups (and indeed the groups themselves) have usually not fared well under the government of the nation that has enveloped them. In the past, and even today in some nations, repressive measures have been taken against minority languages. Even without overt repression, minorities may shift to the dominant language. This shift is sometimes made through voluntary, conscious decision. A group that does not speak the language of government and commerce is disenfranchised, marginalized with respect to the economic and political mainstream. Furthermore, languages other than the languages chosen for government and education may take on a low status in the eyes of a nation's citizens and be denigrated as inferior. Prejudice against "foreign" languages is so strong in the United States, for example, that it is very easy to hear negative comments from "the man on the street" when someone is speaking a different language or speaking English with an accent. Lily Wong Fillmore recently related to me that while she was on jury duty, announcements over the loudspeaker by an employee who spoke grammatically flawless English but with a Spanish accent, produced all kinds of grumbling comments from the jury pool in the waiting room such as, "Why don't they give the job to someone who speaks English!" It takes only one such comment to make someone, especially a child, reject his or her language (Hinton, in press). Because of these

3

attitudes, bilingual families often choose to teach only the majority language to their children, dooming the minority language to oblivion in the new country.

Often, though, the shift is involuntary. Even when a family continues to use a threatened language in the home, the outside environment may be so steeped in the majority language that the child unconsciously shifts languages around school age and no longer speaks the minority language even at home, to the sorrow of the parents (Hinton, 2000, in press).

Because the loss of indigenous languages is tied closely to the usurpation of indigenous lands, the destruction of indigenous habitats, and the involuntary incorporation of indigenous peoples into the larger society (generally into the lower-class margins of that society), language death has become part of a human rights struggle (Nettle and Romaine, 2000). Language choice is part of the right of indigenous peoples to their own land, to autonomy, and to cultural and economic self-determination. To quote from a recent article:

> The decline of linguistic diversity in the world is linked to the world political economy which invades and takes over the territories of indigenous peoples, threatens the ecosystems in which they live, wipes out their traditional means of livelihood, and (at best) turns them into low-caste laborers in the larger society in which they must now live on the margins. (Hinton 1999)

Final extinction of a language may take place within a generation of this disruption, or it may take place more slowly, over several generations; but we can virtually always trace it to this pattern of political, military, and economic takeover. In the 20th century, language death has been speeded up by seemingly benign developments such as television, early-childhood education, and other practices brought to indigenous peoples from the dominant society that increase their level of contact with that society and decrease the domains in which the indigenous language can be used.

This book will discuss languages that are endangered at various levels of severity. The languages we are concerned with all fall into one of the following categories:

(a) Languages still spoken by all age groups, but with a visible decline in the proportion of children learning it at home, and a decline in the domains in which the language is used for communication.

(b) Languages that children are no longer learning at home at all. This could mean that the parent generation knows the language but has ceased using it, or perhaps the grandparental generation is the last generation that knows it. Depending on the characteristics of language loss in a given community, there may be a generation of semi-speakers.

(c) Languages that no one speaks except a few aged individuals.

(d) Languages that have lost all their speakers, so that the only record of them (if any) lies in notes and recordings by linguists. These are beyond being "endangered" and are usually called "dead languages," although L. Frank Manriquez, whose ancestral language, Tongva, has no speakers, "prefer[s] to think of them as sleeping" (personal communication).

Even in the face of the linguistic catastrophe described here, this is also a time of unprecedented efforts on the part of minority peoples to keep their languages alive and to expand their usage. There is now a worldwide movement of indigenous peoples seeking rights to decision making about their own future and, most relevant to our concern here, seeking to save their languages from oblivion. They are searching for and inventing ways and means to reverse language shift (RLS is the acronym coined by Fishman [1991] for the process of reversing language shift). The people in the community and the teachers, linguists, and politicians assisting them are doing pioneering work as they attempt RLS. There are no tried-and-true methods or instructions for RLS that work for all communities. There are no pedagogical materials or trained language teachers to teach most endangered languages, and very few language revitalization programs are old enough to serve as models for RLS. Even some of the most successful programs are able to base much of their success not so much on methodology as on politics, such as the circumstances that allowed Israel to make Hebrew (which was actually long extinct as a language of daily communication) the official language of the country and the language of daily communication. For smaller groups, whose languages will never be able to serve as a language of wider communication outside of the small community of speakers, much inventiveness, energy, and dedication are needed to manage RLS. It is a superhuman task, but one to which an increasing number of people are passionately dedicated.

WHY CARE?

Why does it matter that the linguistic diversity of the world is diminishing? Why should anyone care if indigenous groups shift from their ancestral tongue to a world language? Is it not communicatively beneficial for people in a nation to speak the same language as each other? Is it not the case that languages have been dying throughout human history? These questions are very frequently asked by the general public, and are ably answered in a number of important publications (Fishman 1991; Hale et al. 1992; Grenoble and Whaley 1998; Nettle and Romaine 2000). I will briefly summarize some of the arguments here.

Starting with arguments of the narrowest applicability, the editors of this book, as linguists, certainly share with their colleagues professional reasons for preferring to see linguistic diversity maintained. Linguistic theory depends on linguistic diversity. It is one of the charges of linguistics to understand the range of possibilities within human language and the cognitive models that would account for this. The study of historical linguistics, language universals and typology, sociolinguistics, and cognitive linguistics has been driven by the study of the very indigenous languages whose existence is threatened.

More broadly, the loss of language is part of the loss of whole cultures and knowledge systems, including philosophical systems, oral literary and musical traditions, environmental knowledge systems, medical knowledge, and important cultural practices and artistic skills. The world stands to lose an important part of the sum of human knowledge whenever a language stops being used. Just as the human species is putting itself in danger through the destruction of species diversity, so might we be in danger from the destruction of the diversity of knowledge systems.

Finally, as mentioned above, language retention is a human rights issue. The loss of language is part of the oppression and disenfranchisement of indigenous peoples, who are losing their land and traditional livelihood involuntarily as the forces of national or world economy and politics impinge upon them. Indigenous efforts toward language maintenance or revitalization are generally part of a larger effort to retain or regain their political autonomy, their land base, or at least their own sense of identity.

Despite the fact that the general public should feel they have an investment in the survival of indigenous languages and cultures, what is really important is self-determination: the rights of indigenous peoples to determine their own futures, whether or not they see language survival as an important part of that future. It is only if an indigenous speech community itself desires and initiates efforts toward language survival that such programs should exist or would have any chance of success (see Ladefoged 1992).

WHY THIS BOOK?

This book is about the various ways in which people are working to keep their languages alive or bring them back into use. It is not aimed at any kind of equality of geographic representation; indeed, we focus primarily on North America, with only some of the most important programs elsewhere in the world being brought in. Rather, it is aimed at representing the principles and methods of language revitalization. We would like the general reader to understand the issues of language loss and revitalization, but our main goal is for this book to serve as a reference for individuals and communities who are interested or active in the revitalization of endangered languages.

This volume contains a number of ideas for how people can work to bring their languages back into use. Each chapter concerns some aspect (or aspects) of language revitalization as presented by someone directly involved in the program being written about. In addition, each chapter has two main purposes: to display some particular principles and methods of language revitalization and to show an actual program of revitalization in progress. Each section will be introduced with an overview of the particular principles or methods featured in the chapter(s). It is our ultimate hope that this book will provide individuals and communities working on language revitalization with ideas about what works well and how to design programs for their own communities.

In this chapter I will go over some of the important general principles of language revitalization.

THE BIG PICTURE: STEPS TOWARD LANGUAGE REVITALIZATION

I use the term "language revitalization" in a very broad sense. At its most extreme, "language revitalization" refers to the development of programs that result in re-establishing a language which has ceased being the language of communication in the speech community and bringing it back into full use in all walks of life. This is what has happened with Hebrew. "Revitalization" can also begin with a less extreme state of loss, such as that encountered in Irish or Navajo, which are both still the first language of many children and are used in many homes as the language of communication, though both languages are losing ground. For these speech communities, revitalization would mean turning this decline around.

Even when almost all families are still using a language at home, there might be danger signs, such as the loss of domains of vocabulary. The Havasupai bilingual education program that was put into place 25 years ago was designed for children who were native speakers of the language but who were showing signs of language contraction—that is, they tended not to know certain domains of vocabulary or certain aspects of grammar, or to lack formal speaking or storytelling skills. The goal of revitalization in that case was to remedy the children's incomplete learning.

In many cases, the language is almost or completely extinct, and the community that wants to revive it is so small or the resources so meager that the community may settle for smaller goals—for instance, producing language-learning programs and materials without the goal of complete fluency or re-establishment of the language as the main language of communication. Another alternative for such deeply endangered languages has been simply to assure its continuation through one or two speakers per generation, who learn the language from the last native speakers through mentored programs such as California's Master-Apprentice Language Learning Program (Chapter 17).

The goals of a language revitalization program must depend on the situation in which the language finds itself. How large is the speech community? Are the speakers or potential learners geographically together or scattered? What level of political power do they have? Do they have a nation that could come to see this as the national language, or are they a tiny minority in a multilingual nation? What kinds of resources are there? Are there still native speakers? What is the age of the youngest speakers? Is the language well documented? Does it have a long history of writing? Are there colleges or universities where the language can be learned? Are there trained language teachers who can teach the language? What kind of monetary resources are there? What is the level of desire on the part of the community for language revitalization?

While some of the speech communities in this book have large populations and optimal resources, many more have tiny populations and minimal resources. No matter which end of the scale a language is on, language revitalization is complex and difficult; but it is also always possible, at least to some degree. A small, scattered community with few speakers, no trained personnel, and limited resources may not be able to achieve as much as a large speech community like the Māoris of New Zealand, nor to reach its goal so quickly. But some level of revitalization is still possible, and as certain levels are reached, new ones may become reachable. All that is really needed for language revitalization to begin is a minimum of one person who is dedicated to the cause. That one person can do a great deal with no support from the community: find out what documentation exists; get to know living speakers; learn the language, or as much of it as possible from the resources available, if not already a speaker; develop learning materials that others can use (in the researcher's lifetime or later); try to develop community interest through meetings or language gatherings; and incorporate the assistance of linguists to document the language or help interpret existing documents. Community support may come later, after the prime mover has accomplished something the community can trust. Even if it does not, that one interested person can produce something of value that future generations may appreciate more than that person's peers.

Fishman (1991) has designed eight steps toward reversing language shift (RLS). They are based largely on the Hebrew RLS model and other large-scale examples of language expansion and include steps that many indigenous languages can never hope to reach, such as his step 1 (he designed the table to be read from bottom to top), making the language the language of national government. As Fishman points out, where a speech community begins depends on how complete language loss is. For example, his step 8 (reconstructing the language and designing programs for adult acquisition) might not be necessary for a language that shows some decline in the number of speakers but is experiencing nothing as drastic as having no children learning at home. For the purposes of this book, we would like to make a modified model of steps toward language revitalization that expands on earlier steps and focuses less on the steps that can bring a language into national use. (We also number the steps in the opposite direction so that you can read from the top down!) I must emphasize here that the order of many of these steps may differ according to the circumstances, and some steps may be conducted simultaneously. For example, step 1 (language planning) might in fact take place after some of the later steps have already begun. In fact, what often happens in language revitalization is that a few dedicated individuals begin activities at some later step, such as learning the language from elders (step 3) or teaching the language to their children at home (step 7), which then provides inspiration to the community as a whole, whereupon language planning might begin to take place. We should also point out that for many small communities, a realistic goal might be no more than to reach step 3 or 4. It may well be that some languages will survive from generation to generation only through one or two individuals in each generation who take the initiative to learn it.

Step 1. Language assessment and planning: Find out what the linguistic situation is in the community. How many speakers are there? What are their ages? What other resources are available on the language? What are the attitudes of speakers and non-speakers toward language revitalization? What are realistic goals for language revitalization in this community?

Step 2. If the language has no speakers: Use available materials to reconstruct the language and develop language pedagogy (see Chapter 32 on the Native California Language Restoration Workshop).

Step 3. If the language has only elderly speakers: Document the language of the elderly speakers. (This may also take place at the same time as other steps.)

Step 4. Develop a second-language learning program for adults (see Chapter 17 on the Master-Apprentice Program). These professional-age and parent-age adult second-language learners will be important leaders in later steps.

Step 5. Redevelop or enhance cultural practices that support and encourage use of the endangered language at home and in public by first- and second-language speakers (see Chapter 7 on Cochiti and Chapter 24 on Irish).

Step 6. Develop intensive second-language programs for children, preferably with a component in the schools. When possible, use the endangered language as the language of instruction (see Chapter 11 on Māori and Chapters 12 and 13 on Hawaiian).

Step 7. Use the language at home as the primary language of communication, so that it becomes the first language of young children. Develop classes and support groups for parents to assist them in the transition (see Chapters 12 and 13 on Hawaiian).

Step 8. Expand the use of the indigenous language into broader local domains, including community government, media, local commerce, and so on (see Chapter 24 on the use of Irish on the radio).

Step 9. Where possible, expand the language domains outside of the local community and into the broader population to promote the language as one of wider communication, regional or national government, and so on (see section on Hebrew in Chapter 31).

To reiterate, some steps (e.g., step 9) may be outside the possible or desired goals of small indigenous communities, and some of the earlier steps (except language planning) may not be needed for communities where language loss is in the early stages. Enterprising individuals and organizations might do work at later steps first, with the community as a whole only later beginning a step-by-step process of revitalization inspired and heartened by the work of the first individuals. Some individuals and communities might have less ambitious goals; they may not even have in mind the goal of developing new fluent speakers. Such communities might wish to have some part of step 2 as the ultimate goal: the gathering of written and taped resources, the development of minor learning materials, and the transmission of a few basic words and phrases to the community.

APPROACHES TO LANGUAGE REVITALIZATION

Looking at language revitalization programs around the world, we find many different approaches. Most of them fall into one of five categories: (1) school-based programs; (2) children's programs outside the school (after-school programs, summer programs); (3) adult language programs; (4) documentation and materials development; and (5) home-based programs.

School-Based Programs

Many school programs around the country are now involved in the teaching of local endangered languages. There are three main types of school-based language programs: teaching an endangered language as a subject (like a foreign language), bilingual education, and full-scale immersion programs. Different goals, benefits, limitations, and results characterize these three types.

Endangered Language as a Subject

Probably the most common form of language teaching in the schools is teaching it as a subject for a limited amount of time each day. This is not a good way to create new fluent speakers, but it is often all that is possible in a given situation. Schools have a structure and a required agenda that allows language teaching only a small role compared to those played by the more favored subjects of math, reading, and so on. Programs allowed a time slot in the general school day

range from as little as half an hour a week to as much as an hour a day.

An hour a day of language, if taught with the appropriate methodology, can bring children a long way toward fluency. Even half an hour a week, although it will do little toward the development of fluency, can at least result in the important development in children's minds of a sense of appreciation for the language. Teaching the language as a subject has done a lot in many communities to help erase the shame that generations of people have felt about their language and has created a readiness and eagerness in young people to learn their language and develop more intensive programs for revitalization. An example of a good language-as-subject program can be found in Humboldt County, California, where the public school system has a policy of teaching the local Native American languages in schools with a large native population. Tolowa, Hupa, Karuk, and Yurok are all taught in various of the schools. These languages can now serve to fulfill the high school foreign-language requirement (a bad name, but a good policy) for graduation.

In every type of program, there are advantages and problems. The language-as-subject program has two disadvantages: there is usually not enough exposure time to bring a student to fluency, and the program does not create any real situation for communication. Foreign languages are generally taught with the expectation that the students will someday put the language to practical use through interaction with other speakers, ideally in the country where the language is spoken. In the case of endangered languages, there may be no such place. When there is no speech community using the language, then any program that teaches the language must also concern itself with creating a situation in which the language can actually be used.

However, such problems do not detract from the excellent advantages of a language-as-subject program. The Humboldt County program, for example, has helped a generation of children become proud of their linguistic heritage and develop at least some degree of conversational ability. The children may themselves create the situation in which the language can be used; indeed, even when speaking English, children can be heard inserting certain phrases from their language that they learned in school. Many Native American teenagers—that most critical group—in Humboldt County are extremely proud of their heritage and their language. In contrast to what their parents felt as teenagers, I have heard this generation of teenagers say that the children at school think it is really "cool" to know their language. Children with such positive attitudes will be tomorrow's leaders in language revitalization.

Bilingual Education

Many Native American language programs got their start under Title VII bilingual education funds. Some of these programs have been in existence since the late 1970s. The communities served best by bilingual education programs are those where the language is still spoken by children; in fact, if the language is not spoken by children entering school, it is hard to find funding with Title VII, since those funds are used primarily for schools in which a portion of the children lack full English skills. Bilingual education in the United States has been plagued by uncertain funding, inadequate opportunities for teacher training, and negative posturing by politicians, and as a result it has not been as effective as it would have been with better support. However, many excellent programs have developed in spite of these problems, and among them are a number of well-conceived and well-executed programs for Native Americans. A major difference between bilingual education and teaching language as a subject is that in bilingual education, a portion of instruction is actually done in the minority language. Bilingual education therefore takes on the role of being a language of instruction, and for a number of programs for endangered languages, this has resulted in the development of new domains of use for the language that are brought about by school requirements: a writing system (if one does not already exist) and written materials are developed in order to teach the children to read in their languages, and ways of talking about math and science and world affairs are developed. For endangered languages, this often means the development of new vocabulary for topics that were never before discussed in that language. All this means that settings and situations are provided in which actual communication can take place in the language. A good bilingual education program is ideal, for it can result in true balanced bilingualism—generally the main goal for people seeking to revitalize their ancestral language within a dominant culture that speaks another language.

Bilingual education as envisioned by the American government has a number of limitations beyond those placed on it by poor funding and training and the lack of moral support. One is that it is not usually oriented toward teaching the endangered language to those who do not already know it, since the main goal of federally funded bilingual education is for everyone to learn English and then switch to it as the main language of education (the "transition model"). A number of good programs, however, are aimed at making children bilingual in both languages, and even teaching the minority language to children who do not know it. Also, successful language learning can take place within a bilingual education program if there are only a few children who do not know the language within a general environment of children who do. The programs aimed at total bilingualism are best funded and best developed when the other language is also a world language, such as Spanish or French—languages for which there are plenty of teaching materials for all school subjects and plenty of teachers fluent in the language, and for which there is plenty of financial support. It is much more of an uphill battle to create a full-scale bilingual education program if the language has few speakers and few written materials and has not been previously used in the educational domains.

Like other programs, bilingual education for endangered languages also has the disadvantage that the language has little reinforcement from the family and community. While bilingual education creates a situation in which the language can actually be used for real communication purposes, those purposes are oriented directly to the classroom; there is little motivation for children to use the endangered language on the playground or at home if it is not being used there already. But certainly, where most children already know and use the minority language, a well-taught bilingual education program can serve to reinforce language learning that is already taking place at home. In this sense, bilingual education is a potentially better tool for language maintenance than for language revival. (I have also seen some bilingual education programs—the transition model among them—that actually exacerbate language loss. Language loss can also be the unintended result of a poorly planned program that hopes to assist in maintenance.)

These paragraphs about what constitutes "good" bilingual education will be read with ire by opponents of bilingual education in the United States, who believe that any program that assists in the maintenance of any language other than English is to be abhorred. Bilingual education is a hot political issue, and even though its opponents do not focus their energies against the endangered indigenous languages but are rather arguing against the maintenance of Spanish and immigrant languages, the fact is that the politicization of bilingual education makes it difficult to find and retain funding for programs that are focused on language maintenance and revival.

Immersion Schools and Classrooms

A model that is being used increasingly in the United States and elsewhere is the full-immersion program, where all instruction in the classroom is carried out in the endangered language (see Chapter 14). There is no doubt that this is the best way to jump-start the production of a new generation of fluent speakers for an endangered language. No other system of language revitalization has such complete access to so many members of the younger generation (who are the best language learners) for so many hours per day. More and more programs worldwide have immersion preschools that teach children to communicate in the endangered language, and for a number of programs it has been possible to develop an immersion schooling system all the way through high school and even into college. Hawaiian and Māori are two languages discussed in this book (Chapters 11–13) that have developed a whole generation of new speakers through this type of program.

By providing sufficient exposure to the language to produce fluent speakers as well as a venue for using the language in real communication, immersion schools solve many of the problems discussed above with respect to the other types of school programs. In the immersion schools, the presence of the target language is so strong that children tend often to use it with each other outside the classroom as well as in.

The immersion schools and classrooms also must overcome certain limitations and obstacles. Educational laws and regulations make it difficult to found immersion schools: in order to permit Hawaiian language immersion classes, Hawai'i had to change a state law mandating English as the only allowable language of instruction. Any community that has an immersion school in mind must realize that it will entail years of legal wrangling and figuring out ways to comply with all the local and state regulations. But it can be done—and a growing number of successful immersion schools attest to that fact.

As indicated earlier, having children who know a language is not enough; they must also use it robustly with others if the language is to continue. Problems develop if the immersion classroom is in a school where other classrooms are in English, for in those cases English is the language of the playground, and children become used to talking to their peers in English. Developing that habit does not bode well for hopes that these children will grow up to use their language in the home, even if they know the target language fluently.

The school is a specialized setting that makes inflexible demands in terms of subject matter and styles of interaction. When a language is chosen as the language of instruction, that language must be developed to accommodate the needs of education. Thus, a language that might never have been used to communicate such things before must develop vocabulary for math and science, as well as discourse styles that fit the situation. (For example, giving oral book reports or writing essays may never have been done in the language before.) Developing new vocabulary and discourse styles is not that hard, but it does change the language. People who wish to revitalize their language because of a desire to return to traditional culture and values must be aware that language revitalization does not automatically bring people back to these traditional modes of thought. If the language is learned solely in school, then it is school culture and school values that are learned along with it. Even when a conscious effort is made to teach traditional culture and values, the schoolroom agenda imposes its own culture on the students.

Another problem is that for some families and communities, devoting all education to the endangered language may seem like too much; they fear that children will not get sufficient English-language education to keep up in the higher grades or in college. This is a constant debate in communities where immersion schools exist. But this level of intensity in language teaching may be the only thing that works in turning around language decline. Wilson and Kamanā put it

very well: "The philosophy that has brought our movement most of its success establishes the priority goal as the continued existence and strengthening of a linguistically and culturally defined community. The 'Aha Pūnana Leo sees academic achievement, especially achievement higher than that of the dominant society, as an important tool in reaching our priority goal. But, high academic achievement is of itself not the goal" (Wilson and Kamanā, this volume, page 147).

In fact, even the immersion classroom is not sufficient unto itself to turn around language death: it is essential that the families play an active role as well. Students whose families are unwilling or unable to reinforce the language at home do not fare as well as students whose families actively use their language. Thus, the successful immersion programs also usually have a family component in which parents are asked to learn the language in night classes, to volunteer in the immersion classroom, and to reinforce at home the lessons the students learn in school.

Language and Culture

Language and culture are closely intertwined. One important reason many people want to learn their ancestral language is that they want to regain access to traditional cultural practices and traditional values. It is often said that language is the key to and the heart of culture.

And yet, one does not automatically gain the culture by learning the language. Language is a very changeable form of behavior, and if language is taught outside of and without reference to the traditional culture, then that language will be devoid of the traditional culture. Let us take as an example the teaching of a language in the classroom using immersion methods. It is normal to talk about the objects and practices in the immediate environment, and so, if the classroom is designed to reflect the mainstream culture, as classrooms usually are, the language will be taught in such a way that children learn how to talk about classroom objects and classroom activities. A language learned outside of its traditional cultural context will lack the ability to reflect traditional culture.

This is an obvious enough point, although sometimes the subtleties of "classroom culture" work against culturally appropriate language learning in unexpected ways. For example, in most indigenous cultures, the art and genres of traditional storytelling are an exceedingly important part of traditional culture. Yet rarely can classroom teaching do an adequate job of helping children learn these oral arts. A number of factors can make it difficult or impossible for a classroom-based language revitalization program to do an adequate job of teaching traditional storytelling. Traditional storytelling may have constraints, such as only being done at night, or only in certain ceremonial contexts. In addition, traditional tales may be very long, precluding their full presentation in the classroom setting, and they may have scatological or sexual content considered inappropriate to the classroom.

There are at least two lessons to be learned here. One is that if a community engages in classroom-based indigenous-language instruction, it must work actively to bring indigenous culture into the classroom and to change the classroom culture to meet indigenous culture halfway. This includes bringing traditional objects into the classroom, teaching traditional subjects, designing the shape of a classroom or school to fit traditional culture and values, leaving the classroom altogether for field trips or instruction in more traditional settings, and arranging hours and holidays around traditional ceremonial structure. The most successful school-based language revitalization programs often create separate schools, bypassing the mainstream public school system altogether in order to have sufficient power to do culturally appropriate language teaching.

The other lesson to be learned is that classroom-based language instruction can never be the sole source of serious language revitalization. Schools are limited in what and how much they can teach of the indigenous culture, and they are also constrained by having to fulfill the educational requirements of the dominant society. School personnel may have insufficient knowledge of traditional language and culture and may even be hostile to the presence of the indigenous language and culture in the school. Even if the school is friendly and willing, language revitalization must also have strong components in the broader community and in the home. Much of culture must be learned in the home, in a ceremonial context, or in the field—not in the classroom.

Children's Programs outside the School

Many communities develop programs outside the school either to supplement school programs or to be completely independent from the schools. After-school programs have developed in some cases, although in the United States there are many more after-school programs for immigrant languages than for indigenous languages. While children are often tired and less attentive at this time of day, a well-designed after-school program (especially one that combines language with recreation) can help children develop skills in the target language.

One popular kind of revitalization program that is offered outside the school is summer programs for children. These take the form of summer language schools or language camps. Since they take place while children are on summer break from school, they can last as long as all day and be very intensive. They therefore have advantages over after-school programs, which must fit into a short time frame and have the added disadvantage that the children come to them tired, after long days at school. An excellent summer program for the Cochiti language is described in this volume by Regis Pecos and Rebecca Blum-Martinez (Chapter 7). A great deal of language can be learned in a two- or three-month summer

program; however, what is learned may soon be forgotten if the language is not reinforced during the school year. But an intensive summer program reinforced by a nonintensive school program might have quite excellent long-term results. Reinforcement may come as well or instead by the family, keeping the knowledge active and helping the child develop further.

Adult Language Programs

One common kind of program is evening classes for adults or families. In practice these are usually held once a week, and although they rarely involve immersion, they can of course be taught in that manner. As mentioned before, the best school programs have a family component that is often a weekly evening class.

In Hawai'i, a group on Oahu recently received a grant for a community recreation program to be run in Hawaiian in which regular events such as volleyball and cookouts were held where only Hawaiian was spoken. This kind of program, where immersion-style learning is combined with other activities, is especially promising for endangered languages, since the language has to be brought into real communication situations again if it is to survive. A program such as this takes language learning outside of the classroom situation and puts it into daily life.

A program in California that has had good results is the California Master-Apprentice Language Learning Program, run by an intertribal organization, the Advocates for Indigenous California Language Survival (Chapter 17). In this program, the last elderly speakers of California Indian languages are paired with young relatives who want to learn the language; they are taught immersion-style techniques of language teaching and learn to speak in their language together one-on-one. It is stressed that rather than doing "lessons" most of the time, the team should do activities together—cooking, gathering, housework, taking a walk or a drive—and communicate at all times in the language during these activities. In this way, as with the Oahu community recreation program, language learning takes place in the context of real communication, thus performing both functions of a revitalization program—teaching the language and bringing it into use in daily life.

Documentation and Materials Development

To many communities now, language teaching and learning is the essential goal, and documentation is only secondary, or frequently ignored altogether. They reason that a language is dead if it is just recorded, with no living speakers. "Preserving" a language through documentation is seen to be like pickling something, rather than keeping it alive and growing. Nevertheless, for communities whose languages are deeply endangered—that is, there are no children or young adults speaking it—it is essential that a program of documentation accompany any other measures being taken. For those languages, a day will come, and soon, when there are no native speakers left alive. The people who have devoted themselves to language learning in the last days of the native speakers' presence can never learn everything the native speakers know. Even the biggest and most active revitalization programs, such as those for Hawaiian and Māori, which have large numbers of new speakers, find that the new generation speaks with a different kind of intonation from the old native speakers. In addition, the programs make tremendous use of sound recordings of Hawaiian as spoken by these elders, especially a large set of recordings of radio interviews conducted with older Hawaiians by Larry Kimura over a span of many years. Many of the old genres and old vocabulary may be lost or insufficiently taught. As thorough documentation as possible of the last native speakers will be a critical resource for future language learners. And documentation is even more important in the absence of a revitalization program. Many linguists and anthropologists in the first half of this century worked with the last speakers of dying languages in the United States (and elsewhere) to record all they could of them at a time when communities had little or no interest in maintaining their ancestral languages, and these speakers knew that working with the scientists was their only hope of passing on their knowledge to anyone. The linguists and anthropologists made a great effort to record as much as possible of the vocabulary and grammar of endangered languages and also to record traditional tales and ethnographic texts. In many cases, this documentation is all that is left of the language. The publications, field notes, and recordings made by these speakers and researchers, now being used by new generations avid to learn what they can about their languages, are a rich source of material that can be invaluable to language revitalization programs—indeed, often they form the only basis on which revitalization can begin.

Certainly the beginning stages of any revitalization program must include finding out what kind of documentation of the language exists. There are great archives, such as those of the Smithsonian Institution in Washington, D.C., the American Philosophical Library in Philadelphia, and the Bancroft Library at the University of California, Berkeley, that have millions of pages of linguistic materials. But smaller local archives such as those at county museums may also have rich holdings. In response to the surging interest in language revitalization, clearinghouses are beginning to develop where teaching materials on various languages and catalogs or references to archival holdings around the world may be found. Two of these are the ERIC Clearinghouse on Languages and Linguistics in Washington, D.C., and the recently established International Clearing House for Endangered Languages at the University of Tokyo. More clearinghouses are being planned as of this writing.

Programs to increase accessibility of archival materials to native communities now exist, such as the "Breath of Life, Silent No More" California Indian Language Restoration Workshop at Berkeley, where California Indians whose ancestral languages are extinct are invited to come for a weeklong program to show them how to find materials on their languages and how to work with them for language revitalization purposes (see Chapter 32). Another excellent program, though now dormant owing to loss of funding, is the California Indian Libraries Collection, which copied linguistic and ethnographic materials from the University of California archives and placed them in county libraries in the vicinity of the communities the collections came from. Accessibility is also being increased by the microfilming of unpublished field notes. Many of the linguistic collections at the Bancroft Library are now on microfilm, as are those at the Smithsonian Institution and elsewhere. Another major project in archives around the world has been to transfer old sound recordings to more accessible formats. The wax-cylinder recordings made by anthropologists at the University of California at the turn of the century were transferred to audiotape in the 1980s. The Smithsonian Institution is expected to finish the transfer to audiotape of J. P. Harrington's vast audio collection of Native American languages in 2001. In the future, we will see big projects to digitize recordings and put them on CD. We will also see some of the large printed or audio collections put on the Internet, so that immediate access will be possible to anyone, anywhere, who has a computer. Even now, materials on endangered languages are increasingly common on the Internet (Chapter 26).

Older documentation is invaluable, but more documentation is still needed. Some languages have less documentation than others, and no language has ever been documented in its entirety—an impossible task, given human beings' huge capacity for constant linguistic creation. There are also frustrating gaps in the documentation by social scientists. Missing almost always is material on the rules and patterns of interaction. How people greet each other, how they carry on a conversation, how they joke and tease, how they apologize, or how they express emotions—this information is rarely present in the field notes and recordings. And since videorecording is relatively new, most of the documentation of endangered languages lacks the visual component of communication. At present, visual communication is a growing field of research, so there will someday be important video archives to match the audio and written archives; but as of now, relatively few speech communities have been studied in this way, and for many it will soon be too late.

It can be very beneficial for a language revitalization program to have the help of linguists to document their language. This can be done without any cost to the community by a linguist doing a research project, or, if the community prefers to have complete control over the materials, it can hire a linguist as a consultant. Since a research linguist may have very specific goals which may not be compatible with broad documentation, it is generally preferable to hire one as a consultant so that the community can determine the agenda of study. It is also possible, where the financial aspect of a revitalization program is not strong, to get a linguist to work for free as a trade: the linguist can do his research project part time and spend the rest of the time doing documentation useful to the community.

But documentation need not be done only by professionals. The community can do its own. Chapter 21 discusses some of the principles and methods of such documentation.

Development of Teaching Devices: Books, Audiotapes, Videotapes, CD-ROMS, and the Like

The development of books and audiotapes that teach the language and of learning aids such as videotapes and CD-ROMs is an important component of language teaching, as an aid to immersion programs, as a way of increasing community interest, and often, as the only alternative available to some people. Many language activists are working alone or in small groups. There may be insufficient community involvement to develop classes, or else the descendants of speakers of the target language may be scattered geographically. Often the development of pedagogical materials is the best language activists can do under the conditions they are working in. The development of language teaching materials for use both by interested people now and by future generations can be a great gift to the community's posterity. Dictionaries are of use even to native speakers, who, because of nonuse or the limitations of their background, may be lacking vocabulary in specific domains. Guided lessons that motivated students can use on their own can be a great way to set someone on the track of language learning. Reference grammars are an important resource for teachers planning classroom language lessons. Well-made videos and other visually oriented learning materials can keep a child's interest and attention during lessons.

As with language teaching, the development of such materials generally demands some prior training on the part of the person developing them. Besides the obvious need for technological expertise in making videos and CD-ROMs, linguistic training or consultation with a linguist or language-teaching specialist may be necessary in order to produce a good reference grammar, dictionary, or book of language lessons. The language data from which such references are developed must of course come from native speakers or, lacking those, from linguistic documents (publications, tapes, and field notes) found in archives.

Family-Based Programs at Home

When a revitalization program results in a large and growing percentage of families using their ancestral language as their home language, so that children are learning it as their first language, then it is time to celebrate and take it off the "endangered" list. Hebrew is the only language in the world with a revitalization program big enough and advanced enough to have reached that stage. Hawaiian and Māori are now at the stage at which Hebrew was about 75 years ago: at this time they are being used in only a few homes in which the parents are second-language learners, most of whom learned Hawaiian or Māori as college students. The school immersion programs are less than 15 years old; the "lead groups" who have spoken their languages since preschool are still in high school. It is strongly hoped that a sizable number of these students will make Hawaiian or Māori the first language of their homes, but it is still too early to see whether this will happen.

Beginning to use an endangered language as the first language of home is a big commitment, because it may mean that one's children will be less proficient in the national language. The potential role of the endangered language within the nation can play a large role in a parent's decision whether to commit to using the language exclusively at home. As the national language of Israel, Hebrew is now the language of schools and daily life, so it is now a boon to a child's well-being in the society to teach him Hebrew. If Hawai'i's independence movement were to result in a break from the United States, the importance of English there could conceivably decline, as Hawai'i would look to increase its economic ties with Polynesia and Asia. Hawaiian, though still the language of a small minority, already plays a symbolic role in the independence movement and could be increasingly important. Such considerations no doubt help Hawaiian families make their decision when they contemplate using Hawaiian in the home with their children.

But for small minority languages in localities where political and economic independence from the larger nation seems impossible, parents may have a harder time deciding to bring back the endangered language as the sole language of the home, because of their fear of potentially handicapping a child in his or her fluency in the nation's mainstream language.

Raising Bilingual Children

In most contexts in which endangered languages exist, parents with an interest in bringing their ancestral language into the home might be more comfortable with the goal of raising a fully bilingual child than with raising the child to be dominant in the endangered language. It is especially comforting to be reminded that recent research shows that bilingual children may have certain cognitive advantages over monolingual children, so bilingualism may be beneficial to a child's development.[1]

Although there are billions of bilingual people in the world—it has been suggested that over half the population of the world is bilingual—deliberately raising a child bilingually turns out not to be an easy thing to do. Most people who grow up bilingual either do so because of excellent language teaching in the schools (as in much of Europe) or, more commonly, because they simply are reared in a situation where one language is used in the home and another in some other major language-learning situation (such as in the school or on the streets). Having the home be responsible for the development of both languages is more difficult.

In fact, in most situations where a language is truly endangered, meaning that it is not spoken as the main language of the community anymore, if parents focus on using the endangered language in the home, the child will "automatically" learn the main language of the general environment anyway. Certainly this is the case for Hawaiian. Even when families use Hawaiian in the home and send their children to a Hawaiian immersion school, there is enough English all around them—in the marketplace, at the playground, among family friends, and so on—that the children learn English simultaneously. If parents try to do something like spend "equal time" on the two languages, it is the endangered language that will suffer, for unlike the mainstream language, the endangered language receives little or no reinforcement outside the home. Since children do a great deal of language learning outside the home, the parents, if their goal is bilingualism for their children, should spend relatively little time on the language that is dominant in the general environment and concentrate instead on speaking in the endangered language.

The most common mistake that parents make who are trying to raise bilingual children is to use the dominant language for the main language of communication and then try to consciously "teach" the other language, which ends up with children learning the same thing they learn in American elementary schools: numbers, colors, and a few animal names. If a parent is not fluent in the endangered language, then perhaps this is all he or she can hope to do. But if the parent is fluent, then that must be the language of communication between the parent and child, either at all times or during a significant amount of time. Some parents designate certain times for certain languages—for instance, "Today is Thursday, so we speak Gaelic. But Friday we'll speak English." Again, the endangered language should get more time than the majority language.

One Parent, One Language

A fairly common method of attempting to raise bilingual children is for one parent always to speak to the children in one language and the other parent always to speak in the other. A recent study on this method (Dopke 1992) documented a number of families in Australia and found that few of them were successful. The children always learned English—that was not a problem—but many of the children stopped speaking the other language at some point in the learning and became at best "passive speakers"—understanding in part but not producing the language. The families that *were* success-

ful in raising fully bilingual children had at least three things in common: the minority-language parent spent at least as much time with the child as did the majority-language parent; the parent using the minority language refused to accept a response from the child in English (there was nothing punitive about this; the parent would just say something like "What?" until the child responded in the other language); and there was at least some reinforcement from outside the home, such as relatives or friends who spoke the language.

If a community is active in language revitalization, the one parent–one language approach might work out well. So placing the child in a school program that teaches the endangered language or giving him or her ample opportunity to speak the language with elders might provide sufficient reinforcement to allow continuing bilingual development. Often, of course, the one parent–one language approach is the best that a household can do, if only one parent knows the language in the first place.

WAYS TO ENCOURAGE AND DEVELOP THE USE OF AN ENDANGERED LANGUAGE

The heart of a language is its native speakers. In general, the main direct cause of language death (which is itself the result of other factors) is that at some point the native speakers stop using it as their means of communication. Most of the time the cessation of use of a language is not owing to a conscious decision. It is more like the cessation of a heartbeat: when trauma or disease or deterioration stresses the body beyond that which life can tolerate, the heart stops beating, and death ensues. In the same way, the stresses and demands of the dominant society and language eventually lead to the cessation of use of the endangered language.

For a person in danger of dying, the first job of medics is to get the heart beating again. For an endangered language, the first job is to get the native speakers speaking it again.

There are a number of reasons why it is difficult for native speakers to speak their language, and the difficulty becomes greater the longer the language is silent. The factors that silenced the language in the first place are still in operation. Most problematic is the absence of communicative situations in which the language can be used meaningfully. In particular, when most people in the community do not know the language, no one in a speaker's circle of daily contacts is able to understand the speaker or respond. Another major problem is that as the length of time that its speakers have not spoken it increases, they begin to lose their competency; they start feeling self-conscious and are afraid to make an error, especially in front of other speakers. Alternatively, the last speakers may not have learned the language fluently in the first place and may have stopped speaking because of criticism or ridicule from other speakers. I have been to meetings of Native American tribal language committees whose goal is to save the language and where the committee consists primarily of elderly native speakers—yet through all the talk about how to save their language, no word of the language is uttered. On discussing this with them, they generally say that they feel shy about speaking the language around each other because they have not spoken it for so long that they feel they have forgotten a lot, and they might make a mistake.

How, then, can the heart of the language begin to beat again, however tentatively? How can the speakers be encouraged to use the language again?

A person who knows a language will use it if he or she is spoken to in that language. It is the learners who must bring the native speakers back into language use. In a language revitalization program, perhaps the most important first step of second-language learning is to teach the learners things they can say to speakers. Simple greetings and conversational openers are important. This creates a tiny place where the language can be spoken again. This is just a first step, though; a native speaker cannot continue the conversation beyond the greeting if that is all the learner knows. It is very important for learners to practice everything they learn on speakers, both for the sake of learning and for the sake of encouraging the speakers to use the language. The fear of error is somewhat lessened when a native speaker talks with a learner, for the speaker surely knows more than the conversation partner, and the learner would not dare to criticize—nor, indeed, would most learners even recognize an error from the speaker. (It is the learner's own fears of error and of ridicule that are strongest in this situation.)

A part of this encouragement from learners can come from learning and using certain phrases, such as "Speak to me in our language" or "Say that in our language." In Cochiti, children in a summer immersion program have learned how to remind people to speak Cochiti by saying so whenever they hear a Cochiti speak English. They say in Cochiti, "I'm not white, I'm Cochiti. Please talk to me in Cochiti" (Chapter 7).

Another way to encourage the speakers to use their language is, of course, to get them to teach it. Whether or not a speaker actually knows anything about how to teach, the speaker is the one who has the real information that must be taught and certainly should be a part of any teaching situation. (See below for teaching methodologies that involve native speakers.) Even if the speaker is not part of any formal teaching situation, a learner can simply ask the speaker to teach him. The learner can elicit words and phrases, ask the speaker to tell a story, or simply ask speakers to teach something of their own choice.

There are also more formal ways to get speakers to use their language. Traditional ceremonies, led by speakers, are often a natural place to use the language. In less traditional situations such as community meetings, speakers can be asked to begin the meeting with a prayer or a few words in the language.

Some communities encourage speakers to use their language through community events such as potluck dinners honoring the speakers at which the speaker is asked in advance to give a speech in the language, and by encouraging or even insisting on no English from speakers and learners alike. In the California Master-Apprentice Program, one activity that is suggested for teams is to hold a dinner for the elders who speak the language and have the apprentices go to all the homes of the elders to be invited and invite them to the dinner (speaking only the target language during the visit).

Sadly, most communities begin to attempt to revitalize their language only when no one speaks it anymore except the oldest generation. Obviously, the best time to start is before the language has ceased being spoken in the home. But failing that, if the parent generation still knows the language, then one important challenge is to help interested families get the language back in their home again. Family education is vital in this case; teaching families how to bring their native language into the home in such a way as to produce bilingual children would be of great benefit.

In sum, this must be one of the key goals in a language revitalization program in communities that still have native speakers: to get the speakers using their language again.

LANGUAGE CHANGE

One inevitable fact about language is that it is always changing, whether we want it to or not. Even a conservative speaker who thinks he or she is speaking just like the previous generation still has some observable differences from his or her elders. Many studies of English and other languages have been done showing the small variations from generation to generation that result over the centuries in considerable change. Change may also be very great from one generation to the next, such as when massive borrowing from one language takes place. Over half of the vocabulary of English, for example, comes from other languages—one of the main characteristics of modern English that makes it exceedingly different from the Old English of a thousand years ago. There are also major changes over the centuries in pronunciation and grammar.

As for endangered languages, young speakers often exhibit many differences from older speakers, owing in part to their bilingualism and possibly to their dominance in the mainstream language, which means that, because of insufficient exposure, they may have learned the endangered language only partially. The grammar and pronunciation might be simplified in younger speakers, and many domains of vocabulary may be replaced in their speech by English. Frequently the discouragement they feel over criticism or ridicule by older speakers makes them give up on speaking the language altogether.

Varieties of Language

Language revitalization programs may involve many varieties of the language. First of all, a decision must be made as to which variety (or varieties) of a language will be taught in second-language programs. A more conservative version than that spoken by the generations described above who have been so influenced by the dominant language of the society may be preferred. A thriving language usually has many dialectal and even ideolectal variations, but in a classroom it would be deeply confusing to try to teach all these variations, even if the staff knew them. On the other hand, settling on one variety could have the unwanted result of disenfranchising some of the native speakers. If there are speakers who speak differently than each other, it is important for everyone in the community to understand that there is not just one "right" way to speak and that the variations that occur among the speakers are the vestiges of healthy language variation. Often an endangered language has a social past where different villages spoke different dialects, or different clans had different ways of saying things. As in the case of the languages of Native Americans of the United States, whose original geographic and social systems have been destroyed and whose survivors all live on a single reservation, the social underpinning of the language differences has disappeared, but the language differences themselves still survive. As one talented learner of Hupa (a Native American language of northern California), Gordon Bussell, once told me, "Every elder I speak to has a different way of saying some things, and they all tell me the other ways are wrong. I've just learned to try to talk the same way as whomever I'm speaking to." Such compromises may be the best solution in this situation. In any case, disagreements over which variety is the "correct" form of a language are worse than useless—they can destroy morale and short-circuit a revitalization program. Tolerance of variation is essential.

"Dialect merging" is the natural linguistic result of the social merging of previously separate speech communities. We have seen such mergers in American English as people from different dialect areas moved west and came together in new communities. Language revitalization can also result in a dialect merger. A frequent historic event for Native Americans has been for separate communities to be joined together on a single reservation. Often the last speakers of languages come from different dialect backgrounds and have differences in their speech, as illustrated above in the case of Hupa. It will not be long before Gordon Bussell and the other Hupas who have been learning with him will be the ones who carry on the language to the next generation—in fact, they are already running immersion summer programs for Hupa children. Gordon's own speech will be an amalgam of what he has learned from the different native speakers, and the dialect merger will be complete.

Vocabulary Development

In general, an endangered language which is not used as the main language of communication will be behind the times in its ability to express modern culture. Even someone who knows a language fluently might go into a department store and find that there is no name for most of the objects for sale there. Immersion and bilingual education programs that take place in the schools may find that there are no words for many of the topics being taught there; higher math, chemistry, and physics may be subjects never before discussed in that language. This is a problem not just for revitalization, but for any language that is expanding into new domains. The developing countries of Africa, Asia, and the Pacific have taken on this problem and created a whole field, often called "language engineering," to discuss vocabulary development and other issues in language expansion. Of course, even the international languages, such as English, are constantly developing new vocabulary for new concepts.

Thus one of the most controversial (but at the same time one of the most fun) challenges of language revitalization may be vocabulary development. In many situations, the development of new vocabulary is rather incidental and can be done informally or individually. For example, in the California Master-Apprentice Language Learning Program, where a single learner works with a single speaker, as they bring the language into new communication situations, they can decide themselves how to approach new concepts. But for more major programs, the vocabulary needs may be great enough and the program large enough to demand setting up a committee to make these decisions. The Hawaiian immersion schools have a Lexicon Committee that determines new words, which are needed in large numbers as advanced school curricula are developed. They put out a *Dictionary of New Words* in a new edition each year that is sent out to all the classrooms and used religiously by the teachers.

Development of new words can be controversial because the language being developed might express certain values or traditions that could be lost if the language is changed. The revitalization of Hebrew was controversial from the beginning because of its long role as the sacred language of Jewish religion. To some, the expansion of Hebrew into secular life was blasphemy, and the development of vocabulary for mundane and morally impure ideas was shocking. Those Native American languages that survive only in ceremonial contexts have taken on the same sacred connotations that Hebrew did, so their use in non-sacred contexts is similarly debated. Even if the language is not seen as carrying only sacred connotations, it is very often seen as the carrier of traditional culture and values. If the language is used to express mainstream culture and ideas, then perhaps it has lost the traditional values that it was thought to contain. Some members of the community will argue that the endangered language should be used to express traditional ideas and the mainstream language to express mainstream ideas. Some older Hawaiians argue this when they see the *Dictionary of New Words,* with thousands of vocabulary items not present in the language as they know it. It is reported that some Māori native speakers say the same thing of Māori children being educated in immersion programs: "They speak Māori, but they just spout English concepts!"

Another challenge and constant debate in revitalization programs is what the technical principles of vocabulary development ought to be. Should words be borrowed, or should they be created through indigenous processes such as compounding or descriptive phrases? Since endangered languages are fighting for survival against the mainstream language of their country, borrowing from the mainstream language is not normally desired. In fact, the development of new vocabulary by indigenous processes can be an answer to the problem of maintaining traditional values. New terms can be developed that evoke native traditions—for example, the Karuk word for "wristwatch" is a phrase that translates "little sun worn on wrist," thus reminding us that the traditional way to tell time is by the sun (Hinton and Ahlers 1999). On the other hand, it has been argued by the Lexicon Committee for Hawaiian that technical scientific terms are international terms, not specifically English; they are mostly developed out of Latin and Greek roots in any case. So a good deal of the Hawaiian technical vocabulary consists of "Hawaiianized" borrowings, the international technical terms being adapted to the Hawaiian sound system.

New Genres

Developing languages add more than just new vocabulary: they also add whole new genres of speech. A language that had previously not been written will, if used in the schools, develop such genres as readers, essays, poems, or short stories. Oral book reports, plays, and formal debates may enter the language. Outside of school contexts, the language may be used for court proceedings or the writing of tribal or even national constitutions.

Pidginization

I mentioned above that in contracting languages, there may be generations with partial knowledge of the language, that lack some domains of vocabulary, and that use nontraditional grammatical constructions influenced by the dominant language. This can also be true of people learning the endangered language as a second language. Second-language learners are likely to have an accent and at various stages in their learning will put together sentences with all kinds of grammatical errors. Foreign-language teaching theory has developed the term "interlanguage" for the kind of mixed grammar language learners create when they use their new language, which may contain elements of their native language or perhaps just very simplified structures that lack the grammatical elements of either language. This is just as true of learners of endangered languages. One of the main differences between foreign-language learning and the learning of endangered languages is that there may come a time—or it may already be the case—when the endangered language has no native speakers at all, and whatever the learners know and use will be what the language *is* from then on. This kind of language change is akin to pidginization. In intense language-contact situations, often an entire speech community begins using a language that is everyone's imperfectly learned second language (a pidgin), and the children born to that community grow up speaking this very changed form of speech (at which point it is technically a creole). Sometimes such creoles develop into languages of nations. For example, Tok Pisin (from "talk Pidgin"), a creole that arose out of a pidginization of English, is now an official language of Papua New Guinea and has been so thoroughly developed that it is used in all levels of government, education, and the language arts.

It may seem that language revitalization resulting in a greatly changed language is undesirable. Certainly native speakers would think so. However, if a language is close to extinction, many people are willing to settle for what they can get. I am fond of a statement made by Terry Supahan, a language learner and teacher of Karuk (northern California). He says, "I'm interested in communication, not in preservation," meaning that he is willing to make all kinds of errors so long as he can just get his point across. He wants to use the language and hear it used by others, even if it is butchered. He sees perfectionism as a bar to language use, a deterrent to revitalization. In a similar vein, Cody Pata, a Nomlaki language learner (central California), has no native speakers to work with at all and is depending on linguistic documentation to learn his language. In a recent workshop, he wrote out and recited a "Pidgin Nomlaki" prayer (his term), consciously using English wherever he did not know the Nomlaki word or structure. His goal is to insert more and more Nomlaki as he learns more, but in the meantime he would rather use "Pidgin Nomlaki" than simply not be able to communicate in Nomlaki at all.

SOME FINAL POINTS

Successful language revitalization programs have a number of key characteristics, among them *persistence, sustainability,* and *honesty with oneself.*

Persistence means not taking no for an answer. Steven Greymorning (see Chapter 23 on Arapaho) wanted to make an Arapaho version of Disney's movie *Bambi*, but Disney Studios repeatedly refused until Greymorning finally won them over. Hawaiians were told they could not have immersion schools because it was illegal to educate children in any language but English, so the Hawaiians lobbied until they got the law changed. Communities are told over and over again that native speakers cannot teach the language in the schools because they do not have the credentials; the persistent communities have usually found a way to get around these rules. Often the greatest resistance to language revitalization comes from within the community itself, where factionalism, jealousy, negative attitudes toward the endangered language, and a propensity to constant criticism are frequently a threat to progress of any effort. As the language learner and educator Terry Supahan says, "You have to develop a thick skin." Going on with the program in the face of barriers and negativity is an essential prerequisite to its success.

Sustainability is the setting up of a program so that it can keep on going. It is common for language revitalization efforts to make a small contribution and then run out of energy or money and disappear. Burnout of key personnel is an ever-present danger. It is important for the program's prime movers to discover ways to keep it growing, keep new people coming in, and make it not completely dependent on its founders' continued involvement. The program needs to evolve to meet new conditions. If a second-language learning program is successful in getting people to know the language, what can be done to create conditions in which they can continue to actually *use* the language? Can the learners be trained to become teachers? Can the program expand to other communities? How can it continue to be funded? All these are questions that a program's personnel must ask themselves constantly.

But it must also be pointed out that if a program does end, due to loss of funding, personnel, or energy, it has not by any means been a wasted effort. It has surely been a positive experience for all involved and has left a legacy that can be used in future revitalization efforts.

Honesty is crucial, because we want so badly for our efforts to succeed that it is not always easy to stand back and see if what we are doing is really working. It is important to look critically at the program and see what it is actually accomplishing and what problems it has. Are the learners really learning the language as well as they could? Are the materials that are being developed really useful? How can the program improve? Should some directions be abandoned? Should new directions be taken? What is the next goal? Good ongoing programs, no matter how successful they are, never stop asking these questions.

Notes

1. We asked the educational linguist Brian Bielenberg to assist us with the literature on the cognitive advantages to bilingualism. He summarized it so well that I would like to quote him at length here:

> A good list of the early work on the benefits of bilingualism is given in Hamers and Blanc 2000. A lot of the findings discuss how bilinguals are able to analyze language as an abstract system earlier than monolinguals. Others claim that bilingualism promotes creative thinking. For studies which attempt to demonstrate a stronger link between bilingualism and cognitive abilities, one must turn to the work of psychologists like Ellen Bialystok. Bialystok's main claim is that bilinguals have greater metalinguistic skills that allow them to talk about or reflect on language. Such skills, she argues, are useful for learning how to read and to use more academic oral language in schools (Bialystock 1991).
>
> Another good source of review on this topic is Diaz and Klinger 1991. They present a series of studies that demonstrate that children's bilingualism is positively related to concept formation, classification, creativity, analogical reasoning, and visual-spatial skills. Following their presentation of studies showing cognitive advantages, Diaz and Klinger propose a model to explain the cognitive advantages of bilingualism. The studies they cite which focus on cognitive abilities include Hakuta and Diaz 1985, Diaz 1985, and Diaz and Padilla 1985. These studies make use of a number of widely accepted nonverbal tests of cognitive ability such as the Raven Progressive Matrices. The authors also cite Bialystok and others whose work has demonstrated increased metalinguistic knowledge. The positive effects of bilingualism on metalinguistic abilities include early word-referent distinction, sensitivity to language structure and detail, detection of ambiguities, syntactic orientation in sentence processing, and control of language processing.
>
> Overall, I think that these studies, combined with the results of late-exit bilingual programs, make a convincing argument for verifiable cognitive advantages of bilingualism. I certainly would not be raising my son bilingually if I did not believe them.

References

Bialystok, Ellen. 1991. Metalinguistic dimensions of bilingual language proficiency. In *Language processing in bilingual children*, ed. Ellen Bialystok. Cambridge: Cambridge University Press.

Diaz, R. M. 1985. Bilingual cognitive development: Addressing three gaps in current research. *Child Development* 56: 1376–1388.

Diaz, R. M., and Cynthia Klinger. 1991. Towards an explanatory model of the interaction between bilingualism and cognitive development. In *Language processing in bilingual children*, ed. Ellen Bialystok. Cambridge: Cambridge University Press.

Diaz, R. M., and K. A. Padilla. 1985. The self-regulatory speech of bilingual pre-schoolers. Paper presented at the April meeting of the Society for Research in Child Development, Toronto.

Dopke, Suzanne. 1992. *One parent, one language: An interactional approach.* Amsterdam: John Benjamins.

Fishman, Joshua A. 1991. *Reversing language shift: Theoretical and empirical foundations of assistance to threatened languages.* Multilingual Matters.

Grenoble, Lenore A., and Lindsay J. Whaley. 1998. *Endangered languages: Language loss and community response.* Cambridge: Cambridge University Press.

Hakuta, K., and R. M. Diaz. 1985. The relationship between degree of bilingualism and cognitive ability: A critical discussion and some new longitudinal data. In *Children's language*, vol. 5, ed. K. E. Nelson. Hillsdale, NJ: Erlbaum.

Hale, Kenneth, Colette Craig, Nora England, LaVerne Jeanne, Michael Krauss, Lucille Watahomigie, and Akira Yamamoto. 1992. Endangered languages. *Language* 68: 1–42.

Hamers, Josiane F., and Michel H. A. Blanc. 2000. *Bilinguality and bilingualism*. 2d ed. Cambridge and New York: Cambridge University Press.

Hinton, Leanne. 1999. Teaching endangered languages. In *Concise encyclopedia of educational linguistics*, ed. B. Spolsky. Oxford: Elsevier Science.

———. 2000. Trading tongues: Loss of heritage languages in the United States. *English Today*.

———. In press. Involuntary language loss among immigrants: Asian-American linguistic autobiographies. In *Proceedings of the 1999 Georgetown University Round Table in Language and Linguistics.*

———, and Jocelyn Ahlers. 1999. The issue of "authenticity" in California language restoration. *Anthropology and Education Quarterly* 30, no. 1 (March), 56–67.

Krauss, Michael. 1992. The world's languages in crisis. In Hale et al.

Ladefoged, Peter. 1992. Another view of endangered languages. *Language* 68: 809–11.

Nettle, Daniel, and Suzanne Romaine. 2000. *Vanishing voices: The extinction of the world's languages and the global biodiversity crisis.* Oxford: Oxford University Press.

Diversity in Local Language Maintenance and Restoration: A Reason for Optimism

ANNA ASH

School of Languages
Cultures & Linguistics
University of New England
Armidale, Australia

JESSIE LITTLE DOE FERMINO

Department of Linguistics
and Philosophy
Massachusetts Institute of Technology
Cambridge, Massachusetts

KEN HALE

Department of Linguistics
and Philosophy
Massachusetts Institute of Technology
Cambridge, Massachusetts

Before explaining our optimism, we should perhaps mention the factors which have led many to be pessimistic about the possibility of local and minority language maintenance. As Michael Krauss has pointed out repeatedly, we stand to lose half of the world's 6000 languages during the 21st century, and at the end of that century, most of the remaining languages will be endangered, to be lost in the subsequent century (Krauss 1992).

This is not the only time in history when massive loss of language has occurred. From studies of linguistic diversity in modern hunting and gathering societies, it is reasonable to suppose that between 100,000 and 10,000 years ago, the inhabitable world came to be fully occupied by small, linguistically distinct communities speaking well over 15,000 languages. The modern distribution of language families is strongly at odds with this picture, however. In the modern period, large regions are now occupied by language families whose time-depth is as little as 5000 years or less. This means that hundreds, even thousands, of languages were replaced in the course of the expansion of a few languages which subsequently differentiated to form the established modern families, including Indo-European, Elamo-Dravidian, Afro-Asiatic, Austronesian, Sino-Tibetan, Uto-Aztecan, Chibchan, and Oto-Manguean, among others. Archaeologists have provided much evidence that this pattern of replacement is due primarily to the development and expansion of agricultural societies, fueling the process of "farming dispersal," in the terminology of Colin Renfrew (1994).

The factors at work in our own waning half millennium are of a different and more drastic sort. Whereas the early expansion of agricultural and pastoralist societies created large regions occupied by a single linguistic family, those same regions subsequently became linguistically diverse through the natural processes of language differentiation, giving rise to large, internally diverse families. That is not the case in the modern period, the period spanning the last 500 years. With certain exceptions, the situation now is that linguistic diversity is simply being lost without languages being replaced. The forces at work in this period belong, we suppose, to the process Renfrew terms "elite dominance," or, more bluntly, "military, political, and economic dominance." For us now, these forces are inherent in the patterns of political and economic domination which have their origins in the European invasion and exploitation of the western and southern hemispheres. While we justly bemoan the loss of linguistic diversity over the last 500 years, we must realize that the situation of local languages is no less ominous now than at any other point in history. It is in fact more desperate now than before. We do not exist in a condition of economic justice in which people who choose to do so can speak a local language and pass it on to their children entirely without regard for any economic consequences. To be sure, individuals and communities do accomplish this, but it is typically at a cost. The pressure to use the dominant language, and even to abandon one's own local language, is quite generally overwhelming and virtually irresistible. Many reports of language shift attest to this (cf. Ladefoged 1992). Language shift is often perceived as the only rational choice for the economic well-being of oneself and one's family.

How can there be reason for optimism about such a situation?

19

There is reason for optimism because local language communities all over the world are taking it upon themselves to act on behalf of their imperiled linguistic traditions in full understanding of, and in spite of, the realistic perception that the cards are stacked against them. There is, in effect, an international movement in which local communities work in *defiance* of the forces pitted against their embattled languages. It has something of the character of a modern miracle, if you think about it—while they share the goal of promoting a local language, these groups are essentially independent of one another, coming together sometimes to compare notes, but operating in effective separation.

Two factors in our optimism are the very existence of the movement itself and what is sometimes decried as a flaw in the movement: the feature of independence, the fact that local language projects operate separately from one another. But this is a strength, in fact, a true reason for optimism. It is the natural consequence of the fact that local conditions are very particular and, in the final analysis, unique. Programs in support of local languages necessarily address local conditions. The sharing of materials and ideas among language projects and the use of consultants in relevant fields (e.g., linguistics, education, and computers) are good and often absolutely necessary, of course, but the structure of a local language program is determined by local considerations. We have seen no exceptions to this, neither in places we have worked—Australia, Central America, and North America—nor in places we have visited or read about, including Europe, China, Northern Ireland, North Africa, and Polynesia. Realism is no less essential in this regard than in relation to the challenges confronting the movement as a whole.

To emphasize this point, we will briefly describe four cases of local language support projects. They represent a tiny sample of the diversity of conditions and responses which characterize the local language maintenance movement. Despite differences among them, they have one feature in common: they do not attempt to tackle the grand problem of global language loss. Rather, they function to secure a position of dignity for their local languages in terms of local exigencies. They also agree in recognizing that knowledge of a local language is in no way incompatible with full mastery of a dominant national or regional language. The four cases are we examine are Lardil of Mornington Island, North Queensland, Australia; Tuahka (Sumu) of Eastern Nicaragua; Wampanoag (Massachusett) of southern New England, United States; and Irish in Belfast, Northern Ireland. They will be discussed in relation to five factors: (1) the present condition of the language; (2) projects initiated: their history, results, and prospects; (3) resources available to the community; (4) sociopolitical and economic factors bearing on the effectiveness of the projects; and (5) decisions and agreements which required discussion in the community. We begin with Lardil of North Queensland.

THE LARDIL LANGUAGE PROJECT

Lardil is the traditional language of the Lardil people of Mornington Island, which is the largest island of the Wellesley group in the southern Gulf of Carpentaria (see Map 2.1). It is roughly 65 kilometers long and varies in width from 10 to 26 kilometers. Other Aboriginal peoples of this area that speak languages closely related to Lardil are the Yangkaal from Forsyth and Denham Islands and the Kayardild from Bentinck and Sweers Islands. Since around the 1940s, most of these people have been based on Mornington Island, together with some Yukulda people (also known as Kangkarlida) from nearby areas of mainland Australia.[1] The total population of Mornington Island is around 1000 Aboriginal and 100 non-Aboriginal people.

Yangkaal, Kayardild, and Yukulta are technically dialects of a single language, while the closely related Lardil is clearly a separate language within the small family to which the group as a whole belongs.[2] The family is called Tangkic, after the shared term *tangka* 'person', following a common practice in language-group nomenclature. It was first classified as belonging to the large Pama-Nyungan superfamily, or phylum, which predominates in Australia. On the face of it, Tangkic belongs typologically to that group, being a suffixing and head-marking language with rather standard Pama-Nyungan features. But evidence has since been brought forward in favor of the view that it is a separate family belonging instead to the diverse non-Pama-Nyungan collection of language families extending from the Wellesley Island area westward across northern Australia to the northwest coast in the state of Western Australia (Evans 1995, 30–39). Tangkic is therefore twice distinguished: it is the easternmost non-Pama-Nyungan family, and it is a non-Pama-Nyungan family boasting primarily Pama-Nyungan typological characteristics.

The Present Condition of the Language

No children are now learning Lardil as their first language. This has certainly been the case since the 1950s (and may have been true even earlier) and is a result of assimilationist policies and practices affecting Mornington Island, as well as most of Aboriginal Australia, throughout most of Australian history. At the present time, English is effectively the language of the island. Hence, this situation may be described as one calling for language revitalization—adults and children alike need to learn more Lardil if the language is to be maintained.

Most people who speak Lardil are in their 50s or older and divide into two groups. The first is a small group (6 or 7) of people 70 years old or older who speak "Old Lardil," with the full Wellesley Island case and concord systems and the original Lardil system of truncation and augmenta-

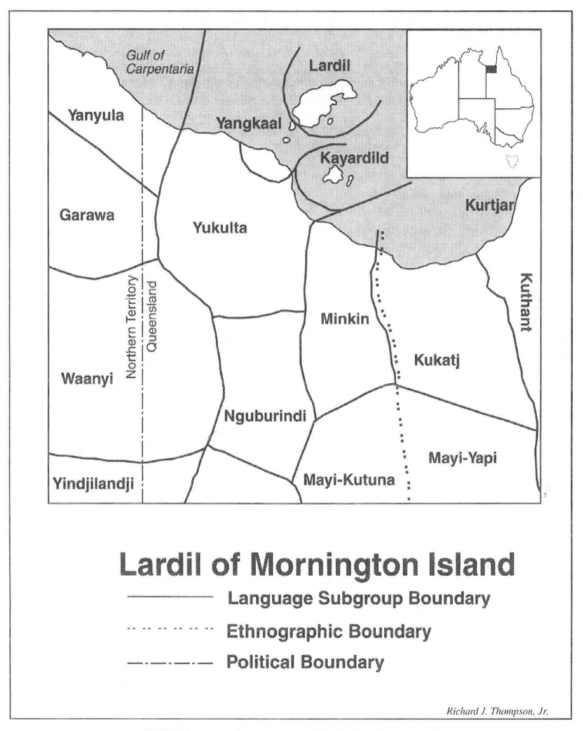

Lardil of Mornington Island

———————— **Language Subgroup Boundary**

– · – · – · – · **Ethnographic Boundary**

– · — · — · — **Political Boundary**

Richard J. Thompson, Jr.

MAP 2.1   Lardil of Mornington Island, North Queensland, Australia

tion in nominal and verbal phonology. These few are the only people who regularly communicate fully in the Lardil language, and this is not really in everyday contexts, but rather on special occasions like dance festivals, church ceremonies, and funerals. The second group consists of perhaps

30 people in their 50s and 60s who speak "New Lardil," characterized by absence of the original case and concord systems and adoption of a regularized nominal and verbal morphology.

While Lardil people, speakers and nonspeakers alike,

generally have an extensive Lardil vocabulary covering the names for animals, fish, plants, material culture such as tools, and kin terms, they communicate now primarily in a local variety of Aboriginal English which shows some influence from Northern Territory Kriol and includes the use of Lardil expressions that people know. In addition, some people are also speakers of standard Australian English and utilize this form in such contexts as school, council office, meetings, and dealings with non-Aboriginal people. The rest of the community (about 400 people) speaks English and has in addition some knowledge of Lardil kinship terms, which are regularly used in Mornington Island English.

Projects: History, Results, and Prospects

A renaissance of Lardil culture occurred in the mid-1950s and progressed through the next two decades, and some steps were taken then to document the Lardil language. However, no formal language maintenance program was undertaken until 1981. The first short-lived project, the preparation and distribution of a dictionary, was the idea of an outsider and had some support from members of the community. The dictionary was made, but the project foundered, and the dictionary languished uncopied and undistributed for 15 years. In the mid-1990s Lardil's situation was seen as very serious, and the community itself undertook to revive the dictionary project and to initiate the development of materials to teach Lardil to adults as well as schoolchildren.

In 1995, the Language Projects Steering Committee of Mornington Island, known officially as Ngakulmungan Kangka Leman ("our language") was established. It is made up of Lardil language experts and representatives from a number of local organizations, including *Muyinda* (male elders); *Yuenmanda* (female elders); *Woomera* (dancers); the Mornington Shire Council; and the School Language Program. The central aim of Ngakulmungan Kangka Leman is to ensure that language revitalization activities reflect the needs and wishes of the Mornington Island community.

Anna Ash was employed in 1996 by the Mornington Shire Council and Mornington Island State School to coordinate the publication of the *Lardil Dictionary*. During this time there were regular meetings with Ngakulmungan Kangka Leman, who were involved in many decisions having to do with the dictionary, including the choice of orthography, copyright, size, cost, print size, overall layout, choice of cover illustration, and whether to include information about Damin, a sacred language based on Lardil. In July of 1996 four other linguists (Ken Hale, David Nash, Norvin Richards, and Jane Simpson) met on Mornington Island for the final checking of the dictionary, which was based on Hale's draft from 1981. The *Lardil Dictionary* was published in 1997 and is available from the Mornington Shire Council.

Ngakulmungan Kangka Leman discussed the question of

what else could be done toward the revitalization of Lardil. Committee members recognized that while the school had a language program, there were few resources supporting language learners in the general community. A decision was made to apply for funding from the Australian Institute for Aboriginal and Torres Strait Islander Studies (AIATSIS) to produce a learner's guide to Lardil, consisting of a booklet and audiotapes. Community discussion about the proposed learner's guide emphasized the importance of the audio component:

> Young people can listen to the person talking, pronouncing the words properly. But when you read it in the dictionary, some learners might be a little bit puzzled up, but when they listen to it on tape, they can catch on properly. . . . They need the tape and the book as well. (Kenneth and Juliana Jacob)

The learner's guide was produced and given the title *Merri Lardil Kangka Leman* (Listen to the Lardil Language).

In designing the learner's guide, a domain approach was adopted—that is to say, it was organized around themes or areas of life relevant to the Lardil people. The first draft contained an introduction on how to use the guide and six lessons: the sounds of Lardil, useful expressions, people, family, the islands, and the sea. The proposed themes reflected the importance of the land-sea dichotomy in Lardil life and cultural beliefs. The language committee agreed with the proposed thematic breakdown and emphasized that stories and conversations should be included.

The issue of Old and New Lardil, as described in the dictionary, was discussed. People agreed that we should teach New Lardil, as that is the language more commonly used in the community. However, some old forms were recorded. For example, the base forms of monosyllabic verbs rather than the full forms were sometimes used in the negative imperative—Old Lardil *dine* rather than New Lardil *dithane* 'don't sit'. In other areas the learner's guide used New Lardil forms, which tend to be simplified versions of Old Lardil. For example, in Old Lardil there is an accusative marker and relatively free word order. Today the accusative ending is not always used, but a regular (subject-verb-object) word order conveys who is doing what. In areas such as this, it is possible that Lardil has been influenced by English grammatical principles.

The audiotape was recorded with four principal Lardil-speaking consultants. It covered vocabulary lists, sentences illustrating points of grammar, some conversations, stories, and useful expressions. Some rehearsal was needed to ensure that the conversations utilized relatively simple grammar. There was successful elicitation of the plain form of the verb, the perfective pre-verb, and four out of nine types of verbal inflection: the imperative, negative imperative, future, and negative future forms. Other inflections were either not used or recognized or were used inconsistently; for example, rather than the Old Lardil sequential imperative, two imperatives were used. With nominal inflections, the genitive and the origin suffix were consistently used, but it was not possible to fully elicit the locative, allative, ablative, and instrumental. More research is needed, but the tendency seems to be to use separate words—for example, instead of the locative ending people used a separate word such as *wirde* 'inside'. Further research is required in order to draw firm conclusions about the true nature of New Lardil.

Ash, who had been given a fellowship in the linguistics department at the University of New England (Armidale) for the duration of the project, returned there in order to utilize a sound laboratory. Ten hours of field tapes were edited down to about two hours, using Sound Edit Pro on a Macintosh computer. Copies of the tapes were made. In addition, the draft booklet was extensively revised to match the audio version, and comments on the grammar were added. On her return to Mornington, Ash returned copies of the guide to the community for checking. First, everything was checked with the main consultants, and after some minor changes to the booklet, 50 copies were produced. These were quickly snapped up, so another 40 were made and distributed. Copies were given to all local organizations, including the school, council, church, hospital, Aboriginal Health Unit, men's and women's groups, local radio station, youth center, outstations, and representatives from all Lardil family groups. In 1999, the resident linguist did another print run.

The learner's guide is structured as follows. Generally the audio component consists of graded lessons which begin with a short conversation or story, followed by a selection of vocabulary items and example sentences for practice, each illustrating a new point of grammar. The first lesson describes the sounds used in the Lardil language; these are compared to English sounds, and several example words using the sounds are given. The second lesson provides some "everyday words" or useful expressions. Some basic vocabulary is introduced, including some terms for the pronominal system, kin relations, flora and fauna, and other appropriate cultural knowledge, like terms for tools and hunting techniques. Finally, people hear two stories from Hale's recordings from the 1960s; while these are in Old Lardil and therefore may not be fully comprehensible to all learners, they provide valuable culturally rich examples of Lardil speech and are enjoyed by many, particularly more fluent speakers. For the vocabulary, sentences, and useful expressions, people hear the English version first and then the Lardil translation, working on the principle of going from the known to the less known. However, the conversations and short stories are heard in their entirety, first in Lardil, then in English. While not all grammatical constructions used in the stories and dialogues are fully explained in the commentary, it was considered important that learners be exposed to more-naturally occurring speech. It is evident that people are sharing the tapes among their extended families; also, children have commented on the guide's content to the school linguist.

In addition to the items mentioned above, the booklet also contains some commentary on grammatical points such as verbal inflections, using lots of examples and a minimum of technical vocabulary. This was not included on the tape, as it was thought it might be distracting. The booklet also has drawings by community members, including children, which stimulates further interest in the learner's guide.

Resources Available to the Community

Human and material resources are essential to any language maintenance program, of course. In the Lardil case, speakers of the language, including the current mayor of Mornington, are eager to have their knowledge used in the service of the program. In the realm of material resources, linguistic documentation of Old Lardil from the 1960s forms the initial basis for the dictionary and companion sketch-grammar. And in the course of the actual preparation of the dictionary, New Lardil usage was documented (and dated) to the extent possible. In addition, there is a wealth of material from an anthropologist who has worked on Mornington for 30 years. Those materials will greatly enrich the body of Old Lardil, facilitating the production of new learning materials. While New Lardil will prevail in the development of learning materials, new data from Old Lardil will contribute to the program, since New Lardil forms are largely predicated on those of Old Lardil.

A number of community organizations contribute in various ways to Lardil language maintenance. A major role is played by the Woomera Aboriginal Corporation, which organizes tours throughout Australia and overseas involving the performance of Lardil dance and song and the organization of cultural workshops; elders are also working with Woomera and the linguist Cassy Nancarrow to compile an extensive song register and book of songs. Within the community, Woomera coordinates dance festivals, children's dance classes, and "culture camps." The camps are held out bush (i.e., outside Gununa, the town in which most Mornington Islanders live), and they encourage intergenerational language use in the course of activities such as hunting, craft making, singing, dancing, and listening to recordings of Lardil songs and stories. Families visit their traditional country (outstations) whenever possible, and this activity has a great potential to contribute to the learning and use of Lardil. The Muyinda Corporation of male elders manages the production and sale of artifacts, crafts, and paintings, and it facilitates training sessions where skills are passed on from elders to young people. The Lardil language with English translations is used in marketing these items, appearing in catalogs and information sheets which accompany the artifacts and paintings. The Aboriginal Health Unit has produced posters about health issues in Lardil and English. Around town, the Lardil language is used in street signs and signs for various institutions such as shops, the hospital, and the canteen. Lardil is used occasionally in notices promoting events and in the local newsletter.

In 1977 Mornington Island State School hired the linguist Cassy Nancarrow to coordinate their language program. Lardil, as the language indigenous to the island, has been taught at various times in the preschool, primary school, and high school. It is hoped that later other languages represented in the local population will be taught. The resident linguist has also initiated language lessons in the community. The aim is to give all children the opportunity to learn the local language and to participate in cultural events that encourage its use. Teaching the program at the school encourages a positive attitude toward local languages and cultures, and children's self-esteem is increased when their previous language knowledge is acknowledged and supported (Nancarrow 1997, 5).

Several Lardil speakers come into the school to work with the linguist in providing weekly lessons. Children are taken out on bush trips to "story places" (significant sites) to learn more about language and culture in the appropriate country; some overnight camping trips have provided good opportunities for the children to hear Lardil spoken. Also, indigenous language materials are produced locally which can be accessed by the whole community, such as storybooks, games, puzzles, worksheets, posters, and video- and audiotapes which utilize the Lardil language. Elders have been employed using funds from the Aboriginal and Torres Strait Islander Languages Initiative Program, run by the Aboriginal and Torres Strait Islander Commission. At this stage, funding restrictions permit the program to operate only for about half of the school year.

Community meetings that have to do with cultural matters may also stimulate the use of Lardil; a discussion about traditional clan boundaries and the launch of the Lardil dictionary were two occasions on which Lardil was used by the older people present. The process of recording Lardil for the learner's guide led to further use of the language. At night we would sit around the fire recording a description in Lardil of the day's hunting. Following this the speaker would often start talking to the children in Lardil, telling them to bring things such as the billy, meat, tea, or more firewood. The young people responded to his requests, and with some encouragement from his wife, they repeated words and sentences and answered questions about their language names until someone made a mistake, which would be met with general laughter.

It is worth asking why it took 30 years to produce the first published Lardil language material for use by the Lardil people. We think that the main factor in its completion was impetus from the community itself. The dictionary project, for example, languished because it was not really a community project until 1995. As Mithun (1994) remarked in connection with the successful Mohawk language maintenance

project, "[I]f the community has the idea itself, there are successes." The Lardil School Program and the learner's guide are entirely community projects, building on what already exists in the community.

Sociopolitical and Economic Factors

Mornington Island is a shire of the state of Queensland. This means that a certain amount of funding is available for local programs, including the compilation and production of materials, such as the dictionary. But this status also leads to tensions. The shire has a council, which in the case of Mornington is Aboriginal in composition but functions on the advice of a deputy clerk from outside the community. Many see this as a symbol of imperialism and the usurpation of Aboriginal authority, and since the council controlled the funding, the language project was naturally affected. As mentioned earlier, an alternative group, entirely Aboriginal, was established under the name Ngakulmungan Kangka Leman (the steering committee). This group had the great advantage that it was invested with authority by the Aboriginal community of Mornington Island. Its views had to be taken seriously, driving home the point that decisions having to do with "things Aboriginal," as its chairperson forcefully framed it, could be taken only by an Aboriginal body, not by one which functions as an arm of the state of Queensland. Decisions having to do with the Lardil language, therefore, were decisions to be made by the steering committee, an Aboriginal body open to all Lardil people.

Decisions and Agreements

Once an agreement to move forward with a language project had been made, decisions which had to be taken in the Lardil case included, among others, the problem of a standard orthography. It had been decided back in 1981 to use /b/ and /d/ rather than /p/ and /t/ for the bilabial and apical stops. The use of /th/ for the interdental stop (alternating with fricative) and /ng/ for the velar nasal were accepted as far back as 1960. But there was enormous disagreement about the velar stop. Some wanted /g/ and some wanted /k/. The latter had been chosen in 1981 to reserve the use of orthographic /g/ for the velar nasal digraph /ng/. And the original dictionary of 1981 was written that way. To use /g/ for the velar nasal would require extensive revision, even in the electronic version. It was not a simple matter of substitutions; phonological distinctions were at issue. When a dispute arose about this, great groans came up from the people charged with preparing the final computerized version. But the issue was going to be decided by the steering committee; outsiders could present arguments, but the decision would be the committee's. The meeting about this was long and tense, because people simply had preferences: "It sounds like 'g' so why write 'k'?"; "I'm used to reading 'k,' and I don't want to change." A respected teacher finally broke the deadlock, mercifully in favor of /k/, by stating her own preference and that of several students who had been working with her using the 1981 version of the dictionary.

Another decision that had to be made was whether Damin, the special initiates' vocabulary, should be included in the published dictionary. Damin is a lexicon based on abstract semantic principles, once used publicly but only by advanced initiates, men of *warama* status. It is a wondrous product of human intellectual toil and the jewel in the crown of the Lardil people. It was included in the unpublished 1981 dictionary, but the committee decided in 1996 that it should be left out of the published version. They felt that its publication would detract from its special position in Lardil culture, its status as something to which a person should *earn* access.

An especially problematic issue was the matter of copyright. Who would hold the copyright to the dictionary—the shire council, or the steering committee? This question, which strikes at the core of the issue of Aboriginal authority, could have delayed publication indefinitely. After discussion, however, it became very clear to all that the steering committee, though unfunded and unincorporated, had the proper authority and should hold the copyright. The committee remains unincorporated. Funding awarded to it for the learner's guide was administered by the council.

Although each local language situation is unique, there are commonalities, general rubrics which all communities must deal with. These include the five just enumerated for the Lardil project. The details of the Lardil case are not replicated in any other community, and the Lardil language program will necessarily be worked out in a manner which deals appropriately with the specifics of the Lardil situation. In broad outline, however, the factors which impinge on Lardil also impinge on other languages of the category termed "local" here (we use this term, instead of "minority," in deference to the sentiments of many people who object to the latter designation in reference to languages which are indigenous to a region). The system of five "factors," though incomplete, can function as a framework for discussion of local language situations generally and for comparison among them. We turn now to the situation of the Sumu languages of Eastern Nicaragua, giving special attention to the Tuahka dialect of Mayangna (Northern Sumu).

TUAHKA (SUMU)

"Sumu" is the name applied to a group of closely related languages belonging to the Misumalpan family. Sumu is distantly, but obviously, related to Miskitu, the indigenous *lingua franca* of a large region in eastern Nicaragua and Honduras (see Map 2.2). There are two extant Sumu languages, Mayangna (Northern Sumu) and Ulwa (Southern Sumu). Mayangna has at least two "variants," Panamahka and Tu-

ahka. Both Ulwa and the Tuahka dialect of Mayangna were neglected in the early years of the Sandinista government of the 1980s, when the Autonomy Project began to plan and implement bilingual education programs. In both cases, this was because the term "Sumu" was believed to adequately embrace those speech communities as well as the much larger Panamahka community, for which a bilingual education program was developed. The story of Ulwa has been told in a number of places, but that of Tuahka is still unfolding. We will confine our remarks to that group.

The Present Condition of the Language

The situation of Tuahka, as spoken by some 300 residents of the town of Wasakin in the RAAN (Región Autónoma Atlántico Norte [North Atlantic Autonomous Region]) of Nicaragua, differs diametrically from that of Lardil described above. While Lardil must be classed as moribund, having no young speakers (cf. Krauss 1992), Tuahka would seem to be in excellent condition, judging by its speaker population, which includes the children of Wasakin and all individuals in that town who consider themselves to be Tuahka. The problem is the position of Tuahka among the languages of the region where it is spoken: it is at the bottom of a hierarchy containing not one but two other languages and a dialect.

Spanish
|
Miskitu
|
Panamahka
|
Tuahka

This subordinate position is generally associated with unidirectional bi- or multilingualism, a phenomenon commonly observed in socioeconomic structures of the type prevailing in the RAAN. Norwood (1993) has discussed this arrangement from the point of view of Mayangna generally. Mayangna speakers are generally multilingual, speaking Mayangna, Miskitu, and Spanish. In the case of Tuahka, its speakers are bidialectal as well. While multilingualism, in the abstract, is certainly a good thing, it presents a certain challenge in the unidirectional case, that is, the case in which the number of languages a person knows depends upon the person's position in the hierarchy. If one is at the top, one is typically monolingual; people at the next level down are bilingual, and so on. The language which is lowest in the hierarchy is, of course, highly vulnerable in relation to the forces which encourage language shift. In part, this is because language shift is virtually effortless, owing to the effects of multilingualism, and given in addition the usual socioeconomic pressures, the effort to maintain a language or dialect like Tuahka requires a special commitment, to say the

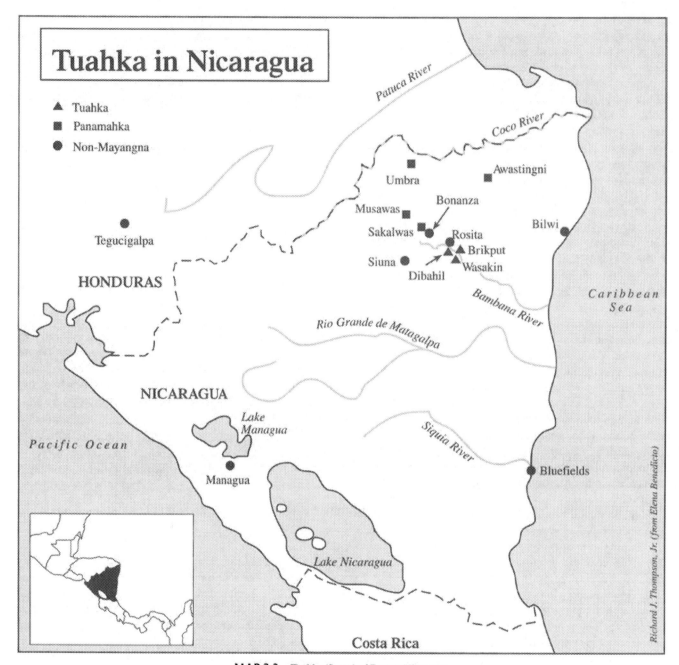

MAP 2.2   Tuahka (Sumu) of Eastern Nicaragua

least. Precisely this situation brought about the imperilment of the related Sumu language Ulwa, when, in 1950, a lumber business imported Miskitu-speaking workers to Karawala. The switch to Miskitu as the principal language of the town was easy, because of bilingualism. But it was largely responsible for the present circumstance in which children are no longer learning Ulwa, and for the sense of urgency expressed by Ulwa speakers involved in the effort to revitalize it. Thus, while Tuahka must rank on Michael Krauss's scale as "safe" in terms of its speaker population, it is perhaps no

less endangered than Lardil, a language which boasts only middle-aged and elderly speakers.

Projects: History, Results, and Prospects

In the mid-1980s, bilingual education programs were instituted for the indigenous languages of the Atlantic Coast, first for Miskitu and then for Sumu. These programs were part of the Autonomy Project being developed by the authorities on the Atlantic coast and the Sandinista government. The Sumu Bilingual-Intercultural Education Program (PEBI-Sumu, now called PEBI-Mayangna) understandably picked the majority dialect, Panamahka, as the form of Sumu to be used for instruction and for the preparation of readers and other school texts, which now exist for the first through fourth grades. Since there was to be but one Sumu bilingual education program, this left Southern Sumu (Ulwa), a distinct but closely related language, entirely out of the picture; the children of Karawala would be served by the Miskitu program. More to the point for this discussion, Panamahka's sister dialect, Tuahka, was left with no formal standing in the program. This made sense at the beginning, when bilingual education was being designed to serve as many children as possible within the severe economic constraints affecting all aspects of life and government during the war years. Not only would two Sumu (i.e., Mayangna) programs have been insupportable in terms of both economics and manpower, the necessary room to "experiment and find one's way" in a new and unfamiliar enterprise would have been excessively crowded by the inevitable friction and competition between two partially distinct, partially interwoven, experimental undertakings. It seemed a much better idea to proceed with Panamahka, which would serve a majority of students and provide the linguistic uniformity that would simplify the process of developing the bilingual program in its initial years. Still the issue of Tuahka remained unresolved. It has been a bone of contention since the mid-1980s, when bilingual education was initiated on the coast.

In the course of a language workshop in 1994, one of many held in support of the bilingual education programs on the Atlantic Coast, a letter was passed to one of the linguistics instructors asking why Panamahka received all the attention. Could not something be done about Tuahka? The source of the letter was an influential teacher from the Tuahka town of Wasakin; she was also an important member of PEBI-Mayangna. The two linguists involved in the workshop had a meeting with this teacher and concluded together with her that it was important to begin to do something in relation to Tuahka. It was agreed that at the beginning of 1995 a research project would be undertaken in which three Tuahka speakers and three linguists would do (1) a preliminary survey of the grammar, using as a guide Susan Norwood's 1987 grammar of Panamahka (now published as Norwood 1997) together with unpublished materials on Ulwa grammar, and (2) a preliminary study of the lexicon, using the model of the Panamahka and Ulwa dictionaries (McLean-Cornelio 1996; CODIUL/UYUTMUBAL 1989). This project would also train the three Tuahka speakers in the construction of dictionary entries, with the understanding that a dictionary would be the first production. The project was carried out in Rosita, the headquarters of PEBI-Mayangna, in January 1995. At that time a preliminary study of Tuahka verb morphology was made and materials for a demonstration "dictionary" were obtained. A small amount of funding

was left to help support further work on the dictionary, and plans were made for additional Tuahka language workshops in 1996 and 1997. The first of these focused on further work on the grammar and the dictionary, and the second focused on the development of technical vocabulary in Tuahka.

Resources Available to the Community

The resources available to the Tuahka community consist not only in the strong speaker population, including people of all living generations, but also in the existence within that population of teachers and *técnicos* (support staff) who have experience working in the Mayangna Bilingual-Intercultural Education Program, headquartered in Rosita, near Wasakin. Three people in this category are involved in the Tuahka language project.

The existence of a grammar and small dictionary of Panamahka (Norwood 1997; McLean-Cornelio 1996) must be considered a resource available to the Tuahka project, inasmuch as these works provide the essential outlines for eventual comparable works on the Tuahka dialect. In addition, there are a large number of school texts in Panamahka; these are also a resource for Tuahka, since the lessons learned in their planning do not need to be relearned, particularly in view of the fact that Tuahka as well as Panamahka speakers were involved in the preparation of the Panamahka texts. Tuahka differs sufficiently from Panamahka to warrant special investigation of its grammar and lexicon.

In addition to the Panamahka materials just mentioned, there now exists a demonstration "dictionary" of Tuahka, short in terms of number of entries but more ample in terms of material included in each, together with documentation of the basic elements of verbal and nominal morphology.

Sociopolitical and Economic Factors

The Mayangna peoples live predominantly in the interior of the RAAN. Both Panamahka and Tuahka have been subordinate to the Miskitu for more than three centuries; they owe their isolation to the expansion of the Miskitu—beginning in the late 17th century, when English commercial enterprises forged military and commercial alliances with them—out of the Cape Gracias region and westward into Sumu-held territory. The Miskitu interaction with the Sumu people is strongly evident in the languages, whose relationship displays the telltale marks of Miskitu predominance. The layer of early and intimate borrowings from Sumu into Miskitu are of the type found typically when a dominant group absorbs into its community large numbers of the subordinate group as wives, children, and servants; and the more recent layer of borrowings from Miskitu into Sumu is of the type which flows from a dominant to a subordinate group, including as it does large numbers of assimilated English loans as well as a number of recent technical terms of native origin, including some that were originally Sumu, borrowed back into that language. This Miskitu-Sumu relationship is a fact of RAAN politics. One of the benefits of the Autonomy Project, however, was the establishment in law of a status, that of "semi-official language," for each of the principal indigenous languages of the Atlantic Coast, including Mayangna. This status is reflected concretely in the Mayangna Bilingual-Intercultural Education Program.

The exact position of Tuahka under the semiofficial umbrella afforded by the autonomy law is not altogether clear. It qualifies by virtue of being Mayangna, but it must still contend with the issue of its subordinate status in relation to its sister dialect Panamahka, with its 9000 to 10,000 speakers. The most pressing issue for the development of a Tuahka language project has to do with funding. Strictly speaking, there is no funding within the normal channels for a Tuahka project. This is true to an extent for the Mayangna bilingual education program itself; there is governmental support for that, to be sure, but it is meager, especially since the change of government in 1990. And the Mayangna program has had to rely heavily on aid from nongovernmental organizations (NGOs) to develop and publish its school textbooks. If the Tuahka project is now integrated within the general Mayangna program, it will have official status; but without substantial aid from outside, this will place an extra financial burden on the PEBI-Mayangna, already under great stress.

Decisions and Agreements

It is to the credit of the director of the PEBI-Mayangna that despite the obvious difficulties entailed, he recognizes the validity of the Tuahka position. The program is working toward the goal of integrating Tuahka into its operation so that the schoolchildren of Wasakin will have the benefit of both materials and instruction in their native dialect. A Tuahka-speaking *técnico* has been engaged, with outside funding, to train teachers in the use and development of written materials for first grade. The precise nature and extent of Tuahka language integration in the education of the schoolchildren of Wasakin is, at this point, still a matter of discussion. Many factors enter into the decision, the role of Panamahka and Miskitu being an important consideration. Much more is written in those languages than in Tuahka, and some of the literature is important in the religious life of the region. It is conceivable that educational materials in Tuahka will assume a position similar to that described by Rickford (1997) in his discussion of AAVE "dialect" readers in East Palo Alto, California—that is, as a means of relatively quick and painless access to the basic skills of reading and writing and, therefore, to subsequent literacy in the languages of the local linguistic hierarchy. A final question which must be asked is whether the traditional bilingualism and diglossia of Tuahka speakers will be affected by a change in school policy toward Tuahka. If so, how will it be affected, and does it matter?

MASHPEE WAMPANOAG

The Mashpee people have lived in southeastern Cape Cod, Massachusetts, in a region which bears their name, for more than 350 years of recorded history and for an unknown period before (see Map 2.3). The language their ancestors spoke, called Wampanoag (also Natick, Massachusett, and Massachusee), belongs to the southeastern subdivision of the eastern branch of Algonquian, which includes Western Abenaki, Narragansett, and Mohegan-Pequot, among others. Within Eastern Algonquian, Wampanoag can be identified as an n-dialect—that is, it reflects non-final Proto-Algonquian *l and *θ as /n/, in contrast to /r/, /l/, or /y/, as in some of the other Eastern Algonquian languages. This feature has been a shibboleth of New England Algonquian from the very earliest period of European contact, the word for 'dog' being regularly cited as a characteristic of different languages and dialects: *anum, arum, alum,* and *ayum.*

Wampanoag was once spoken (with dialectical variation) over a geographical range stretching from the tip of Provincetown, Massachusetts, to Narragansett Bay, Rhode Island. The main boundary to the west was the Blackstone River in current-day East Providence, Rhode Island. The territory also included two small islands off of Rhode Island.

Despite the variety of names by which the language is known, it is properly termed Wampanoag, given the geographic provenance of the majority of the native written source material and the fact that three of the Wampanoag communities which contributed to the corpus of material are still surviving today as Wampanoag communities in Massachusetts: the Aquinnah Wampanoag Tribe (Aquinnah, formerly Gay Head, on Martha's Vineyard), the Herring Pond Wampanoag Tribe (Plymouth), and the Mashpee Wampanoag Tribe (Mashpee). These tribes comprise the Wampanoag Nation and are the only surviving tribes which have shown continuous Wampanoag cultural community since the dates of the native written documents. The Wampanoag Nation once numbered some 69 separate tribal groups. Their territory covered 194 present-day towns. The Massachusett people became a part of the larger Wampanoag confederation just prior to the period of King Philip's War. There is no longer a Massachusett tribe.

The Present Condition of the Language

Wampanoag is no longer spoken. Thus, its condition is at the most dire point on the scale formulated by Michael Krauss. The few people who know phrases and texts in the language have learned them from written sources or have learned to recite them from older relatives. There have been no fluent speakers for a century or more. The nature of the program that is needed for Wampanoag is therefore that of a reclamation project, and it is just such a project that is being undertaken by members of the Wampanoag Nation.

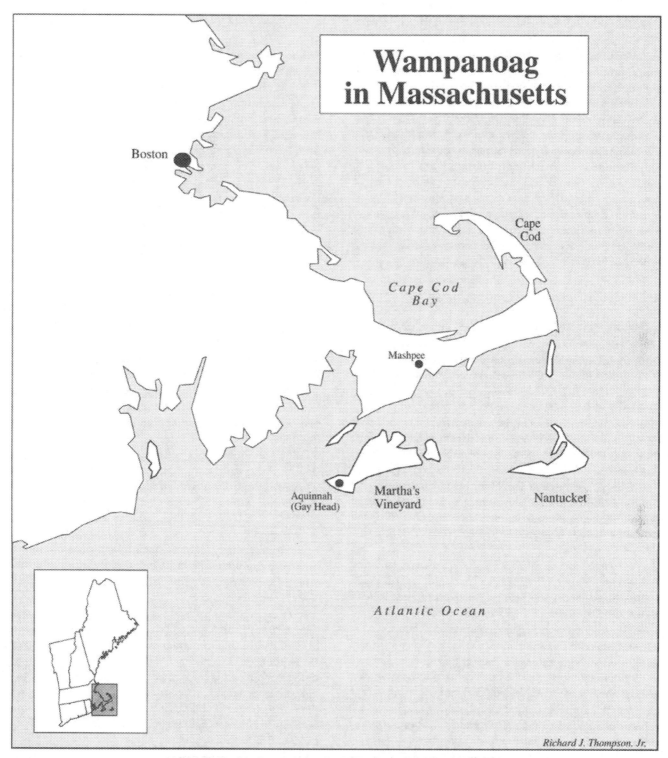

Richard J. Thompson, Jr.

MAP 2.3   Wampanoag (Massachusett) of Southern New England, USA

However, Wampanoag is in the enviable position of having some of the best early records in North America. In the 17th century, a grammatical introduction and the two testaments of the Bible were prepared by the linguistically gifted John Eliot ([1663] 1685, 1666). And, most important, native speakers wrote the language and set down for posterity certain extremely valuable texts in it, including the *Massachuset Psalter* (1709) and the documents assembled in *Native Writings in Massachusett* (Goddard and Bragdon 1988). Included in this latter work is an excellent and detailed grammatical sketch based on the language of the native writings and informed both by other period materials and by Goddard's unparalleled knowledge of Algonquian linguistics. There is also a dictionary compiled in the early 20th century by Trumbull (1903).

From the point of view of documentation, Wampanoag is in reasonably good condition. However, the materials that exist are extremely difficult to use—individual forms are difficult to read because of variations in orthographic usage, and the process of establishing full paradigms (verbal and nominal conjugations and declensions) requires hours of searching in the original documents as well as much comparison with other Eastern Algonquian languages (Delaware, Abenaki, Passamaquoddy-Maliseet, etc.). It is a matter of much detective work. In short, a great deal remains to be done to prepare for a full-fledged Wampanoag language program.

Projects: History, Results, and Prospects

Several projects have been initiated in recent years to revive Wampanoag. A promising new one is that of the Wampanoag Language Reclamation Committee, composed of members of the Aquinnah tribe (Gay Head, Martha's Vineyard), the Mashpee tribe, and the Assonet band (Wattupa). The idea of a reclamation project began to receive serious consideration in 1993 with a meeting between Jessie Fermino, of the Mashpee tribe, and Helen Manning, of the Aquinnah tribe. There seemed to be substantial interest in language reclamation, as demonstrated by a language survey completed by members of the Wampanoag community.

The committee met monthly to explore the possibilities of language reclamation as well as the resources available in the formation of such a project. During the project's three-year planning stage, the committee met with Kenneth Hale of the Massachusetts Institute of Technology, Kathleen Bragdon of William and Mary College, Philip Lesourd of Indiana University, Steve Pierro and Rita Pierro (both Micmac speakers), and Brian Myles of the Falmouth Institute. The aim of these consultations was to gain a clear view of the issues facing the community in undertaking such a project and to form an overall plan to carry out the project's goals.

First and foremost was the obvious need to train at least one community member as a linguist. Funding to hire a linguist was not available—the many hours of research and development required would not permit it—and besides, any real chance of reclamation has to be considered a lifetime's work. A Wampanoag linguist was the obvious choice, owing to the fact that this person would remain in the Wampanoag community permanently. Fermino was identified as the appropriate candidate for this and for the role of project director. She first began her studies and her research program as a fellow in the Community Fellows Program at the MIT Department of Urban Studies and Planning in 1997 and subsequently entered MIT as a graduate student in the Department of Linguistics and Philosophy. This seemed the best way to proceed: taking the study of the Wampanoag language as a serious responsibility, one to be approached systematically, not haphazardly.

It is Fermino's opinion that being born and raised Wampanoag may give one the moral right to claim the language, but not the right to produce work which is only "somewhat accurate." Receiving formal linguistic training from the predominantly nonnative world of Algonquian linguistic academia is a necessary piece of healing the broken circle of language. Both Wampanoag and nonnatives share the responsibility for the loss of the language's use; both groups work for restoration. The circle completes itself.

Serious and difficult linguistic questions must be addressed in order to produce a standard body of Wampanoag material capable of functioning as a sound foundation for a language program, one that satisfies the needs inherent in the various options which the Wampanoag people will wish to consider. The principal problems include (1) reconstruction of the phonological properties of lexical items in Wampanoag (i.e., their pronunciation); (2) reconstruction of the morphological alternations of nominal and verbal bases (in particular, determination of the inflectional base where it is obscured by truncation); (3) securing for as many nouns and verbs as possible their full inflectional paradigms; and (4) reconstruction of the major syntactic features of Wampanoag.

There are in fact two aspects to the Wampanoag Reclamation Project: research and materials development, and teaching the structure of Wampanoag to members of the community. While the second depends upon the first, it is necessary that the two go hand in hand, because that is what the community has requested. The research component will result in a dictionary and grammar of Wampanoag which can be used by informed lay people within the community and which can serve as the foundation for training a corps of Wampanoag teachers.

Even at this early stage of the project, it is possible to prepare accurate lessons which teach certain important features of Wampanoag and to communicate to students a fascination for its remarkable structure. And this is the modest purpose of the teaching program at this point. Formal Wôpanâak language classes began in April 1998. The class schedule was two nights per week, one hour per class, and its participants included both male and female students with an age range of 27 to 74.

Material for the classes has been prepared in an orthography which is both consistent and as close as possible to the writing system of the original documents. The adjustments made include consistent use of the grapheme {ô} for the long back nasal vowel [ã:] and {â} for its oral counterpart [a:], as in Wôpanâak for Wampanoag. The long high front vowel [i:] is written {ee}, reflecting 17th-century usage. Following a common practice in Eastern Algonquian orthographies, the grapheme {8} is adopted for the mid-high back long rounded vowel [u:]; and the grapheme {u} is adopted for the short central schwa vowel [ə]. The 17th-century geminate graphemes {tt, pp, kk, . . . }, indicating shortness of a preceding vowel, are written single {t, p, k, . . . }, eliminating a redundancy in the original system. Finally, the digraph {ty} is used for the palatalized reflex of certain occurrences of Proto-Algonquian *k, as in *weetyu (wôm)* continuing Proto-Algonquian *wi:kiwaHm 'house, wigwam'.

Wampanoag vocabulary and structure are taught in the form of sentences illustrating the essential principles of its grammar. The classes began with nominal constructions and progressed gradually to the much more complex verb system. Among the features of Wampanoag taught in the first two years were the animacy distinction in nouns and animacy agreement in both transitive and intransitive verbs; prepositions and the locative case; the distinction between dependent (inalienable) and independent nouns; obviation (placing in secondary status one of two third-person arguments occupying the same domain); the person hierarchy and person and number marking in nouns and verbs; the inverse construction; the preterit tense of the verb; the polar (yes/no) interrogative; the basic order of constituents; and variations in word order. These are properties which are quite obvious in actual Wampanoag forms, and the distinctions are rather intuitive, even for the beginner. Other features of the language (the conjunct, the subordinative, double-object constructions, and the absolute-objective distinction) are much more subtle, and their introduction must be delayed, partly because of their complexity but primarily because they must still be studied—they are not well enough known as yet.

It is the belief of the Wampanoag that their language is not merely a means to communicate one's thoughts. It was given to them by their creator as one of many gifts and responsibilities. For Wampanoag, it is the language their creator would prefer them to use in prayer and ceremony, something they have not done for six generations. They also hold the knowledge that whatever they do as people will have an effect on the seventh generation of as-yet-unborn Wampanoag.

In using the early documents written by Wampanoag families six generations ago, the people have a chance to close this circle during the seventh generation. They will be the grandchildren of the current generation.

One of the teaching methods Fermino has used is the opportunity for each student to compose prayers in Wampanoag. This seems to have a profound effect both on the individual creating the prayer and on the community as a whole. The prayers are not expected to be elaborate at this point, but they are still very beautiful and expressive. The Wampanoag community has had the opportunity now, at community events and ceremonies, to hear its language of origin in the form of prayer, with some people hearing it for the first time. For the purpose of creating prayers the class learned the transitive animate 1–2, 2–1, that is, first-person subject acting on second-person object, and vice versa.

Poetry is another medium for learning and using Wampanoag. Several poems have been written using the lexicon and syntax acquired in class. The poetry is not only a very strong teaching tool in that it requires a great deal of original thought and grammar for the student, but it also serves as a vehicle for healing some of the pain people feel over the generations of disuse of the language.

Object identification and discussion are also used in the class. After the first four months of classes, Fermino noticed that people were able to retain and write down thoughts and ideas learned during class, but actual speaking was very difficult. At that point the class decided to work with some object identification requiring the use of the transitive inanimate paradigm. Everyone in class was asked to gather objects or photographs of things that they could speak about in Wampanoag. They placed the objects and photos on tables and then went around the room and taking turns saying things like "I [or you, or we, etc.] see a ____." ; "Do[es] you [or I, or he/she, etc.] see a ____?"—in both present and preterit tenses. Content questions were exercised as well: "What thing[s] do [or did] you [or I, or he/she, etc.] see?" This was interactive, so that the group would then answer the speaker if a question was asked. Initially this was very difficult for people to do. They were afraid of being laughed at and of not making the correct sounds. The students helped each other sort out any mistakes of grammar or pronunciation. People seemed to become more comfortable with speaking aloud the more they practiced this.

Many of the lessons have involved the students translating phrases and sentences written in Wampanoag to English and vice versa. This seemed to work well. Students met independently for one hour per week and assisted each other with the translation work. The most common error found in this exercise seems to be the proper use of obviation.

Fermino did encounter certain problems in teaching. One is that of teaching full verbal paradigms without overwhelming people. A solution was to work on each inflection for a couple of weeks and then expand a bit further every two weeks thereafter. This sounds reasonable enough, but it proved to be difficult to keep everyone moving at the same pace. There is also the problem of the acceptance of Wampanoag syntax. Some of the students had not been exposed to a language other than English, which by comparison to Wampanoag is rather impoverished morphologically. In addition, students have a natural tendency to want to apply English grammatical constructions, and some effort is required to enable them to see that Wampanoag constructions are not "wrong" where they differ from English, that is, to understand the principle that each language is right, natural, and logical.

These first Wampanoag classes make it clear that there is a need for a more systematic approach to the curriculum.

Fermino is considering looking at other Algonquian languages which have a curriculum in order to apply an overlay system of some sort that would allow the lexical and syntactic items to be supplanted with Wampanoag. Passamaquoddy seems to be a good place to start. In addition, people need a variety of learning methods in order to keep up their enthusiasm for the work. Although several different exercises have been used with each lesson, more learning tools need to be created for the students. For this task, Fermino will consult with other teachers who are working on language acquisition or revitalization projects.

Resources Available to the Community

Since there are no native speakers of Wampanoag, the linguistic basis of the program will come from historical records of the language. The quality of these records will determine the range of options available to the community. In the case of Wampanoag, the situation in this regard is remarkably good. The undisputed treasure of southern New England Algonquian linguistics is the Eliot Bible of 1663 (the first Bible in any language to be published in the western hemisphere), together with later works within the Eliot tradition, particularly those by native speakers. A second treasure resides in the fact, little known to people of this day, that literacy was a feature of Wampanoag life in the 17th and 18th centuries, and a respectable number of documents survive. Mercifully, this material was assembled in a wonderful two-volume work by Ives Goddard and Kathleen Bragdon (1988). This was fortunate indeed, since it provided a foundation upon which the research phase of the Wampanoag project was able to begin with dispatch.

Fermino, as the codirector of the Wampanoag Language Reclamation Project, has assumed the task of preparing language materials. She is learning linguistics as she proceeds to assemble materials, and she is consulting with other linguists who have expertise in Algonquian linguistics, including those who have worked extensively with Eastern Algonquian languages—for example, Passamaquoddy-Maliseet and the two Delaware languages. These living Eastern Algonquian languages are considered a resource for the project, as are the detailed comparative and descriptive studies of Algonquian languages and the Proto-Algonquian reconstructions now available. Where possible, these sources are used to help refine nominal and verbal entries in the lexicon Fermino is compiling.

Sociopolitical and Economic Factors

The Wampanoag project has in its favor the fact that it is evolving in a traditional-style cohesive human community in which members are for the most part secure in their knowledge of their position and relationships. The Wampanoag tribes and bands have been cohesive social entities through-out recorded history, despite such contrary legal decisions as that reached in Judge Skinner's court in 1978 to the effect that the Mashpees were not a tribe during the period relevant to their claim to land alienated from them. Legal reverses of this sort do not diminish the Wampanoag sense of community and common heritage. Part of the Wampanoag heritage is the Wampanoag language, and that raises the question of rights to it.

The question of who has rights to a particular linguistic tradition is often difficult to resolve and in some instances retards or even stops the development of an effective project. The Mashpee, Aquinnah, and Assonet communities are unquestionably descendants of people who spoke Wampanoag. There are other groups in southern New England, however, whose linguistic heritage, while technically not Wampanoag, is closely related to it. The Mohegan-Pequot, the Narraganset, and the Mahican, for example, spoke a closely related form of Eastern Algonquian, but their descendants have few recorded materials appropriate for a revival program. The Wampanoag Reclamation Committee has taken an inclusive attitude on this issue and is meeting with other Eastern Algonquian groups in southern New England to discuss ways in which the Wampanoag model can be used.

Decisions and Agreements

A major decision which must be taken in any language revitalization project is the degree or extent of revitalization contemplated as a reasonable and desired goal. In the Wampanoag project, the extent desired is maximal. Optimally, there will be people who speak Wampanoag fluently, having learned it as children. This is a remote goal, to be sure, but it is not impossible. It entails, among other things, (1) developing materials comparable to those used in standard foreign-language classes which actually produce speakers competent enough to use the language in all interactions with other people; (2) bringing as many people as possible, preferably couples, to this level of competence; and (3) parental use of Wampanoag consistently with and around children from birth onward. The compilation of the linguistic basis for this—lexicon, grammar, and language courses—will be a lengthy process, but it can involve members of the community (through learning games and activities, as well as actual research) while it is actually going on. By the time fully efficient language courses are ready to be taught, many people in the community will be pretty familiar with basic principles of Algonquian grammar.

BELFAST IRISH

The scenario just considered for Wampanoag would seem utopian in the extreme if there were no precedents for it. A contemporary example is that of Modern Irish in Belfast, Northern Ireland (see Map 2.4). This is not, to be sure, the

Ireland

Ireland

Great Britain

Donegal

Northern Ireland (U.K.)

Belfast

Leitrim

Sligo

Carrick-on-Shannon

Monaghan

Cavan

Mayo

Roscommon

Longford

Louth

Irish Sea

Meath

Galway

Westmeath

Dublin

Dublin

Offaly

Kildare

Atlantic Ocean

Laois

Wicklow

Clare

Carlow

Kilkenny

Limerick

Tipperary

Wexford

Waterford

Kerry

Cork

Cork

Richard J. Thompson, Jr.

MAP 2.4   Irish in Belfast, Northern Ireland

revival of a language no longer spoken, but the two situations bear important similarities. This account is very brief and is included because the case of Belfast Irish has certain parallels with the Wampanoag project.

The Present Condition of the Language

When the Belfast initiative began in the 1960s, Irish had not been spoken there for many years. And in Northern Ireland generally, Irish had ceased to be spoken in the previous decade. This means that the people carrying out the project would have to acquire Irish as a second language, as in the Wampanoag project.

Projects: History, Results, and Prospects

In the 1960s a group of 11 families decided to raise their children as Irish speakers in a supportive environment (Maguire 1990). This goal is remarkable when considered in light of the actual situation of the parents undertaking to achieve it: they live in a monolingual English-speaking city, and they are not themselves native speakers of the language but instead had to become competent speakers as young adults. In this respect, they faced a situation like that of the Wampanoag people, who are proposing to revitalize that language.

To quote from Maguire's *Our Own Language* (1990),

> Community members were motivated by the recognition that the creation of a socially cohesive speech community was necessary if they were to have any chance of bringing up Irish-speaking families in Belfast. This project proved successful. Not only did the community of eleven families survive the pressures of being rooted in an English-speaking society. In addition, it exerted a significant impact upon the surrounding neighborhoods, contributing to a wider shift towards bilingualism. Furthermore, the Shaw's Road Community inspired other community enterprises throughout the North, particularly in the area of Irish medium education.

The families created the cohesive community they determined would be necessary, in part, by buying or building houses in a contiguous area, at great sacrifice given their economic condition. In the Wampanoag case, by contrast, the cohesive community has been there from the start.

Resources Available to the Community

Irish has been written longer than English, and the study of Irish grammar boasts a long history and an impressive body of work. Modern Irish has a significant number of accomplished grammarians, and a large number of language courses exist for both children and adults, including an entertaining television program covering a respectable range of grammatical structures, vocabulary, and dialogue structure. This is the Irish linguistic heritage, and it is of course accessible to people living in Northern Ireland. Irish is taught in universities there, and in general, it is possible to find a course on the language or to arrange to learn it with a teacher or by oneself. This is a far cry from the Wampanoag situation, where no teaching materials existed but had to be created from scratch.

Sociopolitical and Economic Factors

There are enormous economic pressures working against this project. The very creation of the community involved expenses which were extraordinarily severe for the working families involved, and as the project advanced, and as bilingual children approached preschool age, further expenses had to be faced in order to ensure that their education would proceed in Irish. Furthermore, the tensions which have long existed in Northern Ireland did not afford a very favorable sociopolitical environment.

Decisions and Agreements

The most impressive decision taken by the families which undertook to create an Irish-English bilingual community in Belfast is the very decision to actually undertake that project. But the successes of the project have led to other issues requiring decisions, including the question of the role the established project should assume in assisting new projects that attempt to determine a position for Irish in the education of their children.

AN ENDANGERED LANGUAGES MOVEMENT

For many linguists and anthropologists there is an awareness of the existence now of an endangered languages movement, particularly those of us on e-mail who receive messages and documents from the Society for the Study of the Indigenous Languages of the Americas (SSILA), the Endangered Languages List, the Endangered Languages Fund, Terralingua, and the Foundation for Endangered Languages and through them learn of other organizations concerned centrally with endangered languages, like IPOLA and the language programs of Unesco. The fact is, the potential exists for an international support movement. And this is another reason for optimism, since it gives promise of an eventual structure for (1) the exchange of resources, ideas, and moral support among local language projects; (2) the organization of conferences and workshops for projects wishing to discuss ideas face to face and in detail, and (3) the organization of courses around technical and practical skills, such as the use of computers in linguistic work, curriculum development, and linguistic matters generally.

In addition to the components of this global movement, a system is in place of regional support structures which are able to convene representatives from local language projects within a particular area, like the southwest, where the American Indian Language Development Institute (AILDI) has held workshops at least since 1980. In addition to their support function, established regional organizations such as this are extremely valuable when it becomes necessary to present a united front in relation to national policy, as when AILDI members and others worked on behalf of the passage of the Native American Languages Act.

In all of this, it is important to bear in mind that the real foundation of the endangered languages movement consists in the actual local language programs which develop and grow in individual communities. Each local language program is one among many pillars holding up a larger global movement. When one pillar weakens, this has little effect on the movement as a whole. On the other hand, the experience of the larger movement can give sustenance to individual programs through organizations like AILDI and help them to recover, become strong, and prevail.

In our introduction, we implied that the flowering of local language maintenance and revitalization programs around the world has the character of a miracle, inasmuch as they function separately, for all intents and purposes. But this is wrong—if it were a miracle, we would have little cause for optimism, since miracles do not happen very often. Moreover, to call this phenomenon a miracle is to detract from the contribution of countless people who have struggled on behalf of diversity and essential human rights in the past and in the present. Rather than a miracle, it is a natural outgrowth of years of struggle on the part of people involved in progressive movements of great diversity all over the world. This, in itself, is another reason for optimism. People will continue to struggle to protect diversity and to use that very diversity to ensure a productive and enriched future for their children.

Notes

1. These language names are also spelled Kaiadilt and Ganggalida (Evans 1992).
2. There is an additional language, or dialect, which should be added to the first group, namely Nguburindi, once spoken on the mainland (Evans 1992 and 1995).

References

CODIUL/UYUTMUBAL. 1989. *Diccionario elemental del ulwa (sumu meridional)*. Karawala, Región Autónoma Atlántico Sur [Nicaragua]: CODIUL/UYUTMUBAL; Bluefields: Investigaciones y Documentación de la Costa Atlántica; Cambridge, Mass.: Centro de Ciencia Cognitiva, Instituto Tecnologico de Massachusetts.

Dixon, R. M. W. 1980. *The languages of Australia*. Cambridge: Cambridge University Press.

Eliot, John. [1663] 1685. *The Holy Bible. Containing the Old Testament and the New. Translated into the Indian Language*. Cambridge, Mass.: Samuel Green and Marmaduke Johnson.

———. 1666. *The Indian grammar begun*. Cambridge, Mass.: Samuel Green and Marmaduke Johnson.

Evans, Nicholas D. F. 1992. *Kayardild dictionary and thesaurus*. Melbourne: University of Melbourne.

———. 1995. *A grammar of Kayardild*. Berlin and New York: Mouton de Gruyter.

Goddard, Ives, and Kathleen Bragdon. 1988. *Native writings in Massachusett*. American Philosophical Society.

Hale, Kenneth, Colette Craig, Nora England, LaVerne Jeanne, Michael Krauss, Lucille Watahomigie, and Akira Yamamoto. 1992. Endangered languages. *Language* 68: 1–42.

Krauss, Michael. 1992. The world's languages in crisis. In Hale et al.

Ladefoged, Peter. 1992. Another view of endangered languages. *Language* 68: 809–11.

Maguire, Gabrielle. 1990. *Our own language: An Irish initiative*. Multilingual Matters.

The Massachuset Psalter or, Psalms of David with the Gospel according to John. 1709. Boston: B. Green and J. Printer.

McLean-Cornelio, Melba E. 1996. *Diccionario panamahka: Sumo-español-sumo*. Managua, Nicaragua: CIDCA.

Mithun, M. 1994. Unpublished, untitled talk. Australian Linguistic Institute, La Trobe University, Melbourne.

Ngakulmungan Kangka Leman. 1997a. *Lardil dictionary*. Mornington Shire Council.

———. 1997b. *Merri Lardil kangka leman (Listen to the Lardil Language)*. Mornington Island.

Nancarrow, C. 1997. Mornington Island State School Language Program 1997: Report for Cape York and Gulf Indigenous Languages Program (unpublished report). Mornington Island: Mornington Island State School.

Norwood, Susan. 1993. El sumu, lengua oprimida. *Wani* 14: 53–64.

Norwood, Susan. 1997. *Gramatica de la lengua sumu*. Managua, Nicaragua: CIDCA.

Renfrew, Colin. 1994. World linguistic diversity. *Scientific American*, January.

Rickford, John. 1997. Unequal partnership: Sociolinguistics and the African American speech community. *Language in Society* 26: 161–97.

Trumbull, James Hammond. 1903. *Natick Dictionary*. Smithsonian Institution, Bureau of American Ethnology Bulletin No. 25. Washington, D.C.: Government Printing Office.

PART II

LANGUAGE POLICY

3

Federal Language Policy and Indigenous Languages in the United States

LEANNE HINTON

Department of Linguistics
University of California at Berkeley
Berkeley, California

Language planning and language policy can refer both to plans and policies external to a local group, such as national language policies, and to plans and policies internal to the group, such as community or even family language policies. A family language policy is illustrated by a statement made by an Assyrian father to his daughter: "When you go out the door of this house, you are an American, and you speak English; but when you come in the door, you are Assyrian, and you speak Assyrian" (personal communication). In this chapter I will focus on external language policies, those made by governments and other agencies external to a local language that affect that language. In the chapter on language planning (Chapter 5), I will focus on community-internal planning and policy.

Language policy has often been a tool for the oppression of minority languages, but it can also serve as a tool for their survival and public enhancement. It can be very important for indigenous groups to learn how to affect the language policies of governments and schools. Although language policies have usually been discouraging toward languages other than the national language, a visible pattern can be seen in a number of countries, during the last decade or two, of slowly increasing influence by indigenous peoples on language policies in such a way as to increase the protection of their languages. In view of the centuries of oppression (and worse) that preceded this glimmer of change, some observers call it too little, too late, or even "closing the barn door after the horses have gone" (Schiffman 1996). However, the change toward a friendlier policy is not to be rejected and can help in the quest for language survival.

WHY GOVERNMENTS DEVELOP LANGUAGE POLICIES DISCOURAGING TO MINORITY LANGUAGES

Governments tend to discourage minority languages for many reasons, both pragmatic and symbolic. Pragmatically, the use of a single language makes government's job easier. Official documents and proceedings, education, and so on are all much easier if they can be done in a single language.

But once one language becomes the main language of government and commerce, people who do not speak it are automatically disenfranchised—they are less able to join the economic mainstream and participate in the affairs of nation. This marginalization of language minorities can also be a source of unrest that can lead to problems for the government. And these problems make it easy to see that when a government believes in equal rights of citizens to the social and economic benefits of their society, the presence of minority languages can be viewed as a disadvantage to the minority citizens, and to easy governing as well. Thus, making sure that everyone knows the language of power can be argued to be important for several good reasons.

However, the support of one language over another can also be motivated by an effort to exclude minority groups from power and privilege. The ruling group assures the maintenance of its own power by making sure that its language is accorded special status. For example, English is the heritage of Great Britain, and countries that speak English do so because of the spread of the British Empire. American English is part of the northern European heritage that is now seen by European Americans as the core history, ethnicity, and cultural background of the United States. Many people who support making English the official language of the United States are not interested in minority economic rights at all but are instead fearful that the Spanish language, in particular, is gaining too much ground in the United States and represents a threat to the hegemony of English.

Symbolically, language is seen as a factor in unification or separation. Linguistic minorities see their languages as a symbol of their identity; so too does a nation. A language may become a symbol of patriotism, and minority languages are therefore seen as antipatriotic, a sign of divided loyalties.

As an example of this attitude, we can look at the reaction to an event in the early 1990s in Arizona, when the oath of citizenship during a ceremony for a group of bilingual new citizens was conducted in Spanish. The administrator who allowed this said he had reasoned that it would make the ceremony more meaningful to the new citizens, whose dominant language was Spanish. This created an uproar in Congress, where legislators raged that it was unpatriotic to have the oath of allegiance in any language except English. Many of the bills about official English that have come up since then in Congress include a rider that all oaths of allegiance must be taken in English. Such legislation is obviously not aimed at the benefit of the Spanish speakers but is instead a reaction to this conducting of an official ceremony in Spanish and is based on the symbolic value placed on English as the language of American patriotism.

Nevertheless, government policy toward minority languages is not always negative. The policy of governments may also be neutral or even encouraging of the maintenance of minority languages. I will go over a history of community-external language policies affecting Native Americans, where we will see that language policy has gone through many transformations over the years.

U.S. LANGUAGE POLICIES AFFECTING NATIVE AMERICANS

Before there was a United States of America, Europeans and Native Americans had already had close to 200 years of contact, much of it hostile, with great harm to the natives. War, slavery, massacre, and removal were the main order of the times. The linguistic symptoms of this harm included the demise of many languages. On language maps of North America depicting Native American languages, part of the southeast has a giant blank spot, where languages disappeared so quickly and completely that nothing at all is known about them. An interesting case is the Lumbees of North Carolina, who have no idea what language or languages they once spoke. The sociolinguist Walt Wolfram and his associates have found in working with the Lumbees that their particular dialect of English has certain distinctive features and words that at least distinguish them from the non-Indian population living in the same region—but those distinctive characteristics of English are all that they have left of any lin-

guistic heritage they can call their own. (For more information, see Hutcheson and Wolfram 2000.)

A more "liberal" approach to the Native Americans was taken by the missionaries, who came from religious institutions that had little respect for Indian culture but at least believed the people should survive. In the early days of North American colonization, it was often the case that the missionaries learned to speak the language of the people they came to proselytize. They translated the Bible and their message into the local languages and taught literacy to the Indians so that they could read the Bible. There are many translations into eastern Native American languages of the Bible and other documents that date from the 17th and 18th centuries, including many written by the Native Americans themselves. Besides the missionaries, there were quite a few colonists who learned Indian languages fluently, and some of them became famous as interpreters between Indians and the colonists.

At the time of the American Revolution, government language policy per se was nonexistent. The new government decided to keep it that way, refusing to make English the official language. This was not because the new Americans were thinking about Indian languages, but rather because there were many who spoke other European languages, especially German, and no politician wanted to risk losing the immigrants' allegiance by any insult to their language. Throughout the first century of the new nation, many Europeans coming from nations that spoke other languages had their own independent communities, with schooling in their heritage language. But although the government tolerated minority European languages, its attitude toward indigenous languages was quite different. Those Indians who could attend school were always sent to schools where the language of instruction was English. Otherwise, Indians were simply outsiders. The U.S. census did not even count Indians until late in the 19th century, with the exception of so-called "civilized Indians," those who lived in town rather than on reservations or out in "Indian country."

So until the end of the 19th century, Native Americans were primarily treated as unwanted foreigners, and large numbers of them were pushed ever westward into territory not yet known to or desired by European Americans. What the Indians did out there on the frontier and what language they spoke was of little concern to the U.S. government. As the westward movement of whites advanced, Indians would again and again find themselves evicted, and those who fought these evictions usually died.

BOARDING-SCHOOL POLICY

With the end of the Indian Wars and the closing of the frontier, there was no place left to which Native Americans could be exiled. Treaty making was ended, and assimilating the Indians into the mainstream became the primary government agenda. Language eradication was considered an important part of this program. A system of federally run boarding schools was set up, and children were removed, often forcibly, from their families for schooling, with the express goal of teaching the children European ways and making sure that English became their main language of communication. Old people today can tell many stories about the punishment they received as children in those boarding schools if they were caught speaking their native tongue, whether in the classroom, on the playground, or in the dorms. Those schools that attempted some instruction in the children's native language for the sake of helping them understand the content of the lessons were told that the children would be taken away and support by the government withdrawn from the school. The directives also said that "English only" had to be the policy of both government and parochial schools.

The attitude toward Native American languages and culture that fueled this oppressive language policy is exemplified in a report by J. D. C. Atkins, the federal commissioner of the Bureau of Indian Affairs in the 1880s:

> To teach Indian school children their native tongue is practically to exclude English, and to prevent them from acquiring it. This language, which is good enough for a white man and a black man, ought to be good enough for the red man. It is also believed that teaching an Indian youth in his own barbarous dialect is a positive detriment to him. The first step to be taken toward civilization, toward teaching Indians the mischief and folly of continuing in their barbarous practices, is to teach them the English language. The impracticability, if not impossibility, of civilizing the Indians of this country in any other tongue than our own would seem to be obvious, especially in view of the fact that the number of Indian vernaculars is even greater than the number of tribes. . . .
>
> But it has been suggested that this order, being mandatory, gives a cruel blow to the sacred rights of the Indians. Is it cruelty to the Indian to force him to give up his scalping-knife and tomahawk? Is it cruelty to force him to abandon the vicious and barbarous sun dance, where he lacerates his flesh, and dances and tortures himself even unto death? Is it cruelty to the Indian to force him to have his daughters educated and married under the laws of the land, instead of selling them at a tender age for a stipulated price into concubinage to gratify the brutal lusts of ignorance and barbarism? (Crawford 1992, 51).

Clearly, the possibility of encouraging bilingualism among the natives was not even considered. Indian languages and English were considered to be mutually exclusive. One language had to be traded for the other.

These policies had a strong effect on the children who attended boarding schools. They developed a strong sense that their language was evil or inferior to English. Many saw their language as the reason for their suffering in school (as opposed to blaming the language policies themselves). And the government got the desired result: the children stopped speaking their language in most situations and swore not to teach it to their own children. To quote one boarding school graduate:

> I was eleven years old [when I went to Covelo], and every night I cried and then I'd lay awake and think and think and think. I'd think

to myself, "If I ever get married and have children I'll *never* teach my children the language or all the Indian things that I know. I'll *never* teach them that. I don't want my children to be treated like they treated me." That's the way I raised my children. Everybody couldn't understand that, they always asked me about it in later years. My husband has a different language. He can't understand me but I learned his language much faster. I can talk it too but I never taught my children. That's why they don't know. [My daughter] can understand it, but she can't speak the language. (Hinton 1994, 176)

BILINGUAL EDUCATION

In the latter half of the 20th century, many Native American communities, now more skilled in dealing with the American institutions in their terms, began to demand more control over their children's education, and in the 1970s some tribes set up contract schools, which allowed at least limited ability of local school boards to set policy for their own schools.

The advent of bilingual education in the 1970s marks a period of relatively liberal policy toward minority languages. President Lyndon B. Johnson approved the Bilingual Education Act in 1968 as Title VII of the Elementary and Secondary Education Act, and as a result of a 1974 U.S. Supreme Court decision (*Lau v. Nichols*) and the subsequent "Lau Remedies" announced in 1975 by the U.S. Commissioner of Education, bilingual education was expanded (Crawford 1989). At first bilingual education was aimed not at Native Americans, but rather at immigrant children and native Spanish speakers. However, Indian communities were quick to grasp this opportunity. In its first year of funding, only 5 out of a total of 76 local projects served American Indian students. But within a decade, there were nearly 70 American Indian bilingual education projects funded by Title VII (McCarty 1993).

Bilingual education has its roots in a series of Supreme Court decisions beginning during the civil rights movement. In *Brown v. Board of Education* in 1954, the court ruled that public schools could not deny students equal educational opportunities. This was expanded in the 1964 Civil Rights Act, which said that people could not be denied equal access to services on the basis of ethnic background. These paved the way for the 1974 *Lau v. Nichols* decision that Chinese children being held back in school because they did not know English were being denied equal rights to education. The Court decreed that the schools were responsible for developing English as a Second Language (ESL) or bilingual education programs for these children. The decision resulted in the 1975 Lau Remedies, which provided funding for bilingual education. The Bilingual Education Act had already been passed in 1968, and the Lau Remedies provided a great expansion of service to children who did not speak English.

Bilingual education has been controversial throughout all its years of existence. The main point of disagreement in earlier times was whether bilingual education should have the goal of "transition," where it served language shift to English, or of "maintenance," such that children would emerge from school well educated in two languages. The second view, carried to its extreme, is much more expensive than the first and also strikes at the notion held by many monolingual Americans that the maintenance of any language other than English is unpatriotic. Albert Shanker, president of the American Federation of Teachers in 1974, held to the transition model:

> The American taxpayer, while recognizing the existence of cultural diversity, still wants the schools to be the basis of an American meltingpot. While the need for the child to feel comfortable and be able to communicate is clear, it is also clear that what these children need is intensive instruction in English so that they may as soon as possible function with other children in regular school programs. (Crawford 1989, 39)

The other point of view was well expressed by Santiago Polanco-Abreu, the congressional delegate from Puerto Rico in 1968:

> I wish to stress that I realize the importance of learning English by Puerto Ricans and other minority groups living in the States. But I do not feel that our educational abilities are so limited and our education vision so shortsighted that we must teach one language at the expense of another, that we must sacrifice the academic potential of thousands of youngsters in order to promote the learning of English, that we must jettison and reject ways of life that are not our own.

He proposed

> [t]he establishment of programs which (a) will utilize two languages, English and the non-English mother tongue, in the teaching of the various school subjects, (b) will concentrate on teaching *both* English and the non-English mother tongue, and (c) will endeavor to preserve and enrich the culture and heritage of the non-English-speaking student. (Crawford 1989, 38)

Bilingual education sent local languages in a certain direction: since these were school-based programs and the policy was to teach school subjects in the native language, Native American communities had to develop writing systems and concern themselves with the development of vocabulary and new genres that had not previously been present in the language. New genres such as essay writing and poetry became part of the native-language curriculum. Active programs developed all kinds of reading materials, reference grammars, dictionaries, and workbooks for use by students and teachers. The inclusion of native culture in the curriculum quickly became a concern, for it was clear that if the language was used only to teach mainstream American subjects, the heart and soul of the language would not be there. Furthermore, as many educators perceived, one of the great problems of Native American children is that as an oppressed minority, they develop very low self-esteem (as illustrated above by the quote from Elsie Allen, whose estimate of herself as stupid and inferior was imposed on her by the boarding-school policy which denigrated Indian languages and cultures). Low self-esteem is a major factor in failure at school, and it was considered important to show

children that their local language and culture was just as respectable as the English language and mainstream American culture. By bringing the local language and culture into the classroom, children could be shown that they can grow up bilingual and bicultural, and that their Indian heritage and Indian ways of life were something to be proud of.

Rock Point, on the Navajo reservation, is an example of one way in which such goals were carried out. Primary classrooms were divided in half, with Navajo objects, decor, books, and tapes in one half, and Anglo-American objects, decor, books, and tapes in the other half. Children and teachers alike were expected to always speak Navajo when they were on the Navajo side of the room and English on the other side of the room. The goal was to educate children to be bilingual and bicultural, with pride in their background.

Thus, to Native Americans, bilingual education was seen from the beginning as a tool for language maintenance and the development of cultural pride. However, whether this should be a goal of bilingual education was a controversial topic within the federal government from the beginning. Bilingual education is very expensive, for one thing, attracting the ire of balanced-budget advocates and legislators watching out for their taxpaying constituents. Furthermore, the question of whether bilingual education should be aimed at language maintenance or language transition was immediately raised. The maintenance model's goal is for the child to maintain the first language while developing skills in the second language; the transition model focuses on using the first language only until the child learns English well enough to get along. (This might better be called the "early transition model"; there is also a "late transition model" that is very supportive of the first language, where all schooling takes place in the first language until about fifth grade, at which point English begins to be introduced.) The early transition model is cheaper than either maintenance or late transition, but it usually results in loss of the first language, and many educators argue that it does not serve the student as well as the maintenance model.

Various arms and factions of government and school systems have battled each other over bilingual education ever since its inception, weakening its effectiveness considerably (Fillmore 1992). Funding and other forms of support have been diminished over the years and are constantly in danger. In 1998 California passed the Unz initiative (proposition 227), which virtually outlawed bilingual education. Other states are in the process of preparing legislation or initiatives against bilingual education as well, and this is encouraging to conservatives in Congress who hope to see an end to the program altogether.

ENGLISH-ONLY LEGISLATION

Related to the antibilingual education movement is another strong movement toward adopting English as the official language of many states and attempting to pass an official-English bill in Congress. These movements represent the pendulum swing of the 1980s and 1990s back toward the suppression of language choice. Twenty-three states have adopted English as their official language, although one state was declared officially bilingual: in Hawai'i, English and Hawaiian are co-official languages. In many cases, the state bills are fairly harmless to other languages—they call English the official language much as they might name the official bird or flower. But in other states, the official-language legislation carries with it various restrictions against the use of other languages. Arizona's highly restrictive 1988 law, which said, for example, that all government actions, governmental documentation, and schooling must be English, was struck down by the federal courts. Alaska passed a similar law in 1998, but it has been stayed by court injunction (Crawford 1999).

In Congress, a good half dozen bills are introduced each year that would make English the country's official language. These bills differ in terms of how restrictive they are: some are similar to the Arizona and Alaska bills, some specifically end bilingual education, some repeal bilingual voting requirements, and so on. Below is a summary of the bills that were introduced into the Congress of 1999–2000 (Crawford 1999), though, as usual, none passed. We can predict they will come to the floor again in the next Congress.

106th Congress (1999–2000):

H.R. 123 (Barr), "Bill Emerson English Language Empowerment Act"; the lead version of English-only legislation; referred to Education and Workforce Committee

H.J. Res. 21 (Doolittle), Constitutional English Language Amendment; referred to Judiciary Committee

H.R. 50 (Stump), "Declaration of Official Language Act of 1999"; would also repeal the Bilingual Education Act; referred to Education and Workforce Committee

H.R. 1005 (King), "National Language Act of 1999"; would also repeal the Bilingual Education Act; referred to Education and Workforce Committee.

H. Cong. Res. 4 (Serrano), English Plus resolution; a nonbinding policy statement in opposition to English-only measures; referred to Education and Workforce Committee

S. 667 (McCain), English Plus policy statement as part of a private-school "choice" bill; would also authorize a study of Americans' multilingual proficiencies; referred to Finance Committee

HR 50 and HR 1005 are especially conservative in that they would repeal the Bilingual Education Act. H. Cong. Res. 4 and S. 667, on the other hand, are in opposition to official-English measures.

Interestingly, over the years a split has developed in the way the U.S. government views Native American languages and immigrant languages. In the 1980s, the movement making English the official language of the United States was

growing, boosted by lobby groups such as U.S. English. Michael Krauss relates going into the U.S. English office in Washington, D.C., where he pointed out to S. I. Hayakawa (the founder of the organization) that indigenous languages should enjoy a protected status and should not be lumped with immigrant languages in the eyes of the organization (Krauss, personal communication). Hayakawa agreed. So does much of Congress: attached to each bill that has come up over the last decade to make English the official language, including the one bill that passed in the House in 1996 (only to die again because it did not make it out of committee in the Senate), has been an amendment saying that this bill is not intended to discourage the use of Native American languages. Below is a summary of H.R. 123, as summarized in 1996.

Summary:
Table of Contents:
Title I: English Language Empowerment
Title II: Repeal of Bilingual Voting Requirements
Bill Emerson English Language Empowerment Act of 1996—Title I: English Language Empowerment—
Amends Federal law to declare English to be the official language of the U.S. Government.
States that representatives of the Federal Government have an affirmative obligation to preserve and enhance the role of English as the official language of the Federal Government.
Requires such representatives to conduct official business in English.
Prohibits anyone from being denied Government services because he or she communicates in English.
Requires that all officials conduct all naturalization ceremonies entirely in English.
Directs that nothing in this title be construed to limit the preservation or use of Native Alaskan or Native American languages [italics mine].
Sets forth definitions for purposes of this Act.
Title II: Repeal of Bilingual Voting Requirements—
Amends the Voting Rights Act of 1965 to repeal bilingual voting requirement provisions.

Native groups are not necessarily happy with what they see as another divide-and-conquer ploy, and some, such as the Hawaiian 'Aha Pūnana Leo, have declared this split in language policy to be dangerous to the cause of minority language survival in general. Furthermore, the passage of an official-English bill, many versions of which would bring an end to bilingual education and other programs useful to indigenous Americans, would be deleterious to Native American languages even with an amendment such as that noted above. Nevertheless, we can take it as a good sign that the United States is beginning to see indigenous languages as a part of its heritage to be protected.

During the last two decades of the 20th century, indigenous minorities have begun to become powerful enough to begin effecting a change in language policy in the United States and elsewhere. Despite the conservative counterbalances described above, we see policy changes that are increasingly protective of indigenous languages. In Hawai'i, for example, besides initiating the movement to make Hawaiian an official language of the state, the Hawaiian community successfully lobbied to strike down older laws forbidding the use of Hawaiian in the public schools and clearing the way for Hawaiian language–based classrooms and schools (see the articles in this volume by Warner, Chapter 12, and by Wilson and Kamanä, Chapter 13).

The best sign of the new policy of respect toward Native American languages is the Native American Languages Acts of 1990 and 1992. Robert Arnold was one of several principal parties who labored over the writing and the negotiations that eventually led to the passage of these bills through Congress. The next chapter tells about the history of these two important bills and the kind of work that is necessary to get legislation passed. This represents a key part of the process of language revitalization: working to change official policies that directly or indirectly affect minority language survival.

References

Crawford, James. 1989. *Bilingual education: History, politics, theory, and practice*. Crane.

———, ed. 1992. *Language loyalties: A source book for the official English controversy*. Chicago: University of Chicago Press.

———. 1999. Language policy [database online]. <http://ourworld.compuserve.com/homepages/JWCRAWFORD/home.htm>

Fillmore, Lily Wong. 1992. "Against our best interest: The attempt to sabotage bilingual education." In *Language loyalties: A source book for the official English controversy*, ed. James Crawford, 367–76. Chicago: University of Chicago Press.

Hinton, Leanne. 1994. *Flutes of fire: Essays on California Indian languages*. Heyday Books.

Hutcheson, Neal, and Walt Wolfram, producers. 2000. *Indian by birth: The Lumbee dialect* [video]. Raleigh: North Carolina State University.

McCarty, Teresa L. 1993. Federal language policy and American Indian education. *Bilingual Research Journal* 17, nos. 1–2: 13–34.

Schiffman, Harold F. 1996. *Linguistic culture and language policy*. London and New York: Routledge.

4

". . . To Help Assure the Survival and Continuing Vitality of Native American Languages"

ROBERT D. ARNOLD

Professional staff, 1989–1995
U.S. Senate Committee on Indian Affairs
Washington, D.C.

As 1991 was drawing to a close, the prospect of enacting a bill in Congress to enable American Indian tribes and other Native American organizations to implement policies supportive of Native American languages was very promising. A persuasive record had been established by the Select Committee on Indian Affairs in the Senate, and the bill had been adopted by the Senate without objection and sent to the House of Representatives. But in the House, objections to the bill by a key member threatened to kill the bill. Even though compromises on certain provisions had been agreed to, the bill would have died but for the active efforts of American Indian, Alaska Native, and Native Hawaiian language advocates.

Although the process of shaping and enacting the bill signed into law as the Native American Languages Act of 1992 is the subject of this chapter, that account must be preceded by a discussion and review of its predecessor and foundation, the 1990 Native American Languages Act.

THE NATIVE AMERICAN LANGUAGES ACT OF 1990

The historically important 1990 act repudiated past policies aimed at eradicating Indian languages by declaring, at long last, that Native Americans were entitled to use their own languages. Specifically, Public Law 101-477 declared that "[i]t is the policy of the United States to . . . preserve, protect, and promote the rights and freedom of Native Americans to use, practice, and develop Native American languages" and to "fully recognize the right of Indian tribes and other Native American governing bodies, States, territories, and possessions of the United States to take action on,

and give official status to, their Native American languages for the purpose of conducting their own business."

Other policy declarations in the act were narrower—addressing education—but they were not unimportant, for it was the schools established by the United States in Indian areas that had been the principal means—as the 1868 Peace Commission had urged—of ensuring that the "barbarous dialects" of Indians "be blotted out." These provisions of the act were intended to recognize the right of tribes to use their languages as a medium of instruction, to encourage state and local education authorities to implement the act by including Native American languages in their curricula, to grant appropriate credit (including substitution of a Native American language for a foreign language), and to allow exceptions to teacher certification requirements for Native American language teachers. An implementation provision in the act required the president to direct the heads of federal agencies to evaluate existing policies and procedures in order to identify what changes were required, and to deliver his recommendations to Congress by November of 1991. In its declaration of policy and its findings, the 1990 act's provisions closely tracked the words of a resolution adopted at the 1988 conference of the International Native American Languages Issues Conference. And much of that text had been drawn from a resolution adopted by the Hawaiian legislature in 1987, calling upon the Congress to enact legislation in support of Native American languages.

The Hawaiian resolution was the product of efforts by William Wilson, the chair of Hawaiian Studies at the University of Hawai'i at Hilo, and his wife, Kauanoe Kamanā, both fluent speakers of the Hawaiian language and among the founders of 'Aha Pūnana Leo, an educational program employing the Hawaiian language. Their consistent advocacy

The Green Book of Language Revitalization in Practice   **45**

for a changed national policy—in which they were joined by American Indian language advocates such as Lucille Watahomigie, Ofelia Zepeda, Patricia Locke, Edna McLean, and Joan Webkamigad—was important to the introduction and eventual passage of the 1990 act.

But enactment of the enlightened policy statement was not easily achieved. In 1988 Senator Daniel K. Inouye, a Democrat from Hawai'i, had introduced a joint resolution and steered it through the Select Committee on Indian Affairs, which he chaired, but the Congress adjourned without taking any further action. The following year he introduced (with nine cosponsors) a revised and expanded version of the resolution as a bill (S. 1781), but it was strongly opposed by the Bush administration largely on the grounds that it would require an appropriation of $20 million. After Inouye revised the bill to address administration concerns, however, it was approved by the Senate on April 3, 1990, and sent to the House of Representatives. But in the House, it soon became clear that key members were intimidated by a growing sentiment against the use of languages other than English in America, and they refused to allow the bill out of committee.

Despite a vigorous telephone campaign by Native Hawaiians, American Indians, and Alaska Natives, the bill was dead unless a way could be found to get around the problem of the English-only movement. Inouye's aide and his manager for the bill, Lurline McGregor, a Native Hawaiian who had produced a video program on the revitalization of the Hawaiian language and who was an early and active participant in the shaping of a Native American language policy proposal, discovered that way. Her counterpart in the House reported that the opponents would probably make no objection if the Native American languages bill were incorporated into a bill with a title that made no mention of the word "languages." McGregor looked for a bill that was likely to pass in the closing days of the Congress and that would not face a veto by President Bush.

A bill that I was managing for Inouye met the requirements, so when he took that bill to the floor, he offered an amendment to it that consisted of the entire text of his Native American language bill. Both the amendment and the bill were approved by the Senate, and on the same night, the amended bill was concurred in by the House. When President Bush signed the bill, titled "Tribally Controlled and Navajo Community Colleges, Reauthorizations," on October 30, 1990, he was approving also its Title I, the Native American Languages Act of 1990. The public law as printed, P.L. 101-477, was bewildering to some because the title mentioned only the tribal colleges.

THE NATIVE AMERICAN LANGUAGES ACT OF 1992

No procedural stratagem was required to enact the Native American Languages Act of 1992, but as with the 1990 legislation, objections in the House of Representatives made its fate uncertain as the 102d Congress was drawing to a close.

In introducing what was to become the 1992 act on November 24, 1991, Inouye pointed out the unique status of Native American languages, saying:

> unlike languages brought to these shores by people from east and west, languages indigenous to this hemisphere are spoken nowhere else. Since Europeans first arrived on these shores in the sixteenth century, hundreds of languages have been lost. Each year, additional languages are threatened with extinction.

Inouye went on to describe the 1990 policy declarations and said his bill was intended to be a means of implementing these declarations by authorizing funding for tribes and Native American organizations to establish native-language training programs, to develop written materials, to compile oral records, to establish community language programs, and to construct facilities, if required. He explained that his bill would amend the Native American Programs Act of 1974, a grant program administered by the Administration for Native Americans (ANA), to enable tribes to advance toward economic and social self-sufficiency. The amendment would provide an additional authorization of $5 million (to the ANA's existing authorization of $34 million) for the language grant program. Inouye told the Senate that his bill was modeled upon an earlier bill introduced by Senator Frank Murkowski, a Republican from Alaska, to provide language grants to Alaska Natives, but pointed out that the bill passed in the Senate had made no progress in the House of Representatives.

As with all Indian bills that he introduced, Inouye mailed copies of it, accompanied by his floor statement and a section-by-section analysis, to all tribes and Native American organizations and invited their comments. Although the response to this outreach effort was often disappointing, he received a substantial number of responses that were both supportive and constructive.

Accordingly, Inouye scheduled and chaired a hearing on June 18, 1992, of the Select Committee on Indian Affairs on his Native American language bill (S. 2044) in room 385 of the Russell Senate Office Building in Washington, D.C. In his opening statement, Inouye reported that despite his urging, the Bush administration had failed to implement the review and evaluation required by the 1990 act. He said that act had "become a stimulus for change in some jurisdictions," but that "absent any financial resources, [local] commitment and leadership may not be enough." In other opening statements, Murkowski and Democratic Senator Daniel Akaka of Hawai'i (speaking in part in the Hawaiian language) expressed their strong support for the bill.

The committee then heard persuasive testimony on the bill from tribal representatives and linguists. First was Kenneth Hale, of the Department of Linguistics and Philosophy of the Massachusetts Institute of Technology, who told the committee, "A language is, in fact, the repository of the intellectual wealth of a culture, the product of intellectual labor on the part of a people who speak those languages." Using as an example the verse of the Tohono O'odham, a people with whom he had worked for a number of years, Hale explained that "the form which the verse takes depends in a manner which is inseparable from the form of the language," and that, accordingly, no translation would entirely capture the beauty of the original. To emphasize the importance of language diversity, he said:

> I think that an important human purpose is the fullest use of the mind in creating intellectual wealth or products of intellectual labor. An enabling condition for this is linguistic and cultural diversity, since it is that condition above all others that permits the exploration of the widest range of paths of creation . . . Thus, the loss of a language is a certain tragedy for the human purpose, not just locally, but the human purpose in general. And the loss of a language, if it can be prevented, must be prevented.

A second witness, the director of the Alaska Native Language Center of the University of Alaska, Michael Krauss, compared the imperiled condition of indigenous languages to the condition of endangered biological species and provided a detailed analysis of the status of Native American languages. He testified that in the United States there are 155 such languages spoken or remembered, but he pointed out that perhaps only 20 were still spoken by people of all ages. As a result,

> [a]t the rate things are going, of the present 155 languages, by the year 2000, 45 will be gone; by 2025, 60 more will be gone; and by 2050, 30 more—135 of 155 languages extinct. And will the remaining 20 too be on the road to extinction?

Krauss applauded the provision of the bill that would allow only tribes or Native American organizations to be applicants for funding, pointing out that "you cannot from outside inculcate into people the will to revive or maintain their languages. That has to come from them, themselves." That will is there among the Coquille, the committee learned from a tribal member, Troy Anderson, in his prepared statement. Anderson, who had spent four years compiling what he called a rudimentary dictionary of Miluk, emphasized how multimedia technology could facilitate language recovery and language learning.

From Carl Downing, the director of the Oklahoma Native American Language Issues Development Institute, members learned of the work of the national Native American Language Issues Institute since it was first chartered in 1986 and the institute's support of S. 2044. Quoting a member of the Bad River Band of Chippewa that "to not know one's own language is to be left out," Downing reflected upon his own experience:

> I think this is the position that many of us find ourselves in. We have been raised with a certain amount of culture but because of certain conditions, the desire to buy into the American dream or some other need, we have lost our language. Those of us who are like me feel a very real loss because we do not have that language. . . . And it is through a bill such as this that [it] can be preserved in the future. Without this bill, more languages will be lost.

Greeting the committee in the Navajo language, the superintendent of Leupp Schools in Winslow, Arizona, Tommy C. Yazzie, declared that "[t]he very essence of self-worth and dignity lies in our language." Referring to Indian languages as the "strongest bond that welds Indian societies together," Yazzie said:

> Our traditional songs, prayers, and chants are carefully designed to communicate to the spirit world our petition for daily subsistence, good health, and also harmonious relationships with our four-legged creatures and the human race.

Superintendent Yazzie also translated the remarks delivered in the Navajo language by a school board member, Joe Yazzie, who accompanied him. He said the board member told him that he had witnessed the "deterioration of the family, the social fabric of Navajo life where heretofore the Navajo language had been used to communicate all aspects of social, political, and economic survival" and that he believes "the language needs to be put back into place in many of the school curricula."

The committee also received a resolution of support from the oldest and largest national Indian organization, the National Congress of American Indians. After presenting the resolution, its executive director, Michael J. Anderson, said that nearly every Indian person in the room could relate stories of how their parents or grandparents were punished for speaking their own languages at federal boarding schools. He said that in his own case,

> [b]oth my grandparents on both sides of my family, the Creek side and Choctaw side, were fluent in their language. My grandmother attended a Federal boarding school at Tuscahoma in Oklahoma, which is in the Choctaw area of the state, and with the forced removal of many of the Choctaws that's where many of our Choctaws in Oklahoma remain today. She was not permitted to speak her language at boarding school. . . . That fear of speaking the language in school caused her to have a real fear of teaching my mother the language because she thought that she would have some of the same problems in school as well. So my parents, who also attended BIA [Bureau of Indian Affairs] schools, didn't have that opportunity to learn the language from their parents and also didn't have the opportunity to learn it in school.

The committee also received strongly positive testimony from another important national organization. Representing the National Indian Education Association, its legislative analyst, Karen Funk, called the committee's attention to recommendations of the Indian Nations at Risk task force report and the recently concluded White House Conference on Indian Education, which pointed to the importance of Native American languages to the future of Native Americans. She also told the committee that the need for the proposed grant program was underscored by the large number of applications received by the National Park Service for its limited small grant program.

All of these witnesses provided detailed statements for the hearing record, and several of them made recommendations for changes to the bill. Letters of support for the bill (including dozens from students) were also made part of the hearing record.

But the testimony of one witness was not persuasive. Speaking for the Bush administration, Dominic Mastraquapa, deputy commissioner of the Administration for Native Americans, opposed the enactment of S. 2044, advising the committee that the agency already had the necessary authority to carry out its purposes and that its goal was "sufficiently broad to encompass the purposes of preserving native culture and language." He said, further, that the level of funding was adequate and that no further appropriations were needed. Subsequently, the agency corrected the record by advising the committee that no grants that included language components were awarded in fiscal year 1991.

Recalling the opposition of House members to the 1990 act, which had arisen over the movement to make English the official language of the United States, the committee had sought the views of the organization U.S. English. Although not received by the day of the hearing, the organization's letter, which was made part of the official record, was more supportive than had been expected. Its executive director, William Christopher Doss, wrote in part:

> First and foremost, despite the propaganda circulated about U.S. ENGLISH, you may rest assured that genuine efforts to preserve and maintain our indigenous languages are NOT contrary to the goals of the common language movement. Indeed, efforts to maintain North America's indigenous languages inevitably bolster the arguments to protect the role of our common language. . . . If we do not maintain our linguistic heritage by giving our historically important languages a genuine place in our educational institutions, then how would we expect this heritage to be preserved through the piecemeal officialization of those speakers who have political clout?

Based upon the supportive testimony and recommendations for changes received by mail, Inouye presented a substitute for S. 2044 at the committee's mark-up session on July 2. The substitute included provisions that would encourage tribal governments, at their discretion, to establish partnerships with schools, colleges, and universities; authorize grants to be made for up to three years; limit any funds granted for construction to the conversion of existing facilities; and authorize the use of grant funds for recording equipment and computers required for any language program. After adopting an unrelated amendment to satisfy a member, the committee unanimously approved the substitute and ordered it favorably reported to the Senate, where, on August 5, it was approved by unanimous consent and transmitted to the House.

Once the bill was referred to the Committee on Education and Labor, staff of the Senate Committee on Indian Affairs (including myself as the bill's manager) scheduled a meeting with majority (Democratic) and minority (Republican) staff of that committee. The majority staff, represented by Alan Lovesee, urged that the bill require the Administration for Native Americans to include Native American language speakers and linguists in the development of regulations to implement the act and that the bill designate the Institute of American Indian Art in Santa Fe, New Mexico, as a repository to ensure that materials produced would be properly preserved. Following some discussions over the specific text to be included, we agreed to the amendments.

Minority staff, represented by Lee Cowan, on the other hand, explained that the ranking minority member of the committee was opposed to the passage of the bill. The member, Harris Fawell from Chicago, had told his staff that he saw no reason to appropriate federal funds to help tribes preserve their languages. He persisted in that view even though Lovesee and others pointed out that it was United States policy that had led to the loss of Native American languages, and that federal appropriations had been spent to implement the policy of eradicating Indian languages.

Over the next two months, in a series of meetings with Cowan, Lovesee and I searched for ways to accommodate the views of the objecting member of the committee, for unless we could persuade him to abandon his objections, the bill would not even go to the House floor. Based on what we understood to be some of his specific concerns, we agreed to increase the requirement for local matching funds from 10% to 20%, to disallow grants for construction, and to reduce the first-year authorization from $5 million to $2 million. Even with these concessions, however, Fawell was unwilling to allow the bill to go to the floor.

As these discussions ground on, it was becoming increasingly late in the session, and the bill would die unless acted upon by both houses before the Congress adjourned. Accordingly, we alerted the Hawaiians through Kamanā and Wilson and the office of the Native American Language Issues Institute in Oklahoma, and they in turn alerted others. How many people placed telephone calls to Fawell's office I do not know, but they were many. Only a few days passed before Cowan called me. "Please call off the troops," he said. "We'll let the bill move." The Chicago congressman had reportedly received more calls from Indians and other Native Americans in those few days than in all of his four terms in Congress.

The bill, as amended, was approved by the House on October 2, and we arranged for it to be held at the desk in the Senate, which had begun counting down the days to adjournment. In its new form, it was approved by the Senate by unanimous consent on October 5, just days before the 102d Congress adjourned.

On October 26, 1992, President Bush signed into law the Native American Languages Act of 1992, a bill titled "To Help Assure the Survival and Continuing Vitality of Native American Languages."

PART III

LANGUAGE PLANNING

5

Language Planning

LEANNE HINTON

Department of Linguistics
University of California at Berkeley
Berkeley, California

Like language policy (Chapter 3), language planning takes place at many levels in society. Most books on language planning are about planning at societal governmental levels. In the United States, language policy and language planning at the federal level have a big impact on local speech communities. Often, too, language planning even in smaller organizations, such as in public school systems, may sometimes take place without adequate consultation with the indigenous communities whom these policies might affect. This chapter is not about these external types of language planning, but, rather, about community-based language planning, or "language planning from the bottom up," as Nancy Hornberger labels it (Hornberger 1997).

Language planning is essential for a good revitalization program. This does not mean that a community has to plan before it can do anything else. Often experience in language projects is necessary before people have the knowledge to do good overall planning. In this chapter I will go over some of the steps that are necessary for language planning and some of the components of a good language plan.

Some of the reasons language planning is important are:

(1) The thought processes and research involved in language planning help a community establish reasonable and realistic goals and help find the most effective methods and strategies of reaching those goals.

(2) Language planning helps a community keep an eye on long-term goals and the "big picture" in which various projects take place.

(3) Community-based language planning is a way of making sure that the community, rather than outside agencies such as governments, public schools, and so on, stays in charge of its own language policy. Outside agents may

be an important component in language revitalization and may even help in language planning, but they should not be the ones to determine the future of the language. As one member of the Karuk language committee said, "[T]he very establishment of a committee has been a positive step towards the people's 'ownership' and self-determination about how Karuk will be introduced as a common language" (Sims 1996, 20).

(4) Language planning can help to coordinate what might otherwise be disparate or conflicting efforts by different people and groups.

(5) Good language planning can help to prevent or reduce factionalism and rivalry that might otherwise arise around language and reduce the effectiveness of revitalization efforts.

So important is language planning that the Administration for Native Americans, which distributes $2 million a year in grants to tribes doing language revitalization, now insists that the first grant a tribe must apply for is a "planning grant," and only after carrying out a year of planning can they then apply for an "implementation grant."

Who does language planning? Language planning can be done by a community, a school, a classroom, a family, or even an individual for his or her own language learning. We will assume here that a community is doing the planning, but many of the steps and components would also be part of a school language plan.

Anyone and everyone can do language planning. You do not need a formal committee to do language planning; it can just be done by interested people or at town hall meetings. However, often the task is taken on by a committee, either one formally appointed or an informal committee that is

51

open in membership and formed voluntarily. For a community or school, then, language planning may begin with the formation of a committee of people who are knowledgeable, dedicated, and have a sense of responsibility toward language revitalization. These people may well be the same people who will apply for grants, teach the language, and so on. In some communities the committee may consist of elders, with perhaps some younger prime movers joining in who have an interest in and knowledge of language revitalization. This language committee might simply provide philosophical oversight and suggest general goals in language revitalization, or it might make various decisions and even perhaps manage the implementation of programs. It all depends on the particular structure of a given community and its situation. Each one of the steps below might be either carried out by the committee or assigned to other groups or consultants for implementation. The committee will find itself most effective if community participation is encouraged every step of the way.

PLANNING AS AN OPEN-ENDED PROCESS

One of the first things to know about language planning is that it is an open-ended, ongoing process that continues to take place even during implementation of the program. The Hualapai linguistic and educational expert Lucille Watahomigie teaches in classes and demonstrations that the process of language revitalization involves a cycle she calls a PIE: Planning, Implementation, and Evaluation (Fig. 5.1). You plan what you will do; you implement the plan; you evaluate what you have done; and then you plan some more.

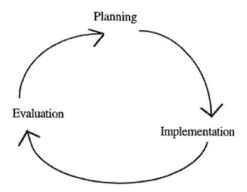

FIGURE 5.1 PIE: Planning, Implementation, and Evaluation (illustration by Lucille Watahomigie)

TYPES OF PLANNING

Hornberger lists four types of language planning and two appraches (1997, 7):

Approaches: One approach is policy planning, and the other is cultivation planning, which will be the main focus here. Within these two planning approaches, Hornberger identifies four types:

(1) *Status planning,* about the uses of language. The possible *cultivation* goals of status planning would include long-term goals involving maintenance and revitalization. For example, setting up the goal of having the language become the main language of daily communication within the community would count as status planning. In the *policy* approach, the planning body might consider, for example, whether the local language should be proclaimed the official language of the community. An example of a policy about status planning is one that was developed by the Cochiti, which stated that the tribal government should provide a model for the rest of the community by using the Cochiti language at the tribal office at all possible times (see Chapter 7).

(2) *Acquisition planning,* about users of the language. Under the cultivation approach, this kind of planning involves the maintenance or reacquisition of the language by members of the community. How will the language be taught, and to whom? Decisions about whether there should be a school-based language program and/or programs to teach adults and families and about what methods will be used to teach the language fall under this type. Under policy, this program might state policies about language acquisition at work, what the language of instruction will be at school and so on. The Cochiti, for example, made a policy that all tribal employees who did not know the language should learn it, and all tribal employees who did know the language should teach it. They declared that the first 15 minutes of every workday would be a gathering for a language lesson.

(3) *Corpus planning,* about language itself. Here planning might include modernization of the language—the creation of new vocabulary or the development of new genres to fit modern communicative needs. For example, the Hualapai schools have developed (written) genres of poetry. Traditionally the Hualapai had stories and songs that exhibited many poetic elements, but the actual writing of poetry did not exist until it was developed in the schools. Hawaiians established the Lexicon Committee to develop and authorize new vocabulary to fit the needs of the classroom in language immersion schools (Chapter 13). The investment of authority in this committee is an example of policy planning. Their work in developing new vocabulary is cultivation planning.

(4) *Writing*, Hornberger's final category, about writing systems. Cultivation planning would include the design and reform of writing systems, and policy planning would include the official sanction of a particular writing systems. The Cochiti developed a policy that their language not be written at all.

STAGES OF PLANNING

An excellent discussion of language planning is found in Brandt and Ayoungman 1988. They include implementation and evaluation as part of the planning process and label the steps as follows:

> There are seven basic stages or phases in the language planning process: the introductory stage; preplanning and research; needs assessment; policy formulation and goal setting; implementation; evaluation and last, replanning. These should not be considered as irrevocable steps, but as necessary stages that need to be repeated as needed. We propose using a *Spiral Model* in which all the stages suggested in the model are reviewed continuously and added to and/or revised. In other words, there is always room for improvements and adaptation, especially as the situation changes. The planning process will take years and should be viewed as a continuous process without a final stopping point, just as the chambered nautilus adds additional chambers as it grows. (Brandt and Ayoungman 1988, 51)

Although Brandt and Ayoungman place goal setting with policy formulation, they also talk about goal setting as a process that takes place previous to goal setting. Goal setting really has a place in various stages of language planning. General and long-term goals might be set quite early in the planning process, but specific short-term goals might take place later, after research and setting language policy. Here I will modify the stages outlined by Brandt and Ayoungman and will discuss goal setting as part of stage 2, and again in stage 6. We talk about stages or steps in language planning, but the order of the steps should not be considered rigid. Each step feeds into all the others.

Stage 1: The Introductory Stage

In this stage, highly motivated people (whom Brandt and Ayoungman call "catalysts") initiate activities, recruit others, and seek community involvement. Committees may be formed at this point, and community meetings might be held.

Stage 2: Goal Setting

What do you want to accomplish? Do you have an overall goal of reversing language shift so that the language be-comes the main language of communication in the community? (Such a goal may take generations to accomplish.) Or perhaps the goal is really something else, such as the maintenance of traditional religion or lifeways, with language as a means to that end. Do you have the goal of developing new fluent speakers? Perhaps the goal is simply to make children appreciate their language and teach them something about it. Perhaps the goal is instead to document the language—to videotape the elders or develop a dictionary. Goals may be lofty or small. If they are lofty, you will need to develop smaller objectives to carry out the larger goal. Think about both short-term and long-term goals and about how short-term goals will help reach the long-term goals. (You may have to redo your goals when you find out what your resources are. Resources and goals are intertwined and feed back on each other.)

Brandt and Ayoungman suggest that the first stage of goal setting is something they call "futuring," which should take place in a community meeting. Here the members of the community are asked to consider and express their ideals for the future of the community, with an emphasis on language, but not leaving out other aspects of life which may ultimately be relevant to language. The ideas can be brought out through brainstorming (see below). Questions to the participants might include:

What role would you like to see the language play in our community?

What abilities or skills (language proficiency, communicative competence) do you want to see?

What characteristics do you want to see in the citizens of our community in the 21st century (thinking especially about those who are young children now)?

What value systems do you want to see in them?

What community contributions do you want to see them make?

What are the most important aspects of our way of life which you want to see continued?

What aspects of our way of life would you like to see changed? (adapted from Brandt and Ayoungman 1988, 65–66)

While many of these questions are not directly related to language, all of them have implications for language planning. For example, if one ideal is that future citizens of the community should be more involved in traditional ceremonies, then a language program should be partly based on ceremonialism, teaching children the language arts they need to participate in ceremonies and, if the language program is to be school based, arranging for field trips or school holidays to support their attendance at ceremonies.

Goals are often set by brainstorming. As Lucille Watahomigie does in classes on language planning (e.g., at

AILDI—see Chapter 29) and as Brandt and Ayoungman describe, planners (hopefully with strong community presence at this stage) can brainstorm together as follows (the same process would be used for futuring, above):

> *Purpose:* to identify and prioritize community goals based upon what has been identified in [the futuring process, above]
> *Materials:* flip chart and markers. Each ideal identified [in the futuring process] should be permanently recorded for later reference and use and possible distribution to participants and others as needed.
> *Activity:* choose a recorder and without criticism place the factors identified on flip charts. Distribute a list of the ideals identified in [the futuring process] to all participants or place it in clear viewing for all.
> (1) Without discussing how ideals should be accomplished, begin a new list of those ideals which community action could clearly affect, and place those which it could not on a separate list. Some general statements may need to be rephrased into more specific goals. Once these have been listed, distribute the list to the participants for step 2.
> (2) Prioritize this list of things into those which are most important based upon group consensus, assigning a rank of 1 to the most important and so on down the line. These now become the goals of the language planning process. (Brandt and Ayoungman 1988, 66)

Since we are talking about language planning, how a language revitalization program could be designed to effect each ideal must be kept in mind. Goal setting will take place on a more detailed basis as subsequent stages are reached. Once you know your resources and needs, for example, goal setting can become more precise and informed.

Stage 3: Preplanning and Research

This is the stage at which planners survey their communities, discover their resources, research their language, and find out what other revitalization programs are doing.

The Language Survey

One of the most important steps in language planning is to find out the attitudes of the people in your community. To what degree are the members of the community interested in language maintenance or revitalization, and what kind of projects would they like to see? While community meetings can tell you a great deal about this, they do not necessarily represent the views of those who do not attend the meetings. The community language survey has the function of helping planners understand the attitudes of the whole community toward the language and language maintenance or revitalization, and individual members' willingness to participate in the process. The language survey can also tell you about the degree of language knowledge and usage in the community. The survey will thus help you learn about the human re-

sources for language in your community—for example, how many fluent speakers there are, how old the speakers are, and how well they know the language.

Surveys might be based on open-ended oral interviews, which are a rich source of information, or, on the other end of the continuum, might be written in a multiple-choice format, which makes them more quantifiable and easier to obtain from large numbers of people. Written surveys are usually anonymous—that is, the respondent does not put down his or her name. This is important for getting honest answers to what could be sensitive questions. You need to include questions eliciting some basic demographic data such as the respondent's age.

Questions about degree of knowledge and exposure to the language might look something like this (although this is by no means the only possible format):

How well would you estimate that you can speak [language name, e.g. Tohono O'odham]?
_____ Fluently
_____ Somewhat well: can make myself understood, but have some problems with it
_____ Not very well: know a lot of words and phrases, but have a hard time communicating
_____ Know some vocabulary, but can't speak in sentences
_____ Not at all

How well do you understand [language name]?
_____ Understand everything someone says to me
_____ Understand mostly, but not completely
_____ Understand some words and phrases only
_____ Not at all

To what extent do you and your family use [language name] at home at the present time?
_____ Always
_____ Sometimes
_____ Never

When you were growing up, how often did you hear [language name] in your home?
_____ Always
_____ Sometimes
_____ Never

When you were a small child (before school age), how often did you speak [language name] at home?
_____ Always
_____ Sometimes
_____ Never

Once you started going to school, how often did you speak [language name] at home?
_____ Always
_____ Sometimes
_____ Never

These are only a few of the questions that could be asked. Depending on your needs, and on the patience of the people you ask to fill it out, the survey may only be a page or two, or it may be many pages.

Surveys of adults often take the form of asking people to

mark on a scale the degree to which they agree with certain statements. For example, some of the questions designed to elicit language attitudes and interest in revitalization might look like this:

It is important for members of our community to know their language.
Agree strongly   Disagree strongly
5   4   3   2   1

An important part of being [e.g., Navajo] is to know the language.
Agree strongly   Disagree strongly
5   4   3   2   1

Our community should make efforts to teach the language to people who don't know it.
Agree strongly   Disagree strongly
5   4   3   2   1

Our language should be taught in our schools.
Agree strongly   Disagree strongly
5   4   3   2   1

It would be a good idea to provide classes for families on how to keep their language in use at home.
Agree strongly   Disagree strongly
5   4   3   2   1

It would be a good idea to develop a writing system for our language.
Agree strongly   Disagree strongly
5   4   3   2   1

I would be willing to assist in a language program.
Agree strongly   Disagree strongly
5   4   3   2   1

You should probably do a pilot test of your survey, because often you will find that some of the questions you ask on the first draft are unclear or objectionable; or you may find, by interviewing people while you administer the survey, that some important questions have been left out.

It may be that you only want to administer the survey to adults; a more thorough approach would be to administer it to all age groups, at least from elementary school on. Surveys for children would have to be rather different from surveys for adults (see Sims 1996).

Administering the survey individually to people while in their presence gives you the best chance of getting a response from everyone. It also allows you to discuss language knowledge and language revitalization in a more open-ended way with people, affording you the opportunity to learn much more than if you only use a quantified written set of questions. Surveys can also be administered to groups and collected on the spot. Alternatively, they can be mailed out; but sometimes this will mean that many will not respond. Following up mailings with phone calls or visits will increase the response rate.

Surveys may of course be of different types than the kind illustrated above. Just to give an example, a large language community serviced by multiple schools might want to use a survey to find out what sorts of language teaching and materials preparation are going on in various schools.

Finding Your Resources and Constraints

What and whom do you have available to help you in the planning and implementation of a language revitalization program? What constraints are there that you need to work within?

Human Resources

Some of the human resources in your community may have been discovered by the initial survey described above. The human resources include:

(1) Speakers—your most important resource!
(2) Community members who have been working with language in one way or another, such as trying to learn the language, teaching it in school, developing materials, and so on. Often individuals or small groups are doing independent work on language, and whenever possible, it is very important to incorporate them somehow into an overall language plan, to avoid factionalization, reinventing the wheel, and other such problems.
(3) Community members with expertise in traditional ceremonialism, traditional medicine, knowledge of plants and animals, native crafts, subsistence on the land, and so on.
(4) Language supporters and advocates within the community—perhaps the tribal council or other governing body.
(5) Experts in the community with skills useful to language revitalization, such as teachers, artists, grant writers, computer experts, and so on.
(6) Associated outside consultants, such as linguists, anthropologists, or education consultants who have worked in your community.

Cultural Resources

What active traditions, ceremonies, and native skills are present in your community? These can be extremely important resources for language revitalization efforts.

Documentation Resources

(1) Linguistic materials and publications on your language
(2) Writing systems developed inside or outside the community
(3) Classroom materials, books, language teaching manuals and curricula, Web sites, CD-ROMs, and other such items that have already been developed in or for your community
(4) Tape recordings, video recordings, and so on, developed by outside professionals or by community members
(5) Useful books, articles, Web sites, and so on, on such relevant topics as language teaching theory and methodology, and a new but growing literature on language revitalization.

Besides identifying these resources, their value to your goals must also be assessed.

Model Programs Elsewhere

While each community has a unique set of resources, needs, and goals that will make its language revitalization program unique, the experience of other communities doing language revitalization can provide a great deal of inspiration. Visits to interesting language programs or communication with the people that work in them can be tremendously educational and helpful in language planning for your own community.

Institutional Resources

Some endangered languages are taught at universities. One can learn Hawaiian at the University of Hawai'i. There are American universities and community colleges that teach Navajo, Ojibwa, Dakota, and other Native American languages. Gaelic can be learned in schools and universities in Scotland and Ireland, Welsh in Wales, and so on. While the very small language communities will not find universities teaching their languages, such institutions may nevertheless be capable of providing assistance in other ways. There may be important archives or clearinghouses that have materials of use to your community. Consultants of various sorts might be available from universities or other institutions. Some institutions may have departments that can be helpful in training, or in developing materials.

Equipment and Supplies

What is available to your language efforts in terms of equipment and supplies, such as computers and software, tape recorders, video cameras, printing capabilities, and the like? The presence or absence of the more expensive items may play an important role in your planning.

Funding Sources

What foundations and granting agencies might be able to fund your projects? Are there community-internal funding sources? Funding is a complex and difficult issue, but we all have to face it.

Constraints

What constraints are there that will affect your language program? For example, Hopi language planners in 1998 identified a constraint against centralized language programs as being that the villages were autonomous and wanted to guard their autonomy by designing their own programs. Dialect differences between villages were another constraint. Thus, although diplomatic coordination of existing programs could be useful, any program that went against the village autonomy and dialect preservation might well prove unsuccessful (class presentation by instructor at AILDI, 10 June 1999).

Many constraints operated in California that resulted in the basic design of the California Master-Apprentice Language Learning Program (Chapter 17). The fact that California has such great language diversity and, in some cases, such small populations speaking these languages means that classes in the languages at universities would be impossible, as would K–12 immersion schools of the sort found in Hawai'i (Chapters 12 and 13).

Step 4: Needs Assessment

Once you know what you have in the way of resources, you will also know what you need. Do you need funding? How much? Will you need to bring in consultants? What kind of training will be needed? What kinds of equipment will have to be obtained? What kind of space will you need? Specifics of a language plan may well be determined by these needs. For example, if your community wants language teaching to take place in the school, but you find that you have no language teachers who are speakers and no speakers who are teachers, you may well need to develop a specific plan for producing speaker-teachers. This may involve teaching present or future teachers the language (which could mean, for example, the establishment of a master-apprentice program such as that described in Chapter 17); or it may involve teacher training for speakers. You may find that there are actual laws that make it difficult to implement a language program. The problem that speakers are usually not teachers may lead you into the realm of lobbying your government for legislative changes allowing speakers special status that can put them on a school payroll. An example of the necessity for legislative lobbying is found in Hawai'i, where a Hawaiian language immersion program could not be established until the state law that mandated that all teaching be in English was changed (see Chapter 13).

Step 5: Policy Formulation

Language policy consists of a set of statements and mandates about language based on philosophy and ideology within the language community. Language policy need not always be a part of planning, and it need not be a formal document, but it may be. A language policy statement could contain some or all of these sections, among others:

(1) A general mission statement about language or language related issues
(2) A statement about the philosophy and value of the local language
(3) A statement declaring the official language(s) of the community
(4) Information on the role and authority of various bodies, including local governing or policy-setting bodies, community members, and committees
(5) A list of prioritized goals

(6) Statements on policies about orthography and literacy (such as acceptance of an official writing system or rejection of writing systems altogether)

(7) Statements about intellectual property rights, copyrights, and so on

(8) Statements about social, cultural, religious, situational, and political constraints that may affect language programs, such as constraints on when traditional tales can be told or in what context certain sacred songs must be sung

Depending on the situation in your language community, it might be important to develop a formal language policy that can be presented to an authoritative body for endorsement (such as a tribal council, school board, or regional or national governing body). However, a language policy may often be written and rewritten for years by planners before it is deemed appropriate to submit it to an authoritative body for endorsement (if ever).

Step 6: Goal Reassessment, and Developing Strategies and Methods to Reach Your Goals

At this stage, the planners are well informed about general community goals, resources, needs, and policies within the context of which a language plan will be implemented. Now is the time to do a more detailed look at goals, and strategies and methods to reach those goals, along with a proposed timeline. Here is where planners will design the nature of specific programs and projects, adopt methodologies, decide on funding strategies, training methods, and so on. Writing proposals and holding training seminars may be taking place at this point.

Step 7: Implementation

Now the program begins! Whatever you have planned now takes place. Materials, reference books, and curriculum are developed. Archives grow. Teaching happens. The community is doing the real work of language revitalization.

Step 8: Evaluation

The people involved in revitalization must evaluate the progress and effectiveness of the program on a regular basis. Evaluation may include such things as the assessment of language proficiency of learners, the amount and quality of materials developed, the degree to which desired groups are involved (such as the elders who are the speakers of the language), and so on. Whatever the community is doing, is it working? Evaluation may take place informally, where people meet to discuss the good and bad points of the program, or it may involve more formal processes such as the administering of tests to students.

Step 9: Replanning

Evaluation of the program leads back to planning. Given that problems were identified in stage 8, how should the program be modified to solve them? Given that successes were identified in stage 8, does this mean that the community is ready to implement a more advanced goal? Replanning will take place on a constant basis once a program is under way.

CASE STUDIES OF LANGUAGE PLANNING

The Karuk Language Restoration Committee

Christine P. Sims (1996) did a study of Karuk, an endangered language of California. The tribe formed the Karuk Language Restoration Committee in 1988; it is open to any tribal members who wish to be involved but has a core group of about ten active members. The committee was established by the members themselves, but in 1993 it was officially sanctioned by the Karuk Tribal Council, who provided limited financial support. Some members are native speakers; several have participated in the California Master-Apprentice Program and are second-language speakers of varying proficiency. These same members have conducted summer language camps, teach the language in the schools and preschool programs, or hold adult language classes. Thus a great many active language revitalization efforts were taking place before the committee began serious language planning.

The committee began a planning process in 1989 that began with an assessment of Karuk language vitality and reasons for its decline. The committee came up with the following general proposals:

(1) Recording the elders

(2) Developing new fluent speakers over an extended period of time

(3) Educating the community about language restoration and cultural preservation

(4) Involving the community in designing and evaluating a Karuk language restoration program

(5) Promoting community participation in activities where the language could be used

Nancy Richardson Steele, a member of the committee, stresses that language planning is an ongoing process. It is never possible, nor is it desirable, to come up with a finalized rigid plan that will then be implemented without any changes. As plans are implemented, it will be found that some ideas work well, some do not. Some projects require a longer or shorter time period (usually longer) than projected. People get burnt out; other people join in with new skills and knowledge. Research and the experiences of other communities present new ideas and possibilities that people might want to incorporate into a plan for language revitalization. Funding for specific projects might be obtained, or perhaps not obtained, which would necessitate rethinking the plan.

In my university, each department is asked to come up with a five-year plan—every year! Thus we are always thinking five years ahead, but our plans change according to our experience in any given year. Language planning could take place along similar lines. Of course, even if a committee develops a five-year plan, it must be based on goals and missions that may be longer term. The major goal proposed by the Karuk language committee is to make Karuk a language that will one day be used again in the daily course of life. Such a goal is known by the committee to be very long range indeed, and five years was seen to be the minimum time needed to make even a slight initial impact on the language situation.

In summary, Sims says this about the role of Karuk language planning:

> Language planning has undoubtedly been an important factor in all of the initiatives that Karuk people have taken. Planning, for instance, has been instrumental in helping individual Karuks identify needed resources for training, creating opportunities for more Karuk people to be involved in language learning, and in learning appropriate methodologies for language teaching. Much of what has taken place within the last few years has been through individual tribal member efforts in carrying out the goals of Karuk revitalization. The Language Restoration Committee provides the authority for the many different efforts being carried out in Karuk language revitalization. And although community-wide collaboration is not always evident and often difficult to coordinate between various communities, the fact that Karuk people are involved in language restoration at the grassroots level is a considerably different approach than what was tried in the past. (Sims 1996, 20)

The Yurok Language Committee

The Yurok Language Committee consists primarily of elders who speak the language and care greatly about its continuation. An example of language planning by that committee which I observed personally serves as a model for how planning can overcome divisive issues. Yurok is one of several languages in northern California which adopted the UNIFON writing system in the 1970s, an alphabet of odd symbols which was introduced by the training staff from the Center for Indian Community Development at Humboldt State University. (See further discussion of UNIFON in Chapter 19.) UNIFON engendered a great deal of controversy and was especially disliked by linguists, in part because for most of the languages to which it was applied, it failed to represent certain distinctive sounds and overdistinguished nondistinctive sounds. The Yurok version of UNIFON was reasonably good in terms of accurately representing its sounds, but it was not based directly on the Roman alphabet, which meant that it could not be typed, it was impossible to enter on a computer without a special font, and people could not readily use their knowledge of English orthography in learning the system. Nevertheless, some people

liked UNIFON precisely *because* it was not based on English and thus symbolized the separate identity of Indian people and the separateness of Indian languages from English. UNIFON was taught to a number of native-speaking elders, some of whom produced some important materials using that writing system. For example, one Yurok elder, Jessie Exline, has produced a very large and impressive dictionary manuscript of Yurok using UNIFON.

The staff who played the leadership role in the teaching and support of UNIFON are no longer at the university. Linguists working with the tribes continue to use Roman-based orthographies in their work, and in some cases young tribal members studying linguistics have become convinced that the Roman-based systems are superior, for the reasons outlined above. Other young tribal members who see UNIFON for the first time are simply horrified by the foreignness of the symbols. So over the years, the languages using UNIFON have one by one abandoned the system and replaced it with Roman-based alphabets.

However, the elders who learned the system did so with great effort and devoted many hundreds of hours to learning and producing materials using it. The abandonment of UNIFON could negate all their work and devalue the products of their efforts. This would create a potentially dangerous situation wherein the elders, who are the most valuable language experts in the community, could become estranged from the younger generation of language activists.

The Yurok language committee, many members of whom know UNIFON, met the issue of orthography head on. They discussed all the pros and cons of continuing to use UNIFON as the official orthography, and as a group they decided to work on the development of an alternative system. They invited various linguists in to present potential replacement alphabets and to teach the committee how the Roman-based orthographies correlate with UNIFON symbols. They themselves assumed the responsibility of approving the final choice of a writing system. They also decided that at least for now, future publications would be done in both orthographies.

Thus, careful decision-making averted a blowup between orthography factions, made certain that the elders who knew UNIFON were shown proper consideration and respect, and thus assured continued cooperation between all parties. By inviting linguistic consultants to propose orthographies but keeping the final decision on orthography as the responsibility of the committee, the committee also asserted community control over language policy.

CONCLUSION

Darrell Kipp, one of the founders of the Blackfeet immersion school system in Montana, often cautions people wanting to save their language not to wait until conditions are just perfect. "Just do it!" he says. Planning need not be a hurdle that one must get over before language revitalization can begin. If someone has a particular project she or he wants to do, it can be undertaken without necessarily waiting to see how it fits into a large overall language plan for the community. Nor, as we have seen, should language planning ever be thought of as complete. Constant evaluation needs to go on as action is implemented. A continuous evaluative and re-planning component to a language program can help coordinate different projects within a community, develop funding for them, reduce the intensity of factionalism, and ensure that language revitalization efforts develop effectively.

References

Brandt, Elizabeth A., and Vivian Ayoungman. 1989. A practical guide to language renewal. *Canadian Journal of Native Education*, 16(2), 42–77.

Hornberger, Nancy H., ed. 1997. *Indigenous literacies in the Americas: Language planning from the bottom up.* Mouton de Gruyter.

Sims, Christine P. 1996. *Native language communities: A descriptive study of two community efforts to preserve their native languages.* Washington, D.C.: National Indian Policy Center, George Washington University.

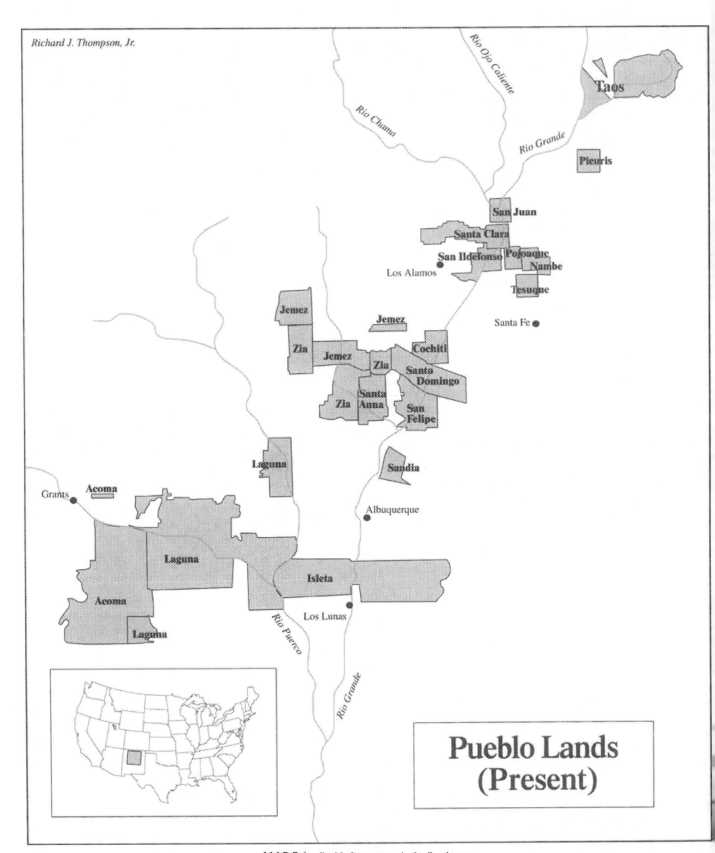

Richard J. Thompson, Jr.

Taos

Pleuris

San Juan

Santa Clara

San Ildefonso   Pojoaque
Los Alamos   Nambe

Tesuque

Santa Fe

Jemez

Jemez

Zia   Jemez   Cochiti

Zia

Santo
Domingo

Santa
Zia   Anna   San
Felipe

Laguna

Sandia

Grants   Acoma

Albuquerque

Laguna

Isleta

Acoma

Laguna

Los Lunas

Rio Puerco

Rio Grande

Rio Chama

Rio Ojo Caliente

Rio Grande

Pueblo Lands
(Present)

MAP 5.1   Pueblo Languages, in the Southwest

Introduction to the Pueblo Languages

LEANNE HINTON

Department of Linguistics
University of California at Berkeley
Berkeley, California

The Pueblo Indians are a group of independent and linguistically disparate communities that got their name from the Spanish explorers. "Pueblo" is the term the Spanish used in their written chronicles to describe the indigenous people who lived in adobe apartment-style houses upon first contact (Christine Sims, personal communication). There are 20 Pueblo communities, counting the Hopis who live in Arizona; all the other current Pueblos are in New Mexico. Four linguistic groups are represented among them: the Tanoan family is represented by the Tiwa language (in Picuris, Taos, Isleta, and Sandia), the Tewa (in San Juan, Santa Clara, San Ildefonso, Nambe, Pojoaque, and Tesuque), and the Towa (Jemez). The Keresan languages go by the names of their pueblos: Acoma, Laguna, San Felipe, Santa Ana, Cochiti, Zia, and Santo Domingo. Zuni is a language isolate, and Hopi is a Uto-Aztecan language.

Spanish explorations of the 16th century were soon followed by masses of military men and church officials who ruled the Southwest with an iron fist. The Pueblo Revolt of 1680 "culminated decades of resentment of religious persecution, demands for tribute payment, involuntary labor, and conflicts between religious and civil authorities who demanded obedience from Pueblo Indians" (Pueblo Indian Cultural Center Web site). This allowed the Pueblos a brief period of autonomy, but one marked by continuing battles with both the Spanish and with other tribes. De Vargas reentered in 1692 with his troops and restored Spanish rule to the Southwest. During this time, the Pueblos suffered devastating losses in battle, and some were destroyed completely.

Spanish rule continued until Mexico gained its independence from Spain in the latter part of the 19th century, and a few years later the Americans took over the New Mexico Territory.

During Spanish and Mexican rule, there was little in the way of language suppression, but there was a great deal of suppression of indigenous religious practices. People were harshly punished for practicing their traditional religion, and Catholic ritual was forced upon the Pueblos. Since most of the church ritual and catechesis was done in Spanish, many Pueblo people became limited bilinguals, with Spanish being used in the church and to a limited extent in trade. As Chris Sims says (personal communication),

> Much like how Pueblos took their native religion "underground" and secretly kept away from the eyes of Spanish authorities, so also did they do this with the language. They in essence kept apart what was native and what they were willing to adapt to in "surface" culture so as to keep the Spanish at bay. The Pueblo secular governments introduced and established by the Spanish for each Pueblo was also a buffer that kept the native religious leadership in position to continue leading their people in indigenous native lifeways, while the secular positions played an intervening role that dealt with outsiders. It is still that way today in many Pueblos.

Indeed, many of the Pueblos have treated their language as "secret," and some of these languages are among the least well described in the linguistic literature because of that philosophy. Related to this is the feeling among many Pueblo people that their language should not be recorded or written, as illustrated among the Cochiti.

Today most of the Pueblos retain a religious structure much like the one they developed under Spanish rule, which combines Catholic and indigenous elements. Under American rule, assimilation policies have dominated, including language suppression, which was practiced through boarding-school policies until just a few decades ago; and as English has come to rule more and more aspects of daily life and as environmental degradation conducted by mainstream culture and the accompanying economic changes have forced the decline of some of the traditional ways that supported the languages, the languages have fallen into decline. Of all the Pueblos, at this point only four of them—Jemez, Santo Domingo, San Felipe, and Zuni—have a large number of children who speak their native tongue on entering kindergarten. For some of the others, language "tip" occurred relatively recently, so that people of parenting age know the language, but not their children; and for still others it occurred somewhat longer ago, so that the native speakers are all of grandparent age.

References

Pueblo Indian Cultural Center. 1997. Pueblo Indians of New Mexico Web site, at <http://www.bhs.edu/wmc/lzc/Pueblos.html>

6

Native Language Planning
A Pilot Process in the Acoma Pueblo Community

CHRISTINE P. SIMS

Department of Education and Linguistics
University of New Mexico
Albuquerque, New Mexico (and Acoma, New Mexico)

In the spring of 1997, a number of Acoma Pueblo tribal members embarked upon a campaign to revitalize concern about Acoma language retention in their community. Envisioning the potential impact of engaging community resources to address this challenge, a plan began to emerge for developing and implementing community-based initiatives designed to stem further Acoma language erosion and to attempt reversal of a critical shift toward English.

Since the initial community discussions of 1997, a series of events has brought together a core group of Acoma speakers who have focused their efforts on building a foundation of understanding about issues of native language loss and revitalization in their community. These initial experiences, which are currently in progress, underscore a number of issues that point to the complex nature of language restoration work in Native American communities. A critical part of this process has involved the collection of data in the community focusing on language use in the community and the present status of the language. This has been used to plan, develop, and pilot Acoma language immersion programs for the community

This essay begins with a background presentation of past historical influences that have helped shape and contributed to the current status of the Acoma language. Some of the key findings from data collected in the community and the events that have influenced community language planning are described. Past efforts to address Acoma language retention are discussed and provide insight into the choices and decisions that have guided efforts in the Acoma community thus far.

THE ACOMA COMMUNITY

Acoma Pueblo is one of 19 Pueblo Indian tribes in New Mexico located in the northwestern region of the state. The Keres language is spoken by six of these pueblos, including Acoma. Members of Acoma and of its adjacent neighbor, Laguna Pueblo, are considered the western Keres speakers. The two tribes are geographically located some distance from the remaining Keres language communities situated further east along the Rio Grande. Some linguists consider the Keres language family to be an isolated language group (Davis 1959) with no known affiliations to other native languages in North America.

The sprawling reservation community of approximately 3,000 enrolled Acoma tribal members is located 64 miles west of Albuquerque. The total tribal rolls are actually greater by at least another 2,000 or so members; however, many families live off the Acoma reservation in nearby towns, where job resources are more readily available (1998 Acoma Tribal Census Records). In a limited sense, the reservation provides some isolation from urbanized centers, although recently the rise in New Mexico's tourism industry and opening of a tribally operated casino off the reservation now brings additional numbers of outside visitors to the pueblo. Most visitors come to see the famous "Sky City," a tourist reference to the Acomas' ancestral village, which sits atop a 350-foot sandstone mesa. Located 15 miles north of the old village are the modern-day villages of Acomita, McCartys, and Anzac. Most tribal members live in these villages, which are closer to the major east-west interstate highway and local schools, and provide access to electricity, natural gas, and running water.

63

The ancestral village of Haak'u (the traditional Acoma name), on the other hand, is occupied by a few Acoma families year round, including individuals who are annually appointed by the *caciques*[1] as the spiritual caretakers of the pueblo. Water, fuel, and food must all be taken to the top of the mesa, as the old village has no modern conveniences such as indoor plumbing, running water, or electricity. Most Acoma families have homes in the modern-day villages but still maintain family homes at the old village as well. Acoma families return to the old village for feast days, native religious observances, and other community events throughout the year.

The gradual move of the Acoma population from the main ancestral village to the three northern villages, beginning in the late 1800s, was influenced in part by the entrance of the railroad that ran directly through the Acoma reservation (Minge, 1976). The railroad provided the first modern means of transportation for Acoma children attending federal boarding schools off the reservation after the turn of the century. It also introduced wage-earning labor to the Acoma male population and created a limited pipeline for manufactured goods and American-made products to enter into Acoma life.

The old village of Haak'u serves as the center for the pueblo's native religious observances, and it is here, when Acoma families come together, that the use of the native Acoma language plays a key part during ceremonies and social functions. This is especially true among older and middle-aged adult generations in the community. During these events the old village is usually closed to the non-Indian public, with some events lasting several days. Thus, Acoma families have the opportunity to engage in the social and ceremonial discourse that is a key aspect of public use of the language and is available for younger generations to observe and hear. With few modern conveniences available in the old village, it is possible during these events to shut out one medium of English language intrusion, namely television. However, unconscious habits of using English have been increasingly observed among native speakers in these settings and threaten to undermine the continued use of the Acoma language for purposes of public and private discourse.

ACOMA GOVERNANCE

Acoma Pueblo is one of the few tribes in New Mexico that has retained a traditional system of governance, meaning that each year the pueblo's secular governing officials, tribal council members, and native religious appointees are made by the religious leaders of the pueblo, namely the caciques. Only men can serve as tribal officials. The secular officials consist of a governor, two lieutenant governors, a tribal interpreter, and a tribal secretary. Additionally, there is a tribal council consisting of 12 men and 3 tribal sheriffs. The titles of several of these offices reflect their origin in the Spanish colonial rule imposed on indigenous people during the 16th century. The offices were integrated over time with the indigenous form of governance, which predated early Spanish contact. Hence, yearly appointment of tribal leaders includes both secular positions and traditional religious leaders. The indigenous societal structure was based upon a cooperative relationship and interdependence of various clans and societies. These groups provided a complex support system of collective responsibility for the well-being of the whole community. Each had some part in carrying out various religious functions and providing for the material needs of the community through collective functions and activities.

Today, Acoma clans still function as the social foundation for a matrilineal society. The role of native religious leaders in appointing secular and native religious positions continues to uphold the sociocultural and socioreligious systems of the pueblo. Thus, appointed secular leaders such as the governor and other tribal officials play an important role not only as public leaders who provide an interface between the tribe and the outside world, but also as protectors of the internal core of traditional governance and native religious leadership.

In the domain of governance therefore, oral Acoma language use continues to be an important part of council deliberations and public meetings involving the community, as well as in conducting the internal affairs of the pueblo's socioreligious life. Within this domain, however, the variance in mastery of formal Acoma discourse is becoming increasingly apparent. Older fluent adult speakers still use the language with ease in these contexts, while younger adults rely on a mix of English and Acoma or on English only. Many in this latter group have not yet mastered the more complex structures of oral discourse, while others simply do not either understand or speak the language.

EARLY SPANISH CONTACT

When 16th-century Spanish explorers and settlers arrived in the Southwest, new cultural, political, economic, and religious influences were introduced and adapted to varying degrees in all of the pueblos, including Acoma. For instance, the economic livelihood of Acoma Pueblo before contact centered upon an agricultural lifestyle. With the arrival of the Spanish, new cultivation tools, domesticated animals, and even new crops added to the agricultural life of the pueblo. Thus, the Spanish names for these items were eventually incorporated into the Acoma lexicon as well (Miller 1960).

Perhaps far more significant, however, was the influence and adaptation of a Spanish socioreligious system imposed upon the Acoma people. In the region's arid desert climate, where cultivation depended on summer rains, a complex native religious system had developed over centuries long before Spanish contact in the 1500s. This native cosmology, which centered upon human beings' relationship with creation, depended upon song, dance, and ritual to ensure that the earth continued to yield its gifts of sustenance season after season. This native religious system, however, was what early Spanish colonial powers tried to dismantle and replace with Spanish Catholicism, often through oppressive and brutal measures. Eventually, over time, Spanish Catholicism did take root among the Acomas. This was also the beginning of Spanish cultural influences that eventually were incorporated into the seasonal calendar of native religious observances. The language of Spanish Catholicism inclusive of prayers and rituals was learned by the Acoma people at that time. Today, Acoma people celebrate saints' feast days and baptismal ceremonies and observe seasonal celebrations such as Christmas, All Souls' Day, and Easter. As extensive as these influences were, the Acomas continued to practice their native traditions and kept their native belief systems alive throughout Spanish colonial rule. This was possible only as a result of the native religion being taken underground and practiced in secret, despite the fact that Acomas outwardly complied with the Spanish imposed religion.

This dual system of religious practice still exists today. Most present-day Acomas practice Catholicism and observe native religious practices as well. Both are openly practiced and embraced by many as a single socioreligious system. There is, however, a marked difference between the aforementioned celebrations originating with Spanish Catholicism and those involving native religious observances. These latter events are usually closed to non-Indians, and there are strict prohibitions on providing information about them to the outside world. Acoma language use in these domains continues to be strongest among middle-aged and older adults of the community. On the other hand, the use of Spanish for Catholic observances has long since been replaced by English as the language for prayers and rituals conducted in church settings.

Over the course of nearly three centuries of Spanish historical influence, some Acomas learned a functional level of Spanish. There was also some limited incorporation of Spanish vocabulary into the Acoma language itself. This occurred primarily in three domains: the government, where the language of Spanish governance and economics was required to communicate with outsiders; Spanish Catholicism, which required the use of language in church rituals, prayers, and songs; and everyday life, influenced by the introduction of new material culture from Spanish colonial life. The internal syntactic structure of the Acoma language remained, on the other hand, relatively intact and free from Spanish influence. This may have been possible because of the selective adaptation of Spanish lexical items and through deliberate separation of the two languages for very different uses and specific functions.

Following the Spanish and Mexican periods of government, the acquisition of New Mexico Territory by the United States introduced an even more rapid pace of new foreign influence and change to the Acoma community, especially in the socioeconomic and education domains (Minge 1976). Expanding Anglo-American interests directly introduced these changes throughout the second half of the 19th century and the early 20th, bringing with them as well a new foreign language: English. This introduction made its most influential mark on the status of the Acoma language for generations born during and after the early 1900s.

ANGLO-AMERICAN INFLUENCES IN THE 20TH CENTURY

In the late 1800s, the Atlantic and Pacific Railway company had begun to build a major east-west railroad line across the country, one which eventually ran directly through Acoma land (Minge 1976). This development alone had a far-reaching impact on the social and economic lifestyle of the Acoma people. For example, in order to lay the tracks and maintain the grades for the railroad, the company offered limited wage labor to Acoma males for the first time. The railroad also influenced a gradual demographic shift away from the old village to the three satellite villages where train stops were eventually located. Outlets and markets for the sale of wool and livestock that could be shipped by rail also prompted a rise in the number of families who began to establish herds of sheep and cattle in addition to maintaining their agricultural subsistence. Railroads also provided a new transportation mode that made it possible for the first Acoma children to be transported to far-off military boarding schools in Oklahoma and Carlisle, Pennsylvania, during the late 1890s (Minge 1976) and to boarding schools in Albuquerque and Santa Fe during the early 1900s.

By the 1920s, the presence of a major automobile route through the reservation opened up other avenues of influence on Acoma families as well. The sale of Acoma pottery to tourists traveling through the reservation opened the doors for increased contact with non-Indians, while creating limited cash outlets for a few Acoma women who sold their wares in roadside stands along U.S. Route 66 (Minge 1976).

UNITED STATES GOVERNMENT EDUCATION POLICIES

Owing to these and other socioeconomic developments, the federal government began overwhelmingly to pressure the Acomas to assimilate into mainstream American society. The situation was exacerbated when federal Indian education policies of the late 1800s and early 1900s forced Indian tribes to begin to send their children to government-run schools (Adams 1995). Forced schooling practices aimed at removing Indian children from the influence of native traditions and culture were carried out through military-type institutions and vocational-training boarding schools established for Indian children far from home (Adams 1995). In 1881 the first Acoma boys and girls left for the Carlisle Indian Training School in Pennsylvania and Chilocco Indian School in Oklahoma (Minge 1976). Later, off-reservation boarding schools were established closer to home, allowing Acoma students to attend schools in Albuquerque and Santa Fe. These places, however, were still distant enough that Acoma children seldom returned home during the school year. By 1883, Acoma reported 30 students enrolled at Carlisle and the Albuquerque Indian School (Minge 1976).

When U.S. government day schools began to appear in the Acoma villages of McCartys and Acomita by 1891 (Minge 1976), tremendous pressure was placed on Acoma families to send their children to school. For a time, this became a source of internal friction, as some elders and traditional leaders viewed the white man's education as a threat to continued Acoma culture (Minge 1976). Some saw the very changes in dress and appearance among Acoma children returning from boarding schools as direct signs of this threat. Others were convinced that the white man's education would benefit their children and that the learning of English and vocational trades would better enable them to deal with the outside world. The acquisition of the white man's language was viewed by some as a necessary part of Acoma survival, and children were urged to learn it at school. Acoma children who had formerly spent their entire adolescent years in family and community settings were uprooted from this familiar environment and placed in formal schooling settings where only English was spoken.

Thus, for the first groups of Acoma children introduced to formal government boarding schools in the late 1800s and early 1900s, education was a cultural and linguistic shock. The Acoma language had been the students' one and only language. They acquired English for school functions under strict, punitive conditions that remain in the memories of many Acoma elders today. Among some Acoma children who were initially taken to military boarding schools back east for long periods of time and at a very young age, temporary Acoma language loss sometimes occurred (Acoma elders, personal communication), as did cultural displacement within the community upon their return to the pueblo (Minge 1976).

Subsequent generations born after the 1920s and who were schooled in boarding institutions closer to home or in village day schools were able to maintain and develop their Acoma language skills, owing to several factors: a strong foundation in the native language, developed during early formative years at home; the continued use of the Acoma language, albeit clandestinely, among Acoma-speaking peers at school; and continued use of the Acoma language in family and community domains that were separate from the school setting. This latter factor was especially important for Acoma day-school students, as it meant that daily exposure to Acoma-speaking adult models could still be maintained throughout the early formative and adolescent years. Many Acomas from these generations are today's bilingual grandparents and great-grandparents of the Acoma community.

Among the young adult Acoma male population born after the 1920s, military conscription and contact with the world beyond the reservation also introduced new influences. By 1950, at least two generations of Acoma men had served in either one of the two world wars or the Korean conflict. Returning Acoma veterans, armed with new skills and the GI Bill, were most likely to seek wage-earning jobs in nearby towns; some also moved away from the reservation temporarily in order to take advantage of vocational training available in distant towns and cities. Thus, the isolation gap between Acomas and American Anglo society began to close rapidly especially after the 1950s as access to American material goods, wage-labor jobs, and transportation became more readily available to more and more Acomas.

As local public secondary schools began to open up to New Mexico Indians after the 1930s and 1940s, more of the Acoma youth were further influenced through increased contact with non-Indian peers, who often made up the majority of students in the local county high school. The first groups of Acoma students attending public high school had to travel to the town of Grants, located some 15 miles away from the Acoma reservation. Acoma students were usually transported from the reservation by local non-Indians who owned automobiles. Secondary-education experiences further exposed older Acoma adolescents to modern influences well beyond the boundaries of traditional Acoma life. By the 1960s a new high school had been built on the nearby Laguna Pueblo reservation where both Acoma and Laguna students made up the majority of the student body. In this same time period, preschool education was introduced to the Acoma Pueblo community. The advent of federal Head Start programs thus introduced English to Acoma children at a much earlier age than previous generations, and access to secondary education for more Acomas meant that more time was spent in English-based education systems.

LANGUAGE SHIFT IN THE ACOMA COMMUNITY

Indications about the depth of language shift that had taken place concomitantly with social, economic, and educational changes in the community began to emerge by the early 1980s as more and more Acoma children entered elementary school speaking English as their first language. By

1997, when surveys about Acoma language use in families and in the community were conducted, results confirmed that there were no children of preschool or elementary school age speaking Acoma as a first language. Furthermore, many Acoma parents in the 20–40 age range were also experiencing difficulty in reinforcing Acoma language use at home, many citing their own lack of understanding or inability to speak the language as a reason for their children not speaking Acoma. A one-year language planning process undertaken in the Acoma community attempted to further identify the extent to which the Acoma language had begun to erode and among which generations language loss was most critical. Various age groups in the community, including school-age children, middle-aged adults, and young adult parents were surveyed.

Table 6.1 presents responses from a sample group of Acoma Head Start parents responding to the 1997 Acoma Language Use Survey when asked about their use of the Acoma language in the home.

TABLE 6.1 Parent Responses about Acoma Language Use at Home (N = 47)

Statement	Percentage of respondents who agree with statement
Acoma is not spoken at home	19%
Acoma is "sometimes" spoken at home	45%
Acoma is spoken "very little" at home	36%

When this sample group was asked to explain their reasons for not speaking Acoma at home, many of their responses indicated that they did not speak or understand the language well enough to use it with their children. A sample of their responses is presented in Table 6.2.

Survey results indicated that over half of the parents in this age group, or 47 respondents, were in their 20s. Table 6.3 shows that almost half, or 49% of this parent group, had grown up in families where English had been spoken (Boynton and Sims, 1998).

TABLE 6.2 Parent Explanations about the Lack of Acoma Language use in the Home

"I tried to, but I can't speak the Acoma language."

"Because I really don't know how to."

"I just speak short phrases."

"Because we're so used to English."

"My children don't understand."

"I don't know how to speak the language well."

"I can barely speak the language."

TABLE 6.3 Head Start Parents' Responses to Acoma Language Use in the Home during their Formative Years (N = 47)

Statement	Percentage of respondents who agree with statement
Parents "always" spoke Acoma	51%
Parents "sometimes" spoke Acoma	26%
Parents spoke "very little" Acoma	6%
Parents spoke no Acoma	17%

For many concerned tribal members, the results of the 1997 Acoma Language Use Survey confirmed what most people in the community already knew intuitively about the status of the language. Signs of language erosion had begun to appear, especially in places like the home, where native language fluency had formerly been strongest. The extent to which language erosion had taken place in various domains and the relative strength and weakness of Acoma language use among different sample age groups became clearer as additional survey data were gathered and analyzed. The data in Table 6.3, for example, further clarified why present-day Acoma language use among Head Start parents at home was so low. This group had been influenced to a large degree by the introduction of English into their homes during their early formative years (Boynton and Sims, 1998).

The response of present-day generations of elementary- and secondary-school Acoma students to the question of what language their parents used most with them at home revealed a similar shift in language use as shown in Table 6.4.

TABLE 6.4 Language Used Most Often by Parents When Speaking to Youth in the Home

No. of Students	Mostly English	Both Acoma and English	Mostly Acoma
Grades 9–12 (N = 136)	23%	71%	6%
Grades 7–8 (N = 74)	22%	70%	8%
Grades 4–6 (N = 103)	13%	78%	10%

Other results from the 1997 survey showed that while a majority of the community viewed Acoma language retention positively, the diversity of proposed solutions for revitalizing the language underscored the complex nature of bringing together a unified cohesive effort to meet this challenge. Furthermore, the need to clarify issues related to community attitudes and understanding of language transmission processes appeared to be just as important as initiating any revitalization effort in the community. The overriding question was where to begin.

BUILDING FOUNDATIONS
OF UNDERSTANDING

Much of the historical background recounted in the previous sections formed the basis of a collective body of information that was gathered in the community during a one-year language planning study funded by the Administration for Native Americans (ANA) under the U.S. Department of Health and Human Services. The collection of historical information and data concerning the present status of the Acoma language served as a critical beginning point for reflection and discussion among members of the pueblo. In addition, data was gathered in both quantitative and qualitative form to determine:

(1) to what extent Acoma language was being used in home and community settings;
(2) to what extent Acoma language use was a part of people's family history;
(3) the general attitude toward the use and value of retaining the Acoma language; and
(4) the interest level of tribal members in learning and teaching the Acoma language.

Qualitative data were gathered, including classroom observations of Acoma children and their use of language in three tribal Head Start centers. This was done to ascertain the quality of Acoma language learning opportunities engaged in by the children in these settings. Interviews with community elders and oral group surveys were also conducted with tribal members and parents. In these interviews tribal members offered their perspectives about native language teaching and learning, thus providing further insight into various sociocultural aspects fundamental to language vitality in the Acoma community.

This latter process was especially critical in providing an open forum for expressing personal views and perspectives about issues related to language loss in the community. Group discussions allowed both fluent and nonfluent speakers to present their viewpoints about past experiences that were sometimes painful reminders of how Acoma language use had been dealt with in the past. For older generations there were the reminders of early forced schooling experiences and memories of humiliation and punishment for speaking Acoma, the only language they knew at the time. Acoma nonspeakers related contemporary experiences that had discouraged them from trying to speak Acoma and described how the lack of understanding from older fluent speakers often resulted in embarrassment or low self-esteem. As well, there were conflicting perceptions about who was to blame for the current status of Acoma language loss and whose responsibility it was to address the issue. Only through open discussion of these and other sensitive topics concerning the language was it possible to move beyond individual and group feelings of guilt and blame. It further al-

lowed a move forward with a positive focus on what had to be done and how an approach could be developed that would encourage the participation of speakers and nonspeakers alike. These concerns also drew attention to how Acoma language teaching needed to be conducted in order to avoid repeating unpleasant language-learning experiences of the past as well as to plan a program that would encompass the different generations in the community.

A yearlong process of learning about language-teaching strategies and appropriate approaches to create needed change in the community began to take place. Throughout 1997 and 1998, a small group of tribal members attended training sessions and native language forums sponsored by the Linguistic Institute for Native Americans (LINA), a New Mexico–based training organization. They also became involved in an ongoing effort to inform the rest of the Acoma community, including parents and the tribal leadership, about Acoma language issues, so that a broader foundation of support and participation could be established. LINA trainers and consultants, knowledgeable about pueblo language communities as well as language acquisition and second-language teaching issues, assisted with many of these training efforts.

It should be noted that building these foundations of understanding took time; they did not develop overnight. These initial efforts also did not immediately bring the entire community together. However, the fact that various members of the community came together as a group to discuss language loss issues gave far more impetus to collaborative commitments at this beginning stage of revitalization efforts. Tribal members who in their various capacities as traditional appointed officers, leaders, elders, and parents represented a small but committed core group that evolved and expanded over a two-year period. As participation of this group in language planning and training sessions continued, so also did their understanding of language issues most critical in their community. The development of this community base proved vastly different from previous school-based efforts in which Acoma language and culture instruction had since languished for lack of community involvement and participation.

EARLY BILINGUAL
PROGRAM EFFORTS

Previous efforts to address Acoma language teaching stemmed from local school-based efforts during the late 1970s through the late 1980s. These efforts were instituted through federal Title VII bilingual programs and focused primarily on the production of Acoma cultural materials to help supplement the regular curriculum in the local Bureau of Indian Affairs (BIA) elementary school located on the Acoma reservation (H. Berendzen, personal communication 1997).

While these early efforts were well intentioned and did

raise awareness of the importance of using Acoma-related materials in the instructional program, the bottom line was that these were transitional programs geared toward the improvement of English and were not intended as native-language teaching programs per se. Moreover, these programs had not produced what was most critical to Acoma language stability and vitality: new generations of Acoma speakers.

Another major activity of these early bilingual program efforts focused on development of a writing system for the Acoma-Keres dialect. With the help of linguists, these efforts resulted in a few Acoma teaching personnel who learned to write the language. Their skills were utilized in producing a limited amount of written Acoma materials for use in the local BIA elementary school. Native language literacy in the school and community, however, never flourished outside this setting. Moreover, the bilingual program and Acoma materials production ceased when federal funding ran out by the late 1980s (Boynton and Sims 1998).

During the 1990s, efforts to provide Acoma language instruction in the BIA elementary school were carried out sporadically and mostly through individual Acoma teacher efforts. In the 1997 Acoma Language Use Survey Report, instructional time devoted to Acoma language teaching was reported as being the result of isolated efforts, with no central focus on developing oral language speakers and no articulated language-instructional curriculum. Moreover, the existing gap between these efforts and the absence of parental and community involvement prevented any cohesive front against continued language erosion on a broader community scale.

A TIME FOR PLANNING

As discussions among tribal members proceeded in early 1997, there was no argument that the community was moving toward a critical point of language loss. However, this had never been substantiated with a body of data that could help place the problem in proper perspective and provide insight into some of the salient social attitudes influencing language transmission processes in the community. To what extent, for instance, did the problem of language loss actually exist among different age groups in the community? Did parents want their children to learn to speak Acoma? What were the expectations of different generations as to the value of teaching and learning the Acoma language? Did Acoma youth have any desire to learn the Acoma language? What had contributed to Acoma language erosion, and what could be done to turn it around?

Answers to these questions and other issues were brought forth in the results of the 1997 Acoma Language Use Survey. Data in Table 6.5, for example, show how Acoma youth responded when asked about the importance of learning the Acoma language.

Adults, as well, indicated a strong interest in maintaining

TABLE 6.5   Students Responding to the Statement: "Learning Acoma Is As Important As Learning English"

Students	Agree	Disagree
Grades 9–12 (N = 131)	93%	7%
Grades 7–8 (N = 74)	91%	9%
Grades 4–6 (N = 104)	88%	12%

the language and often placed high value on its use, especially with regard to carrying on traditional practices, its importance to Acoma identity, and its use as a medium of communication within the Acoma community. These feelings were also frequently expressed by Acoma youth in written survey statements that indicated a desire to be able to communicate with grandparents and parents in the language. Among tribal employees who responded to the survey, the ability to speak Acoma was especially important in work settings when other Acomas are present or when dealing with non–English speakers in the community.

The aforementioned examples were part of a body of data that was used by the core planning group in moving toward specific plans that would address the various language learning needs of the community. It was clear from the survey, for instance, that intensive instruction in Acoma would be needed for youth and young adults in the community. This would be especially critical for those without immediate access on a daily basis to fluent-speaking individuals in their family. Survey results had shown a high level of interest and a desire to learn the language among these age groups, but many respondents had also stated that they had no one to teach them at home. When asked to provide suggestions for how they could learn Acoma best, students ranked the following responses in order of importance.

1st choice: Have parents or family teach students every day
2nd choice: Have language instruction held in the community
3rd choice: Have language instruction offered at school

Acoma parents needed a stronger awareness of their role in speaking Acoma at home with their children. Many students noted that if their parents were speakers of the language, they tended to use the language with them only during certain times, usually in disciplinary situations. Survey results had also shown that many parents of preschool-age children expected their children to learn Acoma, yet they themselves were unable to support this at home because they did not know the language. Parents of Head Start children suggested in the language use survey that parent workshops and training in Acoma language learning would be helpful, as would language classes for parents. Examples of specific suggestions included:

"Teach parents about traditional Acoma parenting practices."
"Hold weekly language classes for parents."

"Have community-wide language teaching by fluent speakers."

"Have parent-child fairs and get-togethers using the Acoma language."

"Have community classes for parents and young children to understand and speak the language."

Middle-aged adults, on the other hand, also stated their need for continuing the development of their Acoma language skills. The 1997 survey results had shown that while many adults in their 30s and 40s had varying degrees of receptive understanding of the Acoma language, they wanted help in mastering more complex oral uses of the language, especially those required in more formal discourse and traditional practices. Tribal employees working in various community service programs also stated that their line of work often necessitated the use of the Acoma language in order to communicate with non–English speaking elders or to make formal presentations to the tribal council or to the community. These adults wanted help from older fluent speakers so that they could explain concepts about health and nutrition, emergency health care, legal matters, and other areas requiring the explanation of specialized or emergency services.

As language forums and meetings continued during the planning year, a deeper awareness about the need for a multifaceted approach began to emerge. Appropriate methods for second-language teaching and information about oral language development were also explored during language-teaching training sessions. The role of native language literacy was examined as well. It was agreed that the time factor related to development of speakers of the language was far more critical than the time it would take to develop literacy materials and train a substantial number of tribal members to teach native literacy. From these and other discussions, a working approach for teaching youth and adults was eventually developed. This approach focused on oral language development as the basis for Acoma language teaching, utilizing fluent community resources to help implement community-based, intergenerational language-learning initiatives.

Active recruitment of fluent speakers also began as plans for piloting an Acoma language immersion camp for youth slowly took shape. These latter activities became an important step in helping fluent speakers from the community understand the concept behind a total Acoma language learning environment in which young learners would be exposed to rich language input from fluent speakers. Less fluent speakers and parents were also actively recruited to help with the logistics of putting together a daily immersion program that was to last for several weeks. It was hoped that by including them in these efforts, the adults would be encouraged to become active participants in language learning alongside more fluent speakers, as well as to begin using the language with their families at home.

ACOMA LANGUAGE IMMERSION CAMPS

In the closing months of the 1997 planning project year, a two-week summer language immersion camp for youth took place. Teams of fluent speakers implemented language immersion teaching that they had learned in training sessions during the course of the planning year. During the summer of 1998, a second language camp was organized on a much broader scale, extending over a period of six weeks. The programs were attended by Acoma youth in kindergarten through grade 12, along with some preschoolers. Over 90 Acoma youth participated in the 1998 summer program. The 1998 summer camp was supported through a collaborative network of various tribal programs that provided financial and in-kind resources and was staffed by a team of 12 Acoma speakers from the community.

In each of the two pilot efforts, Acoma language immersion provided the setting in which youths and adults were involved in daily interactive language learning activities. The teaching techniques utilized by the staff meant that no English translations were used during the three-hour language sessions. Elementary-school-age children were taught in the morning, while secondary-school students were taught in the afternoon. Teams of fluent speakers were assigned to work with small groups of students so that adult models of everyday conversational Acoma could be heard by the students at all times.

The responsibility for helping students understand Acoma rested on the fluent speakers, so that many of the gestures and games and much of the role playing and use of visual aids were important instructional techniques and resources that were used to help children develop a sense of understanding basic conversational Acoma. The aim was not to force language learners to speak Acoma from the start, but to help them develop a beginning level of understanding so that they could interact immediately with fluent speakers and experience a measure of success in their first attempts to learn the language. Helping the children to speak increased only as students became more comfortable with the instructors and felt "safe" within the learning environment created by a team of supportive and attentive fluent speakers.

Teamwork in planning language lessons and age-appropriate learning activities took place at least one to two months before the summer camp began. These planning sessions also continued as critical weekly activities during the summer program and included fluent Acoma speakers, elders, younger adult speakers, and Acoma language teacher trainers. Games that elders recalled playing when they were young were resurrected as ideas for outdoor activities; the social etiquette of Acoma language use in the community and with parents and elders was identified; short stories using puppets and simple Acoma dialogues were created for presentation to the students; and songs, rhymes, and even team cheers for outdoor baseball games were created by the staff and taught to the children. Additionally, field trips to sites holding special cultural significance in the Acoma community were planned. These latter outings afforded the youth an opportunity to spend time with elders, parents, and other adults from the community, listening to them tell about places and their significance to traditional Acoma life.

Parent participation was encouraged and several mothers and fathers did attend the immersion programs with their children. This included both fluent-speaking parents and nonfluent speakers who participated in various language learning activities. Adult participation was particularly significant to students, many of whom commented at the end of the program that it was helpful to know that adults also needed help learning Acoma, and that adults also made mistakes when trying to speak Acoma.

For parents who could not participate in the classes, an introductory information session was held to explain the language teaching approach that was to be used during the immersion program and how parents could help support their children's language learning. These sessions were also utilized to present basic information about children's native language development, the natural progression and stages of second language learning, and practical ideas for reinforcing Acoma language learning at home.

The culminating event of the 1998 six-week immersion program was an evening of Acoma storytelling presented to the community by the students. This program of short skits, complete with puppetry and background scenery created by the children, was presented during the final week of the program. With much planning, coaching, and rehearsing of the Acoma dialogue accompanying student-created skits, the program was presented to an overflowing crowd of parents, grandparents, and community members. On the night of the program, the Acoma language staff explained to the crowd that while fluent Acoma speech was not going to be evident among all the youth, the fact that they were willing to take the risk of speaking Acoma in a public setting was significant in itself. Many parents later expressed their gratitude for the summer program. Some shared positive experiences that had taken place in their families as a natural result of children's introducing Acoma language use back into the home. Apparently, some children took the language games, songs, and routine dialogues learned during classes and had begun to use them with siblings or with parents at home. Elders also voiced their hope that with continued effort and community commitment, these generations could indeed be encouraged to speak Acoma once more.

PILOTING RESULTS AND CONTINUING EFFORTS

The immediate success of the summer language camps was evident in a number of ways. First, there was the overall enthusiasm of the youth participants about the summer program. Informal group surveys conducted with students at the close of the immersion camp showed that four factors were important in their language immersion experiences: (1) the comfortable language learning environment created by the staff, which made language learning fun and stress free, especially when mistakes were made; (2) the interaction of both adults and youth in language learning; (3) the patient modeling of spoken Acoma by adults; and (4) the ready assistance of fluent speakers in helping students understand what was being said in Acoma. Second, among parents of student participants, there was equal enthusiasm expressed about the changes they had begun to observe in their children. For instance, many of the parents noted that the students had begun to develop a stronger bond of relationship and identity among themselves as they learned about clan relationships with other students who were formerly strangers to them. They noted how at the end of the six weeks many of the youth were using each other's Indian names rather than their English names. One parent noted that in her family the games and learning activities children learned during the immersion camp were being introduced to younger siblings at home and that speaking Acoma around the dinner table was becoming more of a family affair as children themselves initiated speaking games with family members. Lastly, several parents commented that their children's enthusiasm about learning Acoma had prompted conscious efforts on the parents' part to speak more Acoma at home, and that in some instances children were the ones teaching their parents Acoma words they had learned in class.

There were also changes in attitude among the native-speaking teachers who participated in the piloting efforts. Program evaluation comments submitted by the staff showed that they had made adjustments in their own initial assumptions about language teaching. Through firsthand observation of children's language learning, some noted that they could see the natural stages and progression of learning that had been spoken about during their training sessions. Many of the teachers commented on how important it was to focus on the learner, to be observant of children's efforts to speak (or reluctance to speak), and to know when and how to step in to help language learners. Former assumptions and expectations about language learning were influenced in a way that suggested that fluent speakers become more sensitized to how they spoke to one another as well as to their growing realization of the collective responsibility for helping others learn the language.

Documented comments and initial observations like these indicated that an emerging awareness about language had begun in the Acoma community. Increased reminders were being made by tribal leaders in public settings urging parents and grandparents to speak to their children in the Acoma language. Adult males who observed training sessions or sat in on some of the summer program sessions also took back information to the tribal council to clarify the immersion approach to other tribal leaders. This dispersal of information among the community and tribal leadership generated powerful testimony and growing support of the approach that had been initiated.

The most significant support for these emerging initiatives, however, came from within the traditional religious domains, where conscious efforts slowly began to help young males with the more formal registers of language use. This was an outcome that the planning and teaching group had hoped would eventually take place as other fluent speakers in the community realized the need to teach the Acoma language. This extension of awareness and responsibility was a critical part of the foundation building initially envisioned as a key link in the effort to establish a community-wide focus on Acoma language maintenance.

FUTURE PLANS

These preliminary outcomes involving data gathering, pilot teaching efforts, and community discussions served as important stepping-stones toward the eventual development of a long-range plan for Acoma language revitalization and retention. The current plan serves as the framework for immediate and future initiatives and provides a guiding source for community involvement and oversight of long-term efforts by an advisory language committee established in 1999 by the Acoma Tribal Council. A major portion of the long-range plan also became the basis for a two-year Acoma Language Retention project, currently in operation and funded by the Administration for Native Americans.

The Acoma Language Retention and Revitalization Plan identifies the most critical needs and long-term goals, including:

(1) Acoma language instruction and training for parents and caregivers;
(2) year-round Acoma language instruction for preschool, elementary-, and secondary-level students;
(3) Acoma language instructor training for fluent speakers employed as teachers and paraprofessionals in tribal Head Start programs, the BIA school, and other schools with significant populations of Acoma students;
(4) Acoma language classes for adults who are nonspeakers or incipient speakers; and
(5) adult language classes for community members and tribal employees in specialized areas.

For each critical area of need, the necessary resources for carrying out training and implementing Acoma language teaching activities have been identified. This plan is used to solicit various kinds of support from tribal programs such as training and implementation costs, instructor stipends, instructional materials and supplies, and use of facilities for language classes.

A major complement to the plan itself is the Acoma Language Advisory Committee. This group serves as the sanctioned planning group responsible for guiding future language initiatives in the community. Their responsibilities include gathering ongoing assessment of existing and future language initiatives; providing community training about language issues and language teaching; ensuring that all future initiatives maintain a central focus on producing new speakers; and reporting to the tribal leadership about the progress being made in meeting long-term language revitalization goals. Many of the original core group members involved in the initial stages described herein now serve on this committee, as does the project coordinator for the Acoma Language Retention Project funded by the Administration for Native Americans.

SUMMARY AND CONCLUSIONS

This description of language revitalization efforts in Acoma Pueblo provides a brief account of events leading to a community-based approach for language maintenance and revitalization. Over the course of the past several years, as various events have unfolded in this community, several stages of development have been critical to these preliminary efforts. These developments did not stem from a school-oriented focus, but rather from community-based support, participation, and commitment, including:

(1) an assessment of language use in the community to identify the vitality of the Acoma language in various domains and across different generations;
(2) the gathering of a cadre of community people committed to broadening an understanding of language issues facing their community;
(3) the recruitment and training of fluent speakers as language teachers in the community;
(4) the implementation of language teaching programs that introduced tribal members to firsthand experiences with native language teaching and second-language learners; and
(5) the development of a long-range plan to create new generations of native Acoma speakers.

As these stages of development evolved, several concomitant internal changes were also noted with respect to perspectives and attitudes of various groups in the community and at various levels of participation, from student participants in language immersion programs, to parents of student participants, to tribal leaders and native speaker teachers. These internal changes suggest that a key part of the initial revitalization effort included factors that were more internal to the process—that is, the expectations and perspective brought together through community dialogue and active participation of speakers and nonspeakers alike.

This allowed for movement of the community toward a deeper awareness and an appreciation of the serious nature of native language erosion. Moreover, the process of building community support provided important foundations for community training, planning, and implementation.

While much of the current literature on language shift often focuses on causes leading to this growing phenomenon among minority and heritage language groups (Fishman 1972; 1991), it may be that understanding the dynamics of individual language communities and how they contribute to the process of language revitalization and maintenance is just as critical. Informed and in-depth understanding about these and other language issues is especially relevant to native heritage language communities concerned about the future of their languages. Continuing efforts to document processes such as those described herein might also lead to further understanding of how native language communities can be best assisted in their efforts to keep their languages alive for future generations.

Note

1. The term *cacique,* first introduced under 16th-century Spanish colonial rule and used to denote an indigenous leader in the New World, may be of Carib origin, according to the Keres linguist H. Valiquette.

References

Adams, D. W. 1995. *Education for extinction: American Indians and the boarding school experience, 1875–1928.* Lawrence: University of Kansas Press.

Boynton, D., and Sims, C. P. 1998. Acoma language retention project plan. Document prepared for the Pueblo of Acoma's 1998 language proposal submitted to the Administration for Native Americans, U.S. Department of Health and Human Services.

Davis, I. 1959. Linguistic clues to northern Rio Grande history. *El Palacio* 66: 73–84.

Fishman, J. A. 1972. Domains and the relationship between micro and macro-sociolinguistics. In *Directions in sociolinguistics: The ethnography of communication,* ed. J. J. Gumperz and D. Hymes, 435–53. New York: Holt, Rinehart, and Winston.

———. 1991. *Reversing language shift.* Clevedon and Philadelphia: Multilingual Matters.

Miller, W. R. 1960. Spanish loanwords in Acoma. *International Journal of American Linguistics* 26, no. 1: 41–49.

Minge, W. A. 1976. *Acoma.* Albuquerque: University of New Mexico Press.

Pueblo of Acoma. 1998. Tribal Census Records.

7

The Key to Cultural Survival

Language Planning and Revitalization in the Pueblo de Cochiti

REGIS PECOS

Governor
Cochiti Pueblo
Cochiti, New Mexico

REBECCA BLUM-MARTINEZ

College of Education
University of New Mexico
Albuquerque, New Mexico

For over 20 years the Pueblo de Cochiti has been involved in a struggle for cultural survival, fighting the many forces that have threatened their beliefs and their way of life. Federal and state policies and institutions have pressured the community to accept and assimilate into an English-speaking, urban, individualistic consumerism, as they have other linguistic and cultural minorities. However, in addition to these threats the Pueblo de Cochiti also faced the monumental tragedy of the loss of their spiritual and agricultural lands. Since the mid-1980s, this community has used most of its financial and human resources to recover those lands so that its people could re-engage in a traditional lifestyle. Part of this struggle has included special attention to retaining and revitalizing the native language, Keres, for the various generations of tribal members. As the forces from mainstream society have encroached on native values and beliefs, the native language has increasingly become the core symbol for a renewed commitment to a traditional Cochiti lifestyle. The significance of the language is further heightened by the fact that it is used for prayer and is the only viable means for sacred communication. Recognizing the inseparability of language and spiritual expression, the leaders in this community have understood that these revitalization efforts are necessary for its survival.

BACKGROUND

The Pueblo de Cochiti lies approximately 30 miles southwest of Santa Fe, New Mexico, and occupies 58,000 acres. West of the Rio Grande River, Cochiti land rises sharply in a series of mesas and canyons which form the base of the Jemez mountains (U.S. Congress House Committee on Interior and Insular Affairs, 1992). Approximately 15,355 acres are designated for grazing purposes and 880 acres for farming. The Rio Grande has always played a significant role in the lives of the Cochiti people. For centuries it was the source of irrigation for the corn, squash, chile, and other crops which were the people's basic food sources.

A notable aspect of life in this community is that Cochiti people have been able to maintain their unique traditional form of government despite enormous pressure from the federal government to change. Rather than moving to a mainstream, constitutional government, the Pueblo de Cochiti has held to a form of theocracy wherein tribal officials are appointed by the religious leadership on a yearly basis. The notion of a servant-leadership is basic to the continuation of this form of government. Leaders *serve* the community for one year by committing themselves to safeguarding traditional beliefs and practices and to the future of the community. This often means that individuals willingly take a leave of absence from their regular employment so that they can give the community their undivided attention. Members of the community, in turn, pledge their commitment to these individuals to assist them in whatever way they can. For this reason, when an individual is asked for his or her assistance by one of the leaders, he or she must respond in the same spirit in which the leaders accepted their responsibilities.

The continuation of this traditional government requires enormous commitment and sacrifice from all adults in the community. Moreover, participating in it requires considerable fluency in the language, in terms both of its everyday uses and of the more formal registers required for governance and religious affairs. Governing principles, and those which guide the traditional courts, are all expressed through the various registers of Keres. For example, in the traditional

75

courts, rather than processing people legally, as mainstream courts do, the underlying principle is to bring tribal members back into good standing by resolving the disputes, and the ability to use a particular register is required for successful resolution. The critical role of language in all governmental and religious functions must be understood. It is the thread that ties together all aspects of traditional Cochiti life.

Furthermore, life in this community revolves around the traditional religious calendar of events, which requires participation from a majority of tribal members. These activities are private matters for tribal members only. Therefore, no details can be offered here, except for the fact that virtually every month, some religious event is taking place. Preparation for these ceremonies takes a considerable amount of time. It is not unusual for both men and women to spend 10 to 12 evenings a month in preparatory activities. Young people may also participate. In these settings, as in those described for the governmental domain, fluency in the language is a necessary skill.

As can be seen by this brief introduction, the Keres language is an essential element for the maintenance and survival of a traditional Cochiti lifestyle. The leaders of this community have long recognized the necessity of safeguarding this way of life. The battles they have fought against the imposition of a foreign form of government, for the reclamation of their lands, and for the right to determine appropriate housing patterns is a testimony to their commitment to their beliefs. The efforts undertaken on behalf of the language which are described in this essay are a critical part of this struggle.

THE LANGUAGE

Cochiti Keres is one of seven dialects of Keresan[1] spoken in New Mexico. It is probably most closely related to the Keres spoken by the neighboring Pueblo of Santo Domingo. Keresan has no known relationship to any other language and so must be considered a language isolate. Several levels or registers are spoken in the community. The most common is the Keres that is used every day for common activities. Older people speak a more complex, formalized Keres. In religious settings there is still a "higher" and more complex Keres, which is reserved for those in leadership positions. Cochiti Keres remains an unwritten language, in keeping with the oral tradition of the community. There is widespread support for keeping it in its oral form, from the religious and secular leaders as well as from the general tribal membership. The oral tradition in this community has been an important element in maintaining its values and traditional way of life. The leaders know that writing the language could bring about unwanted changes in secular and religious traditions.

The vitality of the language has been affected by several important historic events. The first was the drafting and recruitment of many young Cochiti men during World War II. A number of the returning soldiers came back with ideas about changing their community that did not reflect traditional Cochiti ways. In essence, they believed that the way for Cochiti to progress was by assimilating into white society. They sought work outside the community and encouraged their children to go to school and learn English, never realizing the impact this would have 40 to 50 years later.

In 1969, the Cochiti Dam Project was forced on the Pueblo de Cochiti by the Army Corps of Engineers in order to control flooding and the storage of river sediment for those living in the city of Albuquerque. The community has since then suffered severe consequences. Irreparable damage has been done to its economic, cultural, and spiritual well-being. During the first phase of construction, one-third of all traditional farmlands and homes were destroyed to make room for the dam. Then, when the dam was completed in 1975, the Pueblo de Cochiti began to experience serious difficulties with seepage of water onto what was left of their traditional farming lands. At first, 17 acres were flooded. By 1987, virtually all of the farmlands were under water.

This damage was detrimental not only to the economy of individual farmers, but, perhaps more importantly, to group farming and cultural activities as well. The cultural practices surrounding group farming formed much of the basis for the community's spiritual life. The damage to the land had a devastating effect on traditional culture. This in turn further eroded the use of Keres by younger Cochitis. Contact between several generations of people—elders, middle-aged adults, adolescents, and children—was greatly disrupted, affecting the transmission of important cultural information. The loss of these important activities meant the loss of critical opportunities to use the language.

Similarly, in 1969 HUD completed the first of three housing projects, which brought 94 homes to the community. Although individual families have benefited from these efforts, the community has suffered particular repercussions. The location of the homes away from the plaza, the physical and spiritual heart of the community, and situated some distance from each other has discouraged visiting, especially by older people who do not have any means of transportation. Thus they cannot interact with younger members and share their considerable knowledge and language skills. In addition, the introduction of houses intended for nuclear families, with each person having his or her own room, drastically changed relationships among family members. Previously, families shared everything in the home—rooms, household goods, and so on. Once these new houses were built, however, a new concern for individual comfort was injected into the culture. These changes, along with a growing consumerism, radically changed family life in the community and, as a result, the transmission of the native language to younger generations.

During this same period the federal government was promoting economic development activities on Indian reservations. In keeping with this initiative, a group of private investors sought to develop a housing project for non-Indians on Cochiti land. Taking advantage of the dam, they wanted to build a lake and develop a resortlike community around it. Some of the younger, more "progressive" Cochitis, who were looking for ways to help their community develop a strong economy, believed that they had finally found a financial solution for their tribe. However, once construction began, it became apparent that the scope of this project was much larger than had originally been agreed to. Cochiti tribal members would soon become a minority on their own reservation. The threat to an entire way of life was enormous.

Finally, the schools have played a role in the loss of Keres. For many years, the local public elementary school was located within the community, within walking distance of most of the homes. Although children were forbidden to speak Keres during class time, at lunch and during other times when they left the campus, they reverted to Keres, speaking to each other and to the adults they encountered in the community. In the early 1960s the school was moved to a site some six miles away. Additionally, Hispanic children were enrolled in that same school. The result was that there were few if any opportunities to hear and speak Keres during the day.

In the late 1960s, Head Start established a program in Cochiti. Fillmore has discussed the devastating effects this program has had on language-minority youngsters in other communities (1991). It appears that children in Cochiti were affected similarly. Several parents recalled their children's refusal to speak Keres after attending the Head Start program. Many of the young parents whose children currently attend Head Start were some of its first graduates. The fact that so many of them are only English speaking and oriented toward mainstream values further underscores the influence such a program can have on a community.

Each of these events has had a negative effect on the native language. However, none has been more devastating than the building of the dam and the resultant housing development project. Those who were adults at that time suddenly found themselves without a livelihood. They were forced to look for work elsewhere, mostly in the nearby urban centers. Children were no longer needed to assist in the fields and with other agricultural chores. They spent less time with Keres-speaking adults and more time at school with English-speaking peers. Over the years, these changes resulted in a lower community spirit, fewer participants in the ceremonial calendar, and cooler, more distant relationships between tribal members. For adolescents, it was a particularly difficult adjustment. They had grown up traditionally, speaking Keres fluently. They could clearly see the changes that were taking place in their community. Further, they were old enough to understand the pain that their parents and grandparents were feeling over the enormous cultural and spiritual loss of the land.

This was a decisive moment for some of those adolescents, and as they went on to get college degrees, their experiences stayed with them. They had seen the community on the brink of destruction and understood that soon they would be old enough to participate in the decision-making processes that would guide the future of the pueblo. The educational and professional choices that they made were influenced by their desire to return to their community and participate in its future. They acquired mainstream skills and knowledge that would benefit their people: some studied accounting, economic development, and political science, while others became educators. When they were able to return to the community they began to reevaluate what they had learned at the university in light of the traditional knowledge they had been taught at home. As they became reacclimated, their appreciation for Cochiti culture and wisdom deepened.

In 1985, at the same time that many of these young people were returning to the pueblo, the Cochiti Tribal Council took matters into its own hands. The council members successfully fought for the right to purchase the master lease for the housing development and reduce the scope of the project. They also sued the federal government for the damages the dam had caused to their lands. This was an enormous undertaking for a community of 1000 people, one that required great courage, intelligence, and persistence. Seven years later, the Pueblo of Cochiti won their suit in federal court, and Congress appropriated $12 million as a settlement.

For the first time in 20 years, the community was able to look forward to the restoration of their lands and a traditional way of life. Both older and younger tribal members understood the potential significance of this event. Buoyed by their victory, they now turned their attention to other critical issues in the community, in particular to the issue of language loss in the community.

LANGUAGE REVITALIZATION EFFORTS BEGIN

The Cochiti Indian Education Committee (CIEC) and the Cochiti Education Task Force (CETF) met in January 1992 to set educational priorities for the community. Members of both committees had been appointed by the Cochiti Tribal Council to deal with all of the community's educational concerns. After two days of discussion, committee members unanimously agreed to make the revitalization of their language their first priority. After receiving the full support of the tribal council, the CIEC and the CETF began the arduous task of developing plans for revitalizing their native language.

The first step in this process was to develop a full picture of the community—its resources, activities, programs, history, changes over time, and so on. With the help of a consultant, the committee gathered census data, information about tribal programs, employment patterns, the histories of the schools and of housing, and other major matters affecting the community. As the information was summarized, discussions came to center around the effects each of these elements had had on the use of the native language. These discussions were often very emotional. Initially many people felt personally responsible for the community's language situation. Many of the committee members were in their 30s and 40s and were part of the generation of adolescents that had lived through the upheaval caused by the dam. Most of them could remember many of the events that had impacted language use. The intensity of those memories and the opportunity to reflect on the significance of those events led them to better understand the process of change that had occurred in their community. Gradually, as each event was discussed, committee members came to appreciate the larger picture, that is, the fragility of indigenous languages in light of the unrelenting assimilative pressures from the rest of society.

Once this self-study was completed, the CIEC and the CETF began to develop a language survey to assess the vitality of the language in the community. After several drafts, the committee members decided to conduct three separate surveys. The self-study had indicated that language use varied according to age. Therefore, each survey was written with a different generation or setting in mind. One focused on the use of Keres in different public settings among the elderly. The second survey focused on Keres language use in the home among adult parents 30 to 60 years old. The third survey looked at Keres language use among older children and adolescents in school and in social activities.

During the summer months of 1993, all of the members of both the CIEC and the CETF took it upon themselves to conduct the surveys. For the family and adult surveys, names of the heads of households were chosen randomly from a list obtained from the tribe. A total of 50 names were chosen; however, only 29 families were surveyed in all—21% of the families in the community. Given prior experiences with outside researchers, government surveys, and so on, many people were very wary of survey questions. Therefore, great care was taken to match participants with committee members they knew well and trusted. While not all 50 families were interviewed, those who did participate shared valuable information. This information became the basis for guiding the tribal council and the committee members in their work.

SURVEY RESULTS

Generally, the surveys indicated that those adults who were 35 years old and older were fluent speakers. This meant about one-third of the total population were fluent speakers.

Most people in this group learned English several years after entering school. Those who were 60 and older tended to have limited English abilities. In addition, the older people in this fluent-speaker group were able to use two registers: one spoken by all adults and an elder register, which has greater syntactic complexity.

Younger adults ages 25 to 34 had good passive knowledge of the language and were able to communicate in simple language with fluent speakers. Many of the older people in this age range entered school speaking only Keres but lost that ability over the years. Those at the younger end of the spectrum entered school speaking both English and Keres.

Those who were 15 to 24 years old seemed to understand some Keres and were able to use very simple routines, such as greetings and courtesies. These young people may have spoken some Keres as children, before going to school. It is more likely that English was their first language and that Keres was a weak second language.

Children under 15 vary as to the amount of Keres they can understand and the routines they can produce. However, as in the case of every adult surveyed, the children all emphasized the importance of knowing Keres and expressed a strong desire to learn it.

KERES IN THE COMMUNITY

The three surveys conducted in the community also focused on the presence or absence of the native language in various contexts. One of the more surprising findings was that there was no consistent official use of the native language in any public setting. Most elders used the native language with other fluent speakers when they were together. However, when younger English-speaking people were present, most fluent speakers accommodated to their needs rather than the other way around.

In the homes of most Cochitis, it was found that older people consistently used Keres more frequently than younger people. This included using the native language with spouses, children, other relatives, and visitors, and for a wide variety of functions. Younger people used Keres infrequently with their spouses and for limited functions with their children. Most importantly, the surveys indicated that all adults, those living in the homes and those who were visitors, used Keres only occasionally with children.

Children aged 10 to 14 reported hearing very little Keres at school. Most of the Keres the children heard there consisted of simple routines. Some of the older boys attempted to use these routines when they played sports or "hung out" together. The children indicated it was their aunts and uncles who spoke the language most at home. Aunts and uncles were followed by grandparents, and then by parents, in order of frequency. Once again, most of this language consisted of greetings and simple routines.

A Special Note about Keres Language Usage in the Religious Domain

As has been stated previously, the Keres language is essential to Cochiti spirituality, and CIEC and task force members repeatedly returned to this issue while developing the three surveys. However, because the religious domain has remained private, committee members decided to refrain from asking any questions regarding Keres language use in the religious realm. Nevertheless, it was clear from all of the discussion around this topic that these are the settings in which Keres is used almost exclusively and in which all tribal members would hear the most consistent use of complex, fluid Keres (Benjamin, Pecos, and Romero 1996).

Most of these findings were no surprise to CIEC and CETF committee members and served to confirm their own observations. They were helpful, though, in summarizing the situation to the tribal council and to interested community members. Furthermore, there were other very important findings about people's attitudes toward the language. Across all age groups, participants in the survey consistently felt that the native language was extremely important to the survival of traditional government, to religious activities, and to significant milestones in people's lives. Moreover, most respondents indicated a willingness to increase the amount of Keres spoken in their homes by either speaking it more, taking children to classes, or attending classes themselves. The children themselves were overwhelmingly in favor of learning the language: 91% expressed a desire to learn Keres better.

Once these results were presented to the tribal council, the CIEC and the CETF were directed to develop a revitalization plan for the community. This directive coincided with a call for proposals from the Administration for Native Americans (ANA) for language planning. In August 1994, the Pueblo de Cochiti received a $50,000 planning grant from the ANA. Three long-range goals were identified for this planning period: to develop long-range language revitalization goals, to develop an integrated language revitalization plan for the entire community, and to begin building the capacity of the community to direct its own language revitalization plan.

Using tribal funds, a language coordinator was hired and initial meetings were organized with different segments within the community—elders, parents of school-aged and preschool children, youth of different ages, single adults, and so on—to begin discussions on the status of the language in the community. Over the next year and a half, a series of meetings were held with the groups described above. The purpose of these meetings was fourfold: (1) to inform the community about the fragility of the language, (2) to ask the community what the long-range goals for language revitalization should be, (3) to ask the community for suggestions for language-learning activities, and (4) to keep the community informed about the committees' progress. After each

one of these objectives was accomplished, the language coordinator and committee members would report to the tribal council.

Members of both the CIEC and the CETF were very careful to ensure that each segment of the community was informed and involved in each of these steps. This was in keeping with the way in which things are done in the Pueblo. It was also a way of making sure that the project had community support. More importantly, the tribal council approved each subsequent step, thereby giving official sanction to the committees' work.

Four long-range goals were developed as a result of these meetings:

(1) To re-establish the sole use of Keres in traditional activities
(2) To bring older and younger generations together to be re-engaged
(3) To re-establish the use of Keres in the home and in everyday activities
(4) To make the learning of Keres a priority for all children

Furthermore, fluent speakers were identified and asked to participate in a two-month-long training program which involved basic notions of language learning. Sessions were scheduled to meet the needs of the fluent speakers—for example, morning sessions were held for elders and tribal employees, and evening sessions were scheduled for adults who worked outside the community during the day. Several of the CIEC and CETF members also attended these sessions.

At the same time, CIEC and task force members began holding a series of weekly meetings to develop the necessary strategies for achieving the long-range goals. Their concern was to develop language-learning activities which were embedded in culturally appropriate settings. For this reason, they focused more on language learning within the community and less on language learning in the public schools. Similarly, they decided that the basis for all language learning would be the traditional ceremonial calendar. Preparing learners to participate in these activities would insure their incorporation into the most significant events of the community. Moreover, learners would have the opportunity to participate in real, meaningful communication. During those times when nothing was occurring within this religious realm, learners could focus on traditional cultural activities such as pottery, cooking, or handicrafts.

Having conducted the self-study two years before, committee members were aware of the changes that had occurred within the community which had previously supported language learning and retention. In order to undertake widespread transmission of the language, a variety of initiatives were needed that would maintain and revive critical cultural contexts of language use. By recovering and rejuvenating those contexts where several generations are brought together for a common purpose, the language would have a natural environment in which to flourish. They decided, therefore, to try to revive certain traditional community practices such as visiting and community clean-up projects, in order to bring younger learners and older fluent speakers together. Another strategy involved pairing adolescents with elders. Young people could assist elders with strenuous chores such as yard cleaning and in exchange have the elder spend some time teaching them the language. Other traditional practices, such as mentoring or gatherings of gender groups, needed to be refocused on language learning.

In an effort to establish Keres as an official language in the tribal offices, fluent tribal employees had been asked to teach non-fluent employees Keres for 15 minutes every morning before their workday began. This was attempted in mid-1995. The effort had started with great enthusiasm, but fluent speakers soon became frustrated. Unfortunately, they received little training and no follow-up support. Given this experience, CIEC and CETF members wanted to make sure that the next effort aimed at tribal employees was more successful. Therefore, they decided that non-fluent employees would be taught three times a week, for 30 minutes per session, by the language coordinator, who had attended all the training sessions.

Other classes that were planned were evening and weekend classes for adults and for those adolescents who were otherwise committed during the week. Some of these classes could revolve around crafts such as beadwork, sewing, and cooking. Others could be more conventional language classes. Whatever the format, all classes had to focus on traditional Cochiti culture as the content.

In short, these initiatives—visiting, community projects, gatherings, mentoring, and adolescent-elder pairings—all focused on reviving or strengthening structures and practices native to Cochiti culture. Having suffered the terrible effects of importing solutions to solve internal problems, such as the dam, housing, and the schools, CIEC and CETF members were very concerned that native wisdom be the basis for their plans. By starting with these kinds of efforts, committee members were honoring their own culture. Furthermore, because they were indigenous to this community, there was little danger that these initiatives would unwittingly introduce negative or undesirable consequences.

When the committee members turned their attention to the schools, several issues became apparent. Most important was the fact that the pueblo had virtually no input or say in how its children were educated. Children in Cochiti attend five different schools. Preschoolers attend Head Start, located within the community. Elementary and middle school children go to a public school located on Cochiti land but six miles away from the community. High school students have three options: Santa Fe Indian School, Bernalillo High School, and St. Catherine's Indian School. All of these are located at least 20 miles away.

Up until February 1996, the elementary/middle school was the only one to offer any Keres language instruction. Although the district had hired a native speaker of Cochiti Keres, the program had been controlled by non-Cochiti school administrators, who have designed it to fit their own notions of language teaching. Typically children go to a Keres language class for 30 minutes, once or twice a week, and only when there are no conflicts with other school activities. Given this situation, committee members felt that the best option was to develop programs with the community after school or during weekends to meet the needs of the children.

They moved almost immediately to improve the language situation for very young children by hiring a fluent Keres speaker for the Head Start program in February 1996. At the same time, the tribal council mandated that the teaching of Keres be a priority for the Head Start program. The teacher was directed to speak to the children exclusively in Keres and to give the children direct instruction for certain time periods every day. While some progress was made, the issue of control became problematic here as well. The regional director of Head Start would not allow the Keres language teacher sufficient time with the children, nor did she understand the need for a clear and distinct separation between "Cochiti time" and English. So the Cochiti lessons were frequently curtailed, and English speakers would talk to the children during Keres language instruction.

Having heard of these difficulties, committee members were convinced that the only way to ensure the success of these initiatives was to control these programs themselves. They therefore decided to develop a series of activities and classes for children *within the community*. These included offering handicrafts classes through the language, after-school recreational activities such as baseball and basketball led by a fluent speaker, field and camping trips to cultural and religious sites for children led by groups of fluent speakers, and a summer school program conducted entirely in Keres.

In May 1996, with the sanction of the tribal council and a financial commitment to fund a summer school program, committee members began meeting to plan a six-week Keres language summer-school program. Six fluent speakers who had attended the two-month-long training were asked by the governor to participate as teachers in the program. Fortunately, the pueblo also received funding from the Chamiza Foundation for these efforts. The program would be held at the Cochiti community library and the vacant Head Start building, both of which are next to the tribal offices.

Because this was the first large-scale effort in language teaching, the CIEC and CETF decided that the program should start small. The program was designed so that Keres would be used exclusively every morning from 9:00 to 12:00. After lunch, children would attend a recreational program. Unfortunately, there were no fluent speakers to assist in the afternoon sessions, so these were conducted in English. A summer-school coordinator was hired to facilitate all these activities. Keres language teachers met weekly to plan the content of their teaching, focusing on the traditional events that would occur during the summer. Teachers agreed that they would all teach the same content and, whenever possible, follow the same schedule. In order to do this, they decided to meet every morning for a group meeting and two afternoons a week with the language revitalization consultant for group planning. A few days before beginning, 35 children were preregistered for the program—an ideal ratio for the six Keres language teachers.

Initially, maintaining a Keres-only environment was challenging. Teachers reminded each other of the rule, and the summer-school coordinator reminded visiting parents and tribal employees who dropped by. Children were allowed to speak in English, but all adults had to speak Keres or remain silent. During the first few days, some of the children privately asked their teachers to translate for them. However, the Keres-only rule prevailed and was well established by the end of the second week. While it was initially difficult for the teachers, the children soon became acclimated to Keres-only usage because of the teaching strategies and content the teachers used. Children were involved with hands-on, active learning projects in which they frequently went into the community to play traditional games or learn firsthand about their culture. News of the program spread rapidly throughout the community, and by the end of the third week, 99 children had registered. Also notable was the fact that by the third week, many children were producing simple phrases on their own.

One of the more rewarding experiences of the summer was a traditional meal that the teachers and children hosted for the elders of the community. In keeping with Cochiti tradition, children were taught the formal way of inviting people to a meal and were taken in groups to the elders' homes to do so. Boys and girls were involved in every aspect of this event, from chopping wood for the stoves to peeling potatoes and making fry bread. Ample opportunities were planned for children to interact with the elders during and after the meal. When the afternoon was over, many of the elders remarked that it had been "just like the old days," when young and old often gathered together to spend an afternoon or evening talking and laughing together. To reciprocate, the elders hosted a reception for the children on their last day of summer school.

There have been many wonderful outcomes from the success of the summer school, some more obvious than others. Perhaps the most profound change can be seen in the teachers. Having experienced firsthand how to teach the language, they are now the most outspoken proponents of the language revitalization efforts, and they are the first ones to maintain an all-Keres conversation in most of their dealings in the community. During the last week of summer school they made a formal presentation to the tribal council about their

and the children's experiences. The discussion that ensued lasted several hours and included a great deal of praise as council members thanked the teachers for teaching many of their grandchildren. At the end of the discussion, the council agreed to fund a full-time teaching position with tribal funds.

The children too have been deeply affected. Not only have they gained an initial ability to converse in their heritage language, but perhaps more importantly, they now feel more deeply tied to that heritage. Their participation in the traditional ceremonies of the summer was made more meaningful because the children were given a better understanding of the events' significance. Moreover, their spontaneous greetings and simple utterances throughout the community remind fluent speakers that they wish to be spoken to in Keres. Additionally, the children have developed close and loving relationships with their teachers, reminiscent of the way in which many children in Cochiti used to relate to adults.

The fact that the summer-school sessions were held next to the tribal offices, where people pick up their mail, go to the clinic, and attend meetings, and where the elderly eat lunch, means that many people heard and saw the children as they learned. This served to heighten the awareness on the part of many tribal members of the need to speak and learn Keres. Some parents and other interested adults asked when they could have classes like the ones the children were attending. Others dropped in to observe or assist when they could. Some families reported that they had instituted a Keres-only rule at mealtimes. A few described how they had decided to turn off the all-English-language television. Across the community and within individual families, one can see closer, more intimate relationships growing as fluent speakers take the time to share their knowledge. In short, the children's success is the community's success, and many people are now aware of the need to speak Keres publicly and consistently. Furthermore, a number of people now feel confident about learning and teaching the language. This feeling will be critical as the community moves forward with other language initiatives.

FUTURE PLANS AND CHALLENGES

As of this writing, the plans for the fall include (1) an all-Keres room where Head Start and preschool children can spend from half an hour to two hours daily, depending on their parents' preferences; (2) Keres language classes for tribal employees, to be given three times a week; (3) after-school arts and crafts and recreational activities for school-age children; and (4) arts and crafts and Keres classes for adults in the evenings. In addition, CIEC and CETF committee members have committed themselves to providing mentoring to less fluent speakers and to revitalizing the practice of visiting each other and maintaining Keres during these visits. Several community projects such as ditch cleaning, weeding, and painting are planned in which fluent adults are matched with learning adolescents.

All of these efforts will be undertaken either with volunteers or with tribal funds. This allows the tribe to maintain control and to remain faithful to its own values. Moreover, drawing in the different segments of the community—for example, the elders, the tribal council, tribal employees, parents, and children—underscores the fact that the language revitalization project belongs to everyone and therefore all have a responsibility to its continuation.

Future plans include a language nest, where babies and very young children can be cared for by fluent Keres-speaking "grandmothers"; an all-Keres preschool program; a healthy after-school recreational program; more community projects; adolescent-elder pairings; and consistent Keres class offerings after school and in the evenings for adults. These plans for the future will necessarily mean that more fluent speakers will be needed to teach and to lead in the various initiatives that are to come.

The CIEC, the task force, and the leaders of the community understand the commitment required to make all of this a reality. However, they also understand the power of these initiatives for the language learning of their future leaders.

Much of the success that the Pueblo de Cochiti has enjoyed is owed to the fact that the leaders have moved slowly and planned carefully. Above all, they have made certain that every step taken has been consonant with Cochiti traditional culture and values.

Note

1. Keresan is the name used for the language, which consists of seven dialects; "Keres" is used for a single dialect. But this usage has not been consistent.

References

Benjamin, R., Pecos, R., & Romero, M. E. 1996. Language revitalization efforts in the Pueblo de Cochiti: Becoming "literate" in an oral society. In *Indigenous literacies in the Americas: Language planning from the bottom-up*, ed. N. Hornberger, 115. Berlin and New York: Mouton.

Fillmore, Lily Wong. 1991. When learning a second language means losing the first. *Early Childhood Research Quarterly*, (6)3: 323–346.

U.S. Congress House Committee on Interior and Insular Affairs. 1992. *Authorization of funds for implementation of settlement agreement between Pueblo de Cochiti and the U.S. Army Corps of Engineers*. Washington, DC: US GO.

The Navajo Language: I

KEN HALE

Department of Linguistics and Philosophy
Massachusetts Institute of Technology
Cambridge, Massachusetts

Navajo is a member of the Athabaskan family. Like the various Apache languages, it belongs to the Southern Athabaskan (or Apachean) branch of this widespread family. The other members of the family are found in two locations, the largest being the region comprising the interior of western Canada and the interior of Alaska. A smaller group of Athabaskan languages is found in an area on the Pacific Coast spanning the present California-Oregon border.

The Navajo language itself is spoken primarily in northeastern Arizona and an adjacent strip in southern Utah, and in northwestern New Mexico. This area includes the main Navajo reservation. The language is also spoken on the satellite reservations of Ramah, Cañoncito, and Alamo in New Mexico, and also by families located in many cities in the United States, including Albuquerque, Phoenix, Denver, and Los Angeles, for example.

For good reason, Navajo is famous in linguistic scholarship. In the 1980s, the language could claim to have the very best indigenous language dictionary in the Americas. It was produced by the energetic and productive team composed of the Navajo language scholar William Morgan and the Anglo language scholar Robert Young. The 1987 edition of this work (Young and Morgan 1987) remains without question one of the very best Native American dictionaries; it has recently been joined in this exalted position by the new Hopi dictionary compiled by the Hopi Dictionary Project, directed by Ken Hill and Emory Sekaquaptewa, at the University of Arizona.

Much of what Navajo is famous for is displayed in considerable detail in the grammar which accompanies the Young and Morgan dictionary. There is, for example, a complete treatment of the renowned Navajo system of classificatory verbs—that is, verbs whose stems are chosen according to the nature of the subject or object, respectively, of the intransitive or transitive clauses in which they appear (see also Young and Morgan's chapter on training). The Young and Morgan grammar also includes a survey of native speakers' intuitions and acceptability judgments concerning the Navajo third person inverse construction, according to which transitive sentences with third person subject and object are organized in such a way as to ensure that the order of subject and object conforms to the animacy hierarchy (approximately, human > animal > inanimate). In the domain of syntax, the author of this chapter is responsible for the most detailed study yet of two noteworthy aspects of Navajo syntactic structure: the relative clause and the principles involved in the interpretation of clauses with elided noun phrase arguments (Platero 1974, 1982).

Of all indigenous languages in North America north of Mexico, Navajo boasts the largest number of speakers, approximately 100,000 (Young 1983). However, as pointed out by the Navajo educator Dillon Platero, while the number of speakers actually increases each year, the number of nonspeakers within the Navajo Nation is increasing at a proportionally greater rate, and this is a matter of concern for the Navajo people (Zepeda and Hill 1991). Paul Platero has been involved for many years not only as a linguist engaged in the study of the grammar of Navajo, but also, and in fact longer, as a language scholar concerned with the use of the Navajo language in education. His essay in this book is concerned with two issues which are of great importance to the Navajo Nation at this time. One is the quality of language education, whether in Navajo or English, being made available to preschool children within the area defined by the borders of the Navajo reservation. The other is one about which Navajo linguists and educators have been much alarmed in recent years, namely, the circumstance that Navajo, the strongest language in terms of speaker population, is gradually acquiring the most prominent characteristic of endangered languages: to an ever-increasing degree, Navajo children are no longer learning Navajo as their first language. His essay is a report prepared in 1992 for Anita Pfeiffer and Lena Jim of the Navajo Division of Education of the Navajo Nation. It has had an impact on Navajo language education and has been responsible, among other things, for the increased presence of the Navajo language in courses designed for the training of Navajo teachers, and it has been influential as well in creating a favorable attitude on the part of relevant components of the Navajo Nation government toward the recent efforts of Navajo linguists to establish the Navajo Language Academy for the purpose of promoting college-level educational programs in applied and theoretical Navajo linguistics, bilingual education, and first- and second-language acquisition.

An important lesson in Platero's essay is that a language capability study like this must be properly funded so that enough time can be devoted to it to ensure that the appropriate instruments can be prepared and the full range of relevant people can be interviewed, not only the children themselves, but also their families, their teachers, and other people they are regularly in contact with.

References

Platero, Paul. 1974. The Navajo relative clause. Ph.D. diss., MIT.

————. 1982. Missing noun phrases and grammatical relations in Navajo. *IJAL* 48: 286–305.

Young, Robert. 1983. Apachean languages. In *Handbook of North American Indians,* vol. 10, *Southwest,* ed. Alfonso Ortiz, 393–400. Washington, D.C.: Smithsonian Institution.

Young, Robert, and William Morgan. 1987. *The Navajo language.* Albuquerque: University of New Mexico Press.

Witherspoon, Gary. 1977. Language and art in the Navajo universe. Ann Arbor: University of Michigan Press.

Zepeda, Ofelia, and Jane Hill. 1991. The condition of Native American languages in the United States. In *Endangered languages,* ed. R. H. Robins and E. M. Uhlenbek, 135–55. Oxford and New York: Berg.

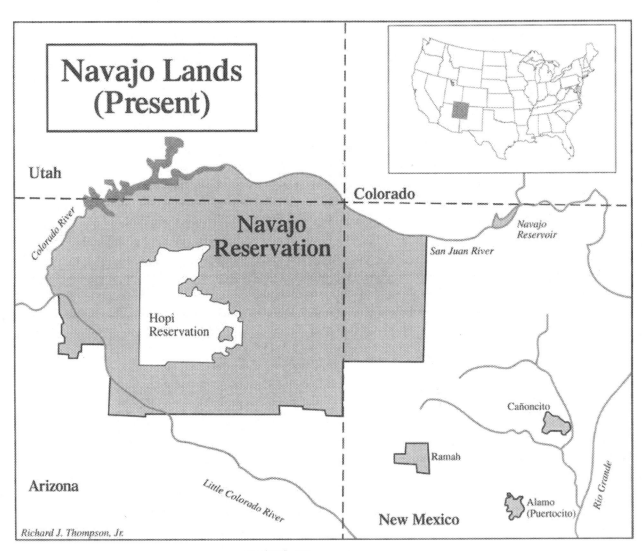

MAP 8.1 Navajo, in the southwest

8

Navajo Head Start Language Study

PAUL R. PLATERO

Tribal Administrator
Cañoncito, New Mexico

The Navajo Head Start Language Study reported on here looked into the Navajo and English language environment in preschools.[1] In this study, efforts were made to assess the languages being spoken by everyone in a typical Navajo preschool. The primary goal was to determine the distribution of children who are monolingual Navajo speakers, monolingual English speakers, and bilingual speakers. Information was sought from children by observation, from their teachers in interviews, and from their parents by interviewing members of the teaching staff.

Navajo preschoolers who are monolingual English speakers were found to make up 54.3% of the 682 children observed in this study; monolingual Navajo speakers made up 17.7%; and Navajo-English bilingual speakers made up 27.9%. No language assessment instrument was used. Rather, the information was gathered from observation and interviews as noted above.

Preschool staff spoke English predominantly, though the staff were Navajo-English bilingual speakers. Parents were also reported to talk to their children more in English than in Navajo. There is almost total immersion in English where the preschools were reviewed.

Teachers lacked essential background in English as a Second Language (ESL) or bilingual education. Additionally, many of the teachers were having difficulty with the English language—the language of instruction at the preschools. Staff "inbreeding" was observed to be a major factor in the circumstance that some teachers did not have all the skills necessary for teaching Navajo children. Teachers were advanced to their positions when openings occurred, without regard to qualifications or lack of them. Although requirements are generally known to apply, adherence to them is lax.

Curriculum materials for the instruction of Navajo language and culture are definitely lacking in almost all the preschools visited. Most materials are teacher generated.

It is recommended in this report that teachers gain further intensive training in ESL, bilingual education, and child development, preferably through college courses. It is recommended that teachers be certified by the states in which they teach and have the appropriate bilingual or ESL endorsements.

It is further recommended that classes support the language of the child even if that means converting the classes into bilingual sessions.

Parents are not involved, according to the teachers. They are encouraged to become deeply involved in the education of their children.

BACKGROUND INFORMATION ON THE DEPARTMENT OF HEAD START

Origin of Navajo Head Start

The Navajo Department of Head Start was set up to serve Navajo children between the ages of three and five within the exterior boundary of the Navajo reservation. The service area is approximately 26,000 square miles and reaches into 12 counties of the Four Corners states (Arizona, New Mexico, Utah, and Colorado).

Each Navajo chapter has one Head Start Center in which one or more classes are held. Some chapters are located in urban areas such as Shiprock and others in very rural areas such as Kaibeto. The number of centers depends on enrollment and facilities. When there are a large number of children qualified for the program that cannot be enrolled in classes owing to limited facilities, the program offers Home-base preschools. Homebase is a program in which a separate teacher travels to the children's homes to teach them.

The program derives its enrollment from a pool of Navajo children estimated by the Navajo Division of Community Development to be 23,411 for 1989, with estimates of 24,588 and 25,197 for 1991 and 1992, respectively. All of these estimates are for children living within the Navajo reservation who are four years of age and under.

Goals of the Department of Head Start

The goals of Navajo Head Start are many. The primary ones are to promote good health and teach readiness skills for school. In summary form, these are:

- To improve the child's health and physical abilities
- To stimulate self-confidence, spontaneity, curiosity, and self discipline
- To enhance the child's cognitive development and motor skills
- To create a positive classroom environment
- To increase the ability of the child and family to relate to each other
- To enhance the child's sense of dignity and self-worth

As part of promoting health among children, they are screened for dental, hearing, and eyesight needs, and they are fed nutritious hot meals and snacks. They are taught to wash their hands before eating, to brush their teeth after meals, and so on.

Navajo preschoolers experience preschool educational activities that lead to readiness skills in language, arithmetic, reading, and writing.

Children Involved in the Program

Eligibility for participation in Head Start is set by federal guidelines which are implemented on the Navajo reservation. One of the primary points of eligibility is low income. Navajo children coming from poverty conditions as defined by the U.S. government number over 11,700, based on projections made from the 1980 census. This amounts to 47% of the total number of children estimated to be in the preschool age group.

The Department of Head Start has received funding for 3,398 eligible children for the school year 1991–92. In this study, thirty-nine preschools were visited where over 822 children were enrolled. On average 9 eligible children were waiting to be enrolled. Owing to budgetary constraints, Navajo Head Start is able to serve only 29% of eligible Navajo children estimated to come from low-income families and 13.4% of all Navajo children of preschool age. It must be noted that the above figures are estimates only, but even so, the number of children needing Head Start services is overwhelming.

Special set-aside slots are reserved for children with disabilities. This group of children has second priority for admission to the program. Others having lower priority are children who come from high-income families as defined by the federal government.

Characteristics of the Preschool Center

Most preschool centers are housed in old trailers or buildings and are usually located in near proximity to Chapter houses. These centers are fenced off and some have playground equipment. Each center devotes close to one-quarter of the poster or display area to Head Start notices, memoranda, class schedules, and other official communication relating to personnel and other policies. The remaining space is decorated with children's work.

The children's activities are assigned to different areas, or corners, devoted to specific interests and skills, as shown in Table 8.1.

These and other interest areas are designed to teach children basic learning skills as outlined in the program's goals and objectives—areas not observed were creative movement, science, health, and nutrition. When children are allowed to select their interest area during free time, they are grouped into various areas in the building while teachers direct activities in certain areas.

The Preschool Staff

Each preschool has a full-time staff of four people: teacher, assistant teacher, cook, and bus driver. The teacher generally is the person in charge and thus supervises personnel and all operations of the center. The assistant teacher or teacher's aide assists with the instructional program and is usually the person in charge in the absence of the teacher. The cook prepares meals and also teaches along with the others when her responsibilities for the day are fulfilled. The bus driver begins and ends the day by transporting children to and from school. His responsibilities also include teaching as well as other transportation-related duties.

In some centers, a foster grandparent is present. The preschool staff usually leaves Navajo language and culture to the foster grandparent to teach by modeling speech and other items. It was not clear whether all centers are encouraged to have foster grandparents involved, but in centers that have them, their role is usually to teach the Navajo language and culture. Additionally, the children's parents may be present to help. Those volunteers usually work under the direction of the teacher.

These four preschool staff members often rotate roles in some centers. In some of the sites visited, the cook of the day turned out to be the teacher, for example. During small-group activities, each of the four persons will be helping children in the various interest areas.

The minimum requirement of the Head Start teacher is

TABLE 8.1   Preschool Activity Centers Observed in This Study

Area	Activity	Materials	Supervision
Block building	Children play in small groups to build, tear.	Cardboard boxes wooden blocks, etc.	Children usually self-directed and on their own. Occasional word of caution from teacher if children became too loud or abusive.
Home	Children play dress-up, housekeeping, adventures, etc.	Stove, broom, household play furniture, dishes, etc.	Usually self-directed
Art	Finger painting, cut-outs and paste-ups, etc.	Paper, scissors, glue, etc.	Always teacher directed
Manipulatives	Puzzles, beadwork, lacing, small blocks, etc.	Puzzles of varying difficulty, beads, laces, small blocks	Always teacher directed
Library	Storytelling	Picture books, jumbo reading books	Most often teacher directed
Navajo culture	Singing, arts and crafts, building hogans	Papier mâché, sticks, etc.	Usually unattended if no foster grandparent is present

to have a CDA endorsement. Many of the staff members do not have CDAs and are in the process of obtaining the endorsement.

DISCUSSION OF THE PRESCHOOL CHILDREN'S LANGUAGE STUDY

Purposes for the Study

In December 1991 the Navajo Division of Education (NDOE) set out to strengthen Navajo education by serving and supporting schools in their efforts to educate Navajo young children. One of its major programs was to train over 1000 Navajo teachers in the very near future. Information regarding curriculum, Navajo and English language usage in the classroom, and teacher training needs were required before NDOE could begin to meet the needs of Navajo teachers.

Authorization of the Study

The executive director of the Navajo Division of Education authorized the study in partnership with the director of the Department of Head Start. It was agreed that the study would take place over a 90-day period that would include preschool center visits, collection of relevant data and information, and submission of a final written report.

A Formative Review

The study was conducted as a formative evaluation, and the report follows that format—that is, this reviewer assumed the role of advisor and troubleshooter for Head Start planners and directors. The main requirement, then, was to observe Navajo children's language in as many schools as time would allow. Visits to preschools included mixing with children and talking with them to the extent allowed by teachers

and schedules. A driver who was familiar with center staffs was assigned to help minimize possible confusion that might arise when some total stranger arrived and said he was there to monitor or observe children. But as reported below, even with a familiar person as a guide, we still experienced problems.

Who Will Benefit from the Study

The information given in this report, particularly the conclusion and recommendations, will, it is to be hoped, be used by all components of the Navajo Department of Head Start. Further, it is hoped that the Navajo Nation, as a nation and as a people, will see why they must be more intensely involved in the preservation of their language and culture. The Navajo Division of Education will be enlightened by the findings, some of which will either confirm or deny their conception of Navajo preschool children and their language. These findings have their most direct impact on parents and their communities. Each preschool center's local parent policy committee and each like parent group in the agency and in the Navajo Nation will also learn from this study.

Information Requested

The information requested was to determine what language (Navajo or English) was used and spoken predominantly across the Navajo reservation in the preschools. No one has previously observed Navajo children and gathered linguistic data from a large pool of communities. Rather than receiving often contradictory reports about Navajo children's language and culture, the administration of NDOE decided that a single overview would be made of at least 25 preschool centers, including at least 5 from each of the five Bureau of Indian Affairs (BIA) agencies.

Under this assignment to review Navajo children's language, a few subdomains of the language were attempted.

Since this study did not collect such linguistic data as speech patterns and samples, no linguistic data are available for further analysis. However, real-time (while it was happening) analyses were done on children's cognitive, semantic, and syntactic development. More time and long-term evaluation are needed, of course, to determine Navajo child language acquisition, cognitive development, and other technical areas. Again, many of these technical areas were observed only cursorily.

Information on the language used by the staff was collected, since this had a direct impact on the children. Some of the data included self-proclaimed Navajo or English language dominance of the staff and observations of language use. Another related area of inquiry was that of teaching and staff training. How many of the staff have had either English as a Second Language (ESL) or bilingual education courses or workshops?

For Decision Makers

The information in the study is provided as a foundation for two other major undertakings that are needed—curriculum development for Navajo preschool children and teacher training. There are sufficient alarming data to indicate that a Navajo and English bilingual curriculum is required, along with professionally trained and certified teachers who have tribal or state endorsements to teach in those areas.

Overall directions for the study came mainly from the executive director of NDOE and support from the director of Head Start. The executive director needed this information in order to explore further refinements and advancement of Navajo Head Start. Both the executive director of NDOE and the director of Head Start believe that the Head Start program did not have a uniform curriculum and that there was confusion about the language dominance of all children in the program. It is not known to what extent the Central Parent Policy Council was involved beyond their approving a position and funds for the study. The evaluator did not meet with this committee at the outset, but he planned to report the study to them orally. During the data-collection phase of this study, five oral progress reports were made with the NDOE executive director and two with the Head Start director at different times.

Constraints Placed on Study

This was a short-term study. Constraints placed upon it included time, weather, distances between schools, and money. What started out as a 90-day agreement ended up lasting only 60 days, reportedly because of a lack of funds. When notice of termination was received, only four days remained in which to write the final report. Additional time was reinstated so that the study report could be completed. Three weeks had originally been allowed for synthesis and analysis of the information gathered, but that time was reduced.

Information from some centers was incomplete or additional visits were needed; accordingly, those centers have been dropped from this study.

Bad weather had a pronounced effect on centers. Some centers delayed school according to the conditions of the local roads, many of which were impassable. Three centers had to cancel classes due to frozen water lines or lack of heat. Long distances between centers also led to short site visits.

There was much discussion among staff members in almost all centers about being merged into the Navajo Division of Education. Since the evaluator felt staff morale had much to do with teaching, he asked to look into this further. But in one of the progress reports, he was asked not to address this particular issue. Consequently, all other areas not directly related to Navajo children's language were left unaddressed.

Preschools Visited

Below, listed under their respective agencies, are the preschools visited in the order of visitations. In this report, each location is considered a center. Note that some places have more than one unit or preschool. These are considered preschools or classes that are part of the center. Thus, preschool I and preschool II are located in the same center, for purposes of this report.

Shiprock

Nenahnezad
Upper Fruitland
Shiprock I
Shiprock II
Two Grey Hills
Sheep Springs

Chinle Agency

Nazlini
Tsaile I
Tsaile II
Tsaile III
Rock Point
Round Rock
Rough Rock
Many Farms
Dennehotso I
Dennehotso II

Tuba City Agency

Kayenta I
Kayenta II
Kaibeto
Inscription House
Tuba City I
Tuba City II
Tuba City III

Fort Defiance Agency

Crystal
Red Lake
Sawmill
Fort Defiance
St. Michaels
Kinlichee
Indian Wells
Dilcon

Eastern Navajo Agency

Crownpoint I
Crownpoint II
Standing Rock
Baca I
Baca II
Cañoncito I
Cañoncito II
Alamo I
Alamo II

Because complete data were not available at some of these sites, some of the preschools were deleted from the final figures and consideration.

Study Design

No instruments were used to collect the data. No time was allowed for the development of any formal measures for staff and children. In retrospect, given the lack of time and funds, it would have been difficult to administer any type of language assessment instrument.

Class Observations

The primary plan used for this study was personal observation of all preschools visited. Observations were made and key findings were recorded in writing. No tape recordings were made. The reviewer followed children while they moved from activity to activity. Sometimes this meant going outside to the playground for free play or fire drills and riding in the bus with children. As much time as needed was spent to get a clear feel for what language the children spoke among themselves and with the center staff. When invited by the staff, the evaluator was a participant observer.

Teacher Interviews

A secondary plan for gathering information and data was by interviews with members of the staff. Usually the person in charge for the day was interviewed.

Selection of Preschools

This evaluator proposed to review centers by random selection. After a brief discussion, it was decided that the Head Start director would select schools for visitations. Although visits by random selection would have been more representative of preschool centers, the time available and distances between preschool sites prevented implementation of this idea. Therefore, a list of schools from the Eastern Navajo Agency was developed, and visitations were arranged from the central administrative offices.

It was decided to make unannounced drop-in observation visits to avoid the possibility of our reviewing specially prepared lessons in Navajo. Drop-in visits were chosen as part of the study design because it was felt that teachers and children would be in their natural daily program if visits were unannounced, thus making it possible for us to collect vital information and data on the language atmosphere. Previously, and apparently when visits were announced ahead of time, the center being visited made special preparations, and consequently all went well. Contacts were made, however, with all agency directors prior to the visit to let them know visits would be made in their area. Exact site visits were not disclosed to any of the directors, however.

Data Collection Procedures

Upon our arrival at a center, the lead teacher was sought out, and introductions were made. Normally our introduction included, "We are here to observe your class, if that's OK with you." Every center was more than glad to receive us, and often we were introduced to the staff and children. Their hospitality was beyond measure. Each center was given the option to refuse us as visitors and observers, but none chose to discourage us.

It is interesting to note that personnel from the agency office who oversee centers as specialists were more uneasy about our presence when they were visiting the same center that day. There were many center visitations that overlapped with those from agency offices. One shocking encounter occurred in a Shiprock Agency preschool center, when our presence was questioned loudly while the children were eating lunch. The verbal challenge was so extraordinary that everyone, including the children, became absolutely quiet, to the point that we could have heard a pin drop. In the seemingly long stunned silence, the driver and I looked at each other and merely said, "We're from Central Office," and a few more words. There were some other uneasy moments, but this was the most disquieting of all. It is possible that the agency specialists were protective of the local centers, and if that is the case, then their attitude is quite understandable. This incident is an example of disharmony and perhaps insecurity among Head Start personnel. This area of personnel interaction is not one authorized for review. Staff morale had a lot of bearing on teacher and staff performance, but the direction we received was, in effect, "Hands off."

FINDINGS

Children's Languages

The overall operation of the instructional component of the Department of Head Start appears to be healthy in those classrooms visited: children are attending classes and learning, the staff members are meeting many of the goals, and so on. There are, however, some serious problems in areas of communication and child language acquisition and enrichment. From the data gathered, over half of the children come to Head Start able to communicate in English, while the remaining children are either monolingual Navajo speakers or are bilingual. Children with Navajo speaking ability are not being served in the language they already know. Even those who are English speakers are not given adequate English language instruction in some cases. Again, while success is being reported from many preschools, there are still problems.

As expected, the language of the classroom is controlled by the teaching staff, including grandparents and other volunteers. Teachers were observed while they were in the process of teaching concepts and reviewing previous lessons. Asking questions of the children was one way of trying to get involvement. The types of questions most often asked required simple yes-no responses. Another type of question, such as "What color is this?" and "What shape is this?" would elicit a single-phrase response.

As one would expect under these circumstances, children would provide simple responses such as "yes," "no," "don't know," or "green." This is certainly true for Navajo as well, although expressing questions along those lines is somewhat more difficult. It takes native Navajo language fluency to ask those questions. One of the reasons is the fact that traditionally, Navajos express those questions ambiguously but in strict context. Variously, those questions could be "Díí haashit'é?" or "Díí haanóolin?" while the questioner pointed to the shape or color concerning which the answer was being solicited. Most often teachers used context-sensitive body motions, such as pointing with the finger or lips. There is no doubt that children are enriched in giving simple one- or two-word responses.

In many of the preschools observed, children's responses were in the form of body gestures such as nodding yes or no or shrugging the shoulders, all of which were acceptable to the teachers. These were most evident in small-group activity circles where those staff members available were helping. Some children did respond with simple answers, but they were the exception.

What was lacking in the majority of the preschools was questions that could bring out more verbal expressions. It takes practice and conscious effort to encourage language development among children. This sensitivity must be instilled in the Head Start teacher. When teachers or others accept body language in lieu of actual verbal expressions, they are subconsciously encouraging and promoting a lack of language.

Children interact linguistically when they are left to themselves; this appears to be more natural. Rather than saying "Teacher, teacher," they simply talk. When children have a choice of which language to speak, they have a preference for English. Most often, when they were left to themselves was during lunch and nap time. Usually during these periods, the teaching staff just took general oversight and perhaps assisted some other children. Not too much time is available for children to express themselves while under the control of the classroom teachers.

Staff Language

At all the sites visited, every full-time staff member spoke English predominantly. When an occasion presented itself for a staff member to talk with a child, that staff member usually adjusted his or her language to the child's specific linguistic needs.

Staff members of the preschools visited talked in English. There was great dominance of English among them. Although 21 of 39 centers reported holding bilingual meetings, they spoke English peppered with Navajo words or phrases. What they spoke to children was pretty much what they spoke to their peers. In other words, a teacher or any other staff member used their language throughout the day, whether that was English dominant, bilingual, or Navajo dominant.

Parents' Language

From teacher interviews, it was determined that almost all of the parents of the children attending the preschools were Navajo speakers. The only exceptions were 12 parents who were non-Navajos and 2 or so who simply had never acquired the ability to speak Navajo at all. In spite of the large number of Navajo-speaking parents, it was reported that many of them spoke almost exclusively in English to their children. Nonetheless, some teachers reported how delighted parents were when their children brought home samples of work done in Navajo or learned to count in Navajo or sing a Navajo song. It is not clear, with the very limited information available, that parents want the schools to teach Navajo to their children instead of taking the lead themselves.

Foster Grandparents' Language

Many of the preschools had "foster grandparents." The reason cited most often for the foster grandparents was to teach Navajo and reinforce Navajo speaking ability for young children. They were used for almost every school activity. Two preschools had monolingual Navajo-speaking foster grandparents; the rest were bilingual. These bilingual foster grandparents spoke mostly English in their official capacity. Parents who were volunteering time most often spoke English.

Issues Regarding the Language of the Preschool

Absence of Language

In a preschool on the western part of the Navajo reservation, the classroom was full of good English-language chatter produced by the children. In large- and small-group activities, some of the children were talking a lot, all in English. It seemed perfectly normal for the children to be talking with each other as well as with the teaching staff. When there is plenty of talk, correct or otherwise, it is expected that children will develop good speech habits.

But in most of the schools observed, there is silence. Some of the silence is so great as to create a feeling of panic. When in small-group activities, for example, a teacher may be helping children to cut out patterns or shapes in preparation for assembling them with glue. There would be silence on the part of the children and the attending teacher. Much of the time may be taken by the teacher repeating simple phrases in English or Navajo to a child. In a 20-minute period, for example, the total amount of speech by everyone in the circle would be approximately 5 to 8 minutes. (This is a best estimate.) There usually are large blocks of time when no one says anything. In a typical small-group activity circle, the silence is usually broken by a single child who is doing most of the talking.

It is often said that Navajo children are taught at home to be silent and attentive. Furthermore, the children are taught that it is the Navajo way and respectful to keep silent. When one does speak, that utterance should be worthy and reflect wisdom and learning. In this context, what does it mean for a child to go to school and be asked to speak up? Even in very traditional settings, children and adults are expected to talk.

Expanding on Children's Speech

Everywhere children are asking for their teachers' approval and encouragement. This happens when children bring completed work to the attention of the teachers. It was observed in many of these preschools that teachers do not expand on the language being used by the children; instead, many simply say "Aah" in response to children's inquiries. Teachers miss an opportunity to take the child's expression and expand on it when the idea is still fresh on his or her mind.

"Good, Correct" Language

Children will learn what they hear subconsciously, and later, when they begin to speak, the things they have heard about language before come to their consciousness. When that happens, as some theories go, we can hear a representation of their subconscious mind. What this means is that what the children learn by hearing is what they will most likely speak in their later lives, if they develop a desire to do so.

In the western Navajo preschool just mentioned and at a few other places, Navajo children were filling the room with English chatter, the type that educationists like to hear. Children there were verbalizing their feelings, expressing them by means of language. This chatter is evidence in linguistic form that the children have developed good speech habits. A continuation of this would further develop communication skills that could lead to their mastery of English or Navajo or both.

Some samples of English that were observed in the field study are listed here to show that many of today's Head Start teachers need further training.

(1) A teacher wanted her preschooler to rotate a shape which was previously cut out by scissors so that the child would see the writing right side up. The child was looking at the shape upside down. She told the child "on the other side." In response the child flipped the work, showing the reverse side. "No, no. Like this," the teacher said, rotating the shape.

(2) Another teacher was telling a boy not to throw cardboard building blocks. "Don't throw it. You're going to hit it with someone."

The total effect this situation has in modeling English for children, the language that is used most predominantly in these schools, is that they may not learn well-formed English.

Context-Heavy Language

Children in most of these preschools are also subjected to very context-sensitive Navajo and English. This is an accepted linguistic practice among Navajo speakers. By such body motions as pointing with the finger or lips and other gestures, Navajos create the right context for the spoken language that follows. Without the proper context, much of the language is ambiguous or without meaning.

(1) A teacher who spoke exclusively in English was telling her children to fold a piece of paper in half, then fold it in half again to create a French fold. She instructed her children, "Fold the paper ear to ear, [pause] ear to ear [pause] and ear to ear."

(2) An assistant teacher was asking a boy not to keep stepping on a girl's foot. "You are stepping on her feet."

(3) "The kids are walking the other way," said another teacher. "Do what the others are doing." She meant, "The kids are walking backward."

DISCUSSION OF DATA AND FINDINGS

The Language the Navajo Preschoolers Talk

From one end of the Navajo reservation to the other, Navajo preschoolers talk predominantly in English while at play or in school. Though many children are reported by their teachers to come as Navajo speakers, the system of the Head Start program converts them into speakers of English or causes them to withdraw into their own separate little worlds.

In this study, teachers' knowledge about their children's speaking and learning abilities was used and relied on heavily.

In studies involving the identification of limited-English-proficient (LEP) children, it was found that teachers' personal knowledge about their schoolchildren was very close to the actual score results of language proficiency testing. From a statistical point of view, their assessment was significantly very close to that derived from the children's overall performance on these tests.

For this study, the very limited amount of time allotted and the lack of a Navajo language assessment instrument did not permit testing of children to find out what the child's language dominance or proficiency was. The next-best remaining options were to either interview teachers or observe a few select children. In this study, both interviewing teachers and observing children were undertaken. And to see first-hand what language children appeared to be more comfortable with, observation was used.

Teachers were interviewed individually, usually at the end of school after the children had left for home. To identify students who were monolingual speakers of Navajo, teachers were asked to identify "Navajo-speaking children who cannot speak or understand English," avoiding the technical term "monolingual." And in general the technical terminology of language studies was avoided, since many of the teachers had not heard them before. Thus, when we were trying to find out how many of the children in a class were monolingual Navajo speakers, the question was better understood if put in this way: "How many of your children speak only Navajo or may have a difficult time understanding English?"

Monolingual Navajo Speakers

The total number of "monolingual Navajo" speakers was 124, or 17.7% of the 682 children observed. In discussions with classroom staff members, there was general consensus that two or three children were actually Navajo-only speakers. They reported that other children could "understand" both languages, but they knew which children needed special assistance in Navajo. The number of children so identified

(98) is thought to be fairly reliable, owing to the special attention teachers have had to give these children and also to the limited number of children in this group.

In time, many of these monolingual Navajo-speaking children have been mainstreamed into English instruction without too great a loss. But there is always the story of the Navajo child who left school because he or she could not "really" understand English, or who "always plays by himself or herself" and is very shy or withdrawn. We heard these stories in almost all the classes reviewed.

The sad part of all this is that Navajo teachers make English the language of instruction although many children would definitely benefit from Navajo-English instruction. Very little time is devoted to Navajo speechmaking for lengths beyond one simple sentence. These sentences are usually for clarification such as *kót'áo* 'like this' and for discipline such as *t'áadoo ánít'íní* 'don't do it'. When these children stay in preschool longer, they tend to become shy and isolated from other children. Staff members can point these children out unhesitatingly.

The few times the children were observed to talk in Navajo, the language reflected competent command of the syntax (grammar) and semantics (meaning) of the language. It was seldom the case that more than one child would be talking in Navajo. The more common communication situation was a single child talking in Navajo while he or she responded to others' English chatter.

One child summed up the whole language problem in her philosophical question in Navajo: "Why doesn't anyone talk in Navajo anymore?"

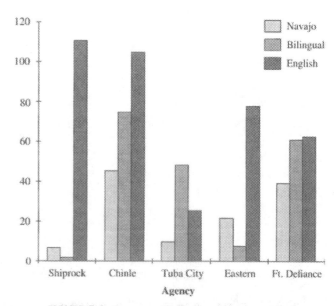

FIGURE 8.1   Language distribution of Navajo preschoolers

Navajo and English Bilingual Navajo Children

The second group of children includes those identified by their teachers as being able to communicate effectively in both Navajo and English. The teachers were asked to identify children who could understand and speak in both languages. Although we were asking about *speaking ability*, many of the teaching staff could make judgments based solely on the children's *comprehension* of both languages. Their responses were typically, "They understand both," or something similar.

In this group, 196 children, or 27.9% of the 682 in the study, were rated by their teachers as being bilingual. This figure for bilingual children is an estimate and is not as reliable as the figure for monolingual children, owing to the manner in which the teachers gave the figures. It appeared that some teachers based their responses upon the children's receptive language skills. They would say something like, "Ten or twelve *understand* both languages." During the study, in only two classes were children heard to be speaking the two languages at length. At other times children would talk almost exclusively in English. The bilingual child does not have the same opportunity as the English-only speakers to use his or her full linguistic capacity, because there are so few children who can communicate in both languages. That opportunity was best provided by the bilingual teaching staff, if they desired it.

Monolingual English Speakers

To identify children who were monolingual English speakers, teachers were asked: "How many of your children are English-only speakers and cannot understand or speak Navajo?"

Teachers have identified 381, or 54.3%, of the 682 children as English-only speakers. Of all the groups of children, this group is the best served. When each class is taught in English throughout the day, one is quickly convinced that the English language is more important than Navajo, even if that means the 124 monolingual children are forced into linguistic isolation. This language, additionally, is reinforced with quality instruction materials that Navajo simply does not have, either for Navajo monolingual instruction or for bilingual instruction.

In sum, Navajo children are taught indirectly that English has a greater value than Navajo. At this critical age, children might be encouraged to shift into English. In many of the classrooms visited, usually fewer than a handful of children do most of the talking. Otherwise, there is a definite lack of language in the classrooms. Teachers fill the room with instructions, but children do not really produce language. They are told in words to be quiet, and the message is reinforced by posters and other labels on the walls of many classrooms.

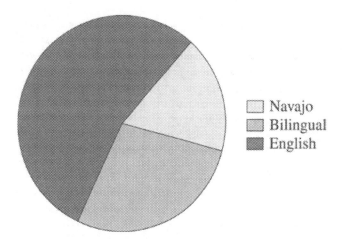

FIGURE 8.2 Navajo area preschool language distribution.
Note: Navajo: 17.69%; bilingual: 27.69%; English: 54.35%

Children have an abundance of sound effects that they used to replace what should be child's talk. It might be the "bilingual" group that does this the most. Also, children communicate by gestures in lieu of speech. Since children do not voluntarily speak in Navajo, this process might be used because it is more generally accepted by all, including the teachers.

The Language the Teachers Talk

All the centers visited had Navajo bilingual teachers and teacher assistants. In the interviews, each was asked to rate the language ability of the staff. All of the respondents said the staff members were bilingual (although some staff members did not specifically indicate they were bilingual, they appeared by observation to be so).

Preschool Staff Meetings

The teachers were asked to rate the language spoken by the staff in their staff meetings. The responses were: 21 bilingual staff meetings, 5 of which leaned toward English and 4 toward Navajo; 6 staff meetings held completely in Navajo; and 2 staff meetings held in English. Ten of the teachers did not indicate what language they used in their staff meetings.

In the few instances in which the staff were observed talking in Navajo, they seemed to be confident speakers of Navajo. When parents came to the classes to pick up children or for other reasons, they talked with parents in either language. Most of the time they were observed speaking English while teaching or visiting with other staff members.

Language Preference of the Preschool Staff

After having visited 39 preschool classes in 26 centers, the conclusion that must be drawn overwhelmingly is that

Navajo teaching staff have a distinct preference for teaching and speaking in English. Whether the teaching staff was well prepared to teach monolingually in English or not, they do teach throughout the day in English. Some of the language samples given above are only representative of the limitations some of the teachers have. In two classes, the teachers appeared to be dominant in Navajo, but they forced themselves to speak English only. This was evident from the many false starts and instances of code switching in which the Navajo language was used to begin an utterance but was quickly replaced with English.

Teachers' Backgrounds

In many respects, the average preschool teacher and teacher's aide appeared not to be well trained in the profession of teaching, especially when children represented a wide range of cultural and linguistic backgrounds, and even when the cultures and languages involved come from only two sources, as in this case. Many of these teachers and their aides had little teaching experience before coming to Navajo Head Start.

Head Start policy about hiring and promotion on an in-house basis has a lot to do with this lack of teaching experience. This "inbreeding" has been a long-standing policy. It has led to people's being promoted to a teacher position without the proper training and credentials. The percentages of teachers and teacher's aides who held CDA certificates were reportedly 85% and 60%, respectively, in the entire Navajo Head Start program. This study did not look at the number of teachers who had a CDA. Had it done so, the results would verify this inbreeding. In other words, many teachers are modeling what they themselves have experienced, which in many cases is very limited. To teach Navajo bilingual children adequately, teachers must have experience and proper training in the areas discussed below.

ESL and Bilingual Training

Teachers were asked if they had had training in ESL. Of the 39 teachers interviewed, only 1 had taken a class in ESL before coming to teach at Navajo Head Start; 1 other had attended an ESL workshop; 28 said they had no background in ESL; and 9 did not know what ESL was.

Teachers were asked also if they had had classroom training in bilingual education, bilingual issues, or teaching the bilingual child. This question had more responses that showed they knew what it meant to teach bilingually. Of the Head Start teachers, 3 had had bilingual education courses, 27 had no such background, and 9 did not respond.

When there are children from different language backgrounds in the classroom, teachers have to extend their communicative skills beyond the language used by the domi-

nant group. In this case, the teaching staff must be able to teach in every child's language, whether the language is Navajo or English. This is not happening in the preschool classrooms that were reviewed. English is spoken almost exclusively even though children who do not understand it are in attendance.

The Language of Parents of Navajo Preschoolers

Navajo preschool children receive their most formative language development from their parents. In spite of this, no provision was included for a more extensive review of the language in the child's home. The only means of obtaining this information was the personal knowledge of the teaching staff, especially the bus driver, who had daily contact with some member of the child's family. Except for a couple of bus rides with the children, we had no other contact with parents in their homes. We met some parents at the centers, but our contact with them was limited because they usually came when observations were in progress in some other part of the classroom.

Navajo-Speaking Parents

According to the teachers, only 12 of the parents who were non-Navajos did not speak Navajo. These parents were Anglo, African American, Polish, Mexican, Italian, and Indians of other tribes. A few Navajo parents did not speak Navajo, though the exact number is not known. All the remaining parents were reported to be good to very good speakers of Navajo. Although teachers were not asked if parents were bilingual, many volunteered this information. Many teachers reported that the parents spoke "a lot of English," or "only English" to their children, which supports the idea that those parents are bilingual.

Parent Volunteers

In a few cases, volunteers were helping to teach children. The parent volunteers and foster grandparents who were observed in this study could seldom be heard talking to or with children. Most of what was heard was English, except in two classes in which the foster grandparents were monolingual Navajo speakers.

From all indications, it appears that parents spoke predominantly English to their children.

Parental Involvement

All teachers said that very few parents expressed interest in their children's education. They generally did not attend parent meetings and seldom came to the class to volunteer.

RECOMMENDATIONS

Language of the Classroom

(1) Navajo children must be supported in the language they already know.

(2) Navajo preschool children must be taught English as a second language if their home or primary language is Navajo.

(3) Language circles must be developed and integrated into the children's daily instruction.

(4) Teachers and teacher's aides should reinforce the child's language acquisition by modeling good, rich language in Navajo and English.

(5) Teachers and teacher's aides must represent a wide variety of language and cultural experiences for Navajo children.

Teacher Training

(6) Training and certification for teachers should include, at the very minimum, ESL, bilingual instruction, child development and psychology, and Navajo language literacy.

(7) Training must be required for teachers in children's acquisition of their first and second languages.

Navajo Language and Culture Educational Materials

(8) Navajo language and cultural materials must be made available in high-quality, colorful reproductions equal in merit to the English-language materials available.

(9) Audiovisual materials for the instruction of Navajo language and culture must be made available.

Parental Involvement

(10) Parents must be encouraged to participate in the language and cultural education of their preschool children.

Personnel Policy

(11) Head Start's in-house personnel policy needs to be reviewed and eliminated or modified in order to ensure that personnel excellence is the primary consideration. Staff must have the necessary qualifications to carry out the responsibilities of the preschool.

Further Study

(12) A longitudinal study should be authorized and funded to assess more accurately the language needs of the Navajo preschooler.

Note

1. This report was done for Dr. Anita Bradley Pfeiffer, Executive Director of the Navajo Division of Education of the Navajo Nation, and for Lena Jim, Director of the Department of Head Start of the Navajo Division of Education of the Navajo Nation. It was submitted on March 23, 1992.

PART IV

MAINTENANCE AND REVITALIZATION OF NATIONAL INDIGENOUS LANGUAGES

9

Introduction to Revitalization of National Indigenous Languages

LEANNE HINTON

Department of Linguistics
University of California at Berkeley
Berkeley, California

There are important differences between the programs for indigenous languages of small communities in small areas of a country versus those that might potentially be "national" or "state" languages. Irish, Welsh, Hawaiian, and Māori are among the "national" or "state" indigenous languages. They have the characteristic of being the only indigenous language of their nation or state, and they all have a historical or potential role in governance. Hawaiian, for example, was the language of government until the coup that deposed the Hawaiian queen. Māori, Welsh, and Irish are all of sufficient importance in their countries that at least some people in government circles know the language even if they are not of the same ethnic heritage. Morgan (Chapter 10) tells the story of the Prince of Wales giving a speech in Welsh; I myself heard a speech in Māori from the New Zealand consul to the United States stationed in Los Angeles, though he himself was of British heritage. Irish is the national language of Ireland, and Hawaiian and English bear coequal status as the official languages of the state of Hawai'i. Each of these languages bears a certain symbolic strength as the language which distinguishes that country (or state) from the rest of the world. In that sense, they are what I will call "national indigenous languages" (even though Hawaiian serves that purpose only for a state within a nation at this point in time), differentiated from official languages or languages of education but of symbolic importance to the states or nations to which they belong.

Owing to British or American imperialism, each one of these languages has become endangered as the power of governance, education, and economics was taken over from the original people by an English-speaking power structure. One by one the functions of these languages were lost, and in ever-broader parts of the land, families who had these languages as their heritage abandoned them for English. The stories of the decline of each of these languages are ably told in the chapters ahead.

But small and large groups alike are fighting in the face of decline to keep their languages alive. The national indigenous languages of which we speak here have a number of important characteristics that provide good resources for revitalization.

(1) The populations that call these their languages of heritage are large, providing a good base from which to draw the necessary professional assistance in language revitalization, such as teachers, linguists, and grant writers, and a large population of learners.

(2) Besides the indigenous population itself, the descendants of the colonizing populations are also inclined to see these indigenous languages as symbolically important and, at present, to have a more positive attitude toward them than is the case with the small language communities; they also have a fair amount of exposure to the language through place-names and loanwords into the local form of English.

(3) Because in each case there is only one indigenous language in the land, financial, political, educational, and professional resources can be focused on that language, in contrast to a place like California, where some 50 indigenous languages still survive. For example, in Ireland, Wales, Hawai'i, and New Zealand one can go to a university and learn the respective languages there, even fluently if the program is good. Such is not possible in California.

(4) For these languages, large-scale revitalization programs can be implemented. Instead of one school, many

101

schools may take part. Instead of a symbolic half hour per week of instruction, entire schools or school systems can be developed with the indigenous language as the language of instruction.

(5) All of these languages have their own relatively long history of literacy, which is not the case with the smaller groups. Thus, these languages have a great deal of documentation and literature.

(6) Even the most ambitious goals of revitalization of these national or state indigenous languages may be reachable. Many of Fishman's stages of language revitalization (see Chapter 1) are not realistic for revitalization of small local languages, but they are potentially attainable by these larger languages. They could become, as they once were, languages of wider communication for everyone in their land.

Because of these issues, revitalization of these national or state indigenous languages is relatively successful, and hope for their future is strong. Although they are in a different league from the smaller languages, they are important to language revitalization everywhere as models and as symbols of hope. Being in the forefront of revitalization and maintenance, these programs can help the rest of the world learn what works and what does not, what succeeds in language teaching, and how to solve the various problems that develop. Language revitalization has not been at all easy even for Hawaiian, Māori, Welsh, and Irish, but they can provide models for how to overcome the many obstacles to realizing their goals. They are capable of bringing state-of-the-art teaching into their programs and of devising even newer and more creative approaches as their situation warrants. The Hawaiians and Māoris, in particular, have been exceedingly generous with their time and knowledge in the service of smaller indigenous groups, being willing to share their methods, their problem-solving successes, and any other useful ideas with any group trying to save its language. Thus, it is to be hoped that the chapters in this section and elsewhere in this book about these national and state indigenous languages will provide everyone with ideas and stimulation that will serve in the development of successful programs for any language, small or large.

Introduction to the Welsh Language

LEANNE HINTON

Department of Linguistics
University of California at Berkeley
Berkeley, California

The Celtic language family, consisting of Welsh, Breton, Gaelic, and other languages, was the dominant family of languages spoken in much of western Europe two millennia ago. But the movement into the area of waves of Roman and Anglo-Saxon conquerors led to the retreat of Celtic languages and eventual extinction of many, leaving only strongholds along the west coast of the British Isles and France. The surviving languages are Welsh, Scots Gaelic, Irish Gaelic, and Breton. Manx and Cornish lack native speakers now but are learned as second languages in the areas where they were once endemic.

Welsh is a member of the Brythonic group of Celtic languages. It was spoken by nearly all the inhabitants until the late 18th century, but since then there has been a steady decline in the use of the language. Industrialization attracted workers to Wales from England, Scotland, and Ireland, and the language of the job became English. There is a strong pattern around the world of the language of the workplace being one of the strongest factors in language shift (Palmer 1997), and so the Welsh themselves began to shift to English, a trend accelerated in the 20th century by English-language radio and television broadcasts and motion pictures (*Encyclopedia Britannica,* 1999). By the late 20th century less than one-fifth of the population could speak Welsh, and they were concentrated in the northern, western, and southern highland areas of the country (see map in Chapter 10). Coastal southern and eastern Wales are, by contrast, heavily anglicized.

Much effort is now being devoted to preserving the Welsh language and culture, with bilingual education, Welsh-language broadcasting, and attempts to maintain the venerable Welsh literary tradition. Of all the Gaelic-speaking peoples, it is the Welsh who have had the most success in keeping their language alive. This chapter tells us why.

References

Encyclopedia Britannica. 1999. S.v. Welsh language. Available at <http://www.britannica.com/bcom/eb/article/9/0, 5716,77919+1,00.html>.

Palmer, Scott. 1997. Language of work: The critical link between economic change and language shift. In *Teaching indigenous languages,* ed. Jon Reyhner, 263–87. Flagstaff: Northern Arizona University, Center for Excellence in Education.

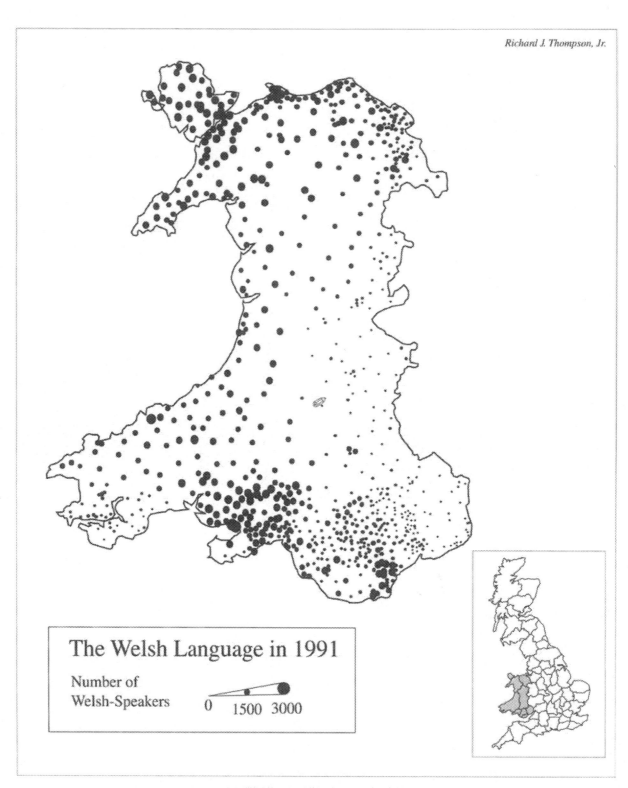

The Welsh Language in 1991

Number of
Welsh-Speakers

0   1500   3000

MAP 10.1   The Welsh language in 1991

10

Welsh

A European Case of Language Maintenance

GERALD MORGAN

Department of History and Welsh History
University of Wales, Aberystwyth

In 1996 I visited Neah Bay on the Olympic peninsula for the Makah Tribal Days, a festival which in some ways strongly resembled a Welsh eisteddfod. In a conversation about language, I drew attention to my own status as a speaker of a European minority language. "How many people speak your language?" I was asked. "About 500,000," I replied. A wry smile. "D'you know how many speak Makah? Twelve!"

Obviously Welsh is not in the same condition as the vast majority of Native North American tongues. With half a million speakers, it is in the top 15% of world languages. Nevertheless, Welsh is in a much less healthy state than, say, Icelandic or Faroese. There may be fewer speakers of Icelandic, but it is that nation's first and virtually universal language: all Icelanders speak Icelandic and are likely to continue to do so. Press, television and radio, education, book publishing—all function overwhelmingly in Icelandic.

Half a million Welsh speakers sounds impressive, but examination shows the number to be less secure than it might seem. In 1911 there were a million, a quarter of whom were monoglot Welsh; today all Welsh speakers are virtually bilingual in English from the age of seven, though fluency varies. The arrival of radio and television ran a language boundary through every Welsh home. Outflow of Welsh-speakers from their heartland areas to the English-speaking areas of Wales and to England and beyond is ongoing, while English incomers have settled in large numbers throughout the Welsh heartland, especially since 1960. This has had the effect of increasing the number of marriages between Welsh speakers and non–Welsh speakers, where English usually has the upper hand. Many homes are occupied by just one person, making dialogue confined to the use of the telephone.

The age weighting of the Welsh-speaking population has for generations been ominous. The percentage of 60-year-olds speaking Welsh has for some generations been larger than the percentage of 10-year-olds. That figure of 500,000 speakers (the standard of whose language skills obviously varies widely) represents about 18% of the total population, but in the censuses of 1961 and 1971 the percentage of young people speaking Welsh was in most areas significantly lower than among the older generations. However, as will be seen below, this situation is changing.

Even when Welsh was the only language of the majority of the population (say, prior to 1840), its domains were restricted. Government, law, and industry—the realm of administration—functioned largely in English. Education, other than for religious purposes, was in English. In a world without press, radio, or television, where government rested lightly on the people, this distortion of domains was not too threatening, though it is evident that the great mass of Welsh-language publishing, both books and periodicals, was religious: there was no fiction or drama, and there were very few books on science, technology, travel, or history.

As a language, Welsh has some interesting characteristics, which it has retained in the teeth of English influence. Noun-adjective order and verbal conjugations resemble French in structure; there are many ways of forming plurals; there is no single word for "yes" or "no"; initial consonants change by complex rules (*cwch* 'a boat'; *ei gwch* 'his boat'; *ei chwch* 'her boat'; *fy nghwch* 'my boat'); and some prepositions are conjugated. But the pressure of English has forced into Welsh not only a considerable vocabulary of loanwords, but also an ever-growing number of calques for functions and expressions which simply were not relevant in an earlier age.

It is hardly surprising that Welsh is in this difficult position.

Wales is a small country, about 200 miles from north to south, and varying in width between about 140 and 60 miles. It has a long land border with England and therefore with a language which had already achieved considerable world status even before the extraordinary development of American cultural hegemony in the 20th century. Wales was never a unitary state; the 13th-century development of a principality ruling much of the country but owing homage to England was nipped in the bud by the conquest of 1282–83, and from 1543 it had to accept (and did so without protest) the English legal and government system. A conquered country, Wales lacked the institutions which gave Scotland a sense of unitary government even after the 1707 union with England took away that country's parliament: Scotland has always had its own laws and legal officers, its own banks, its own national church, and its own universities and education system. Prior to 1872 Wales had none of these things. All it had was its language.

Diversity of dialects is a characteristic of a number of Europe's stateless languages, such as Breton, Irish, and Rheto-Romansch (in Switzerland). It is a situation where the conservative forces of literacy and the centripetal effect of cultural dynamism are weak. Doubtless Welsh—spread thinly, as was the population, over rugged terrain—might have suffered such dialectal extremes had no common form developed. Welsh, however, was fortunate in two ways. During the medieval period a class of professional poets maintained a common literary language which, though it may have been far from common speech, was uniform across the country, and at its best was rich, vigorous, and varied. This class of poets was in decline by the 16th century; the slow process of anglicisation of their gentry patrons, and their own conservatism, made them less and less popular. Not that poetry disappeared—far from it. Instead, poetry became more popular and less professional, using metrical forms borrowed from common European stock, especially, of course, from England.

It was at this point that history played a rare card in favor of Welsh. Initially it was owing entirely to the failure of Henry VIII and his first wife to produce a male heir, and that at the very time when much of western Europe was being convulsed by the Protestant Reformation. Henry's rejection of papal authority in 1532 inevitably brought him nearer to Protestantism, particularly in allowing the publication of the Bible in English in 1535, only ten years after having forbidden it on pain of death. The Tudor dynasty (with the exception of Mary, who reigned from 1553 to 1558) turned England toward Protestantism. But what of Wales? English Bibles and prayer books were of no use. The familiar (even if not well understood) Latin was to be replaced by Anglo-gibberish! And Wales could be dangerous, not only for its local revolts, but as a stepping-stone for invaders; the French had threatened or actually landed in Wales in 1387, 1405, and 1485. Wales had to be made safe for Protestantism.

Two steps were taken. Wales was placed on a basis of legal and political equality with England by two acts of Parliament in 1536 and 1543. The laws were to be uniform and to be administered in the courts in English. This process was less revolutionary than it may seem; English probably was already the language of process in Crown courts in half of Wales. Wales now had representation in the London Parliament. The acts were generally welcomed in Wales, and Welsh people, undeterred by racist jokes, immigrated to England in increasing numbers, while the Welsh gentry became increasingly anglicised in culture and outlook. The second step to secure Welsh stability was to allow the Welsh bishops in 1563 to secure an act of Parliament for the translation of the Bible into Welsh—the only minority language in western Europe to have its own state-authorized vernacular Bible in the 16th century.

Nor was this all. The chief architect of the translation, which appeared in 1588, was not only a fine Biblical scholar but a master of the best Welsh, the poets' Welsh. William Morgan was able to craft a work which, fundamentally, could be understood all over Wales, especially, of course, as the great majority of the population heard it every week. It set a new standard of richness and dignity for Welsh prose. Welsh books had begun to trickle from London's printing presses from 1546, but it was only when the London-Oxford-Cambridge monopoly of printing was abandoned before the end of the 17th century that the number of Welsh titles began to increase significantly. Presses were set up, first in Shrewsbury on the English side of the border, then, in 1718, in Wales itself. Although the bulk of publications were religious, ballads, almanacs, and volumes of poetry were also popular. Ten thousand–copy editions of the Bible in 1718, 1727, 1746, and 1752 sold well, encouraged by the spread of literacy, especially after the establishment about 1732 of the so-called circulating schools of the evangelical parish priest Griffith Jones of Llanddowror (1683–1761).

Jones, a remarkable educationist, brought together a number of current ideas and, with the help of several wealthy Welsh gentry patrons and the backing of the Society for the Promotion of Christian Knowledge, was able to train teachers and support the establishment of local schools wherever the demand arose—and he insisted that in Welsh-speaking areas the teaching of both adults and children should be in Welsh. Although Griffith Jones loved his native language, his movement was entirely devoted to enabling people to read the Bible so that they would be open to salvation. Tens of thousands of ordinary Welsh people learned to read. Not by coincidence, a series of religious revivals began in 1735 which led eventually to the establishment of the breakaway Welsh Calvinistic Methodist Church in 1811, and by the mid-19th century the Welsh people perceived themselves as being overwhelmingly Nonconformist and Welsh speaking. Almost throughout the country, chapels were centers of Welsh-language worship and cultural life.

The reality was more complex. The religious census of 1851 and other statistics showed that while the percentage of Welsh who attended church was double that of England, it was still only half the population—the visible half, so to speak. Moreover, the country was experiencing colossal change under the impact of extractive and basic industry. From 1780 onward south Wales became a major producer of iron (later steel), tinplate, and coal. The overcrowded western rural areas began to bleed population into the industrial valleys. Instead of the roughly even spread of 500,000 people across the whole country in 1801 (the mountainous areas always more thinly populated), by 1871 the majority of the 1,400,000 people were crammed into the southeast, and today (population 2,800,000) the picture is the same.

At first this interior migration was not a threat to the Welsh language. Hundreds of new chapels were established in the industrial valleys, with their attendant Sunday schools and cultural activities, especially the burgeoning choirs. Slightly higher personal incomes meant that the small surplus could be spent on nonessentials, and the Welsh publishing industry flourished as never before, with a vigorous sector of weekly and monthly papers and periodicals. The revived eisteddfod, a competitive festival of music and literature, was successful both at the local and (from 1858 on) at the national level.

However, there were signs that this sea change was not entirely healthy for the language. As in England, religion was less all-pervading in the urban areas than the countryside. The chapels flourished, and the established church (Church of England) underwent a vigorous revival, but it failed to touch a growing segment of the population. The driving force behind the iron and steel industry was investment by English incomers, although coal remained a much more "native" industry, since it was less capital intensive. But nearly all Welsh industry was basic; it produced materials to be used in English factories.

Inevitably, Welsh speakers were perceived to be socially inferior; they ploughed the land, herded the sheep, cut the slate, poured the steel, and hacked the coal, but they did not own the great estates, the quarries, or the ironworks. They had also become, on occasion, ready to manifest serious civil unrest. Industrial riots convulsed the Black Domain, the main coal and iron area of the southeast, culminating in the Chartist Rising of 1839, while the rural areas of the southwest saw the Rebecca Riots of 1839 and 1843–44. The London authorities grew increasingly anxious about Wales.

The key to the problem was seen as education. A massive investigation into Welsh schooling published in 1847 revealed disgraceful inadequacies, though the commissioners were careful to praise the work of the Sunday schools. Their report had a mixed reception; on the one hand they were perceived as blaming the Welsh language and Nonconformity for the ignorance and immorality of the people, but on the other hand Welsh people absorbed the views of the report, and when compulsory schooling was introduced in 1870, not only was the teaching of Welsh entirely absent from the curriculum, even speaking it in the playground was widely discouraged and even forbidden, with little protest from parents. A long-established sense of social and cultural inferiority was reaching crisis point.

Moreover, by the end of the 19th century rural Wales was unable to produce enough recruits for the ever-growing industrial southeast (and, increasingly, the northeast as well). The roaring growth of the coal industry attracted larger and larger numbers of workpeople from England and beyond, so that between 1901 and 1911 Wales was a rare example in Europe of a country of growing inward migration. As the population grew, so did the number of Welsh speakers—but at a diminishing rate compared with population growth. By 1911 almost a million people spoke Welsh, more than ever before—but they were just 49% of the population.

Alongside all these developments, a new and positive cultural movement began to gain ground. Because the Welsh people lacked national institutions, their sense of Welsh identity had depended largely on the language and on the land of Wales. During the 18th century a vigorous sense of Welsh cultural identity developed among a small number of middle-class Welsh people, who collected the evidence of the past from manuscripts and began to establish Welsh societies in Wales's only capital—London. Wales became a popular resort for travelers, artists, and tourists, who rhapsodized over the rugged landscape while deploring the poverty of the Welsh peasantry. During the early 19th century the cultural movement grew apace in Wales itself, with the establishment of regional eisteddfodau and antiquarian societies. The use of Welsh baptismal names, almost entirely abandoned in favor of John, Richard, Ann, Elizabeth, and so on, began to revive from about 1860.

The extension of the franchise in 1867 meant for the first time that a large number of Welshmen (though not, until 1918, women) could vote, and they were increasingly anxious to cast off the rule of the landlord class of politicians in favor of Liberal democracy. Slowly, Welsh issues emerged as distinct matters of concern, especially in the matter of disestablishing the state Church of England, and in education. In 1872 the first college of the University of Wales, at Aberystwyth, was founded. In 1889 Wales was provided, ahead of England, with a network of secondary schools (the equivalent of high schools). A campaign began for the establishment of a national library and museum (achieved in 1909). Welsh was gradually introduced into the school curriculum, though only as a subject, not as a medium of instruction.

Gradually the Welsh were reinventing themselves, not for

the first time in their history. Voluntary organizations—chapel, cultural society, choir, eisteddfod—were additionally sustained by the growing success of rugby football. Invented by English toffs, the Welsh working class adopted rugby and by 1910 had produced teams which could beat all other rugby-playing countries save South Africa. A Welsh-speaking Welshman, David Lloyd George, was the government's chief finance minister, second in authority in all Britain, destined to become prime minister. There was a national anthem, far more inspiring than the thin tune of England, and a national flag, the Red Dragon, with supplementary national symbols in the leek (ancient) and the daffodil (modern). The first university college had become the federal University of Wales, with three colleges before 1900 and more to follow. Poetry, art, and music flourished. Cardiff, the world's largest coal-exporting port, was de facto capital of Wales, though not officially recognized as such until 1955. Politically, the urban and industrial Welsh began to shift from the Liberal party to the Labour party, which developed a strongly centralist attitude toward Welsh matters.

Then history took a terrible turn. The frightful sacrifice of World War I, which saw the slaughter of thousands of Welsh-speaking Welshmen, was quickly followed by economic collapse, which led to the emigration, by 1939, of hundreds of thousands of men, women, and children, a large though unknown percentage of them Welsh speaking. By 1951 the number of Welsh speakers had dropped from 900,000 to 700,000, and the monoglot speakers were being eroded at a much quicker rate. The chapels, both rural and urban, were losing members at a gallop (see Table 10.1).

Before 1950 the British government did not really envisage language promotion as part of its brief. Welsh was taught in schools in those areas where it seemed relevant, but in any case the national government could do little to influence

the curriculum, which was the responsibility of local government. Parents overwhelmingly saw English as the path out of the coal mine and the quarry and into the middle class. Welsh could be left to the Sunday school and the chapels. Classes for adults for learning Welsh hardly existed, and incomers had no encouragement to learn. Apart from place-name signs, the language was virtually invisible—public notices of all kinds, official forms, and government literature were entirely in English. Business, with the rarest of exceptions, was conducted in English. The Welsh language enjoyed no legal status whatsoever. The scene was bleak.

However, between 1918 and the return of war in 1939, straws in the wind began to appear. In 1922 the Welsh League of Youth was established by Ifan ab Owen Edwards to promote the use of the language among young people through voluntary activities. Highly successful in most of its work, the organization still enjoys a high profile among Welsh schoolchildren. In 1925 a minuscule Welsh political party was formed, Plaid Cymru; though it enjoyed no electoral success, it stirred up debate, and it survived the locust years, eventually to reemerge. In the late 1930s petitions were launched for a Welsh parliament and for legal status for the language, which gained broad support but achieved little.

The coming of war in 1939, with its threat of aerial bombardment, brought a new crisis. Thousands of children were sent from English cities to the safety of rural Wales. The arrival of groups of youngsters totally ignorant of Welsh in the schoolrooms and playgrounds of Wales was often traumatic. Many learned Welsh, but others quickly improved the English of their fellow pupils. In Aberystwyth, a small university town on the west coast, Ifan ab Owen Edwards decided something must be done. He exercised the right to found his own school, and it commenced with one teacher (a Welsh speaker, but trained to teach in English) and seven pupils in Edwards' own home.

The experiment became permanent, and after the war local authorities began to establish primary schools in which the main language of instruction was Welsh. This was conceived purely as a defense mechanism—to "protect" the Welsh of children from Welsh-speaking homes from being overwhelmed by the English majority in the relevant districts—namely the industrialized areas of the south and the northeast. By 1953 there were 15 such schools, with 1,000 pupils—but this was still only a tiny percentage of the country's children.

Then two developments began. The northeastern county of Flintshire had a vigorous director of education, Haydn Williams, who succeeded in establishing a chain of Welsh primary schools throughout his district to serve the Welsh-speaking minority. Thus the language was maintained until the child reached the age of 11. But then the pupils moved to secondary schools, which were overwhelmingly English, so that their Welsh-language development was stunted. Williams and some parents saw the need for a secondary (high)

TABLE 10.1   Welsh Speakers in Wales, 1891–91

	Welsh speakers	Welsh speakers as a percentage of total
1891	910,289	54.4 (first year to include a language quesstion)
1901	929,824	49.9
1911	977,366	43.5
1921	922,092	37.1
1931	909,261	36.8
1941	Wartime: no census	
1951	714,686	28.9
1961	656,002	26.0
1971	542,425	20.9
1981	503,520	18.7
1991	508,098	18.6

school which would, while ensuring success in English, teach subjects such as history, geography, and Religious Knowledge through the medium of Welsh, and where the administration and culture of the school would be Welsh.

The school was established in 1955, and to the chagrin of a few and the surprise of many, it flourished. A sister school opened in 1962, and between them they served the county. A third high school was opened in the southeast, north of Cardiff. It was fortunate in having a dynamic principal and grew like a mushroom. Welsh-medium education suddenly became seen as both practicable and desirable, especially since the schools did well in the essential field of public examination results. The primary schools grew apace, as parents who were Welsh but not Welsh speaking sought the restoration of the language which their grandparents had spoken.

The increasing success of these schools, and their numerical growth, should not have been such a big surprise. Despite the major handicap of having no Welsh-language teaching materials, the teachers were largely drawn from among those keen to see their language flourish. Parents *chose* the schools; no one was compelled to attend them. These high schools produced excellent results in English as well as Welsh because the pupils were having double doses of language lessons, with two teachers rubbing in the importance of sentence structure, paragraphing, and spelling.

Growth was slower in the secondary (high-school) sector than the primary, but in 1973 the sixth secondary school was opened at Aberystwyth—the first to be created in an area traditionally regarded as Welsh speaking, but where Welsh-speaking children formed only some 35% of the area pupil body. The success of these schools, and the change of cultural atmosphere, brought about changes in the long-established English-medium secondary schools in the Welsh-speaking areas. Stung by the realization that Welsh-medium teaching was both possible and desirable, these schools began to offer "Welsh streams" where pupils could learn through Welsh while their fellows (all learning Welsh as a second language) were taught in English.

The change in the cultural atmosphere of formal education owed a great deal to other developments, particularly in the nursery-group movement. This provided part-time educational activities for children under fives and has proved an extremely efficient way of teaching Welsh as a second language. The movement, and its mother-and-toddler groups, underpinned the exponential growth of Welsh-medium schooling, especially in the southeast. In 1990 there were 553 nursery groups and 340 mother-and-toddler groups, catering to nearly 13,000 children.

Postwar adult education, largely sponsored by local government authorities, began to include a wide range of classes for learners of Welsh, though since they tended to be weekly occasions, they achieved little in the way of language breakthrough. However, interest in the extraordinary success of

Hebrew in Israel came to the notice of Welsh educationists, and modified versions of the Israeli "Ulpan" immersion programs began to appear first in the summer calendars of the university colleges at Lampeter and Aberystwyth and then, in more diluted form, in their winter programs (so many mornings a week, rather than the all-day arrangement of the summer schools).

Outside the education movement altogether, other developments took place. The founder of the Welsh National Party of 1925, Saunders Lewis, a great Welsh writer but by his own account a failure in politics, was given the opportunity in 1962 to deliver a special lecture on BBC Welsh radio. He appealed to his listeners to resort to civil disobedience in order to achieve legal status for the Welsh language. In response to his appeal, a number of young men and women founded the Welsh Language Society and began to campaign with panache and with a readiness to make sacrifices which made their parents blench. As they occupied post office counters and refused to pay local taxes when demanded on English-only forms, as they pulled down English-only road signs and dumped them in front of police stations, as they refused to pay fines in court and were sent to jail as a result, politicians stood up in droves to denounce them—but gradually the society gained victories. Acts of Parliament gave improved status to the language, so that any transaction in Welsh was legally valid. The post office, reluctantly at first, adopted Welsh for its signs and literature and was followed by the major banks, as well as by most local authorities. At the same time, Welsh cultural activities such as book publishing, the Welsh League of Youth, and the National Eisteddfod began to gain serious financial support from the government, which established a Welsh Office to deal with matters Welsh, with a secretary of state for Wales in the cabinet. The Welsh language was "hot." The BBC was subjected to steady pressure to which it responded by establishing in 1979 a Welsh-language FM radio service which now runs for some 18 hours a day. Welsh-language television, however, was largely ghettoized to unpopular viewing hours, but this was to change, again under pressure.

The initial reluctance of national and local government to understand reasonable demands for improved recognition for the Welsh language drove the young activists to civil disobedience, until it was eventually realized that it would be wiser to listen and, where possible, to act. In retrospect, the turning point seems to have been in 1981. The Conservative government, elected in 1979, promised in the 1981 Queen's speech to establish a Welsh-medium television station, but a few months later it announced a turnabout. At this point it must be understood that although political parties are not on oath in their pre-election manifestos, the promise of action in a Queen's speech is not to be lightly cast aside. Gwynfor Evans, who became the first Plaid Cymru member of Parliament in 1966 but by 1981 was in retirement, announced a fast to the death against the government's decision. The prospect of this gentle, widely respected man's being in extremis was alarming; it would certainly have led to civil unrest in Wales. The government reversed its U-turn, and the Welsh-medium television station was established.

Nor did the politicians forget this lesson. In 1993 the government established a Welsh Language Board with considerable influence to act on behalf of the language in the public realm. Although the board has no powers to impose policies on private companies, most chain stores have introduced prominent bilingual signs on all their premises, and banking services, including telephone banking, are available in Welsh. The board can bring considerable pressure to bear, especially on public bodies, to secure bilingual policies. However, the goal of absolutely equal status has not yet been achieved, and although, by a remarkable turnabout, the Welsh voted for the establishment of a National Assembly, which opened in 1999, the body does not have powers of primary legislation.

It would seem, then, that for a minority language which has suffered severe erosion, Welsh is remarkably well placed, thanks particularly to vigorous campaigning, influential lobbying, and educational change. In education, both Welsh-speaking and non–Welsh speaking children in all but a very few areas can benefit from immersion experiences in preschool groups and then, up to the age of 18, attend schools which have Welsh-medium streams or are dedicated Welsh-medium schools. Higher education is, by contrast, limited to a few courses in three colleges; Welsh itself, history and Welsh history, geography, French, theology, drama, and education are the most frequently taken, though classes are often small. School and college students usually have the right to sit public examination papers in Welsh. If pupils and parents are not interested in Welsh-medium education, then they follow the normal course through school, but (at least to age 14) they are expected to learn Welsh as a second language, though successful acquisition is limited.

The supply of Welsh-medium educational materials, though vastly better than in 1955, is still tiny compared to the English market. A government-funded resources center at Aberystwyth has produced considerable amounts of material in both print and other media, but educational television in Welsh is so expensive that BBC output is strictly limited.

The impact of Welsh-medium education in the anglicized southeast of Wales has been remarkable. The 1991 census registered an increase of Welsh speakers in 1981 of 49% in the populous Cardiff and South Glamorgan area, owing almost entirely to the increase in Welsh-medium education, and all other areas showed some improvement, for the first time in 100 years.

All that having been said, there is little cause for complacency. The dominance of the English media grows ever more powerful and is now boosted by the Internet—though Welsh organizations and individuals have been quick to provide Welsh-language Web sites, and Welsh radio can be heard worldwide. The Welsh-speaking population is becoming increasingly urbanized, tending to move from the countryside, and their places are filled by English incomers escaping from the rat race. In smaller traditional Welsh-speaking communities there has long been a supportive social domain of voluntary groups, with the Young Farmers' Clubs prominent among them. But the farming community, the last Welsh-speaking industry, is rapidly shrinking under economic pressure. A valley which once supported six farms and their families is now farmed by one man and his family; the other five houses have been sold to incomers. On the other hand, even in the urban districts, where Welsh-medium education has been so successful, there is little Welsh-medium social activity attractive to young people that is available to support the linguistic gains made at school. True, there is a lively rock-and-folk Welsh language culture, and several Welsh groups have recently achieved a much wider success. To see thousands of young English people chanting along with Catatonia's lead singer Cerys Matthews, "Every day when I wake up, I thank the Lord I'm Welsh!" is quite extraordinary—but not enough.

There is an interesting dichotomy in the Welsh world of work. In the domains of local and national government and administration, of education, of tourism, and of television and radio, proficiency in Welsh is usually seen as a valuable asset to one's résumé or curriculum vitae. In the domain of industry, on the other hand, Welsh is of little use. The tendency is still for most Welsh manufacturing industries to be branches of larger concerns, with incoming management hiring local labor or bringing in skilled labor from outside, with little regard for the language—sometimes even with hostility toward it.

Harold Carter and John Aitchison, the acknowledged experts on the fortunes of the Welsh language, predict that the success of the Welsh-medium education movement will produce, in the 2001 census, an overall increase in the number of Welsh speakers. But the depth of those speakers' knowledge of the language and its literature, and the range of their skills, may not be so strong. Only 80% of Welsh-speaking couples bring up their children with Welsh as their first language, a 20% leakage unimaginable in a healthy language situation. Dilution of the Welsh-speaking community, by incomers in rural areas and by the very nature of urban community, is still ongoing, still powerful. The wonderful vigor of traditional expression, varying from the biblical to the farmyard dungheap, is also diluted by the overwhelming nature of megalopolitical intercourse.

Nevertheless, the achievements since 1960 have been extraordinary. The Welsh language has a status unimaginable to those of us who remember Wales in 1960. The passion and sacrifice of a few hundred, and the hard work and dedication of many thousands, have, without bombs or assassinations, given civic rights in the language realm not only to the native speakers, but to the many who would like to be able to speak Welsh, who cherish its life even though they cannot share it, and the increasing numbers who have mastered it fluently, and who can once more hear the land speak to them in its own tongue.

References

Aitchison, J., and H. Carter. 2000. *Language, economy, and society: The changing fortunes of the Welsh language in the twentieth century.* Cardiff: University of Wales Press.

Baker, Colin. 1985. *Aspects of bilingualism in Wales.* Clevedon, England: Multilingual Matters.

Davies, Janet. 1999. *The Welsh language.* Cardiff: University of Wales Press. (Although described as a pocket guide, this book gives a valuable summary of the history of Welsh and its present situation.)

Morris, D., and G. Williams. 2000. *Language planning and language use.* Cardiff: University of Wales Press.

Morris Jones, B., and P. A. S. Ghuman. 1995. *Bilingualism, education, and identity.* Cardiff: University of Wales Press.

Thomas, P. W., and J. Mathias. 2000. *Developing minority languages.* Cardiff: University of Wales Press.

Introduction to the Māori Language

KEN HALE

Department of Linguistics and Philosophy
Massachusetts Institute of Technology
Cambridge, MA

Māori is a Polynesian language and, as such, is closely related to Hawaiian, another language which has played an important role in the development and use of immersion programs in language revitalization and maintenance. Māori possesses a history which included a period of extensive use of the written form during the "colonial period." Though Māori was impressive in the level of literacy it achieved, it was not alone in its use of writing in that era—it is an interesting and generally overlooked fact that writing in indigenous languages in places now dominated by English was rather common before the 20th century. The decline in the use of written Māori in the early 1900s, dramatically portrayed in Figure 11.1 of Jeanette King's chapter, has its parallels elsewhere, including, for example, the severe reduction in Cherokee-language literacy, once enjoyed by 90% of the Cherokee population in Oklahoma (Spicer 1969). While writing is not speaking, the loss of a healthy tradition of literacy in a local language represents a decline in the use of the local language. It is part of the general picture and is typically followed by a decline in the use of the spoken language. It is not that the one causes the other; rather, the two are components of the same process of language loss. The number of Cherokees who do not speak Cherokee now exceeds the number who do. And as King reports in her essay, only 18% to 20% of the Māori population spoke Māori fluently in the mid-1970s. This is the condition which gave rise to the Te Kōhanga Reo ("language nest") movement of the 1980s.

Māori has an illustrious history in language scholarship. The dictionary of Williams (1917) is an important and valuable early resource, and through a number of more recent works, the language has contributed much to linguistic theory (Biggs 1961; Hohepa 1967, 1969; Chung 1978;

Bauer 1981, 1993). Māori is known for a number of features, its passive for one. While all Māori words end in vowels, the language has nonetheless inherited from its pre-Polynesian ancestors a set of stem-final consonants, as the final *m* in the verb **inum* 'drink'. But this final consonant only appears if a suffix immediately follows it, as in the passive *inumia*. Otherwise, the final *m* is lost—thus, 'drink' is pronounced *inu* in the active. Some 12 distinct pre-Polynesian final consonants appear in this way in the passive—for example, *kōhete* 'scold' has *t* in the passive, hence *kōhetetia;* *hopu* 'catch' has *k* in the passive, hence *hopukia;* and so on. This has generated some debate in linguistics, beginning with the publication of Patrick Hohepa's dissertation (1967). The theoretical problem has to do with the proper association of the original final consonant in the synchronic grammar of Māori. Hohepa assigns it to the suffix, rather than to the stem, parsing *hopukia* as *hopu-kia,* rather than *hopuk-ia.* The arguments for his ahistorical analysis are very strong. It is in apparent conflict with certain established principles of phonological analysis, forcing a close and critical look at those principles. Tension of this sort is extraordinarily valuable in moving theoretical linguistics forward. It is not only the phonology of the Māori passive that has contributed in this way; its syntax has also been a focus of interest. The use of the passive in transitive imperatives and the strong preference for the passive in the past tense are very interesting typologically. These aspects of the passive, among others, led Hohepa to propose that it was an ergative construction (Hohepa 1967, 1969). This in turn led to important research by others on grammatical relations in Polynesian generally (including Chung 1978 and Clark 1973, 1976).

References

Bauer, Winifred. 1981. Aspects of the grammar of Maori. Ph.D. diss., University of Edinburgh.

Bauer, Winifred, with William Parker and Te Kareongawai. 1993. *Maori.* London and New York: Routledge.

Biggs, Bruce. 1961. The structure of New Zealand Maori. *Anthropological Linguistics* 3, no. 3: 1–54.

Chung, Sandra. 1978. *Case marking and grammatical relations in Polynesian.* Austin: University of Texas Press.

Clark, R. 1973. Passive and surface subject in Maori. Paper presented at the annual meeting of the Linguistic Society of America, December, San Diego, Calif.

———. 1976. *Aspects of proto-Polynesian syntax.* Te Reo Monograph. Auckland: Linguistic Society of New Zealand.

Hohepa, Patrick W. 1967. *A profile generative grammar of Maori.* Indiana University Publications in Anthropology and Linguistics, memoir 20, *International Journal of American Linguistics.* Baltimore: Waverley.

———. 1969. The accusative-to-ergative process in Polynesian languages. *Journal of the Polynesian Society* 78: 295–329.

Spicer, Edward H. 1969. *A short history of the Indians of the United States.* New York: Van Nostrand Reinhold.

Williams, H. W. 1917. *A dictionary of the Maori language.* Wellington: Government Printer.

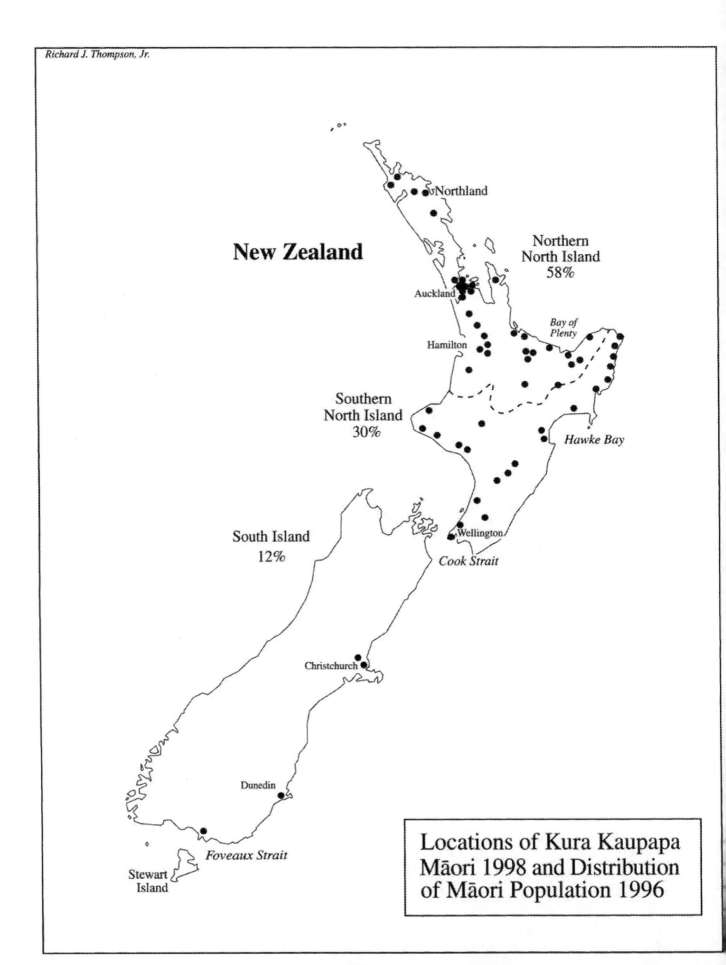

Richard J. Thompson, Jr.

New Zealand

Northland

Northern
North Island
58%

Auckland

Bay of
Plenty

Hamilton

Southern
North Island
30%

Hawke Bay

South Island
12%

Wellington

Cook Strait

Christchurch

Dunedin

Foveaux Strait

Stewart
Island

Locations of Kura Kaupapa
Māori 1998 and Distribution
of Māori Population 1996

MAP 11.1   Kura Kaupapa Māori, in New Zealand

11

Te Kōhanga Reo
Māori Language Revitalization

JEANETTE KING

University of Canterbury
Māori Department
Christchurch, New Zealand

The purpose of this essay is to describe the Kōhanga Reo movement in New Zealand, to attempt to determine some aspects of its success and limitations, and to point out its relevance for broader interests in language revitalization in general.

Te Kōhanga Reo ('the' + 'nest' + 'language', language nest) is an early-childhood language immersion program developed by the Māori community in response to the realization that few children were being raised as speakers of the language.[1] Kōhanga Reo aim to provide an environment where children will hear only the Māori language and will therefore grow up speaking Māori. As might be inferred from the word "nest" in the English translation "language nest," the movement focuses on facilitating language revitalization within the context of the *whānau* (the Māori concept of family).

From its beginnings in the early 1980s the movement had grown by 1998 to include over 600 Kōhanga Reo operating throughout New Zealand. Te Kōhanga Reo has been the spearhead of the language revitalization movement in New Zealand, particularly in shaping new educational options for Kōhanga Reo graduates. For example, bilingual classes in mainstream schools and Kura Kaupapa Māori ('school' + 'philosophy' + 'Māori', Māori-philosophy schools) are now well established in response to the demand from parents for continued education through the medium of Māori.

The growth of Te Kōhanga Reo and other education-based revitalization strategies has required the development from scratch of an infrastructure, the training of staff, and the development of resources. This has involved Māori people in a phenomenal organizational effort. There is an ongoing shortage of teaching resources in Māori as well as of qualified teachers who can teach in Māori. Owing to the speed of the program's development and expansion, to date there has been little qualitative assessment of the achievements and role of Te Kōhanga Reo in the revitalization of the Māori language.

There is a distinct Māori terminology which is used in describing Te Kōhanga Reo and its associated concepts. Many of these words are used in this chapter both to reveal the use of such language by participants and to avoid problems of definition. A glossary is included at the end of the chapter.

The use of these Māori words within the movement serves a number of functions. The main one is to convey concepts for which the Māori word is the most appropriate, there being only a clumsy alternative in English. Other words for which there is a translation, such as *tamariki* 'children', are often used in the English of Kōhanga Reo parents to signal support for the Māori language (King 1995) and also to reflect a Māori cultural outlook.

HISTORICAL BACKGROUND

Māori is one of the small group of eastern Polynesian languages in the very large Austronesian family. Migration by Polynesian ancestors across the Pacific over several millennia led to the settlement of New Zealand in about AD 1000. Over the following 1,000 years several mutually intelligible dialects of Māori developed throughout the country (Biggs 1968, 65). Rarotongan and Tahitian are the languages to which Māori is most closely related (Biggs 1994, 96).

Initial contact by Europeans occurred in 1642 with the arrival of Abel Tasman, followed in the late 1700s by several voyages by James Cook. At this time the Māori population is estimated to have been around 100,000 (Rice 1992, 11).

European whalers, sealers, and missionaries began arriving in New Zealand from about 1800 onward, and Māori was the language of trade and exchange of ideas between the two cultures at this time. In particular, the missionaries, working at first in the northern districts, decided that their task would be most effective if they were to teach and preach to Māori in the indigenous language. To facilitate their use of Māori, the missionaries produced an orthography as well as grammars and dictionaries of the Māori language.[2]

The 20 phonemes of the language (10 consonants and 5 vowels, the vowels having both a short and a long form) were represented in an alphabet by a Professor Lee of Oxford University in 1818, when the Ngāpuhi chiefs Waikato and Hongi Hika journeyed to England (McRae 1991, 4). This orthographical system has remained virtually unchanged.[3]

Teaching of reading and writing in Māori at the mission schools reached a peak in the 1830s (Rice 1992, 143–44). It is argued that at this time there were proportionately more Māori literate in Māori than there were English people in England literate in English (Biggs 1968, 73). Many catechisms and religious texts were disseminated throughout the country as Māori lay preachers took their religious message and their literacy skills to the farthest regions of the land.

The effect of this widespread literacy amongst the Māori was the production of a prodigious amount of manuscript material written in the Māori language. Much of this survives to this day in private and public collections in New Zealand and abroad. In addition, government, church, and Māori presses produced newspapers and periodicals.[4] This written material, ranging in subject from land issues to mythology and poetry, has wider significance as arguably the largest body of writing which survives from an indigenous colonized people produced within a generation of European contact (Orbell 1995, 19, 21).

With the arrival of English settlers from 1840 onward, a colonial government and infrastructure was established. Initially Māori was still the main language of communication between the newcomers and the Māori, with the government employing licensed interpreters to translate letters and documents for official correspondence with the Māori populace. By 1858 a census recorded a total Māori population of 56,000. Until just before the turn of the century, lack of immunity to Western diseases and warfare further reduced the Māori population to 42,000 (Pool 1977, 237).

The progressive change to English as the main language between the two cultures was formalized in the passing of the 1867 Native Schools Act, which made English the language of literacy in schools. The effect of this change was profound: the Māori language was virtually outlawed in schools, and many Māori schoolchildren over the succeeding generations were punished for speaking the language of their home.[5]

The effect of this policy and the changing social climate is demonstrated in the language of letters in the Taiaroa col-

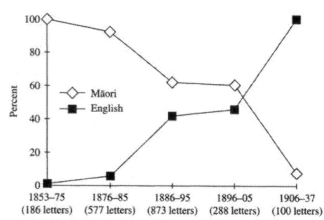

FIGURE 11.1   Percentage of letters written in Māori and English in selected time bands in the Taiaroa Collection. Reprinted with permission from Te Kōhanga Reo National Trust Resource Manual 1985, p. 2.

lection.[6] These 2,084 letters, written by both Māori and government officials, cover the period from 1853 to 1937.[7]

Figure 11.1 shows an accelerated decrease in the use of Māori language after 1885; by 1905 more letters were being written in English than Māori. This trend was led by government ministers and officials, who increasingly wrote in English toward the end of the century, and the replies from Māori began to follow this official lead. This graph illustrates how, for Māori people, English replaced Māori as the language of officialdom and government—the language of power.

However, Māori was still the language of the home and community, with all the estimated 45,000 Māori in 1900 being speakers of the Māori language (Te Taura Whiri i Te Reo Māori 1995a). By the mid-1970s there were about 70,000 fluent speakers of Māori (Benton 1981, 15), but they constituted only 18–20% of the Māori population and were virtually all aged 50 and over. Moreover, there were only a couple of small rural localities where Māori was still the community language.

The gradual shift from Māori to English as the language of the home was linked in various communities to the two world wars, the 1930s depression, urban drift in the 1960s, and the introduction of television (Benton 1991). Those centers of Māori population closest to larger towns and cities were affected sooner than remote heartlands. However, in general, Māori was still the predominant language in most Māori homes until World War II (Te Taura Whiri i Te Reo Māori 1996, 19).

During this time there were also many Māori parents who believed that a good knowledge of English was essential to their children's ability to obtain work and status within the now dominant and pervasive Pākehā (New Zealanders of European background) community. As a result, many Māori parents consciously chose not to speak Māori to their children in the home.

By the 1970s the main domains for the use of Māori were the *marae* (tribal community meeting place) and the church. It was in this decade that the seeds of discontent which led to the current Māori language revitalization movement were sown. Groups of young Māori presented petitions to Parliament and successfully campaigned for Māori to be taught in primary schools (Jackson 1993, 215–18). Although Māori had been taught in secondary schools since 1945 and at university from 1951, it was not until 1977, with the opening of the first bilingual school at Rūātoki, that Māori once again became a language of literacy for Māori children. By 1990 the number of bilingual schools had increased to 17 (Nga Kairangahau 1991, 7).[8]

In 1975 the Ngāti Raukawa tribal confederation launched Whakatipuranga Rua Mano ('generation' + 'two' + 'thousand', Generation 2000), a tribal development program which emphasized Māori language revitalization. As part of this program a university, Te Wānanga o Raukawa, was established in Ōtaki in 1981 to provide degree courses in management and Māori language.[9]

The Te Ātaarangi movement, developed in the late 1970s by Katerina Mataira and Ngoi Pewhairangi, focused on language development for adults, giving them an opportunity to learn Māori as a second language using the "silent method" developed by Caleb Gattegno (Boyce 1995, 9). The Te Ātaarangi method uses only Māori as the medium of instruction and typically involves volunteer tutors working with small groups. Te Ātaarangi continues to be very popular and has tutors throughout New Zealand.

In this climate Te Kōhanga Reo was launched in the early 1980s, to be rapidly followed by Kura Kaupapa Māori and bilingual classes in mainstream schools. These developments are discussed in more detail in the next section.

In 1987 the Māori Language Act made Māori an official language of New Zealand and established rules for its limited use in courts. The Māori Language Commission (Te Taura Whiri i Te Reo Māori) was also set up under this act with a number of functions, including advising on Māori language issues. Te Taura Whiri i Te Reo Māori also certifies interpreters, coins new vocabulary, and promotes excellence in the language through regular Wānanga Reo ('place of higher learning' + 'language', language camps) for those involved in teaching through the medium of Māori (Te Taura Whiri i Te Reo Māori 1996, 12). Wānanga Reo are typically week-long *hui* (gatherings) for adults where only Māori is spoken and are run on marae by the commission as well as other tribal and educational organizations, following a model developed by Te Wānanga o Raukawa in the mid-1970s.

After a successful 1985 claim to the Waitangi Tribunal[10] concerning the Māori language, some radio frequencies were set aside for Māori use with government funding made available for the development and delivery of *iwi* (tribal) stations. The first such station was set up in 1986, and by 1995 there were 23 throughout the country broadcasting in a mixture of Māori and English.[11] A funding body, Te Māngai Pāho, distributes funding to Māori radio broadcasters and also funds a number of television programs in Māori, including a 15-minute, five-day-a-week Māori news program.

The Māori Language Commission designated 1995 Māori Language Year (*Te Tau o Te Reo Māori*, 'the' + 'year/period' + 'of' + 'the' + 'language' + 'Māori'), and this brought government and corporate sponsorship to a number of both once-only and ongoing events and projects focusing on the promotion of the Māori language.[12]

The National Māori Language Survey, undertaken in 1995, found that there are 10,000 to 20,000 fluent speakers of Māori, compared to 70,000 speakers in the 1970s.[13] These 20,000 speakers represent about 4% of the total Māori population above the age of 16.[14] The decrease in the number of fluent speakers since the 1970s is to be expected given mortality rates in the intervening period. Further results show that while nearly 60% of Māori can speak Māori to some extent, the vast majority (72%) are low-fluency speakers. This language survey is to be repeated in 2001.

In 1996 the New Zealand census for the first time included a question about language use in the home; 153,669 Māori (29% of the Māori population) indicated that they knew enough Māori to be able to hold an everyday conversation.[15] This question is to be included again in the 2001 census.

Considering these results, one of the key findings of the National Māori Language Survey was that there should be a focus on improving the language ability of the large proportion of Māori adults who "already have some ability in speaking Māori but have low levels of fluency" (Te Taura Whiri i Te Reo Māori 1995b).

TE KŌHANGA REO AND MĀORI LANGUAGE SCHOOLING

Te Kōhanga Reo had its inception at one of the yearly meetings organized by the government's Department of Māori Affairs from 1979 onward (Government Review Team 1988, 17). At the Hui Whakatauira held in 1981 the concept and name of Kōhanga Reo were developed.[16] The knowledge that most competent speakers were over 40 years old and that language proficiency is most easily acquired by young children generated the idea of forming language nests where the Māori language could be transmitted from the older generation to children and grandchildren. This founding principle of the Kōhanga Reo movement is illustrated in Figure 11.2, which is taken from Te Kōhanga Reo National Trust's Resource Manual (1985a, 2).

The first Kōhanga Reo was officially opened in the Wellington district in March 1982 with funding from the

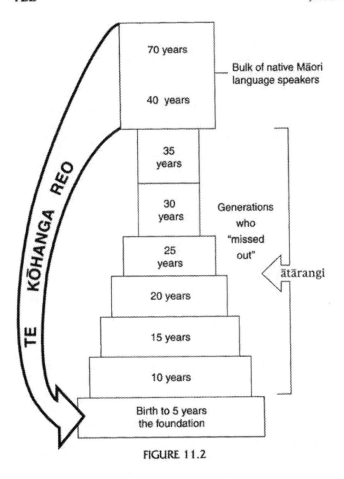

FIGURE 11.2

preschoolers participating in preschool programs were attending Kōhanga Reo.

Within a few years of the movement's beginning, pressure began to build for an extension of Māori-medium and Māori *kaupapa* (philosophy) schooling to continue the Kōhanga Reo experience. Many parents were finding that the transition to mainstream schools was difficult for their children, and the classroom was often not validating the experience that these children were bringing with them.

There were two responses to this need for alternative schooling. One was the development of Kura Kaupapa Māori. These schools have a policy of total immersion in Māori within a Māori philosophical orientation and curricular framework. The first Kura Kaupapa Māori began in Auckland in 1985 alongside a Kōhanga Reo on Hoani Waititi marae. Initially some Kura Kaupapa Māori operated as private schools, but with increased pressure, government funding was gradually secured, and by 1998 there were 60 Kura Kaupapa Māori receiving state funding (see Map 11.1). Students at Kura Kaupapa receive all their curriculum instruction in the Māori language, and some Kura are also now providing secondary level schooling for a total of nearly 500 pupils. In 1998 the 4,505 students attending Kura Kaupapa Māori accounted for 14% of all Māori students undertaking Māori-medium education.

The other schooling option which has developed to cater for Kōhanga Reo graduates is bilingual classes and units in mainstream schools.[19] In 1990, graduates from Kōhanga Reo constituted 40% of bilingual class students (Irwin 1991, 79).

As with Kura Kaupapa Māori, there has been a dramatic rise in the number of mainstream schools which have a bilingual class or unit: from 38 in 1987, to 154 in 1990, to 441 by 1998. The number of students in these classes rose from just

Department of Māori Affairs. As a "flaxroots" (grassroots) initiative it expanded very quickly, as Figure 11.3 indicates.

An initial rapid expansion phase from the beginning of Kōhanga Reo in 1981 to 1985 was followed until 1993 by a consolidation phase characterized by a steady increase in numbers.[17] Thereafter the number of Kōhanga Reo plateaued, suggesting that a stabilization point had been reached. From 1996 to the latest figures in 1998 both the number of Kōhanga Reo centers and the children participating have decreased. In 1996 there were 767 centers, but this figure dropped to 646 in 1998, with the number of children attending also dropping from 14,000 to 12,000.[18] Reasons for this decline are explored in the next section.

The large number of children attending Kōhanga Reo has not meant a decline in the numbers involved in other early childhood options, indicating that "Kōhanga Reo are catering for a client group previously not catered for by early childhood programs" (Irwin 1991, 78–79).

Since 1991 Kōhanga Reo have provided approximately 20% of all early-childhood services and have become the most popular early-childhood option for Māori children. Between 1992 and 1995 an average of 46% of those Māori

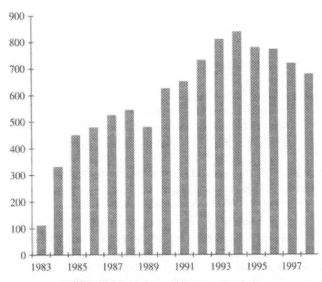

FIGURE 11.3   Number of Kōhanga Reo Centers

under 7,000 to nearly 32,500 between 1990 and 1998. The amount of Māori language used in these classes and units varies from very little to full immersion, but by 1998, 45% of children in these classes were receiving less than 30% of their instruction in Māori. This is one of the main differences between these units and Kura Kaupapa, where pupils receive all their instruction in Māori.[20]

Another difference between Kura Kaupapa Māori and bilingual units is the ethnicity of pupils. Virtually all children attending Kura Kaupapa Māori are Māori, in contrast to the increasing numbers of non-Māori participating in bilingual classes. In 1992, 8% of bilingual class pupils were non-Māori, but by 1998 this had increased to 25%. Most of the non-Māori pupils (84%) are in programs offering less than 30% of the instruction in Māori.

The effectiveness of immersion teaching in the overall goal of revitalization has yet to be studied, and the fact that in 1990 only one-third of immersion teachers in both Kura Kaupapa Māori and bilingual classes were fluent speakers of Māori reflects the continuing need for qualified teachers with a high level of proficiency in the Māori language (Nga Kairangahau 1991, 36). In 1997 there were nine institutions around New Zealand offering teacher training for immersion teachers,[21] but there is still a demand for qualified teachers, which is not surprising considering the huge growth in the number of immersion classes in recent years. The Ministry of Education is now offering grants and other incentives to attract people into Māori immersion teacher training.

Parents of Kōhanga Reo graduates typically choose between a bilingual unit and a Kura Kaupapa Māori for their child's schooling needs. Such decisions often depend on the availability of options and the perceived quality of the program. Some choose bilingual education because of concern that their child may not become competent in English if placed into an exclusively Māori-medium institution, despite research and information to the contrary.[22]

Conversely, some Kōhanga Reo parents choose Kura Kaupapa Māori because of real concerns that their child's ability in Māori will decline if they are placed in a bilingual class within a mainstream school where English is the peer group playground language.

Goals and Details of the Kōhanga Reo Program

The principle aim of Kōhanga Reo is to raise Māori children as speakers of Māori in a whānau environment which will "affirm Māori culture" (Government Review Team 1988, 20). The word whānau traditionally referred to an extended kin group. The meaning of the word has evolved in recent times, and "new kinds of whānau have emerged, modeled on the traditional whānau and its values" (Metge 1995, 17). Kōhanga Reo whānau consist of a range of people,

mostly Māori,[23] and while not all will be related, there are often a number of kinship ties amongst the participants in any one Kōhanga Reo.

In order to achieve the stated aims of Te Kōhanga Reo, the commitment of people to the kaupapa and the whānau are very important. Most Kōhanga Reo make a great effort to ensure that new parents understand that Māori is the only language to be spoken in the Kōhanga, and that parents are expected to provide a Māori-speaking environment at home. Active participation in the whānau's decision making is also required through attendance at the regular whānau meetings. Each Kōhanga Reo is controlled and run by the collective group of teachers, parents, local elders, and members of the Māori community. The whānau as a whole are responsible for the day-to-day administration and running of the Kōhanga Reo.

The particular features of Māori culture that are to be found in the Kōhanga Reo include Māori customs (such as keeping cleaning items for kitchen and toilet facilities separate, not sitting on tables, and so on) and an emphasis on such aspects as whakapapa, whanaungatanga, and tuakana/teina (Ka'ai 1990, 14–15). Whakapapa 'genealogy' forms an important part of mihi (formalized greetings), in which the child learns the importance of their tribal connections. Whanaungatanga (group relationships and support) manifests itself in group responsibility for learning and working together. Tuakana/teina (the role of older to younger) is expressed through leadership roles being given to older children with concurrent responsibilities toward the needs of those who are younger.

Nearly half of all Kōhanga Reo are marae based (45% in 1990), and they typically care for 10 to 20 children, though individual Kōhanga Reo range in size from as few as 5 children to as many as 60 (Government Review Team 1988, 35). Children can attend from birth to age six, although many Kōhanga Reo will not take babies under one year of age, and most children leave to attend school at age five.[24] Most Kōhanga Reo are open on weekdays from 9 AM to 3 PM, and a number provide early and late care.

Most Kōhanga Reo have a range of activity equipment, often with an emphasis on natural materials such as flax, water, and wood. One of the ongoing difficulties facing Kōhanga Reo has been the relative lack of appropriate teaching and developmental resources in Māori. This has resulted in much valuable energy being devoted, often in each individual Kōhanga Reo, to producing play equipment using Māori language as well as to finding visual resources which do not depict white people exclusively.

Kōhanga Reo are funded by the government via Te Kōhanga Reo National Trust through quarterly grants based on the number and the ages of the children on the roll. Most Kōhanga also charge fees above this to cover salaries, teaching resources, utilities, and other costs. The level of this fee is set by each whānau, but it is generally less than other child-care options.

The organizational connections between Kōhanga Reo and Te Kōhanga Reo National Trust have changed several times since the beginnings of the movement, with various numbers of intermediate structural levels. The current structure is for Kōhanga Reo to be grouped into districts, each serviced by a *kaupapa kaimahi* ('philosophy' + 'worker') employed by Te Kōhanga Reo National Trust. In addition, all Kōhanga have computers and are in communication with the National Trust via the Internet.

Te Kōhanga Reo National Trust is a registered charitable trust. Besides administering finances, the other roles of the National Trust are to develop and implement training for kaiako, produce resources, give leadership to the movement, and work in the political arena (the trust is headquartered in Wellington, the seat of government).

The trust board consists of nine representatives from national groups such as the Māori Education Foundation, the Māori Women's Welfare League, and the Māori Language Commission, along with a few invited members. There are no elected members. Thus Kōhanga Reo have no direct influence on national decision making.

Figure 11.3 showed that the numbers of Kōhanga Reo have declined by 173 since a peak of 819 in 1994. Enrollments at Kōhanga Reo have also suffered: from 1995 to 1998 they have fallen from 14,263 to 12,050 despite the fact that overall numbers of Māori preschoolers in early-childhood education services remained about 30,000 during this time.

Frustration at feeling unable to question compulsory requirements of Te Kōhanga Reo National Trust has led some Kōhanga Reo whānau to withdraw from the trust and to continue their operations with funding via mainstream early-childhood provisions. In 1995 there were 25 Māori total-immersion preschools not connected to the Kōhanga Reo movement (Te Taura Whiri i Te Reo Māori 1996, 30).

Other Kōhanga Reo may have closed due to a low enrollment, a lack of whānau support, or difficulties in maintaining either a Māori language environment or an adequate number of qualified staff. A 1997 Education Review Office summary of visits to 100 Kōhanga Reo during 1995 and 1996 noted that 27% of Kōhanga Reo were unable to consistently provide a Māori-speaking environment "because of a lack of Māori language expertise within their Kōhanga Reo" (Education Review Office 1997, 17–18). The decline in numbers of Kōhanga Reo may be a self-pruning of a tree whose branches have grown too far and too fast to be adequately supported by the community.

Training for Kaiako

The original theory that the language would be "fed" to the children in Kōhanga Reo by older native speakers has not always been realized. Initially, the older native speakers, mostly women, needed reassurance that they did not need to "teach" the language in a formal manner and that children would acquire Māori by just listening to it. In addition, many of the better speakers were of advancing years and not always able to sustain the energy required for working alongside young children all day.

Younger adults, many of them with child-care and/or teaching qualifications, have embraced the kaupapa of Kōhanga Reo as part of their own personal reclamation of Māori language. They have brought energy and commitment to the Kōhanga Reo movement.

The skills the two types of kaiako bring with them can complement each other well. The older native speaker can provide a high-quality language environment for both children and parents. But this role can be very draining, particularly if there are no similarly proficient speakers in the Kōhanga Reo.

Those kaiako who are second-language speakers of Māori often have skills and training in providing developmentally appropriate child care. However, it can be difficult for these kaiako who may lack proficiency in Māori to be role models and a resource for parents. It is therefore important to support kaiako and whānau by providing effective programs to keep them motivated and learning.

Within a few years of the beginnings of the movement, Te Kōhanga Reo National Trust had set up 45 training centers to teach and supervise trainees in completing the "Blue Book" training syllabus.[25] This training was required of those who were acting as kaiako in the Kōhanga Reo.

The syllabus consisted of five modules covering *wairua* (spirituality), Māori customs and practices, health practices (traditional and modern), Māori language, and management and administration. The work in these modules was to be completed over 400 hours and required the trainees to undertake much of the learning themselves, drawing on the expertise of their local community. In addition, trainees were required to do 500 hours of practical work in a Kōhanga Reo.

In 1991 this training scheme was replaced by a more comprehensive training called *whakapakari* (strengthening), which has New Zealand Qualifications Authority accreditation. Taking three years to complete, its aim is to provide training in all aspects of child care, culture, and language that a kaiako will need in a Kōhanga Reo.

The 10 units of learning in the Whakapakari training course are:

- The beginnings and history of Te Kōhanga Reo
- The essence and philosophy of Te Kōhanga Reo
- The Māori langage
- The culture of the Māori world
- Teaching and learning
- Human relationships

- Management and administration
- Child development
- Observation and analysis
- Traditional and modern health practices[26]

Those who wish to enter the Whakapakari training must have a reasonably high proficiency in the Māori language. Te Kōhanga Reo National Trust also offers two courses, Te Ara Tuatahi ('the' + 'pathway' + 'first', the first pathway), and Te Ara Tuarua (the second pathway), for Kōhanga Reo adults who have limited language skills; the aim is to bring the participant in three years up to a level where he or she is able to enter Whakapakari training.

Those wishing to enter Whakapakari training must also be working in a Kōhanga Reo and have the support of the whānau. In 1996 there were over 700 people engaged in Whakapakari training,[27] with a key feature of the training being that the whole whānau is involved in supporting the learning of the ākonga (student).

Each unit of work is researched within the Kōhanga Reo using the expertise within the whānau. The unit is then presented to the whānau and then to a group of other local ākonga, each student being supported by three kaitautoko (supporters).[28]

At its best this method of learning involving the whole whānau can substantially benefit everybody participating within a Kōhanga Reo. However, if the Kōhanga has few people with expertise on which to draw, this training process can be frustrating for all concerned.

Whanau

"The Kōhanga is constructed by and constructs such concepts as whānau."—M. K. Hohepa, 1993

The Kōhanga Reo whānau has arguably been one of the strongest forces in the development of the changing concept of Māori whānau in recent times. Since Te Kōhanga Reo began, Metge argues, "there have been signs of increasing participation in whānau, as part of a renewed emphasis on Māori cultural identity" (1995, 17). While traditional whānau are based on kinship ties, the members of Kōhanga Reo whānau are often not related by kinship. Instead, the binding relationship is that of adherence to the kaupapa of Kōhanga Reo. This kaupapa is based on involvement and speaking Māori *i ngā wā katoa, i ngā wāhi katoa* (all the time and everywhere).

The concept of the whānau in Kōhanga Reo has been an important one, particularly at the beginning of the movement. The initial setting up of a Kōhanga Reo involved much work over many years in difficult circumstances. Battling bureaucracy is very time and energy consuming. At one time three government departments maintained an interest in Kōhanga Reo: Māori Affairs, Education, and Social Welfare

(now called Income Support). A strong commitment from individuals was required to make the movement work on both the national and local level, and this was best channeled through group involvement and responsibility in order to offset the real possibility that a few people, usually the kaiako, will burn out.

It is quite usual for those involved with a Kōhanga Reo to talk about taking an issue "to the whānau." The importance and relevance of group decision-making is part of the conceptual construct of the Kōhanga Reo. The Kōhanga Reo is not merely a preschool where one pays for a service. The participants "own" their involvement in a much more tangible way, with the authority vested in the collective, not the individual. The word *whānau* signals a Māori-concept oriented organization which, for many participants, may be their first real link with the Māori community.

The ideal is that each whānau is responsible for raising the skill level of participants in the Kōhanga in areas such as language and management. The benefit is that many people, in particular Māori women,[29] have acquired skills they can and do translate into other employment areas (Government Review Team 1988, 20–26). Whānau involvement in Te Kōhanga Reo has also increased Māori parents' self-esteem (Ka'ai 1990, 8) and encouraged parents who themselves had negative experiences within the school system to effectively pursue schooling options which best suit their children's needs.

But for those Kōhanga Reo that are finding it difficult to provide the linguistic and educationally appropriate environment required for their children, there are few resources for supporting the energies and commitment of the kaiako and whānau. At present Kōhanga Reo are grouped into support clusters, and through this grouping a number of urban Kōhanga Reo have formed very useful and informal relationships of sharing and support with neighboring Kōhanga. But many Kōhanga are still isolated, and the possibilities of cross-fertilization of ideas from other successful Kōhanga Reo are underutilized.[30]

Te Reo Māori—The Māori Language

It is generally agreed that Te Kōhanga Reo is producing a large number of children who can speak Māori. In my experience, most of the graduates from Kōhanga Reo are reasonably bilingual, with proficiency depending on the length of time the child has been in the Kōhanga Reo and the strength of the language environment the child is exposed to, both in the home and in the Kōhanga.

What is uncertain is the level of proficiency being attained by these children and how effective other educational settings are at expanding and enhancing that language base. The tacit aim of the Kōhanga Reo movement has been to produce a new generation of native speakers of Māori, who would, in turn, pass the language on to their children. Whether that aim is being achieved, or is able to be achieved, is yet to be determined; further research is needed "to evaluate the impact of the Kōhanga Reo movement on language retention" (Nga Kairangahau 1991, 42).

In the initial stages, developing a dynamic Māori-speaking environment in a Kōhanga Reo was often difficult. Even if the kaiako and parents were speaking Māori, the children were not always speaking Māori in reply. In the beginning many Kōhanga Reo took in older children, aged three or four, who would typically have virtually no command of Māori and who were already speaking English. The effect of the linguistic dominance of these children often took months, if not years, to overcome.

Reaching a stage where children not only used Māori in response to adult speech, but used it naturally to each other in free play, was a step that often took quite a period of time to achieve from the initial setting up of a Kōhanga Reo. However, once a Māori-speaking environment is achieved amongst the children, it will usually continue, especially if most, if not all, new entrants start before they have acquired any language.

One of the areas which has been somewhat neglected in the effort required to set up the necessary infrastructure for the Kōhanga Reo movement has been the role of parents' language use, particularly in the home. Despite an increasing desire for proficiency among many Kōhanga Reo parents, there is often little Māori spoken to the child at home. In most cases the level of language is not much above that of basic instruction ("Hurry up," "Eat your breakfast") or description or explanation ("That's a nice picture," "We're going now"). Chrisp (1997, 3–4), in describing the importance of making Māori a language of the home, contends that there are few strategies in place to address this difficulty.

As discussed at the beginning of this chapter, the Te Ātaarangi program was independently developed with adult language acquisition in mind, and many parents involved in Te Kōhanga Reo had their first learning experience with this method. Other language learning environments such as night school, polytechnics, universities, and Wānanga Reo are also popular with Kōhanga Reo parents.

The development by Te Kōhanga Reo National Trust of two courses, Te Ara Tuatahi and Te Ara Tuarua, for Kōhanga Reo parents who have limited language skills arose out of recognition of the need to foster and increase the Māori language abilities of those involved in Kōhanga Reo.

In this respect Māori is different from many indigenous languages which are still spoken in the community, but which are not used in the educational setting. In New Zealand, Māori language schooling options are now reasonably well developed, but the use of the language in the home has not advanced in the same dramatic way.

As noted earlier, the 1995 National Māori Language Survey shows a need for courses aimed at increasing the proficiency of the large proportion of Māori who can already speak some Māori. While there is a reasonable range of courses available for adults to learn Māori, few achieve a high level of proficiency. Most begin at the absolute-beginner level and reach intermediate levels.

It is very hard for a second-language learner to continually provide a language environment when there may be few others with commensurate speaking skills. This is especially the case in the home, with television, radio, newspapers, and most adult interaction being undertaken in the dominant language, English. It is not surprising then that "the children educated through the Māori language do not, in general, speak Māori outside of the educational context because they have no societal context for such use" (Chrisp 1997, 4), nor a range of incentives to speak in Māori (Cooper 1989, 159–60).

In order for Māori to truly regain its status as a community language, children need to hear adults speaking Māori, not just to them, but amongst each other. Otherwise Māori will continue to be a language of the Kōhanga Reo and the school, the marae and the church, and not a language in homes.

CONCLUSIONS

Te Kōhanga Reo has been an inspiration to language revitalization efforts both within New Zealand and internationally. The movement has given crucial stimulus to a wider social movement within New Zealand which has gained strength and impetus over the last decade and involves a range of educational institutions, broadcasting media, and political groups (Irwin 1992, 87). That nearly half of Kōhanga Reo are located on marae indicates the link with the resurgence and pride in Māori culture which has permeated many levels of society.

Success of the movement in establishing and developing a model of language revitalization amongst young children is owing to the fact that Te Kōhanga Reo was a Māori community initiative. The movement tapped into Māori values and social structure and brought new generations of parents back into a Māori setting from which they had become alienated.

There have been many difficulties, such as securing funding and setting up an infrastructure, associated with developing organizations such as Te Kōhanga Reo from scratch. It is not surprising to realize, therefore, that overall coordination of effort has often been difficult, and that the personal commitment by kaiako and parents has been immense. But the hard work has made the achievements all the more valued.

Benton's research on the use of the Māori language in the 1970s (1978) found that the main domains for Māori were the marae and the church. Recent research confirms these two domains as the most likely places where one can hear

Māori being spoken.[31] With credit to Te Kōhanga Reo and the consequent Māori language schooling initiatives, we now have a third domain to add—that of the educational setting. This is the crowning success of the Kōhanga Reo movement.

With the development phase complete, the aim for the Kōhanga Reo movement, through Te Kōhanga Reo National Trust, must be to disseminate further appropriate Māori language resources for Kōhanga Reo children by capitalizing on models of good practice already in use within various Kōhanga Reo. And the focus for language planners is to consolidate and improve whānau proficiency in the Māori language, in particular through focusing on strategies which facilitate the use of Māori language in the home.

Glossary

hui   meeting, gathering

hui whānau   whānau meeting

kaiako   teacher(s)

kaumātua   tribal elder(s)

kaupapa   theme, philosophy, worldview

Kura Kaupapa Māori   Māori philosophy schools (school + philosophy/worldview + Māori). These schools have a policy of total immersion in Māori within a Māori philosophical orientation and curricular framework.

marae   tribal community meeting place

Pākehā   New Zealanders of European descent

Te Kōhanga Reo   Māori language immersion preschool ('the' + 'nest' + 'language', language nest)

Te Taura Whiri i Te Reo Māori   The Māori Language Commission ('the' + 'rope' + 'to twist/plait' + object marker + 'the' + 'language' + 'Māori') established under the 1987 Māori Language Act

Te Wānanga o Raukawa   a tribal university in Ōtaki which provides degree and diploma courses in management and Māori language to approximately 700 students per year.

Wānanga Reo   Māori language–intensive hui for adults which are run on marae ('place of higher learning' + 'language')

whānau   Māori concept of family, traditionally referring to a tightly knit extended kin group, but within Kōhanga Reo referring to the group of parents, kaiako, and kaumātua who run the Kōhanga.

Notes

1. See Benton 1981, 23, for a discussion on the use of Māori language in the home before the introduction of Kōhanga Reo.
2. The first book about the Māori language, *A Korao no New Zealand*, was printed in 1815 by the missionary Thomas Kendall (Biggs 1968, 66).
3. The distinction between *w* (semivowel) and *wh* (voiced bilabial fricative) was incorporated beginning about 1840, and vowel length began to be consistently marked in printed Māori from 1960 onward either by use of the macron or through reduplication of the vowel.
4. For more information on Māori manuscripts and newspapers, see McRae 1991.
5. For a personal account see Walker 1987, 164–66.
6. King 1992. The Taiaroa collection is one of the largest collections of personal papers in the Canterbury Museum archives in Christchurch. Much larger collections of Māori material exist in other national archives, libraries, and museums throughout New Zealand.
7. Of these letters, 83% are written by Māori.
8. Since 1990 many of these bilingual schools have become Kura Kaupapa Māori.
9. Accreditation for degrees offered at Te Wānanga o Raukawa was approved by the New Zealand Qualifications Authority in 1993. Two other tribal universities, Te Wānanga o Aotearoa and Te Whare Wānanga o Awanuiarangi, were established in 1983 and 1990, respectively (Winiata and Winiata 1995, 142–45).
10. A government tribunal, instituted in 1975, which investigates cases brought by tribal groups alleging Crown breaches of the Treaty of Waitangi, the founding treaty signed in 1840 between representatives of the British Crown and Māori chiefs.
11. A survey in 1991 indicated that the percentage of Māori language broadcast content from these stations ranged between 20% and 85% (Te Taura Whiri i Te Reo Māori 1996, 40–41), but funding is now given preferentially to those stations with very high Māori language content.
12. See Chrisp 1995 for a discussion on Te Tau o Te Reo Māori. The government, through the Lottery Grants Board, distributed $960,000 in this year to a total of 120 projects, including 88 Wānanga Reo.
13. Statistics are from Te Taura Whiri i Te Reo Māori 1995b and Te Puni Kōkiri 1998.
14. The 1996 census records the Māori population as being 523,371, 15% of the total New Zealand population of 3.5 million.
15. The wording of the question was: "In which language(s) could you have a conversation about a lot of everyday things?" Tick boxes were provided for English, Māori, Samoan, and New Zealand Sign Language, with space for respondents to list other languages they could speak.
16. See Ka'ai 1990, 6, for an account of the genesis of the name "Kōhanga Reo."
17. Obtaining representative statistics for the years up to 1990 is difficult as Te Kōhanga Reo National Trust and Ministry of Education figures are based on different calendar years. Therefore, the apparent decline in the numbers of Kōhanga Reo in 1989 may well not be accurate.
18. Statistics in this section are from the Ministry of Education annual publications "Education Statistics of New Zealand" and "New Zealand Schools."
19. The term "immersion class or unit" is also gaining currency.
20. Differences between Kura Kaupapa Māori and bilingual classes and some implications for the future are discussed more fully in King 1999.
21. David Kingi, Māori Unit, Ministry of Education, personal communication, October 1997.
22. See, e.g., Keegan 1996.
23. Some non-Māori are parents of Māori children. Many Kōhanga Reo allow children who are not Māori to attend, but overall the numbers of such children are few and make up less than 2% of the total (Te Taura Whiri i Te Reo Māori 1996, 30).
24. In 1997 only 5.2% of children attending Kōhanga Reo were under one year of age and only 3.5% were aged five or over (Ministry of Education 1998).
25. Te Kōhanga Reo Trust certificate syllabus, Te Kōhanga Reo Trust 1985b.
26. New Zealand Qualifications Authority 1992, 9.
27. Cath Stuart, district manager, Te Kōhanga Reo National Trust, 1996, personal communication.
28. These are people from the Kōhanga Reo who agree to provide extra support for the student for the duration of the training.
29. Like most preschool organizations, Kōhanga Reo are staffed and supported mainly by women. Māori women in particular have been a strong force in political activism in the past 20 years in New Zealand.
30. There have been no national conferences since 1987, and there was no national newsletter for Kōhanga Reo until the Māori Language

Commission began producing a quarterly bilingual newsletter, *Ko Te Whānau*, in 1998.

31. See Te Taura Whiri i Te Reo Māori 1995b and Te Puni Kōkiri 1998.

References

Benton, Richard A. 1978. *Can the Māori language survive?* Wellington: New Zealand Council for Educational Research.

————. 1981. *The flight of the Amokura: Oceanic languages and formal education in the South Pacific.* Wellington: New Zealand Council for Educational Research.

————. 1991. *The Maori language: Dying or reviving?* Working paper prepared for the East-West Center Alumni-in-Residence Working Papers Series. Hawaii: East-West Center.

Biggs, Bruce. 1968. The Maori language past and present. In *The Maori people in the 1960s*, ed. Erik Schwimmer, 65–84. Auckland: Blackwood and Janet Paul.

————. 1994. Does Maori have a closest relative? In *The origins of the first New Zealanders*, ed. Douglas G. Sutton, 96–105. Auckland: Auckland University Press.

Boyce, Mary T. 1995. *The role of second language learners in Maori language maintenance and revival up to the year 2010: A discussion document.* Wellington: Victoria University of Wellington.

Chrisp, Stephen. 1995. *He Taonga Te Reo: The use of a theme year to promote a minority language.* Paper prepared for Te Hui Taumata Reo Māori (Māori Language Summit). Wellington: Māori Language Commission.

————. 1997. Home and community language Revitalisation. *New Zealand Studies in Applied Linguistics* 3: 1–20.

Cooper, Robert L. 1989. *Language planning and social change.* Cambridge: Cambridge University Press.

Education Review Office. 1997. *What counts as quality in Kōhanga Reo.* Wellington: Education Review Office.

Government Review Team. 1988. *Report of the review of Te Kohanga Reo.* Wellington: New Zealand Government.

Hohepa, M. K. 1993. *Preferred pedagogies and language interactions in Te Kōhanga Reo.* Auckland: Research Unit for Maori Education, University of Auckland.

Irwin, Kathie. 1991. Maori education in 1991: A review and discussion. *New Zealand Annual Review of Education* 1: 77–112.

————. 1992. Maori education in 1992: A review and discussion. *New Zealand Annual Review of Education* 2: 71–91.

Jackson, Syd. 1993. The first language. In *Te Ao Mārama*, vol. 2, ed. Witi Ihimaera, 215–18. Auckland: Reed Books.

Ka'ai, Tania. 1990. Te Hiringa Take Take: Mai i te Kohanga Reo ki te Kura. Master's thesis, University of Auckland, Auckland.

Keegan, Peter. 1996. *The benefits of immersion education: A review of the New Zealand and overseas literature.* Wellington: New Zealand Council for Educational Research.

King, Jeanette. 1992. The Taiaroa collection: A diachronic linguistic analy-sis of selected letters in Maori. Bachelor of arts honors project, Department of Maori, University of Canterbury, Christchurch.

————. 1995. Maori English as a solidarity marker for Te Reo Māori. *New Zealand Studies in Applied Linguistics* 1: 51–59.

————. 1999. Lessons from the Māori schooling experience: Thirteen years of immersion schools. In *Proceedings of the Third Foundation for Endangered Languages Conference, St. Patrick's College, Maynooth, National University of Ireland, 17–19 September 1999*, ed. Nicholas Ostler, 117–24. Bath: Foundation for Endangered Languages.

McRae, Jane. 1991. Maori literature: A survey. In *The Oxford History of New Zealand Literature in English*, ed. Terry Sturm, 1–24. Auckland: Oxford University Press.

Metge, Joan. 1995. *New growth from old: The whānau in the modern world.* Wellington: Victoria University Press.

Ministry of Education. 1985–99. *Education statistics of New Zealand.* Wellington: The Ministry.

————. 1996–98. *New Zealand schools—Nga Kura o Aotearoa: A report on the compulsory schools sector in New Zealand.* Wellington: The Ministry.

New Zealand Qualifications Authority. 1992. *QA News* 12. Wellington: New Zealand Qualifications Association.

Nga Kairangahau. 1991. *Māori education: Current status.* Produced by Nga Kairangahau, Manatū Māori. Wellington: Ministry of Maori Affairs.

Orbell, Margaret. 1995. *The illustrated encyclopedia of Maori myth and legend.* Christchurch: Canterbury University Press.

Pool, D. Ian. 1977. *The Maori population of New Zealand, 1769–1971.* Auckland: Auckland University Press.

Rice, Geoffrey W. 1992. *The Oxford history of New Zealand.* 2d ed. Auckland: Oxford University Press.

Te Kohanga Reo National Trust. 1985a. *Resource manual: Te Kohanga Reo National Wananga, Turangawaewae Marae, Ngaruawahia.* Wellington: Te Kohanga Reo National Trust.

Te Kōhanga Reo Trust. 1985b. *Te Kōhanga Reo Trust certificate syllabus.* Wellington: Te Kohanga Reo National Trust.

Te Puni Kōkiri [Ministry of Māori Development]. 1998. *The National Māori Language Survey: Te Mahi Rangahau Reo Māori.* Wellington: Te Puni Kōkiri.

Te Taura Whiri i Te Reo Māori. 1995a. *Te Tau o Te Reo Māori.* Wellington: Te Taura Whiri i Te Reo Māori.

————. 1995b. *Āe rānei, he taonga tuku iho? National Māori Language Survey 1995: Provisional findings.* Wellington: Te Taura Whiri i Te Reo Māori.

————. 1996. *Toitū Te Reo: Draft consultation document about the Māori language.* Wellington: Te Taura Whiri i Te Reo Māori.

Walker, Ranginui J. 1987. *Nga Tau Tohetohe: Years of anger*, ed. Jacqueline Amoamo. Auckland: Penguin Books.

Winiata, Pakake Calm, and Whatarangi Winiata. 1995. Whare Wananga development in 1993–1994. *New Zealand Annual Review of Education* 4: 137–59.

An Introduction to the Hawaiian Language

LEANNE HINTON
Department of Linguistics
University of California at Berkeley
Berkeley, California

The Hawaiian language, like Māori (previous chapter) and other Polynesian languages, is a member of the Austronesian language family. The Austronesian language family is one of the largest and most widespread language families in the world. It is estimated that this family has more than 1,000 tongues and is spoken by more than 250 million people in the Malay Peninsula; Madagascar; Taiwan; Indonesia; New Guinea; the Melanesian, Micronesian, and Polynesian islands; the Philippine Islands; and New Zealand. The Austronesian language family is about 6,000 years old, and can attribute its present wide distribution to the perfection of open-ocean travel by the ancestors of present-day speakers. Expeditions, explorations, and settlement of islands became a way of life to these adventurous souls, and islands never before visited by humans were settled, often at long distances from each other. Hawai'i is one of the farthest-flung island groups to be settled, being 2,000 miles away from the nearest island group in Polynesia.

Austronesian has been of key importance in historical linguistics. This widespread language family with a multitude of languages on thousands of islands has been a "laboratory" for the development of the comparative method in historical linguistics. Austronesian also has been very important in studying the clues languages can give us about where the homeland of the language family must have been and what kind of culture the speakers of the ancestral protolanguage must have had (Blust, 1995). Scholars such as Peter Bellwood have examined the spread of Austronesian in order to look at issues of importance in human history such as the expansion of agriculture, which Bellwood argues is the driving force behind the spread of this language family and others (Bellwood, 1991).

Today four Malayo-Polynesian languages have official status in four important nations: Malay, in Malaysia; Indonesian (also called Bahasa Indonesia, and based on Malay), in Indonesia; Malagasy, in Madagascar; and Pilipino (based on Tagalog), in the Philippines. Many other Austronesian languages, however, are endangered, and several already are extinct. Hawaiian, which was the language of governance of the independent nation of Hawai'i a mere century ago, now is one of the endangered languages.

The following two chapters about Hawaiian reflect a division in the Hawaiian language revitalization movement that is related to past disagreements in the board of the 'Aha Pūnana Leo, the organization most responsible for the progress of Hawaiian language revitalization. Chapter 13's authors, William H. Wilson and Kauanoe Kamanā, were educated at the University of Hawai'i at Mānoa, studying Hawaiian and linguistics. After teaching at Mānoa (where Chapter 12's author, Sam L. No'eau Warner, was Wilson's Hawaiian language student), Wilson and Kamanā moved to start a new Hawaiian Studies degree program at the University of Hawai'i at Hilo. Warner expanded his interest in Hawaiian through graduate work in English as a Second Language and Education at the University of Hawai'i at Mānoa. He is now on the faculty at that university. Warner's article, which we present first, gives an informative history of events and factors leading to Hawaiian language loss, an overview of the early development of the 'Aha Pūnana Leo until his separation from its board in 1996, general information on sites in the public Hawaiian language immersion program and a discussion of his view of some of the philosophical conflicts that are being addressed within the revitalization movement. He gives special attention to the unique "birth through grade 12" public Ānuenue School with which he has worked extensively, to Ke A'a Mākālei, a community sports program in which he played a founding role, and to a factionalization in the Ni'ihau community on Kaua'i related to philosophical conflicts between himself and the remaining 'Aha Pūnana Leo board members. Wilson and Kamanā's article focuses on the 'Aha Pūnana Leo's work at the preschool level as well as in partnerships that it has developed primarily with the Department of Education and Ka Haka 'Ula O Ke'elikōlani College of Hawaiian Language at the University of Hawai'i at Hilo. These partnerships provide semi-independent schools in the state which, like the Pūnana Leo preschools, have a strong focus on total Hawaiian medium teaching and use a Hawaiian educational philosophy called the Kumu Honua Mauli Ola in addressing the entire family. Their description of 'Aha Pūnana Leo and Ka Haka 'Ula O Ke'elikōlani programs range from the Pūnana Leo preschools to the three partnership schools, and from curriculum and teacher development to graduate education. Wilson and Kamanā also explain the approach toward the place of English in the 'Aha Pūnana Leo's preferred model of Hawaiian medium education.

Perhaps one more thing should be noted about the factionalization described by Warner. Despite the disputes, the overall picture of Hawaiian language revitalization is looking extremely good. But locally, the school at Kaua'i is suffering badly over the split. There are many language revitalization programs smaller and less strong than the Hawaiian system that have foundered due to internal friction. A large program like the one in Hawai'i can surely survive the factionalization, but smaller programs such as those on the American mainland are much more likely to fail altogether when the leadership becomes split and their positions harden against each other. Internal strife is probably the number one cause of failure in smaller language programs. Disagreement is natural and even desired, especially if it involves debate about ways a program can be effective, but if the disagreement hardens into anger and even hatred, the next step is sabotage and possibly the demise of the program. Large-scale programs can handle it; small-scale programs cannot.

The history of Hawai'i and the present resurgence of the Hawaiian language is ably described in the two papers that follow. Of all languages indigenous to what is now the United States, Hawaiian represents the flagship of language recovery, and serves as a model and a symbol of hope to other endangered languages.

References

Bellwood, Peter. 1991. The Austronesian dispersal and the origin of languages. *Scientific American*, July 1991, pp. 70–75.

Blust, Robert. 1995. The prehistory of the Austronesian-speaking Peoples. *Journal of World Prehistory*, I:4, pp. 453–510.

Hinton, Leanne. 1997. Hawaiian language schools. *News from Native California*, vol. 10, no. 4, pp. 15–22.

Ruhlen, Merrit. 1987. *A Guide to the World's Languages. Volume 1: Classification.* Stanford University Press.

12

The Movement to Revitalize Hawaiian Language and Culture

SAM L. NO'EAU WARNER

Department of Hawaiian and Indo-Pacific Languages and Literatures
University of Hawai'i at Mānoa
Honolulu, Hawai'i

INTRODUCTION

On August 5, 1996, Mrs. Josephine Kau'ihailua Kaleilehua Lindsey passed away at the age of 87. A *hulu kupuna*, or precious elder, she was one of the ever-decreasing number of native speakers who was born and raised Hawaiian, whose language and culture experienced from the womb was Hawaiian. Despite 16 years of effort by Hawaiian language educators and the Hawaiian community to revitalize a language threatened with extinction, Mrs. Lindsey's passing is a sobering reminder of how precious and fragile the Hawaiian language and culture are. Although the number of native speakers of Hawaiian is not known, it is believed that there are fewer than 1,000 remaining today. Like Mrs. Lindsey, the speakers of Hawaiian are largely 80 years or older and are the last generation of Hawaiian native speakers, except for one small community.[1] With her passing, we are reminded that language shift (Fishman 1991) can occur swiftly, as it did in Hawai'i. In one generation the Hawaiian language gave way to a local variety of English called Pidgin or Hawai'i Creole English (HCE). Mrs. Lindsey's absence reminds us of how critical are efforts to revitalize Hawaiian.

The year 1996 was also significant because it marked the centenary of the total ban on Hawaiian as a medium of instruction in Hawai'i schools. Three years earlier marked the 100th anniversary of the illegal overthrow of the Hawaiian monarchy. In its place, a group of American businessmen, with the support of a U.S. minister and the Marines, established an illegal provisional government, later renamed the Republic of Hawai'i. One of the results of that was a ban of the Hawaiian language. One hundred years later, President Clinton signed Public Law 103-150 (Scudder 1994). This is an official apology by the United States for its critical role in the illegal overthrow of the Hawaiian monarchy. Both events are significant historical benchmarks of the political, cultural, and linguistic oppression suffered by Hawaiians at the hands of foreigners. One short century saw a rapid decline in strength and prestige of the Hawaiian language and culture (Sato 1991). One by one, the markers of Hawaiian identity as a people have been stripped away, starting with the land, sovereignty, language, literacies (knowledge), histories, and connection to our ancestry. In a sense, Hawaiians have become foreigners in their own land.

During the past 20 years, however, there has been a political and cultural renaissance which has resulted in the movement to revitalize the Hawaiian language through immersion education. This essay will briefly describe the sociolinguistic background of the Hawaiian language and the inception of immersion education in Hawai'i, beginning with the Pūnana Leo preschool program, followed by a more detailed description of the Kula Kaiapuni, the K–12 Hawaiian language immersion program. The second half of this essay describes and examines some interesting issues which have faced the Kula Kaiapuni program since its inception.

SOCIOHISTORICAL BACKGROUND

Hawaiian Society

The Hawaiian[2] people thrived for 1,000 years after migrating to Hawai'i in the eighth century (Beechert 1985). They had developed highly organized social systems, and upon contact with Europeans in 1778, the Hawaiian population was estimated to be 800,000 (Stannard 1989). Hawaiians were economically self-sufficient. They also had a highly

133

developed religious system, which, together with their understanding of the natural environment, nurtured and protected the natural resources from depletion due to overuse. Although unwritten, Hawaiian at that time was a sophisticated language with a long and rich tradition of oral literature. This orature included chants of various kinds (e.g. cosmogonic, genealogical, migrational, and procreational), religious prayers, oratory, histories, myths, and traditional sayings and teachings created and passed down from generation to generation.

Decimation of Hawaiians and Hawaiian Institutions

Initially, contact with Westerners resulted in the death of 80% of the Hawaiian population through introduced diseases (Stannard 1989). The decline continued until 94% of the Hawaiian population had been lost. By 1878, only 47,500 Hawaiians still remained (Schmitt 1968). Foreign influences immediately began to erode the major institutions of Hawaiian society. Ultimately, this process resulted in the replacement of the Hawaiian language by English in the major societal domains of commerce, government, and religion and education. For example, in 1840, a constitution proclaimed by Kamehameha III established a constitutional monarchy, which included a legislature and a judicial system. At its inception, Hawaiian was the primary language of government; however, by the 1870s, official government documents were written in English and translated into Hawaiian (Reinecke 1969).

Disenfranchised from Land and Language

Under pressure of foreign influence, the traditional subsistence system of land tenure was abandoned in favor of a Western system of private ownership. This was brought about in 1848 through the enactment of a law called the *māhele* (division),[3] or division of land. This division of land dramatically changed the socioeconomic picture for Hawaiians. More than 98% of the *maka'āinana* or common Hawaiian people were disenfranchised from the lands on which they traditionally resided and made their livelihood in the growing cash economy. Many Hawaiians found their way to the city of Honolulu, or to sugar plantations.

Hawai'i Creole English Replaces Hawaiian

The importation of foreign workers eventually led to a pidgin Hawaiian as workers of various linguistic backgrounds attempted to communicate with each other (Bickerton and Wilson 1987; Roberts 1993). Subsequently, owing to social pressures against using Hawaiian, a pidgin English supplanted the pidgin Hawaiian as the primary means of communication for immigrants and Hawaiians working on the plantations. The subsequent generation of children of these immigrant populations and Hawaiians systematized the varieties of pidgin English and English that they heard into a systematic, rule-governed language known today as Hawai'i Creole English (HCE).

Influence of Missionaries

Contact with foreigners in the late 18th and early 19th centuries also led to the breakdown of the *kapu* or Hawaiian religious system. This opened the way for the spread of Christianity amongst the Hawaiian people by American missionaries, who arrived in 1820. A basic Hawaiian orthography, developed in 1826, provided literacy to adults and children via missionary schools. Hawaiians embraced literacy with great enthusiasm, and by 1830 some 85,000 Hawaiians were literate (Huebner 1985). By 1850, literacy amongst Hawaiians was said to be universal (Kloss 1977). Hawaiian-language newspapers flourished from 1860 on through the end of the century. Hawaiian oral traditions, which included genealogical as well as other forms of chants, histories, legends, riddles, and various aspects of Hawaiian culture, were documented and circulated amongst the Hawaiian people. Foreign stories, legends, and foreign news items were also translated into Hawaiian and published in weekly newspapers.

English in the Schools

The first English-medium school, Royal School, was founded in 1839 for children of the Hawaiian royal family. In 1840 a constitutional monarchy proclaimed by Kamehameha III established Hawaiian as the primary language of government and provided for the first government-funded public schools, or common schools. In 1848, 99% of 631 common schools were taught through the medium of Hawaiian (Reinecke 1969). English was first introduced in government-funded schools in 1854, and about this time the missionaries, long supporters of Hawaiian for Hawaiians, began to advocate that Hawaiians would need to learn English in order to deal with the outside world. The government began providing more funding (i.e., higher pay) and more positions for English-speaking teachers relative to Hawaiian-speaking ones. This led to a major shift in the language through which children were educated over the remainder of the century.

The Loss of Hawaiian and the Myth of Prosperity

In 1893, after the Hawaiian monarchy was overthrown and the illegal government renamed, the Republic of Hawai'i mandated that English was to be the medium of instruction in schools. This required that all oracy and literacy would be in English. After annexation of Hawai'i by the United States, the Organic Act, signed into law in 1900, mandated that all government business be conducted in English. The Organic Act and subsequent laws of the U.S. Territory of Hawai'i required that English-only be the medium of instruction for not less than 50% of the school day. After the turn of the century, no schools were taught through the medium of Hawaiian.

In Hawai'i, all Hawaiians and part-Hawaiians routinely learned Hawaiian if they were born prior to 1900 (Bickerton and Wilson 1987). It was between 1900 and 1920 that most Hawaiian and part-Hawaiian children, as well as children of immigrants, began to speak (and develop) a local variety of English instead of Hawaiian (Bickerton and Wilson 1987). Some Hawaiians educated during this period recall being physically punished or humiliated for speaking Hawaiian in school. Ironically, many teachers who meted out this punishment were also Hawaiian. At this time, the illusion of future prosperity resulting from the abandonment of Hawaiian in favor of English was inculcated into the Hawaiian people.

As a result, many Hawaiian-speaking parents refused to speak Hawaiian to their children. They would speak Hawaiian only to each other or to other adult Hawaiian speakers. With this came a lack of interest on the part of Hawaiian children in learning their language. The loss of prestige in Hawaiian amongst Hawaiians themselves was established (Sato 1991), and this appears to have been a major factor in the complacency and lack of interest amongst Hawaiians in reacquiring their heritage language in successive generations.

Although Hawaiians began to relinquish the Hawaiian language in the early 1900s, they did not acquire English as their first language. As mentioned earlier, they acquired Hawai'i Creole English, which has traditionally been referred to as "pidgin." Although HCE has been the language commonly used among local residents, it is highly denigrated by those who claim to be Standard English speakers. Over the past 100 years, Pidgin has been used as a marker for socioeconomic discrimination against its native speakers—Hawaiians and various immigrant groups. The empty promise of economic prosperity with the abandonment of the Hawaiian language has not improved the welfare of the Hawaiian people. Not only have the Hawaiian people lost their language and culture, they have also been relegated to the lower echelons of society (see Warner 1999a). Hawaiians have been described as having one of the poorest health profiles of any group in Hawai'i (see Eshima 1996), and they are highly overrepresented in prisons (nearly double the expected number) and highly underrepresented in undergraduate and graduate university programs. In addition, Hawaiians are highly underrepresented as educators at all levels of education (primary through tertiary levels) and as faculty and administrators (see Warner 1999a).

Hawai'i's entrance as the 50th state of the union in 1959 led to vast changes in the economy. Huge amounts of money poured into the islands as developers crowded the beaches of Waikīkī with hotels and other trappings of tourism. Nightlife, cellophane hula skirts, *hapa-haole* songs (songs about Hawai'i with predominantly English lyrics), and gaudy souvenirs began to take center stage. During the 1960s, the mispronunciation of Hawaiian words in songs became the rule more than the exception. Hawaiians were taught that the key to individual prosperity was through tourism—another illusion. In short, the seeds for decimation of the Hawaiian language and culture were sown and largely reaped in one generation.

Hawaiians living during the early 20th century were native speakers of Hawaiian. By the next generation, however, the majority were native speakers of Hawai'i Creole English. This loss is irreparable. With the passing of generations, more and more of the language and the experiences, knowledge, culture, and traditions associated with the language have been (and will be) lost, making subsequent attempts to reclaim and revitalize the language and culture more and more difficult and distant.

THE EARLY MOVEMENT TOWARD REVITALIZATION

Hawaiians today are struggling for a revival of their native language and culture as are other indigenous peoples throughout the world via immersion or native language medium education, such as the Māori in Aotearoa (New Zealand), the Saami in Scandinavia, and other Native American groups in North America.

The Roots of Revival

In the late 1960s, a cultural revolution occurred amongst young Hawaiians. The center of this revolution occurred in the domains of Hawaiian music and dance. Hawaiians suddenly became interested in singing more traditional Hawaiian songs and in learning to dance more traditional forms of *hula*. This led to a renaissance in Hawaiian language and culture which reached its height at the University of Hawai'i in the middle to late 1970s. At that point, as many as eleven elementary Hawaiian 101 classes were offered each semester.

From this first renaissance came a new group of secondlanguage Hawaiian speakers who would become Hawaiian language educators. With this came some significant changes in legislation. During the 1978 constitutional convention, the Hawaiian language, along with English, was designated one of two official languages of the state. In addition, the state was mandated by the new constitution to promote the Hawaiian language, culture, and history. A separate law also designated Hawaiian as the official native language of the state of Hawai'i in 1978. At that time a survey conducted by the state estimated that there were only 2,000 Hawaiian native speakers remaining (William Wilson, personal communication 1978), leading to an awareness of the weakened condition of the Hawaiian language.

By 1982, no better estimates of the native Hawaiian-speaking population existed. The number of second-language Hawaiian speakers graduated by the university was about 150 to 200, a significant increase of L2 (second-language) Hawaiian speakers from the previous 50 years. By that time, there were virtually no children who were first-language speakers of Hawai'i other than those of the Ni'ihau community. Ni'ihau, a privately owned island, had been purchased from the Hawaiian kingdom during the 19th century. It was primarily owing to the isolation of the Ni'ihau community from the outside world that Hawaiian continues to be the first language of this community.

Today, a part of this community now resides on the island of Kaua'i, and their children also continue to speak Hawaiian as their first language. This is true despite generations of Ni'ihau children being enrolled in English medium schools on Kaua'i and having been subjected to transitional bilingual education programs. The purpose of such transitional bilingual programs was to speed up the students' acquisition of English so that they could be mainstreamed into regular English classes.

Thus, by 1982, it became apparent that if Hawaiian were to survive as a living language, a generation of Hawaiian speakers would have to be born. Spurred by the news of the Kōhanga Reo, (Māori language immersion preschools), a small group of Hawaiian educators and community members set about to create similar "language nests" in Hawai'i.

The Pūnana Leo

The Pūnana Leo ("language nest") are total immersion preschools for children between the ages of two and five years old. The first Pūnana Leo center was opened on September 4, 1984, in Kekaha, Kaua'i by the 'Aha Pūnana Leo (Organization of Language Nests). The next two were opened in April 1985 in Hilo, Hawai'i, and in Kalihi, O'ahu. The 'Aha Pūnana Leo ('APL) is a nonprofit, educational organization established in 1983 by a small group of Hawaiian language educators. The volunteer governing board of the 'APL consisted of eight members from the islands of Hawai'i, Maui, O'ahu, and Kaua'i. The initial purpose of the organization was to establish and operate Pūnana Leo schools with the overall goal of revitalizing and perpetuating the Hawaiian language and culture through the creation of new generations of native Hawaiian–speaking children.

Early Difficulties

The opening of the first Pūnana Leo schools was not an easy matter. The Supreme Court of the United States twice ruled (in 1927 and 1946) that the Territory of Hawai'i had no jurisdiction over foreign language schools in Hawai'i, such as Japanese- and Chinese-language schools. This meant that such schools were not subject to any state regulations, such as staffing and building code regulations. However, the state's Department of Social Services and Housing (DSSH) insisted that the Pūnana Leo be subject to all state regulations. Their argument was that since Hawaiian was not considered a foreign language at the University of Hawai'i (a change which only occurred in the mid-1970s, reflecting the growing consciousness of Hawaiian at the university), any school teaching Hawaiian could not be exempted as a foreign-language school. In effect, since Hawaiian is the only indigenous language of Hawai'i, only language schools teaching Hawaiian would ever be subject to state regulation.

The DSSH then argued that the Pūnana Leo should be subject to state regulation because it was unlike typical foreign-language schools in Hawai'i. For example, Japanese-language schools were typically two-hour programs serving children between the ages of 5 and 11. They were conducted after the completion of the regular English elementary school day. Specifically, the DSSH argued that State of Hawai'i regulation was necessary since, first, the Pūnana Leo children were too young (under 5 years old) compared to elementary-school children, and the Pūnana Leo hours of daily operation (approximately 10 hours per day) were too long. It was pointed out that the laws of the State of Hawai'i (1) defined a child as anyone under the age of 18, with no special provision that children under 5 be treated differently and that (2) there was no special provision requiring state regulation beyond a certain number of hours. The DSSH representatives then attempted to argue that it was the combination of the young age and the long hours of operation that made regulation necessary. This interpretation, of course, was also not supported by statute. Finally, the DSSH argued that the method of teaching (i.e., language immersion) was not a true method of language teaching, such as grammar-translation, used in other foreign-language schools in Hawai'i. Although it was pointed out that immersion was, in fact, the most successful of modern language-teaching methods, one with which Canada had had nearly 20 years of experience, DSSH officials insisted on holding the Pūnana Leo to all state regulations.

In order to assure that the buildings were up to code, state regulations placed significant financial and staffing restrictions on the establishment of Pūnana Leo schools. These included space requirements for classroom and fenced playground areas, ramps and bathroom railings for handicapped students, paved parking areas, and so forth. Staffing regulations required that teachers obtain college certification in early-childhood education (ECE). This meant that native speakers of Hawaiian, who were predominantly over the ages of 60 and 70 at the time and were not likely to be able to go to college and obtain ECE certification, would be ineligible to teach at Pūnana Leo. On the other hand, those who were able to obtain such certification were unlikely to be speakers with native-speaker competence in Hawaiian.

Legislative Action

The first attempt by the 'APL, with the assistance of the American Civil Liberties, to change the law affecting state regulation in 1984 was unsuccessful. Despite this, the first Pūnana Leo was opened in September 1984 in Kekaha, Kaua'i. The second attempt in 1985 resulted in a compromise after lengthy public hearings and testimony from the Hawaiian community (Pūnana Leo parents and parents-to-be) and university faculty with expertise in language education in Hawai'i and abroad.[4] This compromise exempted the Pūnana Leo from all staffing requirements given that they would comply with all other DSSH regulations. Under these conditions the second Pūnana Leo, in Hilo, Hawai'i, and the third, at the Kalihi-Moanalua Church on O'ahu, were opened in April 1985. To this day, the Pūnana Leo is the only language school subject to regulation by the State of Hawai'i. The financial restrictions resulting from this regulation still makes the establishment of new Pūnana Leo difficult. By contrast, in 1993, only six Pūnana Leo had opened their doors, while in Aotearoa, over 600 Māori Kōhanga Reo had been established.

Enrollment

By 1999, eleven Pūnana Leo served 209 children. Three are located on the island of Hawai'i (in Hilo, Waimea, and Kona), two on the island of Maui (in Wailuku and Lahainaluna), one on the island of Moloka'i (in Ho'olehua), four on the island of O'ahu (in Kalihi, Wai'anae, Kawaiaha'o, and Ko'olauloa), and one on the island of Kaua'i (in Puhi). Demand for the program typically exceeds the number of openings in the program. On O'ahu, for example, there were times during the program's first years when more than 200 children were on the waiting list.

Funding

Initially, funding for the program came from tuition, donations, and fund-raisers. The major fund-raiser has been annual Hawaiian music concerts, such as Ho'omau (Perpetuation) on the island of O'ahu. Alu Like, a federally funded organization to assist Native Hawaiians, was very supportive in the first years of the program, providing funding from six months to a year to train new staff. Similarly, the Hawai'i Committee for the Humanities also provided support early on. In 1985, the Pūnana Leo also received a one-year grant from the Office of Hawaiian Affairs,[5] although conditions of the grant only enabled the receipt of about 60% of the $54,000 appropriated.

Since 1990, however, the 'APL has received federal funding. Initially this was about $1 million in federal funding per year. These funds were primarily used to increase salaries of the teachers, to provide tuition subsidies to Pūnana Leo parents, to provide better equipment for the schools, to develop Hawaiian language curriculum, and to establish new Pūnana Leo schools. Subsequently, the governing by-laws of the 'APL were changed to broaden the purview of the organization to all matters related to Hawaiian language, culture, and education. In 1995, 'APL was selected to receive approximately $4 million per year in federal funds from the Native Hawaiian Education Act. The additional federal money was to allow the 'APL to develop curriculum and various educational and teacher training programs for the Pūnana Leo and the Kula Kaiapuni (Hawaiian Language Immersion Program) and to provide scholarships for students attending universities. By 1997, this amount was increased to about $7 million. More recent reports released in 1999 indicate that the 'APL received $18 million in federal funding in that year.

By and large, the existence of a Pūnana Leo school in a particular area has led directly to the establishment of a DOE Hawaiian-language school in the same or nearby area. This is a natural consequence of parents' desire to have their children's education in Hawaiian continued. Further, the entrance of Hawaiian-speaking children in the DOE Hawaiian Immersion classrooms (kindergarten and higher) has had profound effects on the acquisition of Hawaiian by non-Hawaiian-speaking children.

THE HAWAIIAN LANGUAGE IMMERSION PROGRAM

The Papahana Kaiapuni Hawai'i[6] (Hawaiian Language Immersion Program) or, as it is more commonly called, the Kula Kaiapuni (Hawaiian Immersion Schools), was begun with the realization that the language and culture of Hawai'i's indigenous people would not survive another generation without the creation of new generations of Hawaiian native speakers. It was obvious that the small numbers of children from the Pūnana Leo preschools would not be able to maintain their Hawaiian language ability without the opportunity to continue to learn and speak Hawaiian through the elementary, intermediate, and high school years.

Alienated from the process of education of Hawaiian children through the sociohistorical context previously outlined, indigenous Hawaiians have largely been absent as teachers and administrators in the Hawai'i school system ever since Hawaiian was outlawed as a language of instruction in the schools 100 years before.

Once established for the purpose of education of Hawaiians exclusively, the public school system has largely failed Hawaiians, an experience not unlike that of other indigenous peoples worldwide. Documentation has shown that Hawaiian students' performances on English standardized testing statewide is amongst the lowest of all Hawai'i's major ethnic groups (Kamehameha Schools Bishop Estate 1993). Thus, in addition to goals of language regenesis, Hawaiians are beginning to realize their stake in the education of their own children through the Hawaiian immersion program (i.e., that education is a key for their children's livelihood and that there is a need to improve the education of Hawaiian children in both the Kula Kaiapuni and the State of Hawai'i DOE public schools).

The Kula Kaiapuni was implemented by the State of Hawai'i Department of Education as a pilot program in 1987 at the request of the Hawaiian community, parents, and teachers. The program was seen as a means for children graduating from the Pūnana Leo Schools to continue their education in Hawaiian while serving to afford other children the opportunity to learn Hawaiian. It is voluntary: parents choose to place their children in the program. Although it is open to all ethnic groups, not surprisingly, approximately 95% of the students are ethnically Hawaiian (Carol Wilhelm, personal communication 1998). Thus far, one-third to one-half of most kindergarten classes have tended to be Hawaiian-speaking children (typically those from the Pūnana Leo).

In general, the enrollment of such Hawaiian-speaking peers has had a profound effect on the language acquisition of English-speaking children first entering the Kula Kaiapuni classroom, in large part because the Hawaiian-speaking children provide new learners with many more models to learn from. Further, Hawaiian-speaking peers provide evidence to the beginning learners that the language can actually be learned by children. Children typically begin speaking Hawaiian in the first half of the year. Not surprisingly, acquisition is significantly slower for those classes in which fewer than one-quarter of the students are Hawaiian speakers. Research conducted in 1999 by Warner and Sismar (forthcoming) indicates that non–Pūnana Leo students have some significant advantages in the acquisition of Hawaiian with respect to their Pūnana Leo peers, a fact not heretofore acknowledged. Thus, under typical conditions in the Kula Kaiapuni today, it would seem that both Pūnana Leo and non–Pūnana Leo children can have significant benefits and advantages from their differing experiences in Hawaiian.

In general, the demand for the program has exceeded the number of children accepted into the program. Formerly, children were enrolled on a first-come, first-served basis. In 1996, the official position of the DOE was that a lottery system at each site was to be used to select children who would be allowed to enroll in the program. This led to a suit by the Office of Hawaiian Affairs against the State of Hawai'i in that year on the grounds that the State had not lived up to its constitutional mandate to support Hawaiian language, culture, and history. This suit was settled this summer where the State ($800,000) and the OHA ($400,000) would provide funding to the Kula Kaiapuni program for five years.

Early Support for the Program

In 1987, the state superintendent of the Department of Education, Charles Toguchi, was very much interested in the concept of magnet schools. A magnet school was to have a particular academic focus, such as in drama or science. Students specifically interested in that particular content area could apply to matriculate in that school regardless of their school district. A school for Hawaiian language seemed to make sense and gained his immediate support. Changes in state law resulting in the treatment of Hawaiian as one of two official languages of the state, and amendments to the state constitution (Article 10, Section 5) in 1978 calling for the promotion of the Hawaiian culture, language, and history in Hawai'i public schools, lent support to the establishment of the Kula Kaiapuni.

Additional support of the initial proposal to establish a pilot Hawaiian immersion program for K–1 students in 1987 came from the community. For example, a parent of two Pūnana Leo students testified in Hawaiian that "there is a critical need to preserve and restore the Hawaiian language—a national treasure and resource—with its heart and spirit intact." He said, "If the language is to live and thrive, it must be taught in Hawaiian—not another language" (Enoka Kaina, Board of Education testimony, July 23, 1987; my translation). The State of Hawai'i Board of Education, which is charged with setting DOE policy, comprised 13 voting members at that time, 5 of whom were Hawaiian. This body also supported and passed a policy to allow the establishment of the Hawaiian Language Immersion Program in 1987.

Evolution of the Program

Thus, in September 1987 the pilot program (for kindergartners and 1st graders) began at two sites, Waiau Elementary on O'ahu and Keaukaha Elementary on Hawai'i. There was a combined enrollment of nearly 40 children. After the first year, a program evaluation indicated that the children were doing well (Slaughter et al. 1988). The board of education approved an extension of the pilot program to grade 2, and over the years the program has been expanded little by little. This has been the result of much debate and testimony by parents, community members, and educators. In 1989 the board of education approved the Hawaiian Language Immersion Program as a limited K–6 program with transition to English during the upper elementary grades.

In a paper presented as part of the initial proposal to the State of Hawai'i Board of Education (BOE) to expand the Hawaiian immersion program to the secondary level, Warner (1990) proposed and argued for a Hawaiian immersion K–12 model. While based on the Canadian French "super-immersion" schools (Genesee, personal communication 1990), the Hawaiian immersion model strengthened the use of Hawaiian in the program, limiting formal English instruction to one hour per day from grades 5 through 12. The elements of this model were implemented subsequently.

In 1990, the BOE also approved the delay of formal English instruction to grade 5.

In February of 1992, the BOE approved the motion, thereby

1. providing one hour of English instruction per day for the grade 6 classes,
2. extending the program to grades 7 and 8 for 1993 and 1994, respectively,
3. providing one hour of English instruction per day for grades 7 and 8, and
4. extending the Hawaiian Language Immersion Program from kindergarten through grade 12 at two sites, one on Oʻahu and the other on Hawaiʻi.

In September of 1992, the BOE approved the extension of the Hawaiian Language Immersion Program to grade 12 with one hour of English instruction per day at each grade level beginning at grade 5.

(State of Hawaiʻi Board of Education, 1994)

The French super-immersion model was really based on French-medium schools in which children who were native speakers of English were enrolled from kindergarten through grade 6. In this model, formal English instruction was introduced at grade 4 for only 30 minutes per day (Genesee, personal communication 1990). This was the strongest model of immersion with respect to the children's acquisition of French. Moreover, as reported by Genesee (1987) for other total early immersion models of French, standardized testing in English indicated these children's competency in French increased with no detriment to their English skills.

In the Hawaiian model, Hawaiian is the medium through which students receive the entire curriculum, including language arts, mathematics, science, and social studies. In general, an attempt was made early on in the program's history to follow a literacy-based program of instruction where children learn literacy and other skills through Hawaiian. Thus, children received a great deal of exposure to literature (books and various print materials). Today, however, it appears that there is no one method which predominates the immersion program. In addition to literacy-based approaches, also included are more traditional skills-based approaches, which emphasize learning the alphabet before teaching reading, and eclectic variations as teachers see fit.

As previously mentioned, English instruction is introduced in grade 5 and is limited to one hour per day through grade 12. The model of English instruction may vary from site to site in the program. For example, in the first year in which English instruction was implemented in the Kula Kaiapuni (1991–92), two different instructional methods were used at the two lead sites. The first involved teaching English (to L1 [first-language] English-speaking children) through the medium of Hawaiian, similar to foreign-language instruction. The second advocated instruction through the medium of English, similar to first-language instruction. Further, a number of sites utilize a model of reading and writing across the curriculum, where English instruction would include literature as well as content-area materials (such as social studies) in English.

Program Goals

Over the years, program goals have been developed and later refined and articulated. The Hawaiian immersion program goals, adopted in 1994, are to develop a quality education program which will assist students in:

1. Developing a high level of proficiency in comprehending and communicating in the Hawaiian language.
2. Developing a strong foundation of Hawaiian culture and values.
3. Becoming empowered individuals who are responsible and caring members of our community.
4. Developing knowledge and skills in all areas of the curriculum and attaining the Foundation Program Objectives of the Department of Education.

(State of Hawaiʻi Department of Education 1994)

The current goals reflect less of a focus on the attainment of equal proficiency in English than earlier versions of the program's goals, although this is most likely included in the phrase "all areas of the curriculum." These goals differ markedly from those of French immersion programs for English-speaking majority-language children in Canada. In those schools, parents choose to enroll children in French immersion programs primarily for the purposes of enrichment and economic gain.

It should be noted that before the actual implementation of the program in 1987, certain DOE officials wanted the design of the program to exclude the teaching of reading and writing in Hawaiian to the children. The argument was that Hawaiian was originally an oral language and that the program would be less expensive since English books could be used and Hawaiian texts need not be produced or translated. Of course, this argument ignores the fact that virtually all languages, including English, were oral languages first. It also ignores the fact that Hawaiians were extremely literate once the concept was brought to Hawaiʻi. Because reading and writing were viewed by the Hawaiian community and educators as a key to language perpetuation, this suggestion was not supported. Literacy would enable children not only to access a large body of native Hawaiian literature already documented and in existence, but to access and take part in the creation of a new body of literature in the present and future. They would also not be limited to the oral mode of communication.

Program Growth and Expansion

By 1999, the total enrollment of the Kula Kaiapuni program was 1,543 in grades K–12 (Wilhelm 1998), with 8 additional children enrolled in a newly established Lei Ānuenue preschool at the Ānuenue school site. These totals combined with the Pūnana Leo enrollment of 209 students throughout the state meant that 1,760 students were being taught through the Hawaiian language. In addition, in the spring of 1999, the oldest children at the two lead sites (Ānuenue and Nāwahīokalani'ōpu'u) became the first students to graduate from the Kula Kaiapuni. A number of these students were intending to enroll in college. For example, four of the six graduates from Ānuenue are currently attending a four-year university (two students) or community college (two students).

The First K–12 Kula Kaiapuni

In 1995, the eldest students at the two lead sites were to enter the 9th grade. On O'ahu, these students attended 7th and 8th grade classes conducted on the Waiau Elementary campus as an extension of the Kula Kaiapuni o Waiau (K–6 Waiau Hawaiian Language Immersion School), thanks to the support of Principal Diana Oshiro and the school administration. In order to accommodate the needs of new high school students, the Kula Kaiapuni at Waiau Elementary was relocated to Ānuenue Elementary School in Pālolo. Intended as an interim site, Ānuenue thus became the first K–12 in the state. The new site was a former elementary school used to house various DOE offices. The majority of these offices were relocated during the year. However, grades 7 through 9 had to be taught in one-third of the dining hall during the entire 1995–96 school year until the offices could be relocated. Whereas most Kula Kaiapuni programs are of the "schools within school" model (i.e., a school with an English stream and a Hawaiian stream), Ānuenue and Nāwahīokalani'ōpu'u (grades 7 through 12), in Kea'au, Hawai'i, alone do not offer an English stream.

In addition, in 1998–99, the Kula Kaiapuni 'o Ānuenue (Ānuenue Kaiapuni School) became the first and only Kula Kaiapuni program that serves children from birth through grade 12. This is because the program enrolled eight children in its new Lei Ānuenue preschool program. These children were predominantly those of teachers and the school community. Unlike the Pūnana Leo, which enrolls children from ages two through five, Lei Ānuenue enrolled children from birth through age five. The staff included a Hawaiian native speaker from Ni'ihau and an L2 speaker of Hawaiian with certification in early childhood education. Because of the combination of native speaker input and the fact that many of the children have one or two fluent Hawaiian-speaking par-

ents at home, this is undoubtedly the strongest Hawaiian-language preschool today.

The oldest students at the lead site on the island of Hawai'i had been taught during the previous two years in an office building in downtown Hilo, Hawai'i. This site was renovated with funds from the 'APL. In 1995, these children (grades 7 through 9) were relocated to a new school site in Kea'au, Puna, Hawai'i. The site, Nāwahīokalani'ōpu'u, was a former private school and was purchased by the 'APL with $2.1 million received from the Office of Hawaiian Affairs (OHA) (see Wilson and Kamanā, this volume). Administratively, the school is part of Hilo Intermediate School of the state DOE.

Currently, children on Maui, Kaua'i, and Moloka'i have reached the intermediate grades as well. The lead classes at Pā'ia School on Maui were sent to a middle school program for grades 6 through 8 at Kalama Intermediate School. They are now attending King Kekaulike High School. The lead classes on Kaua'i in the 1998–99 school year were sent to Kapa'a Intermediate School, located directly adjacent to the Kapa'a Elementary School site.

Kaiapuni Teachers

Teachers in the schools are typically second-language speakers of Hawaiian who have graduated from the university with a teaching certificate. All of these speakers are English- or HCE-dominant speakers. The majority of these teachers have certification from the Department of Education. In the early years, a number of secondary certified teachers were allowed to teach in the elementary grades. On occasion, some uncertified teachers have taught in the immersion schools due to a shortage of teachers.

Most Hawaiian immersion schools have been successful in hiring a native speaker as a part-time teachers' assistant or resource person (typically for less than 20 hours a week). A few schools have managed to hire more than one. In the latter case, native speakers often provide storytelling or hands-on Hawaiian cultural lessons such as food preparation or handicrafts through the medium of Hawaiian. They also provide needed language and cultural models for the children.

At present, there is a growing need for teachers certified in various content areas in the secondary grades. Because of this, there seems to be a natural trend in the secondary and upper elementary program design where teachers with a particular specialization will teach a specific content area to several grades. For example, a secondary science teacher would teach the sciences, a mathematics teacher would teach the mathematics courses, a social studies teacher the social studies courses and possibly the language arts courses, while an English teacher would teach English to a number of grades (7, 8, 9, 10, 11, and/or 12) on a rotating schedule. In this design, each teacher would have a number of different class preparations for children in the different grades. This model has been implemented for upper elementary children in grades 4, 5, and 6 and for some intermediate and high school students at Ānuenue School. Here children rotate through classes taught by teachers specializing in Hawaiian language arts, social studies/English, and mathematics. The problem in high school, however, is a difficult one because, in a sense, the qualified teacher needs to gain skills in three fields of university study, namely Hawaiian language, a content field (science, mathematics, social sciences, etc.), and educational certification. Moreover, science teachers would require knowledge of a number of sciences.

Only recently have the Hawaiian community (students and their parents) and the general community become aware that there is some economic value in the market for skilled speakers of Hawaiian in the teaching profession. Further, only recently has funding become available to support students seeking teaching careers in the immersion program. As such, the numbers of teachers being graduated each year from the universities have not kept up with the demand for them, although the gap is being reduced each year. As this has been designated as a shortage area by the DOE, over the years teachers without certification, or without sufficient language proficiency, have at times been hired.

In 1998, the University of Hawai'i at Mānoa (UHM) established the first teacher preparation program specifically aimed at preparing Kula Kaiapuni teachers. The program is a collaboration between the College of Education, the Hawaiian language faculty of the Department of Hawaiian and Indo-Pacific Languages at UHM, and Ke Kula Kaiapuni 'o Ānuenue of the Department of Education. This program is conducted at the Ānuenue campus site, providing student teachers with hands-on experience. The first 15 teachers from this program were graduated in the spring of 1999. The second cohort of another 15 students is scheduled to graduate in the spring of 2001.

SOME CRITICAL ISSUES IN HAWAIIAN LANGUAGE IMMERSION

Despite the impressive gains and numbers of children and adults learning Hawaiian, numerous barriers and problems stand in the way of reversing language shift in Hawai'i. As it is impossible to describe them all, I will merely point to a few major areas of difficulty.

Domain

One of the major problems in reversing language shift is that the primary means of the children's acquisition of Hawaiian is the school. While the Kula Kaiapuni is necessary and undoubtedly the most important vehicle at this point in time, it in itself is not sufficient to reverse language shift. Perhaps the most important reason for this problem is that the

language of the school has been fairly restricted to the academic domains of language use. Even youths and adults learning Hawaiian in classes ranging from high schools to universities and community colleges as well as adult education primarily receive instruction restricted to academic domains. Hawaiian immersion students (Pūnana Leo and Kula Kaiapuni children) often shift to English when speaking to one another on the playground or when speaking to one another about popular topics, such as music (for instance, MTV), cartoons, and various other social phenomena which are largely available to the community through English. There is generally a direct relationship with respect to age and the amount of English spoken (i.e., the older the child the more English he or she is likely to use).

If Hawaiians harbor any genuine hope of reviving the language, it must be revived in domains outside as well as inside the classroom. A language cannot be perpetuated in a single domain such as the school or the church. Children will need to be able to communicate their feelings, hopes, opinions, and thoughts in Hawaiian in all domains of life if the language is to truly survive. Planners for indigenous or native languages should be aware of this from the start and work to build various domains into their models and strategies for language and cultural regenesis from their inception.

Wong (1995) has advocated the need to expand into other domains in the general community such as in the areas of sports. Warner (1999b) described the Ke A'a Mākālei project, a federal grant from the Administration for Native Americans, in which such alternative programs for learning Hawaiian in and through sports were implemented. One of the most successful programs was the establishment of Hawaiian-speaking softball teams. These teams included men-only and combined teams (men and women or coed teams) which competed in various leagues in the community. Although the grant was already completed by then, the softball teams were still running throughout 1999. Participants tended to include athletes who played softball but never spoke Hawaiian before. Many of these were men who already held full-time jobs and would never consider taking a Hawaiian-language course at the university. Also, some participants were university second-language learners of Hawaiian who were also athletes.

The lexicon for the sport was created or adapted from two sources. The first was baseball terminology printed in Hawaiian newspaper articles from earlier in the 20th century, and those not available were created. Although just a start, the ultimate goal is the creation of Hawaiian-speaking sports teams and, eventually, Hawaiian-speaking leagues for children and adults alike so that the speaking of the Hawaiian language in sports becomes a norm.

Another example of domain expansion in the community is the result of a new generation of Hawaiian-language playwrights who are now beginning to produce Hawaiian plays for public performance. While these tend to embody forms of traditional *hula* (dance) and *oli* (chant) already available in the community, the speaking of only Hawaiian in plays written by Hawaiians about Hawaiʻi is one of the most exciting new areas which children and adults alike can appreciate.

Overall, there is a continual need to create new venues and avenues in the general society so that speaking and hearing Hawaiian again becomes a norm in Hawaiʻi. It is unlikely that Hawaiian can survive if children shift to English or HCE (Pidgin) every time they want to talk about sports, music and MTV, or comic-book heroes, to badmouth someone, or to leave the school grounds.

CENTRALIZED OR COMMUNITY CONTROL

Another important issue facing the Kula Kaiapuni came to a head in 1999. The controversy was related to power and the notion of who should control community schools: one private organization which would have centralized control over all (or a number of) schools, or the local communities. Since 1996, the ʻAPL has embarked upon a course of action intended to privatize or consolidate control over the Kula Kaiapuni program (K–12) under the auspices of the Ka Haka ʻUla O Keʻelikōlani, the College of Hawaiian Language (CHL) of the University of Hawaiʻi at Hilo (three faculty of whom are on the executive board of the ʻAPL) and the ʻAPL. For example, in 1996 (Senate Bill 3166), and 1998 (House Bill 2719 and Senate Bill 3513), legislation was introduced aimed at transferring administrative control over all (1996) or some (1998) of the DOE Kula Kaiapuni schools to the Office of Hawaiian Affairs (a semiautonomous agency of the State of Hawaiʻi), which would then contract the ʻAha Pūnana Leo to administer the program or schools (see Warner 1999a).

Since 1996, local communities have resisted privatization under the ʻAPL consortium. Not one Kula Kaiapuni has opted to become a laboratory school. In fact, in 1999 the Molokaʻi community testified overwhelmingly against a proposal floated by one of the trustees, Clayton Hee, whereby OHA would have purchased a defunct hotel, the Pau Hana Inn, which would have been renovated and turned into the Kula Kaiapuni high school for that island. It would have been operated as a "laboratory" school under the College of Hawaiian Language of the University of Hawaii at Hilo and the ʻAPL. Owing to overwhelming testimony against the proposal, it was voted down five to one by the OHA trustees.

Similarly, several meetings were held on Kauaʻi during 1999 in which Niʻihau community members on Kauaʻi discussed the issue of having their school, Ke Kula Niʻihau O Kekaha (the Niʻihau School of Kekaha), become a laboratory school under the CHL and ʻAPL. This school was located in a newly renovated building known as the Kekaha Armory. Renovation had been achieved through OHA and other private funding. This Kula Niʻihau O Kekaha is not a Kaiapuni school, as it serves students whose native language is Hawaiian. It is, rather, a Hawaiian-medium school whose purpose may be more closely related to language maintenance. Administered by the ʻAPL for over five years, the school had not been asked if they wished to operate as a laboratory school under the CHL and ʻAPL prior to 1999.

When the question was finally brought to the fore, the Niʻihau community split on the issue. The longtime teachers of the Kula Niʻihau O Kekaha did not wish to be a part of the laboratory school under the CHL and ʻAPL. They were given the choice of supporting the ʻAPL and continuing to teach as part of the Kula Niʻihau O Kekaha at the armory or not supporting and leaving. As a consequence, the Niʻihau teachers who preferred not to be a part of the HCE and ʻAPL laboratory school left.

As a consequence, they and 24 children (roughly 50% of the children from the Niʻihau community in Kekaha) met from September 1999 on at a public park in Kekaha. They worked for no pay, with almost no books or curriculum materials. After a period of time, these children were no longer provided school lunches either. Despite this, they continued to attend classes in the park. The group of Niʻihau parents who chose to have their children participate in the laboratory school continued to send their 24 children to the Kekaha Armory as usual, although new teachers were selected from the Niʻihau community to replace the ones now in the park.

Some have characterized the split in the Niʻihau community as a family feud. Others have argued that it is a matter of differences in educational philosophy—that the Niʻihauan teachers and families in the park want their children to learn English during a small portion of the day (30 minutes to an hour) early in the program (i.e., as early perhaps as kindergarten and 1st grade). The ʻAPL, on the other hand, argued that the Niʻihauans needed to stay with their program and receive all their instruction in Hawaiian. English instruction was to begin later, typically in grade 5. Although there is physically sufficient room for both programs in the Kekaha Armory, attempts to find a compromise so that both schools could conduct classes in the Armory were not successful. ʻAPL argued that allowing one group of Niʻihau children to speak English during part of the day in the building would lead to the loss of Hawaiian in the other Niʻihau children.

In reality, this controversy is not owing to a family feud nor a difference in philosophy. It is a struggle for power. Similarly to the Molokaʻi community, who rejected control of their school by outsiders, the Niʻihau teachers and families in the park have gone one step further, deciding that they should actually be the ones to control their own educational destiny. The ʻAPL, on the other hand, is attempting to maintain the control they have maintained over the Niʻihau school for more than five years. For the families in the park, this is an issue of local control and community empowerment. From their point of view, the 'APL is a foreign corporation from a distant island controlled by foreigners.

Elama Kanahele, one of the teachers in the park and one of the original teachers at the first Pūnana Leo preschool, likened their struggle to the lyrics of the song "Kaulana Nā Pua" (Famous Are the Flowers), written in protest of the illegal overthrow of Lili'uokalani, the last reigning monarch of the Hawaiian kingdom in 1893. The lyrics are: *'A'ole mākou a'e minamina i nā pu'u kālā a ke aupuni. Ua lawa mākou i ka pōhaku, ka 'ai kamaha'o o ka 'āina* (We do not wish for the piles of money of the government. We are satisfied with the stones, the amazing food of the land [i.e., we would rather eat stones than take your money]) (Elbert and Mahoe 1970) (Elama Kanahele, personal communication 1999). An interesting question to ponder is how many of the Ni'ihau families in the armory would continue to support the 'APL if the roles were reversed. That is, how many of them would continue to support the 'APL and send their children to a park every day for over a year? Would they be satisfied with *pōhaku* (stones), the amazing food of the land?

In view of the actual situation, one might wonder: why would teachers prefer to teach in a park with no pay, no books, and no curriculum? More astonishingly, why would parents choose to send their children to a park under these conditions? Why would this small community stand up to an organization with millions in federal, state, OHA, and private funding? Perhaps part of the answer can be found in a letter sent to the DOE Board of Education Committee on Special Programs in 1997. The letter was signed by the executive director and four other members of Hanakahi Hawai'i, the parent organization from the Kula Kaiapuni 'o Nāwahīokalani'ōpu'u, on the island of Hawai'i. This parent group requested that their school be assigned an on-site DOE administrator because "the 'Aha Pūnana Leo, landlords of the school site have unofficially placed themselves in charge and have begun setting policy for the school," and this "has resulted in a number of negative situations occurring this school year 1996–1997." One of four reasons cited for their request was:

> Although it is constantly stated that, "our parents run our school," the reality is that only a few parents (those with ties to the "'Aha Pūnana Leo") make all the decisions, behind closed doors and the other parents are expected just to comply without complaint. If parents do verbally disagree with a policy decision made by the "'Aha Pūnana Leo" staff, they are ridiculed and put down in front of other parents. If changes are requested by non-"'Aha Pūnana Leo" parents, they are ignored. In addition to this, the children of those parents are systematically discriminated against thruout [sic] the day.
> (Kapuni Reynolds et al. 1997)

At present, it does not appear that the issue of community empowerment (or disempowerment) versus centralized control is likely to be resolved any time soon.

CONCLUSION

The emergence of the Kula Kaiapuni is a tremendous opportunity for the Hawaiian people. It is not only an opportunity to revitalize and perpetuate the Hawaiian language and culture, whose seeds of extinction were planted 100 years ago. It is also an opportunity for Hawaiians to create and develop schools to educate Hawaiian children in Hawaiian ways. It is an opportunity for Hawaiian students to learn their language, culture, stories, and histories. The program has grown over the years but still faces serious problems, some of which have been briefly touched on here. It is hoped that other native, indigenous, or minority peoples involved in language revitalization and perpetuation can be more circumspect and look below the surface in order to avoid some of the internal and external struggles that Hawaiians have had to endure. Despite these difficulties, Hawaiians are awakening. I remain hopeful.

Notes

1. Ni'ihau is a small, privately owned island. A small community of Ni'ihau families on Ni'ihau and Kaua'i still speak Hawaiian as their native language; it is the only remaining community whose members use native Hawaiian as their day-to-day language of communication.
2. For the purposes of this paper, a "Hawaiian" is defined as anyone descended from residents of the islands before 1778, the year in which Captain Cook arrived in Hawai'i.
3. This māhele, or division, is often called "The Great Māhele" by English speakers, but the term 'great' was never included in the Hawaiian.
4. Non-Hawaiian scholars such as Fred Genesee (a visiting professor at the University of Hawai'i at Mānoa) and Charlene Sato and Michael Long of the University of Hawai'i at Mānoa Department of English as a Second Language, added their voices in support of the Hawaiian educators and community to change the law.
5. The Office of Hawaiian Affairs is a semi-autonomous agency of the state government. It was established through the Constitutional Convention of 1978 and is charged with serving and bringing about the betterment of the Hawaiian people, its primary beneficiaries.
6. This is the name on the last report from the State of Hawai'i Department of Education, although the name is not used in the community as widely as the Kula Kaiapuni.

References

Beechert, E. D. 1985. *Working in Hawaii: A labor history.* Honolulu: University of Hawai'i Press.

Bickerton D., and W. H. Wilson. 1987. Pidgin Hawaiian. In *Pidgin and Creole languages: Essays in memory of John E. Reinecke,* ed. G. Gilbert, 61–76. Honolulu: University of Hawai'i Press.

Constitution of the State of Hawaii as amended by the Constitutional Convention, 1978, and adopted by the Electorate on November 7, 1978. 1979. Honolulu: Constitutional Convention 1978.

Elbert, S. H., and N. Mahoe. 1970. *Nā Mele o Hawai'i Nei: 101 Hawaiian songs.* Honolulu: University of Hawai'i Press.

Eshima, M. 1996. *Native Hawaiian data book, 1996.* Honolulu: Office of Hawaiian Affairs.

Fishman, J. 1991. *Reversing language shift: Theoretical and empirical foundations of assistance to threatened languages.* Clevedon: Multilingual Matters.

Genesee, F. 1987. *Learning through two languages: Studies of immersion and bilingual education.* New York: Newbury House.

Huebner, T. 1985. Language education policy in Hawaii: Two case studies and some current issues. *International Journal of the Sociology and Language* 56: 29–49.

Kaina, E. 1987. Testimony in support of Hawaiian Language Immersion Program. Testimony presented before the State of Hawai'i Board of Education, July 23, 1987, Honolulu, Hawai'i.

Kamehameha Schools Bernice Pauahi Bishop Estate, Office of Program Evaluation and Planning. 1993. *Native Hawaiian educational assessment, 1993.* Honolulu: Kamehameha Schools Bernice Pauahi Bishop Estate.

Kapuni Reynolds, H., R. L. Poepoe, J. Kauoha, C. Ioane, and H. Weller. 1997. Letter to the Board of Education Committee on Special Programs. Request presented to meeting of the Board of Education Committee on Special Programs, March 24.

Kloss, H. 1977. *American bilingual tradition.* Rowley, Mass.: Newbury House.

Reinecke, J. 1969. *Language and dialect in Hawaii: A sociolinguistic history to 1935,* ed. Stanley M. Tsuzaki. Honolulu: University of Hawai'i Press.

Roberts, J. E. 1995. Pidgin Hawaiian: A sociohistorical study. *Journal of Pidgin and Creole Languages* 10, no. 1: 1–56.

Sato, C. J. 1991. Sociolinguistic variation and language attitudes in Hawaii. In *English around the world: Sociolinguistic perspective,* ed. J. Cheshire, 647–663. New York: Cambridge University Press.

Schmitt, R. 1968. *Demographic statistics of Hawai'i, 1778–1965.* Honolulu: University of Hawai'i Press.

Scudder, R. C. 1994. *Apology to Native Hawaiians on behalf of the United States for the overthrow of the kingdom of Hawaii.* Honolulu: Ka'imi Pono Press.

Slaughter, H. B., K. A. Watson-Gegeo, S. L. Warner, and H. Bernardino. 1988. Evaluation report for the first year of the Hawaiian Language Immersion Program: A report to the Planning and Evaluation Branch. Department of Education, State of Hawai'i.

Stannard, D. 1989. *Before the horror: The population of Hawai'i on the eve of western contact.* Honolulu: Social Science Research Institute, University of Hawai'i.

State of Hawai'i Board of Education. 1994. *Long-range plan for the Hawaiian Language Immersion Program.* Honolulu: State of Hawai'i Department of Education.

Warner, S. L. 1990. The delay of the formal introduction of English in the Hawaiian Language Immersion Program until grade five. Unpublished paper submitted at the request of the Hawaiian Language Advisory Council to the Committee on Hawaiian Affairs, State of Hawai'i Board of Education.

———. 1999a. Kuleana: The right, responsibility, and authority of indigenous peoples to speak and make decisions for themselves in language and cultural revitalization. *Anthropology & Education Quarterly* 30, no. 1: 68–94.

———. 1999b. Hawaiian language regenesis: Planning for intergenerational use of Hawaiian beyond the school. In Huebner, T., and Davis, K. (eds.), *Sociopolitical Perspectives on Language Policy and Planning in the USA,* 313–332. Philadelphia & Amsterdam: John Benjamins.

Wilhelm, C. 1998. *1998–99 fact sheet.* Honolulu: State of Hawai'i Department of Education.

Wong, Laiana. 1995. Alternative Avenues in Hawaiian Language Community. Paper Presented to American Anthropological Association, November 18, 1995.

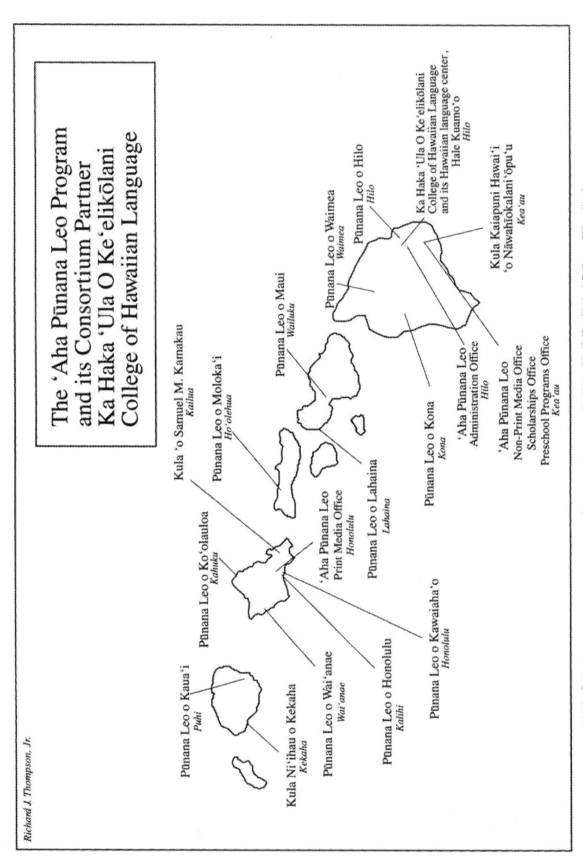

Richard J. Thompson, Jr.

The ʻAha Pūnana Leo Program
and its Consortium Partner
Ka Haka ʻUla O Keʻelikōlani
College of Hawaiian Language

Pūnana Leo o Kauaʻi
Puhi

Kula Niʻihau o Kekaha
Kekaha

Pūnana Leo o Waiʻanae
Waiʻanae

Pūnana Leo o Honolulu
Kalihi

Pūnana Leo o Kawaiahaʻo
Honolulu

Pūnana Leo o Koʻolauloa
Kahuku

ʻAha Pūnana Leo
Print Media Office
Honolulu

Pūnana Leo o Lahaina
Lahaina

Kula ʻo Samuel M. Kamakau
Kailua

Pūnana Leo o Molokaʻi
Hoʻolehua

Pūnana Leo o Maui
Wailuku

Pūnana Leo o Kona
Kona

ʻAha Pūnana Leo
Administration Office
Hilo

ʻAha Pūnana Leo
Non-Print Media Office
Scholarships Office
Preschool Programs Office
Keaʻau

Pūnana Leo o Waimea
Waimea

Pūnana Leo o Hilo
Hilo

Ka Haka ʻUla O Keʻelikōlani
College of Hawaiian Language
and its Hawaiian language center,
Haie Kuamoʻo
Hilo

Kula Kaiapuni Hawaiʻi
ʻo Nāwahīokalaniʻōpuʻu
Keaʻau

MAP 13.1   The ʻAha Pūnana Leo program and its consortium partner, Ka Haka ʻUla O Keʻelikōlani College of Hawaiian Language

13

"Mai Loko Mai O Ka 'I'ini: Proceeding from a Dream"
The 'Aha Pūnana Leo Connection in Hawaiian Language Revitalization

WILLIAM H. WILSON
Ka Haka 'Ula O Ke'elikōlani College of Hawaiian Language
University of Hawai'i
Hilo, Hawai'i

KAUANOE KAMANĀ
Ka Haka 'Ula O Ke'elikōlani College of Hawaiian Language
University of Hawai'i
Hilo, Hawai'i

Having established Hawaiian-medium programs from preschool through graduate school, Hawai'i has the most developed movement in indigenous language–medium education in the United States. This movement has as its beginning, and still its most quickly moving stream, the partnering of government and community resources under the leadership of the non-profit 'Aha Pūnana Leo. While the *'i'ini*—the dream, the heartfelt desire for language revitalization—is familiar to many indigenous people, what is often unfamiliar is the specific actions taken by groups such as ours in proceeding from such a dream toward actual language revitalization. We hope that the following information on 'Aha Pūnana Leo programs may be useful to others who share our deep 'i'ini for continued language life and trust that anything not useful will be put aside.

The leadership of the 'Aha Pūnana Leo consists of a board of unpaid volunteers who are Hawaiian-speaking educators seeking to revitalize Hawaiian as the daily language of their own families and communities as well as of others pursuing the same goal. These educators, we among them, have strived to reverse what has for decades been the standard philosophy for integrating Hawaiian language and culture into education. In the standard philosophy, Hawaiian language and culture are seen as something to use in facilitating achievement of the actual priority goal: academic parity with the dominant society for a "poorly performing minority group."

The philosophy that has brought our movement most of its success establishes the priority goal as the continued existence of strengthening of the Hawaiian *mauli,* or life force, which allows for the continued existence of a Hawaiian people. The 'Aha Pūnana Leo sees academic achievement, especially achievement higher than that of the dominant society, as an important tool in reaching that priority goal. But high academic achievement in and of itself is not the goal. The success of the 'Aha Pūnana Leo has been the development, organization, and strengthening of what it terms *honua*—environments where only Hawaiian is used and the Hawaiian mauli is fostered. These honua presently include schools, offices, personal relationships, and homes. For the 'Aha Pūnana Leo, these honua are essential for the continuation of communities that greatly value a common identity stretching generations into the past and which is being prepared to stretch generations into the future.

Described below is the current core involvement of the 'Aha Pūnana Leo—its base system of Pūnana Leo language nest preschools, its three model K–12 schools, and its support system, including administration, curriculum development, human resource development, telecommunications, scholarships, and site development. Besides the above programs, 'Aha Pūnana Leo current core involvement includes its consortium with Ka Haka 'Ula O Ke'elikōlani College of Hawaiian Language at the University of Hawai'i at Hilo and work with Hawaiian language teachers elsewhere, especially some in the College of Arts and Sciences at the University of Hawai'i at Mānoa and various Hawaiian-language immersion schools. The consortium with Ka Haka 'Ula O Ke'elikōlani extends Hawaiian-medium education through graduate school and provides a key link for the 'Aha Pūnana Leo to additional resources.

Because this configuration of 'Aha Pūnana Leo core involvement is part of a larger interrelated Hawaiian language movement in which the 'Aha Pūnana Leo participates, other Hawaiian programs will be included in the discussion when

147

mutual influences are especially important. The full range of Hawaiian language programs in Hawai'i, however, is beyond the scope of this essay. We will begin with some background information and proceed to the primary focus of this essay, which is the development and delivery of Hawaiian-medium education through the 'Aha Pūnana Leo and Ka Haka 'Ula O Ke'elikōlani. We will then close with some of the philosophical beliefs that have sustained the 'Aha Pūnana Leo and played a role in its success.

BACKGROUND

Hawai'i's history has placed Hawaiian in an especially strong position for language revitalization. As detailed in Wilson 1998a and 1998b, Hawai'i's primordial base is that of an isolated island chain distinguished and united by a unique Polynesian language and culture. Its initial century of sustained contact with the global expansion of European culture was as the Hawaiian monarchy, a multiracial nation using Hawaiian both as a lingua franca and as an official language of government. The past century has been roughly divided in half between a period as an American territory and one as an American state. Through the entire 20th century, however, Hawai'i has been politically controlled on a local level by multiracial speakers of either Hawaiian or Hawai'i Creole English who identify with the indigenous culture. Thus, through all these periods of history, Hawaiian has been accorded special legal status.

In spite of these advantages, Hawaiian has suffered political persecution and the effects of low sociocultural associations. Indeed, Hawaiian has a native-speaker profile worse than that of many other languages indigenous to the United States. For example, a recent count of traditional native-speaking elders born before 1930 by the 'Ahahui 'Ōlelo Hawai'i, an organization that holds an annual conference of Hawaiian-speaking elders, resulted in no more than 200 (Hailama Farden [president of 'Ahahui 'Ōlelo Hawai'i], personal communication, 2000). This figure is less than .01% of an estimated 220,000–240,000 Native Hawaiians now in Hawai'i and less than .002% of the island population of some 1,000,000–1,200,000. A number of these elders could be described as semispeakers who are actually more comfortable in English than in Hawaiian. Yet one small isolated island—Ni'ihau—has retained first–language-dominant fluency in Hawaiian for all ages for its entire tiny population of 134, with strong multiage Hawaiian fluency also in its satellite community of about 287 on the neighboring island of Kaua'i, and others located elsewhere in Hawai'i and the world numbering about 76 ('Īlei Beniamina [Ni'ihau community member], personal communication, 2000).

In 1981 Richard Benton, in his study of the status of Pacific Island languages, predicted that Hawaiian would be the first Polynesian language to be totally replaced by a European language.[1] Yet today Hawaiian is in a better position than many other Polynesian languages which are being replaced by English, French, and Spanish. The Ni'ihau population is growing and regaining language domains that were being lost at the same time that it is expanding into new uses. And there is also now a new non-Ni'ihau category of young native speakers. These consist of some 20–50 children under the age of 18 who have been raised in homes where Hawaiian is either the sole or a major language of interaction between children and second-language-learner parents. Of course, the Hawaiian of these children is even more threatened than Ni'ihau Hawaiian since they all are part of neighborhoods and extended families where everyone else speaks a form of English. The development and strengthening of this new population, like the strengthening of the Ni'ihau population, is closely related to increased attention to the Hawaiian language in education.

Hawaiians have long identified language shift with schooling and the forced closing of Hawaiian-medium educational institutions at the turn of the 20th century. The first generation of Hawaiian parents whose children were affected by forced English-medium education frequently insisted on the sole use of Hawaiian in the home and scolded their children for using English with other Hawaiians (Ka Leo Hawai'i, oral interviews). They also made efforts to maintain Hawaiian-medium education in the Sunday school programs of the Hawaiian-medium churches that they controlled, maintained Hawaiian-language newspapers, controlled electoral politics through their language, and campaigned to restore Hawaiian-medium education ("Olelo Hawaii," Ka Puuhonua [Hawaiian newspaper], 20 January 1917).[2]

Efforts through the schools to reverse the loss of Hawaiian began in the 1920s with second language–style courses legislated by the Hawaiian-controlled territorial legislature, then through the legislatively mandated inclusion of elders in schools in the 1970s, and most recently by Hawaiian-medium immersion education, which began in the 1980s with the Pūnana Leo. At present, every student in the Hawai'i public school system learns a few Hawaiian terms (beyond the many they already know from Hawai'i Creole English) in required courses in Hawaiian culture and history as well as in a greatly weakened elder-resource teacher program in the elementary schools. In 1998, perhaps 2,500 students were enrolled in at least one Hawaiian language course in public and private high schools annually, with another 2,500 at the college level. An additional 1,850 were enrolled in Hawaiian-medium education classes from the preschool level through high school.

Contemporary Hawaiian-medium education at the University of Hawai'i at Hilo began when we were hired in the late 1970s to establish a bachelor of arts degree in Hawaiian studies. The university agreed to our stipulation that if we were to come to Hilo, courses for the degree would be taught at the upper-division level entirely in Hawaiian. The program for this bachelor's degree, which was first awarded in 1982, grew to include the Hale Kuamo'o Hawaiian Language Center in 1990. In 1998, the academic program and the Hale Kuamo'o were organized as their own college, named Ka Haka 'Ula O Ke'elikōlani. Initiated along with the college were a master of arts program in Hawaiian language and literature and a teacher certification program, both taught entirely through the medium of Hawaiian. All activities of these entities are conducted through the medium of Hawaiian.

While working toward the establishment of the Hawaiian-medium bachelor's degree, we also established a "Hawaiian-medium family" with the birth of our first child in 1981. This led to a very personal interest in Hawaiian-medium education at the earlier levels, an interest that was strengthened by our relationship with 'Īlei Beniamina and Paul Williams, who were teaching in a bilingual program established in 1979 for Ni'ihau children temporarily or permanently resident on the nearby island of Kaua'i. The Ni'ihau bilingual program focused on transition out of Hawaiian, a feature with which both Beniamina and Williams were dissatisfied. The fact remained, however, that the Ni'ihau bilingual program demonstrated that provisions could be made for education specifically for Hawaiian speakers. Beniamina and we wanted our children to be able to receive Hawaiian language–tailored education through Hawaiian-medium schools of the sort that had existed in Hawai'i during the 19th century. When the new degree in Hawaiian studies was initiated, Beniamina came to Hilo to pursue it, along with teacher certification, and we spent considerable time discussing how Hawaiian-medium education might look in the future.

Also in 1982, when Beniamina enrolled in her first courses in Hilo, the state superintendent of education made a visit to Ni'ihau school itself, where Beniamina's mother was the head teacher and all staff were also Ni'ihauans. The superintendent criticized the school and the diglossic use of English reading and writing in the school surrounded by oral use of Hawaiian, and he demanded that the district office develop a plan to change the school. Wilson sent a letter to the district superintendent offering his assistance in developing a plan where Hawaiian would be made a medium of education and English taught as a second language. Copies were provided to Beniamina, her mother, and Tīmoti Kāretu (the head of the Kōhanga Reo Trust), then on sabbatical at the University of Hawai'i at Hilo from Waikato University. Beniamina and Kāretu joined us and Byron Cleeland, an English, Hawaiian, and French language teacher on Kaua'i, in helping the Department of Education to develop the plan. It was after a visit to Beniamina and Williams's Ni'ihau bilingual program on Kaua'i with Kāretu and Cleeland that those of us then on Kaua'i (Beniamina, Cleeland, Kamanā, Kāretu, Williams, and Wilson) decided to ask our Hawaiian lan-

guage teacher Larry Kimura and Wilson and Kimura's student Sam L. Warner to come to Kaua'i to discuss establishing private Hawaiian-medium preschools. Kimura had been especially keen on the idea of such schools after hearing of the very recent establishment of the Kōhanga Reo (translated from the Māori as "language nest") in New Zealand. We then established our organization with the name 'Aha Pūnana Leo (translated as "language nest gathering"), honoring in our group's name the initial work that occurred in New Zealand.

Later, in 1983, Hawaiian-medium education progressed with the approval by the Board of Education of the plan to allow Hawaiian-medium education on Ni'ihau. We also legally registered the 'Aha Pūnana Leo as a nonprofit organization and established our first Pūnana Leo site in Kekaha, Kaua'i, to serve the Ni'ihau population with others on a space-available basis. The following two Pūnana Leo, located in Hilo and then Honolulu, also focused on building around a core of existing Hawaiian-speaking children, this time of second-language-learner parents—basically our own children in Hilo and the Kawai'ae'a, Kaina, and Honda children in Honolulu. Thus, from its initiation the 'Aha Pūnana Leo has focused on developing education for native speakers of Hawaiian and the expansion of the native-speaker group by including other families interested in developing children who are dominant-Hawaiian speakers rather than simply teaching Hawaiian as a second-language skill.

After the Board of Education passed its new policy for Ni'ihau School, it discovered that a turn-of-the-century ban on teaching through the medium of Hawaiian remained on the books. Wilson and Beniamina then sought help from legislators such as Senator Clayton Hee, a Hawaiian studies graduate and now chair of the Office of Hawaiian Affairs, to remove the legal barriers to Hawaiian-medium public education. Beniamina led the effort to remove the ban on public education in Hawaiian which directly affected the Ni'ihau population. At the same time the entire 'Aha Pūnana Leo board and its parents, in bills developed by Wilson, sought legislative relief from legal obstacles to Hawaiian-medium private preschools and child care (see Warner, this volume). The legislative changes in public education aimed at the Ni'ihau community benefited not only Ni'ihau children, but all children in Hawai'i, opening statewide access to public education through Hawaiian.

After a three-year struggle the legislative changes were made, and the 'Aha Pūnana Leo began efforts to open new, now-legal preschool sites. However, the Department of Education did nothing to implement the law providing for Hawaiian-medium public education. On Ni'ihau, the local public school practice of using Hawaiian informally was now free from intervention, but no state support was given for Hawaiian materials. Furthermore, the Hawaiian-medium education needs of the new group of native speakers of Hawaiian such as our own children and other fluent speakers of Hawaiian matriculating from the now fully legal Pūnana Leo were completely ignored. Although in Honolulu some of these children, such as Kanani Kawaiʻaeʻa, were assigned by the Department of Education to bilingual education classes, in Hilo a boycott kindergarten that we came to call Ke Kula Kaiapuni Hawaiʻi (the Hawaiian Surrounding Environment School) was established in a room adjoining the Pūnana Leo O Hilo preschool program. We prepared to be arrested for our children's nonattendance at a public or private school if public Hawaiian-medium education was not provided our children. In the legislative session of that year, 1987, we introduced resolutions in the legislature for the Department of Education to implement the new law, and Senator Clayton Hee persuaded his former Senate colleague and then new Superintendent of Education, Charles Toguchi, to support the opening of Hawaiian-medium education in the public schools on the Kula Kaiapuni Hawaiʻi model in both Hilo and Honolulu. That summer the Board of Education approved this action and termed the program the Hawaiian Language Immersion Program. The first Pūnana Leo children then entered the public schools, taking the name Kula Kaiapuni Hawaiʻi from the Hilo site with them. That Hawaiian name spread to other sites, often in a shortened form, Kula Kaiapuni.[3]

Ironically, public Hawaiian-medium education gradually became codified as a program by the Department of Education for nonspeakers of Hawaiian rather than for Hawaiian-speaking children for whom the legislation was initiated (SB 2463–86, committee reports). The Hawaiian Language Immersion Program eventually received a coordinator position, an advisory council, and special funding, all lobbied for by the ʻAha Pūnana Leo and parents of children in the program. And yet, the suggestions of the advisory board and coordinator regarding special consideration for native speakers of Hawaiian were ignored by the Department of Education. Furthermore, the special funding was not extended to programs serving Niʻihau children, the explanation being that since all the children served were native speakers, they did not qualify for Hawaiian language immersion support. An ʻAha Pūnana Leo contention that Hawaiian speakers have a right to education through Hawaiian led to the filing of a suit by the Office of Hawaiian Affairs, at the request of the ʻAha Pūnana Leo. In the meantime, boycotts and demonstrations were used to assure new Hawaiian Language Immersion Program sites that would accommodate the Hawaiian-speaking children being produced in a growing number of Pūnana Leo throughout the state as well as all other children desiring to enroll in Hawaiian immersion programs. Four of the 11 Hawaiian Language Immersion Program streams began with boycotts in this way. Other sites began at the last minute under the threat of a boycott.[4]

As the ʻAha Pūnana Leo and the Hawaiian language programs of the University of Hawaiʻi at Hilo grew, the two entities formed a consortium to coordinate their activities, make maximum use of resources, and jointly seek grants. Funding has been obtained primarily through programs not originally designed for language revitalization purposes but which allow for the pursuit of particular goals without specifying a particular language. In writing our grants we focus on how our language revitalization program provides a unique means of reaching other goals. Our first major grant was with the Native Hawaiian Education Act, introduced by Hawaiʻi's congressional delegation, especially Senator Daniel Inouye. The consortium has developed into a core of educational programs, along with support programs and administrative offices, that includes eleven preschools and three model K–12 schools (designed to also include infant and preschool components). Map 13.1 shows the statewide locations of these schools as well as the support offices. Besides administrative offices, the support offices include curriculum development offices, telecommunication services, and a scholarship program for college students who pursue Hawaiian language either as a major field or in conjunction with another major.

The consortium partners are united in their philosophy and mission, which have been codified in a philosophical statement in Hawaiian called the Kumu Honua Mauli Ola. Within that philosophy, offices and programs serve as honua—distinct places where Hawaiian can thrive as a living language. Hawaiian is used as the language of operation in these offices as well as in the direct delivery of educational programs. While the administrative structures serve only the core educational programs of the consortium and its 800 or so students, most of the support programs serve all Kula Kaiapuni Hawaiʻi students, all second-language students of Hawaiian, all Hawaiian language and culture schools and organizations, and all individuals interested in the Hawaiian language. Thus, the consortium also provides books, videos, radio programming, computer services, newspapers, or scholarships to another 5,000 to 7,000 people in Hawaiʻi and elsewhere. Participation in the core programs is open and growing, and additional support and coordination are provided through outreach to other indigenous communities pursuing indigenous medium education.

CURRICULUM AND OUTCOMES

The core programs of the ʻAha Pūnana Leo are distinctive in that priority emphasis is placed on the maintenance and strengthening of the Hawaiian mauli in contrast to the emphasis on academic achievement simply for its own sake. This does not mean rejection of academics or isolation from other languages and cultures. On the contrary, academic knowledge is seen as an important tool in strengthening the mauli and providing new domains in which it can flourish. Indeed, the ʻAha Pūnana Leo seeks academic achievement above the norm found in English-medium schools and, as will be seen later, has been fairly successful in this regard. Similarly, in 'Aha Pūnana Leo programs, foreign languages and English are to be actively pursued in order for students to interact with those outside the community and to bring in new resources and knowledge to be adapted to the needs of the mauli. Interaction with those outside the community should bring honor and further support for the mauli. Such interaction includes competing in the areas of academics, sports, the arts, and service to the general population, but always as distinctive Hawaiian speakers with a distinctive Hawaiian upbringing and cultural approach.

The result of this philosophy is a stubborn insistence on total use of the indigenous language in in-group communication, a strong applied orientation in curriculum, and a sense of urgency to integrate Hawaiian language and culture into contemporary Hawaiian life. The philosophy is further accompanied by proactive efforts to confirm that Hawaiian language and culture can be, and must be allowed to be, used in contemporary Hawai'i on an equal basis with English language and culture for those choosing to do so. At the base of this thinking is a conviction that full use of Hawaiian on a basis equal to English will provide benefits equal to, or better than, those provided by the current monolingual-English orientation of Hawaiian speakers and latent Hawaiian speakers.

This philosophical orientation has grown out of the observation of the strength of the Hawaiian mauli among Hawaiian-speaking kūpuna and the Ni'ihau population compared to those not raised in the language. In the context of the extremely mixed racial background of the current Hawaiian population and strong Anglo-American ethnic assimilative forces in Hawai'i, the Hawaiian mauli is seriously threatened. For example, in a 1998 survey of Hilo High School, students were asked to designate 1 of 13 ethnicities with which they most identified. The largest ethnicity was Hawaiian at 26.1%. However, 24.9% of all students who indicated primary identification with a non-Hawaiian ethnicity also indicated that they had Hawaiian ancestry. Thus, while 51% of the students in the school were legally Native Hawaiian, essentially half of these Hawaiians identified strongly with another ethnic group.[5]

THE PŪNANA LEO LANGUAGE NESTS

The original concept of the Pūnana Leo language nest was to recreate an environment where Hawaiian language and culture were conveyed and developed in much the same way that they were in the home in earlier generations. Parents were told that this was not a school in the *haole,* or Anglo, sense, but a means to revitalize the language and to recreate, as much as possible, a traditional extended family in which children interacted with family members through Hawaiian. This family orientation was further reinforced by the schools' requirements of family participation, which was necessary to

keep them operational, and the ongoing political challenges faced by Pūnana Leo parents in establishing Hawaiian-medium education in both the public and private sectors.

As much as we wanted to recreate the extended family arrangement, it was very difficult to recreate the traditional activities, the typical life experiences of elders, in ocean and mountain areas. We decided to bring these activities to our programs as best we could through field trips, gardens, and cultural materials. We decided to use a physical boundary around the school that would define it as a Hawaiian space in contrast to an English space, and to insist that everyone, including parents and visitors, use only Hawaiian language and culture within that space.

We also realized that we needed a daily routine during the period the children occupied the space. Kamanā obtained early childhood certification and took a leave from the University of Hawai'i at Hilo to develop the program. She felt that the Montessori methodology had features that would support and facilitate our desire to use natural materials and experiences from the Hawaiian environment and steer away from commercial preschool materials. Other features of the curriculum that she developed focused consciously on Hawaiian family experiences, behaviors, and values—the proper way to interact with adults and other children, actions toward food and animals, spiritual interactions, and the important role of music and dance. Much, however, came from the fact that Hawaiian ways of acting were ingrained for our initial teachers, both native speakers and nonnative speakers, as they had been raised in traditional Hawaiian families.

A typical Pūnana Leo begins with 10 to 12 children aged three to five and has a school day from 7:30 to 5:00 Monday through Friday from September through July. The multiaged group allows for the retention of a number of children each year who help transmit the language to incoming students. Enrollment growth to 20 after the first year is common, and we have had up to 30 children at some sites. State regulations make it difficult to bring children under the age of two to a center such as a Pūnana Leo, and the 'Aha Pūnana Leo has not had the resources to serve children under three on a regular basis. We have experimented, however, with what we call Hui Hi'i Pēpē ("Baby Embracing Clubs") where mothers, along with their children from infancy to three, join with a teacher to learn Hawaiian and simple teaching strategies in preparation for the children's entering the Pūnana Leo. These have been successful but again are difficult to run given our present human and financial resource base.

The Pūnana Leo day begins with parents dropping off their children. There is a first circle in the morning, where the children participate in various activities such as singing and chanting, hearing a story, exercising, learning to introduce themselves and their families in a formal manner, discussing the day, or participating in some cultural activity. This is followed by free time, when children can interact with different materials to learn about textures, colors, sizes, and so on, and to use the appropriate language based on models provided by teachers and other children. Then come more structured lessons, which can include prereading and premath skills, social studies, and the arts. This is done in both large and small groups. Children then have outdoor play, lunch, and a nap, then story time, a snack, a second circle, and outdoor play until their parents come to pick them up again.

From the very first day a child enters the Pūnana Leo, only Hawaiian is used. When children do not yet understand, teachers and older children simply help them move through the daily routine. The routine provides a context for rapid understanding, and the group of fully Hawaiian-speaking second-year students provides a language-rich environment. The new children are also required to memorize formulaic statements such as asking permission to leave the lunch table, to go to the bathroom, and to carry out other daily activities. They are also instructed on how to introduce themselves and learn many songs. These memorized bits of language provide a base upon which to build spontaneous speech and interaction with the other children in Hawaiian on the playground and during free-choice activities. Usually children are using only Hawaiian in the Pūnana Leo within three to four months.

Another feature of the curriculum is family learning. All parents in Pūnana Leo are required to support the program through tuition (currently based on income), eight hours of in-kind service at the Pūnana Leo, attendance by a family member for at least one hour a week in a Hawaiian language class at the Pūnana Leo or elsewhere, and attendance at a monthly parent meeting. These features of the program are designed to further the goals of Hawaiian language revitalization which is an evolutionary process for families and requires demonstrated commitment and constant learning and involvement in self-governance.

Literacy in Hawaiian is a well-established feature of the lives of Hawaiian elders, many of whom learned to read Hawaiian at a very early age by chanting consonant-vowel combinations. When the Pūnana Leo began, this tradition was adapted to contemporary modifications of the orthography and taught to the children. At that time, however, there were no children's books in Hawaiian. So parents created books for their children using photographs of the child pasted to construction paper with a few lines written underneath. A number of English books that the Pūnana Leo thought appropriate were also brought to the school and "read" in Hawaiian, that is, shown to the children with the teacher providing narration in Hawaiian for the book's illustrations. This led to the next stage, which was to translate the story and paste the Hawaiian into the book over the English. Translation was not literal and even sometimes deviated considerably from the English in order to assure that Hawaiian culture and values, rather than haole ones, were emphasized.

Mathematical skills begin in the morning circle, where students count off the days of the month to the appropriate date and learn the names of the week, which are number-based in Hawaiian. They also learn patterns and number skills in independent work with pebbles, shells, seeds, and commercial plastic materials that are to be arranged creatively, graded in size, or ordered in numbered groups. Learning about the natural environment and cultural use of that environment forms the basis for science. Traditional Hawaiian culture, as well as information on the culture of the children's many other ancestors through song and stories, provides the basis for social sciences. Materials on the natural and indigenous cultural world of Hawaiʻi are difficult to obtain commercially and teachers and parents initially drew pictures and provided materials themselves. Even when materials on Hawaiʻi and Hawaiian culture are available commercially, the perspective is typically not from the Hawaiian culture, where the symbolism and association are often totally different from the haole perspective. This perspective is an essential feature of the Hawaiian language, culture, and worldview and must be integrated into all facets of teaching, including teaching about other cultures.

The Pūnana Leo is designed to matriculate children into Hawaiian-medium public schools, but because the state has not always been forthcoming with a Kula Kaiapuni Hawaiʻi in areas where a Pūnana Leo has been established, from its very inception the ʻAha Pūnana Leo has on several occasions had to declare a Pūnana Leo a public kindergarten and even 1st-grade site and then provide all instructors and materials for such programs. These boycott Kula Kaiapuni Hawaiʻi have always eventually been incorporated into the public school system as part of the Hawaiian Language Immersion Program.

Since its initial boycott program, the Pūnana Leo has developed a wide variety of original preschool, kindergarten, and early-elementary-school materials. These materials deal with traditional Hawaiian literature, the natural environment of Hawaiʻi, contemporary Hawaiian life, and other cultures. Among the topics are the origin stories of the Hawaiian islands and people, the mixture of different racial strains among the children, traditional food preparations, typical contemporary home and community life among Hawaiians, traditions and literature relating to animals and plants, assimilated Hawaiian cultural activities (including quilting, Hawaiian Christianity, and Hawaiian cowboy culture), the lives of other peoples in Hawaiʻi and throughout the world (especially indigenous peoples), and songs on topics ranging from pets to vacant lots, urban birds, and welcoming guests.

PŪNANA LEO CURRICULUM OFFICES

Today the ʻAha Pūnana Leo has two offices producing curriculum. One focuses on print curriculum, including original books, matching cards, posters, and translations of foreign language books (mostly English, but other languages as well). There is a gradation of printing, ranging from simply printing computerized translations on adhesive-backed paper to be provided to parents for them to paste into commercial books to machine-copied original books printed in different colors, to commercial products, including joint publishing with other language groups to provide commercial products in two or more languages. This office also prints materials for parents to use in establishing Hawaiian in the home such as labels for household items and cards on how to answer the telephone and write checks in Hawaiian. The 'Aha Pūnana Leo print media center is closely coordinated with the curriculum development efforts of the Hale Kuamo'o Hawaiian Language Center of Ka Haka 'Ula O Ke'elikōlani. The two centers have delineated separate responsibilities in terms of grade levels but also work in consortium, sharing university faculty, advanced student proofreaders, and other technical expertise along with the 'Aha Pūnana Leo's rapid publication, technical, and distribution system. Curriculum development is described in more detail later in the section on Ka Haka 'Ula O Ke'elikōlani.

The other 'Aha Pūnana Leo materials production office focuses on nonprint media, including videos of traditional activities, exercise, and other follow-along videos for children; animated traditional stories; and documentary information to use in work with parents and the community. These materials are often shown on cable and even commercial television in Hawai'i. Other aspects of the nonprint media include a Hawaiian radio program sponsored by the 'Aha Pūnana Leo and the extensive computer system, which it provides through a consortium with Ka Haka 'Ula O Ke'elikōlani (discussed below).

ACCOMPLISHMENTS OF THE PŪNANA LEO LANGUAGE NESTS

The most important accomplishments of the Pūnana Leo are its language revitalization accomplishments. The first of these has been the development of strong Hawaiian communicative and behavioral fluency among its matriculating five-year-old students. This fluency is further accompanied by personal self-confidence and a worldview that Hawaiian should be the normal language and daily culture of interaction for Hawai'i. Pūnana Leo students then come to see themselves, their parents, their peers, and other respected adults and children as seeking to restore this language for themselves and their community. The existence of the Pūnana Leo has encouraged and supported families who are raising their children in a totally Hawaiian-speaking home environment even before they reach the Pūnana Leo. Enrollment priority is given to such families as part of a system of basing enrollment on both cultivated and uncultivated involvement in Hawaiian language and culture.

Hawaiians in general, and those Hawaiians intensely in-

terested in language revitalization in particular, are spread throughout the general population of Hawai'i. The 'Aha Pūnana Leo has always opened its new sites based on a group of such families gathering together to request the establishment of a school, rather than simply opening a site at a particular location and advertising for enrollment. Typically, these families live in a number of adjoining elementary school districts but are drawn together by their strong Hawaiian cultural orientation and not infrequently by other points of communality, such as coming from the same family, cultural organization, or place of work.

While the 'Aha Pūnana Leo system of enrollment priorities runs contrary to the standard government criteria based on race, blood quantum, place of residence, and income level, the 'Aha Pūnana Leo enrollment priorities are essential for the traditional Hawaiian family orientation and language revitalization goals of the 'Aha Pūnana Leo.[6] Running the program on Pūnana Leo priorities has been made possible by combining government and nongovernment funding. In spite of 'Aha Pūnana Leo's rejection of blood quantum, income, and even race as determining enrollment in its programs, over 90% of students in its programs are of Hawaiian ancestry, with perceptually a higher average blood quantum than the Native Hawaiian population as a whole, and a high enrollment of those with low incomes.

The second language revitalization accomplishment of the Pūnana Leo is the development of an interconnected group of young parents involved in language revitalization. These young adults are learning Hawaiian (or increasing their knowledge when they are already speakers), using Hawaiian in formal public situations sponsored by the Pūnana Leo and gradually extending the use of Hawaiian in their private lives as well. Furthermore, the Pūnana Leo is producing parents who are experienced in providing in-kind and governing assistance to a joint language revitalization effort and are excited about the results that they have produced.

The third language revitalization accomplishment of the Pūnana Leo has been to produce statewide receptivity to the actualization of values and laws that provide for the broad public use of the Hawaiian language. This has been accomplished by establishing high-quality programs attended by families who are proud of their use of the Hawaiian language and who are using the language publicly. Families speak Hawaiian with their children in supermarkets and find that they are congratulated for doing so by individuals of all ethnic backgrounds; Pūnana Leo children are invited to sing in special programs in public malls, where their in-school procedure of using only Hawaiian in all introductions and explanations is not only allowed, but supported; Hawaiian-speaking children are also invited to participate through Hawaiian in the inauguration of officials in both the Hawaiian and the general community, where their presence emphasizes Hawai'i's strong identification with its indigenous roots. Most importantly, the Pūnana Leo provides a reason for the establishment of official use of Hawaiian in the state's public school system.

The language revitalization accomplishments of the Pūnana Leo are its most important, but the individual accomplishments of the Pūnana Leo families who make up the program give it its strength. As individuals, Pūnana Leo children matriculate into elementary school with a good body of formal Hawaiian cultural knowledge, including songs, chants and dances, traditional stories, history, and environmental knowledge that enhances their identity as Hawaiians. These cultural skills have the same value for personal development as the study of haole art and culture has for children of haole cultural orientation in haole-oriented preschools. The Pūnana Leo students also master many of the same skills children learn in haole preschools, including fine and gross motor skills, group interaction skills, literacy readiness, and an introduction to a broad range of academic areas, but from a Hawaiian base.

LOSS OF SOME STUDENTS TO OTHER SCHOOLS

The academic and cultural strengths of Pūnana Leo children have made Pūnana Leo graduates attractive to prestigious private schools in Hawai'i, and a few of our students have entered such schools immediately after preschool. Another group of students left Hawaiian-medium education at 6th grade, again primarily to attend private schools, where they often have to take an entrance test in competition with students from English-medium private and public schools. At the very least, the acceptance of these students into these schools and their subsequent accomplishments in such schools have shown that attending preschool and elementary school in Hawaiian does not harm students. Indeed, it could well be argued that the Pūnana Leo program provides an academic advantage. Another group of students enrolled in Hawaiian-medium intermediate and high school programs and then left to attend public school programs that offer a much larger variety of choices in terms of courses, resources, and social activities that is better tailored to their individual interests and talents.

Hawai'i has one of the highest private school attendance rates in the United States, with a strong tradition of enrollment of Hawaiians. Historically, these schools have frequently developed from boarding schools with strong English-language assimilation orientations that had a number of other similarities with the early boarding schools attended by American Indians. One of these institutions, Kamehameha, remains restricted to students of Hawaiian ancestry, and competition to enroll in this highly regarded college preparatory school is very keen. It is thus significant that Kula Kaiapuni Hawai'i students have a high rate of acceptance for enrollment into Kamehameha; indeed, 45% of those who applied to Kamehameha from the first cohort of Kaiapuni Hawai'i students were accepted, although not all enrolled.[7] Hawai'i is also rather small and densely populated, which allows high school students to move among the various public schools for academic and athletic purposes. It is therefore quite notable that families whose children enroll in it, even those who have been accepted by private institutions, are quite loyal to Hawaiian-medium education. This loyalty has been rewarded by the 'Aha Pūnana Leo by providing enrollment priority in its preschools to those with siblings who all continue in Hawaiian-medium education.

Because enrollments and academic performance are crucial in justifying the development of a new program, especially for the lead classes opening a new grade every year, loss of students to other schools creates considerable anguish during the period when a stream of students has not yet reached the 12th grade. The program has now had its first graduates, and furthermore, not one of the current 11 streams of Hawaiian-medium education has been denied vertical expansion owing to lack of sufficient students. Indeed, a number of students who have left the program have returned.

REVITALIZATION DIFFICULTIES WITHIN STANDARD PUBLIC SCHOOLS

Hawai'i's experience in integrating language revitalization into the public school system exemplifies difficulties discussed by Fishman (1991) for his type 4b schools, which are outside the control of the language revitalization community. Conflicts over management and language of operation have been serious obstacles to the maintenance and development of public Hawaiian-medium education as a language revitalization movement. Of the schools operating standard Hawaiian language immersion elementary programs, all but the K–12 stand-alone school Ke Kula Kaiapuni 'O Ānuenue began as Hawaiian streams within English-medium schools, and even Ānuenue is a collecting point for students from such streams on O'ahu Island at the higher grades. Furthermore, in spite of state recognition of the value of a fully fluent Hawaiian-speaking administration and staff, all standard Hawaiian Language Immersion Program sites to date have been administered by non-Hawaiian-speaking principals under non-Hawaiian-speaking district superintendents. The Hawaiian Language Immersion Program thus faces a problem in that its administrators lack full understanding of, and full participation in, Hawaiian language revitalization goals.

Principals have sometimes come to feel that the Hawaiian streams in their schools are an imposition, that the academic goals of their schools are being compromised by the Hawaiian stream, that the students in the Hawaiian-medium programs are being harmed socially by being educated solely in Hawaiian and solely with other Hawaiian speakers, and that

Hawaiian has little value in today's world other than for limited cultural events and purposes. Principals often have difficulty perceiving of Hawaiian as a general language of interaction, not only within the overall structure of the school, including the office, playground, cafeteria, and school assemblies, but even in the program-specific meetings of the Hawaiian Language Immersion Program faculty.

While contemporary Hawaiian-medium education in the public schools resulted from pressure from both members of the Ni'ihau community and Pūnana Leo families for legalization of use of Hawaiian in the education of their Hawaiian-speaking children, the Department of Education rapidly moved the focus of its Hawaiian Language Immersion Program from Hawaiian-speaking students to non-Hawaiian-speaking students. The initial year that parents of Pūnana Leo children were allowed to have their children educated in Hawaiian, the Department of Education stipulated that the Pūnana Leo would have to recruit other families into the program to assure that the standard teacher-student ratio would prevail. Since then all Hawaiian Language Immersion Program kindergartens have been approximately half non–Hawaiian speaking.

Because the initial group of English speakers was recruited by the 'Aha Pūnana Leo, the program began with strong solidarity among all families for language revitalization goals. Once Kula Kaiapuni Hawai'i became more solidly a part of the Department of Education, new policies relative to enrollment in the Hawaiian Language Immersion Program emerged. One policy placed priority on place of residence within the boundaries of the host English-medium school service area over entrance into the public school system as a Hawaiian-language speaker. This policy has had the effect of denying Hawaiian-speaking children living outside school boundaries the right to education through Hawaiian, a right the 'Aha Pūnana Leo sees as protected, along with other aspects of Native Hawaiian cultural practices in the Hawai'i Constitution, and one of the basic arguments used in lobbying the state for the initial opening of the Hawaiian Language Immersion Program.[8] Ironically, programs in public schools typically have been opened only after political pressure is applied by Pūnana Leo parents living on a particular side of an island. Once a program is opened, however, some Pūnana Leo children have then faced being denied enrollment owing to residency considerations. Fortunately, parental pressure, including demonstrations on occasion, has always resulted in the expansion of classes to accommodate all interested in the program, including Hawaiian-speaking children living outside school boundaries. However, parent lobbying and demonstrations for busing of children living outside the school bus routes of the regular service area boundaries have to date been unsuccessful. The 'Aha Pūnana Leo has been able to access grant funding to support busing in some years for some schools, notably Ke Kula Kaiapuni 'O Ānuenue, which faces the greatest busing difficulty. Other Hawaiian entities such as the Office of Hawaiian Affairs and Lili'uokalani Trust have also provided occasional support of this type.

The issue of mixing Hawaiian-speaking and English-speaking children and families is one of accommodation and assimilation. Language revitalization involves the accommodation and assimilation of English speakers to Hawaiian, as they have chosen to join the Hawaiian program. The nature of Department of Education operations has tended to reverse the focus. Instead of providing regular instruction to the Hawaiian-speaking children and giving the English speakers special help with Hawaiian, the language and educational growth needs of the Hawaiian-speaking children have often been put on hold while the entire class focuses on the need of the English-speaking children to learn some Hawaiian. The Pūnana Leo children have been expected to accommodate to this environment, which includes use of English outside class and sometimes even in class. As a consequence, in these situations, both the Hawaiian and the academic preparation of children from the Pūnana Leo begins to weaken and lapse. The Pūnana Leo parents have also been expected to accommodate and assimilate to the English-medium school culture, where parent education and involvement are much diminished and English is used in all communication with parents. Lack of attention to parent education by the department has resulted in new parents' putting their children in the program in kindergarten, sometimes simply as a novelty, without fully understanding the purposes, goals, and design of the program. Soon these parents, who are not oriented to language revitalization, are complaining about the focus on Hawaiian and expressing a desire for more English. Hawaiian Language Immersion Program sites too often have had conflicts erupting within parent groups and with the school administration relative to the program and its goals.

The lack of strong support for the primary position of the Hawaiian language in the enrollment of students in the Hawaiian Language Immersion Program has a parallel in teacher and staff hiring policies in the Program. Hawai'i's public schools still make no special provisions for Hawaiian fluency for teachers hired for the Hawaiian Language Immersion Program. Principals follow standard hiring practices and only use Hawaiian fluency as a criterion for hiring when two candidates are equal in certification status and seniority. This has led on occasion to the hiring of teachers with little or no functional ability in Hawaiian and the release of fluent non-certified teachers who have demonstrated skills in teaching. Principals sometimes assign the least fluent teachers to kindergarten "where the Pūnana Leo children can teach them Hawaiian," or even have teachers use English in kindergarten to "ease children into Hawaiian" or allow the use of English for "the harder subjects."

All of these practices and other features that subordinate the position of Hawaiian within the Department of Education weaken the program's language revitalization goals. The subordination of Hawaiian also has a negative effect on student achievement. The sites with the greatest student achievement are those with the strongest Hawaiian language orientation and Hawaiian language fluency and literacy skills among teachers, a situation that has parallels in New Zealand Māori-medium education (Tīmoti Kāretu, former Māori language commissioner, personal communication, 1999). In spite of the strong evidence provided administrators relative to the academic achievement of programs that are highly oriented to the Hawaiian language, administrators have a difficult time overcoming ingrained preconceptions that not only undervalue that which is Hawaiian, but also see things Hawaiian (especially when they are used in place of things English) as an impediment to achievement.

These ingrained feelings of many in the Department of Education that more emphasis should be put on English than Hawaiian have also been supported by the professional evaluation team that the department hired upon the initiation of its Hawaiian Language Immersion Program. The recommendation of the evaluation team after the first year of the program was that it begin transition to English at 20% of the day in the 3rd grade and then 50% of the day from grades 4 to 6 (Slaughter et al. 1988). This recommendation was met by stiff resistance from families oriented to 'Aha Pūnana Leo philosophy who wanted full Hawaiian-medium education through grade 12. After the second year of the program, and after receiving important input from the Canadian immersion expert Dr. Fred Genessee of Montreal's McGill University, the evaluation team changed its recommendation to include full Hawaiian immersion education until grades 5 and 6, where English would be used as a medium of instruction for as little as 45 minutes per day in a variety of subject areas focusing on English literacy. Genessee's 1988 positive evidence from Canadian immersion, which was reiterated in a paper written by Sam L. Warner for the Board of Education in 1990, along with extensive annual lobbying by parents strongly oriented to language revitalization who were determined to maintain full Hawaiian-medium education through grade 12, had an effect on the Board of Education. The board's policy decisions eventually went beyond the recommendations of the evaluation team. In 1992, in a series of motions, the board voted to allow full use of Hawaiian through grade 12, the teaching of English for one hour a day beginning in grade 5 without restrictions on use of Hawaiian as the medium of instruction in the teaching of English, and the establishment of two totally Hawaiian-medium school sites, one in Honolulu and the other in Hilo. Later, the evaluation team reverted to recommendations that the decision to introduce English in the 5th grade be reconsidered, that the value of establishment of single Hawaiian-medium sites be reconsidered, and that English be used as a primary medium of instruction from intermediate school on (Slaughter et al. 1994, 1997). The evaluation team was also consistently crit-ical of teaching English through the medium of Hawaiian, such as occurs at Ke Kula 'O Nāwahīokalani'ōpu'u, insisting that such an approach could not work well in spite of the evidence to the contrary.[9]

THE QUESTION OF ENGLISH

The question of English has thus been the primary political issue in the Hawaiian Language Immersion Program. The strongest language revitalization stance has been to demand reestablishment of full Hawaiian-medium education to assure a means of quality academic and cultural development for Hawaiian speakers and a means for others to assimilate to the Hawaiian-speaking community, where English would be a highly developed second language taught in accordance with the latest internationally developed methods. The most conservative stance has been to defend maintenance of the position of English as the dominant language of education, even for first-language speakers of Hawaiian, as a means to assure quality academic preparation and access to an English-dominated society on a level similar to that of Anglo-American native speakers of English, possibly with some form of Hawaiian as cultural enrichment. The lines of struggle between these two positions were even evident in the Hawaiian and English names assigned to the program. Kula Kaiapuni Hawai'i was chosen to indicate that the program was totally Hawaiian in all aspects of instruction, staffing, and administration, with preference for native-speaker children and strict requirements of parents. Kula Kaiapuni Hawai'i was used for the 'Aha Pūnana Leo boycott program before the official adoption of the term Hawaiian Language Immersion Program. The term "immersion" was adopted in Hawai'i from programs in Canada and the continental United States designed primarily for second-language learning by majority language–dominant speakers learning a minority language, rather than minority students reestablishing an educational system through their nearly exterminated traditional language. Furthermore, most of these traditional immersion programs transition to majority language programs in intermediate and high school, which contrasted with the desire of language revitalization advocates for full K–12 Hawaiian-medium education. It is therefore important that if the word "immersion" is used for programs such as Kula Kaiapuni Hawai'i, indigenous immersion be clearly differentiated from foreign-language immersion (for learning languages unconnected to the personal identity of students) and also heritage immersion (for immigrant groups with thriving languages elsewhere).

The 'Aha Pūnana Leo language revitalization position of supporting and creating new native speakers was advanced through the activism of parents in the political arena, while the transition and second-language enrichment positions were taken by lower-level Department of Education staff and provided support by the reports of the evaluation team. The delineation of the struggle was rather clear from the beginning, given the historical context of the politically based closure of Hawaiian-medium schools and the four years of political struggle in the legislature to get into the public schools. The lines were further clarified when the department staff member given charge of the program stated to us who were preparing curriculum on our own that this program, like some others in the past, was a political creation and destined to end in a few years. Further instructions from this individual that Hawaiian literacy was not to be taught showed a determination to limit the development of Hawaiian, as did the restriction of special state funding of the program to the hiring of an evaluation team, with no funds for materials development. The lack of funding for materials for the use of Hawaiian in Ni'ihau school thus was also applied to the new program for Pūnana Leo graduates, but the 'Aha Pūnana Leo obtained private funding and developed materials anyway and provided them to the schools against the wishes of the official in charge.

While the evaluation team may have seen its role as to assure maximum success in both language learning and academics, they found themselves in the middle of the political battle by insisting in their first-year recommendations that the program be recognized as "bilingual" in their report's discussion of "transition to English." This produced very real fears that the replacement of Hawaiian with English, which was already occurring with the Ni'ihau children in the bilingual program on Kaua'i, would be reproduced with the Pūnana Leo children. These fears never completely disappeared and resulted in an ongoing struggle with the evaluation team to assure the maintenance of Hawaiian as the full medium of education. This led to further efforts in the political arena which were ultimately successful in assuring full Hawaiian-medium schools.

Consistent Board of Education and Superintendent of Education support of full Hawaiian-medium education has been important in that it has allowed parents, such as those oriented to 'Aha Pūnana Leo philosophy, to seek full Hawaiian language revitalization and maintenance for their families. Such support has not precluded support for teaching Hawaiian as enrichment for other families. The reality of the Department of Education has been that even though the state policy calls for full use of Hawaiian, principals have allowed the use of English at earlier grades and in the teaching of some subjects. We believe, however, that if state policy did not allow full use of Hawaiian, full use of Hawaiian would not occur in the public schools. Regardless of the policies of the Board of Education, the only fully state-established totally Hawaiian-medium site has been Ke Kula Kaiapuni 'O Ānuenue on O'ahu. Ānuenue also remains the only fully state-established program offering totally Hawaiian-medium education in intermediate and high school. All other Hawaiian language–medium intermediate and high school

programs overseen by the Department of Education are streams within large English-medium schools consisting of a number of courses taught through Hawaiian that supplement a predominantly English-medium program of requirements and electives. All separate sites other than Ānuenue using a totally Hawaiian medium for a K–12 program were initiated by the 'Aha Pūnana Leo and are operated in partnership with the state as described below.

The issues and resource needs involved in serious revitalization of Hawaiian as a community language and even Hawaiian language–medium teaching for enrichment purposes require major changes that are difficult to make in a large statewide system in which Hawaiian-medium programs serve but a tiny fraction of students. The Hawai'i State Department of Education is to be commended for providing recognition and shouldering support for three different population groups within the listed purposes of its Hawaiian Language Immersion Program: (1) native speakers wishing to maintain their language, (2) those wishing to integrate into the Hawaiian-speaking population, and (3) those wishing to learn Hawaiian as a second or third language along the lines of foreign-language learning (Long-Range Plan of the Hawaiian Language Immersion Program, 1994). Much of the conflict in Hawaiian-medium education might be reduced by development of differentiated programs of choice focusing on the needs of these three populations as well as parental desire for Hawaiian relative to English, for example, strongly Hawaiian–medium programs, programs that are partially Hawaiian medium and partially English medium, and programs that are English medium with strong Hawaiian-as-a-second-language courses. The 'Aha Pūnana Leo has always tried to work together with the department to assure that shared goals of the two institutions for programs serving all three populations could be met in moving Hawaiian-medium programs forward. More recently, this has led to an effort to develop new structures that could accommodate the distinctive features of families oriented strongly to language revitalization in groups (1) and (2) above within the context of state funding and the 'Aha Pūnana Leo as an administrative entity along the lines of Fishman's 4a schools.

While supporting the desires of those who wish to remain in the standard structure as streams in English-medium schools, or who wish to create alternative structures focusing on enrichment through Hawaiian as second language, or who wish to pursue other methods, strategies, or structures, the 'Aha Pūnana Leo has focused on and pursued the creation of a new, more highly language revitalization–oriented model for those families who desire it. This cooperative model, involving the partnering of the state Department of Education, the Ka Haka 'Ula O Ke'elikōlani College of Hawaiian Language, and the 'Aha Pūnana Leo, is based somewhat on the experience of the American Indian contract schools and charter schools in other states. Movement toward that structure is illustrated by Ke Kula 'O Nāwahīokalani'ōpu'u and programs reproduced along the same lines at Ke Kula Niʻihau O Kekaha and Ke Kula ʻO Samuel Mānaiakalani Kamakau. As these structures are stabilizing, efforts are being made to include external experts in educational methods who wish to assist in further developing academic and other goals. But such development is always done with the understanding that the framework of language and culture revitalization is not to be compromised.

NĀWAHĪOKALANIʻŌPUʻU LABORATORY SCHOOL

Ke Kula ʻO Nāwahīokalaniʻōpuʻu represents a milestone in the struggle of the ʻAha Pūnana Leo to assure the realization of federal and state laws recognizing the right of Native Hawaiians to choose Hawaiian as the daily language of their families and to extend that into government-supported education. At Nāwahīokalaniʻōpuʻu there is an explicit understanding that use of the Hawaiian language has priority over use of English within the context of, and with the support of, Hawaiʻi's compulsory education system. The school further validates the claim of the ʻAha Pūnana Leo that it is possible to have high achievement recognized on an international level within the context of an institution where such achievement is second in priority to linguistic and cultural survival. Indeed, as we will see later, academic achievement at Nāwahīokalaniʻōpuʻu is higher than the Native Hawaiian norm in the English-medium public school in its service area.

Ke Kula ʻO Nāwahīokalaniʻōpuʻu is an institutionalization of the boycott schools that the Pūnana Leo has run in order to assure state provision of education through Hawaiian. The initiation of Ke Kula ʻO Nāwahīokalaniʻōpuʻu differed from the typical boycott school in that it began at the intermediate school level when the Department of Education did not provide a separate Hawaiian Language Immersion Program site in Hilo, as promised by the State Board of Education in conjunction with the establishment of Ke Kula Kaiapuni ʻO Ānuenue on Oʻahu. More importantly, however, Nāwahīokalaniʻōpuʻu changed the paradigm in that the state provided resources for the running of the school in spite of the fact that it was located on property controlled by the ʻAha Pūnana Leo, and its daily operations were developed primarily by the ʻAha Pūnana Leo rather than exclusively by the State Department of Education. The powers of the ʻAha Pūnana Leo within Nāwahīokalaniʻōpuʻu have been further facilitated by the state legislature's declaring Nāwahīokalaniʻōpuʻu "and other sites as appropriate" as the laboratory school program of Ka Haka ʻUla O Keʻelikōlani College of Hawaiian Language and requiring that Ka Haka ʻUla O Keʻelikōlani work in cooperation with the ʻAha Pūnana Leo.

The distinctive administrative powers of the ʻAha Pūnana Leo and Ka Haka ʻUla O Keʻelikōlani vis-à-vis the Department of Education have facilitated curriculum content at Nāwahīokalaniʻōpuʻu that is more language revitalization–oriented and distinct from the English-medium school norms than that at other Hawaiian-medium sites. However, because Nāwahīokalaniʻōpuʻu is still in transition from a Department of Education school to a full University of Hawaiʻi laboratory school, it must follow the standard Department of Education curriculum guidelines and requirements in its choice of course offerings. Furthermore, because of its small size, all students at Nāwahīokalaniʻōpuʻu must take the same courses, with prescribed courses in place of electives. The school has felt that a college preparatory curriculum would best serve the interests of Hawaiian language revitalization by having Hawaiian speakers highly educated to protect and develop their community. This includes excellent skills in English, but English from the perspective of a second rather than a first language. The school also has distinctive block scheduling of 80-minute classes, a longer school day, uniforms, and an applied focus for all students through its sustainable-environment program in agriculture, aquaculture, horticulture, and animal husbandry.

The college preparatory focus of Nāwahīokalaniʻōpuʻu has been lessened by a number of the required department courses such as guidance, community service, and practical arts, whose content the ʻAha Pūnana Leo and Ka Haka ʻUla O Keʻelikōlani administrations feel can be systematically covered through the everyday activities of the school. Also vexing to language revivalists is the classification of Hawaiian language arts classes as second-language courses. Yet Nāwahīokalaniʻōpuʻu has been successful in establishing the Hawaiian language as the medium for all courses and its use as a factor in grading in all courses.

The curriculum materials used at Nāwahīokalaniʻōpuʻu are produced primarily by the Hale Kuamoʻo Language Center of Ka Haka ʻUla O Keʻelikōlani and by the teachers themselves. Indeed, curriculum development is a primary responsibility of those hired at the school under the ʻAha Pūnana Leo. Reference materials are primarily standard English ones, although at present the library at Nāwahīokalaniʻōpuʻu has fewer than 200 books, and the materials available to teachers in their classrooms are very basic. On the other hand, the school makes extensive use of technology and the highly developed Leokī Hawaiian computer system, described below. In addition, the sustainable-environment site includes an *imu* (traditional ground oven) and other outdoor equipment necessary for the production and preparation of traditional Hawaiian foods and arts as well as an extensive traditional agriculture and indigenous-species environmental complex. The focus on application of knowledge to daily life is important from a language revitalization perspective in that students are being prepared to make their homes in the local community and make their contribution to it and its economy as Hawaiian speakers. This focus contrasts with the typical situation in Hawaiʻi private and public schools, where students are encouraged to open their horizons to the "whole world" (in actuality, only to the possibility of living in other states). Those with academic talent are often discouraged from studying Hawaiian topics, areas often viewed as parochial and restrictive, and encouraged to pursue further education without any preparation for them to return to the community. One result of such practices has been an extensive brain drain in the Hawaiian community.

ACADEMIC SUCCESS OF NĀWAHĪOKALANI'ŌPU'U

The priority focus of the 'Aha Pūnana Leo and Ka Haka 'Ula O Ke'elikōlani on language revitalization has not had a negative effect on student achievement, including achievement in English. Indeed, the opposite seems to be the case. In the 1998–99 school year, the 77 students of Nāwahīokalani'ōpu'u were counted among the 1,737 students at Hilo High School, yet this small group (34 of whom were actually intermediate school students) garnered a disproportionate number of academic and other achievements in the Hilo area. For example, of the 100 prestigious Bank of Hawai'i Second Century Scholarships offering up to $10,000 per year for four years of college for outstanding 10th-graders statewide, Nāwahīokalani'ōpu'u students received two. Nāwahīokalani'ōpu'u students took first place in a statewide computerized stock market game, and a Nāwahīokalani'ōpu'u student was chosen to be the vice president of the statewide Native Hawaiian Youth Legislature. Nāwahīokalani'ōpu'u students won the Hilo High musical talent contest for both 1997–98 and 1998–99, and Nāwahīokalani'ōpu'u students were a major presence on Hilo High athletic teams, with two of its girls' volleyball players named to the island all-star team in 1998–99.

Perhaps most significant is the fact that all five members of Nāwahīokalani'ōpu'u's first senior class were also admitted as concurrently enrolled high school students at the University of Hawai'i at Hilo; only one other student from Hilo High School was allowed to attend university classes while still in high school that year. By their junior year of high school, the entire class had completed all but two courses needed to graduate under Department of Education regulations. The students enrolled in two courses each in the fall semester and one course each in the spring semester. During the 1999–2000 year, Nāwahīokalani'ōpu'u students continued to excel, with early enrollment in university and community college courses extended to the junior year, and students won a number of additional academic, artistic, and athletic awards.

There has always been concern outside Nāwahīokalani'ōpu'u that the school's students would have difficulty with English, especially scientific and mathematical language. It thus may have come as something of a surprise to detractors that all five of the initial seniors passed the university's English composition assessment examination. This same examination often presents considerable difficulty to graduates of Hawai'i's English-medium public high schools, especially Hawaiian students. Furthermore, the Nāwahīokalani'ōpu'u seniors reported no difficulty using English in their college courses, which have included such subjects as political science, agriculture, mathematics, horticulture, Hawaiian, and Japanese. Their grades bore this out—virtually all As and Bs, with only a single student earning a C in a single class. All seniors continued on to college.

The success of these Nāwahīokalani'ōpu'u seniors in functioning in a college environment in English supports the contention of the 'Aha Pūnana Leo that much of the poor achievement of Native Hawaiian youth in English-medium schools is owing to resistance, conscious or unconscious, to the subjugation in Hawai'i's schools of Hawaiian identity and culture to haole identity and culture. Certainly, the reason for Native Hawaiian difficulties in school elsewhere cannot be owing to their Hawaiian cultural backgrounds. The first class of Nāwahīokalani'ōpu'u seniors has been educated totally through the Hawaiian language and from a very explicitly Hawaiian cultural base. They received training in English for only one course per semester beginning in the 5th grade, and all their English instruction since then has been through Hawaiian. Furthermore, two of the students were essentially monolingual speakers of Hawaiian until elementary school.

MORE ON THE QUESTION OF ENGLISH

Because the 'Aha Pūnana Leo approach to teaching English as a second language has been so much at odds with the suggestions of the Hawaiian Language Immersion Program evaluation team, it may be appropriate to discuss the philosophical basis behind the 'Aha Pūnana Leo approach. The 'Aha Pūnana Leo provides an environment for those who seek to change their families and communities—that is, it seeks to reestablish Hawaiian as the first language of families and communities with high-level skills in other languages. This approach is based on the practices of small countries and regions of countries such as the Netherlands and its Frisian region, and Denmark and its Faeroe Islands. In these countries and regions daily activities including education are carried out in the respective local language. The local schools produce high levels of academic achievement, including a high level of literacy in English as a second language, often with a third language learned as well. Such a model is legally recognized for Native American languages, including Hawaiian, in the Native American Languages Act (see Arnold, this volume). In following this approach, the 'Aha Pūnana Leo has sought to support and establish schools and associated communities that, as much as possible, reproduce the model of full use of the indigenous language as a first language, even if the community has not completed the process of reversing language shift from English back to Hawaiian. The Department of Education and its evaluation team have stressed the fact that the majority of students in Hawaiian-medium education are first-language speakers of English and that the current situation in their communities is English dominance, if not in terms of daily community interpersonal interaction, then at least in terms of the larger organization of the political units of their society. The evaluation team focus has thus been on maintaining the status quo, with the addition of fluency in Hawaiian as a second language for enrichment rather than reversing language shift.

The 'Aha Pūnana Leo, however, is making progress in reversing the positions of English and Hawaiian in its offices, homes, and schools. The first step in doing so is to change attitudes. The successful teaching of English through Hawaiian has considerable importance in solidifying such attitudes in students, teachers, and families. Furthermore, this attitude toward language revitalization—that English is a useful tool for dealing with those outside the community—contrasts with the sort of negative attitude that one sometimes hears expressed in monolingual English–speaking Hawaiian communities relative to English—that English has been forced upon the community by outsiders and that to speak its standard version well is a sign of acceptance of a sort of defeat. A survey by the Department of Education evaluation team itself gave evidence for a more positive attitude toward learning English among Hawaiian immersion students than among students in English-medium programs (Slaughter et al. 1997).

STANDARDIZED TESTS AND THE COMMUNITY SERVED

The achievements of Nāwahīokalani'ōpu'u students must also be understood within the context of their community. The Hilo area has a household median income about $14,000 lower than the state average, over twice as many households on public assistance than the state average, and over 10 times the number of children considered at risk than the state average. The Hawaiian Language Immersion Program feeding Nāwahīokalani'ōpu'u is located at Keaukaha Elementary, a school serving primarily children from Keaukaha Hawaiian Homelands, an area reserved for lessees of half or more Hawaiian ancestry. Keaukaha Elementary students generally perform below average at Hilo High School and have a below-average percentage of students who continue on to college and an above-average percentage of students who drop out. No students have dropped out of school from Nāwahīokalani'ōpu'u, although some have transferred to other schools for various reasons. There is strong interest in attending college among all students at Nāwahīokalani-'ōpu'u, even though most of the children come from families whose parents had not attended college prior to enrolling their children in the program.[10] Indeed, over one-third of the students come from economic circumstances that qualify them for free school lunches, and a few have learning disabilities that would qualify them for special assistance in the English-medium schools.

The scores of Nāwahīokalani'ōpu'u students on standardized tests, as shown in Figure 13.1, have not been as impressive as the coursework they have completed in high school and college, but they still compare well with the scores from the English-medium schools which the students would otherwise attend. In general, standardized test scores of Nāwahīokalani'ōpu'u students have a lower percentage of students in the below-average category and also sometimes a lower percentage of students in the above-average category than the national average. There is, however, considerable variation between the classes, which can be accounted for in part by the exaggerated role of individuals in determining class averages in classes of fewer than 20 students. It should be noted that a comparison of Nāwahīokalani'ōpu'u students with Hawaiian students at Hilo Intermediate School and Hilo High School would likely show a greater difference in scores because Hawaiians at these schools often have lower scores than do other ethnicities on such examinations (Carole Ishimaru [Hilo High School Vice Principal for Nāwahīokalani'ōpu'u], personal communication, 2000). At Keaukaha Elementary School, which is predominantly Hawaiian, chil-

	Below average (%)	Average (%)	Above average (%)
National average (all grades)			
Reading	23	54	23
Math	23	54	23
Grade 10, Hilo High			
Reading	22	59	19
Math	24	60	16
Grade 10, Nāwahīokalani'ōpu'u			
Reading	0	80	20
Math	0	60	40
Grade 8, Hilo Intermediate			
Reading	32	48	20
Math	31	57	12
Grade 8, Nāwahīokalani'ōpu'u			
Reading	23	69	8
Math	23	69	8

FIGURE 13.1   1996–97 SAT scores for Nāwahīokalani'ōpu'u

dren in the Hawaiian Immersion Program stream generally score higher than those in the English-medium stream on the 6th-grade SAT even though the Hawaiian-medium students have no formal exposure to English until reaching their one-hour daily 5th-grade course in English language arts.

The fact that standardized examinations are administered in English and are based on North American cultural contexts may reduce the number of Nāwahīokalani'ōpu'u student scores in the above-average category. This possibility was a significant factor in Ka Haka 'Ula O Ke'elikōlani College's arguing for the university to admit Nāwahīokalani'ōpu'u students on the same criteria as foreign students, who are not expected to score well on American standardized tests and yet usually perform well at the university. The fact that standardized examinations do not test what is taught as higher-level knowledge at Nāwahīokalani'ōpu'u—traditional Hawaiian oratory and literature, the application of science and mathematics to agriculture and aquaculture, and unique features of Hawaiian life and society—may be another factor in reducing the percentage of above-average scores on standardized examinations. Another possible factor is that Nāwahīokalani'ōpu'u is a new school just beginning to develop, where students from a wide range of abilities are accommodated in a single class and the teaching staff is mostly young people, some of whom have yet to complete certification or even a bachelor's degree. As the school grows and develops, development that includes a plan to integrate juniors and seniors into Hawaiian-medium general education courses to be offered in the Ka Haka 'Ula O Ke'elikōlani College of Hawaiian Language, the number of students scoring above average on standardized tests may increase. Among the areas that are targeted for development is methodology for teaching English to Hawaiian speakers, including improved methods of teaching spelling, an area of weakness reported in Canadian immersion that has also occurred in Hawaiian-medium education. Increased fluency in Hawaiian, however, remains the highest priority, and special work is needed in this area with incoming intermediate students.

MAULI AND THE ISSUE OF CULTURE AT NĀWAHĪOKALANI'ŌPU'U

The 'Aha Pūnana Leo does not consider its revitalization efforts to be confined to the use of Hawaiian vocabulary and sentence structure. Hawaiian language is seen as but a part of a fuller aspect of cultural continuity and individual identity described as mauli. Some features of mauli are covered by the English word "culture," but mauli also includes worldview, spirituality, physical movement, morality, personal relationships, and other central features of a person's life and the life of a people. Furthermore, while the English term "culture" often denotes something that can be separated from life and demonstrated, mauli is seen as something that is al-

ways a part of a person and his or her way of living and also of a group of people and its way of living. In this sense, language and mauli are closely related, as language is always with us in the thought processes in which we view the world and act out our thoughts. The Kumu Honua Mauli Ola educational philosophy thus sees language as the essential feature in maintaining and increasing the strength of the mauli and keeping culture from being simply the public display of physical articles and activities which lack the soul of being truly lived as part of daily life in contemporary Hawai'i.

The mauli-oriented view of Hawaiian culture found at Nāwahīokalani'ōpu'u, along with the use of Hawaiian language and culture approaches to teach what are popularly, and we would say incorrectly, identified as non-Hawaiian areas, such as mathematics and science, have led some in Hawai'i to state that Nāwahīokalani'ōpu'u is a Hawaiian language program but not a Hawaiian culture program. Such a view accepts the Western categorization of language as separate from culture and can be related to the fact that the easily observed physical manifestations of Hawaiian culture at Nāwahīokalani'ōpu'u are not distinctly separated from what appears to outsiders to be non-Hawaiian features. The situation is similar to that of early efforts by some photographers of Hawaiians. The Hawaiian person might be asked to replace "unauthentic" clothing such as a mu'umu'u, the Hawaiian woman's dress adopted after Western contact, with a more "authentic" pā'ū or sarong. The "authentic" clothing might, however, be used in a Western way, for example, as a costume provided to be worn by several people and with colors chosen for their eye appeal, while the "unauthentic" mu'umu'u it replaced would have been worn in a Hawaiian way, including kapu or restrictions on its use and handling and possibly color symbolism unique to that person's family.

The morning assembly at Nāwahīokalani'ōpu'u is an example of how "culture" is integrated as part of the mauli of Nāwahīokalani'ōpu'u. Students and staff line up at the front of the school and begin with a number of chants. The chants are then followed by the singing of Hawai'i's state song, "Hawai'i Pono'ī," while the students face the Hawaiian flag, and an address is given in Hawaiian to students regarding the activities of the day. Students and faculty are wearing uniforms, with the males to the right and the females to the left. The only thing obviously Hawaiian to an observer would be the chant and the language. However, the alignment of students and teachers follows Hawaiian traditions regarding the concepts of male and female space as well as genealogical ordering. A dried lei above the hallway dividing the two groups has significance as the piko or navel of the school, which is associated with unique events in the school year. Even the physical location of the flag has meaning within Hawaiian traditions.

Furthermore, use of uniforms does not simply follow a trend seen in other states, but is related to Hawaiian concepts of unity in body decoration sought in activities of importance, be they in the traditional Hawaiian school, called the *hālau* or in contemporary manifestations of that ideal in family dress in a *lūʻau* for special occasions. The words spoken, both in the chants and in the address to students, furthermore, contain references to oral traditions and Hawaiian beliefs in addition to the simple remarks regarding the day's activities. These words also provide access to multiple meanings or *kaona* that exist at a deeper level of the symbolic structure of the activities opening the school day.

The mauli approach to student interaction found at the opening of the day at Nāwahīokalaniʻōpuʻu is included in all activities of the school, including classroom teaching of standard subjects. While not readily observable by those unfamiliar with the symbolism and thinking behind how courses are taught, this mauli approach is the essential cultural feature of the running of the school. This is not to say that the more stereotypical features of Hawaiian culture are not part of Nāwahīokalaniʻōpuʻu. All students learn Hawaiian hula and Hawaiian music as well as Hawaiian crafts and participate in the cultivation of traditional Hawaiian foods and their preparation. Furthermore, students learn traditional Hawaiian poetry and literature along with studies of their own genealogies and those of important Hawaiian *aliʻi* or chiefs. Students also participate in field trips to culturally important sites outside the school that are related to these activities.

The cultural features of Nāwahīokalaniʻōpuʻu, however, are not learned as "culture" in the sense that Hawaiian culture is a clearly delineated separate class or extracurricular activity in other schools. Chant, music, dance, crafts, and the natural world are instead integrated into the full life of the school. Along with opening the school day, chants are used to ask permission to enter a particular area and to welcome visitors. Traditional foods are prepared to feed gatherings of students and parents at the school. The craft of making feather leis is taught so that students will be able to prepare a lei that will be worn by seniors at graduation, with different parts of the lei symbolizing particular aspects in the ceremony. Traditional musical instruments are made for particular dances with special meanings relative to the school and its community, beyond the purpose of simple musical accompaniment.

In contemporary Hawaiʻi, where much of Hawaiian culture has been used commercially either to entertain tourists or to provide educational insight into the physical appearance of precontact Hawaiʻi, Nāwahīokalaniʻōpuʻū's approach to Hawaiian culture is often difficult to place within the typical public understanding of Hawaiian culture. Furthermore, Nāwahīokalaniʻōpuʻū's incorporation of cultural features from 19th-century Hawaiian life, such as Hawaiian stringed-instrument music and the muʻumuʻu, and indeed its teaching of mathematics and science in Hawaiian as in the early Hawaiian-medium schools, seems un-Hawaiian to some who come from a perspective that only precontact Hawaiian cul-

ture involving stone tools, wood, and bark cloth is truly Hawaiian.

The mental placement of Hawaiian culture in an "uncontaminated" past focusing on the outward physical manifestations of the culture rather than its inner meaning runs directly counter to the concept and practice of *mauli ola*, or living mauli, cultivated at Nāwahīokalaniʻōpuʻu. Such a Western representation of Hawaiian culture is also in direct opposition to a Hawaiian tradition of viewing activities, materials, and meanings from a genealogically developed perspective which gives them an origin in a history of named ancestors from the beginning of time. This genealogical perspective is how Hawaiian culture has been passed down through the generations and how significant changes that occurred in precontact as well as postcontact times were integrated into the lives of the people in a Hawaiian manner. The Hawaiian-speaking elders in Hawaiian families, including those of Kamanā and other members of the ʻAha Pūnana Leo board, themselves approached everything that they did, from maintaining the family laundry to attending church, from Hawaiian medicine to family celebrations, in a distinctive Hawaiian manner. This distinctive Hawaiian manner, the Hawaiian mauli, uses indigenous and introduced materials in an integrated fashion based on Hawaiian beliefs and evolving family traditions that are quite distinct from Western beliefs.[11]

REVITALIZATION PROGRESS AT NĀWAHĪOKALANIʻŌPUʻU

The academic and other achievements described earlier are not the reason for Nāwahīokalaniʻōpuʻū's unique existence. Instead, they are by-products of the effort to maintain and strengthen the Hawaiian mauli using especially the unique powers inherent within the Hawaiian language. Language and culture revitalization is a much more difficult and complex goal than academic achievement. Nāwahīokalaniʻōpuʻu still has a considerable way to go before reaching its goal of full natural use of Hawaiian as the preferred language of students and their families in all aspects of their daily lives based in the Hawaiian mauli. At present, Hawaiian is the full operational language among faculty and staff at Nāwahīokalaniʻōpuʻu. The two exceptions are Department of Education staff members who do not normally interact directly with students, but who are fully supportive of the language revitalization goals of the school and who bring important skills to the school which are unavailable at present among fluent Hawaiian speakers. Hawaiian is used as the language of all teacher meetings and by the secretary and support staff. Hawaiian is also used in formal school assemblies with parents where the minority of parents who understand the language fluently translate for those who do not. All students at Nāwahīokalaniʻōpuʻu make full use of Hawaiian in all formal aspects of their education, such as use of the language in class, assemblies, and speeches, but English still dominates their peer-group interaction in most situations as well as in their family life, with the exception of a few totally Hawaiian-speaking families. Teachers at Nāwahīokalani'ōpu'u have indicated that the difficulties experienced in maintaining Hawaiian in an elementary program that is a stream within an English-medium school have a subsequent impact on the use of Hawaiian at Nāwahīokalani'ōpu'u as students matriculate from such a program to a totally Hawaiian campus. An effort is therefore being made to develop a small elementary program to model practices that would strengthen peer-group use of Hawaiian and Hawaiian mauli, practices that could be copied by other elementary schools, as well as providing a strong Hawaiian-speaking core group for the intermediate and high school program in the future.

Currently, where Hawaiian is most often used at the initiation of students is not on campus, but in Hawaiian cultural situations such as when students visit the taro-growing area of Waipi'o, the island of Kaho'olawe, and other cultural excursions. This shows that the Hawaiian language is increasingly being identified as an essential feature of Hawaiian culture among these students. Students report that they feel that speaking Hawaiian is more natural in such situations than in their daily lives, an indication that students are still affected by a worldview that highly marks Hawaiian language and culture as not part of the normal day-to-day activities of contemporary Hawaiians. A movement toward use of Hawaiian in ordinary activities of daily life is evident among some graduates of the school, perhaps in imitation of their young college-age teachers who use the language with each other in all situations outside of school. Students also use Hawaiian when they are with each other in unfamiliar social situations where Hawaiian seems to bind them together and distinguish them from outsiders. Siblings who speak Hawaiian at all times at home also use Hawaiian at all times with each other regardless of the activity or the presence of others, but code switch to English with others in the same group even when all are Nāwahīokalani'ōpu'u students and thus capable of using Hawaiian. This shows the strong influence of establishing Hawaiian as the language of the family in the expansion of Hawaiian to the normal language of peer groups as well as the present predominance of English-speaking families. The 'Aha Pūnana Leo and Ka Haka 'Ula O Ke'elikōlani College are anxious to develop programs to help families wishing to use Hawaiian in the home to implement such practice and a model elementary program for children from Hawaiian-speaking homes.

The consortium partners are also anxious to develop a Hawaiian-medium boarding program at Nāwahīokalani-'ōpu'u to serve students already moving to Hilo to participate in the school from islands and communities where there are no fully Hawaiian-medium schools available for intermediate and high school. Among these students are some from Moloka'i whose parents had requested the 'Aha Pūnana

Leo and the Office of Hawaiian Affairs to jointly start a K–12 full Hawaiian-medium school like Nāwahīokalani-'ōpu'u there at a small abandoned hotel site. This request was denied by the Office of Hawaiian Affairs after it heard testimony from other parents who planned to attend a partially Hawaiian–medium model intermediate/high school to be housed at Moloka'i High School, as well as community members who wished to see the hotel used for other purposes (see Warner, this volume). After the initial year of partial Hawaiian-medium courses at Moloka'i High School, an expanded group of parents and teachers again approached the 'Aha Pūnana Leo to establish a stand-alone site similar to Nāwahīokalani'ōpu'u on that island.

KE KULA NI'IHAU O KEKAHA: A SCHOOL FOR NATIVE SPEAKERS

There is already an elementary program under the direction of the 'Aha Pūnana Leo and Ka Haka 'Ula O Ke'elikōlani College in partnership with the Hawai'i State Department of Education. Ke Kula Ni'ihau O Kekaha serves a very distinctive population of children who are native speakers of the Ni'ihau dialect of Hawaiian and who live either periodically or permanently on the adjoining island of Kaua'i. The program was established in response to a 1993 boycott supported by the 'Aha Pūnana Leo and modeled on that used in the case of Nāwahīokalani'ōpu'u to induce the Department of Education to provide public Hawaiian-medium education in cooperation with the 'Aha Pūnana Leo. The boycott followed over a decade of discussion of Hawaiian-medium education in the Ni'ihau community led by two 'Aha Pūnana Leo board members, Ilei Beniamina of Ni'ihau and Byron Cleeland, the director of the Pūnana Leo on the island of Kaua'i. These discussions were reinforced by several years of practical experience of Ni'ihau community members in the 'Aha Pūnana Leo summer Hawaiian-medium programs on Kaua'i for Ni'ihau and Kula Kaiapuni Hawai'i students.

Like Ke Kula 'O Nāwahīokalani'ōpu'u, Ke Kula Ni'ihau O Kekaha is a public school program that follows the Department of Education guidelines relative to curriculum. The Department of Education provides a single teacher, while the 'Aha Pūnana Leo provides additional teachers, staff, and resources. The elementary school curriculum in the Department of Education is rather broad, allowing considerable flexibility in incorporating the unique features of the Ni'ihau community. The program includes some intermediate students and has plans to include high school students.

Ke Kula Ni'ihau O Kekaha receives all the curriculum materials used in the other Hawaiian-medium schools but has tried to adapt its curriculum to the distinctive features of the home language and culture of its students, especially as lived on Ni'ihau. Because much of the terminology in

Hawaiian-medium education was coined only recently, the language used in Hawaiian schoolbooks is unfamiliar to many in the Niʻihau community. A decision was made to try to develop materials of their own to use in addition to what has been provided. Funding was procured and non–Hawaiian speakers were hired to develop lessons, which were then translated into Hawaiian by the teachers. The teachers found these lessons unsatisfactory and began developing a curriculum totally on their own that was more closely related to the lifestyle of their island. Their original materials placed a strong emphasis on fishing, the ocean, and self-sufficiency for an environment where there is no running water, electricity, or telephone system, nor are there any commercial services. This curriculum is providing much better results. As the school progresses, the teachers, students, and community are also becoming familiar with new terminology found in the statewide Hawaiian-medium texts. Indeed, daily usage of new Hawaiian terms is now spreading more rapidly in the Niʻihau population than elsewhere.

On Niʻihau itself students do not take standardized examinations, and Ke Kula Niʻihau O Kekaha has been following that precedent. The main indicator of success in the past has been the high level of student attendance. Recently the ʻAha Pūnana Leo engaged the Pacific Regional Educational Laboratory (PREL) to assist with the evaluation of educational progress at Ke Kula Niʻihau O Kekaha after working with the organization in the development of a self-study for Nāwahīokalaniʻōpuʻu. Although this effort has just begun, there are indications that some of the children enrolled in the program are reading above grade level in Hawaiian. There have also been reports that a student who matriculated from the program to the local high school received an A in English her first semester away from the school. The certified teacher at the school is Byron Cleeland, who, besides being a board member of the ʻAha Pūnana Leo, has taught for over 20 years in the Hawaiʻi public school system. Another ʻAha Pūnana Leo board member, Ilei Beniamina, has also been very active in the school, particularly in program and staff development. As the only Niʻihauan with teacher certification and experience teaching from elementary through the college levels, Beniamina has long had unique credentials with both the Niʻihau and the larger community. Integration with Ka Haka ʻUla O Keʻelikōlani College provides an avenue for additional support for adult education and other services to the students of the school that also tie in with Beniamina's efforts through her permanent position at Kauaʻi Community College.

SPECIAL LANGUAGE FEATURES

Language issues have special relevance at Kekaha beyond the typical Hawaiian-medium program. Many adults are somewhat uncomfortable in English and aware of their own difficulties in interacting in English with the world outside Niʻihau. In order to ensure that their children learn English, a sector of the Niʻihau population on Kauaʻi has always kept its children in English-medium schools even though they are often assigned to bilingual programs with immigrant students and teased by other local students. On Niʻihau itself, all formal schoolwork and recitation is still in English, while teachers use Hawaiian for giving directions, explanations, and class discussion. A considerable number of the students at Ke Kula Niʻihau O Kekaha attend both Niʻihau School and the program owing to frequent moving between the two islands. Because of the concern for learning English in the community and because Niʻihau School teaches English from kindergarten, the initial English class is taught at Kekaha in grade 4 rather than grade 5, as in other Hawaiian-medium schools.

The current generation of Niʻihau children have been much more quick to pick up English (Hawaiʻi Creole English) in the areas where they live on Kauaʻi. On Kauaʻi, exposure to English-speaking children, businesses, and television provides much support for English development, while for children who do not attend school in Hawaiian, Hawaiian is supported only in the home and church. Indeed, some children of Niʻihau ancestry on Kauaʻi do not regularly use Hawaiian. Even on Niʻihau itself, modern technology is providing increased exposure to English at the same time that the community is spending more time on Kauaʻi. Thus Ke Kula Niʻihau O Kekaha provides an important means for maintaining Hawaiian for its students.

Differences between Niʻihau Hawaiian and the Hawaiian spoken in other schools have also played a role in curriculum development at Ke Kula Niʻihau O Kekaha. The school has a policy of maintaining and strengthening the Niʻihau tradition of use of Niʻihau dialect as the primary spoken language and standard Hawaiian for formal registers such as use in church and with Hawaiian speakers from other areas. Niʻihau children are very fluent in informal registers of the language but less familiar with the formal forms of the language used by their own elders and the formal language found in documents from the 19th and early 20th centuries. The language used elsewhere has been revived from these very documents, from taped interviews of elders who are no longer living, and from limited contact with people who are now mostly semi-speakers of other dialects of Hawaiian. Because the formal registers of Hawaiian were weakened on Niʻihau and informal registers were weakened on other islands, there is increased cooperation between Niʻihau and non–Niʻihau speakers of Hawaiian in reestablishing the full range of the language.

The strengths that Ke Kula Niʻihau O Kekaha exhibits in Hawaiian language are indicative of the mauli of the school as a whole. A distinctly Hawaiian worldview with distinctly Niʻihau variations within that worldview distinguish this school from all other Hawaiian-medium programs. Ke Kula

Niʻihau O Kekaha has made it possible for this mauli to blossom outside the structures that constrain it in standard Department of Education programs.

UNIQUE OPERATIONAL CHALLENGES

As the last community that has maintained a totally unbroken chain of Hawaiian from antiquity, Niʻihau has a special role in the efforts to revitalize Hawaiian and has been the priority community for the ʻAha Pūnana Leo since its inception. As indicated earlier in this essay, the history of the ʻAha Pūnana Leo has been closely tied to an effort to legalize use of Hawaiian in the public school on Niʻihau Island itself, a struggle led by one of ʻAha Pūnana Leo's founding members, ʻĪlei Beniamina of Niʻihau. Furthermore, the first Pūnana Leo preschool was established in 1984 at Kekaha on Kauaʻi in order to serve Niʻihauans, and there have been a succession of ʻAha Pūnana Leo special summer programs for Niʻihau children and older students in the Kekaha area over many years, frequently combined with children from Kula Kaiapuni Hawaiʻi.

During the time when ʻAha Pūnana Leo Niʻihau programs were funded at a relatively low level and during the four years that Ke Kula Niʻihau O Kekaha was located in a single classroom, ʻAha Pūnana Leo Niʻihau programs drew little attention from those who had differences with the programs or with those organizing them. Things changed when the ʻAha Pūnana Leo sought major funding to provide Ke Kula Niʻihau O Kekaha with its own site on the model of Ke Kula ʻO Nāwahīokalaniʻōpuʻu. The new site was needed because the single classroom that the Department of Education provided became increasingly inadequate for the multiage group of students it served. The ʻAha Pūnana Leo learned that the state was abandoning a small National Guard building across from Kekaha Elementary School and that this could be obtained for the program if the property were transferred to the Office of Hawaiian Affairs by the governor and state land board, with the specification that the property be rented to the ʻAha Pūnana Leo for Ke Kula Niʻihau O Kekaha. The transfer process took over a year, after which ʻAha Pūnana Leo then renovated the front half of the building for an elementary program and began to plan for expansion for an intermediate and high school program.

The new building and its resources and employment opportunities drew interest from those in the Niʻihau and greater Hawaiian community not formerly involved in Ke Kula Niʻihau O Kekaha, and enrollments grew as high as 47. The sudden explosion of new resources and visibility, however, led to community conflicts over hiring and the use of lead-contaminated scrap materials from the renovation of the school. These conflicts, along with a recent split in the Niʻihau church, political divisions, and changes within the Office of Hawaiian Affairs, and a whispering campaign by detractors of the ʻAha Pūnana Leo, resulted in an effort to take over the newly renovated building and place it in under the control of a dissident group. (See Warner, this volume, for a discussion of this issue from the point of view of a detractor of the ʻAha Pūnana Leo and supporter of that transfer.)

The dissident group is led by a president who is a Niʻihauan who raised his children as non–Hawaiian speakers outside Kauaʻi and who had only recently returned to Kekaha. Its secretary is a non-Niʻihauan and a faculty member currently associated with a faction of the University of Hawaiʻi at Mānoa that has been very hostile to the ʻAha Pūnana Leo since the unanimous dismissal of Sam L. Warner from the ʻAha Pūnana Leo Board in 1996 (see Warner 1999 and this volume). The dismissal was related to a pattern of outlandish attacks on other board members and a reversal of support of the basic principles and philosophy that served as the foundation of the ʻAha Pūnana Leo.

A widely publicized feature of the dissident group's plans in trying to take over the Ke Kula Niʻihau O Kekaha building and further renovation funding for it has been to change the Hawaiian character of the site to one in which English is much more dominant—indeed, 100% English and 100% Hawaiian, as it was expressed in one of its written statements. In order to draw support for their plan, the dissident group walked out of Ke Kula Niʻihau O Kekaha, claimed the name of the school as their own, and began to attend meetings of the Office of Hawaiian Affairs at the invitation of trustees opposed to Clayton Hee, a trustee who has been a strong supporter of Hawaiian language and the ʻAha Pūnana Leo.

The walkout involved 2 teachers and 16 students. This group's numbers have fluctuated up and down as some of its students left to enter the English-medium schools and as others from elsewhere, including preschool-age children, joined them during the 1999–2000 school year. The group refused use of a classroom and other facilities at Kekaha Elementary School, registered themselves as home schoolers, and moved to the old boycott site of Ke Kula Niʻihau O Kekaha, a public park.

Enrollment of compulsory school-age students who have remained at Ke Kula Niʻihau O Kekaha has also fluctuated between 19 and 26, depending on the migration patterns from Niʻihau as well as 4 to 12 additional preschool-age students in Pūnana Leo program at the site (ʻĪlei Beniamina, personal communication, 2000). These remaining Niʻihau families have indicated their resolve to remain with Ke Kula Niʻihau O Kekaha as a partnership public school and to keep it a totally Hawaiian-medium program, with English taught as a second language. The ʻAha Pūnana Leo has indicated to them that it will continue to support the remaining families with the program even if the Office of Hawaiian Affairs steps in to prevent the ʻAha Pūnana Leo from using the building they renovated. There has also been a consensus among the

'Aha Pūnana Leo and the remaining families that students who were removed from the program will be welcomed back if their families choose to return after trying an approach with more use of English.

The 'Aha Pūnana Leo has provided complimentary Hawaiian books to the dissident group for the Hawaiian component of its program, as it does with all Hawaiian-medium programs. The 'Aha Pūnana Leo has further stated that it is not opposed to those who wish to initiate a separately operated program that places more emphasis on English, but such a program is distinct from Ke Kula Ni'ihau O Kekaha and should seek a separate name and site rather than attempting to replace Ke Kula Ni'ihau O Kekaha and its program of total Hawaiian use at the current Ke Kula Ni'ihau O Kekaha building site.

The controversy over the building that houses Ke Kula Ni'ihau O Kekaha has taken some energy away from the program's planned services, especially in the area of parent and staff education. Progress is being made in these areas, however, with training in educational techniques used in the Pūnana Leo and Nāwahīokalani'ōpu'u as well as efforts to establish programs for parents and staff to expand their strengths and develop new talents. Those who have remained at the school have been strengthened by the experience, although the effect on the community as a whole has been negative.

The larger aspect of the situation at Ke Kula Ni'ihau O Kekaha is that the effect of disgruntlement aimed at a language revitalization group or a politician who supports language revitalization is a negative aspect of operations that language revitalization groups must deal with. Another feature that plays a negative role is fear in minority communities regarding the dominant language and allegations, even false ones, that children in language revitalization programs are performing at a lower level in the dominant language than children from the same minority program are in English-medium programs. The negative effects of such disgruntlement and fear are especially evident in times of expansion to include new participants or participation at higher grade levels.

KE KULA 'O SAMUEL MĀNAIAKALANI KAMAKAU

The most recent expansion of the model or laboratory school concept is Ke Kula 'O Samuel Mānaiakalani Kamakau, located on a third island, O'ahu—specifically, on the opposite side of the island from Honolulu. Initiated in early 2000, the school is named after the 19th-century Hawaiian scholar Samuel M. Kamakau, whose extensive writings in Hawaiian are a primary source of knowledge about the traditional culture and history of Hawai'i. Kamakau has developed under the direction of two members of the Hawaiian

language faculty at the University of Hawai'i at Mānoa, Makalapua Ka'awa and Kawehi Lucas. Besides the 'Aha Pūnana Leo and Ka Haka 'Ula O Ke'elikōlani College, the school has received support from the College of Languages, Linguistics, and Literature of the University of Hawai'i at Mānoa.

Kamakau has been designed as a Hi'i Pēpē (parent-infant program)/Pūnana Leo program for preschool through grade 12. Enrollment is by family, and those who have enrolled have generally sought out the program owing to a desire for an even stronger Hawaiian language and culture focus than that available in the schools in which their children were previously enrolled. Classes are multiage. The present lead class is in the 9th grade. The school operates on a theme of Native Hawaiian health, with integrated lessons based on that theme. As in Pūnana Leo preschools, parents are required to take Hawaiian language courses or courses through Hawaiian. The association with Ka Haka 'Ula O Ke'elikōlani has allowed parents to receive college credit for their courses.

In the few months of its existence the school has concluded some important partnerships with local Native Hawaiian health providers and others involved in health which are providing additional resources for the program. One of the purposes of the school is to develop curriculum materials and teacher training opportunities with a focus on Native Hawaiian health that can be shared with the greater Hawaiian language–medium education community.

KA HAKA 'ULA O KE'ELIKŌLANI COLLEGE OF HAWAIIAN LANGUAGE

Owing to its large Native Hawaiian population and the significance of its physical features in Hawaiian creation traditions, Hawai'i's second largest city, Hilo, has long been a center for Hawaiian linguistic and cultural activism. Among the proponents of the Hawaiian language associated with Hilo was Luka Ke'elikōlani, governor of the island of Hawai'i in the mid-1800s. Although she was quite fluent in English and, as the wealthiest person in the kingdom in her day, frequently did business with the foreign community, Governor Ke'elikōlani refused to allow anyone to address her in English. She also insisted that only Hawaiian be spoken with her son. An especially memorable event in Hilo was when she used her high ali'i rank and genealogical connection to the fire goddess, Pele, to stop a lava flow just outside the city limits.

Ka Haka 'Ula O Ke'elikōlani ("Royal Standard of Ke'elikōlani"), the College of Hawaiian Language at the University of Hawai'i at Hilo, strives to reestablish the Hawaiian language and culture usage exemplified by its namesake. One of three colleges within the University of Hawai'i at Hilo, it is the first to have a graduate program and the only one administered through a language other than English. Also distinctive is a mandate from the state legislature to work with entities outside the University of Hawai'i system, including the State Office of Hawaiian Affairs, the 'Aha Pūnana Leo, and the federal government. The private-public partnership with the 'Aha Pūnana Leo has been extremely valuable to the college in its efforts to reach its language revitalization goals and in establishing the structure of the college, including its Hawaiian studies academic programs, Hale Kuamo'o Hawaiian Language Center, its outreach efforts, its laboratory school program, and its teacher education program. Similarly, the Office of Hawaiian Affairs and the federal government have played important roles in establishing and funding programs of the college, often through partnership with the 'Aha Pūnana Leo.

CURRICULUM PRODUCTION FOR HAWAIIAN-MEDIUM SCHOOLS

Since the initiation of the Pūnana Leo program, the University of Hawai'i at Hilo and its graduates have been a primary source of curriculum for Hawaiian-medium schools. With the establishment of the 'Aha Pūnana Leo, Hilo often served as a location for the weekend camp-together meetings of the organization, including its first special curriculum development project. In 1984 and 1985, Kamanā took a two-year leave from her university position to develop the Pūnana Leo program and curriculum. The teachers she trained were primarily native speakers and college students either freshly graduated or still taking courses. In 1986, when the Pūnana Leo in Hilo was boycotting the Department of Education by setting up its own Hawaiian-medium kindergarten, Kamanā provided the direction for its teachers and curriculum.

Initial curriculum development efforts were expanded with a summer program in Hilo in 1987 through a private grant to the 'Aha Pūnana Leo to create materials for the transition into the Department of Education. This summer program received assistance from Dorothy Lazore, the pioneering Canadian Mohawk immersion educator, who suggested curriculum goals and ways to attain them for the initial public school Hawaiian-medium classrooms. The Hawaiian-speaking team, consisting of most of the present faculty of the College of Hawaiian Language, took Lazore's ideas and put them into the context of Hawai'i's natural and cultural environment. Larry Kimura, the founding president of the 'Aha Pūnana Leo, then secured a federal grant to give Pūnana Leo and Kula Kaiapuni Hawai'i teachers inservice summer teacher and curriculum development training through Hawaiian at both the Mānoa and the Hilo campuses of the University of Hawai'i. This grant provided summer teacher training and curriculum development from 1988 through 1991. Finally in 1990, the Hawai'i state legislature funded the establishment of the Hale Kuamo'o Hawaiian Language Center at the University of Hawai'i at Hilo.

From the beginning, the Hale Kuamo'o and 'Aha Pūnana Leo closely coordinated their development of curriculum and avoided duplication of translations to assure the maximum benefit to teachers. Nineteenth-century Hawaiian-medium textbooks were not usable, as they were sorely outdated (for example, a geography book showed the Mississippi River as the western boundary of the United States). But the earlier texts did provide inspiration and some vocabulary terms. Larry Kimura moved from the University of Hawai'i at Mānoa to the University of Hawai'i at Hilo with the establishment of the Hale Kuamo'o, a center which he had envisioned, and took on the task of translating the standard state mathematics curriculum. Kalena Silva and Wilson worked on science with Kimura, and the entire faculty did projects in Hawaiian language arts, social sciences, and culture, along with some exceptionally talented students.

Keiki Kawai'ae'a, a founding parent of the Pūnana Leo O Honolulu and the pioneering Kula Kaiapuni Hawai'i teacher on Maui, was hired as the educational specialist and full-time manager for the Hale Kuamo'o. Kawai'ae'a further strengthened the coordination of curriculum development with the Kula Kaiapuni Hawai'i classrooms through her contacts in the schools and her personal experience. When the 'Aha Kauleo Advisory Council was formed for the Hawaiian Language Immersion Program by the state Department of Education, Kawai'ae'a was appointed as chair of its curriculum committee, which coordinated all curriculum development statewide with the larger Hale Kuamo'o and 'Aha Pūnana Leo efforts.

TECHNOLOGY AND LEXICAL EXPANSION

Kawai'ae'a also brought Keola Donnaghy from Maui to start a Hawaiian-language computer system, which is now the most sophisticated computer system anywhere in an indigenous language. Based on Macintosh computers (chosen for their ease of use by children and technologically unsophisticated language-materials writers), Donnaghy's Leokī system links all Pūnana Leo and Hawaiian-medium schools and Hawaiian language program offices statewide in a free system provided totally through the Hawaiian language with appropriate unique Hawaiian spelling symbols, icons, and directions. The system contains chat rooms, central calendars of events, a dictionary, and folders for the different entities and interest groups within the Hawaiian language revitalization community. There is also provided in the Leokī system a means for teachers and the general public to quickly order curriculum materials. Most recently, Donnaghy provided a Hawaiian version of Netscape Navigator, which provides students with limited library resources with a means to search the Pūnaewele Puni Honua (the World Wide Web) in Hawaiian. An employee of the 'Aha Pūnana Leo, Donnaghy is stationed at the Hale Kuamoʻo and provides technical stability and direction for the entire Hawaiian language revitalization movement.[12]

Moving Hawaiian into new domains has required a huge amount of new vocabulary. From the beginning of the ʻAha Pūnana Leo, the Hawaiian language has been the fortunate beneficiary of Larry Kimura's visionary work in collecting and coining new terms. Before the first Pūnana Leo opened, Kimura was working to develop a list of appropriate vocabulary to use with new activities and materials to be found in the schools. Sometimes native speakers, especially Niʻihau speakers, would have terms that had not been documented, for example, ʻōwili 'photographic film' (literally, "twisted coil"), or would clarify terms already listed in the dictionary, such as pēheu 'mumps' (listed in the dictionary as "soft, flabby, sagging, as fat flesh; swelling or protuberance, as on cheeks or neck").

When we moved into our first group curriculum project with Dorothy Lazore, Kimura arranged for a late-afternoon meeting every day to have translators and native speakers discuss and decide upon new terms which he recorded. His next step was to organize a formal lexicon committee composed mostly of native speakers with representation from different parts of the island chain. But Kimura also included in the committee younger Hawaiian language teachers from the university who were doing the translations. The elders in the committee found that their contribution was primarily in the area of clarifying older terms. They had difficulty with the newer terms for concepts and technology with which they were unfamiliar. The university-trained translators then began meeting on their own to deal with these modern technical terms. This younger group developed into the present standing Lexicon Committee chaired by Kimura. The process of approval of new terms includes documenting all submissions to the committee, first readings, and final approvals. A joint project of the ʻAha Pūnana Leo and the Hale Kuamoʻo, the Lexicon Committee publishes annually an updated book of recently coined or documented terms with both a Hawaiian-to-English and an English-to-Hawaiian section. The book, Māmaka Kaiao (The Burden Pole of the Dawn), currently has some 4,000 entries.

The Lexicon Committee focuses on producing terms of practical use to the growing Hawaiian-speaking community—at present mostly classrooms and offices serving schools. These terms are meant not to supplant traditional terms but to allow Hawaiian to move into new fields of use and grow as a living language. Every effort is made to create new words that tie in to Hawaiian traditions—for instance, the word māuiili 'equinox' is related to the name of a famous ancestral hero, Māui, who slowed the movements of the sun. The committee also tries to model new words on established older vocabulary. Thus the traditional term kālaimanaʻo 'philosophy' ("thought carving") has led to kālaiʻōlelo 'linguistics' ("language carving"), kālaimeaola 'biology'

("living-thing carving"), and kālaiōewe 'genetics' ("lineage-continuant carving"). While it supports developing vocabulary from indigenous Hawaiian roots, the committee is not adverse to borrowing, especially from other Polynesian languages—thus naʻinaʻi 'lowercase [letter]' and maʻaka 'uppercase [letter]' are derived from the Tahitian and Rarotongan words, respectively, for small and large. When terms relate to an area outside Hawaiʻi, efforts are made to borrow from languages indigenous to those areas—thus kokeiʻa 'prairie dog' and ponī 'skunk' from the Ute language of southern Colorado.

The biggest difficulty the committee has faced is in developing Hawaiian equivalents of terms that are from categories that seem to go on endlessly—Latinate scientific terms for chemicals, species, and so on, and the names of places outside Hawaiʻi. These are a problem for all modern languages participating in the global society. The committee has been torn in two different directions regarding the development of Hawaiian terms in these categories. One direction is to continue composing terms based on Hawaiian roots, and the other is to borrow the international term. The native-roots position has proven to move much too slowly, and although the committee has approved native-root terms, especially for very common things such as the stomata of a leaf, pukahanu (literally, "breathing hole"), it has often also adopted many terms from the international lexicon. The borrowing position is designed to allow students to move between Hawaiian, English, and other languages in the scientific area, especially in the written forms of these languages.

An extreme view in terms of borrowing and one frequently adopted by teachers and students who are first-language speakers of English is to use the terms as in English and move on. These individuals simply pronounce and write "sodium bisulfate" or "Bulgaria" as they are pronounced and written in American English. For first-language speakers of Hawaiian, a similar process takes place, but of course their pronunciation of the borrowed term is more distinctly Hawaiian and differs from individual to individual according to how well he or she is able to pronounce English. There is a sentiment in the Lexicon Committee that Hawaiian should have its own pronunciation and spelling of international terms, one distinct from the English pronunciation and spelling in the same way that the French, Spanish, and Japanese versions of international terms are written and pronounced differently from the English versions of the same words. This has been accomplished by developing a formula for the adoption of international terms from English spelling rather than from English pronunciation. The formula consists principally of inserting vowels in consonant clusters and at the end of words, with some letter changes, and the invention of equivalents of some common scientific endings. Thus "sodium bisulfate" is sodiuma bisulufahate and "Bulgaria" is Bulugaria.

Hawaiianization of the spelling of scientific words is similar to the solution adopted by missionaries in adapting foreign words in the Bible, such as *Iosepa* 'Joseph', *Betelehema* 'Bethlehem', and *nāhesa* 'snake' (from Hebrew *nachash*). This solution was expanded by the Hawaiian people in newspaper reporting in the 1800s. Because some of the borrowed consonant sounds are not native to Hawaiian, there are usually at least two possible pronunciations of these borrowed biblical, scientific, and geographical terms. One pronunciation uses the borrowed English consonant sounds, and the other assimilates those consonant sounds to indigenous ones, which are then pronounced variably according to dialect. Through this process over the last century, spoken Hawaiian has borrowed a number of consonant sounds from English. In some instances this borrowing process has also established minimal pairs such as *berena* 'communion wafer' versus *pelena* 'cracker', both originally the same word, derived from the English term 'bread'.

ISSUES IN ADAPTING WRITINGS AND TAPES OF NATIVE SPEAKERS

Reworking older materials has been a means by which much curriculum has been produced. Hawaiian is very fortunate in having a very large amount of older written materials as well as much taped material. As with vocabulary development, we have faced two schools of thought in the use of older written documents. At one extreme is the opinion that these materials should be changed as little as possible to retain the form in which they were created, avoiding mistaken interpretations by contemporary readers. At the other extreme is the opinion that the materials should be completely rewritten to meet the needs and comprehension of the young children in the schools. This way the language and culture in these materials can be actually passed down to the students rather than simply read without understanding.

The Hale Kuamoʻo has taken more or less a middle ground. All older written material used by the Hale Kuamoʻo is reformatted in modern orthography. Efforts are also made to fill in gaps when a word, sentence, or page is missing or damaged. The Hale Kuamoʻo has also, in its less conservative efforts, produced glossaries for such texts that provide explanations for terms and idioms. Among the decisions that must be made are the pronunciation, meaning, and grammatical classification of words for which no living resource authority exists. This task is carefully done by very experienced language professionals supported by proofreaders.

The Hale Kuamoʻo has probably been a bit too conservative in its approach to old texts, and as a result some of its reformatted older works have sat unused in the schools. It is not uncommon for whole sections of texts to be quite obscure, especially to young teachers, not to mention elementary, intermediate, and high school students, who thus become frustrated trying to read them. Often these passages

can be clarified by providing information on older customs, extinct species, genealogical connections, historical happenings, and so on. The Hale Kuamoʻo has included endnotes in some materials, but not extensive ones. It has also produced some rewritten materials for contemporary readers incorporating explanatory information as part of the narrative and context. This process requires high-level skills beyond those required for simply reformatting materials and has so far been done only on a limited basis.

Taped, rather than written, materials have been more commonly used for "rewriting" older materials for contemporary purposes. The many pauses, self-corrections, and asides require modification for written purposes, so there is less concern with maintaining the exact form of the original. Adaptations of audiotapes also include use of short taped selections of natural conversation by native speakers on various cultural and historical topics which are used as aural introductions for lessons and models for pronunciation, vocabulary, and grammar. Videotapes of interviews and semiscripted cultural activities have also been developed, but primarily by the 'Aha Pūnana Leo rather than the Hale Kuamoʻo.

TEACHER TRAINING FOR HAWAIIAN-MEDIUM SCHOOLS

Teacher training has been an area of concern since the initiation of the 'Aha Pūnana Leo and an activity in which the University of Hawaiʻi at Hilo Hawaiian program has been very much involved. All teachers other than the few native-speaking teachers have learned the language over the years in courses in various universities and community colleges in the state. Beyond standard Hawaiian language and culture courses, university Hawaiian studies programs initially focused primarily on further developing language and culture skills appropriate to be taught to Pūnana Leo preschool- and elementary school–age children.

Certification of teachers has always been an issue for Hawaiian-medium education. Initially the Pūnana Leo preschools were effectively barred from legal establishment by requirements that its teachers be certified through English language– and culture–based early-childhood training provided by colleges. This was unattainable for our native-speaker teachers, who often had maintained the language by being isolated from haole education. However, in 1986 lobbying by Pūnana Leo resulted in a legal change that exempted teachers in preschools taught through Hawaiian from certification requirements. From its inception, the Pūnana Leo has encouraged its teachers to expand their knowledge of other approaches to education by assisting its staff in enrolling in haole culture– and language–based early education programs. The Pūnana Leo is concerned, however, that its teachers not be overly influenced by haole approaches to early childhood education and has also encouraged learning from other countries and cultures, especially when they align with Hawaiian culture and values. The main focus of Pūnana Leo preschool teacher training, however, has been on internally run in-service training. Similar in-service training is available to teachers in Kula Kaiapuni Hawai'i through the Hale Kuamo'o at the College of Hawaiian Language.

Certification has remained a major issue for the public school Hawaiian Language Immersion Program. The initial two elementary Kula Kaiapuni Hawai'i classrooms were opened as combined kindergarten and 1st grade classes with teachers who had already been certified. Neither teacher had the ideal qualifications of full training in Hawaiian and early childhood education. One, Puanani Wilhelm, was a Hawaiian studies major certified to teach second-language courses at the high school level, while the other, Alohalani Kaina, was an elementary school teacher who had had two years of college Hawaiian and also had children in the Pūnana Leo with whom she and her husband were using Hawaiian at home. As the program grew, it became increasingly difficult to find teachers who combined Hawaiian and state certification qualifications, even to the level found in these initial teachers. Principals leaned toward hiring teachers who met the certification criteria and downplayed the Hawaiian qualifications; Pūnana Leo philosophy–leaning parents downplayed certification and stressed Hawaiian qualifications. Parents actually drove out some teachers with very obvious deficiencies in Hawaiian.

The University of Hawai'i at Hilo Hawaiian studies major had been approved as an area of certification for second-language teaching before the initiation of the Pūnana Leo. Graduates of the program entered the university's English-medium education department for further training, which culminated in student teaching in high school courses in Hawaiian language taught through English. The initiation of the Kula Kaiapuni Hawai'i presented the opportunity to begin specialized training for Hawaiian-medium schools which we proposed to begin with student teaching. When in 1990 two Hawaiian studies graduates in the university's education department approached the department regarding student teaching in Hawaiian, they were initially refused. Evaluation of student teaching was considered impossible because the department did not have any Hawaiian-speaking faculty. This barrier was overcome by the offer of Kamanā, in the Hawaiian studies department, to provide interpretation services to the education department for all on-site visits and the offer of the students to write all lesson plans in both Hawaiian and English. The education department then agreed to allow student teaching through Hawaiian but also told the students that they were greatly damaging their employment prospects by refusing to student teach in English. Nāko'olani Warrington, the one student who decided to student teach through Hawaiian, received the University of Hawai'i at Hilo education department's award for elementary student teacher of the year.

As more Kula Kaiapuni Hawai'i opened, it became increasingly difficult to obtain trained teachers, and the ad hoc solutions of bilingual lesson plans and voluntary interpreters became increasingly burdensome. Furthermore, Kula Kaiapuni Hawai'i were not satisfied with the standard English-medium teacher training; they desired something more closely tailored to Hawaiian cultural perspectives and taught through Hawaiian itself, a position that was finally officially articulated by the 'Aha Kauleo advisory council to the Department of Education. In addition, with the establishment of Nāwahīokalani'ōpu'u, a number of talented undergraduate students joined with Kamanā and other experienced teachers in developing the intermediate and high school program. These university students became the nucleus of what was to become the Kahuawaiola Professional Teaching Certificate Program of Ka Haka 'Ula O Ke'elikōlani.

Initial plans for a Hawaiian-medium teaching certificate offered through the Hawaiian studies department began in 1994. Moving the program forward through the university structure was difficult until a Hawaiian-medium teacher training program was mandated by the 1997 state legislature in the legislation establishing the College of Hawaiian Language. An official pilot program began that year, and the certification was given final approval by the university administration in early 1999 as the Kahuawaiola Professional Teaching Certificate Program. The final step now underway is a self-study in conjunction with the state Department of Education, which should lead to full teacher licensing by the year 2000. Eleven students have graduated from the program and await news regarding Department of Education licensing.

The Kahuawaiola Program is designed to meet the special needs of teachers in Kula Kaiapuni Hawai'i and also to serve teachers in English-medium schools who are teaching Hawaiian language and culture and/or serving students from strongly Hawaiian cultural backgrounds. The program is taught entirely in Hawaiian and draws primarily Hawaiian studies majors as students. Entrance requirements include a bachelor's degree, four years of Hawaiian with a grade point average of 2.75 in the last two years, and, for non-Hawaiian-studies majors, at least two additional college courses in Hawaiian culture. Majors from outside Hawaiian studies are recruited, and double majors are especially encouraged. Before entering the program, a student must have completed either 50 hours of teaching through Hawaiian or 75 hours in curriculum development.

All students, regardless of the level or program in which they are to teach, take the same set of courses but with instruction designed to allow students to focus on their own particular needs. Thus, during the mathematics strand, students preparing for elementary mathematics, high school mathematics, or high school Hawaiian language in an English-medium school all work on projects designed to tie in mathematical principles and the Hawaiian culture to their particular specialization. For example, such students might develop a unit on traditional Hawaiian children's jingles relating to numbers for kindergarten, the geometry involved in the construction of Hawaiian terraced taro gardens for high school, and a unit on special numeral groupings and number symbolism for a high school language class. The initial core credits are offered over the summer in a live-in, totally Hawaiian-speaking environment using the dormitories and classrooms of Ke Kula 'O Nāwahīokalani'ōpu'u.

After completing the core courses in the summer, teachers proceed to a school of their choosing in the state, where they work for the entire school year with an experienced Hawaiian-speaking teacher. The experienced teacher and a site-visiting faculty member from Ka Haka 'Ula O Ke'elikōlani provide direction and grading for this on-site training. In addition, while they are doing their student teaching, participants enroll in 2 three-credit seminars. The first seminar deals with the day-to-day strategies and problems of teaching through Hawaiian. The second deals with broader issues faced by Hawaiian-medium schools and programs. These seminars are taught through interactive television using sites within the statewide University of Hawai'i system.

To receive the certificate, teachers must also pass a base-level Hawaiian fluency examination that is provided as part of a one-credit course. The examination consists of five sections. Oral fluency is tested through an interview following the guidelines of the American Council on the Teaching of Foreign Languages. Transcription of taped natural conversation of elders and answering written questions in Hawaiian on the content of such tapes is used to test listening comprehension. Teachers need to be able to translate English materials into Hawaiian for their classrooms, a facility tested through a translation exercise, usually using English newspaper articles. Skill in using older written Hawaiian materials is tested through a section calling for rewriting a selection from such older materials in contemporary Hawaiian orthography. Finally, there is a composition section tested through writing in Hawaiian on an assigned topic provided on the day of the examination.

The preparation of teachers in Kahuawaiola follows the Kumu Honua Mauli Ola educational philosophy adopted by Ka Haka 'Ula O Ke'elikōlani and the 'Aha Pūnana Leo. The philosophy is based on Hawaiian traditions and includes attention to four aspects of knowledge or skills: *ka 'ao'ao pili 'uhane* (the spiritual or intuitive aspect), *ka 'ao'ao 'ōlelo* (the language aspect), *ka 'ao'ao lawena* (the physical and body language aspect), and *ka 'ao'ao 'ike ku'una* (the traditional knowledge aspect). This is to be conveyed in a *honua* or specific location which becomes more permeable to outside influences as the student grows in age and wisdom, and

through three focal points of human interaction: *ka piko 'ī*, or point of spiritual/intuitive connections; *ka piko 'ō*, or point of inherited, genealogical, and externally initiated connections; and *ka piko 'ā*, or point connecting one to relationships and materials created or adapted by a person himself or herself. This last point of connection allows for the integration of contemporary non-Hawaiian knowledge such as science and computers into the system, which is then passed on as traditional knowledge though the *piko 'ō* in the same way that earlier generations of Hawaiians integrated the horse, quilting, and the guitar into their lives in a distinctive Hawaiian manner and then transmitted them to their descendants.

A major challenge for the Ka Haka 'Ula O Ke'elikōlani has been in convincing the teacher education establishment that preparing teachers from a Kumu Honua Mauli Ola perspective can produce teachers who can educate students on a level comparable to that provided by standard Western teacher education approaches. While the teacher education establishment has shown genuine interest in the academic and other achievements of students at Nāwahīokalani'ōpu'u and the unique results of implementation of the Kumu Honua Mauli Ola, there is still considerable skepticism regarding the Kahuawaiola program and its being taught by faculty whose degree qualifications lie primarily, but not exclusively, outside traditional Western education. We are hopeful that licensing will be granted to allow a number of years' demonstration of the value of the strongly Hawaiian approach of Kahuawaiola. In this regard it is important to note that a fully licensed program to prepare teachers for Hawaiian language immersion classrooms already exists at the University of Hawai'i at Mānoa, where Hawaiian language teaching and literacy training from the Hawaiian language program is integrated with English-medium pedagogical training within the College of Education there using faculty with more standard education backgrounds. The Kahuawaiola program, like other 'Aha Pūnana Leo and Ka Haka 'Ula O Ke'elikōlani programs, seeks to establish a more radically distinct indigenous approach to education in its belief that closer alignment with Hawaiian tradition will provide greater benefits for schools with a strong Hawaiian language and culture revitalization orientation as well as for Hawaiian students in English-medium schools who could benefit from teachers with a strongly Hawaiian approach to education.

MASTER OF ARTS PROGRAM

A number of the teachers at Ke Kula 'O Nāwahīokalani'ōpu'u have been simultaneously enrolled in both the master of arts in Hawaiian language and literature and the Kahuawaiola Professional Teaching Certificate Program. The 33-credit master's degree, begun in September of 1998, is at present being offered on a cohort model. Because all nine students have also been working full time, only two required courses are offered per semester. The coursework is modeled on standard foreign-language master's programs, but again with a distinctive Hawaiian base. Included is a course on the history of the Hawaiian language and literature and an introduction to research methods, both taught the first semester. These are followed by courses in various aspects of Hawaiian linguistics and literature, including the performance of literature through chant. The breadth and depth of recorded Hawaiian literature allows for courses on such subjects as traditional Hawaiian literature, ethnological and historical narratives, European-influenced Hawaiian literature, and applied Hawaiian chant. Enough materials exist in each of these areas that the courses can be offered in several different subcategories. The program also requires all students to write a thesis in Hawaiian and to earn three credits through educational interaction with an ethnic group outside Hawai'i involved in language revitalization.

The focus on language revitalization and application to the community distinguishes our master's program from foreign-language master's programs. Students are encouraged to choose as their thesis topic any area in which data are secured through Hawaiian or for which Hawaiian-speaking communities are being created. Thus, student thesis topics chosen the first semester include formal language devices in Hawaiian poetry; the traditions of *akule* fishing in Hāna, Maui; the development of the genre of Hawaiian language film and video; and Hawaiian language substrata in Hawai'i Creole English. During discussion periods in the master's courses, students relate the topic of study to their field of interest. Students also use the expertise of non-Hawaiian-speaking faculty on campus in developing their thesis.

BACHELOR OF ARTS PROGRAM

The Master of Arts in Hawaiian language and literature and the Kahuawaiola Professional Teaching Certificate are built upon the bachelor of arts in Hawaiian studies. The 43-credit bachelor's program was originally designed by Wilson from a vision statement developed by a committee headed by the program's senior member, the late Hilo language, culture, and hula revivalist *kupuna* (elder) Edith Kanaka'ole. The program has two tracks. Track 1, Continuing the Culture, is taught entirely within the Hawaiian studies department and focuses on language, linguistics, performing arts, and traditional culture. This track is taught entirely through Hawaiian at the upper division level and requires four years of Hawaiian language. Track 2, Monitoring the Culture, also requires four years of Hawaiian language and six additional credits taught through Hawaiian, but the remainder of the credits are taken in courses taught through English outside the department, in anthropology, political science, biology, history, and other fields.

The language courses that are the heart of the bachelor's program are the most intense in the state of Hawai'i. The hour-long classes meet 5 days a week for 30 weeks per year, not only at the first two levels, but all the way through fourth year. The methodology used focuses on grammar and translation, with weekly quizzes and speeches. Grammar is taught using Hawaiian terms and a system developed by Wilson and Kamanā using the metaphor of an octopus. By the second year all language-skills course instruction is through Hawaiian, and by the third year, students are taking content courses in Hawaiian.

The nearly 20-year old bachelor of arts in Hawaiian studies and the affiliated minor and two subject certificates are now being considered for revision. In recent years, students have come to the program with less personal experience in Hawaiian lifeways and therefore desire a stronger cultural focus. Students also need to understand the language and culture revitalization in which they are participating as a historic and social process. The weakening of the traditional Hawaiian lifestyle has also made students more vulnerable to generic Western stereotypes of indigenous identity which urgently need to be addressed. Finally, the B.A. program needs to address the phenomenon of students entering Ka Haka 'Ula O Ke'elikōlani with high fluency in Hawaiian as graduates of Hawaiian-medium schools.

Many of the changes needed for the B.A. program are expected to be developed in a new general education program of Ka Haka 'Ula O Ke'elikōlani. Previously, Hawaiian studies majors participated in the College of Arts and Sciences' Western-based general education program. A new Ka Haka 'Ula O Ke'elikōlani general education program is being discussed as focusing on a Hawaiian and language revivalist view of the world. Some of these general education courses would be made available through Hawaiian to accommodate fluent Hawaiian speakers and could be enrolled in by advanced high school students still attending Ke Kula 'O Nāwahīokalani'ōpu'u. Changes to the major itself will likely target improving methods of language teaching and expanding Hawaiian-medium courses in Track 2, focusing on the social and natural science areas of the Hawaiian world.

All of these changes, however, require additional personnel and funding.

EXTERNAL CONNECTIONS

The 'Aha Pūnana Leo and Ka Haka 'Ula O Ke'elikōlani have long held a philosophy of working with others involved in language revitalization. From the very beginning, the 'Aha Pūnana Leo has had a close relation with New Zealand Māori language revitalization, benefiting especially from a close relationship with Tīmoti Kāretu, the current head of the Kōhanga Reo Trust and the former commissioner of Māori language. Within Polynesia, Ka Haka 'Ula O Ke'elikōlani serves as the permanent secretariat of the Polynesian Languages Forum, a body consisting of delegates from 14 Polynesian countries that was established through the initiative of Kāretu. Relationships with Polynesia have now extended to 'Aha Pūnana Leo– and Ka Haka 'Ula O Ke'elikōlani–sponsored school visits, student exchanges, and joint printings.

Relationships with American Indians, Alaska Natives, and Aboriginal Canadians have also been very strong. As recounted earlier, Dorothy Lazore, who pioneered Mohawk immersion in Canada, played an important role in the crucial year in which Pūnana Leo students matriculated into the public Hawaiian Language Immersion Program. She later hosted an important visit to her program for 'Aha Pūnana Leo and Kula Kaiapuni Hawai'i teachers. Even earlier, Lucille Watahomigie of the Peach Springs School Hualapai Bilingual Program hosted Kamanā, introducing her to the Native American Languages Issues (NALI) Institute network and methods of curriculum development. This led to the 1993 NALI conference's being hosted by the 'Aha Pūnana Leo and the University of Hawai'i at Hilo, assisted by the Office of Hawaiian Affairs and the Kamehameha Schools, and to increased assistance to native peoples in North America following the total indigenous language–medium model. These relationships have led to assistance with teacher training, curriculum development, and joint printings with Piegan Institute's Blackfeet schools, the Washoe Washiw 'itlu Gawgayay school, Sealaska's Tlingit immersion program, and many others.[13] More recently we have expanded our horizons to contacting European regional languages. We see such contacts and mutual assistance as important in strengthening the overall effort of language and cultural revitalization and maintenance on a global level. The strengths of the 'Aha Pūnana Leo in Hawaiian-medium education have resulted in the 'Aha Pūnana Leo's having the unique privilege of being chosen as the indigenous peoples' exhibitor in the area of education at Expo 2000, the millennium world's fair held in Hanover, Germany.

CLOSING THOUGHTS

I ka 'ōlelo nō ke ola; I ka 'ōlelo nō ka make. "In language rests life; in language rests death." This traditional saying has served as the cornerstone of the 'Aha Pūnana Leo in its belief that the Hawaiian language, the actual use of the language, and what is said in the language hold the key to the survival for a distinctly Hawaiian society. The converse of the saying is that replacing Hawaiian with other languages, using other languages regularly in place of Hawaiian, and using foreign words to define Hawaiians is the road to eventual extinction for Hawaiian society. The 'Aha Pūnana Leo, therefore, strives to use Hawaiian in all its activities, utilizing other languages to interact only with those who are not able to function in Hawaiian. No matter how rudimentary

their knowledge of Hawaiian, individuals are expected to use the language within the 'Aha Pūnana Leo system and to constantly improve their level of proficiency. Furthermore, the language is not to be put in a lower social position by switching to English in conversations with another Hawaiian speaker simply because nonspeakers are present. The programs described in this article strive to reflect the ideal that the Hawaiian language and culture are the priority.

Hawaiian culture and sayings are often characterized by dualities. The second part of the above saying could be interpreted to mean that too much emphasis on words can lead to death. Indeed, in Hawaiian culture, words are used sparingly and there is much emphasis on action. *Huli ka lima i lalo, piha ka 'ōpū; huli ka lima i luna, piha ka 'ōpū i ka makani.* "Turn your hands down to work, and your stomach will be full giving survival; turn your hands up in supplication to others, and your stomach will be filled with the wind of words alone." In spite of its belief in the crucial role of language, the 'Aha Pūnana Leo also believes that in order for the language to survive, its speakers must work very hard and reach a higher level of achievement. In the Hawaiian ethic, work is motivated by a need to produce in order to be able to share on a large scale.

Within the 'Aha Pūnana Leo system, we do not wait for others to help us. And no matter how fluent one is in Hawaiian, or how educated in either the Hawaiian or the Western sense, one is expected to work as part of a group for the basic needs of the group and to share with others for the good of all. The programs described in this article seek to reflect the ideal that action—not academic credentials, not blood or background, not even native-speaker status—but action, especially coordinated action as in a Hawaiian family, brings language and culture revitalization. Without such action, we have nothing to share but our observations, our fears, and our dreams.

The actions described above grew out of dream for a revitalized Hawaiian language. It is easier to understand where that dream has taken us by personal observation of results of the language revitalization movement here in Hawai'i. We hope, however, that the words of this article will be of some value, especially to those who may never visit our programs. With that hope, we also note that there are many circumstances in the world and even in Hawai'i. Many other perspectives and approaches to language revitalization and to Hawaiian language and culture besides ours exist. We offer what has been done by one particular coordinated group of people to which we are honored to belong and to contribute—the 'Aha Pūnana Leo and its consortium partner, the Ka Haka 'Ula O Ke'elikōlani College of Hawaiian Language.

Li'ili'i kahi lū'au me ke aloha pū. Lawe i ka mea maika'i, kāpae i ka mea maika'i 'ole.

"The bit of cooked taro leaves before you is small but we offer it with aloha. Take that which is valuable to you; put aside that which is not."

Notes

The title of this article is taken from 'Aha Pūnana Leo's mission statement, which has been translated as:

> "The Pūnana Leo movement grew out of a dream that there be re-established throughout Hawai'i the mana of a living Hawaiian language from the depths of our origins. The Pūnana Leo family initiates, provides for, and nurtures various Hawaiian language environments, and we find our strength in our spirituality, love of our language, love of our people, love of our land, and love of knowledge."

While taking responsibility for any errors in this article, we would like to recognize that "proceeding from the dream" has occurred because of the Pūnana Leo family, an intricate web of people who work, teach, and participate in the various programs described in this article because of that *aloha* or love described at the end of the mission statement. We would like to dedicate this article to them.

1. There is a concerted interest in developing immersion programs such as those in New Zealand and Hawai'i in other parts of Polynesia. The most recent meeting of the Polynesian Language Forum described later in this article was held in April of 2000 in Rapa Nui (Easter Island) in conjunction with the inauguration of a preschool and first grade Rapa Nui immersion program. Subsequent to the forum, the French Polynesian government announced that it planned to establish immersion pre-schools for the five Polynesian languages in that country.

2. Fishman (1991) downplays the role of schools in language maintenance and revitalization compared to the home and community associations. We note, however, that in spite of early twentieth-century home and community use of Hawaiian, the effect of the forced English medium schooling and the anti-Hawaiian language philosophy promoted in it was profound on the first generation to be educated entirely in such schools. While sufficiently fluent in Hawaiian to interact with parents, and sometimes with their peers (with whom, however, many preferred English), the first generation forcibly educated entirely in English typically used only English with their own children. It is our feeling that Fishman has de-emphasized the role of schools too much, especially since they play a crucial role in cultivating attitudes among children regarding language shift and reversal of such shift. Fishman himself acknowledges that in today's society, where both parents typically work and families are more fragmented, a system of full services to families centered around their children, such as what is being developed within the 'Aha Pūnana Leo and its schools, provide a form of community that can facilitate language revitalization. See *The Encyclopedia of Bilingualism and Bilingual Education*, especially the section "language revival and reversal," for additional ideas on the role of schools in language revitalization in today's world.

3. From the initial efforts to change legislation banning Hawaiian medium education in 1984, a few Hawai'i legislators posed questions regarding federal policy relating to Hawai'i's official recognition of Hawaiian. Subsequent to establishment of Hawaiian medium education in public schools, there were further statements by professional educators, including the evaluator of the Hawaiian language immersion program, to the effect that being an American required English to take precedence over Hawaiian. It was this subordination of Hawaiian to English as if it were an immigrant language, and the indignity felt by parents at this treatment, that resulted in the initial contacts by Wilson with Lurline McGregor of Senator Inouye's staff to investigate the possibility of clarifying that American policy did not require such subordination. Interest by Senator Inouye's staff in this issue was followed by efforts by Wilson in drafting a legislative proposal and bringing it with others, especially Ofelia Zepeda, before interested American Indian and Alaska Native communities through the Native American Languages Issues Institute and through other means. These efforts eventually led to the Native American Languages Act of 1990 and the clarification that federal policy does not require the subordination of Hawaiian and other Native American languages to English in schools. (See Arnold this volume.)

4. Recently, the new superintendent of education, Paul LeMahieu, has been working with the Office of Hawaiian Affairs and others to address these issues without going to court and thus there is some optimism that these issues will be resolved.

5. In support of the contention that use of Hawaiian strengthens identification with Hawaiian ethnicity, the statistics on ethnic identity were quite different for Ke Kula 'O Nāwahīokalani'ōpu'u. While Nāwahīokalani'ōpu'u is administered by the state with Hilo High, only one student there with Hawaiian ancestry did not state Hawaiian as his or her ethnicity of primary identification.

6. Different state and federal funding sources have requirements such as one-half Hawaiian ancestry, any amount of Hawaiian ancestry, low-income status, single-parent status, and residence in certain geographic areas. The realities of Hawaiian families are that they include Hawaiian as well as non-Hawaiian children, children of various blood quantum including some whose 50% quantum cannot be legally verified—and children of unique Hawaiian categories such as *hānai* (children adopted by Hawaiian tradition rather than by law), whose legal parents have different residences and incomes than those of their hānai parents. Another reality is that there are Hawaiian children brought up in families with minimal Hawaiian cultural continuity, including single-parent homes where the parent is non-Hawaiian or in cases of adoption into non-Hawaiian families. In such cases the 'Aha Pūnana Leo programs provide a means for access to other Hawaiians and development of Hawaiian mauli. However, a central tenet of the Kumu Honua Mauli Ola is that one must not deny one's own genealogy and history but integrate it as an essential part of the mauli that one exhibits.

7. Kamehameha is going through a period of change, including an evaluation of its role in Hawaiian language and culture teaching and partnering with the state and private entities in the education of Hawaiian children throughout the Hawaiian Islands. Both the 'Aha Pūnana Leo and Ka Haka 'Ula O Ke'elikōlani have been invited to provide input into ways that Kamehameha might be able to better serve the Hawaiian community in these areas. There is therefore a possibility that the resources of this important private Hawaiian entity will become involved in Hawaiian medium education. We are hopeful that this will be the case.

8. The state constitutional provision that protects the use of Hawaiian language by children in their daily lives, including the considerable time spent by them in required public education, is article XII, section 7, traditional and customary rights, as follows:

> "The State reaffirms and shall protect all rights, customarily and traditionally exercised for subsistence, cultural and religious purposes and possessed by ahupua'a tenants who are descendants of native Hawaiians who inhabited the Hawaiian Islands prior to 1778, subject to the right of the State to regulate such rights."

9. The Nāwahīokalani'ōpu'u method of teaching English through Hawaiian follows the internationally accepted language minority revitalization practice of providing greatest emphasis on the language with the weakest position in the general society. It is similar to the Welsh method called *trawsieithu* successfully used in Welsh language schools there (*Encyclopedia of Bilingualism*, 594–595). The Hawaiian Language Immersion Program evaluation team has looked primarily for direction in Canadian and American second language and immigrant bilingual programs where language revitalization is not the goal. There are language revitalization and maintenance models in other countries, especially Europe and New Zealand, that should be investigated by those involved in Hawaiian and other indigenous language revitalization. Even these should not preclude the development of innovative models especially suited for the unique situations of individual languages such as Hawaiian.

10. A number of parents have attended college since enrolling their children at the Pūnana Leo. The Pūnana Leo Hawaiian language study requirement often leads parents to attend Hawaiian language classes at the university level after completing parent classes at the Pūnana Leo site. This then leads to taking other classes in other fields. A large portion of the 'Aha Pūnana Leo staff is derived from parent volunteers. These parents especially have gained much university experience from the program because of 'Aha Pūnana Leo requirements that its staff complete four years of Hawaiian and the support that the organization provides in paying for such courses and providing time off for further university study for its employees.

11. The Western focus on the outward manifestations of Hawaiian culture creates the possibility of something that is physically or outwardly Hawaiian in the Western sense, but inwardly is not. Similarly, something may be outwardly Western, yet inwardly Hawaiian. The mauli focuses on the inward sense. This facet of Hawaiian identity is recognized in the Kumu Honua Mauli Ola, which notes that both *'ike ku'una* 'traditional knowledge' and *'ōlelo* 'language' have the potential of communicating falsehood as compared to the *'ao'ao pili 'uhane* 'spirituality/intuitive knowledge' and *lawena* 'physical movement/body language', which do not communicate falsehood. Thus even the use of Hawaiian language or the performance of Hawaiian dance can be done in a non-Hawaiian manner. However, the way in which one acts or conveys oneself spiritually cannot hide one's true mauli. Spirituality is seen as distinct from *ho'omana* 'religion'. Indeed, it is possible to have Hawaiian religion without Hawaiian spirituality, and Christian religion with Hawaiian spirituality. An example of the latter is the type of Hawaiian Christianity that grew up after the overthrow of the traditional Hawaiian temple religion in 1819. Most of today's elders as well as the Ni'ihau community grew up with such a religious background conducted in Hawaiian using the Hawaiian bible. The way in which these elders manifest Christianity is quite distinct from haole Christianity. An example of something outwardly Western but inwardly Hawaiian in Hawaiian Christianity is observing the Sabbath by not fishing but explaining it by saying that the ocean must also rest in respect of the Sabbath.

12. The computer address for Leokī and its bulletin board Kualono is <http://www.olelo.hawaii.edu/>. The 'Aha Pūnana Leo also has a separate site at <http://www.ahapunanaleo.org/>

13. Among these programs, Piegan Institute's Blackfeet Cut-Bank Language Immersion School is the most developed along lines similar to the Pūnana Leo. A very useful resource for those interested in American Indian language revitalization through schools is the recent publication by the school's founder Darrell Kipp entitled "Encouragement, Guidance, Insights, and Lessons Learned for Native Language Activists Developing Their Own Language Programs."

References

Arnold, Robert. To help assure the survival and continuing vitality of Native American languages. In this volume.

Baker, Colin, and Sylvia Prys Jones. 1998. *Encyclopedia of bilingualism and bilingual education.* Clevedon, England: Multilingual Matters.

Benton, Richard A. 1981. *The flight of the Amokura: Oceanic languages and formal education in the South Pacific.* Wellington: New Zealand Council for Educational Research.

Fishman, Joshua A. 1991. *Reversing language shift: Theoretical and empirical foundations of assistance to threatened languages.* Philadelphia: Multilingual Matters.

Hilo High School. 1998. Focus on learning: A self-study, 1998–99.

"Ka Leo Hawai'i" [Hawaiian language radio talk show], 1970s and 1980s. Hale Kuamo'o, Kulanui O Hawai'i Ma Hilo.

Ke kuamo'o o Ke'elikōlani. kau hā'ulelau. 1998. Hilo: Hale Kuamo'o, Kulanui O Hawai'i Ma Hilo. puke 8 helu 1.

Kipp, Darrell R. 2000. *Encouragement, guidance, insights, and lessons learned for native language activists developing their own tribal language programs.* St. Paul, Minn.: Grotto Foundation.

Legislative Reference Bureau/State of Hawai'i. 1998. Hawaiian demographic data: 'Ehia Kānaka Maoli, Susan Jaworowski, researcher.

Māmaka Kaiao. 1998. He puke hua 'ōlelo Hawai'i hou. Hilo: Hale Kuamo'o, Kulanui o Hawai'i ma Hilo.

"Olelo Hawaii." *Ka Puuhonua,* 20 January 1917.

Papa Ho'olālā Hikiāloa—'Elima Makahiki 1996–2001. Hilo: 'Aha Pūnana Leo.

Slaughter, Helen B., Karen Watson-Gegeo, Sam No'eau Warner, and Haunani Bernardino. 1988. Evaluation report for the first year of the Hawaiian Immersion Program: A report to the Planning and Evaluation Branch, Department of Education, State of Hawai'i.

Slaughter, Helen B., Sam L. No'eau Warner, and Waldeen Kahulu Palmeira. 1989. Evaluation report for the second year of the Hawaiian Language Immersion Program: A report to the Planning and Evaluation Branch, Department of Education, State of Hawai'i.

Slaughter, Helen B., Morris K. Lai, Sam L. No'eau Warner, and Waldeen Kahulu Palmeira. 1990. Evaluation report for the third year, 1989–1990, of the Hawaiian Language Immersion Program: A report to the Planning and Evaluation Branch, Department of Education, State of Hawai'i.

Slaughter, Helen B., and Morris K. Lai, with Sam L. No'eau Warner and Waldeen Kahulu Palmeira. 1991. Evaluation report for the fourth year, 1990–1991, of the Hawaiian Language Immersion Program: A report to the Planning and Evaluation Branch, Department of Education, State of Hawai'i.

Slaughter, Helen B., with Morris Lai, Louise Bogart, Jennifer Leilani Basham, and Dannie U'ilani Bobbit. 1993. Evaluation report for the first cohort to complete sixth grade in the Hawaiian Language Immersion Program: A report to the Hawaiian Language Immersion Program, Office of Instructional Services, and to the Planning and Evaluation Branch, Hawai'i State Department of Education.

Slaughter, Helen B., with Morris K. Lai, Louise Bogart, Jennifer Leilani Basham, Dannie U'ilani Bobbit, and Waldeen Kahulu Palmeira. 1994. Evaluation report for the sixth year of the Hawaiian Language Immersion Program: implementation and selected outcome indicators, grades K–6, 1992–1993: A report to the Hawaiian Language Immersion Program and to the Planning and Evaluation Branch, Department of Education, State of Hawai'i.

Slaughter, Helen B., with Robert Keawe Lopes and Chelsea Kalei Nihipali. 1997. Evaluation report of the ninth year of the Hawaiian Language Immersion Program, school year 1995–1996: A report to the Hawaiian Language Immersion Program Department of Education, State of Hawai'i.

Stansfield, Charles W. 1996. *Test development handbook: Simulated Oral Proficiency Interview (SOPI).* Washington, D.C.: Center for Applied Linguistics.

State of Hawai'i Board of Education. 1994. Long-range plan for the Hawaiian Language Immersion Program—Papahana Kaiapuni Hawai'i.

State of Hawai'i Legislature. 1986. Committee reports on SB 2463–86.

Warner, Sam L. 1990. The delay of the formal introduction of English in the Hawaiian Language Immersion Program until grade five. Unpublished paper submitted at the request of the Hawaiian Language Advisory Council to the Committee on Hawaiian Affairs, State of Hawai'i Board of Education.

———. 1999. Kuleana: The right, responsibility, and authority of indigenous peoples to speak and make decisions for themselves in language and cultural revitalization. *Anthropology and Education Quarterly* 30, no. 1: 68–94.

———. No'eau. I Mana Ka Lāhui, I Mana Ka 'Ōlelo: The movement to revitalize Hawaiian language and culture. In this volume.

Wilson, William H. 1981. Developing a standardized Hawaiian orthography. *Pacific Studies* (spring): 164–181.

———. 1998a. I ka 'ōlelo Hawai'i ke ola, "Life is found in the Hawaiian language." *International Journal of the Sociology of Language* 132: 123–37.

———. 1998b. The socio-political history of establishing Hawaiian medium education. *Language, Culture, and Curriculum* 11, no. 3 [special issue on indigenous community–based education]: 325–38.

Zambucka, Kristin. 1992. *The high chiefess: Ruth Keelikolani.* Honolulu: Green Glass Productions.

PART V

IMMERSION

14

Teaching Methods

LEANNE HINTON

Department of Linguistics
University of California at Berkeley
Berkeley, California

INTRODUCTION

Language revitalization usually must include as its largest task the teaching and learning of the endangered language as a second language. Second-language teaching (a cover term for what of course could for some individuals be the teaching of a third, fourth, or fifth language) is a big industry throughout the world, and a large body of literature exists on the research and documentation of effective teaching methods. People who are going to teach a language seriously would be well advised to read some of this literature or undergo training in good methodology. A few of the many excellent books available on the topic of language teaching and learning and that can give you some good ideas on how to teach or learn a language are Asher 1977; Brewster and Brewster 1976; Brown 1987; Hadley 1993; Krashen and Terrell 1983; and Richards and Rodgers 1986.

Most of the literature on language teaching methods is about either the teaching of foreign languages or the teaching of English (or other national languages) to immigrants. Teaching endangered languages has important differences from teaching foreign languages or ESL, and someone who is going to teach an endangered language must keep those differences in mind and adapt whatever is read to the specific situation at hand—some information will be useful, some will not. (For a discussion of some of the differences between teaching foreign languages and teaching endangered languages, see Hinton 1999.)

MODELS AND METHODOLOGY: A BRIEF ACCOUNT OF INDIGENOUS LANGUAGE TEACHING IN THE UNITED STATES

Informal Language Classes

In the effort to maintain and teach a language which is no longer being learned at home, speech communities have often started the process with informal gatherings of speakers and nonspeakers. I remember, for example, when I was a graduate student, going to weekly small gatherings with Ted Couro, then one of the few remaining speakers of Northern Diegueño. The gatherings were run by Couro and Margaret Langdon, a linguist who specialized in that language. The participants included some Diegueño young people and some other locals with an interest in the language, and the sessions consisted mainly of elicitation of words and phrases from Couro, with Langdon writing them on the board and the participants copying them down. The Hupas have a similar Wednesday evening get-together—a few native speakers, a few young Hupa second-language learners and interested tribal members, and sometimes one or two linguists. As with the Northern Diegueño sessions, the Hupa sessions tend to be informal language reminiscences by the speakers and elicitation of vocabulary by the learners, who often write the words down as they hear them.

These informal language classes are meaningful gatherings, and participants get great pleasure out of them. They are also potentially useful for documentation of the language. However, they are not a way for someone to learn to speak the language. Learning to speak the language can only come through intensive exposure and practice to connected speech and real conversation.

Bilingual Education

Classroom teaching of endangered languages was extremely rare until the advent of bilingual education in the United States and elsewhere in the 1970s. Given that the schools were one of the main instruments by which indigenous languages were purposely eradicated by governments, the previous lack of presence of indigenous languages in the classroom is tragic but not surprising. As discussed in Chapters 1 and 3, the civil rights movement of the 1960s and related political events resulted in a slow but strong liberalization of educational policy, one aspect of which was the development of bilingual education. While bilingual education was originally conceived by legislators as applying mainly to immigrant groups and Spanish-speaking populations, it also created a flowering of opportunity for indigenous languages to enter the classrooms for the first time. However, the main thrust of bilingual education from its inception was the teaching of classroom subjects in children's native language, not the teaching of the language itself. Thus bilingual education flourished mainly in communities where children spoke the language at home. Teaching school subjects in the language necessitated language engineering: many indigenous languages had no writing systems, so orthographies, literature, and curriculum materials, as well as new vocabulary and genres of writing such as essays and poetry, had to be developed. Thus new genres and literature were developed even as spoken language was in decline in indigenous communities. From the outset, those speech communities whose languages were in decline used this opportunity to try to teach the language to children who did not know it, but the bias of bilingual education was often toward the written word, and there was little training available to the teachers in language teaching methods. In fact, inadequate training has been a problem that has plagued bilingual education among the smaller language groups for years. Speakers of indigenous languages of the United States or of immigrants who had a minority language heritage in the old country (such as the Hmong and other minority groups from Asia, or indigenous people from Latin America) rarely had teaching credentials. Usually they were only teachers' aides, a status that gave them little or no authority over curriculum and little access to relevant and useful training programs. Sometimes actual damage was done to the health of the language through bilingual education programs. As an example, colleagues and I have on a number of occasions observed bilingual education classes in communities where the children were quite strongly bilingual in their language (let us call it language X) and English by the time they reached kindergarten age. Adults were concerned, though, about attrition of indigenous vocabulary among the children, who often used English rather than language X for such things as numbers, colors, kinship terms, and so on. Thus it was considered a priority to make sure the children learned these terms in language X. A teacher's aide (a fluent bilingual) often ran the class but spoke mostly in English and gave the words only as translations from English. This meant that the children were hearing much more English than language X during the class and were also learning the words in terms of English concepts. For example, language X might use different words for "grandmother" depending on whether it is the mother's side or the father's side, but only one set would be taught, so that the children learned to use the same word for both, as in English. The end result is that the children were learning English concepts, and language X only provided alternative labels for these concepts. This is a much better lesson about English than about language X!

Despite these problems with some indigenous language bilingual education programs, there were also many programs that were excellent, such as the Hualapai program and the Rock Point Navajo bilingual education program, among others. (For a good description of the excellent Hualapai program, which was chosen as a model program by the government, see Watahomigie and McCarty 1997, and see Crawford 1997 for an excellent description of good bilingual education practices in general, along with the political forces acting against them.)

But in general, because of the transitional emphasis of government policy and the assumption that the ancestral tongue is learned at home, the development of effective language teaching methods for indigenous languages was not supported under bilingual education, and most programs for indigenous bilingual education have found that it has not stopped the erosion of the language from the community.

Immersion

The old methods of foreign language teaching used to be the "text and translation" methods, where students learned to read, write, and understand the grammatical structure of the language, but did not learn to speak it. During World War II, the U.S. government had a great need for American military personnel who could speak the languages of the countries in which they were stationed, and whole new methods of intensive, orally based language teaching were developed. Since then, orally based language teaching has slowly begun to enter the school system, as at least a part of the foreign language curriculum (although a great many schools are still using the old "text and translation" methods only—change is slow). Since the late 1970s, when changes in immigration policy allowed a great influx of new immigrants to the United

States, intensive and effective methods have also been developed for the teaching of English to children in the schools. ESL (English as a second language) is now a specialty in which future teachers can receive a degree. (Again, many schools lack the resources for effective English teaching; good methodology is available in general, but training programs and funding to pay for well-trained ESL teachers is missing in many schools.)

There is now a huge body of literature on second-language teaching methods, but mostly on the languages of the national majorities—for instance, English, Spanish, and so on. Nevertheless, much of the theory and methodology of teaching world languages can also be applied to endangered languages.

IMMERSION SCHOOLS: INTRODUCTION

A model that is being used increasingly in the United States and elsewhere is the full immersion program, where all instruction in the classroom is carried out in the endangered language. There is no doubt that this is the best way to jump-start the production of a new generation of fluent speakers for an endangered language. There is no other system of language revitalization that has such complete access to so many members of the younger generation (who are the best language learners) for so many hours per day. There are an increasing number of programs worldwide where immersion preschools teach children to communicate in the endangered language, and for a number of programs it has been possible to develop an immersion schooling system all the way through high school and even into college. Hawaiian and Māori are two languages discussed in this book that have developed a whole generation of new speakers through this type of program.

The main activity of any language revitalization program is to teach people the language who have not learned it as a first language. The question of how to teach the language to others is one of the central questions in program design. Most of us have had the experience of being taught a foreign language as a subject in elementary or high school, but—and this is especially true if we attended public schools in the United States—if that was our only exposure to the language, we came away knowing very little. My own experience with learning Spanish began in elementary school, where we all got paper nameplates with Spanish versions of our first names on them and learned colors, animals, and the numbers from 1 to 10. In high school we focused on Spanish grammar and reading and on answering test questions involving grammar and reading comprehension. Neither of these experiences taught me to understand what a native Spanish speaker was saying or to carry on a meaningful conversation in the language. It was not until I went to South

America for a year that I felt as if I had really learned how to speak and understand Spanish. What happened that year was that I was immersed in Spanish. The language was all around me all the time, and if I wanted to communicate anything to anyone, I had to do it in Spanish. This was a kind of sink-or-swim immersion. Even better would have been structured immersion, which I experienced years later in French immersion classes at the University of California at San Diego and at Aix-en-Provence. In both these immersion situations, learning to converse was treated quite differently from learning to read. Conversation was taught entirely in immersion style: the teachers spoke only in French, and students had to respond in French. Taped lessons added more exposure time, but in the conversation component we learned everything by ear, not by reading it. In order to understand the tapes, a written English translation was provided; but we never saw them written in French. We learned to "shadow" the tapes: we would practice saying the taped excerpt along with the speaker until we could keep up. Grammar was not explained to us in the conversation section of the class; even though we understood what a given sentence meant, we did not necessarily know which word meant what, or even where one word stopped and another began. Like first-language learners, we assimilated the information that allowed us to understand and construct connected speech without prior conscious analysis. We also received separate lessons in grammar, but the grammar lessons allowed us to recognize constructions we were already using rather than showing us constructions for the first time.

The main point to be made here is that the way most of us have been taught languages in the public schools has not provided a very good model for an ideal language-learning program. Many attempts at teaching endangered languages have had disappointing results because of poorly developed teaching methodology. The programs involve overly repetitive review of a small range of vocabulary or spend too much time "explaining" the language in English rather than actually using the language, or depend too much on writing things down rather than aural learning, or never get to the point of teaching people how to talk in complete sentences or how to communicate about real things.

In recent decades there has been a great deal of research on effective language teaching. Reading some textbooks for future teachers who are learning how to teach bilingual education or ESL or methodological texts on foreign language teaching will show some of the teaching theories and methods that can help a good language teaching program get off the ground. But there is no absolutely set program that will work for all languages. Endangered languages, in particular, may have certain restrictions on resources, opportunities, and cultural conditions that will place specialized demands or present specialized opportunities for teaching. And because the languages we are concerned about are endangered, time is also of the essence. Rather than waiting until the best possible program has been thoroughly planned in advance, it is often best to just start right away with whatever knowledge and resources are available and learn, plan, and grow as you go.

Teaching the Language in the Schools

There are many school programs around the country now that are involved in the teaching of local endangered languages. There are three main types of language programs: teaching an endangered language as a subject (like a foreign language), bilingual education, and full-scale immersion programs. Different goals, benefits, limitations, and results characterize these three types.

Immersion schools solve all the problems discussed above for the other types of school program: they provide sufficient exposure to the language to produce fluent speakers, and they also provide a venue for using the language in real communication. In the immersion schools, the presence of the target language is so strong that children tend to use it with each other outside the classroom as well as in.

The immersion schools and classrooms also have certain limitations. Because of educational laws and regulations, immersion schools are not easy to found. Hawai'i had to change a state law mandating English as the only allowable language of instruction in order to allow the Hawaiian language immersion classes to exist. Any community who has an immersion school in mind must realize that it will involve years of legal wrangling and figuring out ways to comply with all the local and state regulations. But it can be done—and there are a growing number of successful immersion schools to attest to that.

As indicated earlier, it is not enough for children to know a language; they must also use it robustly with others if the language is to continue. Problems develop if the immersion classroom is in a school where other classrooms are in English, for in those cases English is the language of the playground, and children become used to talking to their peers in English. Developing that habit does not bode well for hopes that these children will grow up to use their language in the home, even if they know the target language fluently.

The school is a specialized setting that makes strong demands on subject matter and interaction style. When a language is chosen as the language of instruction, that language must be developed to accommodate the needs of education. Thus a language that might never have been used to communicate such things before must develop vocabulary for math and science and must develop discourse styles that fit the situation. (For example, giving oral book reports or writing essays may be things that have never been done in the language before.) Developing new vocabulary and discourse styles is not that hard, but it does change the language. People who wish to revitalize their language because of a desire to return to traditional culture and values must be aware that language revitalization does not automatically bring people back to these traditional modes of thought. If the language is learned solely in school, then it is school culture and school values that are learned along with it. Even when a conscious effort is made to teach traditional culture and values, the schoolroom agenda imposes its own culture on the students.

Another problem is that for some families and communities, devoting all education to the endangered language may seem like too much—they fear that children will not get sufficient English-language education to keep up in the higher grades or in college. This is a constant debate in communities that have immersion schools. But this level of intensity in language teaching may be the only thing that works in turning around language decline. In fact, even the immersion classroom is not sufficient unto itself to turn around language death: it is essential that the families play an active role as well. Students whose families are unwilling or unable to reinforce the language at home do not fare as well as students with active families. Thus, the successful immersion programs also usually have a family component in which parents are asked to learn the language in night classes, to volunteer in the immersion classroom, and to reinforce at home the lessons the students learn in school.

To make a final general point about language revitalization in the classroom setting, the classroom is the most efficient place to teach the target language, but no classroom program is sufficient unto itself; it must be accompanied by family commitments and other community programs. One reason that Māori and Hawaiian programs have worked so well is that their school programs have developed out of grassroots community movements that include other components to language revitalization. A number of families who were second-language learners of their ancestral languages chose, even prior to the establishment of the schools, to raise their children in the language at home. Bringing the language back as the first language of the home is the true heart of language revitalization. No school can make that happen; only families can. However, the schools can play a vital role in helping to make that transition to home speaking possible. They can provide a new generation with the fluency to make such a transition possible, and since the fear of having their children enter schools without knowing the language of the school was one of the main reasons that previous generations switched to English at home in the first place, just knowing that their children will go to a school where the ancestral tongue is the language of instruction will make it safe now for parents to speak it to their children at home.

Other Kinds of Immersion Programs

Schools are not the only place where language immersion can take place. Where language programs in the schools are impossible or insufficient, after-school programs may be created. While children are often tired at this time of day and less attentive, a well-designed after-school program (especially one that combines language with recreation) can help children develop skills in the target language. Intensive summer language programs for children are increasingly utilized to supplement school programs, or if school programs are impossible, to do instead of them. A great deal of language can be learned in a two- or three-month summer program; however, what is learned is soon forgotten if the language is not reinforced during the school year. But an intensive summer program reinforced by a nonintensive school program might have quite excellent long-term results.

Another common kind of program is evening classes for adults or families. In practice these are usually held once a week and rarely involve immersion; but of course they can be taught in that manner. As mentioned before, the best school programs have a family component that is often a weekly evening class.

In Hawai'i, a group on O'ahu recently received a grant for a community recreation program that would be run in Hawaiian: they are holding regular events such as baseball and cookouts where only Hawaiian is spoken (see Chapter 12). This kind of program, where immersion-style learning is combined with other activities, is especially promising for endangered languages, where the language has to be brought into real communication situations again if it is to survive. A program such as this takes language learning outside of the classroom situation and puts it into daily life.

A program in California that has had good results is the California Master-Apprentice Language Learning Program, run by the Advocates for Indigenous California Language Survival (Chapter 17). In this program, the last elderly speakers of California Indian languages are paired with young relatives who want to learn the language, and they are taught immersion-style techniques of language teaching and learning to do together, one on one. It is stressed that rather than do "lessons" most of the time, the team should do activities together—cooking, gathering, housework, taking a walk or a drive—and communicate at all times in the language during these activities. In this way, as with the O'ahu community recreation program, language learning takes place in the context of real communication, thus doing both jobs that a revitalization program must do—teaching the language and bringing it into use in daily life.

There are a number of talented individuals who have completely managed their own language learning. One of these is Loren Bommelyn, who decided as a young man that he wanted to learn his ancestral language, Tolowa, fluently. He managed his learning program by asking the elders how to say things, by then practicing those things with the elders and on his own, and later by the ingenious method of deciding to say everything in Tolowa before saying it in English, no matter who he was talking to. This way he both practiced his language extensively and also found out what he did not

know yet; he would then ask the elders when next he was with them. His technique involved a rather brave act, for it tended to create a strange interaction between himself and other people, many of whom were not Tolowa and none of whom knew the language (other than the few elders that he had taken on as his teachers)—but when there is no way to learn within a real communication situation, this unique method works very well. By this means, Bommelyn created an immersion situation for himself even when the language was not spoken by anyone else around him. And the end result was that he has become a fully fluent speaker—one a good 50 years younger than any other fluent speaker of Tolowa.

SOME BASIC TEACHING METHODS

There have been many theories and methods of second-language teaching developed in recent decades, most of them related to language immersion techniques. There are many different models, but most of them share basic similarities. We find the key factors in successful language teaching and learning to be:

(1) If the goal is to develop oral competence, the main methods of teaching should be oral (rather than written).

(2) Language lessons should be "immersion" style, where the target language is used solely, without English translation. Still, the learners must be able to understand, at least partly, what is being said, through contextual clues. Thus the teacher must use gestures, miming, actions, pictures, and so on, to make himself or herself understood. (This is called "comprehensible input.")

(3) Learners need to be engaged in real communication efforts, rather than just hearing and spouting language. Learning lists of words alone does not help a person learn how to communicate. (For example, you do not just teach students a list of kinship terms; once you show them the vocabulary, you immediately engage them in communicative activities such as having them ask each other to tell who their family members at home are.) Communication-based teaching and learning leads to much more thorough learning of vocabulary and of grammar. Let me give an example. In Havasupai, while it is possible to learn kinship terms as nouns, if they are used in conversation they often occur as verbs. For example, the word *jita* translates as "mother," but that word alone would almost never be heard. If you want to say "she is my mother" in Havasupai, you cannot translate that from English word for word; instead, you say "ñaj jita'wi"—literally, "I 'mother' her" (which perhaps makes more sense if it is translated something like "I call her mother"). A construction like this is so different from English that special attention must be paid to it. It

is obvious that just learning the nouns for kinship terms is not enough to allow a learner to actually use that vocabulary in meaningful conversation. The only way to learn meaningful conversation is to engage in it.

(4) Repetition without repetitiveness: one formula is the "20 × 20 rule": that a learner has to hear or use a word 20 times in 20 different situations before he or she masters it. But just saying a word 400 times does not do the job. Classes should always have a review component, and old vocabulary must be included in activities that also practice new vocabulary. Thus, if last week's lesson was about numbers and this week's is about kinship terms, some activities can include practice with both—for example, asking each person how many brothers and sisters they have.

(5) Activities, active physical work, and games related to the vocabulary or phrases being learned help the learning process in many ways, by making it more interesting, keeping up the attention level, associating words with actions, and so on.

(6) Comprehension precedes production. That is, a student first understands a word and then starts being able to say it. For comprehension, there are two stages: first, coming to understand what the teacher is saying (because of nonverbal cues, etc.); and then coming to recognize the word or sentence without the verbal cues being present. For example, the teacher may say "Stand up!" and make gestures with her arms that make the students understand what they are expected to do, and they then do it. After a while, the students will recognize the word without any nonverbal cues. Production also has two stages: *mimicking* and true *production*. A student may be able to mimic what the teacher says right after the teacher says it, but may not yet be able to dredge the word up from memory without that immediate cue from the teacher. Later, a student can say the word voluntarily without the teacher's saying it first; that is true production. Activities regarding new material should keep this in mind: the first presentation leads to *understanding*, and later activities test *recognition*. Mimicking may begin with the first presentation, but only after recognition will true production finally develop. While all four stages of learning can be practiced during a single lesson, the final stage, long-term *retention*, may take longer. A student may forget in-between lessons, and it may take a lot more practice in review before he or she can retain the material for the long term.

The teacher provides practice and tests comprehension through activities involving commands (which the students then perform) and yes-no questions (e.g., pointing to her ear and asking "Is this my nose?" and students answering "yes" or "no"). *Mimicking practice* can be given by instructions such as saying in the target language "Say 'nose,'" or asking either-or questions such as "Is this my ear or my nose?" (students answer "ear" or "nose"). *Production practice* is exemplified by *wh*-questions: "What is this?" (the student must answer with the appropriate word), or "What am I doing?" and so on. Various activities and games can be designed for practicing and testing either comprehension or production.

(7) Teaching grammar can be implicit rather than explicit. There is much debate in the literature and among learners about the role of grammatical analysis. Should students be taught explicitly about grammatical terminology and taught things like "To form the past tense, add such and such a prefix"? Or should they instead be taught implicitly, without grammatical terminology, so that they will acquire the patterns inductively, and often unconsciously, through mere exposure to them? The latter is the way children learn their first language, and there is a great deal of good evidence that a second language can be learned the same way. But some adults prefer explicit grammatical analysis and get frustrated and uncomfortable without it. And since a positive attitude is also important to the learning process, sometimes a teacher must cater to a learner's desires. For this reason explicit explanation of grammatical processes might sometimes be necessary, but in fact the real learning takes place through exposure and use, not through memorizing a stated rule.

Many endangered languages have no grammatical analyses available anyway, or perhaps only linguistic grammars, which are not geared the same way that teaching grammars would be. The only speakers who are available to teach the language may not have any explicit grammatical knowledge (that is, they may not know what counts as a noun, verb, or relative clause, or what a prefix or suffix is), even though they have mastered the grammar of their language as native speakers. Thus they may not be able to explain the grammar very much. It is therefore important to remember that grammar can be taught without explicit grammatical analysis. See Chapter 18 for a detailed example of how to teach grammar implicitly.

(8) Criticism discourages learners from speaking and participating and thus discourages them from learning. Praise and positive forms of correction enhance the learning process.

Planning Lessons

For most (but not all) endangered languages, teachers are pretty much on their own with regard to planning what they will teach and how they will teach it. There are few or no books or materials available to them from which they can work. Teachers must use their imagination and their ingenuity to develop effective language courses.

TABLE 14.1   Approaches to Lesson Planning

Vocabulary	Grammar	Situations
Numbers	Plurals	Everyday life:
Colors	Past, present, future	Greeting people
Kinship terms	Case (object, subject, etc.)	Shopping
Animals	Adjectives	Talking on phone
Plants	Word order	Planting garden
Clothing	Transitive and intransitive verbs	Cooking
Seasons, months, days	Irregular verbs	Driving car
Weather and astronomical terms	(etc.)	Traditional life:
Kitchen utensils		Language usage for a particular ceremony
Household objects		Traditional crafts
Actions (stand, walk, give . . .)		Prayer
(etc.)		Traditional medicine
		Traditional cooking
		School life:
		Sharing
		Reading and writing
		Math, history, and other subjects
		Hanging up coat
		Washing hands
		Using bathroom
		Snack time
		Playground activities
		(etc.)

The first stage in lesson planning is to figure out what exactly you plan to teach in a given lesson. There are at least three ways to come up with ideas on topics: the vocabulary-based approach (e.g., animals, colors, numbers); the grammar-based approach (e.g., adjectives, plurals, word order); and the situationally based approach (e.g., greetings, talking on the phone, making a basket). Table 14.1 provides a few of the many ideas that will come to mind depending on which approach you take.

When planning a course, a language teacher should probably use all three approaches. Thinking about vocabulary sets is useful for beginning classes, but you run out of inspiration very soon. Thinking of lessons in grammar is also of limited productivity (though it can be important). When thinking about lessons in terms of grammar, it is very important to think about the grammar of the particular language being taught. For example, some languages might have no noun plurals but would perhaps have ways of marking on the verb if more than one participant is involved. Some languages have no simple past separate from present tense. Some languages have verb stems that change in form depending on what affix is added. Some languages have special obligatory affixes for things an English speaker would never think of—such as evidentials, which are affixed to verbs in statements

in order to communicate how the speaker knows what he is stating: whether he saw it, inferred it from indirect evidence, heard it from someone else, or learned it in some other way. Thus, what is important to teach in the way of grammar differs from language to language.

Thinking in terms of situations is the most fruitful of the three strategies. Besides the everyday activities that most people do and the traditional activities that may be part of your community heritage, a given speech community might have other situations specific to it: perhaps the community does cattle ranching, or herding of some domesticated animal, or horseback riding and packing, or perhaps it has a timber industry. Whatever is important will provide a situational base of interest for language learning. Each situation will provide inspiration about what vocabulary and what grammar is necessary to master in order to communicate.

One reason situationally based teaching is so beneficial is that what is learned is immediately usable in real communication. If the teaching is taking place in a classroom, for example, everything you do in the classroom can be done in the target language. If you call roll, instead of having students answer "Here!" in English, find an equivalent phrase in the target language to teach them to use instead. If the teaching is being done on a one-on-one level with adults (Chapter 17), a coffee-serving ritual might be developed, so that students learn how to say all those things we say around coffee, such as, "Would you like a cup of coffee?" "Do you want cream?" "No, I drink it black," and so on. Terry and Sarah Supahan (Chapter 15) write that before planning a lesson they ask themselves what it is that they want their students to communicate—what the function of the language is that they want their students to learn. Once they have answered that question, then they can have a clear idea of what to teach. Arviso and Holm's essay in this volume (Chapter 16), gives excellent exemplification of situationally based classroom activities done in the target language (in this case, Navajo).

Each lesson should have:

(1) a review component (possibly embedded in (3));
(2) presentation of new vocabulary, phrases, and/or grammatical constructions, perhaps tied to a particular situation (also possibly embedded in (3)); and
(3) communicative activities allowing practice of the new items (and review of old items); these activities should first test comprehension of new material and then go into production practice.

So after you have decided on the topic you will be teaching (such as animals, plurals, traditional cooking, or some other subject), plan the following:

(1) specifics of vocabulary, phrases, and so on;
(2) specific activities you will do, making sure that some of them are for comprehension and some for production; and
(3) props you need for the activities.

Sample Lesson: Clothing

Initial Presentation and Practice

(1) Indicate your own clothing and that of students, while saying in the target language, "I'm wearing a shirt." Continue to say sentences containing "shirt" while going around the room and indicating several shirts. "Julia and Marv have on pants. Who else has pants? Mary has a skirt. Joanne has a dress. These are shoes; those are sandals . . ." and so on.
(2) Comprehension: Right from the beginning of the presentation, get students active too by having them point out who else has on a skirt, and so on.
(3) If you have done colors in a previous lesson, insert a review component by asking "Who has blue pants?" "Does anyone have brown pants?" and so on.
(4) Production: Ask students questions that demand the use of the new vocabulary in their answer, such as "Is that a shirt or a jacket?" "What is this?" (while indicating a piece of clothing). "What is Julia wearing?" or "Julia, what are you wearing?"

Possible activities (do not do all of these in one lesson, just choose two or three at most before going on to some other topic. These are just a few ideas out of dozens of possibilities; think up your own, but always ask yourself how they will be useful in enhancing the practice and use of the target language):

(1) Do commands relating to clothes (props: bring extra-large clothing of various types): "Julia, put on this jacket" (help her put it on if she doesn't understand). "Marv, put on these pants." After students understand the command, you can start leaving out the nonverbal cues, while saying, "John, put on a shirt." "Mary, put on a dress," and so on. (If someone does not understand right away, put the nonverbal cues back for him or her.)

Other commands could include: "Julia, take off the jacket"; "Fold the jacket"; "Give the jacket to Marv"; "Hang the jacket up on this hanger" (props: jacket, hanger). This exercise gives practice in comprehension.
(2) Clothes-washing activity (props: clothes, laundry tub, soap, pitcher, clothespins, clothesline): In this activity, the teacher can improvise a lot; the goal is to get the students to hear long sequences of connected speech, including but not limited to clothing words. Even if they do not follow every word, nonverbal cues will make the gist of everything understandable. The patter, along with nonverbal cues and activities, could go something like this (all in the target language, of course):

"This is a clothesline. Mary, would you help me hang it up over here? Thank you. I brought a washtub. John, bring that washtub over to this table. Put it down on the table. That's good. Now we can pretend to put water in the washtub. Julia, would you take this pitcher and pour in the water? [said while gesturing to Julia to get her to come take pitcher and pretend to pour in water]. This is soap. Julia, put some soap in the washtub. Marvin, get that jacket and bring it over here. Marv, get the pants, shirts, and dresses and bring them here. [Pick one up, smell it, and make a face.] Eew, that shirt's dirty! Put them in the tub. Good. Stay here now and we'll wash the clothes together. Scrub them well. Now wring everything out. Wring out that shirt; good; now put it aside. Wring out that jacket; put it aside. Wring out those pants; put them aside. . . . Now we'll hang the clothes up. John, Mary, here are some clothespins; take these clothes to the clothesline and hang them up. Hang up the skirts. Hang up the dresses . . ." and so on.

[Later]: "OK, everything is dry. Julia, Marv, take down the clothes. Marv, fold these pants. Julia, fold the dresses. Mary, fold the shirts [etc]."

Note: In an informal program like the master-apprentice program, instead of pretending to wash clothes, the teacher and learner can really wash clothes together.
(3) Vocabulary race (props: large sheet of paper on wall with pictures of different articles of clothing on it): Divide

children into two lines by some criterion, for instance, people born from January to June versus those born from July to December; the front of the line is 15 feet or so from the picture. When the teacher calls out the name of an item of clothing, the front two children race to the picture and try to touch their finger to the correct one; the first one to touch it wins a point for his or her team. Then they go to the back of the line. This is a fast game that gets children's heart rate up, which is good for overcoming afternoon sleepiness. This exercise is for comprehension practice.

(4) Memory: In this old game, a bunch of cards are lying spread out face down on the table, and players take turns turning up two cards. If the cards are the same, they get to keep the pair. This can be adapted to the learning of nouns: for example, you could make pairs of cards with the names of items of clothing and other vocabulary the students have been learning. An added task would be that students get to keep the pair only if they can name the item depicted.

(5) Paper dolls (props: sets of paper dolls): This is good to do with kids, but boys will not like it unless they can play with paper dolls of G.I. Joe or some other action figure. In the right atmosphere, adults will enjoy this too. Hand out paper dolls and scissors—probably one set of paper dolls and two pairs of scissors to each pair of people in the class (if you have a big class and little money for paper dolls, the groups can be larger). Tell everyone to "cut out a dress," or "cut out a skirt," or "cut out pants," and so on. Have people dress their paper doll and then tell you what it is wearing. While people are cutting things out, go around the room engaging the students in simple conversation about the clothes, saying, for example, "Show me a skirt," testing comprehension, or "What is this?" (pointing to a piece of paper doll clothing), testing production. This is mostly comprehension practice but also can involve some production, depending on what questions the teacher asks.

(6) Clothing musical chairs (props: chairs in a circle with students sitting on them. There needs to be one fewer chair than there are people.): This game allows students to actually speak, whereas most of the other games above test their comprehension rather than production. Whoever is "it" (probably the teacher will be the first "it") stands in the middle and has to say in the target language some item of clothing and perhaps its color, like this: "Everyone wearing white socks get up!" (For beginning students it could be something simpler, like "White socks!") So everyone wearing white socks has to get up and find another chair (they are not allowed to sit back down in the chair they just vacated). Meanwhile, the person who is "it" also tries to grab one of the chairs, so most likely another person will end up being "it." Then that person says, for example, "Everyone wearing a skirt get up!" and so on.

(7) Have students mill about and ask each other "What are you wearing?" This gives production practice.

Grammar note: A given language will have different kinds of grammar that will show up in a lesson like this. In some languages, nouns will take different forms depending on whether it is the subject or the object. So in "Put on the dress," the word for "dress" in the target language may, for example, have a suffix. Thus the activities above will teach people how to use words with these suffixes on them. Other languages may have other things going on. In Havasupai, for example, you cannot just say "I'm wearing [pants, a dress, shoes, etc.]." There is no word for "wear." You must instead turn the word for "pants" or "dress" or "shoes" into a verb. For example, *mahño* is "shoes," but "I'm wearing shoes" is *ñaj mahñok'wi,* literally "I'm shoe-ing." So for people learning Havasupai, the grammar implicit in the lesson would be that of turning nouns into verbs.

Depending on the length of time a class meets, the illustrated lesson on clothing terms may just be one out of two or three topics that would be focused on during class time.

Inexperienced teachers having to make up their own curriculum often focus too much on the teaching of nouns, when the core of real language tends to be in the verbs. No one can utter a sentence without a verb in it. There are many ways to make sure that your teaching involves verbs.

(1) If you do have a noun-based lesson (such as clothing), make sure that your practice and activities involve a lot of full sentences, such as actions that can be done to clothes (putting them on, taking them off, washing them, hanging them up, folding them, etc.).
(2) Think about verb-based lessons, such as various actions people can do.
(3) Situationally based lessons involving conversational development will always be verb-focused in large part.
(4) Some teachers base a whole lesson or series of lessons around a story. The teacher can tell the story using pictures or props (e.g., puppets) to make the story understood. Students can do projects around the story such as turning it into a play, which they later perform. Stories give students good exposure to long stretches of connected speech that contain lots of verbs.

The above are just a few ideas for classroom activities and lesson development. Other ideas can be found in many essays in this book. Read up on methodology and use your imagination. Make sure your lessons are active, interactive, entertaining, and rich in the target language. English should be barred from the classroom.

When the Teacher Is Not Fluent

Unfortunately, for endangered languages of small speech communities, especially those that only have a few speakers (and those few elderly), the people who end up teaching in the classroom are usually not fluent speakers. Of course, every effort should be made to have fluent speakers as teachers, but we have seen many instances where this is not possible. Rich immersion-style teaching cannot be done if the teacher is not fluent.

If there are speakers of the language who for one reason or another cannot be the teachers, a number of strategies can be used to enrich the learning situation.

(1) Have a fluent speaker as a teacher's aide or visitor, and plan with that speaker various ways in which they can actively participate, using the full richness of their language. For example, the speaker and teacher could prepare a storytelling lesson, with the teacher making pictures or props to go with the story. Or the speaker might teach songs to the children (if it is culturally appropriate to do so) or do sessions based on traditional crafts. The teacher may have to work with the speaker first to train him or her in ways to be understood without reverting to English.

(2) Hire a speaker as a consultant to the teacher to help the teacher prepare lessons. A nonfluent teacher will never be able to teach the language as effectively as a fluent one (assuming the fluent speaker knows the principles of teaching), but by working closely with a fluent speaker, there can still be fresh materials for each class session, and the teacher can remain a step ahead of the students.

(3) The teacher is honor bound to increase his or her fluency level as much as possible. Thus the teacher must expect to spend a great deal of time outside the classroom learning the language. If there are no formal classes anywhere, the teacher must do this through any available materials and working closely with native speakers. A learning program like the master-apprentice program (Chapter 17) is one way an adult can learn the target language from a native speaker. The teacher might learn from the speaker during school terms between classes, and/or he or she could do intensive summer sessions with the speaker.

Chapter 15 is a lovely discussion of excellent teaching methodology through immersion principles, taught by teachers who when they started out were not fluent in the Karuk language. They have done all the suggestions above, have created an excellent language teaching program, and in the process have continually become more and more proficient in Karuk.

When Immersion Is Impossible

Immersion of any sort may simply be impossible for the teacher, if he or she does not know the language well and it is difficult or impossible to get the assistance of a fluent speaker. In that case, what the students learn will have to be more limited. It is common when the teacher is not fluent to fall back on teaching vocabulary items alone, so that students learn to name things but not to put those names into sentences. We strongly recommend that even without immersion, communicative practice be a strong component of the language teaching sessions if at all possible. The teacher can learn and then teach pattern commands fitting some of the activities shown above for the lessons on clothing, for example, "Give me the X," "Pick up the X," and "Put down the X." Also, the teacher can learn and teach questions relevant to a particular vocabulary set, such as "What is this?" or "What are you wearing today?" Knowing just a few commands and questions gives the interactive basis needed for interesting exercises and practice routines for the class, and once students learn how to utter these commands and questions themselves, they have the potential to use the language in communicative situations.

Even if nonfluent teachers decide they must focus on vocabulary for most of the class time, they might be able to develop some specific communicative goals for themselves and their class. Here are just a few out of hundreds of possibilities:

(1) Greetings could be done in the target language. Many languages have no words for "hello" or "goodbye," but every language has greetings of some sort, such as telling people it is good to see them again, announcing that you are leaving now, and so on.

(2) It is very empowering for a student to learn how to introduce himself appropriately in his language. In Navajo, for example, students would learn how to introduce themselves according to their ancestral clan affiliations. In some cases, one may just learn how to say in the target language, "My name is X, and I come from Y."

(3) A ritual that could be done in every class would be to ask someone what the weather is like today. There might be just a few weather terms that are taught to the class—sunny, raining, foggy, cloudy, windy, hot, cold—and each day a different student could be asked to say which of those terms applies to the weather today.

(4) Some kind of communicative question-answer sequence could be developed for every lesson on vocabulary. For example, I have already suggested "What are you wearing?" as a good question to ask students so that they can practice saying clothing terms. If you can, teach the students to answer in sentence form in the target language—for example, "I'm wearing pants and a shirt." If you are doing colors, each student could be asked to name the colors he or she is wearing. Other kinds of questions would be "Who is wearing blue?" or "Do you have blue on?"

CONCLUSION

Immersion methods of teaching have been most successful in teaching endangered languages. However, one of the problems with conversationally based immersion methods is sometimes that although conversational proficiency is developed, grammatical correctness lags behind. One of the major differences between the teaching of endangered languages and foreign-language teaching is that the students learning an endangered language are probably going to one day be the only speakers of that language. Thus any kind of error in grammar, pronunciation, communicative practices, and so on will actually become part of that language in the future. There is therefore a more solemn responsibility for the teachers to teach, and the learners to learn, the language as completely, as competently, and as correctly as is humanly possible. This is not said to discourage anyone from doing what they can even if they know it is not perfect. Rather, it is important not to be complacent about what is being taught. Evaluate frequently, add new components to the program whenever possible, and realize that every success is a step, and never the last step.

References

Asher, James J. 1977. *Learning another language through actions.* Los Gatos, Calif.: Sky Oaks Productions.

Brewster, E. Thomas, and Elizabeth S. Brewster. 1976. *Language acquisition made practical: Field methods for language learners.* Colorado Springs: Lingua House.

Brown, H. Douglas. 1987. *Principles of language learning and teaching.* 2d ed. Englewood Cliffs, N.J.: Prentice-Hall.

Crawford, James. 1997. *Bilingual education: History, politics, theory, and practice.* 3d ed. Los Angeles: Bilingual Education Services.

Hadley, Alice Omaggio. 1993. *Teaching language in context.* 2d ed. Boston, MA: Heinle and Heinle.

Hinton, Leanne. 1999. Teaching endangered languages. In *Concise encyclopedia of educational linguistics,* ed. B. Spolsky. Oxford: Elsevier Science.

Krashen, Stephen D., and Tracy D. Terrell. 1983. *The natural approach: Language acquisition in the classroom.* Englewood Cliffs, N.J.: Prentice-Hall.

Richards, Jack C., and Theodore S. Rodgers. 1986. *Approaches and methods in language teaching: A description and analyis.* Cambridge and New York: Cambridge University Press.

Watahomigie, Lucille J., and Teresa L. McCarty. 1997. Literacy for what? Hualapai literacy and language maintenance. In *Indigenous literacies in the Americas: Language planning from the bottom up,* ed. Nancy Hornberger. Berlin and New York: Mouton de Gruyter.

The Karuk Language

LEANNE HINTON
Department of Linguistics
University of California at Berkeley
Berkeley, California

The Karuk language is spoken in Northern California, along the upper reaches of the Klamath River. Karuk is a Hokan language, and, along with its neighbors Yurok (Algic) and Hupa (Athapaskan), has been famous as a test of the Sapir-Whorf hypothesis. The Sapir-Whorf hypothesis states that thought is governed by language, so that speaking a different language is not just a matter of words and grammar, but rather a whole different worldview. Karuk, Yurok, and Hupa are from three different language families, and yet they share a striking amount of their culture—so much so that William Bright wrote, "Aboriginal Karok culture was essentially the same as that of the neighboring Yurok and Hupa tribes" (Bright 1957, p. 1). Bright was in company with A. L. Kroeber, who stated essentially the same claim in 1925: "The Yurok shared this civilization in identical form with their neighbors, the Hupa and Karok" (Kroeber 1925, p. 5). If the Sapir-Whorf hypothesis is to be believed, how could three totally unrelated, totally different languages represent what appears to be the same worldview? In a later article, William and Jane Bright began to examine this problem in detail, and found a way to salvage the Sapir-Whorf hypothesis, by showing that in fact the languages had converged in some very important ways (Bright and Bright 1965, 1976). One example is that Karuk shares with Yurok a similar system of spatial orientation. The two languages both refer to cardinal directions according to their relationship to the river—instead of terms like "north, south, east, west," they use terms translatable as "upriver, downriver, towards the river, away from the river." In this way both languages reflect the same conceptual structure. Bright and Bright found other such conceptual similarities in some of the other languages of the area. They also pointed out that there seem to be cultural differences between the language groups that make them less similar than previously claimed.

Related to the river-oriented cardinal directions is another interesting feature of Karuk: Karuk has a very large class of directional suffixes with highly specific meanings. The following is a list of suffixes from Bright 1957 (p. 95):

-mu 'thither'

-raa 'hither'

-rupu 'hence downriverward'

-unih 'down from a considerable height; hence uphillward'

-uraa 'up to a considerable height; hence uphillward'

-faku 'hither from uphill'

-rôovu 'hence upriverward'

-várak 'hither from upriver'

-sip(riv) 'up to the height of a man or less'

-ish(rih) 'down from the height of a man or less'

-kath 'hence across a body of water'

-rina 'hither from across a body of water'

-kara 'horizontally away from the center of a body of water'

-rípaa 'horizontally toward the center of a body of water'

-kara 'into one's mouth'

-rupaa 'out of one's mouth'

-rámnih 'into a container'

-ríshuk 'out of a container'

-vara 'in through a tubular space'

-kiv 'out through a tubular space'

-rúprih 'in through a solid'

-rúprav 'out through a solid'

-fúruk 'into an enclosed space'

-rúpuk 'out of an enclosed space'

-vrin 'in opposite directions'

-tunva 'toward each other'

-várayva 'here and there within an enclosed space'

-thuna 'here and there in an open area'

For example, the word 'throw' is *path*, and *paath-kúrih* would be 'to throw into water'; *páath-raa* is 'to throw upwards from downhill'; *paath-rámnih* is 'to throw into (a basket)'; *paath-ríshuk* 'to throw out'; *paath-rôovu* 'to throw upriverward'; *paath-rúpuk* 'to throw outdoors'; and so on. This is, of course, just one of the many delightful aspects of the Karuk language.

Northern California is very active in traditional cultural practices. The Karuks, like other tribes in the region, are deeply involved in summer ceremonies that last many days and nights.

Some of the ceremonies are being reactivated now after decades of nonpractice. Basket makers and regalia craftspeople are increasingly active in their work on the intricate basket hats, head-dresses, necklaces, and skirts made from shells, bear grass, pine nuts, and other natural ingredi-ents. Northern California regalia is among the most beautiful forms of clothing in the world. Karuk song-making is active still, and becoming more so. So many people want to dance that even the elders are complaining that the dance pits get too overfilled with people nowadays.

Besides cultural maintenance and revitalization, the tribes of the region are strongly commit-ted to language revitalization. There has been an almost 30-year history of teaching Karuk in the classroom, first as part of bilingual education, which tended to focus on writing, and now with a more oral approach, which has the goal of creating functional proficiency among students. The Karuk tribe has a language planning committee, an official writing system, and an increasing amount of language materials. They have participated in master-apprentice programs (see Chap-ter 17), classroom education, and language-documentation programs. A number of talented Karuk tribal members have been active in language teaching, teacher training, and the develop-ment of the language arts in recent years, among them Nancy Steele (a trainer and consultant to the Karuks and other tribes in language revitalization), Julian Lang (an artist, playwright, and scholar who has created plays in the Karuk language), and Terry Supahan and his family, who have been especially active in bringing good teaching techniques to the classroom. All of these people have not only been involved with the revitalization of Karuk, but also with consultation for other tribes in the area and around the nation on language teaching methods and curriculum and other aspects of language planning and revitalization.

Despite this activity, or perhaps guiding it, is the knowledge that the last native speakers of Karuk are now very old, and number less than a dozen. The language began to lose ground with the arrival of U.S. government oversight and boarding schools. With no large body of land now, people live scattered throughout the territory their tribe once controlled, and the few remaining speakers live hundreds of miles apart from each other (Sims 1996). We can only hope that the continuing dedicated efforts of the talented people dedicated to language teaching and revitaliza-tion will bear fruit and keep the language from disppearing from the face of the earth.

References

Bright, William. 1957. *The Karok Language.* University of California Publications in Linguistics, vol. 13.
Bright, William, and Jane O. Bright. 1965. Semantic structures in Northwestern California and the Sapir-Whorf Hy-pothesis. *American Anthropologist* 67:5, part 2, *Formal Semantic Analysis,* ed. Eugene Hammel, pp. 249–258. Reprinted in *Variation and Change in Language: Essays by William Bright,* ed. Anwar S. Dil, pp. 74–88. Stanford: Stanford University Press, 1976.
Kroeber, A. L. 1925. *Handbook of the Indians of California.* Bureau of American Ethnology Bulletin 78. Washington: Smithsonian Institution.
Sims, Christine P. 1996. *A Descriptive Study of Two Community Efforts to Preserve their Native Languages.* Washington, D.C.: National Indian Policy Center.

MAP 15.1 Karuk in California

15

Teaching Well, Learning Quickly
Communication-Based Language Instruction

TERRY SUPAHAN

Community Development Consultant
The Shivshaneen Company
Orleans, California

SARAH E. SUPAHAN

Director, Indian Education Program
and Native Language Coordinator
Klamath-Trinity Joint Unified School District
Hoopa, California

Ten years ago, following the death of a family member who was one of only a dozen fluent elders of the Karuk language, we began to research ways to make Indian language learning quicker and easier. We knew we had to find teaching methods for the Karuk language, and other Indian languages, so that they would once again be used on a regular basis and not die with the elders. And we knew we had very little time left.

Ten years ago we were not entirely sure just what we might learn from foreign language instruction. As we talked with professionals in the field (principally Humboldt State University's foreign language professor James Gaasch; the Berkeley sociolinguist Leanne Hinton; and the teacher and director of the Redwood Area World Languages Project [RAWLP], Karen Elfers), it became clear that a successful method of language instruction worked for all languages. Although it was a new idea for us, we started to believe it could work for Native American languages as well.

At Karen Elfers's invitation, we began to attend RAWLP meetings and training opportunities. Soon we were welcomed into this dedicated and professional group as project team members. In the summer of 1993 we organized a two-week summer institute which was attended by many language teachers, including six Native American–language instructors funded through the Klamath-Trinity School District (representing the Hupa, Karuk, and Yurok languages).

It was through RAWLP, and most intensely through the institute, that we learned the communication-based instruction (CBI) method and the five-step lesson plan. This California state framework-based method has now changed the way we teach.

COMMUNICATION-BASED INSTRUCTION

The CBI method involves the use of the targeted language in all instruction, in context, and in ways that communicate. It means that language instruction is to be relevant to students. We found that our desire not to emphasize the written form of Native American languages over the traditional, oral form was validated through this method, especially for younger, elementary-school children.

CBI has as its focus natural communication between people. Our lessons consist of language which communicates things important to Karuk life, whether that means a long time ago or today. This concept may seem simple, but in a discipline that has in the past been taught by translating a written sentence of one language into another language, it is revolutionary.

Before we teach a lesson we ask ourselves what is it we want our students to be able to communicate. What is the function of the language? Do we want our students to be able to have a phone conversation in the language with their peers? Do we want them to be able to understand a traditional Karuk story told in its original language? Do we want them to be able to use the language in the classroom? In their home? At a ceremonial dance? Once we know what the function or purpose is, then we work backward from there to design lessons that will lead students toward that end.

A CBI lesson also involves the use of a great many visual props, such as pictures and photographs, to show what we are referring to in the language. We also use real props. For a unit on the process of making acorn soup, we pack into each classroom a whole box of the things we use in our own home to prepare acorns: rocks and hammers for cracking them open, mortar and pestle for grinding, sifting basket, leaching basket and cloth, and cooking rocks. When we teach a story about Panther, our panther hide comes with us. When a story involves articles of clothing, we bring in a laundry basket full of pants, shirts, socks, and coats.

We also involve the students in hands-on learning. During the unit on acorn preparation students crack enough acorns to feed the whole school. To better tell a story about Coyote and the animals, students make puppets for a puppet show and backdrops for a play. To learn items of food and how to count money in Karuk, students act out situations in Karuk restaurants and stores. When learning to say a Karuk jump-rope rhyme, we bring in the rope, move the desks out of the way, and get everyone jumping.

A CBI lesson always includes a great deal of modeling. When we teach greetings and conversational language to our students we spend a portion of every class greeting each other and carrying on conversations—modeling what we will later have the students do. At first the students watch the two of us carry on several "telephone" conversations with each other using the handsets from two phones. Eventually they begin holding conversations with us and then with each other. It is important to note, however, that this method never forces students to produce speech before they are ready.

CBI takes into account the fact that language is first learned by listening to others talk. As babies many of us learned English as our first language. We learned as we listened to others talk to us and around us. Of course, when we first tried to speak, what came out was mostly babble. Soon we learned enough to know what our parents were telling us. We could respond to their directions, but we could not yet say much ourselves. Later we could respond with one or two words, then simple sentences, before we were old enough, and fluent enough, to express our own ideas.

This same process is true for learning another language. Initially there is a time of listening, called a "silent" or "receptive" period. Later, when we are ready, we produce short, simple words that we eventually attempt to combine into phrases of language. Following that, a spiral of learning takes place as we learn more language or learn language in other contexts. This learning spiral will lead to fluency as long as we have practice and encouragement.

Encouragement is vital. We always try to model proper speech as it has been modeled for us, rather than to embarrass or put down students if their early attempts at language production are inaccurate. There is nothing more devastating to the learning process than being told you are wrong the first time you attempt to utter a word.

If we are at a point in the classroom when we expect a student to be able to respond or create speech and they cannot with any accuracy, we know not to push them. Instead, it is an indication to us as teachers that we must back up and offer more instruction. One simple tool we use to determine the readiness of our students to produce speech themselves is called "comprehension checks." These checks are not only used to instantly assess a student's progress but can be used to introduce new vocabulary as well.

Simple comprehension checks proceed in the following order. We will use an example about birds, in English.

Statement: This is a robin. This is a blue jay.
Question: Is this a robin?
Expected response: Yes [or "No"].
Question: (holding up a picture of a blue jay) Is this a robin or a blue jay?
Expected response: Blue jay.
Question: (holding up a picture of a robin) What is this?
Expected response: A robin.

CBI'S FIVE-STEP LESSON PLAN

CBI lessons are organized into five steps. Step 1 is called *setting the stage.* This step is somewhat optional, but it is intended to provide a look at what the upcoming language lessons will be about and to motivate students to learn. We often do role-playing in Karuk concerning what our students can expect to learn in later lessons. Sometimes we dramatize a Karuk story that we will be teaching, *completely in the language.* We do not yet expect our students to know all of the vocabulary in the role-playing or story, but it gives them an idea of what they *will* be learning in an entertaining way.

Step 2 is *comprehensible input.* In this step, vocabulary is introduced in a comprehensible way—provided in context and in a way that students will understand. If we want them to learn the name of basket materials, we show them the actual plant material as we tell them what it is in full sentences: *Páy uum panyúrar* 'This is bear grass', *Páy uum tíiptiip* 'This is woodwardia fern'. At this point we also use hands-on learning techniques sometimes called total physical response, or TPR: *Áfishi pa panyúrar* 'Touch the bear grass', *Úusip pa tíiptiip* 'Pick up the fern'. It is important for students to hear the vocabulary repeated again and again, but in different ways to keep it interesting. Because we teach beginning Karuk language, a majority of our class time is spent providing new input.

Step 3 is *guided practice.* During this part of our lessons we guide students in activities which give them the opportunity to practice the language presented. We often play games at this stage. Not only are games a good way to practice language in a non-threatening way, but they are fun. The more enjoyable the class, the faster we feel everyone learns.

Step 4, *independent practice,* is a time for students to use what they have learned to generate their own language. The teacher is always close at hand for any necessary assistance, but the teacher is no longer the center of the classroom—the student is.

Finally, Step 5 is *assessment*. Assessment can take many forms and may be an ongoing process, as with the use of comprehension checks. We personally use assessments only to check students for understanding, although other teachers devise assessments to grade students' progress (at the elementary level we grade only on participation).

The five steps are used as a strategy to help us organize our lessons. The steps remind us that there is a process we can follow to learn or teach a language. We cannot expect students to know a part of language until we as teachers have first modeled it many times and then given our students an opportunity to practice it, first with our assistance and then on their own.

Truly, the strength of the method lies in the success we have seen in our students. We knew we must be doing something right the very first year when we observed our elementary school students on the Little League baseball team using the Karuk language, on their own, during a game. We are continuously amazed that when we come back to teach each September, the students are right where we left them in June. With the CBI method, the 10-week vacation appears not to affect their language retention. What we have learned through our teaching we have been able to apply to our work in directing language camps and in the Master-Apprentice Language Learning Program as well.

CLASSROOM INSTRUCTION WORKS WITH OTHER PROGRAMS

We recognize that classroom instruction is only one facet of an overall language restoration effort. Our instruction would not be possible if it were not for our work with a fluent elder, our great-aunt, Violet Super. Because we are not yet fully fluent, we still have to rely on Auntie's knowledge as a resource for our lesson planning. We are in fact constantly learning right along with our students. In the beginning we were barely a few words ahead of the students. Now in each lesson there may be only one or two new phrases of vocabulary we must learn. But our teaching could only come about with our continuous work in the language with Auntie. The Advocates for Indigenous California Language Survival Master-Apprentice Language Learning Program formalized this process, and now individual tribes have adopted the program themselves. The goal of the program is to create an immersion experience for one or two language learners with a master speaker, similar to what we try to do in the classroom. Through this program, representatives of a younger generation can accelerate their learning and can eventually become the resources needed to continue classroom instruction.

Nine years ago, after our first year in the classroom, we realized that parents were being left out of the language learning process. Because we wanted language learning to be family based, we organized the first of many language immersion camps for tribal families. During the camps children and adults were able to learn together and to continue to practice the language in their homes. Later, in addition to language camps, we started teaching through the local colleges, holding weekend courses that again welcomed children and adults to learn together.

The structure of the CBI method and the five-step lesson plan included in our language education efforts has allowed us to combine the best from both modern and traditional sources of knowledge. We feel that this method is having a real, positive, and—we hope—lasting impact on the rejuvenation of the Karuk language.

The Navajo Language: II

KEN HALE

Department of Linguistics and Philosophy
Massachusetts Institute of Technology
Cambridge, Massachusetts

Navajo has occupied a special place in bilingual education in the United States of the latter half of the 20th century. Rough Rock Demonstration School was begun in 1966 and quickly became an important symbol and example of the promise inherent in the notion that the education of school-age children is most effective if it crucially involves their native language. This proposition is unchallenged and unquestioned, of course, where the young children in question speak the dominant language of the country. It would be preposterous for public schools to teach English-speaking American children in any language other than English. In fact, no idea to the contrary would ever enter anyone's mind.

But Rough Rock Demonstration School took this very conventional and reasonable idea, that children should be taught in their own language, and implemented in a way which, at the time, was radical, not at all universally approved of, and extraordinarily exciting on the educational scene of this country at the time. Here, children were to be taught in Navajo—their own language, to be sure, but one utterly different from the English that had always predominated in education throughout the country and in all Navajo schools. Rough Rock Demonstration School was nothing less than inspirational, and its name came eventually to be heard on the tongues of educators as far away as central Australia, where, in like manner, Aboriginal children deserved to be taught in their own languages.

It should be pointed out that there were periods of linguistic enlightenment preceding the 1960s. The Navajo language became rather famous during World War II with the renowned code

199

talkers. The war years also saw the publication of Robert Young and William Morgan's *The Navaho Language* (1943), probably the best dictionary of a native North American language at the time, as well as the extraordinary monthly newspaper *Ádahooníłígíí*, published well into the 1950s by Young and Morgan. This publication is a jewel in the body of written literature in Native American languages, and its discontinuation was then and is now justly bemoaned by its readers and by those who are now directly involved with Navajo-language literacy.

The dictionary and newspaper were part of a general program of literacy in Navajo; there was also a Navajo literacy campaign during the postwar years, and a number of children's books were published in this period. A period of neglect ensued in the 1950s, however, representing a shift away from progressive language programs. This coincided, temporally at least, with the general shift in the federal government toward the infamous policy of "termination," which, if fully carried out, would have ended federal responsibility toward Indian nations and effectively destroyed their sociopolitical and economic integrity. Although the disastrous consequences of termination were evident within a decade or so and the policy was mercifully reversed, many noteworthy programs were casualties of the period, including the Navajo-language newspaper and the effort to spread literacy in Navajo. Although they were interrupted for a time, these progressive and promising efforts should be kept in mind when considering later developments, because some of the enabling foundation for them was laid in the 1930s and 1940s. Of particular importance is the linguistic foundation, including a firmly established and linguistically sound Navajo orthography, a superb dictionary of Navajo, and a sizable body of written material in the language.

It took nearly a decade for these enlightened Navajo language programs to recover from the regressive trends of the 1950s and for a newly invigorated tradition of Navajo language and education to realize its philosophy in the form of a school that actually taught children in a bilingual education program, achieving superior results in the mastery by those children of the oral and literate use of both Navajo and English (Emerson 1983; McCarty 1998). Rough Rock Demonstration School is a community-controlled contract school, its educational services being contracted for by an established school board made up of people from the local community (under the provisions and guidelines of Public Law 93-638). Its example was followed by a number of other contract schools, including the outstanding Rock Point school, where Wayne Holm, coauthor of the following essay, worked for approximately a quarter of a century.

Community control has been the keystone, the sine qua non, of these remarkable institutions. The tradition represented by Rough Rock Demonstration School, and others like it, is guided in large part by the idea that a Navajo child's education should involve his or her native language, that is to say, Navajo. Moving now to a later period, and to different places, this important relationship—between the Navajo pupil and the Navajo language—must sometimes take on a different character and may require a different educational response. As we see in Paul Platero's chapter (Chapter 8), Navajo is not necessarily the dominant language of a Navajo school-age child.

In the following essay, Wayne Holm and Marie Arviso describe the situation found in the Fort Defiance School, where two-thirds of Navajo elementary-school children are dominant not in Navajo but in English. The educational response to this situation has taken the form of a Navajo language immersion program. It becomes clear in this discussion that the full measure of the

Fort Defiance situation is somewhat more complicated and alarming than that which might be remedied in this way alone, since the very nature of linguistic abilities must be addressed ultimately for both languages, in order to bring academic (classroom) ability in line with conversational ability. The integration of these two abilities was an inherent feature of the development of the bilingual program of Rock Point.

References

Emerson, Gloria J. 1983. Navajo education. In *Handbook of North American Indians*, vol. 10, *Southwest*, ed. Alfonso Ortiz, 659–71. Washington, D.C.: Smithsonian Institution.

McCarty, Teresa L. 1998. Schooling, resistance, and American Indian languages. In *Indigenous language use and change in the Americas*, ed. T. L. McCarty and O. Zepeda, *International Journal of the Sociology of Language* 132, 27–41.

16

Tséhootsooídi Ólta'gi Diné Bizaad Bíhoo'aah
A Navajo Immersion Program at Fort Defiance, Arizona

MARIE ARVISO
Former Principal, Ft. Defiance Elem. School
Ft. Defiance, Arizona

WAYNE HOLM
Education Specialist
Division of Diné Education
Window Rock, Arizona

BACKGROUND

Fort Defiance Elementary School was, at the time the Navajo immersion program began, a large, around 900-pupil K–5 elementary school, one of two elementary schools (and one small satellite school) in the Window Rock Unified School District along the Arizona–New Mexico line in northeastern Arizona. The school draws children from at least four Navajo chapter-communities: the emerging reservation town of Fort Defiance itself, the Sawmill chapter to the northwest, and parts of the Red Lake chapter to the north and the St. Michaels chapter to the southwest.

Tséhootsooí 'rock' + 'area' + 'yellow' + 'the one that' may mean something like "rock-edged meadow." Near where Bonita Creek debouches from the Defiance Upwarp on its way to Black Creek, the army established a fort in 1851 intended to "defy" the Navajos. After the Navajos came back from some years of concentration camp–like relocation in eastern New Mexico (1863–1868), Fort Defiance became the seat of the Navajo Agency. Here, in 1869 or 1870, the first on-reservation school was set up in makeshift quarters at the agency.

Fort Defiance was the site of one of a small number of relatively large boarding schools built on Navajo land by the Bureau of Indian Affairs before the turn of the century. When the Navajo Area was grouped into five agencies, Fort Defiance became the seat of one of those five agencies, while the Area Office was sited at nearby Window Rock. The Bureau until several decades ago was almost a government within the government, with not only education functions, but also health, road, land management, and a number of other functions. As an "agency town," there were, in addition to the school, hospital, and offices, also a few churches and trading posts.

A small "accommodation" school was built at Fort Defiance in the late 1930s or early 1940s. This was a state-and-county-supported public school for the non-Navajo students in the community: the children of Bureau employees, traders, missionaries, and others. A small number of Navajo children, usually employees' children, were sometimes allowed to attend these schools. These were the beginnings of the public school system at Fort Defiance and the Reservation.

The 1950s witnessed one of those massive every-few-decades shifts in national Indian policy. To over-simplify: the "Indian problem" was seen to be that the Indian kept himself aloof from his white brothers. The "solution" was to throw the Indian into the arms of those brothers. Thus public schooling became the educational policy, "relocation" the economic development policy, and "termination" the long-range legal-political policy.

The Navajo Reservation was divided into school districts much the same way 19th-century Africa was divided—by drawing straight lines on the map to divide up the territory (and the relatively few tax resources, such as the railroads and natural gas pipelines). While respecting state and county lines, these lines usually had little to do with the topography of the land and almost nothing to do with Navajo political boundaries, that is, the chapter (community) boundaries.

In Arizona, this resulted not just in the extension of reservation peripheral city districts into parts of the reservation (as happened in New Mexico and Utah), but also in the creation of a number of new completely on-reservation districts: Window Rock, Ganado, Keams Canyon, Tuba City, Kayenta, and Chinle.[1]

The public school system mapped the entire Reservation as did the Bureau school system; the one was laid down as if the other did not exist. The working rule of thumb—approved by the Navajo Tribal Council—was that if students *could* attend a public school as a day student, they *should*—otherwise they could attend a Bureau school. Thus the once day-and-boarding Bureau school system became an almost-all-boarding school system. And the mostly one-community Bureau schools became mostly multicommunity schools, taking in from a number of other communities those students who could not or would not attend a public school.

In this way, the current lack of alignment between schools and communities became institutionalized. From a chapter's point of view, its children attend a number of different schools, often different kinds of schools (public, Bureau, contract, grant, or mission). From a school's point of view, its students came from a number of different communities.

To fund the transition from Bureau to public schools, relatively large amounts of federal money were made available—at least in the early years of the transition. PL 815 funds enabled the districts to build or enlarge public schools; PL 874 ("Impact Aid") provided operating funds. In the early 1950s, the public school at Fort Defiance was one of the first of the new PL 815–built public schools.

By 1986 the school at Fort Defiance was a 900-plus-pupil elementary school (with a small satellite school at Sawmill). The Fort Defiance school and the 600-plus-pupil school at Window Rock fed into the Tse Ho Tso Middle School and thence into the Window Rock High School.

Fort Defiance had by then become an emerging reservation town. Although the Bureau school had been closed, the Indian Health Service hospital and clinic and the various agency offices remained. There were a post office and now some tribal offices as well. An electronics assembly plant provided a significant number of jobs. Newer, cash-based convenience stores had replaced the older, credit-based trading posts. But other than gas stations and convenience stores, most small businesses were by then in Window Rock, seven miles away. With improved roads and better transportation, most people shopped in the border town of Gallup, New Mexico—some 30 or more miles away.

In addition to the homes of the older, livestock-based, original Fort Defiance families, there were by then single homes of wage workers who had moved in from other communities. There were also several public housing areas and trailer parks.

Fort Defiance was by then becoming a small, more or less unplanned town. The population consisted of older land-based families, older salary-based families, and a number of younger, newer families attracted to Fort Defiance by jobs there, in nearby Window Rock, and even in Gallup.

In the emerging reservation town, social class had begun to be as important as, or perhaps more important than, eth-nicity or degree of traditionalism. There were a small number of middle-class Anglos: educators, health-care workers, other professionals, and business people. There were a growing number of Navajo professionals. There were both land-based Fort Defiance people and a growing number of more or less urban or urbanizing people—people who might have ties to the land in other communities but not in the Fort Defiance area. Although extensive livestock holdings might make land-based people more middle class–like, most land-based people near Fort Defiance had relatively small holdings. There was a tendency for town-based professionals to look down on town-based nonprofessionals, and for both to look down on more rural people. The term "John" was used by teenagers as a somewhat derogatory term to refer to people who were rural, poor, and/or traditional.

THE PROGRAM

The above is an oversimplified picture of the Fort Defiance school and the communities it served as they were in 1986. There were in Fort Defiance itself a growing number of children who had more or less grown up "in town" and whose ties with their parents' home communities—and the language and culture thereof—were becoming more and more attenuated.

Marie Arviso was a Navajo from the Mariano Lake community in Eastern Navajo. She came to the then-new Window Rock School District in 1964 and there had conducted what many felt was one of the more successful public school–based bilingual programs. In time, she became the principal of the very large Fort Defiance Elementary School.

Wayne Holm was an Anglo married to Agnes Dodge, a Navajo. They had been at Rock Point—the site of a community-controlled K–12 school—for about 25 years. In 1981 they had both received Fulbright fellowships to go to New Zealand, where they had been stationed at Ruatoki, then the leading Māori immersion school in the country. They came to Window Rock when Agnes Holm assumed the directorship of the Navajo North Central Association.

Upon coming to work at Fort Defiance, Holm was asked to conduct a survey of the language abilities of the students (as a way of bringing the school into compliance with Arizona law). Louise Lee and Holm tested all of the kindergarten and 1st grade students and most of the 2nd graders by mid-fall. The results were somewhat surprising. Perhaps only one-third of the kindergarten entrants had even passive knowledge of Navajo. (Only fifteen years earlier, Spolsky and Holm had found that approximately 95% of Navajo six-year-olds spoke Navajo upon entry into school.) In Fort Defiance in 1986, fewer than 1 in 20 was a reasonably fluent speaker of Navajo. Despite a very supportive Navajo principal (Arviso) and a Navajo-majority teaching staff, it was

	+N	−N	0N
+E	+N/+E	−N/+E	0N/+E
−E	+N/−E	−N/−E	0N/−E
0E	+N/0E	−N/0E	—

FIGURE 16.1

obvious that even those children who spoke some Navajo were reluctant to do so in public—on the playground or in the halls or cafeteria.

Even more surprising were the measures of English language abilities. Remember, two-thirds of these children spoke *only* English. But many of these students did not test well in English. Had they spoken some Navajo, they would have been classified as LEP—limited English proficient. But they spoke only English. They were relatively weak in their only language!

In determining children's abilities as strong, weak, or nonexistent in Navajo, and strong, weak, or nonexistent in English, we classified children by their combinations of competence in the two languages (see Figure 16.1). We found that most were weak in English, their only language, or were weak in both English and Navajo. But however weak they were in English, most were even weaker in Navajo.

This was contrary to the "folk linguistics" of the time (unfortunately still common in some places). Even some educators tended to feel that most children could be strong in only one language: that being strong in Navajo made one weak in English, and vice versa. But these children were not alingual or semilingual. They were quite fluent in English and could interact well enough to get whatever they wanted in English.

We felt that the theories of Jim Cummins, an Irish-born, Canadian-based student of bilingualism, better explained what was going on. He posits what he later came to call "conversational" and "academic" language abilities. Conversational language abilities are those used in cognitively less demanding and more highly contextualized situations; we sometimes called it "playground language." Academic abilities are those used in cognitively more demanding and less contextualized situations; we sometimes called it "classroom language."

Put simply, conversational language is the language of situations where people are engaged in familiar recurring experiences in which others know what they mean from context. Academic language, then, is the language of relatively new or changing situations where one has to supply considerable context. In school, for example, it is the language of expository writing, reading comprehension, math word problems, and so on.

But academic or classroom language should not be thought of as only the language of the school. It is involved

in the ability to explain things to others: to summarize, compare, generalize, predict, and so on. Thus, we would explain the relative success of the Rock Point program by saying that, by developing *academic Navajo* abilities, that program was also developing *academic English* abilities. But relatively few of the Fort Defiance children came to school with what could be called academic Navajo abilities.

Fort Defiance had had, in the 1970s and into the 1980s, a relatively successful transitional bilingual program—so successful, Arviso said, that the LDS "home placement" program used to select many of these children for placement off-reservation. But, by the mid-1980s, it was becoming apparent that this program was no longer appropriate. The school no longer had any sizable number of Navajo-dominant speakers coming into the school. By then, most of the kindergarten entrants spoke English better than they did Navajo—or they spoke only English, though not necessarily well.

It was becoming increasingly obvious that neither the "developmental" Rock Point type nor the earlier "transitional" Fort Defiance type of bilingual program would be appropriate in the changed and changing language situation at Fort Defiance, and that something more like the Māori immersion programs might be the only type of program with some chance of success. Arviso approached the district with a proposal that we find out if there were enough interested parents to start such a program.

Window Rock and Fort Defiance had a reputation for apathy about the increasingly rapid loss of Navajo. Many people seemed to feel that it was their English-language abilities that enabled them to find work there—this despite the fact that a number of those positions required, at least on paper, that the speaker be bilingual.

We identified some 48 candidates: kindergartners who had at least some passive knowledge of Navajo. Most of these had *only* passive knowledge. Lee and Holm went out to talk to parents. Arviso and Holm thought that if as many as half of the parents agreed, there might be enough students to set up a single immersion kindergarten. To our great surprise, 46 of the 48 parents signed up their children. Some asked us why this had not been done earlier. Others scolded us for limiting the program that first year to kindergartners.

We did not feel that we could claim—as we had concerning Rock Point, some years before—that these children would necessarily do better academically. We were more concerned that the children come to identify and value themselves *as Navajos*. We said that in an environment which tended to devalue Navajoness, we wanted to help these children experience success in school *through* Navajo. We said that by the end of the 5th grade, these students not only would be doing as well academically as those children instructed only in English, but they would also have come to talk, understand, read, and write Navajo.[2]

We designed an initial immersion program with progressively less Navajo as the child moved up through the grades.

- Kindergartners and 1st graders would be taught all, or almost all, in Navajo.
- The 2nd and 3rd graders would be taught a half-day in Navajo and a half-day in English.
- The 4th and 5th graders would have a minimum of an hour's instruction a day in Navajo.

Participation was to be voluntary, and parents would have to re-enroll their children each year.

We would be fantasizing if we claimed that the program was implemented exactly as we originally blocked it out. As with all living programs, this one tended to grow and change as we learned from both our successes and our mistakes. (And, of course, it has continued to evolve; it is conducted somewhat differently in 1999 than it was in, say, 1989.)

We were fortunate that there were at Fort Defiance a small cadre of experienced bilingual teachers who rather quickly made the transition to the somewhat different requirements of immersion teaching.[3] That first year Les Allen and Alma Lewis were the kindergarten classroom teachers. Complying with parents' wishes, we added Lettie Nave's Navajo-and-English class as a third class. It used a somewhat different model: the language of instruction and interaction was basically English, but there was considerable use of Navajo.

Remember, most of these children spoke little or no Navajo. We taught them, when they were not able to communicate with the teacher, to say "Shikáá anilyeed!"—"Help me." Thereupon the child said what he or she wanted to say in English. The teacher gave this back to the child in Navajo, breaking it into phrase-sized chunks if need be. After the child repeated what had been said in Navajo, the teacher responded (in words or actions) as if the child had just said this on her or his own. That is, the child was actively *expected* to communicate in Navajo, even if he or she needed help in doing so.

Children are amazingly adaptive. Many soon learned to "chunk" their communication in English. Or to ask another child for help. Or, in time, to ask only for the word or phrase he or she needed in Navajo: "Diné k'ehjí, X haash yit'áo ádídííniil?"—"The Navajo way X, in what way are you going to say it?"

The first few months were scary. We as teachers expect to communicate. When we see that we are not communicating, the tendency to slip back into English is very strong. But Les Allen, Elena White, Alma Lewis, and Sarah Watchman persisted. Navajo does not have a large body of secular music or dance as Māori does. We found that we had to begin with whole-group activities. (We have since found out that other immersion groups have had to do the same.) But it was not until after Christmas—perhaps six weeks after we had started—that we noticed students beginning to use "survival Navajo" phrases with relative freedom.

The program was based on small-group work. While there was some whole-group work, most of the work was done in half-class groups, or (when other people could be recruited) in one-third-class groups. The children would move from one group to another roughly every 20 minutes. Those who profess to be horrified by such an "unnatural" approach would do well to read—and think about—some of Lily Wong Fillmore's studies, in which she concludes that if "real" communication is what is needed to acquire a second language, then we had better go with instructional models that provide the most real communication, even if they are not the most trendy model. Given that the immersion staff was almost the only source of Navajo in the school setting, this approach seemed best suited to the situation there at Fort Defiance.

All communication, interaction, and instruction was done in Navajo. Teachers and aides tried to use Navajo even on the playground and in the dining room. In time, the teachers trained the office staff to talk Navajo to them on the public-address system. Visitors to the classroom were first addressed in Navajo; teachers switched to English only if the person obviously could not talk Navajo. Here Arviso's frequent visits to the classroom, or greetings to children outside, helped legitimate the use of Navajo in the school setting.

We did conduct two "periods" in English a day. Holm came in to teach math in English, and Darlene Ashley came in to teach "concepts" in English. Although they stayed in the room for an hour, they worked with each one-third-class group for only 20 minutes. While they were teaching in English in one corner, the teacher and the aide were conducting lessons with the two other one-third-class groups in Navajo. Thus, in a school day of five hours, each child had roughly 40 minutes of one-third-class group instruction in English. Holm and Ashley were the only ones who spoke in English; when they left the room, they took the English language with them. (Of course, Holm complicated things by speaking Navajo to children in informal interaction outside of his math-in-English classes. We came to feel that it did not hurt to appear to "favor" the weaker language.)

As at Rock Point, we started with a "stripped-down" curriculum: talking, writing, math, and a catchall of content subjects. The following year, most of these children re-enrolled in the 1st grade. Here, we taught initial reading in Navajo. The arrangements were much the same as those for kindergarten described above.

Eventually, in the 2nd and 3rd grades, we tried to pair two classrooms side by side. Half of the children were in the all-in-Navajo room, half were in the all-in-English room. The two groups of children would change places—and teachers—at midday.

In the 4th and 5th grades, we tried different arrangements to try to get the children an hour of half-group instruction in Navajo. Arviso left the year we started the 4th grade; while the program did continue, we were never able to fully implement the 4th and 5th grades as planned. As noted earlier, the curriculum was a stripped-down one.

Talking

At all grades, we used and expected a lot of what we have since come to call "situational Navajo": those Navajo sentences[4] that might be expected in frequently recurring situations throughout the school day.

While we did quite a bit of choral-like speech and responses in the opening exercises in kindergarten, we began early on to require more individualized language. The first activity each morning was something we called "talking time." Here children were asked to give a brief account of something they had done since school let out the day before. Where needed, children were given help in doing so. The group might then be asked what the person had done; they had to respond with the appropriate third person singular person verbs corresponding to the first person singular forms the speaker had used. In time, children were invited—and taught—to ask questions of the speaker about what had been said. These had to go beyond what the child had actually said and required the use of the appropriate second person singular forms.[5]

In the 2nd grade, these accounts sometimes led to written newspaper article–type summaries or the development of group-written stories. (Since then, Holm has also come to advocate turning more of these accounts into "playlets," because while accounts are usually in the perfective mode, playlets are in the imperfective mode usually used in face-to-face encounters.)

Writing

Holm and Gayle Barfoot observed process-writing programs in other schools, and Holm began adapting some of these techniques to Navajo. (Given the relative paucity of Navajo-language materials in print, it will always be necessary for children and staff to collectively create a lot of their own materials.)

As early as kindergarten, children were encouraged to use invented spelling in labeling pictures. After leading the child to talk about the picture, the teacher would sometimes write a word or phrase for the child. In both written and oral work, we tried to focus on verbs and verb phrases. Navajo has an extremely intricate and complex verb system. Many programs tend to teach children only nouns and a few (adjective-like) neuter verbs; but without verbs, one cannot really communicate very much in Navajo.

By the end of kindergarten, some children were writing sentences or even small sets of sentences to make up stories. From the 1st grade on, we used process-writing methods: writing, reading, revising, and so on. Holm typed and photo-copied some of the 1st graders' booklets using the Navajo fonts then available on Apple computers.[6] In time, Maggie Benally began typing up some of the 2nd grader's booklets. By the 3rd grade, Emma Dixon had children typing their own booklets.

In the 2nd grade, we had children start writing in English (while continuing to write in Navajo). While they had more trouble with the idiosyncrasies of English spelling than with Navajo, most of the things they had learned in Navajo transferred well.[7]

Phonics

The use of invented spelling was only part of the reading and writing program. The other half was the use of Navajo phonics materials Holm had devised at Rock Point based on the Russian work of Zhurova. Despite the length and morphological complexity of Navajo verb forms, almost all words can be analyzed as being strings of CV or CVC syllables. Perhaps somewhat mechanically, children were taught to analyze syllables into their constituent sounds, relate letters to these, and resynthesize the sounds into syllables. In theory, the use of invented spelling in communication and expression situations and the precise use of the highly phonemic orthography should, in time, converge. We felt that they did: by 2nd grade, children could write almost any word they knew or could retain in short-term memory.

In the 2nd grade, we added phonics in English, emphasizing of necessity the more morphophonemic nature of English phonics. The English phonics segment was intended to precede the introduction of given spelling patterns in the reading-in-English materials. The idea was that children should already be able to sound out any possible one-syllable word of the form they were expected to encounter that day.

Reading

Of course, in a process approach to writing, there is a great deal of reading of one's own, and other's, work. But we also used reading materials.

We started children reading in the 1st grade in Navajo. This was an act of faith for many parents, and some became apprehensive. Starting in the 1st grade, we made use of the Native American Development Center (NAMDC)[8] materials: *Chaa', Ch'al, Náshdóí (Beaver, Frog, Wildcat)*, among others, together with the related workbooks. Since the lower-level books were already out of print, we had to make photocopies of them locally.

We tried to use these materials in ways that would maximize the amount of talking that children would do about what was going on in the story they were reading. Other books from the NAMDC materials were used all the way up into 5th grade.

We started reading in English in the 2nd grade using the so-called Miami Linguistic Readers, a phonics-based reading program intended for ESL students. We wanted a program that built on what the children had learned in Navajo, one that made English seem more like Navajo. Separating the phonics and the comprehension activities, we led students to retell stories from notes and then to tell and then write summaries of those stories.

Late in the 3rd or early in the 4th grade, we switched to the reading materials used elsewhere in the school. We used cooperative learning approaches in which we separated factual- and inferential-type questions. Pairs were expected not only to answer factual questions but to also cite the source of their answer. Since this involved more or less convergent thinking, we only checked to see if other pairs had other answers. With more inferential questions, pairs were expected to justify their answer by talking through their reasoning. Here, since this was more divergent thinking, we asked each pair for their answer. Almost all answers were accepted as long as they could be justified and were not explicitly contradicted by the story. Starting as early as the 2nd grade, we tried a variety of techniques intended to enable the children to recount the story (orally or in writing).

Cumulative retelling, or written summaries at the end of a story that unfolded over several days, emphasized not trying to remember everything but becoming aware of what was and was not important. Children sometimes had to be shown how one goes about "throwing out" notes on events that turned out not to have advanced the story. Perhaps, just perhaps, children can be taught how to determine what is important, what the "main ideas" are.

Math

We taught math in both Navajo and in English. But these were very different maths.

Math in Navajo was taught using what we call the Stern-Willink approach.[9] This involves the use of so-called Unifix materials: 3/4-inch plastic cubes that can be joined or separated in ways resembling the operations of the base 10 number system. Children were expected to be able to talk through what they were doing, one step at a time: moving blocks while explaining what they were doing, and only then writing down what they had done in arithmetic notation.

Math in English focused on using the workbooks associated with the texts used elsewhere in the school. Using an instrumental enrichment approach, children were expected, before working a given page, to explain what they saw on the page, what was expected of them, and their strategy. Here the academic English of the directions was as important as "doing" the page appropriately. Students might be asked to talk through a few problems as a group. Individuals might be asked to talk their way through at least one problem before working the page and another after doing so.

Content Subjects

Teachers taught health, social studies, science, and other subjects by having the students do things and then talk and, where possible, write about what they had done.

Some teachers were particularly good at conducting a series of activities in which students first talked about, and then wrote about, those activities. These were turned into booklets which were shared first with other students and then with parents.

The common denominator in almost all instruction was that we attempted to get as much explicit talk and writing as was reasonably possible from a given activity. We attempted to test student mastery formally or informally; we tried to convey—by actions more than words—that we really did expect each child to perform at his or her level of competence.

BEYOND THE CLASSROOM

The School Day

Meals

Kindergarten and 1st grade teachers ate with their students. Teachers in the higher grades usually did not. The dining room was overcrowded; it took several shifts to feed everyone. Under these circumstances, it was hard to use Navajo with the students. The kindergarten and 1st grade teachers tried to do so. In the first few years, students reported that when they tried to talk Navajo in the dining room some of the other children laughed at them. This seems to have been less of a problem in subsequent years.

Recess

Again, because the school playgrounds were overcrowded, it was difficult to use Navajo at recess. While teachers in the primary grades went to recess with their students, teachers in the upper elementary grades did not. Even if primary-level teachers tried to stay with their students, there were often children from several groups competing for the same play equipment; teachers attempted under these circumstances to talk Navajo with children, but this was often difficult.

Speaking Navajo on the playground was almost impossible in the upper elementary grades. Some teachers took recess duty while others did other things, and students in the upper grades intermingled in competing for the limited play equipment. It was not possible to use much Navajo on the playground.

Specialty Classes

Students went to various specialty classes such as library, music, computer, counseling, and, in a few cases, special ed or gifted-and-talented. In most cases, while teachers might talk with students in Navajo while in transit, Navajo was seldom used in these classes because few of the teachers were Navajo speakers and/or the immersion students were mixed with monolingual English-speaking students.

The one exception was the music teacher. Not only did she use some Navajo, at least one year she put on a musical all in Navajo for the whole school in which immersion students had most of the leading parts. This single action did a great deal to raise the prestige of Navajo-speaking students. One of her students—a 5th grade girl in the immersion program—created a small sensation by singing the national anthem in Navajo at the evening ceremonies at the huge Navajo Nation Fair that year.

Programs

While the school had an "Indian Day" in the fall and again in the spring, this often involved aspects of other tribes' culture and usually involved little spoken Navajo. Still, there was some.

Expectations

While teacher expectations were not consciously a part of the curriculum, they had much to do with the relative success of the program.

More-traditional Navajo expectations of children were that they would work hard and act responsibly—in adultlike ways. Anglos tend to expect children to act in more childlike ways. In schools in the emerging Navajo towns, Navajo children are coming to act less and less like traditional Navajo children. More-traditional parents tend to perceive such behavior as self-indulgent and irresponsible. At worst, children come to exploit the gap between parental and teacher expectations. That is, more-traditional Navajo parents come to think that the children are behaving as their non-Navajo teachers expect or allow them to; non-Navajo teachers come to think that the children are behaving as Navajo parents expect or allow them to. In time, both parents and teachers come to accept that "that's the way things are."

One of the somewhat unexpected consequences of the program was the degree to which the children came to act more like traditional Navajo children—particularly within class. The children came to sense that Millie Allen or Pat Johnson *expected* them to act responsibly. Les Allen needed only quietly say "ge'," and a child would pause to think what he or she was supposed to do. Betty Moore or Sadie Yazzie would explain to children what they were expected to do—and most children would do it.

This is not to say that children became docile or passive. If anything, most became even more active participants in their own education. They talked. They kidded one another or the teacher. But, unlike many of their peers, most knew when

to stop. Anita Pfeiffer once described such instruction (at Rock Point) as being "like breathing": in Navajo-mediated instruction, children seemed to "inhale" (concentrate) and "exhale" (relax) quite naturally. Knowing how to participate responsibly in their own education and genuinely respecting their teachers, students were at once more focused and more relaxed.

Of course, most of these children did not come from more-traditional homes. Many of the teachers did. But in a sense, these children had been self-selected: they would not have been in the program if their parents had not felt strongly about Navajo ways of life. And most of the children seemed to sense the continuities between their teachers' and their parents' expectations.

Training

Arviso would point out that considerable training was involved in the development of this program.

- While most of the teachers had some experience in writing Navajo, many did not feel confident that they could write accurately whatever their students said. We spent considerable time the first year learning to write Navajo accurately and well. This is absolutely essential where one has to expect students and teachers to produce most of their own reading materials.

- The first summer, the teachers spent considerable time working out which verbs they felt were most important—in what we would now call "situational Navajo"—and then writing out the basic conjugations of these verbs. (Given the extreme complexity of the Navajo mode and aspect system, it sometimes difficult for many otherwise fluent Navajo speakers to stick to the same conjugation in real-life situations.) While teachers did not necessarily refer to the resulting book, the experience of compiling it seemed to help them maintain the degree of verb control necessary for effective "sheltered Navajo" instruction.

- As none of us knew much about process-writing, Holm and Gayle Barfoot spent some time studying English-language programs elsewhere which Holm then adapted to writing in Navajo.

- We adopted a number of the Stern-Willink procedures (from Rock Point) to the teaching of math in Navajo by "talking things through" with manipulatives. (While Millie Allen and Pat Johnson did some interesting things with oral word problems, we did not go as far as we should have in "talking through" and schematicizing word problems.)

- Although we did carry forward some of the learning-to-read-in-Navajo activities from Rock Point, we did not do as much as we should have. We did develop new materials to facilitate the transition from Navajo orthographic expectations to those of English orthography.

- And while some of us did do some serious work on curriculum one of the last summers Holm was there, we did not do nearly as much in the area of community-based research-oriented Navajo social studies as we now would. (There has since been considerable work on both curriculum and standards.)

The point that Arviso wishes to make is that whatever we did not do, we did do a lot of ongoing in-service training. And such training is absolutely necessary if a native-language program is to succeed. Good intentions simply are not enough. Appropriate materials and day-to-day techniques must be consciously developed.

Coming in and out of different teachers' classes to teach the English portions of the program, Holm was able to demonstrate some of the kinds of instruction we wanted. Almost all of the teachers were better teachers than he was; in most cases they went on to develop and improve on these initial attempts. With Arviso's active participation and support, we were able to meet together to develop and refine new activities and techniques. There were dead ends. There were things that did not work. There were things that we should have done that we did not do. But there was enough mutual respect and enough collegiality to enable people to work together effectively.

Parents

The program was voluntary. It depended upon continuing parental support. Here we try to give some idea of some of the things that were done involving parents, students, and staff.

Enrollment

The program was voluntary from the start. We felt that, given what we assumed to be the prevailing apathy about Navajo language, only voluntary participation would be possible.

While others might disagree, we felt we tried hard not to "oversell" the program. We said that these children would do at least as well in English as the children in the monolingual program by the 5th grade. And that they would learn to talk, understand, read, and write Navajo—something the other children would not.[10]

We discouraged parents who did not feel that they would be in the district through 3rd grade, telling them that the delay in starting to read in English would probably be misinterpreted elsewhere. We insisted that there had to be someone in the home who could and would talk Navajo with the children in the evening. A number of non-Navajo-speaking parents who enrolled their children got grandparents, aunts, uncles, even babysitters to do so. And children had to be re-enrolled each year.

Some parents became concerned, particularly at the end of the kindergarten year, when they realized that their child would not learn to read in English until the 2nd grade. The parents' decision to keep the children in the program was an act of faith, and indeed some parents did not re-enroll their children as 1st graders. Sometimes parents changed their minds in the middle of a year. While we encouraged parents to stay with the program through the 3rd grade, we did not retain any child against his or her parents' wishes.

Many of the parents' dedication to the program was moving. Some parents were non-Navajo-speaking Navajos; they did not want their child(ren) to be "deprived" as they felt they had been deprived. A few were non-Navajos. Some were the children of education or health professionals, potential opinion makers who gave the lie to the assumption that Navajo language programs were only for the less-English-speaking, more rural poor. One girl prevailed upon her mother not once but twice to bring her back to the program when job opportunities took the mother to other communities.

"Homework"

Taking a page from the some of the British programs, we tried to insist that some adult spend some time talking with the child in Navajo each evening after school. A number of teachers sent the child's work for the day home with the child. The child was expected to talk this over with an adult—in Navajo—and the adult was expected to initial that he or she had done so and return the child's work the next day. While we cannot say that all parents did do, many did; the response was heartening. (On a recent visit, Holm overheard 3rd graders talking about *hooghan binaanish*—a calque for "homework.")

Parent-Teacher Meetings

The program held quarterly parent-teacher meetings just after the end of the quarterly grading periods. These consisted of potlucks, demonstrations, and discussions.

Some people had told us that while parents might come to a dinner, it was not realistic to expect parents to provide the dinner. But in more than five years, we never lacked for food. Children came and ate with their parents; teachers helped serve and then ate with parents and children.

A central part of most potluck meetings were "pick-up demonstrations" by teachers and students. Selecting a common theme—talking or writing or reading or math—teachers were asked to do pick-up demonstrations: five-minute segments of something they had been doing in class which would show parents what they had been doing. The "master of ceremonies"—usually Les Allen—commented on the demonstrations to help parents see the continuity from grade to grade. The fact that teachers could and did conduct such demonstrations with whichever children happened to be there that evening may have done more than anything else to make the programs credible.

The final feature of many potluck meetings is what one might call testimony: parents talking about what they were doing to help their child(ren) acquire and use more Navajo outside of school. Hearing other parents helped parents support one another. And hearing this can only have helped the children present.

Although the immersion program never constituted more than one-sixth of the total enrollment—at its largest, approximately 160 of more than 900—there were almost always more people at the potluck meetings of the immersion program than there were at the schoolwide parent-teacher meetings. We began to realize that the apparent apathy about the Navajo language in the Fort Defiance community was only apparent—that we had reached a number of those parents who had been "bucking the tide" in trying to give their child(ren) some appreciation of what it meant to be Navajo in the late 20th century. The very fact that they were bucking the tide and were aware that they were doing so made them all the more determined. Arviso feels that parents saw in the program an opportunity to "parallel" the two cultures.

Participation

Although we have no data other than that of attendance at potluck meetings, we do feel that the parents in the immersion program tended to be more involved in their children's education. Having eaten together and visited together, parents no doubt felt more comfortable about coming in to talk to members of the immersion staff than they might have otherwise.

While we cannot claim that the program necessarily caused this, we do feel that it did at least serve as a catalyst. Arviso feels that parents were responding to the increased opportunities to become meaningfully involved in their child(ren)'s education. We came to realize that many of the parents who placed their child(ren) in the immersion program were also some of the people who were most concerned about their child's education. But they also tended to be people who had moved beyond the conventional wisdom of the last three or four decades of being "Navajo *or* educated." They tended to be people who, concerned about the social problems that they saw many deculturating children were having; they wanted their child(ren) to be both "Navajo *and* educated."

AFTERTHOUGHTS

The Dénouement

Arviso retired in 1990. A new superintendent had come in the preceding year; that year there were a new principal and assistant principal, neither of whom were Navajo.

At the end of that year, the superintendent said he was still undecided as to whether or not the immersion program would be continued into the 5th grade (the highest grade in the school). He professed to be concerned that the children in the program would be unable to do middle-school work unless they were switched into an all-English program in the 5th grade.

At an emotional meeting with parents at the end of the school year, the superintendent finally agreed to allow the program to continue. We gathered all the data we could lay hands on and presented them to the board. At a subsequent board meeting, the board called for the continuation of the program.

On local writing assessments, both the 4th and 3rd grade NI (Navajo immersion) students outperformed the ME (monolingual English) students. Some of the best writing in the school came from NI students. This should not have been so surprising since the NI students, writing in both languages, did more writing than most ME students.

On measures of performance on math in the computer lab, the 4th grade NI students outperformed the ME students.

On the standardized achievement tests given by the school:

- The NI students had scored somewhat lower in reading than the ME students but appeared to be closing the gap. (That is, starting to read in English at the 2nd grade, they had been behind then but were closer at each succeeding grade.)
- The NI students scored slightly lower on some language subtests and slightly higher on others. (So-called language tests have more to do with written than oral English.)
- The NI students scored almost 10 percentage points higher in math.

While we would have liked to see the 4th grade students doing better in reading, we were confident that they would close the gap by the end of the 5th grade. The next group, then 3rd graders, were doing even better than the 4th grade had the year before and seemed likely to close the gap by the 4th grade.

Thus it would appear that Navajo immersion had not hurt these students. They were doing almost as well as, or better than, the ME students. And they had learned quite a bit of Navajo.

We found that on the rather crude tests of oral English, the NI students were comparable to the ME students, which should not have been surprising since analysis showed that the remaining NI students had been roughly comparable to the ME students as kindergartners. That is, these children started with roughly the same amount of English as the ME students did.[11]

All of the NI children showed some progress in Navajo. Surprisingly, of some 40 4th graders who had entered school as Navajo speakers but had received monolingual-English instruction, only three scored as high or higher as 4th graders than they had as kindergartners. That is, most Navajo speakers under monolingual instruction seemed to have actually *lost* some Navajo language ability.

Holm left the school in 1992 after a six-month hassle that ostensibly had nothing to do with the program.

Problems

We got the impression that those children who were getting active support from someone at home were moving toward near-native proficiency for their age. Those who were not seemed reasonably competent in school routines but varied in their ability to go beyond those routines. There were a few surprising children who, despite strong support but limited language opportunities outside of school, seemed to be approaching near-native proficiency for their age.

But if we were to start over, we would try to find ways to enable children to expand their use of verb forms beyond just those needed to get a particular task done. Too many children still seemed reluctant to go very far beyond what had been given. And making reasonable guesses about verb forms you have not heard is critical to really acquiring a language.

Parental Choice

One of the unusual features of this program was and is that of choice. Parental choice is the source of both some of the strengths and some of the weaknesses of the program.

We realized at the outset that, given the assumed apathy about Navajo and distrust of Navajo-language programs, only a voluntary program had any chance of success. Having come from Rock Point, Holm needed some time to realize that below the surface of apparent resigned acceptance of the loss of Navajo, there *was* concern; that beneath all the apparent anglicization in the emerging Navajo town, some parents were exploring and finding less obvious ways of being Navajo; and that we had in a sense reached just those people who had been struggling in their own way to bring up their children as Navajos, people who felt that the school's assistance in all this was both welcome and overdue.

Despite the departure of Arviso and then Holm and the relative lack of on-site administrative support, the program continues. Though some have left or gone back into monolingual English classrooms, there is a core of superb Navajo-language teachers. And parents continue to enroll younger siblings, cousins, or relatives of children who had gone through the program. Surely the fact that participation is voluntary, as well as the fact that parents have had to struggle to maintain the program, has led to its continuation.

And yet, the fact that the program has been voluntary has also been a source of weakness. It would appear that whatever success the children and their parents may have felt, we do not seem to have fully convinced some key opinion makers and decision makers within the school. It is our impression that most of the Navajo teachers came to accept if not boost the program, but that some of the non-Navajo teachers and some of the administrators may not have. We feel that the administration has allowed the program to continue because of the good teachers in it and the strong parental support for it. They have received some favorable publicity for doing so. But it is our impression that some still perceive the program as being one for poorer, more rural, limited-English-speaking children—this despite the continued participation of many more middle-class and/or more urban children in the program. Not really understanding the program, the administration has continued to cut resources for the program and to increase English-language demands upon the staff.

Although the school conducted weekly (or even less frequent) "pull-out" classes in Navajo culture for children (in English), there has been a big gap between the instruction the children in the Navajo immersion program and those in the monolingual English program have received. There is a problem in schools where some of the children receive instruction in Navajo which actually enables them to communicate in the language and others do not, particularly in schools where the students in the Navajo language classes are mostly rural or poor or both—which was not the case at Fort Defiance. Unless (or even if) the Navajo program is superb, the fact that most Anglos and many Navajo middle-class students are in the monolingual English program leads many people to conclude that it is language (rather than social class) that enables the monolingual English students to do better in schools whose curriculum is stacked in favor of middle-class, English-speaking students.

And those students will have been denied the opportunity to acquire Navajo at a time when it would have been considerably easier for them to do so. (Not easy, just easier.) It is not unusual for bright, socially aware Navajo high school and college students to come to wish they could talk Navajo. But by that age it is very difficult for all but the most determined to acquire anything like near-native ability.

We agree with the 1984 Navajo Nation Education Policies, which call for Navajo-language instruction for all children in all grades in all Navajo schools. We would argue that young adults can choose whether they will use Navajo, whom they will use it with, and what subjects they will discuss in Navajo. But making the participation of young children in serious Navajo-language instruction a matter of parental or school choice denies the children themselves the opportunity for that later choice. By the time they come to *want* to talk Navajo it will be—for most of them—too late.

Unfortunately, to date, only a handful of schools have taken those policies seriously. And until or unless they do, it will be extremely difficult to establish serious school-wide Navajo-language programs. Certainly a voluntary program for some is better than no program at all.

In the early 1990s, districts began to implement a 1989 Arizona State School Board rule which added "Foreign or Native American Language" as a required subject in grades 1–8. Districts could choose the language and the type of program. But they were expected to add such instruction in at least one more grade each year until the language was being taught in all grades by the year 2000. Like other schools in most of the 11 Navajo-majority Arizona public school districts, Fort Defiance has struggled to do so with no additional monies in an era of tighter budgets and increased (English-language) expectations.

In theory, this might be an excellent solution: a two-tier program in which all children will participate in either a basic Navajo-as-a-second-language program or in a more intensive Navajo immersion program. The problem is that despite the best efforts of some of those actually trying to deliver such programs, we are nowhere near delivering adequate Navajo-as-a-second-language programs in most Navajo schools. Most children who enter school with little or no Navajo are not acquiring enough Navajo to enable them to actually communicate in the language. Relatively few children who enter school with some Navajo are continuing to develop those abilities—at least not through the efforts of the school—despite the best efforts of some very hard-working teachers. Too many teachers and administrators still do not realize that one can achieve excellence *through* two-language education. And too many teachers and administrators still do not realize the time and effort and resources that it will take to do so.

The education policies of the Navajo Nation, passed in 1984, call for all children in all schools to be taught in Navajo. Not *only* in Navajo but *also* in Navajo. Not taught *some* Navajo but taught *through the medium of* Navajo. Currently, while we may be moving slowly toward that goal, young children are shifting ever so much more quickly toward English only, though often an English which may be adequate for the playground but not necessarily for the classroom. And an increasing number of children cannot hear the discourse about cultural and family values that goes on in Navajo. It is a slow but desperate race against time, apathy, and free-floating nostalgia.

A problem still on the horizon is the trickle-down of Goals 2000 to Navajo schools. Schools, districts, and states need to define their goals and objectives, teach toward those objectives, assess the children's mastery of those objectives, and modify their programs in light of those results. We would argue that Rock Point was—and, we hope, still is—doing just those things, and in two languages. Fort Defiance is moving toward doing so.

Our concern is that if they find that children are not doing well in reading, math, and science, schools will be inclined—or forced—to give up instruction in or through Navajo as not contributing to the mastery of the state-defined objectives. It is going to take extremely strong and dedicated school people—and parents—to continue to argue that schools can be both excellent *and* Navajo.

AN UPDATE ON THE NAVAJO IMMERSION PROGRAM IN DECEMBER 1999

We think it important to conclude this paper with an up-to-date description of the Navajo immersion program. No program stays the same; there have been ongoing changes since we left the school, and at least some of these changes should be noted. It was not possible to get back to school staff before this section was written in December 1999; most of this material comes from Holm's observations from recent years.

The program is now in its 14th year. The 1999 graduates of Window Rock High School included some of the first Navajo immersion students of 1986–87. While no attempt has been made to track these students (neither of us is with the district now), we do know through personal contacts that a number of the girls have had the traditional kinaaldá (puberty) ceremonies—something not usually done by those living in town. And that at least some of these students are now in college.

The district built a new primary school several years ago. What was the K–5 Fort Defiance Elementary School is now divided between the grade K–2 Tse Ho Tso[12] Primary Learning Center and the grade 3–5 Tse Ho Tso Intermediate Learning Center. The two centers have separate campuses a mile or so apart and are administered by separate principals. One person—who also teaches—is responsible for the Navajo immersion programs in both schools.

There have been significant new links with other programs. Concerned about Navajo school entrants' lack of Navajo, the then Navajo President made Navajo the language of instruction in the Navajo Head Start centers in 1995, in which almost 4000 children were enrolled. (The Head Start program is the only school program directly controlled by the Navajo Nation.) Implementation has been slow, but both the Sawmill and the Fort Defiance centers are among the pilot "full immersion" centers. Some of these students are beginning to feed into the immersion program at Fort Defiance.

Recognizing the abilities of the Navajo immersion teachers at Fort Defiance, the Diné Teacher Education Program, a Kellogg Foundation–funded Navajo-language teacher training program at Diné College–Tsaile, has been placing some of its student teachers with cooperating teachers in the Navajo immersion program at Fort Defiance.

An attempt is being made to implement a parallel Navajo immersion program at Window Rock Elementary School, the district's other elementary school. That program is now in its second year.

And Navajo is now a required subject in the grade 6–8 Tse Ho Tso Middle School. It appears that Navajo is taught there more as a foreign language than through immersion. But students are now being grouped by ability: the immersion students are often able to go into advanced placement Navajo classes, for which they receive high school credit. Thus, students in the Window Rock district are now required to take some kind of Navajo from kindergarten through grade 8.

Navajo has been and remains an elective at the high school level.

In 1999 the Navajo Nation set new requirements for the Manuelito Scholarships, the most prestigious of the Navajo Nation's ambitious scholarship programs. This will phase in requirements that will require Manuelito scholars in 2004 to have had at least two semesters of high school Navajo language instruction, a semester-long Navajo government class, and at least one semester of other Navajo-related coursework.

A number of universities in the area now accept Navajo as meeting their foreign language requirements.

That is the good news. Unfortunately, not all the news is good. The program has had strong support from the district office—particularly from the Navajo assistant superintendent. But the district is committed to site-based management, and the program has been conducted under principals who have not always understood it. The separation of languages by teacher was an early casualty. In many cases, teachers were expected to teach both Navajo and English. As Arizona has moved toward increasing "accountability," teachers in the NI program have been expected to have their students do as well on English as the students in the ME classrooms. The good news is that they have managed to do so. In 1998 and 1999, the NI students were said to have done better on the SAT than the ME students at most grades 2 through 5. But this may have come at a price. The school again has a Navajo principal—the first since Arviso left in 1990. It is to be hoped that she will be able to better support the program.

A potentially serious problem is the low enrollment in the program. The district has seldom "advertised" the program; it has depended over the years upon word-of-mouth recommendations by the parents of students in the program. In 1998 and 1999, the school limited enrollment to a single group of around 20 kindergartners. Given the relatively high mobility in the district, and the fact that it is difficult to enter the program after the 1st grade (because the children cannot read in Navajo), this could cause the school to run out of students in the higher grades. Limiting the enrollment in the program has also sidelined some of the most effective immersion teachers.

The division of Fort Defiance Elementary School into two smaller schools has caused other problems, as has the failure to place a full-time person in charge of the program. The program has always been more difficult in the upper elementary grades with the time crunch of a more complex curriculum and the demands for mastery—in English.

Arizona, like many other states, is implementing statewide accountability testing. In 1999, approximately 60% of 10th graders failed the first administration of the 12th grade writing test, and approximately 90% failed the 12th grade math test. The failure rate was considerably higher in Navajo schools.

In spring 2000, 3rd, 5th, 8th, and 10th graders were to be tested in reading, writing, and math—all in English. While students may take one of these tests in Spanish, there are no Navajo-language versions, and there would be few takers if there were. Schools in which students do not do well will be expected to modify their curriculum and practices. Given the relatively poor performance of most Navajo schools, we can expect some to seriously consider throwing out Navajo language and culture classes—even though these are required by the Navajo Nation and Arizona's own foreign and Native American language mandate.

Anticipating this, the district has endeavored to align the curriculum of the district—and that of the Navajo immersion program—with the state standards. Students in the Navajo immersion program are not taking Navajo as a "foreign language" so much as they are endeavoring to meet state standards *through* Navajo. Whether or not this will be enough to survive remains to be seen. But Native American language programs that do not do so will be much more vulnerable.

Unfortunately, aligning with the state foreign language requirements has the unfortunate consequence of concentrating on the written language—which is what the state will be able to test. There is the danger of having students spend too much time on reading and writing materials they do not quite understand.

Proposition 227, the so-called California Unz initiative, was passed by California voters in the summer of 1998. This would place all "English language learners" in a mandatory one-year (only) "sheltered/structured English Immersion" program. Despite the apparent failure of the program in California—it now appears that as many as 93% of the California "English language learners" were not reclassified as being fluent in English at the end of their first year—an even more draconian version of the initiative is being carried for signatures in Arizona. While "Arizona Unz" (now labeled "Proposition 203") purports to be aimed at "immigrants," the initiative if passed would also affect long-resident Hispanic and Native American students. It would make it impossible to give meaningful Navajo language instruction to the many Navajo students who are classified as "English language learners." Passage of this initiative in 2000 might allow a program such as the Navajo immersion program to continue as a program for Anglo and middle-class Navajo students who are reasonably proficient in English. It would preclude the participation of the many Navajo students who are not proficient in English upon entry to school. All this for a simple-minded, one-year-only version of an English-only program that did not work very well as a multiyear program in the century from 1870 to 1970.[13]

Notes

1. Some of these districts have since subdivided to create additional on-reservation districts.

2. At the outset, Holm somewhat naively thought that because of the considerably more English most children spoke, this might happen by the 3rd grade. He later modified this to 5th grade. This is more consistent with Cummins's figure of the five to seven years it seems to take to acquire academic proficiency in a language. But later developments seem to have borne out the earlier assumption.

3. There are significant differences between native-language *bilingual* and native-language *immersion* teaching. In the first, it can usually be assumed that the children know the language fairly well. The problem is mainly one of selecting and using relatively "technical" education terms in Navajo. In the latter, one is trying to teach the language *through* teaching skills and content in that language. One has to, so to speak, keep one eye on content and one on the language through which that content is being taught. One has to select high-utility verb forms and try to use those rather consistently. One has to actively expect the children to use that Navajo, waiting when necessary for them to do so. One might think of it as teaching "sheltered Navajo." Good bilingual teachers do not necessarily become good immersion teachers—certainly not right away.

4. Almost any statement including a verb *is* a sentence in Navajo because the pronominal element is included as a prefix. We now try to avoid verb-less utterances as much as possible.

5. First person singular forms are "I" forms; second person singular forms are "you" forms; and third person singular forms are "he/she/it" forms. In Navajo—somewhat like Spanish—these involve different forms of the verb. But because of the number of prefixes that may precede the stem and the rather complicated verb morphology, one form is not as readily predictable from another to those just learning the language.

6. The Navajo orthography requires only two characters not found on most English-language computer fonts: the voiceless ł and the so-called nasal hook ˛. (Many fonts already have the acute accent used to mark high tone in Navajo.) But since vowels are marked for tone and cavity (as well as length), the number keys at the top of the keyboard are utilized to give the twelve "marked" vowel letters. While the fact that there are more marked than unmarked vowels in Navajo poses problems for adult typists, children learning to keyboard do not know that it is hard to type Navajo. There is a great deal to be said for teaching children to type in the native language early. One of the biggest disincentives to doing the amount of revision needed to write well is the chore of writing everything again (and again). In writing out the old mistakes, children often write in new ones. With a computer, one only changes what one wishes to change; the rest remains the same. This makes children much more willing to revise, and it teaches them to do so in English as well.

7. While some people noted that some letters had different sounds in the English orthography than in the Navajo orthography, we would say that this was a relatively minor problem. A more serious problem is the occurrence of what one might call the use of letter diacritics in English. In Navajo, one can usually analyze letters-to-sounds left-to-right with very few problems. But in English, the sound associated with many vowel letters is determined by consonants or vowels which follow that letter. If this was taught explicitly in English (in the 2nd and 3rd grades), however, the Fort Defiance children seem to have had relatively little difficulty in learning to sound out words in English. We would argue that the very high phonemic regularity of Navajo leads children to expect—and find—the underlying phonemic regularities in English that many Navajo children learning to read in English first may not become aware of. The more morphophonemic nature of the English orthography does not become apparent until children start encountering more complex words.

8. The NAMDC is a Title VII–funded materials development center located in Albuquerque. With the commercial development of more Spanish-language materials, these centers were (unwisely, we think) defunded.

9. This is an approach originally developed by Catherine Stern but much expanded and systematized by Elizabeth Willink at Rock Point.

10. When, in 1989, the Arizona State School Board made "Foreign or Native American Language" the ninth required subject, we felt that this would allow parents to choose their child's Navajo-language program—not *whether* their child took Navajo but *how* the child would do so. The district has been moving toward parallel programs.

11. We pulled together what information we had on rather short notice. Thus we know that those students still in the NI program then had originally placed at about the same level in English (as kindergartners) as the remaining ME 4th graders. What we did not have time to ascertain was whether this had been true of *all* students upon entry. Unfortunately, we did not have time to research this, owing to the rather high mobility in the school. Given the common (but mistaken) perception among ME teachers and the administration that the NI students tended to be rural, poor, and less English-speaking, it is also unfortunate that we do not know more about entry-level abilities of the two groups. Still, what we do know about the entry-level abilities of the remaining students five years later should be reason for caution. It would appear that these students differed less in English language ability than they did in their parents' *attitudes* about the Navajo language.

12. The district spells this as three words, Tse Ho Tso. While naming schools in Navajo was a forward-looking practice when the district adopted the name, it is unfortunate that the district has not since corrected the spelling to Tséhootsoo or Tséhootsooí. Navajo is a tone language in which both tone and vowel length are marked. Writing Navajo syllables as separate words seems to imply the limitations of speakers when it in fact reflects the limitations of nonspeakers.

13. Although Prop. 203 received no more than 20 percent of the vote in any Navajo precinct, it passed by a 2-to-1 margin in the state. In a courageous opinion, the state attorney general said that Prop. 203 is now the law of the state, and it is not to be interpreted as preventing Indian LEP students from receiving instruction in their native language.

Richard J. Thompson, Jr.

Tolowa
Karuk
Chilula
Yurok
Shasta
Modoc
Wiyot
Hupa
Northern
Paiute
Whilkut
Achumawi
Chimar
Wintu
Mattole
Nongatl
Atsugewi
Sinkyone
Yana
Lassik
Wailaki
Nomlaki
Maidu
Cahto
Yuki
Konkow
Washo
Pomo
Patwin
Lake
Miwok
Nisenan
Wappo
Coast
Miwok
Plains Miwok
Northern
Paiute
Sierra
Miwok
Costanoan
Owens
Valley
Paiute
Yokuts
Mono
California
Shoshoni
Esselen
Salinan
Tubatulabal
Kawaiisu
Chemehuevi
Chumash
Kitanemuk
Tataviam
Serrano
Mojave
Gabrielino
Juaneño
Halchidhoma
Luiseño
Cahuilla
Cupeño
Diegueño
Quechan
Cocopa

California Languages (Pre-Contact)

MAP 17.1   California languages, pre-contact

17

The Master-Apprentice Language Learning Program

LEANNE HINTON

Department of Linguistics
University of California at Berkeley
Berkeley, California

California's Master-Apprentice Language Learning Program is a program that teaches native speakers and young adults to work together intensively so that the younger members may develop conversational proficiency in the language. It is designed to be a one-on-one relationship between the "master" (speaker) and the "apprentice" (language learner), who together constitute a team. In this article, I will describe how the program works in California and then discuss how it can be adapted to other locations and situations. Further information on the master-apprentice program can be found in Hinton 1997.

California may have more dying languages than any other place in the world. Close to 100 languages were spoken here before the missions began their northward march in the 18th century. The missions of Baja California and California del Norte virtually enslaved the population and brought diseases that wiped many communities out. California had just emerged from the mission era and was settling down to a ranch-based life, with the Indians filling the role of a peon class, when a quick series of events changed the scene once again: Americans arrived, the Mexican-American War ended up with California going as booty to the United States, and the Gold Rush created one of the biggest migrations in the history of the world. In the new order of things, Indians were enslaved, killed for bounty, or massacred by posses. Then, late in the 19th century, government agents came to make treaties with the Indians, but once the agents were back in Washington, the 80-some treaties that had been developed were tabled permanently, sealed, and never acted on. Survivors of the holocaust of the 19th century found themselves without land and were often unrecognized by the federal government and thus unable to receive aid. The boarding-school system of the 20th century then kicked in. California

Indians survived all these horrors, but by the dawn of the 20th century, most California Indian languages were either extinct or moribund. Of the original 100 or so languages, 50 are now extinct, and the other 50 are spoken only by a few elders. At last count, only 4 of these 50 languages have more than 100 speakers. 12 California languages have somewhere between 10 and 60 speakers; 13 have 6 to 10 speakers; and 21 have fewer than 5 speakers.

There has been considerable documentation of California languages by anthropologists and linguists, starting from the beginning of the 20th century. In the 1970s, with the development of federally funded bilingual education programs, a number of bilingual education programs were established in California, resulting in the development of writing systems and language materials. But none of these efforts slowed the steady loss of native speakers, and none succeeded in bringing about fluency in indigenous languages for second-language learners.

The benefits to language learning of language immersion and of specific methods such as "total physical response" (TPR) were obvious by the 1980s. Immersion schools were developing in Hawai'i and elsewhere that had great promise for the survival of indigenous languages. But California did not have the resources to plunge into these methods. Native speakers were few, old, and generally untrained in language teaching methodology. The younger California natives who had become teachers and teacher's aides in bilingual education were generally not fluent, and language teaching could rarely go beyond the level of simple vocabulary and rote phrases. Nor were there any university classes in California where young adults could get intensive training in their languages. Native California's tremendous and admirable diversity of languages puts us at a disadvantage: unlike the Hawaiians, the Māoris, the Welsh, and the Irish, California's Indians have no one language that can become the symbol of indigenous rights or an official state language, nor is there one language into which human and financial and university resources can be poured. Where, then, could young Indian language teachers learn the language they were supposed to teach? Where could parents learn the language they wished their children to learn? How could these dying languages ever be transmitted at all?

The answer lies with the elders themselves, the last native speakers. The key needed to be found to unlock the door between the speakers and those who wanted to learn. The master-apprentice program was developed to overcome the obstacles that were characteristic of the California situation so that the missing generations of young adult speakers that are so crucial to language transmission could become proficient in their language.

The master-apprentice model takes ideas from TPR, conversational competence models, linguistic elicitation techniques, the use of technology in language learning, and just plain common sense to create a successful language-learning situation for teams. The main principles are:

(1) No English is allowed: the master speaker must try to use his language at all times while with the apprentice, and the apprentice must use the language to ask questions or respond to the master (even if he or she can only say "I don't understand").

(2) The apprentice must be at least as active as the master in deciding what is to be learned and in keeping communication going in the language.

(3) The primary mode of transmission and learning is always oral, not written.

(4) Learning takes place primarily in real-life situations, such as cooking, washing clothes, gardening, taking walks, doing crafts, going to traditional ceremonies, and so on.

(5) The activity itself along with other forms of nonverbal communication will provide the context in which the language can be understood by the beginning learner.

HISTORY AND ADMINISTRATION OF THE MASTER-APPRENTICE PROGRAM

The master-apprentice program was developed in 1992 by the Native California Network (NCN) on the basis of a suggestion by Julian Lang (a Karuk speaker). Its initial design was created by Leanne Hinton, Nancy Richardson, Mary Bates Abbott, and others in close communication with each other. Since then, the program design has been fine-tuned based on the experiences and contributions of

the participants. Further refinement of the program has taken place as a result of a set of advanced training workshops given by the California Foreign Language Project and attended by most of the people who are trainers for the program. It has been administered throughout its seven years of existence by the Advocates for Indigenous California Language Survival (AICLS), which was originally an advisory committee to NCN. AICLS has now become a project of the Seventh Generation Fund. The master-apprentice program has been supported over the years by a number of foundations: in recent years, the Lannan Foundation has been the main funder.

A total of 65 teams have gone through the program with AICLS for one or more years or are enrolled as of this writing. Twenty different languages have been taught in this program (see Figure 17.1).

TEAM SELECTION AND ADMINISTRATION

Each year, application forms are sent out to our mailing list, to tribal offices, and to the journal *News from Native California*, which is widely read by California Indians. Teams apply (not individuals—the potential master and apprentice must find each other before applying) and are selected by the AICLS board. The most important criteria for selection are, for the master, fluency, and for the apprentice, demonstration of prior interest in learning and teaching the language. Other factors include how close the master and apprentice live to each other and, for advanced teams, whether

NORTH

Karuk	15
Hupa	8
Wintun	3
Maidu	2
Pomo (Central and Northern)	3
Washo	2

CENTRAL

Mono	3
Chukchansi	2
Choinumni	1
Wukchumni	5

SOUTH

Fort Mojave	4
Chemehuevi	2
Kiliwa	1
Kumeyaay	2
Paiute	2

FIGURE 17.1   Tribe Number of Teams. From Hinton 1999

they completed the necessary hours of language work in previous years. Teams are allowed to reapply for a total of three years in the program. There is no doubt that they could benefit from even longer participation, but room needs to be made for new teams. It is always hoped that teams will continue on their own after three years, since they now know the method.

Each member of each team is given a stipend of $3,000 for 360 hours of language immersion work. The apprentice is asked to keep a log of their work that describes their activities and what sorts of language learning took place. After each 40 hours of work, the log is sent in to the master-apprentice coordinator (currently Audrey Osborne of the Choinumne tribe), and checks are then sent to the team for those 40 hours. While paying the master for his effort and time seems only right, there are certainly pros and cons to paying apprentices. One might argue that apprentices should, if anything, be paying for this learning opportunity, and that they need to be learning not because of money but because of extreme dedication to the cause. However, the practical side of the issue is that often this stipend can make the difference between an apprentice who works full time and thus is too busy or exhausted to take full advantage of the program versus an apprentice who can cut back on work hours and devote himself more fully. Also, we ask the apprentices to take on some responsibilities beyond language work: it is the apprentice who must fill out the logs, send them in to the coordinator, and be responsible for making sure payments arrive.

TRAINING

Given the scattered geographic circumstances of the California natives, the teams have to work mostly alone. Thus the initial training for the teams is really the core of the program. The teams come together before beginning their work for a weekend training program, which is usually held at some rural retreat that has housing and food service. The gathering begins on a Friday evening, at which time we all get to know each other, and the teams talk about themselves, their previous experiences with their language, and their goals. Experienced teams talk about what they have accomplished so far, the problems they have encountered, and solutions they have found.

Principles of Immersion

On Saturday morning, the training begins in earnest. There are generally three or four trainers, at least one or two of them advanced apprentices or masters from previous years. This description is for a typical training, but details differ from session to session. We begin by giving an overview of the master-apprentice methodology. Since the goal is for all communication to take place in the target language, we begin by showing people how communication can take place even when the apprentice does not know the language at all. To demonstrate this, we pass out cards to the participants with directions written on them (in English) for some task that the participant must get someone else to do. Examples:

"Get someone to give you a dollar."
"Get someone to sit on someone else's lap."
"Get someone to tie someone else's shoelaces together."

These tasks are to be communicated and performed without any English. People do not have to use language at all to begin with, although the masters are encouraged to use their target language; but the main point is that the task is to be communicated through the use of gesture and mime. This exercise is usually accompanied by great hilarity and demonstrates the ease with which communication can occur without a common language.

Various other exercises may be done to practice miming and use of the target language. We find that one of the difficulties teams have at the beginning of their work together is that the master speaker, who has probably not been using the language on a regular basis for many years, has difficulty getting back into the habit of using the language at all. There are many exercises that can be done that involve the master's speaking. One exercise we assign sometimes is to give out large cards that have pictures of a sequence of activities on them, such as the stages of chopping wood and building a fire, making and serving coffee, saddling a horse, putting on one's shoes and socks, washing one's hands, and so on. The teams are then given about 10 minutes to practice together: the master is to develop a set of verbal commands in the language which the apprentice then carries out through miming. After the teams demonstrate the results, we explain that this is a dry run for something we expect them to do together a lot at first: for the master to give commands and the apprentice to carry them out. The apprentice, if he or she is a rank beginner, may say very little, and the master will do most of the talking. We point out that this is an opportunity for the master to get the apprentice to do a lot of work! Washing clothes, digging a garden, and cooking a meal can all be great language lessons. Get your apprentice to wash your car for you! Just be sure you are talking to him as he does it ("Wipe on, wipe off").

Besides showing the master the skills of nonverbal communication and language teaching through commands, we also discuss other principles of immersion, such as the need for repetition and review, the use of vocabulary in complete sentences, and the application of vocabulary to different situations. We mention the rule of thumb that a new vocabulary item must be heard and practiced 20 different times in each of 20 different situations (for a total of 400) before a learner will master it. We call for patience on the part of the master, and point out the stages of learning that an apprentice must go through:

Comprehension

(1) Understanding what is being communicated (through the nonverbal part of the communication, even if the apprentice doesn't understand the words yet)
(2) Recognizing what is being said (i.e., actually understanding the language being used)

Production

(3) Mimicking what is being said (i.e., producing an utterance by copying what the master has just said—can theoretically precede comprehension)
(4) Producing the utterance without prompting
(5) Using the word or phrase creatively in spontaneous communication (advanced knowledge)

It is important for both master and apprentice to realize that learning takes lots of repetition and review. We all remember speakers getting mad at learners in previous kinds of language classes, saying, "I taught that word to you yesterday. How come you can't remember it?!" The 20×20 rule is an important lesson for the teams to remember in order to learn patience.

Active Learning

The next stage of the training is directly oriented toward the apprentice. We tell apprentices that they need to take a leadership role in their own training. It will often be the apprentices who decide what direction to take their learning, who plan out what activity to do on a given day, and who remind the masters to speak in their language. During the weekend training, the beginning apprentices learn how to ask questions in the target language. The first questions are whatever the best translations are of "What is this?" and "What am I doing?" as well as "Say that again" and "Please say that in our language." We give the teams time to decide how to ask these questions, and then have the apprentices practice learning new vocabulary and phrases from the speakers, using props or moving about the room. Since more advanced teams are usually attending the same training session as the novices, they practice with more advanced questions that lead to more complex answers. Examples of complex questions would be "What is this used for?" "How is this made?" "What shall I do next?" "Tell me a story," and so on.

This section of the training is also a good time to talk about how languages and the use of those languages differ from each other. Even a simple sentence like "What is this?" may be different in surprising ways when translated into another language. Some languages have different words for "this," depending on whether the object is big or small, round or long, or soft or hard, or on whether the person is touching it or pointing to it. Also, it may not be polite to ask direct questions in one's language—one might instead have to circumlocute the question in some way, such as saying "I wonder what this is."

During meals, teams are often given assignments—for beginners, it might be to learn the names of a few items on the table; for advanced teams, it might simply be to spend lunch talking to each other in their language only.

Activities as Language Lessons

After teaching the basics of immersion and of active learning, we demonstrate and then have the teams practice doing everyday activities as language lessons. Advanced teams or trainers demonstrate an activity such as setting a table, with the speaker talking it through (usually giving commands) while the learner does the actions. For novice teams, the learner may simply do the tasks silently, but once they know how, learners should ask questions to increase the speaker's input. Our talented apprentice-turned-trainer Matt Vera, before his untimely death in 1998, used to demonstrate playing the clown in order to get more language out of his teacher. His teacher would say, "Put the plates on the table," and Vera would simply put them in a pile until his teacher would amend his command to "Put one at each chair," at which point Vera would put them *on* the chair, forcing the teacher to say, "No, put them on the table—one here, one here, and one there." Then Vera might put them in their correct locations but upside down, forcing the teacher to say, "Turn the plates right side up!" and so on.

If table setting is the demonstration, we then have all the teams do it themselves, one team at a time, each in their own language. More advanced teams may turn the tables (no pun intended) and have the apprentice tell the master what to do. Afterward, we talk about what activities are done during the day—getting up in the morning, brushing teeth, making and eating breakfast, and so on—and how each one of those can become a language lesson. Teams who live together often practice talking about their dreams when they get up in the morning. If the apprentice and master do not live together, there are still many activities they can do together—making coffee, going on a drive, doing various kinds of crafts together such as basket making, fishnet making, or quilting, or going "out on site," as some teams call it, to traditional locations. The importance of doing both traditional and modern activities together is stressed. On the one hand, most people's desire to learn their language is related to a desire to get back meaningful traditional values and wisdom, which means that doing traditional activities is of key importance. On the other hand, language revitalization can be defined as successful only if the language is used as a language of everyday communication, and since everyday communication takes place mostly in the context of modern living, then the language must be used in that context. This also brings up the problem of vocabulary for modern items. Since the California languages have not, in general, been used for daily communication for a long time, there are no words for many modern items. At all points during the training we leave periods for discussion, and this is one of the areas that gets the most discussion. Frequently the master-apprentice teams are the only people using the language, and it is therefore up to them to figure out how to talk about modern items. We discuss the various options they have available to them if vocabulary creation becomes necessary—borrowing and nativizing pronunciation versus using the traditional ways of naming new items that have been used in the past (such as descriptive phrases or semantic extension), and so on. The philosophy and politics of the coinage of new terms varies from language to language and from group to group, and each team has to venture its own way in this difficult task. It is one of many ways in which language teaching and learning is very different for endangered languages than for the world languages: the learners and teachers are also by necessity language engineers, a rather frightening and controversial role.

Tape Recording

We stress oral language over written; many of us have had experience with language classes where the effects of learners' writing things down has been detrimental to language learning. Writing words down diminishes the amount of language being uttered in any given unit of time and also diminishes interaction and real communication. Words put on paper are less likely to be put in the brain. And going back to the notes and then pronouncing what is on the paper almost invariably leads to atrocious pronunciation. At the same time, we recognize the apprentice's need to make a record of new utterances for the sake of practicing later. We believe that tape recording the utterances is the best way to make that record. Then the learner can rehear the language rather than just look at imperfect visual traces of it. The tapes can be listened to in the car or in bed at night even after the lights are out. They can form the main source of repetition and practice by the apprentice, thus saving the master from "repetition burnout." The apprentice can say the utterances after the taped version, or even "shadow" them—speaking along with the utterance. Furthermore, the tapes will someday be a priceless record of the speech of these last native speakers.

We give some hints about good recording techniques, good labeling, and good storage and security. Some people simply record everything they do, but this can result in an overload of tape with long, boring silences and disorganized pieces of language that may not be easily found again. It is better to devote a part of each session, perhaps toward the

end, to review what was done during the day and record a tighter version of the new vocabulary and phrases.

The Typical Language Session

Nancy Richardson Steele, our most talented trainer, is an experienced language educator and has trained since the beginning of the program. However, she did not know her ancestral tongue (Karuk) fluently. She therefore decided to become an apprentice herself and is now in her third year of apprenticeship to Leland Donahue. In the process of her own apprenticeship, she learned how difficult it is for teams to stay immersed in the language at all times—it is in fact virtually impossible for beginning teams. She thus developed a model of a typical session that goes something like this. The details will differ depending on where the team works together and other variables.

(1) Advance preparation: At your last session, you should have made plans for the next session, and the master and apprentice may each have things they need to prepare in advance—gathering props, arranging for a car, thinking about necessary vocabulary items, and so on.

(2) The apprentice might begin with a phone call to confirm that this is a good time for the apprentice to come to the speaker's home. (Some of the early lessons the team has together would involve learning how to do such a conversation in your language.)

(3) Arrival: Greetings and small talk (devote early lessons to how to perform a greeting, talk about the weather, about what you have been doing since you last saw each other, etc.).

(4) On-site prep work: Whatever your next activity is going to be, you may need to prepare for it—both in the way of gathering needed materials and discussing vocabulary. You might be preparing for some activity around which language will be used, such as making coffee; or you might be preparing for just talking about some conversational topic you have in mind. For new teams, some of the preparation may involve speaking in English; but the goal should be that eventually even prep work will be conducted in your language.

(5) "Immersion sets": Once the planning and preparation for the activity are complete, start the real work of actually conversing in your language. At first, you might find that an "immersion set" will only last a few minutes, after which you might need to do further preparation. Try to aim for something like 20 minutes; then, if necessary, relax into English for a few minutes, talk a little about the immersion set; then do another 20 minutes. This is "structured immersion," where the apprentice is learning new words and phrases related to the lesson and practicing with them.

A session might cycle through points (4) and (5) several times for each activity, and there might be several different activities in a session, especially if it is a long one. The team might start out making coffee as a regular first activity (*every* activity should be a language lesson), then they might have some kind of project they are doing together such as making a fishnet or working on a vegetable garden, and then they might have certain topics they want to go over together, such as how to do a telephone conversation, or weather, or saying prayers at a particular ceremony, or vocabulary around horseback riding, and so on. If the master needs to go shopping that day, that becomes a language activity too; much can be discussed about the environment while the team drives or walks to a store, and much can be said about the objects being bought or the activities or physical appearance of the people in the store.

(6) "Unstructured immersion": Each session should also have some unstructured immersion, where the team is doing real communication about real things, or just talking about whatever they want to talk about. This allows the apprentice to use language knowledge already mastered, and also allows the team to explore new conversational areas they might not have explored before. Unstructured immersion can occur during the same activities that you might be doing structured immersion with, or it might be a period when the team is just sitting around relaxing.

(7) Tape recording: Devote some time toward the end of each session to recording the new material that was learned that day and preparing practice tapes for the apprentice.

(8) Planning for next time: Make dates for your next session (though ideally the team has regular times all set up), and plan the activities and topics you will deal with then. Decide what each of you will need to do to prepare for these activities and topics. (This might be in English; keep in mind the constant goal that someday even the planning will be in your language. Anything you *can* say in your language, do so.)

(9) Leave-taking. Say your goodbyes. Let the very last words you say to each other be in your language.

The 10 Points of Language Learning

The teams are given a manual that can be used to guide them through the first few weeks of language work together (Hinton et al., in press). The core of the manual is the "Ten Points of Language Learning," most of which have been discussed above (see also Yamamoto, this volume). In the manual we go into each point in detail; here I will just give the main headings:

10 Points for Successful Language Learning
(1) Leave English behind.
(2) Make yourself understood with nonverbal communication.

(a) actions
(b) gestures and facial expressions
(c) pictures and objects

(3) Teach in full sentences; teach in conversations.
(4) Aim for real communication in your language.
(5) Language is also culture: do traditional activities when possible, and remember that your language and the way it should be used will be different from English.
(6) Focus on listening and speaking, rather than writing and grammatical analysis.
(7) Activities for master and apprentice to do together.
(8) Do audio- and videotaping.
(9) Be an active learner.
(10) Be sensitive to each other's needs; be patient and proud of each other and yourselves!

Language Demonstrations by Advanced Apprentices

Sometime during the weekend, each continuing team is expected to give a demonstration to show something they have learned. By the end of the third year, we hope to hear speeches 10 minutes or more in length from the apprentices. These are tremendously inspiring to everyone at the conference.

Cultural Sharing

On Saturday evening, we unwind with informal "cultural sharing," where people tell stories and sing songs, around an outdoor fire if weather allows. Since participants are from all over the state, there are many different song traditions and many different kinds of stories to share. Often the stories are in English, but we love it best when a speaker talks to us in his own language.

Assessment

Each team undergoes an assessment at the beginning and end of each year during breaks in the training sessions. The assessment is given in a private room, and as we have usually done it, it has two parts:

(1) A set of questions is given to the master (written in English), which he or she then relates to the apprentice in their language. The questions range from simple to complex, starting with something like "How are you?" "What's your name?" and "Where do you live?" and ending with questions as complex as "Tell me something that happened to you when you were a child," or "What would you like to be doing 10 years from now?" The master only asks questions until the apprentice does not seem to be understanding and then stops. Meanwhile, an assessor (one of the trainers) is writing down how well

the apprentice seems to understand and the characteristics of the answers. Recall that some 20 different languages are involved in this program, and in most cases the assessors do not understand any of them. We listen not for grammatical accuracy, but rather for seeming fluency. We record whether the apprentice uses one-word answers or whole sentences, how long the apprentice speaks, and whether the apprentice pauses frequently and has many false starts or produces a flowing stream of words. Afterward, we ask the master to translate what the apprentice said and to give us his or her evaluation of the apprentice's grammatical accuracy.

(2) In the second part of the assessment, the apprentice chooses a picture out of a collection of options. The pictures are old photographs of California natives doing activities in interesting surroundings, and paintings by native artists. We choose complex photos and paintings that are open to interesting interpretation. The apprentice is then asked to talk about the picture, sometimes being prompted with questions by the master, and the assessor again writes down the fluency and length of the description. Again we ask the master to translate after the apprentice has finished.

The assessments are videotaped, with the idea in mind of someday comparing early assessments with later ones.

PHONE MENTORING, LOGS, AND SITE VISITS

Once the training session is over, the teams go home and put into practice what they have learned. They have to work without regular oversight, and everything is usually a lot harder to do than people think it will be. People feel foolish trying to communicate nonverbally when they have a language in common (English) that would make communication instantaneous. People get frustrated at not understanding or not being able to make the other person understand, or at their slow progress at learning. The master may have his own ideas about language teaching that do not involve immersion. One or both members of the team might have full-time jobs and families and other responsibilities and be exhausted a good deal of the time, so that devoting the necessary time to language learning turns out to be more difficult than they realized. There are all kinds of difficulties ahead for the teams, and they need mentoring. In a situation like ours, where the teams live all over the state, there is no way that they can get together with trainers on a regular basis; but we have a staff person (the master-apprentice coordinator) who is in charge of mentoring them at least once a month by telephone and visiting them at least once a year. Furthermore, the teams need to turn in logs on a regular basis to get their stipends, and these logs are reviewed by the staff person as further input on how well the team is progressing and what kinds of problems they might be having. Sometimes, for example, the logs show that they are focusing too much on vocabulary and not enough on connected speech, or that they have started to get stuck in the same activity over and over (e.g., just going to Bingo twice a week!). The staff person needs to discuss these things with the team and help them find ways to get beyond whatever obstacles might be impeding their progress.

On the site visits, the master-apprentice coordinator or other representative from among the trainers will be able to see the team in action. The team is asked to conduct a session as they usually do so the coordinator can see ways in which they might need some assistance. He or she can point out times when they lapse needlessly into English, discuss possible activities that the local environment provides opportunities for, and give them pointers on how to develop their language usage more richly.

RESULTS

The desired result of the program is that by the end of three years, the apprentices will be at least conversationally proficient in their language and ready to be language teachers to other people. However, never could we expect an apprentice to be so fluent as to equal the ability of the master. Preferably, the master and apprentice develop a lifelong relationship (if they did not already have one), and the master will also be involved in all the future language activities of the apprentice.

Here is a list of some of the teams and what they are doing now (from Hinton 1999). As you will see from this list, many apprentices have gone on to do language teaching or training other master-apprentice teams.

Karuk: Terry Alford (apprentice) and his grandfather Lester Alford (master). This talented team worked on language in the outdoors, hunting together and walking the hills, so that Lester could teach Terry not only the language but also traditional knowledge about hunting and gathering and about spirituality. Terry learned how to speak very well, and although he is presently working full time at an unrelated job, he tries to use the language when he can, at least on weekends. To our great sadness, Lester passed away in December of 1997.

Karuk: Terry Supahan and family (apprentices) and Violet Super (master). Terry, his wife, Sarah, and their children have all made a great effort to learn their language from their great-aunt Violet Super and from other sources. Terry and Sarah teach Karuk at the local school and have also run summer camps and made videos, books, and teaching materials. Their twin daughters are just graduating from high school now and are deeply involved still in language learning as well as tribal ceremony. One of the twins, Elaina, has gorgeous, intricate regalia that she made herself for the traditional dances. She continues to work with her aunt as an apprentice, and comes to language conferences.

Karuk: Nancy Richardson Steele and Leland Donahue (Junie). Nancy and Junie have a very close working relationship and friendship; Junie sometimes says he cannot imagine working with another apprentice, although there are many Karuks who hope to change his mind about that. Nancy has a long and intensive background in language education, starting with bilingual education in the late 1970s. She has been involved with AICLS in various ways since its inception and is the top trainer in the master-apprentice program. Yet she had never had the chance to really learn Karuk fluently until she herself signed up as an apprentice. Now her Karuk is tremendously improved, and her understanding of how to best train the teams has increased too. Nancy will always be an important force in Karuk language revitalization.

Hupa: Danny Ammon (apprentice) and Calvin Carpenter (master). Danny is quite fluent and teaches at the Hupa school, where he gives classes in the Hupa language half time and in math half time. He has participated in Hupa summer language camps and has trained other master-apprentice teams at training workshops. Danny has a Web page that includes some very informative material about the Hupa language. He is speaking to his two-year-old daughter almost solely in Hupa and has strong hopes of being able to raise her to be a fluent native speaker of the language.

Hupa: Gordon Bussell (apprentice) and Jimmy Jackson (master). Gordon speaks quite fluently, although he says he has far to go still, and even though his status as an apprentice in the program is over, he continues to study with anyone who will teach him. Gordon teaches Hupa at school and in summer camps. Gordon, Jimmy, Calvin Carpenter, and others also have a weekly get-together with anyone else who is interested in learning and teaching more about the Hupa language. Gordon is presently the president of the AICLS board and has worked as a trainer in master-apprentice training workshops in California and for programs developing outside of California. He and I have gone to Alaska together twice to train for Athabaskan programs there. Since Hupa is also an Athabaskan language, Gordon is fascinated with the languages and participates in much trading back and forth about cognate vocabulary.

Yurok: Georgiana Myers (apprentice) and Georgina Trull (master). Georgina Trull is an excellent, eloquent speaker of Yurok and a member of the Yurok Language Committee, which has been working on perfecting the writing system and planning for language revitalization. Her granddaughter Georgiana Myers is the youngest of the apprentices, still in high school as she completes her third year of apprenticeship. Yurok is being taught in the school, but Georgiana, spending 10–20 hours per week with her grandmother beyond school hours, serves more as a teaching assistant than a student in the school classes.

She talks about the language and about how her peers feel about the language in a way that gives real hope for the future. She and her friends all think that the Yurok language is "cool" and are proud to use it with each other and within earshot of everyone. Young people in previous generations grew up with exactly the opposite opinion of their native languages, and feelings of shame about their language played a big role in its decline. To have the teenagers of the present generation feeling proud of their language and motivated to learn it is wonderful to behold.

Pomo: (Hopland): Betty Verdugo (apprentice) and Cynthia Daniels (master). Betty is currently involved with the tribal council and is advocating for the development of a language program. She works with her own family, teaching them words and activities she has learned. Cynthia Daniels is currently teaching her language in community classes.

Yurok: Barbara McQuillen (apprentice) and Ida McQuillen (master). Barbara now works as the master-apprentice coordinator for the Yurok language program, which now runs its own master-apprentice teams. Barbara also helps with the language classes. Ida, having worked with Barbara for three years in MALLP, since trained a second apprentice with the Yurok program. We are sorry to say that Ida passed away in March of 1999.

Wukchumne: Susan Weese (apprentice) and Eddie Sartuche (master). Susan is on the AICLS board as an alternate and was active in the Wukchumni language preschool until it closed (we hope temporarily), and she speaks in Wukchumni to her grandchildren. Eddie worked with three apprentices at once for a three-year period. He is part of a language class now taught weekly by a number of Wukchumni elders and helps with language in the preschool curriculum development. Eddie still works with anyone who wants to learn and is also learning himself from a more fluent older speaker.

Wukchumne: Debra Fierro (apprentice) and Eddie Sartuche (master). Debra was the teacher at the Wukchumni language preschool for as long as it was able to stay open.

Wukchumne: Yolanda Chambers (apprentice) and Eddie Sartuche (master). Yolanda is teaching her grandchildren Wukchumni.

Yowlumne: Christina Martinez (apprentice) and Jane Flippo (master). Jane is one of the few people in California who speak the language on a daily basis, with her relative Agnes Vera who lives next door. Christina is an unusually talented language learner. Her work is not related to her language, but she is one of a couple of members of the younger generation of younger Yowlumnes who, given the opportunity, will make a good teacher and carry the language forward. Christina still actively attends language conferences and comes to do research on her language occasionally in the archives at the University of California, Berkeley.

Yowlumne: Kerri Vera (apprentice) and Agnes Vera (master). Kerri has learned a great deal of Yowlumne from Agnes, her grandmother, who is among the most talented language teachers in the program. Agnes has helped in training both for MALLP and for programs such as the recently developed Comanche master-apprentice program in Oklahoma. Kerri gave an impressive talk in Yowlumne at the end of her third year. She has taught community language classes with Agnes and would make an excellent teacher if the Yowlumnes ever establish an immersion preschool or another school program. Before Kerri, Agnes taught her son Matt Vera for three years. Matt was a real leader in language revitalization and not only learned the language proficiently but also worked to develop a writing system and learning materials. He even became the lead teacher in the Wukchumne preschool. (Wukchumne is a different but related language that Matt learned on the job, working with Wukchumne speakers and using his knowledge of Yowlumne-Wukchumne sound correspondences.) Tragically, Matt died in 1998 owing to complications from injuries in an automobile accident.

Paiute: Donna Thomas (apprentice) and Norma Nelson (master). Donna has an education center for language development. With the help of Norma, she is presently working with a group community language class.

Mojave: Sylvia Arteaga (apprentice) and several masters. Sylvia has worked extensively on learning Mojave and has also taught extensively. She runs after-school classes and summer classes and has even begun to work with apprentices herself.

Chemehuevi: Nora Vasquez (apprentice) and Gertrude E. Burns (master). Nora and Gertrude now teach community language classes together.

BENEFITS OF THE PROGRAM

As can be seen from the list above, the program does what it is supposed to do—it trains young professional-age adults in the language so that they can go on to teach it themselves. There is no California tribe with the resources to do what Hawai'i has done—create an immersion schooling situation stretching all the way from preschool to a master's degree—but some California groups have at least established immersion preschools or state-of-the-art language teaching programs in public schools.

The principles of immersion, once learned, have a basic commonsense basis, and it does not demand any special location, equipment, or curriculum.

Besides being able to bring people to conversational proficiency, the program has many other benefits. For one thing, it involves the elders in positive ways, reducing the generation gap felt by so many Native Americans who have struggled with the enormous cultural changes of the last century, and bringing people back in touch with their roots. School-based programs often end up excluding the elders, who may not be able to participate in such school-based skills as teaching reading and writing or any of the school subjects in the language. The culture of the classroom is fundamentally different from traditional culture and from the daily life of elders, whereas the master-apprentice program takes place right inside the daily life of the team. In the master-apprentice model, the knowledge of the master is of direct and immediate use to the learner and does not have to be mediated by classroom constraints and demands. The positive benefits to the self-esteem of the elders themselves are often notable; sometimes elders even tell us they are getting better health reports from their doctors lately, which they attribute to their work with their apprentices.

Since the master-apprentice program teaches effective language-teaching and language-learning methods, apprentices not only are potentially able to learn the language well enough to teach it, but also learn a methodology that they can then use in their own teaching. This improvement in the quality of school and evening classes is another benefit of the model.

Another benefit is that it is a relatively simple model. Once teams understand the basic methodology, they can work independently from any professional assistance. They do not have to depend on the constant presence of any professional such as a professor or other professional teacher or consultant in order to carry out the program. This also means that the program can be spread by relatively informal, grassroots means.

SOME PROBLEMS

Some problems to watch out for are:

(1) The model is simple conceptually, but it is difficult to carry out practically, because it demands a great deal of time, energy, dedication, and faith on the part of the teams. Only about one-third of the teams that start out in the California program end up completing three full years, because people often find that this program on top of the demands of their daily lives is just too much for them.

(2) Owing to the particular administrative and financial history of this program, it is not year round, but only lasts for about half of each year. This has both good and bad points. The flexibility of how many hours per week the teams spend together (at least 10, but up to 20) allows some teams to have an intensive learning period for 3–4 months (which works when, for example, the apprentice is a student or a teacher with summer vacations that can be devoted to language), while others might prefer to spread out their learning period for a longer period of time. But what would be ideal for the purposes of language learning would be for them to work on a year-

round basis. We always tell teams at the training that the months they are working within the program are just a training period for what we hope will be a year-round teaching and learning relationship between master and apprentice.

(3) The emphasis on oral learning is to be desired, given the purpose of the program. However, even though documentation and the development of written teaching materials are not part of the program, they should not be ignored. Most alarming is that fact that our valued elders will be leaving us one day; a number of masters have already died since the program was developed. Even the apprentices themselves, though younger, are far from immortal—as of this writing, two apprentices have passed away during the years of the program. One day, all too soon, there will be no native speakers left. We hope that by then there will be apprentices who will carry the language forward, but in any case, a great deal of the language knowledge of the elders will be gone. At that time, all the apprentices and other language activists will have for the possibility of further learning will be whatever documentation has been made of the language. We want the teams to remember that. The tape recordings we teach them how to make will be especially valuable—priceless—and this means that they should record as much as they can of their teacher, not just what they learned that day, but stories, songs, all the verbal arts that their teacher is willing to impart. Translations of the texts and explanations in English about their history, meaning, and function will also increase their worth to future generations. It also means that they need to think about long-term preservation of their recordings. They need to make sure that the originals are stored safely, that copies are made in case something happens to the originals, and that someday the tapes (either copies or originals) be archived somewhere for the sake of further permanence.

THE SPREAD OF THE MASTER-APPRENTICE MODEL

The master-apprentice model has spread to various places around the country. AICLS trainers have trained groups in Oregon, Nevada, Arizona, Alaska, Wisconsin, and Oklahoma; and within California, a number of tribes have gone on to get grants that involve a master-apprentice component of their own. Some funding agencies describe the master-apprentice model in their materials, and some agencies focus primarily on immersion schools and master-apprentice programs in their language funding.

We have been careful not to try to claim "ownership" of the program. Although the trainers for the program have done training workshops for other programs elsewhere in the country, we are also happy to hear that people who have learned the program from us are doing their own training in their own or other communities without further involving us. The goal is for the master-apprentice model to spread wherever it can be useful.

References

Hinton, Leanne. 1997. Survival of endangered languages: The California Master-Apprentice Program. *International Journal of the Sociology of Language* 123: 177–91.

———. 1999. The advocates. *News from Native California* 12, no. 3: 8–12.

Hinton, Leanne, Matt Vera, Nancy Steele, and the Advocates for Indigenous California Language Survival. In press. *Keep your language alive: A common-sense approach to one-on-one language learning.* Berkeley, CA: Heyday Books.

18

Linguistic Aspects of Language Teaching and Learning in Immersion Contexts

KEN HALE

Department of Linguistics and Philosophy
Massachusetts Institute of Technology
Cambridge, Massachusetts

There are at least five "degrees of immersion" which can be identified in categorizing the various monolingual situations in which a person may acquire a language. The first degree is the most favorable. It corresponds to the situation in which a child learns a language within the context of his or her family. Virtually everyone experiences the first degree of immersion, since this is the environment in which one's first language is learned.

The second degree of immersion would be that corresponding to the situation in which preschool and kindergarten children are cared for and instructed by people who speak to them always and only in a particular language (referred to here as "L") during the period when the children are in the school environment. Where L is not the child's first language, this is indeed a lesser degree of immersion. The exposure to L in this second degree of immersion is extremely valuable and often leads to native-like mastery of the language, but it is not as full and consistent as the first-degree immersion situation characteristic of the acquisition of one's first language. Nonetheless, it is in many communities the most promising environment for language revitalization. This second degree of immersion, depending on the nature of the education framework in which it functions, can in principle be extended to the elementary, secondary, and tertiary school years (see, for example, Chapters 10, 11, and 12 on the Hawaiian and Māori immersion programs). In principle, therefore, the second-degree immersion program can lead to the circumstance in which a learner achieves a mastery of L essentially equivalent to that of a native speaker, that is, a command of L virtually indistinguishable from that of a person who learned the language in the first-degree immersion situation.

The third degree of immersion can be realized in a num-ber of different formats. An important one is that in which two people, one a native speaker of L, the other a learner of L, spend their days together speaking only L. Where the speaker and the learner are able to spend a great amount of time together, even an adult lifetime together, this can also bring a learner to a level of competence functionally equivalent to that of a native speaker. Typically, however, such associations are more short-lived, resulting in a level of mastery which, though significant, is generally much less than that of a native speaker. This is essentially the situation involved in the master-apprentice immersion program (see Chapter 28). We place this at the third degree because that amount of exposure is typically less here than in the second degree, and certainly less than in the first degree. There are exceptions, of course, of couples (a speaker and a learner) who spend their lives speaking the language together, the learner becoming almost as competent as the native speaker, functionally at least. This learning environment is also found in a relationship which might not occur to one as at all relevant to a discussion of immersion. This is the relationship between a linguist or anthropologist and his or her informants, or language consultants, the former being the apprentices, the latter the masters. Typically, of course, this relationship begins with the use of two languages, the apprentice's language being used to elicit forms in the language of the master, but in many cases, the work shifts to the master's language entirely. In these cases, the master-apprentice model is operating, to all intents and purposes.

Our suggested fourth degree of immersion is the "content course," in which L is used as the language of instruction in a series of lessons whose content is something other than the language itself—for example, biology, math, geography, philosophy, and so on. This is similar to the second-degree

227

immersion situation, but the amount of contact is less. While the subject matter of the course is not L itself, the purpose of the course is both to teach the subject matter and to teach the language as well, through the example of its use in explaining the course content. To say that this is the fourth degree of immersion is not to say that it is less important or less valuable than higher degrees, because in many present-day communities, the fourth-degree immersion situation is the only realistic possibility within the general immersion class of language-learning situations. Furthermore, the fourth degree is a good language-learning environment, fully worthy of the immersion label.

The fifth and final degree in our classification of immersion environments is the monolingual language class. In some variants, this is virtually indistinguishable from the fourth-degree learning situation. In the monolingual class, L is used exclusively, generally in a conversational setting and often around a particular topic—a movie, a *telenovela* or soap opera, food, the news, and so on. This model is common in contemporary conversational language classes.

The degree of immersion has interesting implications for training. I will consider here the training required to ensure that the learner acquires the structural features of L—that is, its sound system, morphology, syntax, and semantics. In general, the higher the degree of immersion, the less attention needs to be paid to the structure of L. That is to say, less attention has to be given specifically to teaching structure in the first and second degrees. In fact, little if any attention has to be given specifically to grammar in the first and second degrees, since these are full and rich immersion environments. In the best of circumstances, the learner is exposed to all the data needed to acquire L in the manner of a first-language learner, and where the learner is an infant or young child, he or she has the great advantage of being able to make use of the special language-learning capacity of children. The first degree, and to some extent the second degree, are "natural" language learning environments and are normally not specially constructed for the teaching of structure, although, as is well known, in many societies mothers and other close kin will present children with carefully edited models of a standard form of L, often adjusted in accordance with their perception of what is appropriate to their age.

The situation is very different for the lower degrees of immersion, where the contact with the language is less. This is especially true of the fourth and fifth degrees, where the teacher must have training not only in teaching methods, but also specifically in the structural features of L. The reason for this is obvious: since the exposure to the language is limited, special measures must be taken to ensure that the structural features of L are adequately covered, especially those features which are in some sense "characteristic" of L— those features which one must acquire in order to be able to say that one is actually speaking L and not some diluted or modified version of it.

By way of illustrating the point just made, I present part of a fourth-degree immersion lesson in Miskitu, the indigenous lingua franca of eastern Nicaragua. The content of the lesson deals with certain aspects of the geography of Nicaragua. Although the written version of the text does not show this very well, the oral classroom version, aided by various props, such as a map of the country, and pictures, makes it clear to the students what is being said in the lesson, even if their command of the Miskitu is still incipient. Embedded in the text are a number of Miskitu constructions, of course, but this lesson is constructed in such a way as to give special attention to a particular construction which figures prominently in the grammar of the language. The lesson is of course monolingual in Miskitu, but for present purposes the lecture will be given in translation as well, in parentheses; stage directions are also given in English, in square brackets.

WAN TASBAYA 'Our Land'

[pointing to map]
    Naha kuntrika sika Nicaragua.
    'This country is Nicaragua'.

    Bara naha kuntrika sika Honduras.
    'And this country is Honduras'.

    Nicaragua kuntri sirpi sa.
    'Nicaragua is a small country'.

[pointing and signaling "two" with the fingers]
    Nicaragua pîs wal brisa.
    'Nicaragua has two parts'.

[pointing to the western part]
    Naha pîska sika Pasipik Kus.
    'This part is the Pacific Coast'.

    Bara naha pîska sika Atlantik Kus.
    'And this part is the Atlantic Coast'.

[pointing and indicating sizes]
    Atlantik Kus târa sa, kuna Pasipik Kus sirpi sa.
    'The Atlantic Coast is big, but the Pacific Coast is small'.

[pointing at the Coco River]
    Nicaragua wihki Honduras wal lilapas ra âwala kum bâra sa.
    'Between Nicaragua and Honduras there is a river'.

    Âwalka ba lika Wangki mâkisa.
    'The river is called the Wangki [Coco]'.

[indicating large size]
    Wangki ba âwala târa sa.
    'The Coco is a large river'.

[pointing at houses and villages on the Atlantic Coast]
    Miskitu uplika nani ba Atlantik Kus ra twisa.
    'The Miskitu people live on the Atlantic Coast'.

    Upla ailal Wangki âwalka ra îwisa.
    'Many people live on the Coco River'.

[pointing to Waspam on the Coco River and indicating large size]
    Naha tâwanka sika Waspam. Tâwan târa sa.
    'This town is Waspam. It is a large town'.

Waspam uplika nani ba Miskitu sa.
'The people of Waspam are Miskitu'.

Waspam tâwanka Miskitu tâwanka kum sa.
'The town of Waspam is a Miskitu community'.

This is part of the "lecture portion" of a lesson on the geography of Central America presenting part of the content of a course on Nicaragua. It is monolingual and could be addressed to any audience learning Miskitu, particularly one that has had some exposure to Miskitu through earlier lessons. In actual practice, courses on Miskitu are addressed to non-Miskitu people living and working on the Atlantic Coast, such as people from the Pacific Coast or foreigners, including families, hence both children and adults. Apart from the information which is given about Nicaragua, there is of course a linguistic point to be made. Thus, the course has the dual purpose of teaching about a part of Central America and, more important, the Miskitu language. In this lesson, the main grammatical question is, what is the difference between the two forms which nouns take in Miskitu? That is, what is the principle governing the use of the forms given in the left-hand column and those given in the center column below?

pîs	*pîska*	'part, piece'
kuntri	*kuntrika*	'country'
âwala	*âwalka*	'river'
upla	*uplika*	'people'
tâwan	*tâwanka*	'town, community'

In these examples, the morphological difference is quite clear: the ending *-ka* is present in the forms of the center column, and it is absent from the forms of the left-hand column. But this is not the point of interest here. Rather, we need to understand *when* to use these different forms. This is an important feature of Miskitu grammar.

The teaching method implied in the fourth-degree immersion environment is based on the idea that principles of grammar are to be *discovered* by the learner. They are not told to the learner explicitly. Direct teaching of grammar is avoided, unless it becomes necessary for some reason. The hope in this program is that the discourse will be rich enough in examples of the two nominal forms to permit the learner to "figure out" the principle involved.

The principle is revealed in the following pair of sentences:

Naha kuntri târa sa.
'This is a big country'.

Naha kuntrika târa sa.
'This country is big'.

In the first sentence, the subject is the word *naha* 'this', and the remainder is the predicate. In the second sentence, the subject is the sequence *naha kuntrika*. The essential point is that in this use, the noun is "in construction" with a preceding element (in this case, the demonstrative *naha*). And the grammatical principle involved here is that a noun appears in the "construct state" if it is in a construction with a preceding element. In the first sentence, the noun appears in the "absolute state" *kuntri*, because it is a part of the predicate and therefore is not in construction with the demonstrative *naha*. The structural relationships involved in the two sentences are:

Subject	Predicate
Naha	*kuntri târa sa*
this	country big is
Naha kuntrika	*târa sa*
this country	big is

There is a more natural way to express these assertions, utilizing one of the topicalization particles *lika* or *sika* in the equational or identificational construction, in which the subject (on the left) is clearly set off from the predicate (on the right). The position of this particle clearly indicates the structural difference between the two sentences:

Subject	Particle	Predicate
Naha	*lika*	*kuntri târa.*
this	[topic]	country big
'This is a big country'.		
Naha kuntrika	*lika*	*târa.*
this country	[topic]	big
'This country is big'.		

Here the particle *lika* partitions the sentence into a subject and a predicate. Structurally, it indicates clearly what does and does not "go with" the subject. Thus, its position shows clearly that *naha kuntrika* is a single constituent, a nominal construction, whose head noun must appear in the construct state.

The use of the particles *lika* and *sika* would quite naturally be introduced in the course lectures themselves, and they could be used as the basis of an ancillary lesson of the type we have referred to as the fifth-degree immersion environment, that is, a monolingual lesson devoted specifically to the Miskitu construct-state construction. Further evidence to help the learner is given in the following forms:

Subject	Predicate
Naha na	*kuntri târa sa*
this [proximate]	country big is
Naha kuntrika na	*târa sa*
this country [proximate]	big is

Here the demonstrative is accompanied by the proximate marker, an enclitic element indicating that the entity referred to by the phrase is located near the speaker (spatially or psychologically). This gives us a handy way to see whether or not the noun is in construction with the demonstrative. If it is, then the proximate enclitic will follow the noun, as in the second sentence. As expected, the noun is in the construct state there, hence it has the form *kuntrika*. By contrast, in the first sentence, the noun *kuntri* is part of the predicate, and the proximate enclitic directly follows the demonstrative. The point of this lesson could be illustrated further by sentences using the non-proximate demonstrative and enclitic, as in:

Subject	Predicate
Baha ba	*kuntri târa sa.*
that [non-proximate]	country big is
'That is a big country'.	
Baha kuntrika ba	*târa sa.*
that country [non-proximate]	big is
'That country is big'.	

The partial lecture cited above is not enough, actually, to permit all participants in the class to discover the principle involved in the Miskitu construct state construction, since it is necessary to have an understanding of the relevant aspects of constituent structure, reflected in part by the manner in which the clauses are partioned into a subject or topic, on the one hand, and a predicate in the other. These principles must also be learned. In an actual class, or sequence of classes, more evidence would have to be given. In addition, the interactive component would engage the students in using the construct and absolute forms of nouns. For example, in comparing the sizes of different countries, the instructor might say:

Nicaragua kuntri sirpi sa.
'Nicaragua is a small country'.

Rusia lika kuntri târa sa.
'Russia, on the other hand, is a large country'.

The instructor might then say:

Âni kuntrika târa sa ki?
'Which country is large'?

to which the following is a possible, and even true, answer:

Rusia kuntri târa sa.
'Russia is a big country'.

In the question, the noun is in the construct state, because *âni kuntrika* 'which country' forms a constituent, that is, a single nominal construction, in which an interrogative determiner (*âni* 'which') precedes the noun (*kuntrika* 'country'). In the answer, however, the word preceding the noun *kuntri* is the subject of the sentence and it is not "in construction" with *kuntri,* which consequently appears in the absolute form, as expected.

The example of the Miskitu construct state is presented to illustrate the fact that learning Miskitu as a second language, as would be the case in a fourth- or fifth-degree immersion situation, involves the acquisition of a structural feature of the language which is in a sense definitive of it—if one acquires Miskitu, one necessarily acquires the construct state. But at these degrees of immersion, it is not possible simply to assume that the learner will pick up the principles underlying the grammar of the construct on the basis of a "natural and essentially random corpus" of the language. By contrast, this expectation *is* reasonable in the first and second degrees of immersion, because there the "accidental corpus" is large enough to virtually guarantee that the learner will eventually have the data needed to acquire the construction and the associated morphology (*-ka* in the examples given, though this is just one of the forms it takes).

At the fourth and fifth degrees of immersion, a somewhat artificial environment must be created, one in which the structural properties of the language are brought forward often, and in a context which reflects as clearly as possible the meaning of what is being said. To learn the Miskitu construct state, one must not only learn to create the correct morphological form of a noun appearing in that construction, but also learn the syntactic structure associated with it. In an immersion situation, that is, a monolingual environment, one needs to learn what the construction "means"—its associate semantics—and since no one is going to tell the learner what it means, the learner must figure it out on the basis of what he or she hears. All of this requires data, and in the lower degrees of immersion, these data must be made to appear frequently and in a context rich enough to reveal adequately the form and meaning of the construction.

It is for this reason that teachers at the fourth and fifth degrees of immersion must have the training that will ensure that they are consciously aware of the special structural properties of the language being taught, L. It is not enough to be a fluent speaker of L; it is necessary to make *conscious* appeal to its grammar in order to plan the revelation of its special structural and grammatical properties in sufficient abundance to guarantee their acquisition. In some cases, inevitably, the teacher will have to resort to explicit explanations of grammatical forms and constructions. This also requires training, of course. In effect, the teacher is a language scholar, or linguist, in relation to L.

The remarks just made assume that the training burden falls exclusively on the teacher, not the student. This may not be the case, however, in all instances. It can be the student, rather than the teacher, who brings the necessary training. This is sometimes true in the master-apprentice relationship, where it is often the student who must have conscious awareness of what he or she needs to learn in order to acquire the language. Here the student may not be aware of the special properties of L, but a background in linguistics, or experience with learning other languages, will be useful in discovering its structural features. This is essentially the situation in which a linguistic or anthropological field worker operates in learning a new language in the field.

What is it that must be given special attention in teaching and learning a language in the fourth- and fifth-degree immersion environments? Many aspects of a given language are so richly forthcoming in an immersion situation that it is unnecessary to give them any extra attention, above and beyond the usage inherent in the situation itself, unless, of course, mistakes persistently appear in the learners' speech. For example, the standard unmarked verb-final word order of Miskitu is evident at every turn, only deviations from it deserve special attention. And, for the most part, the segmental phonology and accentual system of Miskitu are likewise evident at all points. Sufficient usage alone will guarantee acquisition of Miskitu phonology—though, to be sure, special practice in pronunciation may be required. However, all languages, so far as we know, have certain "special features" that deserve attention at the lower degrees of immersion. A small subset of such features for Miskitu includes:

(1) Verbal inflection
(2) Nominal inflection
(3) Subject obviation (switch-reference)
(4) The causative construction
(5) The transitivity alternation

For the most part, languages will differ in the features belonging to this special category—hence my use of the label "special." These features are special because they belong to the parametric and language-specific inventory of elements and constructions. They are not directly attributable to the universal properties of the human linguistic capacity, only indirectly so. It is not surprising, therefore, that they must be specially learned. And in the case of the lower degrees of immersion, they must be given special attention, or so I contend.

Miskitu is not alone, of course, in having verbal inflections, but the particulars of the Miskitu system must be learned, and the system is sufficiently rich to require special attention. The same is true of the nominal system, whose inflectional complexity is expressed in the possessive construction. This latter is built upon the construct state, illustrated in earlier paragraphs. The Miskitu construct is, in its details at least, quite unique to that language and clearly deserving of special attention.

Subject obviation (switch-reference) is pervasive in Miskitu usage, but it is easy to miss. Many second-language learners of Miskitu have failed to acquire it, since it must be consciously taught at the lower degrees of immersion. It is exemplified in the following pair of sentences:

Yang	âras	ba	atk-i	dakak-amna.
(I	horse	the	buy-PROX	feed-I.will)

'I will buy the horse and (I will) feed it'.

Yang	âras	ba	atk-rika	dakak-ma.
(I	horse	the	buy-OBV	feed-you.will)

'I will buy the horse and you will feed it'.

In the first sentence, the proximate suffix -i (glossed PROX) indicates that the subject of the verb to which it is attached is the same as the subject of the second verb (for this reason, the suffix can also be glossed SS, for "same subject")—*yang* 'I', the first person singular, is the subject of both verbs. In the second sentence, by contrast, the obviative suffix -rika

(glossed OBV, or DS for "different subject") indicates that the subject of the first verb is different from that of the second verb. In that sentence, *yang* 'I' is the subject of the first verb, while *man* 'you' is the subject of the second verb (the independent second person pronoun *man* is actually omitted, being embodied in the verbal inflection, -ma [second person future]).

The Miskitu causative is based on the obviative variant of the switch-reference system. It is shared by the other Misumalpan languages but is otherwise virtually unique among the languages of the world. The causative verb itself is drawn from the set of so-called light verbs, verbs of abstract semantic content, including *yâb-* 'give' and *mun-* 'do'. The second of these is exemplified in the following:

Yang	âras	ba	mun-rika	plap-bia.
I	horse	the	do-OBV	run-it.will

'I will make the horse run'.

Superficially, the causative has the same form as the obviative member of the pair of simple clause-sequencing examples cited above. But there is an important syntactic difference between the two constructions. The clause-sequencing construction is just that, a sequence of clauses each representing a separate proposition arranged in some sort of logical sequence, knitted together by means of the subject obviation construction. The causative, however, is a syntactically integrated complex clause representing a single proposition. This difference is reflected in the grammar of the two constructions and, for a second-language learner, it takes some time to understand what is going on in this aspect of Miskitu grammar. Again, this is something that can be missed entirely if not given special attention.

In many languages of the world, perhaps most, there exist verbal pairs, one member of which is intransitive, the other transitive. The morphological details differ from language to language, as expected. In English, the alternation is morphologically unmarked, hence *break* intransitive and phonologically identical *break* transitive. The Miskitu equivalent of this verb also alternates, but the alternation is morphologically marked, thus *kri-w-* 'break (intransitive)' beside *kri-k-* 'break (transitive)'. Apart from simply learning this alternation and its associated morphology, there is the problem of learning how it is constrained, that is, of learning which verbs participate in the alternation and which do not. This is a principled matter, governed by principles of a universal character. But it is not a simple matter to teach this to second-language learners in an immersion setting, as opposed to a setting in which grammatical principles are taught explicitly. The reason is that the evidence for the constraints on this transitivity alternation is negative and hence unlearnable. In most cases, it will become obvious eventually that the verbs which participate in the alternation—that is, those seen to do so in a sufficiently rich linguistic context—belong to a class which can be characterized semantically as involving a change in state (e.g., from whole to broken, in the case of Miskitu *kri-w-/kri-k-*). This is "learned" on the basis of positive evidence, and it can be reinforced by another bit of positive evidence, that is, the fact that an intransitive verb like *krat-w-* 'snore', which is not a change-of-state verb, usually takes, as its "transitive partner," the productive syntactic causative form *mun-ka krat-w-aia* 'to make snore'. We can predict, then, that there is no Miskitu verb *krat-k-* 'snore (transitive)'. This is correct. And we also predict the lack of any transitivity alternation of the form **plap-w-/plap-k-* 'run'. These observations can be made by a second-language learner in an immersion environment, but the linguistic context must be quite rich in examples, a circumstance which can only be ensured if the teacher consciously contrives to make it so. It should perhaps be mentioned that the facts pertaining to the Miskitu transitivity alternation, in particular the constraints on it, are only partially "learned." Here, and elsewhere as well, it is reasonable to assume that at some point in a learner's exposure to a sufficiently forthcoming linguistic sample, the principles involved are grasped in part through a process that could be called learning and in part through something that the learner (even the second-language learner) already knows by virtue of being an organism endowed with the human capacity for language. Be this as it may, the linguistic context must be appropriately rich to permit mastery of the system.

At the level of second-language learning, which is my primary concern here, languages are notoriously unequal in the matter of difficulty. While Miskitu is relatively "learner friendly," many other languages erect impressive, though ultimately surmountable, barriers for the second-language learner. Navajo is such a language, as are other members of the Athabaskan family to which it belongs. I will use Navajo as another example of my general point about lower-degree-immersion learning environments. A small selection from the large set of special features of Navajo is set out below:

(1) The verb word
(2) Obviation and the inverse
(3) The animacy hierarchy
(4) The internally headed relative clause
(5) Classificatory verb stems

For the second-language learner of Navajo, mastery of the verb word is a long and arduous process, and it must be a constant focus of attention in the immersion settings of concern here. The Navajo verb word is not like that of French, say, or even that of Russian. While these also take time to learn and are to some extent challenging, the process consists essentially in learning regular inflections, an inventory of irregular forms, and, in the case of Russian, the aspectual pairs and the rather daunting system of accent placement. By contrast, the Navajo verb word is a "compressed phrase," containing within it not only the verb stem and a rich system of inflectional morphology, but also adverbial, aspectual, and relational elements which, in languages like English, are expressed by means of separate words and phrases (including adverbs, aspectual verbs, particles, and prepositional phrases). I use the informal locution "compressed phrase" here to reflect the fact that the components of a Navajo verb word are not simply arranged agglutinatively like beads on a string, but rather accommodated within a word-sized package in great measure through the effects of an impressive array of morphological and phonological processes which often considerably obscure the morpheme boundaries between them. It is this latter circumstance, as much as any other, that makes the Navajo verb a formidable and quite wonderful challenge. As an example of this, we cite the inflected verb word *ch'éénísh'nil* 'I released them (as horses), I got them back out (of some enclosure)'. The elements contained in this word are listed below:

(1) *ch'í-* [adverbial] 'out, outward (horizontally)'
(2) *ná-* [adverbial] 'back (to previous state or position)'
(3) *n-* [mode] 'ni-conjugation marker'
(4) PERF [aspect] 'perfective'
(5) *sh-* [person] 'first person singular'
(6) *d-* [voice] 'passive, middle, reflexive'
(7) *-nil* [perfective stem] 'move/be (of plural entities)'

For present purposes, one can say that these components are grouped as follows within the verb word:

    [ch'í-ná-][n-PERF-sh-][d-nil]

They do not appear as such, obviously. Instead, certain morphophonological principles apply, resulting in the actual pronunciation. Let us consider first the pair [d-nil], consisting of the stem *-nil* and the reflexive *d-*. The stem itself is in the perfective form—if the verb were in the imperfective, the stem would take the form *-nííł*. The reflexive voice marker *d-* appears here not because the construction is reflexive in the usual sense; rather, it is an "event or state reflexive," reflecting a *return* to the state of affairs described by the verbal theme—in this case, the condition of being *out* or *uncontained, free*. In this use, the d-voice marker is functioning in concert with the "reversionary" adverbial prefix *ná-* 'back (to previous state or position)'. This cooperative arrangement is common but not altogether regular, and it must be learned for each verb. Phonologically, the *d-* prefix is not realized as such before the initial consonant of a stem (only if the stem begins in a vowel does the *d-* appear as phonetic [d]). In this verb, the so-called "d-effect" takes place, so that the sequence /dn/ is realized phonetically as ['n], the glottalized apical nasal. Moving leftward in the verb word, the combination [n-PERF-sh-] requires a number of comments. This combination amounts to the first person singular of the perfective mode, in the form it takes before the voice element *d-* (if this were absent, the first person prefix *sh-* would be deleted). The morpheme representing the perfective aspect is represented by PERF because it is not a uniformly definable affix. Here, it is essentially non-overt, giving us the sequence /n-sh/, to which i-epenthesis applies, inserting the vowel [i] between the two consonants, resulting here in the syllable [nísh], with high tone acquired automatically through tone-spreading from the vowel of the prefix immediately to the left. The full story of the Navaho verb word would, in addition, include an account of the selectional relationship between the mood marker *n-* and the adverbial prefix *ch'i-* 'out (horizontally)'. Finally, the leftmost pair, *ch'í-ná-*, exemplifies a somewhat idiosyncratic process whereby the combination fuses to *ch'éé-* in certain environments, including that in which the combination immediately precedes certain (conjunct) prefixes of the form CV, as here (compare the imperfective where this fusion fails to take place: *ch'ínásh'nííł*).

This example is a rather ordinary one for Navajo; many verbs are much more complex, and some are actually simpler. I give this example to demonstrate the impressive task, and adventure, that presents itself to the student who embarks on the journey of acquiring the language. In the normal course of an immersion program, of course, the analytical details informally set out in the preceding paragraph would not be explicitly "taught" to the learner. In the immersion setting, the linguistic context will have to be extraordinarily rich. And at the fourth and fifth degrees of immersion, the teacher will have to create, consciously, a linguistic context capable of revealing the internal structure of the Navajo verb word in all of its rich diversity, all its variability from verb to verb, and, at the same time, all of the shared features which will function as "cornerstones" and "safe havens" in the difficult work of mastering the system.

Turning to the area of sentential syntax, we illustrate another special feature of Navajo. In transitive sentences in which both the subject and the object are third person, the object appears in the *obviative* form if the subject precedes it (indicating that the subject occupies a higher position in the syntactic structure). This arrangement is reflected in the object agreement morphology internal to the Navajo verb word—the obviative object agreement is represented by the prefix *yi-*, as in the following example:

Łį́į́'	dzaanééz	yi-ẓ-tał.
horse	mule	yi-PERF-kick.

'The horse kicked the mule'.

The obviative construction is the "unmarked" or normal form of a transitive sentence in which the subject and the object are both third person. It places the second of the 2 third person arguments in a semantically subordinate position, while the subject assumes the more prominent "topic" position.

If the object is elevated to the topic role, it is represented by the normal third person object prefix *bi-* and, in addition, it is advanced to a higher structural position, at the front of the sentence. This object-advancement construction is sometimes called the "inverse":

Dzaanééz	łį́į́'	bi-ẓ-tał.
mule	horse	bi-PERF-kick

'The horse kicked the mule'.

The meaning remains the same, essentially, except that *dzaanééz*, the mule, is now the primary topic, as it would be, for example, in the corresponding passive in English, *the mule was kicked by the horse*.

In this example, the inverse is freely possible. In other cases, however, this is not so. In (1) below, the inverse is impossible, while in (2) it is obligatory:

(1) | Łį́į́' | tsé | yi-ẓ- tał. |
|---|---|---|
| horse | stone | yi-PERF-kick. |

'The horse kicked the stone'.

(2) | Tsís'ná | ashkii | bi-shish. |
|---|---|---|
| bee | boy | bi-PERF.sting |

'The bee stung the boy'.

This circumstance reflects an animacy hierarchy in the language, placing humans at the highest rank, animals at a lower rank, and inanimates at a lower rank yet. In relation to the use or nonuse of the inverse, the rule is basically:

> Arrange the sentence so that the higher-ranking argument assumes the structurally and semantically most prominent position (i.e., topic position).

If two arguments are of the same rank, the inverse can be used freely to alter the topic-comment relations in the clause. In (1), the horse outranks the stone, so the inverse is not possible, as it would violate the principle. In (2), the boy (corresponding to the grammatical object) is higher in rank than the bee (the grammatical subject). Consequently, the inverse must apply there.

In the realm of complex sentences, the Navajo internally headed relative clause deserves special attention. In many languages of the world, the relative clause is externally headed. That is to say, the head is outside the relative clause itself, either to the left (as in English) or to the right (as in Japanese). By contrast, many languages employ a relative clause construction in which the semantic head is internal to the clause, the latter being nominalized in some manner. Miskitu and Navajo share this type. Consider, for example, the way in which these two languages render the equivalent of the English complex sentence *I will brand the horse I bought yesterday*, where [I bought (it) yesterday] is the relative clause and [the horse] is the head, external to the clause and to its left in English. In the following examples, glossing of the verb forms is in the manner of a translation, not a formal item-by-item glossing:

Navajo:
'Adą́ą́dą́ą́	łį́į́'	nahátnii'-ę́ę	bí'dideeshłił.
yesterday	horse	I.bought.it-REL	I.will.brand.it

Miskitu:
Nauhwala	áras kum atkri	ba	brân-angkamna.
Yesterday	horse a I.bought.it	REL	brand-I.will burn.it

The relative clause is formed on the sentences

'Adą́ą́dą́ą́' łį́į́' naháłnii'.
'I bought the/a horse yesterday'.

Nauhwala âras kum atkri.
'I bought a horse yesterday'.

In the relative clause construction, these are simply nominalized by means of the appropriate determiners (-*ę́ę́* 'the aforementioned' in Navajo, *ba* 'the' in Miskitu), and the semantic head is represented by the relevant argument (*łį́į́'* 'the/a horse' and *âras kum* 'a horse') located *in situ* in its basic object position internal to the dependent nominalized clause.

While this construction is rather easy to get used to, it can be missed or badly misunderstood by a learner whose first language lacks it. In the case of Navajo and Miskitu, languages relatively well documented, explicit recognition of the fact that they possess the internally headed relative clause is remarkably recent in the history of scholarship pertaining to them. In general, second-language learners of Navajo and Miskitu have to have this construction brought to their attention. At the fourth and fifth degrees of immersion, it deserves special attention, without question.

Navajo is renowned for its classificatory verb stems, the final item on my brief list of special features. The phenomenon itself is not unusual, but the extent to which it is developed in Navajo is impressive. So-called handling verbs (verbs of giving, putting, and the like) have received the most attention, though related intransitive verbs of being at rest have also figured in studies of this aspect of Navajo grammar. Essentially what is involved is this: A standard classificatory verb construction consists of a verb theme in which the stem position is occupied by an item drawn from a set of more than a dozen verb stems, each of which has the property that it selects arguments having certain semantic properties and not others (allowing latitude for joking and metaphor). The verb with which we began this discussion of Navajo exemplifies the classificatory verb construction. In its most basic form, omitting inflectional material (and the reversionary adverbial prefix *ná-* as well, for simplicity), the theme of the verb is set out below, with the stem cited in the perfective form:

ch'í-n-nil 'put/let them out horizontally'

The stem -*nil* is the one which is appropriate where the grammatical object refers to plural countable entities. Themes expressing the idea of carrying an entity or entities out horizontally share this structure. Some of them are presented below (with the stem cited in the perfective form). The examples illustrate clearly what is meant by classificatory verb stem.

ch'í-n-łtį́	'carry animate entity out horizontally'
ch'í-n-tą́	'carry slender rigid entity out horizontally'
ch'í-n-lá	'carry slender flexible entity out horizontally'

ch'í-ni-'ą́	'carry solid compact entity out horizontally'
ch'í-n-tjool	'carry non-compact matter out horizontally'
ch'í-n-jaa'	'carry many objects out horizontally'
ch'í-n-yí	'carry a burden, pack out horizontally'
ch'í-n-łtsooz	'carry flat, flexible entity out horizontally'
ch'í-n-ką	'carry entity in an open container out horizontally'

If the use of a particular stem can be said to involve the grammatical relation commonly termed "selection," then here we can say that each stem selects a grammatical object represented by an argument (noun phrase or pronominal element) referring to an entity possessing certain properties, for example, that of being slender and rigid (such as a rifle, stick, etc.), that of being flat and flexible (such as a sheet of paper or blanket), and so on. It is the stem that changes from theme to theme; otherwise these are essentially the "same verb." This is typical for classificatory verb systems. The complexity of the system is only partially revealed here. In addition to verbs of handling, exemplified here, there are also verbs of falling and dropping, verbs of throwing, verbs of eating, and verbs of impact and concussion which enter into selectional relations of this sort. The identity of the selected argument must take into consideration the syntactic structure defined by the verbs as well. The selected argument is regularly an "internal argument" and therefore the grammatical object in the transitive configuration; it may be a subject only in the case of certain intransitive verbs, including those which are related to transitive classificatory verbs.

There is a special wrinkle which should be mentioned here, as it bears directly on the issue of the special features which must be mastered in acquiring Navajo. As noted above, certain verb stems select arguments according to number. The verbs of going or walking illustrate this clearly:

Shí yishááł.	'I am walking along'.
Nihí yiit'ash.	'We (dual) are walking along'.
Nihí yiikah.	'We (plural) are walking along'.
'Ashkii yigááł.	'The boy is walking along'.
'Ashiiké yi'ash.	'The two boys (dual) are walking along'.
'Ashiiké yikah.	'The boys (plural) are walking along'.

The verb stems here are respectively -*ááł* (singular), -*'ash* (dual), and -*kah* (plural). They are selected according to the number of the subject, hence -*ááł* occurs with the first person singular subject (represented by the first person singular pronoun *shí*, and by first person singular agreement *sh-*) and with the singular nominal subject *ashkii* 'boy'. Similarly, the dual and plural stems, -*'ash* and -*kah*, occur with nonsingular subjects, represented by the first nonsingular pronoun *nihí* and agreement *ii(d)-* and by the nonsingular nominal *'ashiiké* 'boys'. All of this is representative of standard agreement relations in Navajo—singular subject with singular stem, nonsingular subject with dual or plural stem. No surprises.

But there are always surprises. We can predict on the basis of the above that the following verb forms are ill formed as they stand, hence the asterisk (*), following the general practice in signaling ungrammaticality:

*yish'ash
*yiidáál

These represent a failure in number concordance. The first form has singular (first person) subject agreement, but the stem is dual. And the second form corresponds to the opposite situation, with first person nonsingular agreement in combination with the singular stem. Spoken in this simple form, these are indeed ungrammatical.

The two verb forms just given do in fact occur in well-formed sentences in Navajo. The first occurs in the comitative construction, and the second occurs in the partitive, as exemplified below:

'Ashkii bił yish'ash.
'I am walking along with the boy'.

Nihí ta' yiidáál.
'One of us is walking along'.

These sentences show us that the principle governing stem choice in the comitative and the partitive is not agreement with the grammatical subject but rather selection determined by the number of participants in the activity depicted by the construction. In the comitative example, there are two actors participating in the activity of walking, hence the dual stem is appropriate; in the partitive, only one walker is involved, hence the singular stem is appropriate there.

TRAINING FOR THE CONSCIOUS TEACHING OF LINGUISTIC STRUCTURE IN FOURTH- AND FIFTH-DEGREE IMMERSION SETTINGS

The Miskitu and Navajo examples cited here represent a small part of what is involved in learning the grammatical structures of those languages. The examples have been discussed only briefly but in enough detail to make clear that the grammatical features of individual languages are complex and must be consciously taught in an immersion environment at the fourth and fifth degrees. To plan adequately for building an immersion environment that will reveal the structural features of a language in sufficient abundance and appropriate sequencing, training in linguistics as well as course design and curriculum development is needed.

Fortunately, there are programs in which it is possible to obtain the necessary training, often in a context which takes into consideration the specific need of indigenous-language communities. In North America, for example, the American Indian Languages Development Institute (AILDI) offers summer courses which have precisely this purpose. For the Americas generally, a number of resources are listed in the Native Languages Revitalization Resource Directory compiled by the Institute for the Preservation of the Original Languages of the Americas (IPOLA). While this publication deals primarily with the Americas, it also includes an international section. For training and support, the nearest university or community college (or a more distant institution, if there is no local one) may well have individuals who are capable and eager to be of assistance. This is true particularly of universities and colleges that have programs committed to the study of indigenous languages and cultures. Such institutions often prove to be the best sources for productive relationships in support of language revitalization programs. It often takes time to establish such a relationship, to find the right individuals, and so forth, but it is an avenue that is well worth pursuing.

Fundamentally, training for teachers at the fourth and fifth degrees of immersion must include a program in linguistics, leading to a good understanding of the basic elements of phonology, morphology, syntax, and semantics. In many cases, the teacher will have to do what amounts to field work on the language concerned in order to plan organized and fully comprehensible lessons around its grammar. This is true not only for teachers who have acquired the language as adults but also for native-speaking teachers, who must bring these aspects of grammar to consciousness—using themselves and other speakers as consultants. Training in linguistics is necessary for this, whether this is acquired in coursework or through self-directed study.

Finally, it must be said that the immersion setting is not always adequate, especially where the time available for study is limited—for instance, as little as three or four hours per week. Direct, explicit grammatical instruction is necessary in this circumstance. It is only necessary to reflect on the fact that the simplest Navajo verb has 180 forms (compared to just 3 highly regular forms in English) to appreciate this point. Only a few of the forms themselves will occur in a class of limited time. One must come to know the general principles for forming Navajo verb words, many of which have several thousand forms. There exists now a manual of nearly 500 pages of explicit rules and exercises for communicating this aspect of Navajo grammar (Faltz 1998), giving an idea of the immensity of the task. Navajo and its Athabaskan relatives are special in this domain, to be sure, but most languages have one or more areas of complexity which may require explicit grammatical instruction.

Reference

Faltz, Leonard M. 1998. *The Navajo verb: A grammar for students and scholars*. Albuquerque: University of New Mexico Press.

PART VI

LITERACY

19

New Writing Systems

LEANNE HINTON

Department of Linguistics
University of California at Berkeley
Berkeley, California

Nancy Hornberger writes,

> In the Americas as elsewhere, it has long been perceived that literacy in the dominant language of the society is linked to power in the society; while anyone or anything indigenous has traditionally been powerless. . . . What the papers in [Hornberger's 1997] volume collectively show, however, is that, for the indigenous communities, indigenous literacies are increasingly seen as providing opportunity and means for empowerment—of indigenous people, their languages and their cultures. Whatever the differences in specific rationales and means of implementation among the cases described . . . , they are united in suggesting that indigenous literacies provide a door of opportunity for those who have been marginalized. (Hornberger 1997a, 360)

This chapter will discuss both the benefits and the pitfalls of having a writing system (Section 1); then, I will discuss the history of writing systems in the Americas (Section 2). Assuming a community wants a writing system, the procedures for developing one and issues surrounding its design will be described (Section 3). In the last two sections, I briefly discuss the teaching of literacy and the use of writing as a tool for native empowerment.

PROS AND CONS OF WRITING SYSTEMS FOR NATIVE AMERICAN LANGUAGES

More and more Native American communities are opting to adopt writing systems for their languages, and finding good uses for them and pride in their existence. Some writers go so far as to say, "Lack of literacy is the most important factor in the deterioration and abandonment of indigenous language" (Salinas Pedraza 1997, 173).

But not all would agree that this is the case. Even though any language can be written, for some communities, developing a writing system might not be the best idea at a given time. The Cochiti pueblo in New Mexico is among those communities who have consciously decided not to write their languages at all (Chapter 7).

Pros

There are certainly many reasons why a community might desire to develop a writing system for their language. Some of these follow.

Pride

There is a strong feeling in the modern world that languages with writing systems are in some way superior to languages without them, and that people who do not have written languages are somehow cognitively impoverished compared to those growing up in a society with writing. Linguists are quick to point out that languages without writing systems are every bit as complicated and expressive as languages with them, so it is incorrect to think that there is anything intrinsic to the language that is inferior if it is unwritten. Some authors have opined that written language leads to more complicated sentences, polished language, and objective thinking than can be present in spoken languages, but this is not true either. It is true that if you compare a written essay to informal spoken English, you will definitely see that

239

the written language is quite different. However, some of the features attributed to written English might be due to the contrast between formal and informal language, rather than between speaking and writing. Wallace Chafe, in a 1981 article, shows that Seneca (an unwritten language) has many of the same features in formal oratory that are often attributed to written speech. He suggests that written language and ritual language have six traits in common which set them apart from colloquial spoken language:

> First, they tend to be more conservative, where colloquial language is more innovative. Second, they tend to be more polished, where colloquial language is rougher. Third, they tend to be more integrated, where colloquial language is more fragmented. Fourth, they tend to be more stylized and constrained, where colloquial language is freer. Fifth, they tend to be more detached, where colloquial language is more involved. Sixth and finally, they tend to be more authoritative in their assertions, where colloquial language is more hesitant. (Chafe 1981, 132)

Thus a healthy unwritten language has genres of speech that have many characteristics usually attributed to written language. Nevertheless, native peoples often internalize the attitude that their unwritten language is inferior to a written language and come to believe that the development of a writing system for their language can increase the status of the language in their own eyes as well as the rest of the world. In this sense, there is truly empowerment through writing, even if it is only the empowerment that comes through a positive shift in language attitudes.

Documentation

For an endangered language especially, documentation is of key importance. At the present time, documentation may be done through audio and visual recording, and these means should definitely be used. But written documentation remains critically important and serves some functions better than audiovisual means (in fact, the most valuable documentation of all is audiovisual documentation with a written transcript). Endangered languages, as they lose speakers, lose also much of the knowledge that the traditional culture has accumulated. Stories, songs, histories, prayers, ceremonies, and traditional crafts and practices are all in danger of dying with the languages. And the unique and wonderful words, sounds, semantics, grammatical structure, and discourse patterns of the language die too. All of these can be at least partially preserved through writing.

For language revitalization, written documentation may be the primary surviving resource from which teachers and language learners may draw. Thus any and all possible recording of the last speakers through writing or other means is essential. Language pedagogy depends in part on the written word: even if oral approaches are stressed and native literacy is not being taught, teachers might depend on a writing

system in their language to be able to create lesson plans and curriculum.

Practical Uses

Within an active society with a thriving language, writing may develop many practical uses, not only for the development of literature, newspapers, language materials, and so on, but also for the uses of day-to-day life—letters, shopping lists, diaries, advertisements, accounting, recipes, and so on. When Cherokee developed its syllabary in the 18th century, it was such a hit in that monolingual society that within a few years mass literacy prevailed and was used for everything listed above and more. Even in bilingual communities where English is the dominant language of writing, practical uses develop for a native writing system.

Expansion of Language (Written Literature and Other Avenues of Expression)

The development of a writing system for a language generally results in new genres for the language, such as children's literature, newspaper journalism, poetry, hymnals, school essays, and so on. For an endangered language, these new genres may produce excitement and interest that can help promote language use. As an example of the promotion of a language through new written genres, the Peruvian Academy of the Quechua Language *(Academia Peruana de la Lengua Quechua)* has instituted the National Cusco Prize for a Quechua Novel, Poem, Story, or Drama, and has given out awards to Quechua writers from all the countries on the west coast of South America (Hornberger 1997b). One author alone, Faustino Espinoza, has written over 40 books in Quechua.

Cons

Written English Serves Most Practical Purposes

In bilingual societies, such as any Native American group in the United States today (who, even if their language survives, will also be fluent English speakers), many practical functions are already fulfilled by English literacy, so that when a community develops a writing system it tends to be used much less often than in the Cherokee case described above, and the spread of native literacy will be much less dramatic. While languages with large populations such as Quechua can develop large literatures, which itself creates a reason for literacy, the smaller language groups will not have the ability to produce large amounts of reading materials. In many indigenous communities that develop writing systems, mass literacy in the native language is never achieved, and if it is taught in school, the students find little reason to use it after graduation.

Loss of Control over When and Where and to Whom Information is Communicated

Often elders and sometimes younger members of the community become concerned over one important consequence of writing: the person whose utterances are written down can easily lose control over who has access to his or her utterances. Much ceremonial and religious information, for example, is secret and if written down could get into the hands of people who have no right of access. On the other end of the scale of respectability, gossip is meant to be told, heard, and then silenced. Even in speaking, there is danger to the original speaker that his or her words can be passed on to people in ways originally unintended, but the written word has an even longer lifespan and can be passed on infinitely through space and time in a way that could be damaging. In our own society, we are legally liable for things we have written, whereas the law is much less able to hold us responsible for things we have said (unless they were tape recorded), because there can be no real proof that we said them. A written contract, for example, is much more binding than an oral contract. There are many things in any society that should not be written, and it is good to consider this fact as literacy develops. It is partly due to this issue of control and secrecy that some communities decide not to adopt a writing system for their language at all.

Written Documentation Freezes and Decontextualizes Language and Language Arts

Written documentation is a hollow shell of a real speech event, since it does not record visual and other concomitants of a performance, nor its context, nor the deep aspects of the *meaning* of the event within a society still actively using it. While this does not mean we should not document, it does point out the limits of documentation. We do not "save" a language or culture by recording it; we preserve it, like a pickle (Hinton 1994). Many activists for native languages say that in the case of a severely endangered language, the main energy of the community should be put into producing new speakers rather than in documentation. I myself believe the two need equal billing: documentation of the last speakers is critical, but this can be done through video and audio recording, which are in some ways more complete than written documentation and are much quicker as well.

Writing May Slow and Impoverish Language Learning

Many people believe that a writing system must be developed before language teaching can occur, and teaching would be through the written word. But one does not learn to speak a language by reading and writing; one learns by hearing and speaking. It is sadly typical for language classes in communities to consist of the teaching of written vocabulary, with the primary spoken language of instruction being En-

glish. In Chapter 14, I discuss the pitfalls of this approach. If people are not already literate in their language, learning how to use the writing system takes further time away from oral language learning; and if there is not yet a writing system for the language, still more time and energy is taken up with its development. Language learners, especially beginners, will usually display very poor pronunciation when they depend on the written word instead of aural input. In a situation where all the speakers of a language are old, it is critically important to devise ways of learning their language and other forms of knowledge, rather than delaying this in order to develop and teach a writing system to the community. The main point here is that whether or not a community wants to have and use a writing system, the community should never decide that documentation and language teaching should wait until after the development and teaching of literacy.

As I write this, a call for papers for a forthcoming conference arrived today with further discussion of the pros and cons of writing systems for endangered languages, written by Nicholas Ostler of the Foundation for Endangered Languages, Bath, England.

> Literacy, the ability to read and write a written form of the language, has often been viewed as a necessary first step in maintaining and promoting use of the language. The introduction of literacy is predicated upon the development of an acceptable written form of a language, a step considered by many essential for:
>
> —the creation of grammars, dictionaries, and teaching materials;
> —the preservation of traditional oral literature in communities where the younger generations lack the patience to learn the texts orally.
>
> However, efforts to develop a written language and instill literacy may encounter cultural obstacles and have unforeseen consequences. For example:
>
> —the development of literacy may, over time, fundamentally alter or interrupt the oral transmission of a community's knowledge and beliefs;
> —the members of the community may resist efforts to introduce literacy due to cultural beliefs about, for example, the spiritual or mystical nature of oral communication;
> —the introduction of literacy may create divisions within the community between the literate and the illiterate that ultimately may have social or economic implications.
>
> Even within communities that are receptive to the introduction of literacy, the development of an acceptable written language may pose challenges:
>
> — there may be difficulties selecting one of several dialects upon which to base the written language;
> there may be problems adapting existing alphabets, syllabaries, or other writing systems to the sound system of the language;
> —the availability of typewriter or computer fonts may force unacceptable compromises in the orthography for the language;
> —the language may lack acceptable vocabulary or syntactic structures to replace in the written language suprasegmental, kinetic, and paralinguistic components of oral, face-to-face communication. (Nicholas Ostler, 15 January 2000, e-mail announcement of Fourth International Conference hosted by the Foundation for Endangered Languages)

THE HISTORY OF WRITING IN "PRELITERATE" SOCIETIES

Ideographic Writing

If writing is defined in a narrow sense as the visual recording of actual language, then no, most small indigenous groups did not have a tradition of writing in the past. In the New World, so far as we know, only the Mayan hieroglyphic system is a true writing system.[1]

Nevertheless, "nonliterate" or so-called preliterate societies have many ways of doing the visual recording of information. Even if a visual recording system does not represent language, it may represent *ideas* quite precisely. The examples on the following pages show three ways that people have kept accounts of history. The first is a Sioux "winter count" done on a buffalo hide, keeping track of key events for 70 years by marking pictures symbolizing the events on the hide (Figure 19.1). The second is a Navajo petroglyph panel describing the campaign of Kit Carson against the Navajos (Figure 19.2). The various symbols represent the various stages of the campaign, the starvation of Navajos making a

FIGURE 19.2 The Navajo record of Kit Carson's 1863–64 campaign. Reprinted with permission from Martineau 1973, p. 96.

stand and their eventual surrender, the death of many, and finally their incarceration at Fort Sumner. (See Martineau 1973 for a complete explanation.) The third is one page from the Nutall Codex, made by the Mixtecs of Mexico (Figure 19.3). This codex is the genealogy and biography of the ancient hero Eight Deer (named for his birth date); this particular page, which is to be read from the upper right corner down, up through the center and down again on the left, is the story of Eight Deer's father's marriages and the birth of Eight Deer and his siblings, and finally of Eight Deer's marriage. (See Nuttall 1975 for a complete explanation.)

Through the use of complex ideographic systems like these, most of the functions of writing can be fulfilled by so-called preliterate societies. Groups without "writing" can still record history, stories, and songs; keep accounts; send bills and letters; make maps; have signatures; and do virtually everything else that we use writing systems for. Unfortunately, knowledge of these fascinating and often artistically and intellectually stunning systems of visual recording are part of the knowledge that disappears with endangered languages.

The Cherokee and Cree Syllabaries

Several groups in North America (as well as elsewhere) developed syllabic writing systems in the early 19th century.

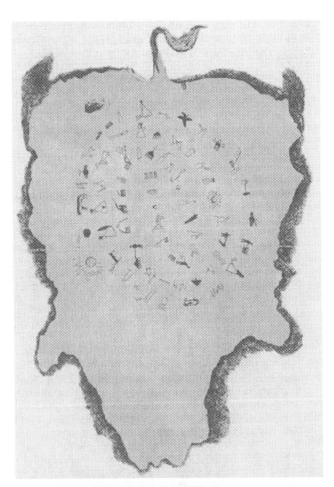

FIGURE 19.1 Lone Dog's winter count. Reprinted with permission from Mallery 1972, p. 267.

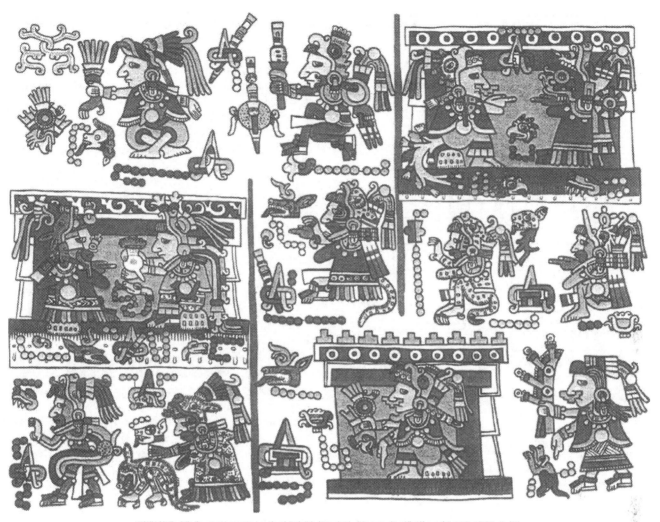

FIGURE 19.3 Mayan hieroglyphics. Reprinted with permission from Nuttall 1975, p. 26.

The two most famous and widespread of these writing systems are the Cherokee and Cree syllabaries (see Figures 19.4 and 19.5), both developed by and for communities who did not know how to speak or read and write English. Thus these syllabaries became the first writing system to be used by the communities. The development of the Cherokee syllabary was completed in 1821 by the great Cherokee intellectual Sequoyah. The Cree system is reputed to have been developed by the Protestant missionary Reverend James Evan, although legend has it that he adapted an indigenous system already in existence (if so, it was probably an ideographic system at the time rather than a syllabary). Both syllabaries are still in use today; the Cree syllabary has spread to several other Algonquian languages in Canada, and also to Inuit (an Eskimo language). The Cree syllabary is especially widespread in Canada, with a large and ever-growing literature. Cherokee literature using the syllabary spreads back over 180 years, to the publication in 1828 of the inaugural issue of the Cherokee newspaper *Tsa la gi Tsu lehisanunhi* or *Cherokee Phoenix,* printed in parallel columns in Cherokee and English. It was the first Indian newspaper published in the United States (Mankiller and Wallis, 1993). Both syllabaries have computer fonts available at various sites (e.g., the Yamada Language Center at the University of Oregon, at <http://babel.uoregon.edu/yamada/fonts>.

Bilingualism and Alphabets

Now that the vast majority of Native Americans know how to speak, read, and write English, there is a very strong impetus toward the use of the Roman alphabet for Indian languages, because of the simple but excellent reason that everyone knows that alphabet. It is estimated that people spend 10,000 hours reading and writing English before they graduate from high school; and only then do we feel that a child could really be called good at it. Most people do not have another 10,000 hours to spend on some totally new system; it is much more efficient to start from what we have already mastered and move out from there. The knowledge of two completely different writing systems is certainly

	Vowels				Finals
	E	**I**	**O**	**A**	**WEST**
	▽	△	▷	◁	
W	▽•	△•	▷•	◁•	ᗪ
P	V	∧	>	<	ˈ
T	U	∩	⊃	⊂	ˊ
K	ᖅ	ᖊ	ᖈ	ᖷ	ˋ
CH	ᖕ	ᖌ	ᒎ	ᒍ	‐
M	ᒣ	ᒥ	ᒪ	ᒧ	ᖯ
N	ᓀ	ᓂ	ᓂ	ᓇ	ᑐ
L	ᕋ	ᕆ	ᕊ	ᕃ	ᖙ
S	ᔅ	ᔋ	ᔆ	ᔥ	ᓐ
SH	ᕻ	ᔑ	ᕬ	ᕽ	ᓷ
Y	ᕞ	ᕤ	ᕦ	ᕔ	+ᕁ
R	ᕰ	ᕐ	ᕑ	ᕒ	ᙆ
TH	ᕛ	ᕦ	ᕝ	ᕟ	ᒼ

$$U° \quad H'' \quad W• \quad Diacritic•$$

FIGURE 19.4   The Cree syllabary.
From <http://www.nisto.com/cree/syllabic/>.

possible; many Cherokees, Crees, and Inuktituts do it, and so do the Japanese and various other nationalities who have more than one writing system to deal with. But most people who do not yet have a writing system developed for their language opt to start from the writing system they have already mastered, rather than try to design a completely new one from scratch; and in the early days of a writing system, when its designers are trying to gain its acceptance in a community, a friendly, familiar-looking writing system gains more friends than one which even a native speaker could not make any sense of at first glance. It is hard enough as it is for native speakers to learn to read the language they have only spoken all their lives. Even some of the Cree and Cherokee literature nowadays is written in both the syllabaries and an alphabetic transcription.

Unifon

Because of their long history, there is a good deal of loyalty to the Cree and Cherokee syllabaries. However, when symbol systems that deviate strongly from the Roman alpha-bet are developed today, they tend to fare less well. The history of one non-Roman alphabet that was adapted to some Native American languages in the 20th century might serve as a case in point. This is the alphabetic code called Unifon, which was invented in 1959 by John Malone, an economist from Chicago. It was intended by its developer to facilitate the learning of English in first-language and second-language classes and to be used as a pronunciation key in English dictionaries. Its symbols include some capital Roman letters and other letters that are not the same as the Roman letters but are based on them. The system is uniquely related to English spelling in that, for example, all symbols that are based on the letter "A" are different pronunciations of sounds that are spelled with the letter "a" in English. Thus the sound of *a* in "*b*at," "*f*ate," and "*f*ather" would each be represented in Unifon by a letter that is based on *A* (Figures 19.6 and 19.7).

Tom Parsons, who then worked at the Center for Indian Community Development at Humboldt State University, adapted Unifon to the various indigenous languages of Northern California with some of his native students, and he and his employees taught this system to native speakers and children. Unifon systems were developed for Hupa, Yurok, Tolowa, and Karuk. Since Parsons did not know the languages himself and was not a linguist, the orthographies initially developed for the languages were insufficient for representing the sound systems; however, some native scholars worked to improve the systems, and in the end some of them were sufficient. This is especially true of the Tolowa orthography, which was much improved by the native scholar Loren Bommelyn.

From the beginning, the Unifon orthographies were disapproved of by linguists, but many native people devoted years to learning and improving them and many publications

D a	**R** e	**T** i	**Ꮸ** o	**Ꮔ** u	**i** v
Ꮡ ga **Ꭴ** ka	**Ꮅ** ge	**Ꭹ** gi	**A** go	**J** gu	**E** gv
Ꮄ ha	**Ꭾ** he	**Ꭿ** hi	**Ꮶ** ho	**Ꮎ** hu	**Ꮙ** hv
W la	**Ꮁ** le	**Ꮃ** li	**G** lo	**M** lu	**Ꮑ** lv
Ꮪ ma	**Ꭴ** me	**H** mi	**Ꮰ** mo	**Ꮉ** mu	
Ꮎ na **Ꮕ** hna **G** nah	**Ꮉ** ne	**Ꮒ** ni	**Z** no	**Ꮖ** nu	**Ꮕ** nv
Ꮷ qua	**Ꮖ** que	**Ꮻ** qui	**Ꮹ** quo	**Ꮗ** quu	**Ꮄ** quv
Ꮜ sa **Ꭴ** s	**Ꮞ** se	**Ꮇ** si	**Ꮝ** so	**Ꮡ** su	**Ꭱ** sv
Ꮣ da **Ꮤ** ta	**Ꮞ** de **Ꮤ** te	**Ꮨ** di **Ꮤ** ti	**Ꮄ** do	**Ꮪ** du	**Ꮫ** dv
� dla **Ꮮ** tla	**Ꮮ** tle	**Ꮝ** tli	**Ꮬ** tlo	**Ꮏ** tlu	**P** tlv
Ꮉ tsa	**Ꮴ** tse	**Ꮣ** tsi	**K** tso	**Ꮫ** tsu	**Ꮯ** tsv
Ꮹ wa	**Ꮾ** we	**Ꮝ** wi	**Ꮠ** wo	**Ꮽ** wu	**6** wv
Ꮿ ya	**Ꮰ** ye	**Ꮵ** yi	**Ꮐ** yo	**Ꮈ** yu	**B** yv

FIGURE 19.5   The Cherokee syllabary.
From <http://public.csusm.edu/public/raven/cherokee.dir/syll.html>.

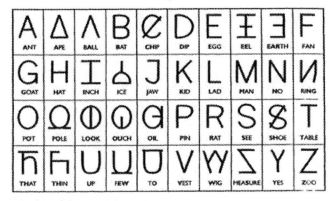

FIGURE 19.6   The Unifon alphabet of 24 consonants and 16 vowels. From Hinton 1994, p. 216 (originally from Culkin 1982).

were developed, so that the communities had a certain sense of loyalty to them. The greatest strain against Unifon, nevertheless, came from within the communities themselves. Once Tom Parsons left the university, there was no one there to teach this strange-looking system, and people of the next age group down, who had not learned UNIFON, were put off by the strange symbols. Linguists, meanwhile, were working with other community members on using standard Roman symbols; Loren Bommelyn himself ended up going to the University of Oregon for a degree in linguistics and decided at that time to abandon Unifon. At this time, all four languages are now being written primarily in a standard Roman alphabetic system.

The Phonetic Alphabet

English has a very strange spelling system: each letter can have several different pronunciations (for example, the *g* in "go," "gentle," "enough," and "though"), and each sound can be spelled in several different ways (such as the sound in "*k*ite," "*c*able," and "ba*ck*"). Unifon is only one of the attempts people have made to solve the inconsistencies of the English spelling system. In the late 19th century, French scholars developed what is now known as the International Phonetic Alphabet (IPA), primarily to assist people trying to learn English pronunciation. This alphabet has been ex-

This is one way to write English.

ᚻIS IZ UNUᚻƎ Ꮶᐱ TU RᐱT IᴎGLIႽ.

ðis iz stɪl ənʌðr wey to rayt ɪŋglɪš

FIGURE 19.7   A passage of English written in the Roman alphabet (English spelling rules), Unifon, and the phonetic alphabet. From Hinton 1994, p. 217.

panded now so that it can write any language in the world according to how it sounds. At the same time that the IPA was being developed in France, another system known now as the Americanist system was being developed here. The two systems have interacted with each other and become fairly similar, with only a few symbols differing. In one version or another, the phonetic alphabet has been used to transcribe the sound systems of most of the indigenous languages of the world. Thus whether or not the speakers of a language are literate, parts of the language itself have most likely been written down by someone.

DESIGN OF MODERN WRITING SYSTEMS BASED ON THE ROMAN ALPHABET

As we all know, Rome was once a great empire. The great empire before Rome was Greece, and the Romans adapted their alphabet from Greek letters, changing some, adding some, and ignoring some of the letters of the ancient Greek alphabet. When Rome brought Europe under its administration, one of the things that happened was that the various languages of Europe adopted the Roman alphabet to write their languages. For many centuries after the fall of the Roman empire, Latin was still the language of learning in Europe, and so the Roman alphabet continued to hold sway. English is one of the languages that adopted the Roman alphabet. With the English language now dominant due to its own empire building, the Roman alphabet continues to spread to other languages, including the indigenous languages of which we speak.

Phonetic Alphabets and "Practical" Alphabets

If a community desires to develop a writing system, one of the first decisions to be made is whether to develop a system that is based on the phonetic alphabet in which scholars have written their language or use a "practical" system, as it has come to be called, which uses primarily English letters rather than the special symbols the scholarly phonetic systems use. There are good arguments both ways. The main arguments for the practical systems are:

- The practical writing systems use letters that can be typed or printed using a standard keyboard or typewriter, so high-tech solutions do not have to be found to put the language into print.
- The practical writing systems look familiar to people, since they are based on the same alphabet as English (or whatever the dominant language is). Thus it is easy to learn and not off-putting to people seeing it for the first time.

However, there are also good reasons for adopting a system based on the phonetic alphabet.[2]

- If linguists have produced a sizable literature for an endangered language, the community may prefer to have a writing system that allows them to read that literature. Adopting a different writing system would make the literature less accessible.
- Since the phonetic alphabet is based on the principle of "one symbol, one sound," the rules of pronunciation will be clear. As we shall see below, a practical system generally also uses the one symbol, one sound principle, but this makes it an orthography that *looks* like English but does not use the principles of English spelling, which some people argue is potentially confusing.
- Since many sounds that might be part of one's language are not present in English, a way must be developed to represent them. As we shall see below, English letters can either be modified or their pronunciation redefined to represent a sound, but the phonetic alphabet already has a symbol to represent that very sound, so why not use it? Redefining the pronunciation of an English symbol might be confusing, and the symbol could easily be mispronounced by a learner.
- While it is true that a standard keyboard does not contain the non-Roman phonetic symbols, phonetic fonts are increasingly easy to obtain through purchase or free downloading from the Web. Looking forward in time a decade or two, it is probable that all computers will use "Unicode," which will include all phonetic symbols as well as the orthographic symbols of most languages of the world.

Several communities have in recent years decided to retain a writing system based on a scholarly phonetic alphabet. In California, the Kashaya Pomos use the phonetic system that the linguist Robert Oswalt used for his publications on the language. And for another California language, Salinan, Joe Freeman is working on the development of a writing system that will allow learners easy reading of J. P. Harrington's linguistic field notes.

"Folk Writing"

Another form of writing that we frequently see is what some linguists call "folk-writing" (Wallace Chafe is the first person I heard use this word in this context), the kind of writing that is done by people who are trying informally to write their language. The two main features of folk writing, for American Indian languages at least, is (1) the frequent use of dashes for syllable breaks, and (2) the use of English spelling rules and even whole words in English to represent

Leave it alone. HeTh-Tha-keh-yeh-chä
Don't hit. Um-AH-WooTch
Why are you hitting? How-wiL-mi-mAh-ThA-Wo-TRO-TRISH
I am going to rest. nAh-KeH-ThA-nÄs-Koh-yeH-HAch-nish

FIGURE 19-8   "Folk-writing."

the syllables of the language being represented. Figure 19.8 shows some examples of handwritten folk writing from a speaker of the Wukchumne language.

This form of writing is usually used by speakers and learners as a memory aid in language classes. It is helpful primarily to the speakers, who can use the written words to remind them of what they taught in the class. It is not at all good for the learners, however, for it inevitably leads to mispronunciation of the words.

Making a Practical Alphabet

Despite the arguments for using a phonetic alphabet that were listed above, it is still the case that the majority of indigenous languages developing writing systems today utilize the orthographic resources of the dominant language of their country. I will now discuss the practical considerations that go into the successful design of a practical writing system based on the Roman alphabet.

Sounds That Do Not Exist in English

One obvious consideration is that there are probably sounds in your language that do not exist in English. The two most likely solutions to this problem are:

(1) to use an English letter but define its pronunciation as being that of the non-English sound in your language. For example, if your language has an s-like sound but is not quite like an English s, you could still use the letter "s" to represent it, but you would explain in a pronunciation guide that it is pronounced differently. A common sound in many Native American languages is a postvelar or uvular stop (it sounds a bit like a "k" but is uttered further back in the throat). In the phonetic alphabet, this sound is represented as *q*, and that letter is often used to represent it in the practical systems as well.

(2) to make up another letter, probably based on an English letter but with extra marks, perhaps. A common set of sounds in Native American languages in the west is known in linguistics as "glottalized stops" or "ejectives." They are sounds like p, t, or k, with an added "popping" quality to them. A typical way of representing these sounds in writing is to add an apostrophe after the p, t, or k, like this: *p' t' k'*.

Digraphs

The typical Romanized practical writing system uses the letters of the Roman alphabet, but also adheres to the one letter, one sound principle described above for the phonetic alphabet. One exception to this is the use of digraphs—two letters—to represent a single sound. English spelling does this a great deal, and that tradition is carried over into the practical systems: thus letter combinations like *th, ch,* and *sh* are commonly used, each one of them standing for a single sound. In phonetic writing, these would be represented by single (non-Roman) characters.

Vowels

English has 14 vowel sounds, but only 5 vowel letters. It solves the problem of how to represent all its different vowel sounds by the use of digraphs (ee, ea, oo, ou, etc.) and by the use of a single letter for more than one sound (such as the *a* in m*a*n, f*a*ther, m*a*ne, etc.). There is no reason to purposefully create a system as complex and irregular as English spelling. Digraphs might be used in some cases, but communities developing writing systems almost never try to use the same single vowel letter to represent more than one sound. Most commonly, the "Roman" pronunciation of vowels is used (the same as Spanish). Thus, *i* would always stand for the vowel sound in "b*ee*t" (or possibly for the sound in "h*i*t"), and so on. The typical pronunciation of the five vowels would be as follows:

a (as in "f*a*ther")

e (as in "p*e*t")

i (as in "el*i*te")

o (as in "ph*o*ne")

u (as in "h*u*la")

Some languages will have somewhat different pronunciations than others—consistency is primarily important *within* a language, rather than across languages. Thus the vowel sounds of Yurok are described (Hinton, ms.):

Letter	Closest English sound
a	between "f*a*t" and "f*a*ther"
e	between "p*e*t" and "p*a*t"
i	p*i*t
o	between "c*oa*t" and "c*o*t"
u	p*u*t

If your language has only five vowel sounds, then you are lucky. If your language has six or more vowels, then you have to figure out what to do for representation of those extra vowels. The Ipai (Diegueño) writing system, developed by Margaret Langdon in the 1970s, has five vowels, but one is quite different from English: it is called "schwa" in phonetic parlance, a sound much like the last vowel sound in the English word "sof*a*." The other four vowels of Ipai were easily represented by *a, i, o,* and *u,* so *e* was left free for other uses. In phonetic writing, the schwa is represented by an upside-down *e,* so the use of *e* was a good choice.

Another possible choice is a digraph. For example, if *a* is used for a sound like the vowel in "father" and *e* is being used for the sound like the vowel in "p*e*t," and your language also has a sound like in English "h*a*nd," that last sound might be represented by a digraph, *ae.* In Yurok, there is a vowel that is exactly like the *er* sound in the English word "h*er,*" and so the digraph *er* is used to represent that sound.

Very common in Native American languages is a distinction between long and short vowels. Long vowels are represented by digraphs in some practical writing systems, and in others they are represented by a colon or other convention. In Havasupai, the word *ha* (with a short vowel) means "water," and the word *haa* (a long vowel represented with a double letter) represents "cottonwood tree." The closely related language Hualapai uses a colon for the long vowel instead, *ha:*.

A third choice for representing a sound that is not in English is to modify a letter to stand for it. Some of the Uto-Aztecan languages have a special vowel sound that is represented in the Americanist phonetic alphabet as a barred *i,* and so many of the Uto-Aztecan practical writing system have adopted the use of barred *i* as well.

Tone, Nasalization, and Voiceless Vowels

Some languages, such as Navajo and Acoma, are tone languages, and some, such as Navajo, have two sets of vowels, one set nasalized and the other nonnasal. (French and Portuguese are examples of Old World languages that have nasal and nonnasal distinctions in vowels; Chinese is an example of a tone language.) Other languages have both voiced vowels and "voiceless vowels," that is, vowels that are whispered. (Japanese is an example of an Old World language with silent vowels.)

The most common way to write these aspects of vowel quality is through diacritics, extra marks that are added above or below letters. The Western Mono orthography developed by Chris Loether and Rosalie Bethel marks voiceless vowels by underlining them. Navajo marks tone by writing accent marks over the vowels and nasalization by a hook under the vowel.

Some of the languages of Southeast Asia, such as Hmong and Vietnamese, have Roman-based alphabets that mark tone by the use of letters at the end of each syllable. Thus in Hmong, *muab* 'give, get' is actually pronounced "mua" with a high tone, while *muaj* 'have' is "mua" with a falling tone, and so on (there are seven tones altogether).

Some languages end up ignoring some of these vowel features. Acoma has both tone and voiceless vowels but does not write any diacritics to mark them. The decision as to whether to write or ignore aspects of pronunciation is something each community must decide for itself. If people are fluent speakers of a language, they only need to recognize a word and then they will know how to pronounce it. Hebrew, for example, does not even write vowels at all, only consonants. Yet it can still be recognized—try a sample of consonantal writing from English, and you will find that a little practice is all that is needed to figure out what is meant:

Prhps ths pssg cn b rd vn thgh ll th vwls r mssng.

Another clue to whether to write an aspect of pronunciation can be taken from Hebrew as well: for nonnative speakers just learning the Hebrew language, for children just learning to read, and for the transcription of new words that a reader is unlikely to know, the vowels are written. If the people most likely to read a Native American language are learners rather than native speakers, then it would be more important to write all aspects of pronunciation.

Consonants

Consonants do not present anywhere near the problem that vowels do, it seems; but even so, there are many consonants not found in English that must be represented somehow in a writing system. Like vowels, consonants not found in English can be represented by:

(1) digraphs (as in the "backed-s," represented as *sr* in Acoma);
(2) new symbols (for example, Havasupai uses a *t* with an extra cross in it for a dental *t*, and the same sound is "d" with a cross in Hualapai); or
(3) diacritics over or under old symbols (e.g., *ñ* in Havasupai, underline *i* for voiceless vowels in Mono).

Differentiation versus Unity in Writing Systems

There are political and social issues involved in the design of writing systems as well as practical considerations. A given writing system might be associated with a certain faction, country, or religious system, which might make it more attractive or less so depending on one's affiliations. I will tell several stories here to illustrate this.

The Havasupai and Hualapai Story

The Havasupais and Hualapais developed their writing systems at the same time. I consulted with both tribes during this development in the mid-1970s; I was especially involved with the Havasupai orthography, but I also consulted frequently with Lucille Watahomigie, the director of the Hualapai Bilingual Education Program and the main designer of the Hualapai alphabet. Lucille and I had agreed that it would be useful if the Havasupais and Hualapais could have the same writing system for the purpose of sharing of reading and curriculum materials. So Lucille and I worked together, debating various symbols and various solutions to orthographic problems. We were each reporting to our tribal councils as we developed the system, so they were well aware of what we were doing. After a couple of months of this interaction, the tribal councils, meeting independently from each other, decreed that they did not *want* identical writing systems. They said they were two separate tribes and they wanted that separateness demonstrated by differences in the writing system.

As a result of this tribal decree, the two writing systems ended up quite different from each other. Wherever the Hualapai and Havasupai committees had different ideas about the best solution to a particular orthographic problem, we simply each adopted our own idea. The systems are not so different as to be completely unreadable, but there are a few symbols that differ—Hualapai has an *ny* where Havasupai has a *ñ*; Hualapai has a *d* with a cross through it for the dental unaspirated *t*, while Havasupai has a *t* with an extra cross through it; and there is one very obvious difference in vowel orthography—Havasupai does not write the predictable short vowel that gets inserted to break up consonant clusters, whereas Hualapai writes it. These differences are political symbols of the separateness of the two tribes.

The Campa Story

A speaker of the Campa language, located in the Amazonian region of Peru, came to Berkeley one year for six weeks to work on his language with a class. The Campa, who are beleaguered by and fighting the encroachment of settlers and various eco-destructive business interests, are a noncentralized group with multiple villages spread over an area of hundreds of square miles and speak a large number of mutually intelligible dialects. Our visiting colleague said that Campa leaders are attempting to unify the Campa politically.

Our colleague had once been trained by a religious organization for linguistic work with indigenous peoples, but had broken with them and had no amicable feelings toward them. In fact, he made various accusations about the organization, believing that they were in league with the government of Peru to "pacify" the Campa and keep them from unifying so that settlement and development of the region could continue. He claimed that one way in which the organization was not acting in the best interests of the Campa was to insist on creating a different writing system for each dialect, so that wherever two dialects differ in pronunciation, they would be represented by different spelling. This, said our friend, was motivated by the desire to keep the villages from unifying. It was his goal that the pronunciation differences between the languages be "leveled" in the writing system to allow better communication, one step toward creating the political alliance the Campa were seeking.

Of course, having spelling reflect pronunciation is the standard orthographic solution that any (albeit politically naive) linguist would be likely to adopt, and I would be loath to believe that the organization in question had any nefarious motives for this policy. Nor would I expect that our friend represented the viewpoint of all the Campa. I present this story not to discredit the organization but to illustrate the political implications of orthographic development—in this case, just the opposite of the Havasupai-Hualapai case, where two almost identical dialects are differentiated in writing.

The Hmong Story

One interesting problem develops when a sizable population speaking a language endemic to one country migrates to another country that has a different writing system. The Hmong are a case in point. Originally a mountain people of Laos, Thailand, and southern China, the Hmong fought beside the Americans in the Vietnam War and faced genocidal repercussions when the Americans withdrew. They died by the thousands both during and after the war, and the survivors fled by the thousands to refugee camps in Thailand and elsewhere. There are roughly 150,000 Hmong people in the United States and many thousands more in Australia, France, and other countries. Several million Hmong people still remain in China, Thailand, and Laos. The Hmong have a number of writing systems. There is a unique demisyllabic system invented by a previously illiterate Hmong named Shong Lue Yang, who obtained it through a vision (Daniels and Bright 1996; Smalley et al. 1990). Associated with particular religious principles, it is used by those adhering to those principles. A Romanized Hmong writing system was developed by missionaries in the 1950s. Other writing systems for Hmong have been developed in the United States and elsewhere. Hmong living in Asia might have writing systems based on Thai, for example, or other non-Roman orthographies. As Gary Yia Lee (1996) says, "We are challenged by the need to adopt a common Hmong writing for all and not the many scripts we now use." Schools offering bilingual education to Hmong children want Roman scripts, partly because they see that learning a Roman script for Hmong will make reading skills more easily transferable to English. But for many Hmong, the main reason for adopting a common writing system is to be able to communicate with Hmong living in other countries. The American, French, and Australian Hmong clearly would prefer a Romanized script, but to what extent can the Hmong still in Asia become part of this worldwide Hmong communication network? These are all thorny issues.

TEACHING READING AND WRITING

Sometimes teachers say of children, "I notice that the kids can't read in our language [whichever indigenous language they are referring to] even though they read English very well," or "I notice the kids get confused when they try to pronounce written words in our language; they pronounce it like English spelling." The reason for this situation is very clear. The students have spent thousands of hours being taught how to read and write English, and few if any hours being taught how to read and write their language. Even though many indigenous writing systems use the Roman alphabet, people's knowledge of English reading and writing will not allow them to automatically read and write their own language. Students still have to be specifically taught how to read and write their own language; and if they are to learn how to read and write as well in their language as they do in English, their language needs to have equal time in the classroom.

WRITING SYSTEMS AS EMPOWERMENT

An example of a fascinating project utilizing new writing systems is CELIAC (Centro Editorial de Literatura Indígena, A. C. in Oaxaca, Mexico.) At CELIAC, three-month courses are offered where the indigenous leaders Jesús Salinas Pedraza and Josefa González teach bilingual teachers, campesinos, and housewives to write in the native languages. They write about anything they want, "using computers to write in their own languages about their lives, their customs, their legends, histories, natural medicine, and so on" (Salinas Pedraza 1997). As of the date of his article, the Oaxaca CELIAC project had trained 121 people, including speakers of 14 indigenous languages in Mexico; Quechua and Aymara from Argentina, Ecuador, Bolivia, and Peru; and one Shuar from Ecuador. Once trained, the participants return to their communities and write and also develop literacy in the home communities.

As Hornberger remarked in the quote that opens this chapter, writing systems can be seen as modes of empowerment. Salinas Pedraza writes:

Etnodesarrollo is the policy that drives some *indigenista* institutions today. The objects of development in *etnodesarrollo* are the various indigenous communities, conceived as total social, cultural, and historical units, that have been marginalized and dominated by the nation state. According to the *etnodesarrollo* perspective, the development of Indian communities across the Americas requires the transformation of national systems of ethnic dominance. Specifically, it requires formal, legal recognition by the nation states of the Americas of their multiethnic, multicultural nature.

History to date shows that this is only possible with direct pressure from the indigenous communities themselves. Economic, social, cultural, and political strengthening of Indian communities will come about only when Indians make conscious decisions to start the process. This is the only way in which we will be able to exert pressure for change on interethnic relations.

This is what we are trying to promote at CELIAC.

(Salinas Pedraza 1997, 175–76)

Notes

1. Until a couple of decades ago, it was still strongly debated as to whether Maya was a true writing system; now it has been proven beyond any doubt. The Inca *quipu* might also have counted as a true writing system, even though knotted ropes may seem like a strange way to write; but the Spanish conquistadores were so ruthless in their destruction of the upper class and the burning of the quipu houses that we have too little evidence left to make a clear determination. We know the quipu represented numbers; what we do not know is whether it could also be used to represent words.

2. I would like to thank Joe Freeman, who is presently designing a Salinan writing system for his community based on the phonetic systems used by linguists, for cogently arguing for his choice with most of these points.

References

Benjamin, Rebecca, Regis Pecos, and Mary Eunice Romero. 1997. Language revitalization efforts in the Pueblo de Cochiti: Becoming "literate" in an oral society. In *Indigenous literacies in the Americas: Language planning from the bottom up*, ed. Nancy Hornberger, 115–136. Berlin and New York: Walter de Gruyter.

Chafe, Wallace L., 1981. Differences between colloquial and ritual Seneca, or how oral literature is literary. In *Reports from the survey of California and other Indian languages* 1: 131–45.

Daniels, Peter T., and William Bright, eds. 1996. *The world's writing systems.* Oxford: Oxford University Press.

Hinton, Leanne. 1994. *Flutes of fire: Essays on California Indian languages.* Berkeley: Heyday Books.

———. 2000. Report to the Yurok tribe on the proposed spelling system for Yurok. Unpublished manuscript.

Hornberger, Nancy. 1997a. *Indigenous literacies in the Americas: Language planning from the bottom up.* Berlin and New York: Walter de Gruyter.

———. 1997b. Quechua literacy and empowerment. In *Indigenous literacies in the Americas: Language planning from the bottom up*, ed. Nancy Hornberger, 215–36. Berlin and New York: Walter de Gruyter.

Lee, Gary Yia, 1996. Cultural identity in post-modern society: Reflections on What is a Hmong? *Hmong Studies Journal* 1, no. 1 (posted on Web at <http://www.como.stpaul.k12.mn.us/Vue-Benson/HSJv1n1Lee.html>.

Mallery, Garrick. [1888–89] 1972. *Picture-writing of the American Indians.* 2 vols. New York: Dover.

Mankiller, Wilma, and Michael Wallis. 1993. *Mankiller: A chief and her people.* New York: St. Martin's Press.

Martineau, LaVan. 1973. *The rocks begin to speak.* Las Vegas: KC Publications.

Nuttall, Zelia, ed. [1902] 1975. *The Codex Nuttall: A picture manuscript from ancient Mexico.* New York: Dover.

Salinas Pedraza, Jesús. 1997. Saving and strengthening indigenous Mexican languages: The CELIAC experience. In *Indigenous literacies in the Americas: Language planning from the bottom up*, ed. Nancy Hornberger, 171–87. Berlin and New York: Walter de Gruyter.

Smalley, William A., Chia Koua Vang, and Gnia Yee Yang. 1990. *Mother of writing: The origin and development of a Hmong messianic script.* Chicago: University of Chicago Press.

An Introduction to Paiute

LEANNE HINTON
Department of Linguistics
University of California at Berkeley
Berkeley, California

KEN HALE
Department of Linguistics and Philosophy
Massachusetts Institute of Technology
Cambridge, Massachusetts

Southern Paiute belongs to the Numic branch of the Uto-Aztecan language family, which extends from the state of Washington as far south as El Salvador in Central America. Southern Paiute and its closest relatives, Ute, Chemehueve, and Kawaiisu, constitute the Southern Numic subgroup of Numic (Steele 1979). It is the language spoken in San Juan, and it is also represented in 10 communities in Nevada, Utah, and Arizona. San Juan itself is a distinct linguistic and ethnic group on the Navajo Reservation.

San Juan is a community where "tip" has taken place (Dorian 1981) in recent years. As Bunte and Franklin report, "The same San Juan Paiutes who called out *wakingu'* to a wandering child or grandchild in 1979 now invariably use the English equivalent, *come 'ere,* speaking to the next generation of toddlers. Speaking English between bilingual Paiute–English-speaking teenagers and adults as well as with children has become habitual in the community." Like other communities that are at this stage of language shift, at one end of the age spectrum there are many Paiute speakers who know very little English, and at the other, many English speakers with little or no understanding of Paiute, presenting the tribe with "serious translation and interpretation problems at the same time that they are beginning to worry about losing the language." Ironically, one of the major factors that have led to language shift has been San Juan's efforts toward being officially recognized as a distinct tribe by the federal government, along with tribal development after the success of these efforts.

San Juan is adopting a three-way language revitalization plan that includes (1) a master-apprentice immersion program; (2) literacy development; and (3) documentation of oral literature and development of Paiute language teaching materials and courses.

Once San Juan gained federal recognition, it had to write a constitution. Significantly, the tribe decided to make this constitution bilingual. This had practical importance given the fact that so many tribal members are not fluent in English, and it was important for all members to approve its final content. It also had symbolic importance, showing commitment to the language. Bunte and Franklin report that "the construction of a Paiute written version has helped to raise Paiute in the estimation of speakers and nonspeakers alike, giving it the cachet of a 'written' language," for example, English. This chapter is primarily about the process of developing this bilingual constitution. The translation process shows some of the important differences between Paiute and English speech and information structure and also shows how the Paiute language is changing to fit the modern information requirements being placed on it.

The Southern Paiute language has an important position in the history of American linguistics because of its role in Edward Sapir's famous paper on the "psychological reality of the phoneme," once required reading in virtually every linguistics department in the country and still quite generally known to linguists here and elsewhere. Sapir's superb linguistic consultant for Southern Paiute, the late Tony Tillohash, wrote his language "phonemically," much to the initial astonishment of Sapir. Thus, for example, when he proceeded to set down the form which in its phonetic realization was approximately [pa:βah], he wrote first /pa:/ for the first syllable and then /pah/ for the second, undoing, so to speak, the phonological rule which "spirantizes" the intervocalic stop consonant /p/, turning it into the voiced bilabial fricative [β]. That is to say, Tony Tillohash was not writing the word in terms of the actual phonetic sounds of which it consisted—the phonetic [pa:βah]—but rather in terms of its underlying phonemic representation, with /p/ instead of the fricative [β]. Southern Paiute was the first of Sapir's four or so examples in his essay on the psychological reality of the phoneme, and it is the example most often used in subsequent years by other linguists to argue for the reality of phonological rules and phonological derivations, that is, processes in which observed surface forms are derived from underlying, abstract, linguistic representations.

References

Dorian, Nancy C. 1981. *Language death: The life cycle of a Scottish dialect.* Philadelphia: University of Pennsylvania Press.

Sapir, Edward. 1933. La réalité psychologique des phonèmes. *Journal de Psychologie Normale et Pathologique* 30: 247–65.

Steele, Susan. 1979. Uto-Aztecan: An assessment for historical and comparative linguistics. In *The languages of Native America: Historical and comparative assessment,* ed. Lyle Campbell and Marianne Mithun, 444–54. Austin: University of Texas Press.

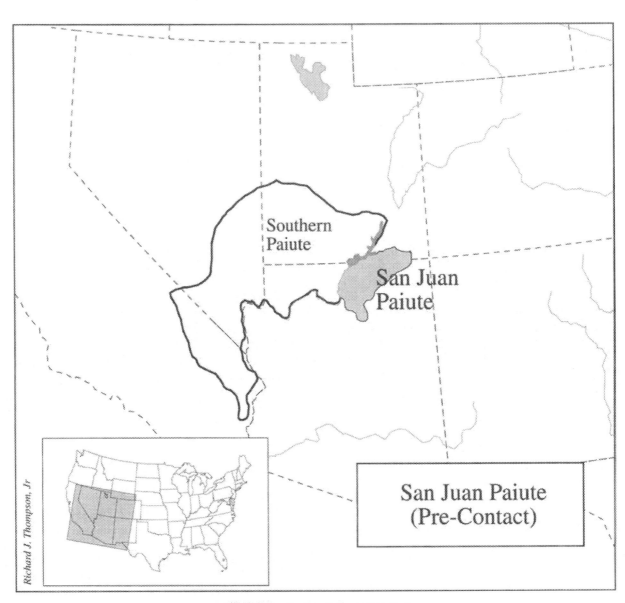

MAP 20.1   San Juan Paiute (pre-contact)

Language Revitalization in the San Juan Paiute Community and the Role of a Paiute Constitution

PAMELA BUNTE

Departments of Anthropology and Linguistics
California State University, Long Beach
Long Beach, California

ROBERT FRANKLIN*

Department of Anthropology
California State University, Dominguez Hills
Carson, California

ankatavats mangwisini, yaeya hee ya he
  ankatavats mangwisini, yaeya hee ya he ya
taxapʉ nukwitʉaxaipʉva
  taxapʉ nukwitʉaxaipʉva
  paava' kanixaiy hyang
  he' yang he' yang hee yang
          Round dance song recorded in 1993, sung by Johnny Lehi, Jr.

Red sun rising yaeya hee ya he
  Red sun rising yaeya hee ya he
At the place where my orphan used to run
  At the place where my orphan used to run
  While dwelling by the water hyang
  he' yang he' yang hee yang

In the fall of 1979, one of the authors accompanied a Kaibab-Paiute friend and colleague on a short visit to the San Juan Paiute settlement of Hidden Springs on the western part of the Navajo reservation. The scene made a lasting impression: parents and grandparents were calling out in Paiute to toddlers; even young people were interacting entirely in Paiute; and a young girl of 11 in long braids doing her homework by lantern light wanted to be shown how to write in Paiute. In contrast, fluent speakers of Southern Paiute in other Paiute communities were at that time primarily middle-aged and older, and no young children were learning the language. To both outside observers and to the the San Juan themselves, it seemed that this San Juan community was one place where the Paiute language would continue to be spoken indefinitely. Nevertheless, today the same San Juan Paiutes who called out "wakingu'" to a wandering child or grandchild in 1979 now invariably use the English equivalent, "come 'ere," speaking to the next generation of toddlers. Speaking English between bilingual Paiute–English-speaking teenagers and adults as well as with children has become habitual in the community, accelerating the language shift from Paiute to English.

As linguistic anthropologists who began linguistic, ethnographic, and ethnohistoric research at the request of the tribe in 1980, we have observed the patterns of language use changing over the years and are presently working with tribal members in an attempt to reverse some of the changes. Although the scenario described above certainly looks very similar to that in other communities where native languages have been irretrievably lost, there are a number of encouraging signs of language strength in the San Juan case. Fluent speakers still have many occasions in which they use the language. Even young children often have passive Paiute skills as well as other special-purpose language skills. The round-dance song at the beginning of this chapter, for example, was sung by an eight-year-old. A number of adult speakers are currently attempting to learn to write in Paiute, and many San Juan have finally accepted that their language could soon be lost if they do not do something.

Ironically, since Paiute is still the primary language of many San Juan tribal members and even members who use English phrases with toddlers often have only very rudimentary English skills, the tribe has to deal with serious translation and interpretation problems at the same time that they are beginning to worry about losing the language. In this chapter, we will examine what has led to the Paiute-English language shift, the attitudes of tribal members toward it, and

*Deceased

the efforts of the tribe and tribal members to deal with both the long-term goal of language preservation and the short-term practical goal of effective interaction and understanding between the English-speaking outside world and Paiute speakers. We will examine the present attempt to integrate these long-term and short-term goals in a comprehensive language program and illustrate the importance of these goals through a discussion of lessons learned while translating the San Juan's new constitution.

CURRENT STATUS OF THE SOUTHERN PAIUTE LANGUAGE

Southern Paiute is the language traditionally spoken by members of the 10 Southern Paiute communities in Nevada, Utah, and Arizona. In the Nevada and Utah communities, only a small number of the oldest members presently speak Paiute. In Arizona, at the Kaibab Paiute reservation, the situation is somewhat better, with a larger number of speakers, including a small number of speakers younger than 50.

Located on the western part of the Navajo reservation, the San Juan Paiutes are the most conservative of the Southern Paiute communities in terms of Paiute culture and traditions. In contrast to the other Southern Paiute communities, where Paiute has not been consistently spoken in homes to children for 25 or more years, Southern Paiute was the language used by speakers in most San Juan political, economic, and social situations until the late 1980s.

At present, Paiute is still spoken between fluent Paiute-speaking adults in many daily contexts in the San Juan community. In fact, Paiute is frequently necessary for fluent conversation, since most speakers older than 50 and even some younger Paiutes speak very little English. In addition, two of the San Juan Paiute Tribal Council members speak virtually no English, so council discussions are generally held in Paiute. When English is spoken at council meetings, it is translated into Paiute.

Due to the increasing number of tribal members who are no longer able to communicate effectively in Paiute, however, communication between tribal members is often neither simple nor effective. Problems occur because of the frequent necessity of translation and the ad hoc nature of such translation, as well as the variable skill of the interpreters. In addition, when interactions include a non-Paiute speaker (a situation that has become common), English is generally used—often without translation into Paiute. Young tribal workers are also frequently frustrated by their lack of ability to communicate with their Paiute-speaking clients.

As noted above, Paiute is rarely spoken to children even when the adult knows very little English. Even among those teenagers who learned Paiute as a first language, most are no longer completely fluent, and only one of the younger children is now learning the language as a first language.

RECENT SOCIAL AND POLITICAL HISTORY

The 1980s and 1990s have been a period of tremendous social and political change for the San Juan Paiute tribe. In the 1970s the San Juan were a distinct community on the Navajo reservation, where they supported themselves with subsistence farming, raising small herds of sheep and goats, and selling Navajo wedding baskets to Navajos and traders (Bunte and Franklin 1987). No San Juan living on the Navajo reservation had graduated from high school; some young adults had never been to school at all and spoke no English. The San Juan Paiutes had no access to any programs that went through the Navajo tribe, including housing and federal food programs. As a tribe which had no formal status with the federal government, the San Juan had no way to gain access to these programs on their own. They had no electricity, indoor plumbing, or telephones, and they lived in one-room homes, most with dirt floors.

In the early 1980s the San Juan became involved in two major endeavors which were to change drastically their relations with the outside world. In 1978 a new bureaucratic procedure was established to allow unrecognized tribes to apply to the Bureau of Indian Affairs for federal recognition. The San Juan, realizing that formal recognition would allow them to gain access to federal programs, began the complicated process of producing a documented petition in 1980. In addition, in 1981 the San Juan discovered that their land, both their present and traditional land, was a part of the contested land in the Navajo-Hopi land claims suit for the 1934 Navajo reservation and with the help of the Native American Rights Fund intervened in the case. The 1980s, therefore, were spent working with outside experts, anthropologists, attorneys, and the Federal Bureau of Acknowledgment and Research (BAR) to document their claims. In 1989 the tribe was federally recognized, and in 1990 tribal members testified in federal district court about their land (Bunte and Franklin 1992). Although they are still working at getting a separate reservation and therefore have not been able to substantially upgrade their housing situation, the 1990s have seen them get funding for tribal offices, including fax machines and computers, and gain access to many economic, health, and social programs. Some San Juan have also acquired GEDs (high school equivalency certificates), jobs, and extra training.

LANGUAGE SHIFT

As a result of this intense interaction with experts, other tribes, and the federal government, all tribal members are now integrated into daily bureaucratic and intertribal dealings in which English is the common language spoken. By contrast, 15 years ago San Juan Paiute speakers rarely had to interact socially with speakers who did not speak Paiute or

Navajo, which, as the lingua franca for the reservation at large, was a second language for many Paiutes. At that time, virtually all San Juan political decision making took place in Paiute. Today, because of the specialized knowledge needed to run a federally recognized tribe, the tribe has had to hire qualified non-Paiute administrators. The tribal manager, comptroller, and director of health and social services, for instance, are all non-Paiute, although two are Indian. For the Paiute tribal members employed by the tribe, English writing and speaking skills are valued over Paiute skills. We should, therefore, not be surprised that a number of the employees are young adults with only passive Paiute language ability.

Another outcome of federal recognition and the jobs and services that followed recognition was a greatly increased access through television and other media to the wider English-speaking environment. As a result of this all-enveloping exposure to English, bilingual Paiute-English speakers frequently feel they must use English if non-Paiute speakers are around, and non-English speakers have begun to understand some English. We have even noted certain Paiutes who previously understood no English at all laughing at jokes overheard in English conversations. All of this has led to a shift in many households toward an English-rather than Paiute-speaking norm so that the language of choice even between bilinguals is often English.

The community is now at a crossroads: they retain the ability to save their language, but if they wait it may soon be too late. At present, approximately one quarter of the San Juan Paiute adults 20 and older speak Paiute with complete fluency as their first language. An additional 25% or more of adults, as well as many teenagers, are partial speakers with varying degrees of fluency. To preserve and revitalize the language, Paiute speaking must again become the norm for the home and at least some other domains. Unfortunately, San Juan Paiutes' mere recognition that this is what is needed or even their strong desire to save the language will probably not be sufficient. One worried San Juan set up a small class to teach preschoolers. However, an emphasis on vocabulary words in the class and the fact that other adults continued to speak English to the children both inside and outside of class prevented any real change in their Paiute skills, and the class was discontinued.

English and the relationships it represents have become too integral a part of San Juan life for the tribe to simply return to the old ways. Paiute speaking which was accomplished unthinkingly and effortlessly 10 years ago now needs to be carefully organized, planned, and encouraged.

PAIUTE LANGUAGE PRESERVATION AND REVITALIZATION PLAN

The tribe is in the process of formulating an ambitious plan for language revitalization through community meetings and networking with a variety of specialists. Although oral language learning in appropriate home and community settings will be the primary emphasis in any language project, the tribe is also interested in training fluent Paiute speakers to read and write their native language. In addition, tribal members are discussing the development of a Paiute language course that would employ learning modules, fluent speakers as facilitators, and multimedia resources. Tribal leaders believe that if they can implement all of these components successfully there will be a real possibility of reinstating the habit and prestige of speaking Paiute in many family and tribal contexts and producing new fluent teenage and young adult speakers who will use the language with the next generation.

An oral language approach likely to be successful with San Juan Paiutes is the master-apprentice approach described by Leanne Hinton (1994). The California master-apprentice project has successfully paired up speakers of California Indian languages with nonspeakers to teach native language skills. Since these skills are passed on orally using only the native language, it has the advantage of not needing literate speakers skilled in classroom teaching techniques. The master-apprentice approach would have the advantage of bringing together the older and younger generations in a program designed to teach Paiute language skills in a natural way to teenagers and young adults. This is important for any San Juan program since few of the speakers have any Paiute literacy skills and many are not English speakers. They would use the communication and teaching skills that they learn in workshops presented at regular social gatherings and training sessions. Another benefit of this approach is that it is successful in getting learners as well as speakers to use the language in varied contexts, including in interactions with speakers and non- or semispeakers not directly involved in the project. In the long term, we believe that this component, probably in conjunction with immersion projects for very young children, has the most chance of changing the underlying culture of speaking, that is, getting the partial speakers and nonspeakers actually communicating in Paiute.

Although reading and writing in Paiute is certainly not traditional, many San Juan Paiutes feel that in order for Paiute to compete with English it must also be used in a written form. The Paiute-speaking population served here includes both speakers who are literate in English and those who do not speak or write English. There is currently a great deal of interest among a number of fluent adult speakers, especially those in their 20s, 30s, and 40s, to learn to read and write in Paiute. There is also one fairly fluent (self-taught) writer. These speakers wish to help provide bilingual materials and to write down some of their knowledge. In addition, after acquiring literacy skills, some of these speakers will be able to help develop written and audiovisual materials.

We have been videotaping and transcribing Paiute oral narratives and songs for a number of years and are currently putting much of the linguistic data into a database program that will provide the basis for a comprehensive dictionary of

Paiute. The tribe is also interested in producing edited videos of storytelling, cartoon versions of traditional stories, and CD-ROM versions of these materials. The collecting of Paiute oral literature and song will continue for its own sake, as the tribe also wishes to preserve as much as possible of its oral and musical traditions and the cultural knowledge that goes with them. However, this collection will also provide important sources for primary and supplementary materials of any Paiute language course and will be a continuing resource for future language and culture programs. We note that other Southern Paiute tribes' attempts to reverse language loss by using language classes alone have not been successful. We believe, however, that when used in conjunction with the project's other components, culturally appropriate classroom instruction can help further the tribe's goal of linguistic and cultural preservation.[1]

THE PRACTICAL NEED FOR A LANGUAGE PROGRAM

Earlier in this chapter, the need for a Paiute language preservation program was presented as self-evident, as indeed it is from community members' perspective. Much of Paiute culture is encoded in its oral stories, songs, conversations, and other genres, and the language itself reflects traditional Paiute life ways and ways of making sense of the world. However, a language is also an important resource for unifying the community, both symbolically and in a concrete way as a medium for interaction.

Although tribal leaders and community elders are primarily Paiute speaking, the fast pace of cultural and linguistic change as well as the reality of creating a modern bureaucratic tribe has produced a situation in which the majority of tribal members are English speaking, and the world the tribe and its members must deal with is English speaking and literacy based. Often, although perhaps not often enough, an interpreter's translation serves to bridge the gap. Even with translations, however, misunderstandings occur. In one recent case, for example, an elder accused a tribal worker of misconduct when actually the elder had simply misunderstood the English explanation for the action. Miscommunication can be caused by a simple lack of common vocabulary or by more complex underlying differences in habits of seeing and talking about the world. From a practical point of view, an effective language program is necessary to ease communication and build understanding between segments of the community.

CREATING A CONSTITUTION IN TWO LANGUAGES

nɨɨn uruh nɨngwutsing san juan southern paiute niaxatɨm washitɨnam uvay 'aɨngwiyu'ngɨpɨxatɨmɨni ara'ay uruxaini ur

shɨɨnɨm ur, nɨngwɨ'a shɨɨnɨm ur, inchɨanɨm constitutioni niaxat nangwa'a ampaxɑpi yunakatɨ, ichu amay:

We the people of the San Juan Southern Paiute Tribe, a federally recognized sovereign Indian Tribe, do hereby adopt this constitution in order to: [literally: We, the people called San Juan Southern Paiute, are federally recognized and our power, our people's power, this our constitution is called the words gathered together, for these things:]

More than any other single element of the San Juan people's transition to modernity, the drafting of a tribal constitution has confronted tribe members with the extraordinary linguistic and cultural problems of English-to-Paiute and Paiute-to-English interpretation and translation. At the same time, since the San Juan eventually opted to draft a Paiute version as well, the constitution process is also playing a surprisingly positive role in the development and future viability of the Paiute language.

In this section, we first describe the particulars of the constitution drafting and translation process. Secondly, we discuss some of the linguistic challenges that community members have faced in the creation of the Paiute version of their constitution. One particularly challenging aspect of this process has centered on the development of an appropriate Paiute lexicon for referring to parts of the constitution itself—"preamble," "article," "section"—and to elements of the new political system—"quorum," "tribal council," "president," "vice president," "regulation," "ordinance," and so on. More difficult yet has been the problem of translating the hierarchical information structure of a formal English legal document, and the related problem of developing ways to express in Paiute complex limits and conditions on legal rules, notably logical conditions of the form, "if either x or y" or "provided that x and provided that y."

The Constitution Process

Most Indian communities in the United States developed their present tribal constitutions and formal systems of tribal government under the auspices of the 1934 Indian Reorganization Act, also known as the Wheeler-Howard Act. When the San Juan Paiute Tribe became a federally recognized tribe in 1990, they entered into the same political reorganization process that so many other tribes had undertaken some 60 years ago.

One key part of this process is the development and ratification of a tribal constitution, something that was quite alien to San Juan political life even very recently. As late as the 1980s, the internal political system of the San Juan was entirely traditional. The unchallenged language of political life, as with community life in general, was San Juan Paiute. Political process was face to face and governed largely by custom; such things as written minutes or written procedural rules played no part in it at all. By contrast, the BIA very strongly encourages newly recognized tribes to adopt a constitution conforming to the Indian Reorganization Act and provides models in the formal politico-legalistic English that characterizes American law and politics. One of the authors (Bunte) has been working closely with the San Juan on the development of the tribal constitution since this process began in the mid-1980s. Also helping the tribe were its tribal attorney and another attorney specializing in tribal constitutions acting as a consultant.

Most of the tribal representatives in the constitution drafting process have limited English language skills at best and many are essentially nonspeakers of English. As a part of the long deliberative process of constructing a constitution, tribal leaders undertook the translation of the constitution into Paiute, section by section as discussions proceeded, to allow the limited– or non–English speakers an in-depth understanding of what they were discussing and voting on. At the same time, the construction of a Paiute written version has helped to raise Paiute in the estimation of speakers and nonspeakers alike, giving it the cachet of a "written" language.

Throughout this process, the tribe has used a San Juan interpreter to translate whatever portions were under discussion at any given point. Johnny Lehi, the tribe's current vice president and also its main interpreter in the Navajo-Hopi-Paiute federal land dispute trial (cf. Bunte and Franklin 1992), agreed to take on this difficult job.[2] Because of the complexity of the English involved and the difficulty of spontaneously translating it in constitution committee meetings, at the tribe's request in 1994 both of us began working with Lehi to draft written translations of portions the tribe was working on. This had an immediate impact. In the first meeting where such a prepared translation was read to the tribal representatives, a number of them remarked afterward that this was the first time they truly understood what the document was about.

Because of his experience as an interpreter, his formidable linguistic intuitions and cultural background knowledge, and his increasing literacy skills in Paiute, Lehi has been a key contributor to our collaborative translation process. His present modus operandi is to write out notes in Paiute on a pad at home and then bring them into our work sessions at the tribal office. Together, we discuss the meanings of troublesome passages, after which Lehi makes the final decision as to the Paiute language to be used.

As required by the 1934 Indian Reorganization Act, the tribe will hold an election to decide whether or not to adopt the constitution. Because so many San Juan adults and elders have limited skills in English, this translated version will be essential for the community discussion that leads up to the vote.[3]

Problem Areas and Resources

Translating the San Juan constitution presented some formidable problems from the standpoint of lexicon. English speakers have had several centuries to develop a vocabulary for labeling the formal political structures and institutions that we are so familiar with. In so doing, English speakers were also able to pillage Greek, Latin, and French to fill in lexical gaps in the domains of politics and law. Like English speakers, San Juan Paiute speakers are also drawing on a variety of resources as they attempt to lexicalize their evolving political landscape. These resources range from neologisms coined over the last 15 years in political discussions among speakers to existing terms which the San Juan used to refer to their own indigenous political process or to describe their relatively rare encounters with non–San Juan institutions. Particularly intriguing is the number of Paiute terms that appear to have been calqued on similar Navajo expressions for similar institutions.

The first domain of terms we want to identify is the self-referring terms used for the constitution itself and its subparts. In the English document, these are used as section headings. They are also used as references when one article or section cross-refers to another, a particularly important role for such expressions. Lehi eventually chose not to translate these terms when they were used in the English as heading and subheading titles, preferring instead Paiute section titles that summarized the content of the section. This proved to be more meaningful in helping San Juan listeners understand the overall structure of the document as they were discussing it. Terms for "constitution," "article," and "section," as well as terms for extra-constitutional law, for example, "ordinances," were still needed because the text often made crucial reference to itself and to extra-constitutional law.

The Paiute term *p'okwatupu* 'that which is written on' is used as an all-purpose term in conversational San Juan to mean not only "paper," but also "book" or "document." Early in the constitution drafting process and the accompanying Paiute discussion, this term developed into a variety of neologisms referring to the constitution's subparts as well as other legal documents. The San Juan constitution includes many examples of this family of lexical terms, including:

p'okwatupu nanaxap'okwatu 'constitution' (literally, "paper[s] together-written")

p'okwatupu 'article' or 'section' (e.g., *ichu p'okwatupu shuukunaxaih* 'in section one')

p'okwatupu nanaxap'okwatu 'aututuniaru 'ordinance' (literally, "papers together-written that tell it better" [or "that go into greater detail"])

The equivalent English terms imply a logical hierarchy of document subdivisions that is not clearly present in the Paiute terms. This bears on the issue of information structure, as noted below.

Even before the process of creating the constitution began in the late 1980s, the San Juan had developed many other neologisms to describe its newly emerging political system. Such terms included another "paper" term for "minutes" as well as the terms for the two district subdivisions in the tribe:

p'okwatupu p'okwatu shuupara'kapipay 'minutes' (literally, "paper[s] written about meetings") *tɨituxwatɨ tɨxakatɨnax* 'Northern District' (literally, "in the uphill measured-off area")

tɨvaituxwatɨ tɨxakatɨnax 'Southern District' (literally, "in the downhill measured-off area")

The terms for the Northern and Southern Districts are especially interesting since the two areas have traditional names that could easily have been used, and furthermore, Paiute does not have terms for north and south. The terms employed here, *tɨi-* 'uphill' and *tɨvai-* 'downhill', were developed and used heuristically for cardinal point directions during federal land claims depositions to accurately translate attorneys' questions about directions (Bunte and Franklin 1992). These terms may have been used in the context of the constitution to indicate that the traditional areas are not exactly the same as the new districts, or simply because the Northern District is based in the higher-elevation Navajo Mountain area and is actually uphill, while the Southern District is in a lower-elevation area, or downhill.

In many other cases, Lehi and the San Juan were able to draw on existing lexical resources. One resource is the traditional Paiute terms for the consensus group decision making that characterized traditional society, for example, for a meeting:

(tangw'a)shuupara'n '[man] meeting in council'
(tangw'a)waixa- '[man] deliberating in council'

These terms and others which are still used are found also in Sapir's Kaibab Paiute texts collected in 1910 (Sapir 1930).[4]

It also turns out that there was a sizable body of Paiute legal and political terminology already being used by the San Juan for referring to Navajo tribal and U.S. political institutions which proved to be applicable to the Paiutes' new system:

namɨ(tangw'a)karɨr 'president' (literally, "first[man] who sits")

ungwávinakwą karɨr 'vice president' (literally, "the one who sits behind him")

tangw'akarɨ/tangw'ayuxwi- 'hold office' (literally, 'man sit [singular/plural]')

(payu)tangw'akani 'tribal administration' (literally, "[San Juan] man house")[5]

(payu)ampaxakani 'tribal court' (literally, "[San Juan] talking house")

p'okwatɨwɨnai(kɨ) 'voting' (literally, "throw a paper [for someone]")

These terms provide us with vital information about the lexical resources regularly exploited by the San Juan in their changing social and cultural environment. Although San Juan generally use the rich morphological resources of Paiute to coin new terms, this last lexical group demonstrates the influence of the Navajo language and Navajo tribal political development on the San Juan political terminology. Navajo-language radio in Tuba City along with informal talk with local Navajos has long been San Juan Paiutes' main source of news about the outside world. This has left an impact on Paiutes' political lexicon. Although some terms, such as the Paiute term for 'court' *ampaxąkanį*, were apparently coined among the San Juan and other Southern Numic speakers, a number of other expressions are calqued on Navajo terms. The following examples give the Navajo expressions that correspond to some of the Paiute terms for the San Juans' modern system:

yá 'ałą́ąjį' dah sidá 'president' (literally, "he sits up ahead for them")

t'áá yikéé' góne' náándzį́ 'vice-president' (literally, "he stands right behind him")

naaltsoos bá 'íiłtsooz 'voting' (literally, "I put a paper in for him")

Translation also proved problematic in the area of information structure. For the purposes of analysis, information structure is understood as the ways that relationships among ideas in a given stretch of oral or written discourse are conceptualized and these relationships communicated to listeners or readers. Formal written documents in English are generally organized hierarchically. This hierarchical structure is often foregrounded through the use of section headings, with roman and arabic numerals as well as capital and small letters to distinguish part-to-whole relationships among sections. Even when such organization is not explicit in the written format, or when the document is presented orally, it is always implicitly there, so that the knowledgeable reader or listener should be able to discover the hierarchical format or outline of the piece. Legal documents, such as constitutions, represent an extreme example of both formality and hierarchical organization. Constitutions, including tribal ones, generally have "articles" and "sections" which are then subdivided even further using various kinds and combinations of numerals and letters as contextual markers.

Paiute, on the other hand, lacking a tradition of formal law or similar linguistic and cultural traditions, has up until now had no equivalent conventions for encoding and decoding discourse in complex hierarchical arrangements. Mythic stories and other narratives, in which one piece of information follows another piece like beads on a string, represent the most complex model for organizing formal Paiute discourse that we know of in the Paiute tradition.[6]

In dealing with this issue, Lehi's main goal for his Paiute translations of the constitution was to structure the Paiute version as close to conventional Paiute information structure as possible, so that Paiute elders would understand. For example, as we noted above, he did not distinguish separate levels of organization with terms such as "article," "section," and "subsection." Instead, he either used the same term for several levels or, more frequently, used Paiute titles that emphasized the content of the section rather than its place in the hierarchical order. Numbers and letters as symbols of the organizational structure also proved unworkable, as these did not convey any useful meaning to non- or only partially literate speakers unfamiliar with these literacy-based conventions.

For English speakers familiar with the conventions of legal discourse, an even more telling difference between the English and Paiute versions is found in the ways listing and logical operations are dealt with in conditions on the application of rules. In legal English, such as that found in constitutions, conditions on rules are frequently organized into lists of two distinct types: those where all member terms must hold true and those disjunctive lists where only one member term need hold true. Since constitutions, like other kinds of legal documents, are expected to provide as much as possible of the necessary information in the words of the text itself, the English version very carefully and explicitly distinguishes these logical operations. In contrast, list making itself is not a commonplace practice in Paiute traditional discourse; and although it is possible to list a set of terms, there is no easy way to distinguish whether all or only one must be included. Nevertheless, by emphasizing the content and the purpose of what is displayed as a list in English and by relying on his listeners' practical knowledge of the world, Lehi has been able to convey the basic meaning of the provisions to community members without relying on logical operators, such as "either/or" and "all of the following," or even formal lists. For example, in the membership section in the English version there is a provision that those who will have full rights as members shall be either those persons accepted as members under the regular membership requirements *or* those who have become members through adoption. In the Paiute version, it is not explicitly stated that only one set of conditions is necessary; the two categories are connected with *uruaxaini* 'also it', which is often used as the equivalent of "and." Of course, the Paiutes' practical knowledge makes it clear that any one person will only fit one of the categories.

Lehi was also able to convey that all of a set of conditions or terms are required; but he generally did this in a manner that emphasized each term in a non-list, non-parallel form. For example, the English version of the Paiute constitution states (article 2, section 2): "The Tribal Council shall have sole and exclusive authority to adopt other persons as members of the Tribe, *Provided,* That at least six members . . . vote in favor of the adoption and, *Provided,* That all persons adopted . . . shall meet at a minimum the following requirements:" In this provision and in others like it, the words "provided that" are used to introduce conditions, each one of which is required. Since these terms or conditions are presented in a list in which each item begins with "provided that," the set of required terms could be extended indefinitely. In addition, note that the statement which precedes the series of "provided that" conditions is the result, or what would be allowed, if the conditions are fulfilled. The Paiute language version, however, is organized quite differently. There is no division of result or outcome from a list of conditions. Instead, the result statement, that is, that the tribal

council will have the authority to adopt, is incorporated into the statement of the first condition:

navaivani yuxwichumu	*navaikumungwani*	*umungwatumutuh*
tribal council	six out of	out of them only
ungah	*haikangukwa'amutuh*	*u'ni*
yes same	say only	it manner
taxapurut'it'akaivach		
shall be allowed to adopt		

'The tribal council shall only be allowed to adopt them when six of them [council members] say yes'.

The second condition is then presented separately:

manoni	*nungwuntsing*	*'um*	*taxapurukwangupi*
all	persons	they	being adopted
ichu	*p'okwatupunax*	*niap'okwapi*	
this	in paper	name written	
aup'atuxw	*uni'mavachuh*		
in accord with it	shall also do it		

'All persons being adopted shall also act according to the enrollment [requirements] in this paper [this section of the constitution]'.

This condition is only connected to the tribal council's ability to adopt through the use of "also," which links it with the previous sentence and, again, through the hearer's common sense. For the Paiute listeners, however, this presentation is more comprehensible than it would be if Lehi attempted to translate the English format more literally.

This careful translation of the constitution is taking place after 16 years of dealing with various attorneys and trying to understand various legal principles, concepts, and processes. Even after all this preparation, the differences in habitual ways of talking about the world result in many difficulties and potential misunderstandings. Nevertheless, San Juan Paiutes have gradually begun to adapt to these new ways of thinking and incorporating both new and conventional ways of talking into their everyday and political discourse. In particular, we have seen that the tremendous changes in the San Juan political system that have taken place in the last 10 years are reflected in the vocabulary needed to describe the political system and its regulations. This political lexicon, which includes traditional Paiute governmental terms, calques from Navajo political terminology, and many neologisms fabricated out of Paiute morphological resources, demonstrates the flexibility and creativity that a vibrant language can reveal in adapting to changing situations.

CONCLUSION

The process of creating a Paiute language version of the San Juan's constitution will not take us back to a 1979 era of Paiute language use. However, the San Juan Paiute Tribe's proposed language revitalization program, together with the constitution project and any other language-oriented project which might be developed, should help tribal members move toward their long-term goal of language preservation, as well as their short-term goal of helping Paiute speakers interact with and understand the English-speaking outside world. The eagerness San Juan are demonstrating for the timely implementation of these projects, as well as the vibrant language use demonstrated by the constitution project, give us hope for the long-term survival of Paiute speaking among the San Juan Paiutes.

Notes

The orthography used here is one developed for Kaibab Paiute by Pamela Bunte and the late Kaibab Paiute elder Lucille Jake. It has been used for educational and other purposes by members of the Paiute Indian Tribe of Utah, by Kaibab, and by the San Juan. Most characters have their IPA values. The following are exceptions or are otherwise worthy of special mention. The apostrophe ['] is the glottal stop. The letter [x] stands for a (usually) voiceless velar fricative; [y] is the glide, as in English; and [r] is a short apical trill or flap. The digraph [ng] stands for a velar nasal, as in English *sing* with no hard *g*; before [k], however, the velar nasal is written simply as [n]. The digraphs [ts, ch, sh] are pronounced as in English; [ʉ] is a high back unrounded vowel; and [ø], a sound that in Southern Ute and San Juan Paiute replaces Kaibab and other Southern Paiute open *o*, is a mid-front rounded vowel often pronounced with noticeable retroflex approximate *r* coloring. A small circle written under a vowel [u̥] means that the vowel is voiceless or whispered.

1. This chapter was completed in July 1996. Due to a number of unforeseen factors, the tribe was not able to implement immediately this ambitious plan. However, the tribe is presently pursuing funding to implement aspects of this plan.
2. Johnny Lehi was elected president of the San Juan Paiute Tribe in 1999.
3. The San Juan Southern Paiute Tribe ratified the constitution in August of 1996 in a tribal election.
4. It is also interesting that some traditional terms are not used: niavihuupara'api 'meeting of chiefs/tribal elders.'
5. *Tangw'a* 'man' is frequently compounded onto many of the San Juan political terms. This could reflect an earlier traditional gender hierarchy or perhaps just be San Juan Paiutes' recognition of such a hierarchy in the United States and in other tribes. The people of contemporary San Juan are extremely gender egalitarian. San Juan women have had a long-standing ability to participate in tribal political life, and from 1969 to 1999 the traditional position of spokesperson and later the present position of president were held by women. Such terminology is clearly not meant literally when used. Its somewhat ambiguous status is attested, however, by its use in joking contexts—as when Evelyn James, the former tribal president (and now the vice president), referred to herself as a man.
6. At the level of sentence structure in Paiute, embedded or subordinated clauses do of course represent a minimal form of hierarchical organization. Even here, however, Paiute grammar does not make fine distinctions of logical versus temporal relations between clauses that English readily makes with *because, when,* and so on (cf. Bunte 1986).

References

Bunte, Pamela. 1986. Subordinate clauses in Southern Paiute. *International Journal of American Linguistics* 52, no. 3: 275–300.

Bunte, Pamela, and Robert Franklin. 1987. *From the sands to the mountain: Change and persistence in a Southern Paiute Community*. Lincoln: University of Nebraska Press.

————. 1992. You can't get there from here: Taking Southern Paiute testimony as intercultural communication. *Anthropological Linguistics* 34 (vols. 1–4 combined; published in 1994).

Hinton, Leanne. 1994. Preserving the future: A progress report on the Master-Apprentice Language Learning Program. *News from Native California* 8, no. 3: 14–20.

Sapir, Edward. 1930. Texts of the Kaibab Paiutes and Uintah Utes. *Proceedings, American Academy of Arts and Sciences* 65, no. 2: 297–536.

PART VII

MEDIA AND TECHNOLOGY

21

Audio-Video Documentation

LEANNE HINTON

Department of Linguistics
University of California at Berkeley
Berkeley, California

In our increasingly technological world, the use of audio-video documentation in language teaching and language learning is more and more popular, and also quite fundable.

AUDIO-VIDEO DOCUMENTATION

Documentation is very important for declining languages, for there may come a day when there are no native speakers left, and documentation will be the only way to learn a language. Many people today have no speakers left for their language, and depend greatly on documentation (see Part IX, "Sleeping Languages"). Any community whose language is endangered should develop a program of language documentation, either with the assistance of linguists or on its own.

Paper documentation is still the most long-lasting and reliable form in which information can be preserved. This is because tapes and compact discs deteriorate over time faster than paper does, and because with the rapid changes in technology, recordings and especially computerized documentation may, unless cared for and updated to new formats over time, end up lost because the computers that held the information have become obsolete. However, paper documentation lacks the actual sound of the language, especially intonation, and the small phonetic details that even phonetic alphabets cannot really record. Also, paper documentation of a language usually lacks information on facial expressions and gestures, and rarely records what a real conversation is like. Furthermore, if a community does not have a writing system for its language and does not have access to a linguist who could write the language, the community people would not be able to do a good job of writing the language down. For these reasons, a community seeking to document the language might decide to devote much of their work to audio and video recordings.

One of the most useful and quickest ways to do good documentation is simply to videotape speakers in a large number of situations—having conversations with each other, telling stories, talking about various topics, singing, doing traditional arts, and so on. To be useful to posterity, these tapes must also be translated. This is much more time consuming and difficult than the videotaping itself. The easiest way to do the translation is to play the tape sentence by sentence and have a speaker orally translate each segment into English while tape recording the translation. One problem that has plagued past documenters is that if the translation is on a different tape or in a different medium than the original document, the two objects tend to get separated from each other over time. With sufficient technical expertise, it is possible to transcribe the translation as subtitles on the tape. But probably before the detailed translation takes place, it would be a good idea to ask the speaker or another bilingual person present at the session to do a rough translation of what he or she recollects was said. That rough translation can be on the same tape as the original document.

Families sometimes do audiotape or videotape documentation of their elders reminiscing. School programs often tape elders that come in to tell stories or discuss topics. Increasingly, communities apply for grants that allow them to document traditional language, culture, and history. Since the main purpose of these documents is to preserve this information for the future, one important question is how to preserve them and keep them accessible for decades to come. There are many woeful tales of families who made tapes of the elders only to have them recorded over by a teenager trying to copy a song off the radio, or who come upon the tape

265

years later only to find it covered with dust and breaking up.

The first stage of preservation is to label the tape, an easy task that is too often overlooked. The name of the person being recorded and the date should be on the tape, and there should be as good an index and description accompanying the tape as possible. Secondly, if possible, a backup copy should be made that will be stored elsewhere. Thirdly, the tape needs to be well stored, not in a metal cabinet (which could demagnetize the tape), but in wood or plastic, in a space that is dry, cool, and dust free.

For long-term preservation of tapes, a stable archive is needed. The archive could be set up in an existing facility in the community, such as a library or local government office. But the security and longevity of the facility housing the archive need to be considered. If there is no place secure in the community, it might be best to set up an agreement with a university or museum to house the originals of the tapes there.

The documentation that exists now of languages with no speakers, and the dictionaries, grammars, and texts (if they are well done) that have been published for endangered languages even when they have speakers, are viewed with great appreciation by communities today. Anyone who now documents an endangered language will also be thanked by future generations. Documentation does not "save" a language in the same sense that revitalization does, but it should be seen as an essential part of any language revitalization program.

COMPUTER TECHNOLOGY

Should You Include Computer Technology in Your Language Revitalization Plans?

With computer technology being so big a part of modern culture, and so new and exciting, people often think that using the computer might be the ultimate solution to language revitalization. However, it is not so easy as that, and it may well be that the computer should not play a big role in a particular program. One has to ask questions as one plans, such as: Will the particular group being served in a revitalization program have access to computers? Is there enough computer expertise in the community to maintain the computers and upgrade the hardware and software regularly and to migrate programs to newer systems as needed? Do the language revitalization goals of the community fit in with computer technology? Are the resources there that are needed to make programs or other software products that will be sufficient to achieve the language revitalization goals of the community? Will the fact that computer technology is nontraditional and reduces human interaction be problematic? It must certainly be kept in mind that any computer project should only be one component of your language revitalization plans, not the whole plan.

Below I will list some of the uses and advantages of computer technology in language revitalization, and also some of the problems and pitfalls.

Uses Of Computer Technology

Development of Materials and Self-Published Books

The simplest use of a computer is to use it for word processing. Word processing is now just about as basic a skill as typing, and most people know how to do it by the time they graduate from high school. (In fact, few young people would be able to use a typewriter nowadays, although they can almost all use a computer.) Desktop publishing may be a little more complicated, but there are many programs available that allow people to learn rather easily how to do books, with illustrations included. Computers make it possible to make attractive, professional-looking books and materials that can be used in language teaching and revitalization programs. (See St. Claire et al. 1999 for a practical guide to self-publishing.)

Online Dictionaries, Grammars, and Other Important Language References

Online dictionaries and other references have a number of advantages over printed dictionaries. As Mizuki and Moll (1999) say with regard to their Tohono O'odham online dictionary project,

> There are several ways that the out-of-print Mathiot dictionary could be made available, and there are many advantages to making the dictionary accessible online. In that format, it has the widest potential availability because people can use it without having to buy it. In addition, an online dictionary allows richer searches than a printed dictionary, which is useful for language learners and language researchers. Computerization of the information in the dictionary also allows for easy conversion from Tohono O'odham to English entries to English to Tohono O'odham entries. In addition, an online dictionary of the Tohono O'odham language provides a higher profile for the Tohono O'odham Nation. (114)

Multimedia Curriculum for Language Pedagogy

In universities and schools around the world, computer-aided language pedagogy is becoming increasingly popular. Computer-based language learning has many advantages. For one thing, if there is a good guided program, strongly motivated individuals can use it to learn the language themselves, without need of teacher or classroom. Computerized language-teaching programs also have frequent tests with immediate feedback that allows a student to progress at his or her own pace and sends the student back to review the appropriate section based on errors the student might make. Perhaps the most important consideration is that sometimes, in cases where there are no more native speakers of a language available to teach, if there are good recordings of speakers and good documentation of various sorts, those resources can be used to develop multimedia curricula, thus allowing a program to continue to use the contributions of the last speakers.

Networking

E-mail and online newsgroups can increase the ability to find people and communicate easily with people who are far away. People working on language maintenance and revitalization for their language may be able to communicate readily with others—for example, both the Maidus and the Karuks have e-mail groups on language that link local language activists and linguists who have worked on those languages, as well as Maidu and Karuk individuals who do not live in the community. Larger groups include the Endangered Languages List. Large spread-out groups like the Navajos can also benefit from online communications.

There is a large and growing number of Web sites of interest for endangered languages and language revitalization. A few of these are described below.

(1) The Society for the Study of the Indigenous Languages of the Americas (SSILA) has a fine Web site at <http://trc2.ucdavis.edu/ssila/default.asp>, with a useful online catalog of language learning materials available for North American Indian languages, an address list of linguists working on Native American languages (with a useful listing by language), and links to other Web sites of interest.

(2) The Native American languages Web site at <http://www.mcn.net/~wleman/langlinks.htm> also has a fine list of publications and materials on specific Native American languages. There are also Web sites on endangered languages all over the world.

(3) The Summer Institute of Linguistics Web site at <http://www.sil.org/> has lists of its extensive publications and available software for language work, and an online version of the *Ethnologue,* a catalog of over 6,700 languages spoken around the world, with basic data about their location and number of speakers.

(4) SILC (Stabilizing Indigenous Languages Conference) has all its conference proceedings online at <http://jan.ucc.nau.edu/~jar/TIL.html>, along with many other kinds of useful information.

(5) James Crawford's Language Policy Web Site and Emporium at <http://ourworld.compuserve.com/homepages/JWCRAWFORD/home.htm> has up-to-date information on policy and legislation about language, including bilingual education, English-only legislation, the Native American Languages Act, and so on.

(6) The National Council for Bilingual Education Web site at <http://www.ncbe.gwu.edu/> has hundreds of publications available for downloading, thousands of references, and constant updates on language research and policy.

(7) The Foundation for Endangered Languages maintains a Web site at <http://www.bris.ac.uk/Depts/Philosophy/CTLL/FEL/> that includes online back copies of its excellent newsletter for downloading.

(8) The International Clearing House for Endangered Languages Web site at <http://www.tooyoo.L.u-tokyo.ac.jp/ichel.html#Redbook> has many links to information on the endangered languages of the world and to papers and conference proceedings on endangered languages.

There are lots more—just do a Web search on "endangered languages," and you will find an enormous number of relevant sites.

Documentation

There is no doubt that the computer is so useful a tool in storing and organizing linguistic documentation of languages that it has almost completely replaced the old "shoebox" of alphabetized material that used to be the linguist's main form of organization. Database programs allow us to find material and sort it according to various parameters. Programs such as Filemaker Pro or Panorama, or the Summer Institute of Linguistics' Shoebox, all have many features that make linguistic organization and analysis of data much easier.

Problems and Pitfalls

General

Some of the negative aspects of the use of new technologies were pointed out at a recent talk by Nick Ostler (1999), who listed them as follows:

(1) Antitraditional, deskilling effects

   (a) Loss of memory, loss of oral traditions as the computer takes over some of their functions
   (b) Loss of traditional occasions
   (c) The fact that computers are a novelty particularly appealing to the young, which can act to make them lose touch with their roots and minimize interactions with the elders, who have much more information about the language and culture than the computer does.

(2) Expense of new equipment and methods

   (a) High initial cost per head
   (b) Rapid change of technology requires frequent upgrade, which is a continuous financial and time drain
   (c) Small communities may not have the resources needed to keep up with high per capita costs.

To sum up, computers and computer programs and CD-ROMs are expensive and antitraditional. Learning language by computer does not teach you much about natural interactive communication between human beings. Related to this is the fact that the computer can do little to help someone learn how to communicate within the context of traditional cultural practices. An easy pitfall is for a language program to get a grant to buy computers and hire a consultant to make some CD-ROMs or programs for the language—and then be left without the money or expertise to upgrade or make repairs or transfer the program or CD-ROM to the next stage of technology. Within 10 years or so, the computers are obsolete and unrepairable, and it is likely that the program cannot be run on whatever new computers are available anyway. So if the community cannot afford its own computer experts to keep things running smoothly, it may not be worthwhile to do this kind of project in the first place.

Online Dictionaries and Other Resources

While it is true that one does not have to buy the dictionary if it is on the Web, buying a dictionary is cheaper than buying a computer. Many people involved in language revitalization do not have computers. A small indigenous community may not be a high-tech place. There may be computers in the administrative centers or schools, but not in people's homes. While a school program may get a lot out of online resources, the community as a whole may nevertheless not be able to access these resources.

Multimedia Curriculum for Language Pedagogy

Computer-based curricula are usually based on written language rather than spoken; voice is possible, but generally as backup for the written version, where one can click on a word and hear it pronounced. Sometimes the computer has a built-in voice that will pronounce what you write; but these are based on English pronunciation (or some other major language), so they mispronounce the words of other languages horribly and cannot make sounds that are not in English. In order to get a similar program that would get the pronunciation of one's own language right, one would have to learn the complexities of sound synthesis or hire a consultant.

Making good multimedia curricula is very labor intensive and time consuming. As Parks et al. (1999) write about an ongoing Arikara project:

> During 1996, the first year of our multimedia language lesson project, we hoped to create a set of lessons that would serve a one-semester course. Those intentions, however, proved unrealistic. There was no model that we could follow for the multimedia lessons, and there was no software program that would easily enable us to create them. In other words, we had to develop our own model, utilizing a new software program and adapting it to our needs. The results of that first year of development were modest: two prototype units. On the surface, those units did not demonstrate much in quantity, but in reality they embodied prodigious research and development by a team of individuals with various computing, educational, and linguistic skills. The White Shield School Board provided additional funding during 1997, and with that support we have been able to complete an elaborate set of 16 lessons. (62)

Thus, making a useful quantity of good multimedia curricula is a very long-term project, not something that can be done quickly. As more models like the Arikara project become available, developing multimedia curricula for endangered languages may become a little easier, but it is still something that one must expect to take years.

Networking

Some newsgroups are active and productive, and some are not. Without an actual project that people might be working on together, small groups tend to become inactive. For the larger newsgroups, flaming and other intimidating verbal behavior can ruin what could have been a nice network. One of the positive points of computer technology, as pointed out earlier, is that people all over can have access to online materials and communications. However, for some communities, this can be a negative, given that some groups do not want outsiders to have access to local language data and language materials.

Documentation

One problem with computerizing linguistic materials is the problem of special characters. Creating special fonts to represent the characters in a particular language is possible but again demands computer expertise which either must be present in the community or else must be obtained through a hired consultant. Sometime in the next decade, a new character set called UNICODE, which represents most of the writing systems in the world (including linguistic symbols), will hopefully become the standard set on computers, in which case most of the special character problems will be over—but there will still be some missing, from community-designed alphabets with unusual characters. (For example, the Havasupai letter *t* with an extra cross on it will probably not be in UNICODE.)

So for now, and perhaps for the future too, special font design may be a necessity for computer documentation of indigenous languages. And this means that every computer involved in the storage or production of data for a particular language has to have that font on it—not hard to accomplish, but sometimes a nuisance. And given that IBM-style and Apple-style computers are so different from each other, if both types of computers are going to make use of the same characters, two separate fonts have to be made, one for each computer.

Sometimes, if a language project involves the use of many special symbols and the online results are expected to be distributed to a widespread audience, substitute symbols are used. The basic character set on computers today is called ASCII, and so one can substitute ASCII characters for the special symbols. For example, the schwa (upside-down *e*) could be written as "@," and the glottal stop as "?" or "7." See the next section below for an example of a project like this. Substitute ASCII symbols have the advantage of being readable on all computers but are of course annoying to read until one is used to it, and impossible to read if there is not a key to go with it.

Some Examples of Language Projects Involving Computer Technology

Many of the computer and multimedia projects that we are aware of are either initiated by linguists or involve linguists working together with community people. Thus these projects have the dual purpose of serving research needs and community needs.

The Tohono O'odham Online Dictionary

Mizuki and Moll (1999) write about a project to put an out-of-print dictionary of Tohono O'odham (Mathiot 1973) online. It is in progress, currently located on the Web at <http://w3.arizona.edu/~ling/mh/lmmm/to.html>:

> Process: The main parts of the process of putting an out-of-print dictionary online are gaining permission of copyright holder, scanning the text, editing the text, and creating the online dictionary (114–15).

The online dictionary is bilingual and designed so that if you enter a word in English, it will give the corresponding word(s) in Tohono O'odham, or if you enter a word in Tohono O'odham, it will give corresponding word(s) in English. There is also grammatical information for the Tohono O'odham entries, and there are example sentences in both languages. Searches can also be made by part of a word rather than a whole word. When relevant, there are links that allow you to go straight to related pages on culture, and so on.

Originally the plan was for the dictionary to be used by researchers and college students. The Tohono O'odham community has little computer accessibility. However, Ofelia Zepeda (personal communication, 1999) thinks that once it is online, it can be taken advantage of by schools and members of the overall population and could become a useful tool to the community.

The American Indian Studies Research Institute

Hooper and Flavin (in Parks et al. 1999, 67–72) write about the American Indian Studies Research Institute (AISRI) at Indiana University, which is engaged in "projects to document several Native American languages and to work with Native Communities in developing language-teaching materials." Some 20 people are employed in this project, which involves the following steps: (1) collecting language data from speakers of Arikara, Skiri and South Band Pawnee, Assiniboine, and Yanktonai Dakota. The proj-

ect includes both data collected prior to this project and more recent oral and written texts, as well as elicited data. Newly collected material is recorded on digital audiotape (DAT), and field recordings are copied onto DAT, with copies also preserved on CD-ROM; (2) both the oral and written data are entered on computer. The sound data from the DAT recordings is entered using Sonic Foundry's SoundForge. The written data are entered into a relational database designed by Microsoft's Visual FoxPro, where each word has an English translation and associated grammatical information, phrasal examples, and other information, along with the name of the associated sound file. This database can be used in various ways, including various search functions and printing possibilities. For example, dictionaries can be printed out from the database in various possible formats. AISRI is also developing software to produce interlinear texts as part of its efforts to process written and oral texts.

This online database can be used in various ways for both research and the development of materials for language preservation and language teaching purposes. Kushner (in Parks et al. 1999, 73–81) describes the use of the database in developing Arikara multimedia language lessons for use in the White Shield School in North Dakota, on the Fort Berthold Reservation. Arikara is spoken by fewer than 10 elders, so it is difficult to impossible to have teachers in the school who actually know the language. The use of multimedia language lessons is a strategy for overcoming this problem. The lessons follow a grammatical approach to instruction: "The linguistic segments are: Written and Spoken sounds, Vocabulary, Conversation, Grammar, and Sentence Patterns. In addition, each lesson has an Arikara Culture segment that describes various aspects of Arikara history, culture, and society. The lessons are fully interactive, employing auditory, visual, and kinesthetic features. Pictures of people, places, items, and cultural artifacts are incorporated into the lessons, as are music and video" (75).

While these lessons are not in themselves sufficient to produce fluent speakers, as immersion methods are potentially capable of doing, Kushner reminds us that immersion is not a viable alternative for many indigenous languages because of the lack of native speakers and environments where the native language is spoken. For languages with good documentation but few or no speakers, multimedia curricula have great potential as a language teaching tool.

The John P. Harrington Electronic Database Project

John P. Harrington is famous in California as the most prolific fieldworker and recorder of Native American languages who ever lived. A famous eccentric who only rarely published, he worked throughout the first half of the 20th century, passionately searching out the last fluent speakers of

California languages and writing down linguistic and ethnographic information on hundreds of thousands of pages. He was an excellent phonetician, of whom the anthropologist A. L. Kroeber once said, "perhaps because he is a young man, he . . . has shown a riotous inclination to indulge in the expressions of fine shades of sounds in the symbols used for them" (Golla 1984, 76). His insistence on extreme detail is now much appreciated, because much of his work was done before the existence of good sound recording, and his phonetic transcription is the closest we can get to knowing the sounds of these languages. He also took thousands of photographs and in later years recorded hundreds of hours of language on aluminum disks, which are now in the process of being transferred to modern sound technology by the Smithsonian Institution. (More on Harrington's life and work can be found in Hinton 1993.)

The Smithsonian, for which Harrington worked, spent years organizing his materials, and most of Harrington's field notes are now available on microfilm. There are 500 reels altogether, each reel holding about 1,000 pages of field notes. Academics and native scholars alike study these notes, and there are many decades' worth of study left to do. For languages which now have no living speakers, Harrington's materials are especially valuable, and a number of native communities and native scholars have lately been collecting the materials and working with them.

Using microfilms of field notes to study a language is inconvenient and difficult. Before the linguistic data can be fully useful or analyzable, it must be transcribed into some other medium, and the computer is of course the ideal medium. The first hurdle to be passed before it can be transferred is Harrington's multitude of special symbols and diacritical marks, many of which are unique to him. The difficulty of such a transfer and the solutions are described above in the section called "Problems and Pitfalls." By using ASCII symbols or sequences, the material can be easily transferred to any computer. When the original characters (if a font can be made available for them) are needed for publication or other needs, a find-and-replace operation can be used to replace the ASCII sequences with the appropriate symbols.

Martha Macri of the University of California, Davis, is heading a project with Victor Golla, Helen McCarthy, and Georgie Waugh to code Harrington's field notes into a flat database program (using Panorama, but any flat database program will do) in order to make them available to tribes, scholars, and other interested individuals. It is a grueling project, one that involves many student employees working over a number of years. So far, one reel of Ajachemem (Juaneño) and two reels of Tongva (Luiseño) have been entered—only 497 reels to go! As the notes are entered, academics and native scholars can obtain floppy-disk copies of the materials to use for their own needs, for research, or for materials development in language revitalization.

Macri and her colleagues are seeking funding to scan the entire corpus of Harrington's field notes so that in the future the coded database can be linked to a visual image of the whole page. Not only will this allow closer examination of the original form of whatever linguistic material might be under study, but it also allows access to drawings, maps, and other graphic material that Harrington included in his field notes. Language-specific CD-ROMs can be developed that have the coded material and the scanned graphic images; thus users have the versatility of the database—where, for example, one could look up all the words referring to plants, or words beginning with a particular sequence of sounds, and so on—along with the reliability and extra information that one gets by looking at the original field notes.

Already the materials for Ajachemem and Tongva have been used by the tribes for such purposes as genealogical searches and support for federal recognition. While the most relevant use of the materials to this book is linguistic, the Harrington electronic database will also be useful for studies in ethnogeography, ethnoscience, archaeoastronomy, ceremonies, and so on. It is also a major source for the study of Old California Spanish, the second language of most of the California Indians with whom Harrington worked, and which he documented quite thoroughly.

Use of the Computer in School: The Hualapai Interactive Technology Model

Schools are likely to have computer facilities and also instruction to students in computer use. One of the aims of American education now is to develop "computer literate" students. It is therefore quite natural for school programs involving indigenous languages to incorporate computer technology into the program. The Hualapai Bilingual Academic Excellence Program (HBAEP) in Peach Springs, Arizona, is an excellent model of combining Hualapai cultural and language studies with high technology (Benally, ms.).

Bilingual education is aimed at supporting the mother tongue in school and teaching subjects in the mother tongue while at the same time teaching English (and other subjects in English). While there are different goals for bilingual education depending on who you talk to, the goal for most indigenous bilingual education programs is to maintain the local language and to educate children to become fully balanced bilinguals. Thus in bilingual education, expanding the mother tongue to develop literacy and the ability to talk and think about classroom subjects, and to combine school skills with traditional knowledge and values, are all important objectives. The HBAEP rejects the assumption that modern technology and traditional learning cannot be combined. The Peach Springs Elementary School has two computer labs, and each classroom has two to five computers, as do the library and offices. The computers are all networked together so that students can link up to the central computer, where they can retrieve, enter, or store information and access the library's online catalog, online encyclopedias, and a wealth of programs and information. Students receive instruction in computer use through Computer Assisted Instruction (CAI) and Computer Managed Instruction (CMI). Teachers themselves, of course, keep lesson plans on the computer and can develop materials on them, as well as receive immediate information on school activities and other announcements. Professional-quality materials have been developed by HBAEP both in English and Hualapai. As Benally (n.d.) writes,

> An added bonus to the use of computers is its inclusion of Hualapai language. Students don't have to limit their computer proficiency to using English language only. The HBAEP includes activities that would allow students to input information acquired through interviews into the computer. This information can be in the Hualapai language. The use of this further reinforces the idea that tribal values and language are compatible to high technology. An individual does not need to give up either for the other.

Various programs and CD-ROMs have been developed and continue to be developed today, in such subjects as Hualapai geology, geography, ethnobotany, and so on.

FURTHER RESOURCES

Many new ideas and models for computer-aided language instruction and documentation will have become available between the time this chapter is written and the time it is published. One promising approach to instructional software is Maxauthor, software created at the University of Arizona with an emphasis on its potential use for the teaching of indigenous languages. Maxauthor can be used to create multimedia courseware for language materials in virtually any language, including video and audio material as well as written material and graphics (Senarslan 1999). As time

goes by, no doubt other such software will become available. For documentation, the Summer Institute of Linguistics has put out excellent software such as Shoebox, which allows the entry of all kinds of linguistic material including full texts with interlinear translations.

References

Benally, A. N.d. Hualapai Bilingual Academic Excellence Program: Parent training manual. Tempe, Ariz., Dzilijiin Consultants. Unpublished manuscript.

Golla, Victor. 1984. *The Sapir-Kroeber Correspondence.* Survey of California and Other Indian Languages, Report 6. Berkeley: University of California at Berkeley.

Hinton, Leanne. 1993. The house is afire! John Peabody Harrington—Then and now. *News from Native California,* vol. 7, no. 1, pp. 4–9.

Mathiot, Madeleine. 1973. *A dictionary of Papago usage.* Bloomington: Indiana University Press.

Mizuki, Miyashita, and Laura A. Moll. 1999. Enhancing language material availability using computers. In *Revitalizing indigenous languages,* ed. Jon Reyhner et al., 113–16. Flagstaff: Northern Arizona University, Center for Excellence in Education.

Ostler, Nicholas. June 4, 1999. New technologies for talking: Lifeline or noose? Talk at the Stabilizing Indigenous Languages Conference, Tucson, Ariz.

Parks, Douglas R., Julia Kushner, Wallace Hooper, Francis Flavin, Delilah Yellow Bird, and Selena Ditmar. 1999. Documenting and maintaining Native American languages for the 21st century: The Indiana University model. In *Revitalizing indigenous languages,* ed. Jon Reyhner et al., 59–83. Flagstaff: Northern Arizona University, Center for Excellence in Education.

Reyhner, Jon, Gina Cantoni, Robert N. St. Clair, and Evangeline Parsons Yazzie, eds. 1999. *Revitalizing indigenous languages.* Flagstaff: Northern Arizona University, Center for Excellence in Education.

Senarslan, Onur, June 4, 1999. Computer aided language instruction in the indigenous languages. Talk at the Stabilizing Indigenous Languages Conference, Tucson, Ariz.

St. Claire, Robert N., John Busch, and B. Joanne Webb. 1999. Self-publishing indigenous language materials. In *Revitalizing indigenous languages,* ed. Jon Reyhner et al., 129–37. Flagstaff: Northern Arizona University, Center for Excellence in Education.

Australian Languages

KEN HALE

Department of Linguistics and Philosophy
Massachusetts Institute of Technology
Cambridge, Massachusetts

The Australian languages which figure in this chapter belong to the great Pama-Nyungan linguistic group, whose member languages are spoken over seven-eighths of Australia, including the western islands of Torres Strait, where Kala Lagaw Ya and its variants are found, throughout Cape York Peninsula and the remainder of eastern Australia (excepting Tasmania), and all of central and western Australia south of an imaginary line extending roughly from the bottom of the Gulf of Carpentaria west to the Australian northwest coast. The region to the north of that line, with certain exceptions, is the domain of the diverse Non-Pama-Nyungan language families. These northern families are distributed over most of Arnhem Land, the Barkly Table Lands, the Daly River area, and the Kimberly region of western Australia. And it has been suggested that the languages of the Wellesley Islands and adjacent mainland are also Non-Pama-Nyungan, including Lardil of Mornington Island and its close relatives, discussed in Chapter 2.

The name Pama-Nyungan is composed of the nouns meaning "person" in the extreme northeast and the extreme southwest, respectively. The genetic reality of this large construct has been called into question (e.g., in Dixon 1980), but more than 30 years of careful and detailed work by the pioneer Australian comparativist Geoffrey N. O'Grady (whose results are represented in part in O'Grady and Tryon 1990) have resulted in a body of evidence which makes it very difficult to deny family status for Pama-Nyungan, in contrast to the more distant and highly diverse Non-Pama-Nyungan families related at something like the phylum level.

Given a random pair of Pama-Nyungan languages, one can generally see that they are related, quickly and without great difficulty. The Western Torres Strait language and the geographically distant Warlpiri of central Australia readily betray their relatedness. Within a matter of seconds, a cursory glance at the material appearing in a short paper on Kala Lagaw Ya (Bani and Klokeid 1976) yielded the following two cognate sets, for example:

Warlpiri	Kala Lagaw Ya	
ngaju	*ngath*	'I'
paji-	*path-*	'cut, chop'

These illustrate the recurrent Pama-Nyungan sound correspondence in which the palatal sound /j/ (like English "j") corresponds to the interdental stop /th/ (like "dth" in English "width"). One must look harder to find correspondences of this type between disparate Non-Pama-Nyungan languages or between one of these and a Pama-Nyungan language. They are there, to be sure, but they are less plentiful and harder to see.

Such comparisons as the ones just cited for Warlpiri and Kala Lagaw Ya are commonplace in Pama-Nyungan, even at great distances. These two languages are separated geographically by as many as 40 tribal territories, each associated with a recognizably distinct linguistic tradition and arrayed along a trajectory from Central Australia northeastward and then north along the Gulf Coast of Cape York Peninsula up to Torres Strait. By contrast with the situation represented by these languages, in the linguistically diverse non-Pama-Nyungan area, even geographically contiguous languages will often fail to present any convincing cognate forms at all on casual inspection and may in some cases give evidence of their relatedness only after being subjected to painstaking study.

Like the overwhelming majority of Pama-Nyungan languages, Warlpiri and Kala Lagaw Ya are suffixing in their morphological structure, and they have a system of grammatical case marking which conforms to the so-called "ergative" pattern. That is to say, the subject of a transitive verb is marked for ergative case by means of a suffix (-ERG), in contrast to the other direct arguments of a verb, that is, the intransitive subject and the transitive object, which are left unmarked:

Warlpiri:
(1) *Kurdu-ngku*   *marlu*   *nyangu.*
    child-ERG   kangaroo   saw
    'The child saw the kangaroo'.
(2) *Kurdu*   *wantija.*
    child   fell
    'The child fell'.

Kala Lagaw Ya (from Bani and Klokeid 1976):
(1) *Moegikazi-n*   *dhangal*   *imanu.*
    child-ERG   dugong   saw
    'The child saw the dugong'.
(2) *Moegikaazi*   *pudhima.*
    child   fell
    'The child fell'.

While the individual morphemes differ, of course, the ergative pattern of case marking is identical in these two languages, a situation which is repeated all over the enormous Pama-Nyungan language area, except for a small region on the northwest coast in which the original ergative languages of the area have developed an accusative case system, with the transitive object, rather than the subject, being the marked argument, and bearing the accusative case suffix.

Warlpiri has the distinction of being one of the few Australian languages having well over 1,000 speakers of Warlpiri heritage. So far as we know, all Warlpiris speak the language, and an almost equal number of non-Warlpiris speak the language as well. It is possible to take courses in Warlpiri at the Institute for Aboriginal Development in Alice Springs, and an impressive dictionary, the largest for any Australian language, is nearing completion under the leadership of Mary Laughren of the University of Queensland and her Warlpiri-speaking colleagues.

The Warlpiri community was one of the first to develop a bilingual education program in the period initiated by the election of the Whitlam Labour government of the early 1970s, a period of great promise in relation to Aboriginal rights, including linguistic rights. The Warlpiri program was first developed at Yuendumu (Baarda 1994). Yuendumu is the location of the Warlpiri Television Project briefly described in Chapter 22.

References

Baarda, Wendy. 1994. The impact of the bilingual program at Yuendumu, 1974–1993. In *Aboriginal languages in education,* ed. Deborah Hartman and John Henderson, 204–13. Alice Springs: IAD Press.

Bani, Ephraim, and Terry Klokeid. 1976. Ergative switching in Kala Lagau Langgus. In *Languages of Cape York: Papers submitted to the linguistic symposium, part B, held in conjunction with the Australian Institute of Aboriginal Studies biennial annual meeting, May, 1974,* ed. Peter Sutton, 269–83. Canberra: Australian Institute of Aboriginal Studies.

Dixon, R. M. W. 1980. *The languages of Australia.* Cambridge and New York: Cambridge University Press.

O'Grady, G. N., and D. T. Tryon. 1990. *Studies in comparative Pama-Nyungan.* Pacific Linguistics Series C, 111. Canberra: Australian National University.

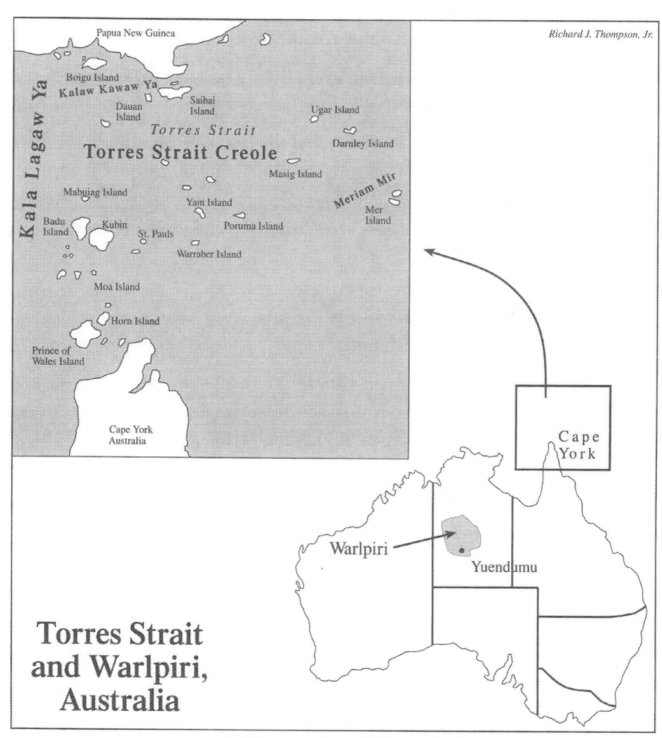

Papua New Guinea

Boigu Island
Kalaw Kawaw Ya

Dauan
Island

Saibai
Island

Ugar Island

Darnley Island

Torres Strait

Torres Strait Creole

Masig Island

Kala Lagaw Ya

Mabuiag Island

Yam Island

Meriam Mir

Mer
Island

Badu
Island

Kubin

St. Pauls

Poruma Island

Warraber Island

Moa Island

Horn Island

Prince of
Wales Island

Cape York
Australia

Cape
York

Warlpiri

Yuendumu

**Torres Strait
and Warlpiri,
Australia**

MAP 22.1   Torres Strait and Warlpiri, Australia

C H A P T E R

22

Strict Locality in Local Language Media
An Australian Example

KEN HALE

Department of Linguistics and Philosophy
Massachusetts Institute of Technology
Cambridge, Massachusetts

BROADCASTING

We are familiar with the thesis that television can be detrimental to local and endangered languages, where the medium is exclusively or largely in English or Spanish, say, and the local language is given little or no time in the programming. The allure of television implicates more than language, of course, but its power can have serious consequences for the continuation of the linguistic and intellectual heritage of a local community.

To be sure, abstractly speaking, both television and radio are, in and of themselves, neutral in this regard. Their effects, bad or good, depend on many contextual factors. And in principle there are good purposes to which these media can be put in language revitalization and maintenance.

Indigenous peoples in various parts of Australia were remarkably prescient in understanding the implications of the impending media onslaught well before advanced technology was in place to transmit an overwhelming deluge of English-laden image and sound into relatively isolated communities in which local languages still flourished. Recognizing the dangers inherent in this inevitable circumstance, they moved to mitigate it to whatever extent possible, by grabbing the mic and confronting the media on their own terms.

As elsewhere in the world, in Aboriginal Australia it is believed with good reason that television in particular "has imposed greater exposure to non-indigenous languages and, perhaps more importantly, has led to a reduction in more interactive pursuits which involved the traditional languages, such as story-telling, singing and dancing and simple campfire conversation" (McKay 1996, 101).

The rational response to this has been the establishment of local programming in diverse Aboriginal and Torres Strait Islander communities by taking advantage of the full range of broadcasting resources, including the Broadcasting for Remote Aboriginal Communities Scheme (BRACS), various regional broadcasting facilities, and both community and commercial broadcasting organizations. Broadcasting in this environment has two major functions, that of securing local control of at least a part of the programming to ensure appropriate cultural and social content and the involvement of people of significance in the communities, and that of providing an opportunity for the use of local languages in broadcasting.

Ironically, it is the very wealth of traditional languages which has hindered full exploitation of this potential. The experience of the Torres Strait Islander Media Association is indicative. Their broadcasts are in Torres Strait Creole, rather than the indigenous languages, for a number of reasons, including the fact that "the broadcast area covers more than one language," "the Creole itself has developed as a significant language of Torres Strait Islander identity over recent years" and would "reach and appeal to more people," and, unsurprisingly, "the level of funding available does not permit the employment of broadcast staff for each language group" (McKay 1996, 102).

By comparison with other parts of Australia, Torres Strait is on the face of it relatively uncomplicated as far as linguistic diversity is concerned. There are two indigenous languages. The Western Island language, called Kala Lagaw Ya (spoken in several regional varieties, including Mabuiag and Kalaw Kawaw Ya, among others), belongs to the large Australian language family known as Pama-Nyungan. The Eastern Island language (Meriam Mir) is of Papuan linguistic affiliation. But what is simple in the abstract is typically complex in reality. The dominant language of the region is the English-based Torres Strait Creole, whose origins are to be found in the Pacific Pidgin English brought to Torres

277

Strait in the mid-19th century by Pacific Islander and European immigrants involved in the commercial exploitation of marine resources such as bêche-de-mer, pearl shell, and trochus. By the end of the 19th century, Pacific Pidgin was no longer a pidgin for many people, being their first language, their *native* language, and thus an established Creole. Its spread to Torres Strait as a whole advanced rapidly in the first half of the twentieth century.

The Torres Strait Islander Media Association did not have a viable option of simply broadcasting in the two indigenous languages for various reasons. Among these are the fact that Torres Strait Creole is now an important element of pan-island consciousness, replacing the tradition of "separateness-in-contact" which once characterized relations between west and east in Torres Strait. Furthermore, Creole is a legitimate indigenous language, born as such on the Torres Strait Islands. An additional factor in the choice of broadcasting language is the circumstance that for many islanders, the indigenous languages are no longer their first languages.

The reasonable desire to serve the widest possible audience has a natural consequence on the linguistic choices of a broadcasting organization. This, combined with economic limitations, can, and usually does, have a marginalizing effect on local languages. Thus, Torres Strait Islander Media Association personnel recognize "not only the power of broadcasting to provide a vehicle for material in indigenous languages and to give status to indigenous languages, but also the power of broadcasting to provide a means for English and Creole to take the 'market share' away from indigenous languages, thus weakening them" (McKay 1996, 81).

In the Torres Strait case, at least, a language seen by Islanders as part of their heritage figures prominently in broadcasting. In other cases, however, the results of this tension have been more serious. The Central Australian Aboriginal Media Association, a pioneer in indigenous language broadcasting, "no longer broadcasts in languages to the extent it once did," and in the Aboriginal (Imparja) television area, "a high proportion of the programming is simply commercial television—in English," prompting one to ask "whether this situation—whether by design or by default—is not actually promoting a shift to English" (McKay 1996, 103).

The problems are not trivial, therefore, for a broadcast organization that seeks to represent the linguistic and cultural diversity of its audience. One response, of course, is to adhere to the principle of economy—that of reaching the largest audience at minimal cost. Australian Aboriginal and Torres Strait broadcasters generally do not accept this philosophy, though economic realities often force them to something amounting to this position in actual fact. Responses by broadcasters in a recent survey mentioned, "in particular, the difficulty of covering all the languages of their broadcast area because funding was not sufficient to employ broadcasters from each language. For many of them, broadcasting even a little in a restricted range of languages was better than only broadcasting in English" (McKay 1996, 102–3).

Thus, spot programming for individual languages is a partial solution to the problem. And the sharing of program material has been a solution to another problem, that is, the Aboriginal language diaspora—the existence of widely dispersed groups representing the same language, a common condition in contemporary Australia. For example, radio programs in Warlpiri and Arrernte produced by the Central Australian Aboriginal Media Association in Alice Springs are used by the broadcaster at Wirramanu (Balgo) in northern Western Australia (McKay 1996, 103).

But this system is fragile. In some instances, spot programming is done on a voluntary and occasional basis, as in the case of the Torres Strait broadcaster Jenny Enosa, who "uses her language (Kalaw Kawaw Ya) from time to time on her own initiative for important announcements," a circumstance much appreciated by her audience (McKay 1996, 80). This example illustrates in rather stark relief the very general condition of dependency in which indigenous languages find themselves in the realm of broadcast media. Minor changes in personnel or funding within a broadcasting organization can have rather drastic consequences for indigenous language programming, often in the direction of reducing it or eliminating it altogether.

However, fragile as this may be, it approaches the condition which could well, given contemporary realities, be optimal for Aboriginal and Torres Islander media development and use. This is the condition of "strict locality," in which media (including printed material, as well as radio and television) are designed and created for dissemination to a particular language audience for the purpose of promoting the use of the language involved and—within reason, of course—without regard to the size of the audience or the economics implicated. As examples of this mode of media creation, I briefly discuss the use of video in the Warlpiri community of Yuendumu, Central Australia (Michaels 1994, 98–124) and the use of newsletters and magazines containing material in Australian Aboriginal languages.

WARLPIRI TELEVISION

The story of Warlpiri media at Yuendumu is not a simple or fully positive one. It implicates old and familiar tensions originating in, among other things, the predictable official state interventions which have beset Aboriginal peoples during the past two centuries. The Warlpiri characteristics of stubbornness and commitment to autonomy and survival, characteristics shared by many embattled local language groups, are precisely those that could, in principle, foster an enduring autonomous local media structure.

Warlpiri media . . . is the product of a struggle between official and unofficial discourses that seem always stacked in the state's favor. This might suggest a discouraging future for Yuendumu Television. Given the government's present policy of promoting media centralization and homogenization, we would expect that Yuendumu will soon be overwhelmed by national media services, including "approved" regional broadcasters who serve the state's objectives of ethnicization, standardization, even Aboriginalization, at the expense of local language, representation, and autonomy. If this scenario is realized, then Yuendumu's community station seems likely to join the detritus of other development projects that litter the contemporary Aboriginal landscape.... We won't know that the experience of television for remote Aborigines could have been any different: for example, a networked cooperative of autonomous community stations resisting hegemony and homogenization. Instead, we expect Warlpiri TV to disappear as no more than a footnote to Australian media history, leaving unremarked its contribution to a public media and its capacity to articulate alternative—unofficial—Aboriginalities.

But something in Warlpiri reckoning confounds their instrumentalization and the grim prophecy this conveys. A similar logic predicted the disappearance of their people and culture generations ago, but proved false. A miraculous autonomy, and almost fierce stubbornness, delivers the Warlpiri from these overwhelming odds and assumes their survival, if not their eventual victory. (Michaels 1994, 101–2)

Warlpiri videotaping was begun in the early 1980s at Yuendumu, by a member of the Japanangka subsection who was responding to the impending arrival of satellite television, asserting that "we can fight fire with fire," in the tradition of the Warlukurlangu (Fire Dreaming) ritual, which now gives its name to the Yuendumu artists' association. Authority for videomaking at Yuendumu was soon transferred to a member of the Jupurrurla subsection, appropriately, since these subsections stand in the kirda-kurdungurlu patrimoiety relation which marks all Warlpiri ritual functions and, more abstractly, symbolizes the pervasive Warlpiri dialectic of the "unity of the opposites." From the very beginning, therefore, to its very core, television at Yuendumu has been a Warlpiri business through and through. And consistent with the Warlpiri character of the business, authority was eventually extended to all eight subsections through an appropriate sequence of training and collegial relationships orchestrated by Francis Jupurrurla Kelly.

If videomaking at Yuendumu is a Warlpiri business, it is a contemporary Warlpiri business, unconcerned with outsider notions of Aboriginal authenticity and the like.

In the case of Jupurrurla's art, the implicit question of authenticity becomes explicit: Jupurrurla, in Bob Marley T-shirt and Adidas runners, armed with his video portapack, resists identification as a savage updating some archaic technology to produce curiosities of primitive tradition for the jaded modern gaze. Jupurrurla is indisputably a sophisticated cultural broker who employs videotape and electronic technology to express and resolve political, theological, and aesthetic contradictions that arise in uniquely contemporary circumstances. (Michaels 1994, 104–5)

Jupurrurla produced a corpus of hundreds of hours of tape for the Warlpiri Media Association. It is not surprising that one of these would deal with the infamous Coniston Massacre, also called "the Killing Time," a notorious event in Warlpiri history. The incident took place in 1929 when a punitive raid—following the murder by Aborigines of a white trapper and dingo hunter—resulted in the slaughter, by police, of as many as 100 Warlpiri men, women, and chil-

dren. The actual death toll varies, but it was a staggering loss for the Warlpiri population of the time. Moreover, the raid wiped out a ritual gathering and the associated intellectual wealth—in the form of verse, design, and choreography—stored in the minds of the slain.

Jupurrurla's video representation of this incident bears no resemblance to what we would expect from Hollywood. It is rather the cinematic representation of an oral account, interested in content unadorned by special technique or fiction. Eric Michaels's report of its production and structure depicts quite well the Warlpiri mode of video production:

The ritual relations between participants were effectively translated by Jupurrurla into those of video production. Because the storyteller was a Japangardi, from the "one side," it was entirely appropriate that Jupurrurla, from the "other side," would be behind the camera. This modeled the in front/behind camera dichotomy after their Warlpiri equivalents. Kirda ("Boss") is on stage, Kurdungurlu ("helper/manager") is behind the scenes. This arrangement was followed throughout the first three scenes, while the fourth includes an innovative deviation from this practice.

Each virtually uninterrupted take was shot on the site where the events of the story being told by Japangardi occurred:

1. the site of Brook's murder;
2. that of his grave;
3. a waterhole where people were encamped for ceremony;
4. a cave in which an old Japanangka hid from police trackers.

In them, Japangardi is first seen from an extreme long shot, his figure appearing to emerge from the landscape. He walks toward the camera, and begins speaking when in medium-shot range.... The effect of these scenes conforms to a ceremonial convention in which certain ritual story-dances do not begin on the dancing ground proper, but are "brought in" from the bush at some distance. The effect is to express the contiguity of such stories and to invoke that corpus of all stories, the Dreaming. More specifically, the relations of stories to land and place are acknowledged by these conventions. Any story comes from a particular place, and travels from there to here, forging links that define the tracks over which both people and ceremonies travel. Jupurrurla models his electronic discourse on exactly such principles. (Michaels, 1994, 113)

The final scene is a taped interview in which Jupurrurla asks certain questions of detail and clarification.

There are no guns, no mounted police dashing around, no fiction as we usually think of it. The only "actor" is the narrator, Japangardi, and he is not an actual figure in the story, except by virtue of being in the same semi-moiety (Japanangka-Japangardi) as the primary Warlpiri protagonist. The video is not for the uninitiated. As Michaels notes:

Reviewing the tape, one is struck by the recurrent camera movement, the subtle shifts in focus and attention during the otherwise even, long pans across the landscape. The superficial conclusion is that we are seeing the effects of "naive" camera work; the preference for landscape is a preference for things that don't move, and are easily photographed: the shifts in focus and direction seem evidence of a simple lack of mechanical skills. Jupurrurla denies this. When asked, he provided a rationale suggesting a meaning in everything his camera does. The pans do not follow the movement of the eye, but movement of unseen characters—both of the Dreamtime and historical—which converge of this landscape: "This is where the police trackers came over the hill," "that is the direction the ancestors came in from. . . ." Shifts in focus and interruptions in panning pick out important places and things in the landscape, like a tree where spirits live or a flower with symbolic value. The camera adopts technical codes to serve a predetermined system of significance in this radically *Yapa* (Aboriginal) sense of mise-en-scène. (Michaels 1994, 114)

Warlpiri people know as much about the "pictures" (movies, the cinema) as almost anyone in the world. And they enjoy them. But there is nothing of the movies in Jupurrurla's Coniston Story, or in any other of his videos. The structure of his videos adheres to a strictly Warlpiri form.

A satellite earth station receiver was installed in August of 1987, introducing live ABC programming to Yuendumu. Jupurrurla began mixing local programming with the incoming signal. Warlpiri News and documentaries were broadcast at 6:30 PM. Tensions developed when Warlpiri News replaced a favorite program of one of the non-Warlpiri residents of Yuendumu and when Jupurrurla decided that "the service would shut off at 10:30 PM, so that kids could go to bed and be sure of getting off to school in the morning. No *Rock Arena*. No late movies," guaranteeing that there would much heated negotiating in the ensuing months (Michaels 1994, 123–24).

Meanwhile, Warlpiri people continued to be involved in their parallel industry of making Warlpiri television, ensuring a continued tradition of strict locality in the use of the media technology of which they had become competent masters.

NEWSLETTERS AND MAGAZINES

Although it is relatively unsung, the printed word is, in potential at least, the most faithful and stable representative of the principle of strict locality in the promotion of indigenous languages in communication. There are, to be sure, issues that arise around writing, and the question of whether or not a particular language should be written is a real one for many communities, leading in some cases to the decision not to use writing. Such decisions are typically well argued and based on fundamental principles of belief and historical experience. On the other hand, many local communities eagerly embrace writing and use it for a wide range of purposes—letters, news bulletins, announcements, signs, instruction sheets and manuals, magazines, books, and others.

The printed word is cheap and in most cases can pay for itself. And it can be tailored to honor the local language, or languages, in a fully appropriate manner.

Like many Australian Aboriginal communities that developed bilingual education programs in the mid-1970s and later, Yuendumu's Bilingual Resources Development Unit produces a magazine at the Yuendumu Community Education Center. The magazine is called *Junga Yimi* (The True Word). It conforms to the strict locality norm in being inexpensively produced and in publishing primarily contributions which come from members of the Yuendumu community (both Warlpiri and non-Warlpiri). It normally appears three times each year, and each issue (ranging in length from 15 to 40 pages) is photocopied and simply stapled together. In recent issues, color has appeared on the cover page, but not inside, which is entirely black-and-white, as earlier issues were in their entirety.

It must be said that *Junga Yimi* usually has more English in it than Warlpiri. But it always has pieces in Warlpiri covering topics of all kinds—community problems, sports, education, Yuendumu news, important events like a trip to Niger by a group of Warlpiri people, trips to the bush, celebrations and social ceremonies, training programs, and training needs, including the need for training in broadcasting. Some issues are devoted to a particular theme, such as, for example, *Junga Yimi* 1998, no. 3, the Warlpiri and English Literacy Edition, featuring interviews at Yuendumu conducted by Christine Nungarrayi Spencer, a graduate of the Yuendumu bilingual education program and later a student in the Advanced Vernacular and English Literacy Course at the Institute for Aboriginal Development in Alice Springs.

The local character of *Junga Yimi* is reflected in part by the fact that it is not read with complete comprehension by outsiders, even outsiders who speak Warlpiri. There is a good reason for this.

Linguistically, each volume of *Junga Yimi* is in effect a time capsule recording aspects of the evolution of modern Warlpiri usage in the contexts of Western education, law, and medicine, and so on. In 1974, at the beginning of Warlpiri bilingual education at Yuendumu, a certain amount of "language engineering" was required. There was in the early years much inconsistency in writing Warlpiri, for example. Comparing the inconsistent conventions of those years with the practices of Nungarrayi Spencer, one sees that some standardization has developed, in the use of hyphens and spaces to alleviate the forbidding appearance of the long words characteristic of Warlpiri, and in the punctuation employed to integrate unassimilated English borrowings into a written Warlpiri text. But these features have to do with the appearance of written Warlpiri and with readability, not with comprehension. Problems of comprehension, which go unnoticed by Yuendumu residents, derive from lexical and grammatical adjustments which have been made over the years. In many cases, even here, there is no problem of comprehension for the "returning Warlpiri." Thus, little difficulty is caused by Nungarrayi's relatively standardized use now of the verb *yirrarni* 'put' for 'write' and the full assimilation of English 'read' as the root element *riiti* in *riiti-mani* 'read'. The realm of quantification is another story, however.

In 1974, the major linguistic expression of quantificational notions in Warlpiri itself was largely by means of the nominal cardinality determiners *jinta* (singular, one), *jirrama* (dual, two), *marnkurrpa* or *wirrkardu* (paucal or lesser plural, three, several), and *panu* (major plural, many). This is not a "counting system," but it enables one to express an exact enumeration, through the universal principle of addition. In "formal" schooling, however, there is need for a counting system, an inventory of expressions including zero and a nonfinite set of cardinality expressions, each of which corresponds to an amount greater by just one (1) than one (and only one) other expression in the set. Efforts were made immediately to address this problem. The linguist engaged to help in starting the bilingual education program was told about a terminology for the playing cards used among Warlpiri stockmen. In consultation with Warlpiri teachers, it was decided that these terms, from ace through 10, could form the basis of a Warlpiri counting system. So, for example, the five was called *rdaka* 'hand', unsurprisingly; the seven was called *wirlki* 'hooked boomerang'; and the eight was called *milpa* 'eye(s)'. These were reasonable names of the shapes of the numbers, but there were two problems, the uninteresting one that they were unstable (in the Warlpiri tradition fostering multiple synonymy), and the interesting problem of actually developing a system of numerals. The first, more trivial problem will account for some failures in comprehension at any temporal remove—thus, a returning Warlpiri who learned *narntirnki* 'curled' for 'nine' in 1974 will in all probability not understand Nungarrayi's use of *kartaku* 'billycan' for the same concept in 1998. But this is commonplace in Warlpiri, where lexical items are regularly withdrawn from use to honor the taboo on the use of the personal name of a deceased, or any word resembling the name or incorporated in it—this, as well as in-law-respect vocabulary, accounts for the proliferation of synonyms (e.g., *yankirri, karlaya, wanyaparnta, pirilyingarnu*, etc., for 'emu'). It is expected that a returning community member will have to learn vocabulary replacements that have taken place in his or her absence, even where the absence is only a year or two.

The second issue, however, implicates a grammatical system. The new numerical terminology was derived from names, the names of playing cards. Inherent in this nomenclature was the possibility of a number system, but it was not a number system in origin, and it had to be "transformed" into a new grammatical category, one functioning both as determiners in noun phrases and as conventional names for numbers. It was necessary, of course, to be able to say things like 'two houses', 'eight horses', and so on. The indigenous determiners (singular, dual, and paucal, described above) can enter into this relation, of course, but the new terms for higher cardinalities really could not. They were names, not determiners. Warlpiri speakers quickly invented a way to do this, creating an ending *-pala* (ultimately from English *fellow*, or its Pidgin counterpart *-fella*), permitting the formation of expressions like *milpa-pala kirntangi-ki* 'for eight months' ('eye' + *-pala* month-Dative). This has now taken on a life of its own in Warlpiri, a fact exemplified in one of Nungarrayi's interviews when she asks: *Nyiya-pala kirntangikinpa yinyangkaju warrki-jarrija?* (How many months

have you worked there?). The formation *nyiya-pala* 'how many' ('what' + *-pala*) is entirely new in Warlpiri grammar, a perfection or filling out, so to speak, of the new quantifier system. The older system had a question word sometimes translated as 'how many', but it was not really a cardinality expression, being rather a discourse-dependent interrogative of the type represented by English 'which'. This is one of several developments in Warlpiri grammar chronicled to some extent by *Junga Yimi* since the initial years of Yuendumu bilingual education.

Like Warlpiri television, *Junga Yimi* is a part of the program to secure for Warlpiri people a "cultural future and a cultural past," to paraphrase the purpose articulated by the Yuendumu videomaker Francis Jupurrurla Kelly.

This holds quite generally for community news magazines. Some of these, like *Mikurrunya*, the newsletter of the Strelley Community School in western Australia's Pilbara region, now exercise students' English literacy skills as much as or more than their writing skills in the local languages, but all retain an indigenous-language component. In its July 1999 issue, in addition to a Nyangumarta crossword puzzle and some children's stories, *Mikurrunya* includes a Nyangumarta eulogy to the late radical organizer Donald W. McLeod, an early and renowned champion of the language and labor rights of the Aboriginal peoples of Western Australia. It is evident from this piece, and from the children's writing as well, that the literary form of Nyangumarta has, so to speak, settled down to a level of consistency and stylistic sophistication quite advanced over that which first emerged in 1960 in McCleod's camp near Roebourne, when the linguist Geoffrey N. O'Grady and the Nyangumarta linguist Monte Hale began to deal with the task of creating a written form of Nyangumarta.

Jupurrurla's purpose would be achieved in grand measure by the development of a written literature in Aboriginal languages, a possibility recognized in the 1988 Pitjantjatjara short story contest promoted by the Anangu Schools Resource Centre at Ernabella, South Australia, through the center's bilingual quarterly magazine *Kurparu* (Goddard 1994). The contest was open to all ages, and the 33 entries received represented five Pitjantjatjara-speaking communities. The panel of four judges was composed of acknowledged expert speakers of Pitjantjatjara, and their criteria were grammar and spelling, seriousness of intent, accuracy of content, and composition. The five prizewinning stories dealt with parental teaching of linguistic elements to babies, a widow, a devil woman, a spearing at Atarangu, and the technique of hunting euros in groups. The winning essays were published in the magazine *Kurparu*. One of the judges added a written Pitjantjatjara commentary on the entries as a whole, suggesting ways in which the unsuccessful writers could improve their writing style, by not changing the subject halfway through an account, by striving for clarity, or by periodically rereading what one has written for intelligibility and coherence. The first-place winner, an essay by Nyurpaya Kaikalu of Amata, compares parental language teaching practices (employing a kind of baby talk) with the phonics method for teaching literacy. It is a respectable piece of Pitjantjatjara literature, well worthy of the name and of an honored position in the Pitjantjatjara chapter of Francis Jupurrurla's global vision of a cultural future for Aboriginal peoples.

CONCLUDING REMARKS

While mass media can overwhelm a local language, effectively pushing it aside, the media notion in and of itself is neutral and potentially positive in relation to indigenous languages, particularly in conjunction with the principle of strict locality. Video and photocopying are now quite cheap, though nothing comes without a price. Stable production of quality materials requires trained personnel, equipment, space, and supplies—all resources for which there may be strong competition within an economically stressed commu-

nity. And independent factors may intervene to block or divert the trajectory of a local language program of media development, as, for example, the subsequent shift away from bilingual education to an "all English" teaching program in the Pitjantjatjara schools of the area where the essay contest just described was conducted. In the final analysis, setbacks like this, a permanent feature of Aboriginal and Torres Strait Islander life, have never really kept people from doing things they are determined to do.

References

Goddard, Cliff. 1994. The Pitjantjatjara story-writing contest. In *Aboriginal languages in education*, ed. Deborah Hartman and John Henderson pp. 316–323. Alice Springs: IAD Press.

McKay, Graham. 1996. *The land still speaks: Review of Aboriginal and Torres Strait Islander language maintenance and development needs and activities*. National Board of Employment, Education and Training, Commissioned Report No. 44. Canberra: Australian Government Publishing Service.

Michaels, Eric. 1994. *Bad Aboriginal art: Tradition, media, and technological horizons*. Minneapolis: University of Minnesota Press.

The Arapaho Language

KEN HALE

Department of Linguistics and Philosophy
Massachusetts Institute of Technology
Cambridge, Massachusetts

Arapaho is a member of the great Algonquian language family, whose members are distributed in Canada and the United States over a region which extends along a north-south axis for a considerable distance over the border separating the two countries, and along an east-west axis extending from far eastern points in the two countries westward to the region where the linguistically diverse northwest begins, in which languages of the Athabaskan, Salish, and Wakashan families, among others, are spoken.

Together with Blackfoot and Cheyenne, Arapaho is traditionally classified as a Plains Algonquian language. This is not a true subgroup linguistically, and today each of these three languages is thought to be coordinate with the individual members of the traditional Central Algonquian group (Cree, Menominee, Fox, Shawnee, and Ojibwa, among others) and with the Eastern Algonquian division as a whole (including Delaware, Wampanoag, Passamaquoddy-Maliseet, Abnaki, Micmac, and others).

There are two Arapaho language communities, the Northern, in the Wind River area of Wyoming, and the Southern, in Oklahoma. The linguistic differences between the two groups are minor (Salzmann 1965). The language represented in Stephen Greymorning's chapter (Chapter 23) is Northern Arapaho.

Arapaho occupies a special place in Algonquian linguistics because of the dramatic changes it has undergone, by comparison with the Proto-Algonquian which was reconstructed by Bloomfield (1946) on the basis of Central Algonquian. In the verb morphology, for example,

Arapaho has extended the use of a participle from the so-called conjunct order to affirmative main clauses. In Algonquian generally, the conjunct is used in certain kinds of subordinate clauses and in questions, while the independent indicative is used in main clauses. This change is shared by the Eastern Algonquian language Micmac, but it is otherwise an innovation in Arapaho. The most noteworthy innovations are in the phonology, however, resulting in such comparisons as the following, between the Arapaho and the Eastern Algonquian language Wampanoag (conjunct):

Arapaho	Wampanoag	
tóó'owún	*ta:kami:yan* (CNJ)	'you hit me'
nonóóhowó'	*na:(w)ak* (CNJ)	'I see him/her'
nonoohóbeθen	*na:wən(ā:n)* (CNJ)	'I see you'
nétʃ	*nəpi:*	'water'
héθ	*anəm*	'dog'
bétee	*məta:h*	'heart'
hinén	*nən*	'man'
hó'	*a:ki:*	'dirt (A), land (W)'
tʃeeb-	*pəm-*	'along' (perlative pre-verb)

Among other things, these examples show that Arapaho /tʃ/ corresponds to /p/ in Wampanoag (and other Algonquian); Arapaho /'/ corresponds to /k/; and Arapaho /b/ corresponds to /m/. In these comparisons, Arapaho is innovative; the bulk of Algonquian languages are conservative here, like Wampanoag, which continues the original Algonquian *p, *k, *m. In the case of Arapaho /θ/, the language appears to distinguish itself by being conservative in retaining the reconstructed Algonquian consonant *θ in its hypothetical original form. In Wampanoag and many other languages, this consonant is continued instead as /n/ (still others have /l, y, r, t/). In verbal morphology, the three Arapaho verbs are in their affirmative main clause forms; these correspond formally but not functionally to the Wampanoag forms. In the latter language the conjunct (CNJ) features in subordinate clause and content questions, as it does in the majority of other Algonquian languages.

Stephen Greymorning's chapter (Chapter 23) is only partly about the Bambi Speaks Arapaho project. It is primarily about the efforts to establish immersion language education for Arapaho children in the Wyoming Indian Schools. There are several lessons that can be learned from the story of this process, including the following:

(1) teaching a language takes time—that is, time out of each school day—and the educational structures in which a local language, like Arapaho, is to be taught must adjust to this circumstance;
(2) in order to achieve this result, there must be evidence, recognizable to the community, to support the immersion concept (e.g., in this instance, evidence of the type marshaled by Greymorning, including a video of the successful Pūnana Leo program in Hawai'i, or the statistics showing decreased absenteeism among immersion class participants, and tests showing actual acquisition of Arapaho forms);
(3) the need for training and careful selection of those fluent speakers who will teach in immersion classes (here the need is not linguistic training, as such, but rather training in providing children with a rich interactive language environment);
(4) the wisdom of promoting public events with local language content;

(5) the need to begin at an early age (i.e., preschool) to guarantee the emergence of a population fluent in the local language; and

(6) the possibility of novel and alternative sources of funding for languages programs, for example, parents themselves as a funding source.

References

Bloomfield, Leonard. 1946. Algonquian. In *Linguistic structures of Native America*, ed. Cornelius Osgood, 85–129. Viking Fund Publications in Anthropology 6. New York.

Salzmann, Zdenek. 1965. Arapaho V: Noun. *International Journal of American Linguistics* 31: 39–49.

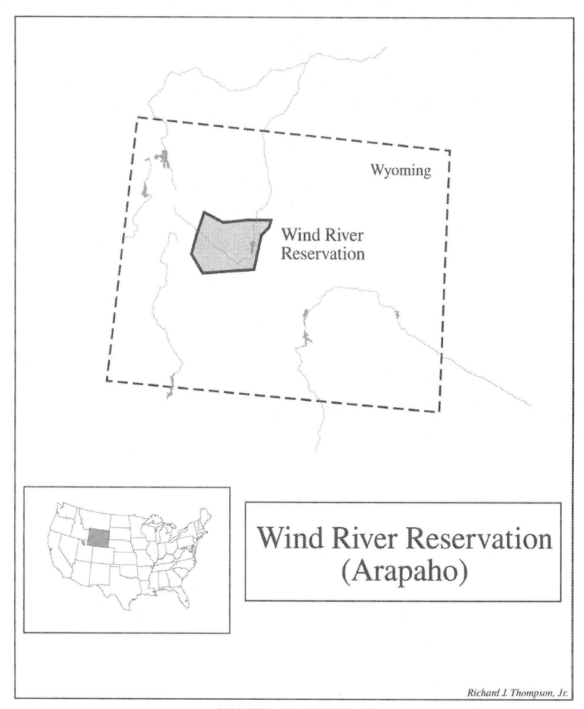

Wyoming

Wind River
Reservation

Wind River Reservation
(Arapaho)

Richard J. Thompson, Jr.

MAP 23.1   Arapaho, in Wyoming

23

Reflections on the Arapaho Language Project, or When Bambi Spoke Arapaho and Other Tales of Arapaho Language Revitalization Efforts

STEPHEN GREYMORNING

Department of Anthropology
University of Montana
Missoula, Montana

BACKGROUND HISTORY AND LANGUAGE MAINTENANCE EFFORTS

As Indigenous North Americans prepare themselves for the challenges they will face in the 21st century, the problems of language loss will stand among some of their greatest challenges because with the loss of language comes an inevitable loss of culture. Typically language loss begins when young adults become bilingual, speaking both the language of their ancestors and the language of the majority culture. The stage that follows occurs when the children of these bilingual speakers become monolingual speakers of the majority language. This pattern continues through successive generations until eventually only the older people speak their ancestral language. At this point the ancestral language has become a minority language, and usually remains so until the last native speaker dies. Long before this occurs, however, the minority language has degenerated through loss of its grammatical complexities, loss of native words that have been forgotten and dropped from the lexicon, and loss through incorporation of foreign vocabulary and grammatical features. As these losses accumulate, they also bring about various cultural losses. While recent governmental attempts have been made to redress the devastating impact that assimilation policies have had upon the languages of Indigenous North Americans, the effort and commitment needed to revitalize endangered languages must come from within native-speaking communities themselves.

In December 1994 I was hired to direct a language revitalization effort on the Wind River reservation in Wyoming. The following will examine strategies used toward this revitalization effort and discuss the steps taken to implement both the first language-immersion kindergarten class and the first full-day language-immersion preschool class for the specific purpose of creating a new generation of Arapaho speakers among children on the Wind River reservation.

The Arapaho language has been classified as a member of the Algonquian language group. In the past century speakers of Arapaho have fallen into three primary tribal groups: the Gros Ventre of Montana, the Southern Arapaho of Oklahoma, of which there are only a handful of speakers remaining, and the Northern Arapaho of the Wind River reservation in Wyoming.

Members of the Northern Arapaho tribe have long been concerned about the rate of language loss that their communities have experienced. Due to influences of missionary boarding schools, Arapaho people were led to believe that it would be detrimental to their and their children's ability to become valued "American" citizens if they continued to speak Arapaho. This resulted in English becoming the standard language of communication, and the Arapaho no longer speaking their language to their children. The effect of this, and the dominance of English in all forms of communication, has led to the steady decline of the Arapaho language.

At the time of this writing, the Arapaho language is identified as a language in serious decline, and if action is not taken to change the language's steady decline into disuse, by the year 2025 the Arapaho language may well be extinct. Table 23.1 illustrates 1996 levels of Arapaho language speaking ability among the Northern Arapaho of the Wind River reservation.

As indicated by Table 23.1, there are approximately 1,000 fluent speakers of Northern Arapaho, all of whom, with one exception, are over the age of 55. By 1978, in an effort to keep the Arapaho language viable, community members had begun to establish adult and youth language programs in the community and schools. In 1992, after observing that the language was still rapidly declining, the community took

287

TABLE 23.1   1996 Levels of Speaking Ability for Northern Arapaho

Speaking ability	Age groups								
	3–4	5–20	21–30	31–40	41–50	51–60	61–70	71–80	80+
None	60	200	138	420	258				
Limited vocabulary	50	1000	690	360	470				
Marginal	15	38			27	74			
Marginally fluent						124 M 151 F	29 M 36 F		
Fluent					1 F	92 M 113 F	157 M 192 F	38 M 45 F	8 M 14 F

M = males, F = females in number of fluent speakers

measures to bring a new vitality to the language. While adult and youth language programs were continued, the community called for a more effective method of keeping the language viable that could produce new speakers of Arapaho among young children.

In the spring of 1992, a community organization called the Northern Plains Educational Foundation was established to oversee planned directional changes of language instruction for the Wyoming Indian School District, a public school system on the reservation. Arapaho language instruction within this school district was being administered by seven fluent speakers who served the total number of Arapaho students from kindergarten to the twelfth grade. As good as this may sound, the downside is that prior to 1994, children from kindergarten to 5th grade received only 75 minutes of Arapaho language instruction per week. This amounted to a total of 45 hours per school year. Interestingly, the school's primary teachers were of the opinion that the language teachers were not competent because the children were not learning the language within the allotted time frame. At the 5th- to 8th-grade levels, about 178 students received 84 minutes of language instruction per week. Although high school students who enrolled in Arapaho language classes received 100 minutes of Arapaho each week, Arapaho language instruction at this level was optional. During the 1993–94 school year, of the 170 students in 9th–12th grade, only 20 took Arapaho instruction. Since the 1994–95 school year, however, this number has shown a small increase, possibly as a result of the Disney production of "Bambi Speaks Arapaho."

In August of 1992, the Northern Plains Educational Foundation approached me to direct an Arapaho Language and Culture Project within a public school system on the reservation. One of the objectives of this project was to arrest the steady decline of the Arapaho language. And so it was that on December 14, after having packed up our belongings, my family and I left Edmonton, Alberta, Canada, where I had been teaching courses at the University of Alberta, to take up a two-and-a-half-year position on the Wind River reservation at Ethete, Wyoming. Fortunately, I did not depart without a well–thought-out strategy and plan of action. At least part of my plan was first conceived during the summer of 1979. It was during this time, while working on the Rosebud Sioux reservation in South Dakota, that I first began to give thought to the idea of using animation as a tool for language learning for children. A year later, after completing a master's in anthropology with an emphasis on language revitalization, I began to examine the merits of language immersion as a tool for second-language acquisition.

THE FIRST STEPS TOWARD CHANGE

As soon as I arrived on the reservation I drafted a letter to Roy Disney requesting permission to translate the movie *Bambi* into the Arapaho language. While waiting for a reply, I began to assess the Arapaho language situation within the school system. Foremost was the realization that whatever knowledge my assessment brought me, I had only about two years to make some sort of impact. I also knew that a single approach to the problem would have little if any real impact. The biggest test, however, was whether the different factions on the reservation could effectively be worked with, and because of this I was hopeful that a project like *Bambi* might work as a catalyst to bring about support from various factions.

As director of a Title V project within the school system, the first obstacle I faced was to try to increase the amount of time allotted for language instruction in the classroom. I decided that the kindergarten represented the best place to initiate change with the least amount of resistance. In a meeting with the elementary school principal, I pressed for an hour of Arapaho language instruction per day as a test model for language instruction. I was allowed to take a team of four Arapaho language instructors into a kindergarten class for the 18 weeks that remained of the second half of the school term. The hour of Arapaho language instruction at the kindergarten level was a significant gain, because prior to that language instruction within the elementary school amounted

Animals (36)

antelope
bear
beaver
bird
buffalo
butterfly
cat
chicken
chipmunk
cow
coyote
crow
deer
dog
duck
elk
fish
frog
hawk
horse
insect/bug
monkey
mouse
rabbit
raccoon
sage chicken
salamander
sheep
snake
wolf
owl
pig
porcupine
spider
turkey
turtle

Phrases (33)

come here
sit down
be still
sit still
listen
stand up
write your name
erase it
move over (sitting)
move over (standing)
are you hungry
yes I am hungry
I am thirsty
pick it up
throw it (an.)
go and get it
let's go
can I touch him
throw it away
can I ride him
can I feed him
give it to me
talk loud
feed him
what is your name
my name is . . .
line up
what are you doing
I am jumping
jump
put it down
come in
quit it

Body parts (16)

body
eyes
ears
mouth
nose
hair
head
elbow
hand
fingers
toes
leg
knee
neck
face
teeth

Foods (14)

apple
bread
butter
corn
bacon
eggs
meat
potatoes
milk
orange
salt
sugar
pepper
water

Clothing (8)

belt
gloves
hat
shirt (men's)
shirt (women's)
shoes
socks
pants

Colors (9)

red
orange/yellow
blue/green
brown
black
white
pink
purple
grey

Miscellaneous word items (24)

box	paper	mountain
cup	snow	grandma
fork	plate	grandpa
chair	river	mother
knife	tree	father
hello	rock	what
spoon	ball	sun
moon	night	day

Numbers (1–30)

Total combined word & phrase count = 170

FIGURE 23.1   Kindergarten Arapaho Language Class after 14 Weeks of Instruction

to only 15 minutes per day. The results of this first effort proved to be dramatic. Where children had been generally assessed at having mastered a vocabulary range of only 15–18 words by the end of a school year, a minimum of 80% of the test class had mastered 170 words and phrases after 14 weeks. This included the ability to count from 1 to 30 and a list of 33 phrases, 16 body parts, 14 different food items, 8 different items of clothing, 9 colors, 36 animals, and the 20 miscellaneous words as illustrated by Figure 23.1.

By mid-April I had received a response from Disney studios suggesting that I contact an individual in their video production department. A letter was immediately drafted and sent. While waiting for a response, an opportune event arose: a conference called Native American Language Issues (NALI). The only catch was that the conference was in Hawai'i, and for this reason alone it appeared as if I would get no support to attend.

When I became aware of the NALI conference in Hawai'i, it seemed like the perfect opportunity to validate what needed to be done next with the language immersion efforts on the Wind River reservation. I submitted my request for travel leave, and two days before the school board was to meet I discovered that my request was not on the agenda. My supervisor was of the opinion that my wanting to go to a conference in Hawai'i would be an embarrassment to the project and I therefore should not make such a request of the school board. It took calling a special meeting of the group that hired me and two hours of discussion before they were sufficiently convinced to allow me to make the request. On the tail of this meeting came another meeting an hour long the following morning with the school district's superintendent to garner his support for my request. With the stage set, I went into that night's meeting feeling fairly confident. Then, right before I was to address the school board, lightning struck. The superintendent got up and spoke to the board on the loss of money that the school district experienced as a result of paying people to attend conferences instead of being on site performing their jobs. It appeared as though my request was doomed, and as my supervisor was telling me I should not make my request, I was called before the school board.

The Wyoming Indian Schools' school board is predominantly native. As I approached the members of the school board I realized that in one way or another they all had some connection to our summer ceremonial lodge. I had been through the lodge three times by then, so I decided to make my request through this shared link. As a result, what I had expected to be a firm denial concluded as a unanimous vote of confidence.

So in May 1993 I traveled to Hawai'i to attend the Native American Language Issues conference. During the conference I was able to videotape several adult Hawaiian students in an immersion class on site at the conference and was also able to visit a Pūnana Leo immersion preschool. My attendance at NALI proved to be instrumental in supplying me with needed resources for negotiating the implementation of a half-day kindergarten immersion class at the Wyoming Indian Elementary.

The NALI conference proved to be even better than I had expected, and I was able to document 18 hours of the conference and surrounding events on videotape. The only disappointing event came when I phoned Disney studios and learned that my request to translate the *Bambi* script into Arapaho had been denied. When I returned to the reservation I quickly mailed off a reply to Roy Disney, taking the liberty of sending him a copy of the letter of denial I had received. Using skills of logic and reasoning, I concluded my letter:

My request was not made in the interest of public entertainment. All I sought was permission to allow the English words from *Bambi* to be spoken in Arapaho to our children in an effort to strengthen the language. How sad it has become. The denial of my request clearly demonstrates that when we can be legally punished for speaking Arapaho in place of English words, because those words are from the movie *Bambi*, we the Arapaho cannot even claim ownership of our language: It would appear that little has changed since the days when the government's boarding schools purged the language from our fathers' minds by punishing them for speaking Arapaho. . . . I find it amazing how the Anglo-European holds such a fascination with Indian culture and yet will idly stand by as our culture slowly slips into extinction: People have done more to save the Florida Manatee than the "American" Indian.

Because I am looking at the face of Genocide I can do no less than continue my efforts. I must continue to believe that somewhere in the Media world there exists a "Moral Conscience" that can not only distinguish there is a difference between helping to preserve the Manatee as a distinct community of animals from helping to preserve the Indian as a distinct community of people, but also be willing to take some form of action. I had hoped that you might understand. (Author to Ron Disney, personal communication, 1994)

I do not know whether this note had any bearing on Disney's decision, but three weeks later I received a phone call from Disney Studios stating they were considering the project and wanted to meet with me in August. We met in New York for about 90 minutes. Disney representatives had planned to use their own voice talents. When I insisted that the language was too difficult and that it was absolutely essential for Arapaho people to speak the parts, serious skepticism was voiced. It was not until I explained that the language had tonal qualities which if not spoken properly could change an innocent word into some vulgarity, that they were finally convinced.

Throughout the summer I had been experimenting with various computer projects, some of which were the creation of an Arapaho talking dictionary that included interactive animation, talking storybooks that incorporated videos of community members and animation, and animated children's songs in Arapaho. I used these new computer tools and the Hawaiian material to try and convince the elementary school principal of the merits of implementing a kindergarten immersion class within the school system.

IMPLEMENTING WYOMING INDIAN SCHOOLS' FIRST IMMERSION CLASS

As the start of another school year approached, with no talk about implementing an immersion class, I was getting worried. I decided to canvas the community with a questionnaire to see if there was any support for such a project. Of the anticipated 60 children that were to start kindergarten, 40 questionnaires came back from parents requesting that their children be placed in an immersion class. The responses worked to get things focused again on the language immersion issue.

It was my good fortune that at the Wyoming Indian Elementary School kindergarten children attend classes all day, versus the standard for the majority of schools in the United States, in which kindergarten students spend only half a day in classes. This variance was used to question why the school's excellent teachers used a full day to accomplish what the rest of the country's kindergarten teachers were doing in a half a day. Amidst complaints and some resistance, a kindergarten half-day immersion class was started in September 1993. After 8 weeks of class, student vocabularies were assessed at 20 words, versus the 14-word vocabulary of other students randomly picked from the nonimmersion kindergarten classes. After 16 weeks, immersion and nonimmersion students were randomly selected from the kindergarten classes and were correspondingly assessed at a 55- and 16-word or phrase vocabulary. By the end of the school year the immersion students displayed an 80-word or phrase speaking ability at the lower end, and a 120-word or phrase speaking ability at the upper end, while nonimmersion students from kindergarten to 4th grade were assessed at a 16-word vocabulary at the lower end and a 42-word vocabulary at the upper end.

At the start of the immersion project it was realized that the strongest possible argument would need to be built if the project had any hope of continuing. This sparked me to compare the immersion children's absentee rate to that of the other kindergarten children (see Table 23.2). The rate of absenteeism was calculated by taking the total number of days' absence for each child in a class in a given month and adding them together, then dividing that number by the total number of child school days in the month (the total number of child school days in a month was calculated by multiplying the total number of children in a class by the total number of school days in the month).

Table 23.2 shows that when the immersion kindergarten student (I.K.S.) statistics are factored from out of the statistics for all kindergarten students (A.K.S.), the absentee rate for the nonimmersion kindergarten classes increased to 8.36%. This increase illustrated that the attendance rate for the immersion kindergarten students was effective in reducing the absentee rate for the entire kindergarten student population. Over the course of the school term, the kindergarten immersion class served as a model which sparked increased interest in Arapaho on the part of teachers and students alike. This increased interest was also reflected at the school's Christmas and spring concerts, which reflected a 60% increase in Arapaho language content in presentations by children in grades K–4. As a result of these positive outcomes, the school administration indicated it would continue to maintain the kindergarten immersion class through to the end of 1997, and possibly beyond.

TABLE 23.2   Absentee Rate for Immersion Kindergarten Students vs. All Kindergarten Students

	Days absent	÷	Total days		Absentee rate
1. (A.K.S.)	94	÷	1,218	=	7.72%
2. (I.K.S.)	(–)15	÷	(–)273	=	5.49%
3.	79	÷	945	=	8.36%

THE QUESTION OF FLUENCY

While considerable debate exists over what fluency means, I choose to approach the term from the position that if individuals think in a particular language and are capable of communicating their full range of thoughts in that language then those individuals are operating at a level of fluency. Furthermore, I do not believe it would ever be claimed that an individual adult, though only possessing the English verbal skills of a five-year-old, was not a fluent English speaker. I would postulate that this individual would most likely be acknowledged as a fluent speaker because English would be recognized as the only voiced language of thought he or she possessed and the only language used to communicate his or her thoughts.

Through my observations of the Hawaiian Pūnana Leo immersion preschools I had calculated that children within the Pūnana Leo were achieving fluency after about 600 language contact hours. This, however, was operating in an environment in which non-Hawaiian-speaking children were entering schools in which 20–30% of the returning children had already achieved fluency in the previous year. Under such conditions I observed that in one of the Pūnana Leo schools, children had only been exposed to about four hours of the Hawaiian language per day, in a five-day school week, and had still achieved an age-appropriate level of fluency in less than five months. This amounted to approximately 400 language contact hours!

The shortfall of the Wyoming Indian public school system's efforts to teach the Arapaho language in the classroom seemed obvious to me: at 75 minutes per week, what could realistically be learned in only 45 hours of language instruction per school year? The kindergarten immersion class, on the other hand, could offer two and a half hours of Arapaho language instruction per day, and over the course of a 180-day academic year this could amount to approximately 450 hours that children could be in contact with the Arapaho language. Thus, with the kindergarten immersion class in place there was a tentative expectation that, if functioning optimally, children could potentially achieve an age-appropriate level of fluency. For the children outside of the immersion class, however, about the best that language classes could offer was to function as a language maintenance program. If this was the best one could hope for, then it logically made sense that if children could gain fluency before they entered kindergarten, then the language program within the school system could function to maintain and perhaps even slowly expand on the children's Arapaho language skills. With this realization, the goal then became to create an Arapaho language immersion preschool.

IMPLEMENTING A LANGUAGE IMMERSION PRESCHOOL CLASS

Starting up an immersion class for preschool children was taking on a major piece of responsibility and represented much more than just getting an already existing school to expand upon its already existing programs. Starting a preschool meant a staff needed to be interviewed, hired, and managed; a site for a class had to be located; a process for selecting children for the class had to be worked out; materials, supplies, and furniture for the class and classroom had to be obtained; a curriculum format needed to be developed; and most importantly, funding needed to be raised to sustain the project for more than a few months. This was a whole new area and a lot of uncertainty existed over the best course of action to take. After several discussions with one of the executives of the Wyoming Council for the Humanities I decided to request funding for a pilot project that would operate from January to May 1994. I was relatively confident that by implementing the project in this way, I could obtain additional funding for another immersion class that would operate over the course of a full academic year. The grant was written for a pilot immersion project to operate Mondays through Thursdays, two hours per day. The $5,000 budget for this project was used for rent, supplies, and second-hand furniture, and to pay the salaries of the two Arapaho language instructors.

A real concern was getting the right people hired for the project. My concern sprang from observing that fluent Arapaho speakers were not speaking Arapaho to children. I was very perplexed by this and over several months of observations I formulated the hypothesis that Arapaho speakers would not engage in anything that even remotely bordered on a conversation with individuals they believed were not capable of addressing them back. Although I explained to individuals that children could not possibly learn Arapaho if people stopped speaking to them, it did not matter how much logic or reasoning I put before individuals, it seemed to have little impact. Speakers might attempt some initial query, but when they got no response they seemed to feel that the exercise was fruitless and silly. It was for this reason that I felt I had to be relatively confident that the people hired as language instructors would carry out the directives of the immersion project.

About six fluent speakers on the reservation loosely made up the "Arapaho Language Commission." This language commission had been set up in the late 1970s, when money was still flowing, as a method of certifying Arapaho speakers as qualified to teach the Arapaho language in the schools on the reservation. When money dried up to pay members of the commission, they became less and less active. By the time I arrived only two of the original members were still available, and they were in a small political battle with a few other individuals trying to position themselves on the commission. For the sake of trying to keep the immersion project apolitical, I decided that I would conduct the interviews myself. Eight people responded to the job advertisement who, I am sure, wondered how I, as a passive speaker, was going to conduct the interviews.

Interviews for the immersion class were set up to ascertain whether the interviewees could competently and comfortably work with children within an immersion environment. As a candidate came in to be interviewed, about 30 minutes was spent explaining how they would actually be interviewed and learning what the individual knew and thought about teaching Arapaho through immersion. The interviews were videotaped and set up so each candidate would spend about 45 minutes in a simulated immersion setting with children. Each candidate had an outline that showed the various activities they had to cover and how much time they should spend on each activity, and all were told that they absolutely were not to speak any English. In spite of the time and detail given to explain the interview process and the importance of not speaking English, it was nevertheless interesting to note that when faced with having to instruct children, some of the best speakers could not get beyond that psychological barrier of feeling that it made little sense to speak to children as if they could understand. As a result, some individuals would either spend extended periods of time saying nothing or would speak to me. This psychological barrier became very evident when a child who knew the routine would cue or prompt the interviewee in Arapaho to let them know the next activity to move on to. In one example, the person being interviewed, who was supposed to ask the children what they were going to play with, fell silent for quite a while, in spite of the fact that one of the children kept saying *niibeetninikotiinoo* 'I want to play'. In another instance the children were supposed to have been told that they were going to eat a snack. After several minutes of silence a child started repeating *heesneenoo* 'I'm hungry'. But it was not until I said *Neh bii3iine* 'Better feed them' that anything happened.

After all of the interviews were conducted, the videotapes were reviewed and a list made of pluses and minuses, representing strengths and weaknesses, for each individual. The pluses and minuses were then added up for each individual, and the candidates with the best scores were offered the job. While the process was quite fair, it did get some flak on the grounds that some people felt interviews should have been conducted by the language commission. My answer to this was that it was clear that everyone interviewed was a fluent speaker. What the interview determined was how well an individual could work with children. From that point on the issue of how the interview was conducted seemed to be over. While things began to gear up for the first Arapaho language immersion preschool class, things began to move forward on the Bambi Speaks Arapaho project.

BAMBI SPEAKS ARAPAHO

In early October I began to put up notices at the elementary, junior high, and high school announcing auditions for the *Bambi* video. The Disney people had wanted me to send them an audiotape of the auditions. I thought that it might be better for me to videotape the voice auditions so they could see the faces of the children. The only problem was that on October 15 only three junior high school girls showed up for the audition. I videotaped the girls introducing themselves and reading the parts for Bambi, Thumper, and Thumper's mother. I rescheduled another audition in two weeks and asked the three girls to spread the word and to bring friends back with them. When the girls returned for auditions they brought with them three more girls, but no others came. I videotaped the six girls reading the parts selected by one of Disney's directors and sent the tape off with crossed fingers, wondering all the while what had happened to all the people. After all, if this were happening in Hollywood parents would have herded their children in like cattle; but then again the reservation was not Hollywood.

By the middle of November I received a call from Disney's vice president of manufacturing and distribution, who told me what I had sent was not going to work. I was expecting to hear that they had decided to scrap the project. When I was told not to abandon hope and to try again I was greatly relieved. It was all too true; the reservation was not Hollywood. The two places represented two different cultures, with each characteristically responding in two very different ways to two very different worlds. I knew the primary characters in the *Bambi* movie and I knew the people around me, so by the middle of January I had selected children to do the voices of Bambi, Thumper, and Flower, and I asked one of the teachers to fill in for Bambi's mother. This time I stuck to the script and sent an audiocassette of the voice auditions. The people at Disney liked what they heard and scheduled a test dub for early March.

One of the questions asked of me was who would pay the cost of renting the studio for the recording sessions in Jackson, Wyoming. While I was well aware that a bill of about $2,000 was relatively insignificant for a corporation like Disney, I also recognized that it represented a measure of good faith on our part, and communicated that we were not simply looking for something for nothing from Disney. I let Disney Studios know that the project I was directing could arrange payment for the recording studio. I also let Disney's assigned director for the *Bambi* project know that the program I directed would also pay the costs of our own transportation, hotel, and meals. Once the formalities were over and done with, we drove the 170 miles to Jackson.

I had originally selected Evan, Roland, and Star for the parts of Flower, Thumper, and Bambi. Roland and Star were in the fourth grade and Evan was in the third grade, and all three were children I was well acquainted with. I selected these students for the parts because their own personalities closely matched the characters they were supposed to represent, and because they were all doing well in their Arapaho language classes. While preparing the children for the recording session I emphasized that they would have to try to follow whatever directions the director would give them. When we started the recording session, the director wanted to switch Star and Roland because Roland was having trouble speaking Thumper's lines. During the recording of Thumper's lines with Star, however, the director ran into a problem. When recording Thumper's lines a part was reached in the script where Thumper had to laugh. The director explained the scene and then when the time came directed Star to laugh. Nothing happened. The director tried the scene again and Star, with a stony expression, said, "No, I don't want to." Nothing we could do could get Star to laugh. The problem worsened as we discovered that none of the children would laugh when directed to. The tension began to mount. I suggested that we try tickling, but both Star and Evan resisted, and even though Roland laughed he fought it all the way. We decided to go back to Star as Bambi and Roland as Thumper, and hoped for the best.

The director flew back to Hollywood late Friday afternoon and was to do the dubbing over at Disney Studios. On Monday morning I received a phone call telling me they all loved it. At this point I was astonished; I knew technology was good but I had not expected that the process would be that fast. I was informed that Disney's executives felt the project warranted moving ahead with plans to dub the entire movie. Still baffled, I asked the director how he had gotten the dubbing done so fast. He told me that the lines fit so well with the animation that it appeared as if the movie had been made for the Arapaho language. The realization then struck me that long before I had received a yes from the Disney Studio, I had spent months trying to find the right translations for the lines and then tested them for mouth synchronization. This was done by turning off the sound and speaking the lines in Arapaho as the English version of the *Bambi* video played. The extra effort had paid off.

I was told that only a small time frame existed within which to work if the video was to be completed before September. The reason for the limited time frame was primarily due to the studio's work to get *The Lion King* completed and out into the theaters. This meant that everyone had to be ready to record the Arapaho version of *Bambi* in April. I also realized that everything needed to move without a hitch if the project's completion was not going to be jeopardized, and that meant a lot of work was still ahead. Once the final approval was given to record the entire movie script into Arapaho, I still had 20 more parts to find speakers for, a recording session to be planned out, transportation and room assignments to be arranged, parent releases to be signed and returned, and approval from the school board had to be obtained before any of this could happen and the project could proceed.

Schedules were arranged to make the most efficient use of time, and the final recording of the entire script proceeded with only minor problems. One of those problems was the result of the director attempting to read the lines in Arapaho. The children would listen and then try to repeat the lines as they had been improperly pronounced. After explaining how the children were being confused, things moved along a little more smoothly. In another instance the director wanted one of the Elders to inflect her lines at the end to show that a question had been asked. I could see that this was causing a problem because the Elder was reluctantly trying to accommodate the request. I finally had to explain that the Arapaho language does not display voice inflection at the end of a question because with Arapaho the question is formed at the beginning of the sentence. Another problem resulted from an instructor being so pleased with a child speaking Arapaho that the child received praise for saying a line, even though it had been spoken incorrectly. This led the director to believe that the line had been properly delivered, and he proceeded to move on to the next line. I had to halt the process and ask for the line to be said again without saying why, out of respect to the Elder. I finally had to request that because the movie was being made as a tool to both spark an interest in learning Arapaho and also as a language-learning device, it was absolutely essential for all children to deliver their lines accurately before they were praised. By the second day of recording the sessions were moving so smoothly that it took only four days for the entire script to be completed.

When the dubbing was complete, people at Disney stated that the finished version exceeded the studio's dubbing standards for voice-to-mouth synchronization of foreign films. The executives at Disney were very pleased, and I was particularly impressed by the attention that Disney Studios had given the project, which once underway was really not much different from any of their other feature films. One of the ways this was illustrated was that while it would have been more economical for Disney to have run all prints off of a video master, it was decided to run the video prints off of a 35mm master. Also, before premiering the movie at a theater near the reservation, Disney brought in upgraded speakers so the sound quality would be at its best for the only two showings the 35mm print version received.

While meeting with the vice president of manufacturing and distribution during the final editing of the video, I learned that Disney Studios had planned to generate five copies of the video for use by the Arapaho people. I explained that five copies would not be very helpful if the end objective was to benefit the Arapaho people and language. When asked how many prints I thought would be needed, my response was a modest 2,500. I observed Miller's expression, which might have suggested that he did not believe what he had heard. When he asked who would pay for the copies, I said the Arapaho people. The vice president of manufacturing and distribution felt that Disney Studios could not ethically ask the Arapaho to pay for the video. I explained that I saw no problem with the Arapaho contributing toward the welfare of their language by individually purchasing videos for their own homes. After all, Arapaho people have purchased many other Disney videos. The difference with purchasing the "Bambi Speaks Arapaho" video was that the money from those purchases could be matched and placed in a special account by the Wyoming Council for the Humanities for the explicit purpose of language revitalization efforts. In the end Disney's representative saw the logic and agreed to the sale of the video.

The final production of the *Bambi* movie dubbed into the Arapaho language has been viewed as a very positive event. Young Arapaho children have been said to watch the video repeatedly and have learned some of the speaking parts of their favorite characters. The fact that the video was produced has also helped in furthering Arapaho language revitalization efforts, one of which has been in acquiring funding from granting agencies to develop and expand upon the Arapaho language immersion project.

THE ARAPAHO LANGUAGE IMMERSION PROJECT

The first Arapaho language immersion preschool class began as a two-hour-a-day, four-day-a-week class that operated from January to May 1994. That first class began with six children in the "L" section of a cafeteria that was used by the Head Start program. Officially the Head Start program was the sponsor of the immersion class. In spite of the strong administrative support, the Head Start instructors teaching in the building made it clear that they would have little tolerance for a program invading their space. After two months the situation had become so stressful we decided we needed to move the class to another location. We moved into a 12 by 18–foot room at the community center. The new site, though cramped for space, had a playground outside, much to the delight of staff and children. In little time we settled in and viewed the new site as our own.

When the pilot project concluded in May 1994, it was obvious that while two hours a day for four days a week was not enough time to have a major impact upon the children's Arapaho language skills, it nevertheless did have the effect of producing limited speaking ability in the children. The children's new-found Arapaho verbal skills impressed family members enough for parents to inquire if the class could extend into the summer. A grant proposal was written for a summer program to operate three days a week for three hours each day on a $2,000 budget. Unfortunately, none of the granting agencies approached would fund the program. In desperation I sought support from two places, the parents and instructors themselves. I explained to the instructors that if they would work the summer program at half the hourly income they had received from the pilot project I believed that the parents would be able to pay their salaries.

It is fairly common knowledge that on the majority of reservations in the United States, unemployment rates are over 75%. On the Wind River reservation the average unemployment rate is about 80%, and during the summer months the unemployment rate may exceed 90%. While some viewed my claim that parents would pay the instructor's summer salaries as unrealistic, when parents were asked to pay summer tuition for their children to attend, their commitment to the project was so strong that they paid readily.

The summer project ran for five weeks, three hours a day, three days a week, on a $500 budget. Each parent paid a $20 tuition fee, and the instructors agreed to work for $5 an hour: It was probably one of the most significant acts of support ever given to a program on the reservation. Before the summer had ended, the Wyoming Council for the Humanities, possibly impressed by the parents' support, agreed to fund the project from September 1994 to May 1995. The 1994–95 project ran three hours a day, Monday to Friday. I was still very much aware that the project needed at least six hours a day if there was to be any hope of developing fluent speakers, but at least the increase in time represented movement in the right direction.

During each of the times I visited the class it was not uncommon for me to hear instructors speaking English. I soon realized that although the instructors knew the project's goals, they still lacked a firm commitment to the methods of immersion. I constantly tried to convince the instructors of the absolute necessity of not speaking English to the children. From their perspective, however, they observed more Arapaho spoken by children than they had ever heard before and were quietly convinced that it was due to their mixing English and Arapaho when they spoke to the children.

As knowledge of the Arapaho language immersion efforts expanded beyond the reservation, more people inquired into whether such a project could happen in their communities. In October 1994, one such inquiry came from a group of Aboriginal elders who had heard about the immersion program and traveled from Australia to learn more about such language efforts by visiting various sites in Canada and the United States. When they arrived at Ethete and saw and heard the children using Arapaho while playing on the playground, they were literally moved to tears.

By April 1995, it was apparent that the goal of producing new speakers among the children was not going to be achieved. The realization made me press even harder for a full-day program. I reviewed the unsuccessful Administration for Native Americans (ANA) grant proposal that I had written in June 1994 and revised it for the implementation of a full-day immersion class for the 1995–96 school year. Though the proposal was again denied, funding proposals written to the Wyoming Council for the Humanities and the Lannan Foundation were accepted.

On September 1995, the Arapaho language immersion class started its third year as a six-hour-a-day class. One of the positions added to the class was a salaried director and curriculum developer position. The immersion project was fortunate to get an individual who had worked with the kindergarten immersion class from 1993 to 1995, so I was fairly confident that we would meet our goal and see the first of a new generation of Arapaho speakers. When classes began I traveled down from Missoula, Montana, to get the immersion class started. The class had been moved over to a large room in a building owned by the Episcopal Mission. When I arrived I was met by the sound of the Arapaho instructors conversing in English. I took the instructors aside and spoke to them to impress upon them the importance of maintaining an Arapaho-only language classroom if the children were going to become speakers. When I left to return to Montana, I departed with the hope that the additional three hours added to the program would make the difference in achieving the program's goal.

Though the new program faced a number of obstacles, we continued to forge ahead. A child could not simply attend the immersion class: parents had to be made aware that they had to be responsible for getting their child to the site as well as for providing for their child's snack and lunch throughout the project year. Fortunately, the reservation community functions as a tightly knit community, so many assisted each other in providing for the children's well-being. As a result of my teaching position at the University of Montana, I was not able to visit the class again until mid-December, but when I did I was very impressed by what I had observed.

On December 18, 1995, about 13 weeks into the project, I traveled down to Ethete to observe the immersion class. My arrival at Ethete and the videotaping that resulted were completely spontaneous and unannounced.

Enrollment in the new immersion class fluctuated between 12 and 15 children. I was able to borrow a video camera, at the last minute, from the elementary school and rushed down to the immersion class to get there by 9 AM. When I arrived at the class only six children were present, owing to a flu outbreak. Between 9 AM and 12 noon, one hour of the six-hour day was filmed. That hour of tape was then edited down to a 20-minute tape, which I planned to use for future funding efforts. The following is a transcription and description of the edited-down 20-minute videotape. Unless otherwise noted, all communication between the Arapaho language instructors and the children was in Arapaho.

Danny's mother says goodbye to him in English. He responds to this with *Heetce'noohobeen* 'I'll see you again'.

Danny: *Neneeninoo Danny* 'I am Danny'.

There is a knock at the door by Daniel, one of the adult language instructors.

Danny: *Ciitei* 'come in'.

Danny repeats after instructor: *tous* 'hello', *nii'ooke* 'good morning', *tooyoo3oo* 'it is cold', and *hee* 'yes'.

Danny: *Kooheinokoh* 'Are you sleeping'? (initiated with no prompting)

A pretaped song is started, and the children sing *heetnee' inonii hinono'eitiit . . .* 'we are going to learn how to speak Arapaho, good morning good morning we are all glad that we are here'.

Danny: *Wohei, ho3o* 'All right, Star' (he is cut off from continuing)

Children sing another song in Arapaho: "Are you sleeping, are you sleeping, brother. . . . "
  Danny is instructed to put on his coat, go out, and knock on the door, which he does. He is then instructed to take off his coat, which he does.
  Danny is instructed to go with Daniel, one of the instructors, where he repeats the days counted on a calendar until the 18th day is reached. He then repeats the 12 immersion-class names of the other children in the class. Before his name is mentioned he gets excited and says *ho3o* 'right there!' (Star is Danny's immersion-class name, which he excitedly states when he sees it on the poster board.)
  A picturebook is brought out and the children identify the following pictures in Arapaho: *siisiikoo'* 'ducks', *he3* 'dog', *wo'oun* 'kitten', *bih'ih* 'deer', *nooku* 'rabbit'.
  There is a knock at the door—children say *ciitei*. Mylan comes in and is instructed to close the door and to take off his coat, which he does. There is another knock at the door and children shout *ciitei*. Alycia comes in. Mylan is told to sit down.
  Alycia, sitting at the table, is asked, "What is your name?" She answers, *neneeninoo Alycia* 'I am Alycia'.
  Mylan is asked, "How many are here?" He counts the number of children present. All children are individually asked to do the same.
  Posterboard drawings are held up, and children as a group say in Arapaho what is on the poster boards. The following is the translation of what the children identified (all the children enthusiastically shouted out their responses in Arapaho).

I am angry, I am crying, I am sneezing, I am singing, I am sad, I am happy, I am hot, I am cold, I am tired, I am laughing, I am brushing (my hair).

Little flash cards are now brought out and children continue in Arapaho: *pants*—when asked, "What color are they?" they answer "red." They continue and identify ducks, calves, train, doll, sheep, bear, and shirt. When asked "What color is it?" they answer "green." They go on to identify tree, airplane, comb, bread, flowers, cup, and milk.
  They now look at cards used to identify weather for the day (this is used in conjunction with the calendar where they are asked, "What is it like outside?") Using Arapaho, they reply: "it is hailing," "it is sunny," "it is hot," "it is raining," "it is cold," and "a cool breeze."
  A book is brought out and the children, using Arapaho, identify the following pictures: frog, man, young boy, water, trees, beaver, little boy, snake, flower, turtle, bugs, ducks (here Alycia says to a boy sitting near her, "You didn't say duck"), kitten, and deer.

Children are instructed that it is snack time, and they get up and eagerly get their snacks.
  Alycia says in English, "I don't have a spoon." She is told how to say *spoon*, which she repeats.
  Alycia is asked by Flora (an adult language provider), "what are you eating?" She is told the word used in Arapaho for Jello® ('it jiggles').
  Alycia is asked by Alvena (another adult language provider), "What are you eating?" She responds using the proper word for Jello®.
  Danny is told the word for the food items he is eating; he repeats them as they are said: crackers, apple, juice.
  Mylan is asked, "What is this?" He responds in Arapaho: juice, orange, crackers. He actually has potato chips; he is corrected and told the Arapaho word for chips, and he repeats the word.

Based on the language development displayed by the children in December, I fully expected that they would be fluent by May 1996. This, however, did not occur. While the children demonstrated an impressive speaking ability, they still did not demonstrate an ability to express their thoughts in Arapaho.

The parent committee had planned a graduation ceremony for the children, and I had been invited. After debating whether I really wanted to drive the 600 miles to Ethete for what I was sure would be a small ceremony, I decided that I should make the trip. As it turned out, the children's graduation ceremony was an impressive event. The parent committee had arranged to hold the ceremony in the community hall. The graduation of those immersion children who would be going on to kindergarten was celebrated by the tribe's drum, the Eagle Drum, and attended by well over 100 community members. The immersion children led the opening prayer, and speeches were given by one of the immersion children and one of the community's teens, who read a speech she had prepared in Arapaho. While the day's event was a significant marker of the children's accomplishments, I was nonetheless aware that the children had yet to attain fluency; I decided to petition once more for federal funding.

KEEPING THE VISION ALIVE

Writing the ANA federal grant and not receiving it remained very frustrating, and I was determined that with my third attempt I would write a grant proposal for the fall of 1996, which I knew could not be refused. I decided to write three grants, one to the Wyoming Council for the Humanities, one to the Lannan Foundation, and one to ANA, in such a way that all three grants would be integrated. The Wyoming Council's grant paid the instructors' salaries for three of the six hours of the Ethete immersion project, while funding from Lannan paid the language instructors' salaries for the other three hours, plus a director's salary. I then used the director to oversee the Ethete project and a second project that I requested funding for from ANA. Writing the ANA grant this way enabled me to show a 50% cash match of the total amount requested of ANA and also allowed me to keep the total amount requested below half of the $125,000 maximum amount allowed per project per year. This as well as a few other strategic pluses proved to make the grant proposal too strong an application to turn down. With three grant applications awarded to fund two immersion classes, the issue of fluency was again the focus of my attention.

Even though the instructors had been exposed to a number of teaching and immersion technique workshops, it was very clear to me that having a program run six hours a day would not necessarily produce fluency, especially when the instructors were not demonstrating strong immersion techniques. What the instructors needed was some very strong training in the principles and methods of second-language acquisition through immersion. Possessing an understanding of how Arapaho people best learned, I knew that even week-long workshops were not going to be enough. If there was any hope of our producing fluently speaking children I would need to hire an immersion training specialist who would train and guide the instructors on a daily basis.

During my last trip to Hawai'i I had met a young California Indian named Pueo who had traveled to Hawai'i and learned the Hawaiian language while working as a volunteer in the Pūnana Leo preschool. I believed him to be capable of providing the guidance the instructors needed. I was prepared to do whatever I could, to offer a salary and a challenge that Pueo could not refuse, on the conviction that the children could be brought to an age-appropriate level of fluency after he had provided the instructors with three months of on-site training in immersion techniques.

At the time of this writing, the Arapaho language immersion project is entering its fourth year. Within this period, the project has expanded from its beginnings as a kindergarten immersion class at the Wyoming Indian public elementary school in 1993 to a two-hour-a-day preschool program in January 1994. Eventually this was expanded to a six-hour-a-day program by September of 1995. Now in its fourth year, the project encompasses a half-day kindergarten program and 2 six-hour-a-day preschool immersion programs in two separate school districts on the Wind River reservation. Although everything is in place for the children to attain fluency, whether this goal is achieved or not now truly lies in the hands of the language instructors of the Arapaho Language Lodge. If the Arapaho Language Lodge Speakers, as they at times are called, achieve their goal, then the next logical step is to spread the immersion class project up through the elementary grades.

Irish

KEN HALE

Department of Linguistics and Philosophy
Massachusetts Institute of Technology
Cambridge, Massachusetts

The Irish language (Gaeilge) belongs to the original Gaelic continuum extending through Ireland and Scotland and now represented by the three major dialects of Modern Irish, by Scottish Gaelic, and by Manx, the revived language of the Isle of Man (Ellan Vannin). These linguistic entities belong to the Q-Celtic (or Goidelic) branch of the Celtic family and are thus distinguished from Welsh, Breton, and Cornish of the P-Celtic (or Brythonic) grouping. This division among the Celtic languages corresponds to the manner in which the Indo-European labiovelar consonant *k^w is continued in the modern languages—as a velar in the first group and a bilabial in the second, accounting for such correspondences as Gaelic *mac* beside Welsh *mab* 'son'.

The linguistic tradition leading ultimately to Modern Irish was present in Ireland in the early centuries AD, when the abundant, manifestly Q-Celtic lithograph Ogam inscriptions were made. Soon after the introduction of Christianity and the Latin alphabet in the fifth century, a strong literary tradition began to develop, culminating in the standardized Classical Gaelic of the Early Modern Irish period—from the mid-13th century to the mid-17th century. What is now called Modern Irish is the language subsequent to that period. The Classical literary language was under the control of a "learned order" of literati and poets who set the standard of literary usage. By contrast with the situation which obtains in present-day Irish literature, manuscripts of the Classical period give no hint of the dialect variation which existed in the country.

The Anglo-Norman invasion marked the beginning of nine centuries of "adstratum contacts between Irish and English which had the most profound effects on the language, from the phonological system right through to a sociolinguistic situation where the continuing existence of Irish is now seriously threatened" (Ó Dochartaigh 1992, 14–15).

The standardized Classical Gaelic held sway until the beginning of the 17th century, when the Irish political structures and interrelations which supported it were suppressed militarily and effectively destroyed. Literary manuscripts after this period—that is, into the Modern Irish period—began to reflect the linguistic features of the three major dialect regions, Ulster, Connacht, and Munster, as do Irish literature and radio broadcasts of today.

Colleen Cotter points out in Chapter 24 that present-day "Ireland is a mostly English-speaking country that nonetheless reveres its heritage language." Native speakers of this heritage are to be found primarily in the three small Gaeltachts mentioned in the previous paragraph. By contrast, the number of people who know Irish as a second language, as a result of the Irish educational system, exceeds that of native speakers. While this disparity might at first blush be a cause for sadness, on reflection it must be considered a triumph and an example for other communities that possess an endangered linguistic heritage. It is an example of what can be accomplished if resources are devoted to language maintenance, or even reclamation (see Chapter 2 for a brief discussion of the West Belfast project). Radio, the focus of Chapter 24, has an important contribution to make in the promotion of a "heritage language."

It is not unusual for progressive projects to find their roots in protest. This is true in the case of contemporary Irish-language radio, whose origin was an unauthorized Irish-language radio station set up by activists in one of the Gaeltachts. In response, the government established and funded Raidió na Gaeltachta in 1972, one of two organizations now broadcasting extensively in Irish, the other being Raidió na Life. The first represents the traditional Gaeltachts, while the second represents the urban Irish. Together, they accomplish important, largely complementary roles in the promotion of Irish within a range of radio programming comparable to what is available in English. On the one hand, Raidió na Gaeltachta promotes traditional Irish linguistic norms, and while it helps to maintain the distinctive features of the three Gaeltachts, it nonetheless fosters cross-dialect comprehension, and consequently a measure of linguistic unity, through the familiarity which daily broadcasts inevitably bring about. Raidió na Life, on the other hand, supports the large number of Irish citizens who are either learning Irish as a second language or who know Irish but have no true Gaeltacht connections or affiliations.

Reference

Ó Dochartaigh, Cathair. 1992. The Irish language. In *The Celtic languages*, ed. Donald MacAulay, 11–99. Cambridge: Cambridge University Press.

24

Continuity and Vitality

Expanding Domains through Irish-Language Radio

COLLEEN COTTER

Department of Linguistics
Georgetown University
Washington, D.C.

Ireland is a mostly English-speaking country that none-theless reveres its heritage language. In Ireland, as in many once-colonized bilingual societies throughout the world, the heritage language (in this case Irish) remains a symbol of national identity but has relatively few fluent speakers. While the language has long been in decline—some Irish citizens declare it already dead (Hindley 1990)—it is nonetheless supported by public and private initiatives, by groups and individuals who work hard to create conditions of vitality. One enterprise that has flourished as a site of language use and language identity has been the media, radio in particular, and more recently, television.

As a language-development mechanism, Irish-language radio is not a new enterprise, but one that has developed in new ways in the past several years, as this chapter will outline.

Radio has been used explicitly for nearly 30 years as a tool for the preservation and growth of the Irish language. (Ireland's example presaged a policy of the European Union's Bureau of Lesser-Used Languages, which endorses incorporating media in any language-preservation program.) This chapter compares the programming and language policy of the two most prominent Irish-language stations in Ireland, one of which attempts to conserve existing linguistic practices (Gaeltacht-based Raidió na Gaeltachta) and the other of which promotes innovative use of language (Dublin-based Raidió na Life). The two Irish-language radio stations provide useful, but different, renditions of the potential language-development practices of a minority language.

Together, the stations work to extend the language into modern contexts, the historical significance of which will be discussed. Using the media as a vehicle, Irish-language broadcast practitioners are engaged in building a social infrastructure in which use of language occurs as a consequence of the activity, rather than in an artificial environment (such as a classroom) that alone cannot sustain language growth. The Irish case provides additional models for endangered languages elsewhere and more fully explicates the potential positive role of media in minority-language development, which to date has not been systematically explored.

THE IRISH LANGUAGE IN IRELAND

The Irish language has been in decline since before the famine of the 1840s, with 10,000–25,000 speakers reporting fluency today, although, thanks to compulsory schooling, there is a significant degree of passive ability. Those who reside in the rural Gaeltachts, located on the northern and western fringes of the country far from Dublin, are primarily bilingual speakers. The Gaeltachts are the historical strongholds of the language and have long been the focus of preservationists.

The modern preservation movement of the last 100 years, initiated in 1894 by the Conradh na Gaeilge, or Gaelic League, has concerned itself with these Irish-speaking rural areas, which are also the recipients of considerable government funding for language development, including *deontas* (grant) monies based on family-member language use. In terms of current language attitudes, having the *teanga ó dúchais*, the native language as spoken in the Gaeltachts, is seen as highly desirable.

Influence on Irish[1] through contact with English and French occurred as early as the late 12th century with the Anglo-Norman invasion. Irish held ground as the vernacular language, enjoying prestige in this domain, until the end of the 15th century (M. Ó Murchú 1985). Several centuries of

British political and linguistic suppression in Ireland had undermined the Irish language by the 17th century. English was the dominant language, and carried the prestige in diglossic communities, as its speakers were the only ones with social power and influence (M. Ó Murchú 1985; Ihde 1994). Political events had by this time eliminated the Irish learned classes, and the domination of the British had reached a high point, extending to social and educational realms. Only 5% of the land was held by Catholics, in the main Irish speaking. The Catholic Church, formerly a stronghold, stopped using Irish.

> English was clearly a desirable key—more and more the only key—to progress. If the church did not adapt itself to this situation, the incipient Catholic middle classes of the towns might be skimmed off, too, in due course, by the Established Church. It behooved the Catholic leadership to meet the demand for education appropriate to an English-speaking world. The Relief Act of 1782, which permitted Catholics to teach, tolled the knell of the old traditional educational arrangements. . . . Henceforth, continental cultural influence in Ireland would wane. (De Fréine 1978, 71–72)

A period of transitional bilingualism during the 18th and 19th centuries resulted in a rapid decrease in the Irish language. Negative attitudes toward Irish, among its uneducated and rural native speakers as well as among both more economically advantaged Irish and English speakers, cemented this stratification (Ihde 1994, 33). The language was seen as defective (judgments Dorian 1981 reports for Scots Gaelic during the same period), with people forgetting, according to De Fréine, that "when people abandon their language, they do so not because it is deficient but because their society is" (De Fréine 1978, 67).

The penalties for speaking Irish were severe.

> Irish speakers commonly became the butt of ridicule and contempt. Parents who knew no English used violence to prevent their children from speaking the only language to which they had natural access . . . *Children admitted to speaking Irish, as a sin, in the confessional* [emphasis mine]. In many places they were forced to wear the notorious tally stick . . . so that they could be beaten later by their parents or teachers for every mark on the stick. . . . When the shift did occur, it generally took no more than a generation to indoctrinate the children with such antipathy to the language that they in turn refused to speak it to their children. (De Fréine 1978, 73)

The combination of socially, physically, and economically punitive factors resulted in a rapid shift away from Irish use and, as a consequence, toward a dialect of English known presently as Hiberno-English, the variety of English spoken by people in Ireland. Thomason and Kaufman 1988 attribute the current distinctive intonation patterns of Hiberno-English, as well as other linguistic features, to the rapidity of the socially motivated shift and to imperfect group learning of the target language. That Hiberno-English currently is a class-linked dialect is one legacy of its origins.

Despite continued penalties for using it, the Irish language of the late 18th and early 19th centuries gave indications of being revived, thanks to a population explosion in the isolated, poor, rural pockets where Irish was still spoken monolingually. But famine, emigration, and political powerlessness decimated these populations and, with them, the language. For example, Máirtín Ó Murchú notes that "no more than 12.66% were Irish-speaking of those who were ten years or under in 1851" (M. Ó Murchú 1985, 28). "These Irish-speaking masses were without economic or political power, and had no means of determining their own destiny" (M. Ó Murchú 1985, 26). Dorian, in her seminal work on the demise of a dialect of Scots Gaelic, refers to the sociologist Michael Hechter's notion of "internal colonialism" (Dorian 1981, 19), which afflicted all of Britain's "Celtic fringe." The concept, in which the power structures of a colonizer society dominate the lives of inhabitants within or near its own boundaries, is applicable to the Irish situation.

De Fréine reads the census data differently and notes:

> The census of 1851 indicates a widespread denial of a knowledge of Irish. . . . Obviously, many who claimed to know English in 1851 did not know enough to bring up their children as English speakers. (De Fréine 1978, 73)

Máirtín Ó Murchú himself observes the complexities of census and other data in determining numbers of speakers as a way of gauging the progress of shift. Even today, it is difficult to get an exact numerical figure for the Irish-speaking population. Hindley (1990), whose book on the purported death of Irish presents a careful, fine-grained analysis of census and *deontas* records, notes problems accounting for the inconsistencies and overgeneralizations of the data, making it clear that the statistics belie the real language situation. He rectifies this limited statistical view by looking at small portions of the picture—notably single parishes or school districts—noting the extrastatistical circumstances that influenced language use in microsegments of the Irish-speaking community. His rationale can also be a rationale for looking at radio data as a product of a bounded discourse community, a media-centered microsegment of the population which is nonetheless linguistically and socially influential in society.

Negative attitudes toward the language and its rural, uneducated users following the famine persisted into the modern day. The speakers' low social and economic status was linked to their use of a disfavored language, making it seem only "logical" to eliminate the language as a first step to eliminating stigmas of other kinds.[2]

While the undisputed economic advantage of knowing English hastened the process of language loss in the last century, at the same time Irish managed to remain strong as a *symbol* of Irish nationhood. Irish was named the first official language when the Republic of Ireland was formed in 1922, linking linguistic pride with national pride, language with nationhood. The de facto use of a language does not always match its intended function, leading some researchers (such as Coulmas 1992) to claim that a language, no matter how lovingly and financially supported, will not persist unless there is an economic reason for doing so. Symbolic value is potent for other affiliations with language, such as national identity, which De Fréine sees rather critically as the sole function of Irish in the 1920s and 1930s:

> Between the World Wars there was no apparent need for the language. It was confidently expected in the years after 1921 that the major problems of Irish life would evaporate in the warm air of freedom. Irish was regarded largely as a fitting badge of nationality. There was, in those emotionally-satisfying years, little need to regard it otherwise: *it performed much the same function as the word Éire on the postage stamps and the national flag over Dublin Castle* [emphasis mine]. (De Fréine 1978, 116)

Language-attitude surveys conducted by the Institúid Teangeolaíochta Éireann (Irish Linguistics Institute) in the mid-1990s indicate that this symbolic-nationalistic link remains strong in the national consciousness.

Despite its strong symbolic value, the Irish language in day-to-day use remains largely restricted to the rural coastal areas that once experienced the full consequences of the famine. The current urban exceptions in Dublin and Belfast, the latter described in Maguire 1986, as well as the "constructed Gaeltacht" in Rath Cairn north of Dublin, have become relevant only very recently. (Indeed, the revitalization of the language in Dublin in these early days of the new century [cf. Cotter 1999], including the emergence of a new variety by speakers who attend the all-Irish schools, is worthy of note and further attention.) Any map that shows the Gaeltachts today makes immediately evident their geographical separation from each other. Of course with cars, roads, satellite dishes, television, VCRs, the Internet, and employment-instigated emigration being a major part of 21st-century Gaeltacht life, Gaeltacht residents are far from isolated from the rest of the world.[3] Because the language has traditionally persisted in areas that accrue low social status or economic prestige, maintaining the language within the sphere of the Gaeltachts becomes problematic. Edwards cites the "paradox of the Gaeltacht": left alone, the area will shrink and no longer be viable linguistically; if something is done, "then the enclave becomes artificial and those within it can take on the appearance of fish in a bowl" (Edwards 1994, 109).

Revival efforts started a century ago have held the erosion at bay in many respects (cf. Kiberd 1996, De Fréine 1978, Hindley 1990, and others), but they have also uncovered other problems that affect preservation efforts. Ironically, the strong dialect group affiliations have created hurdles. None of the three main dialect regions—Ulster in the north, Connacht in the west, and Munster in the south—is considered the standard, and no dialect group has been willing to defer to another for the "honor." For that reason, a compromise standard that rather arbitrarily includes features from all the dialects, known as An Caighdeán, was instituted for education and government functions in the 1950s. The result of that is a variety of the language spoken primarily by native English speakers who do not live in a Gaeltacht, a fact that brings its own influence to bear on the language, since this is the variety that nonnative Irish broadcast announcers will use. Interestingly, while An Caighdeán is used and ratified by the society's institutions, the prestige targets for speakers remain the various dialects of the Gaeltacht (which is contrary to many of the contact situations described in the sociolinguistic literature, including Blom and Gumperz 1972, in which the language of institutions becomes a "high" language with prestige).

Irish "language workers" in the linguistic trenches see the evolution of the language from a different perspective. Pádraig Ó Duibhir, the manager of broadcasting services for Raidió na Gaeltachta, focuses on how far the language came in the late 20th century. In the 1950s Irish was a rural language, Ó Duibhir said. It expanded to the cities in the 1960s and 1970s with internal migration, which forced the language to develop with respect to commerce, trade, and technology (Ó Duibhir, 1994 interview).

The creation of the Irish department at University College Galway, the formation of Údaras na Gaeltachta (the government's Gaeltacht Authority), and increasing participation of Irish bilingual speakers in general social and economic development has "given the language a status" it did not have three or four decades ago, Ó Duibhir says.

Number of Speakers

It is difficult to pin down the number of speakers who use the Irish language, especially since Gaeltacht figures compare differently from the rest of the population. In a recent census, one-third of the overall population described themselves as Irish speakers. Given that Irish is compulsory in school, this is hardly remarkable; it says nothing about the degree of proficiency or use, since census data typically do not attempt to ascertain different levels (cf. M. Ó Murchú 1985). The most recent analysis of 1996 census data indicates that 3% of the population of over 3 million report speaking Irish on a daily basis (Murphy 1999).

Focusing on the Gaeltacht areas, Ó Murchú says, "It is fairly reliably estimated that no more than 25,000 of the Gaeltacht population now use Irish consistently in day-to-day conversation" (M. Ó Murchú 1985, 29). Ó Siadhail supports this figure with pessimism: "The population of the Gaeltacht may now be considerably less than 25,000 with hardly any monoglots remaining" (Ó Siadhail 1989, 2). This contrasts with usage judgments overall: the Gaeltacht population in 1971 was 65,982, with 83.3% indicating that they were Irish speakers; the population in 1981 increased to 75,000, but usage claims declined to 77.4%. However, a survey from the early 1980s indicates the percentage who actually use the language countrywide to be much lower in relation to these Gaeltacht figures (from M. Ó Murchú 1985, 32). Note the high percentage of no. 5:

Actual use	Percentage of users
1. In conversation since leaving school	18%
2. In writing since leaving school	5%
3. Frequently or normally in home	5%
4. Sometimes in home	35%
5. [Listening to] Program in Irish on TV	72%

Additionally, Ó Murchú cites a separate pre-1985 survey that indicates that more Irish-speaking parents than previously are using only English with their children: English only 46.1%; English and Irish 33.7%; and Irish only 20.2%. Given these numbers, and the importance of speaking daily, it seems reasonable to give the 25,000-speaker assessment the most significance.

Of greater interest in Ireland in recent years have been the results of a survey, undertaken by the Institiúid Teangeolaíochta Éireann. For example, results published in March 1994 in the Irish press created a flurry of commentary and discussion. As in earlier surveys, speakers reported a largely passive knowledge of Irish. In contrast with the high percentage of respondents who would watch an Irish-language television program—for which only passive knowledge of the spoken language is needed—the 1993 survey indicates that only 16% of the respondents occasionally or frequently read Irish-language columns in daily newspapers (*Irish Times,* March 22, 1994). (Nonetheless, the ability to read has improved in the past 10 years, the *Times* noted about the survey results.)

Additionally, the 1993 survey indicated that 4% of the respondents listened to Raidió na Gaeltachta daily or frequently, and 11% listened to the station occasionally. These are not trivially small numbers, as only 2% of the respondents indicated "native speaker ability" and 9% indicated an ability to understand and participate in "most conversations." Statistically, all speakers who have a fair to great degree of Irish proficiency—11%—at some time listen to Raidió na Gaeltachta. (This survey was conducted before Raidió na Life started broadcasting.)

The value of the language *symbolically* exhibits no signs of erosion: 73% agreed that "no real Irish person can be against the revival of Irish." Furthermore, attitudes toward the value of the language have improved in the last 20 years.

> For example, while 42 [%] of the respondents in 1973 agreed with the statement, "Irish is a dead language," 31 per cent agreed with it in 1993. Last year, some 45 per cent agreed that Irish could still be revived as a common means of communications, compared with 39 percent in 1973.   (*Irish Times,* 22 March 1994)

IRISH-LANGUAGE BROADCAST MEDIA

Irish-language broadcast media in Ireland are very limited in comparison to the English-language offerings, which also include the BBC and a few cable stations. According to typical schedules published in *RTÉ [Raidió Teilifís Éireann] Guide,* Ireland's equivalent to *TV Guide,* in the late 1990s, the Irish national stations offer five minutes of *nuacht*—news in Irish—daily on their English-language networks and a longer current-events program weekly in addition to documentaries or special programs. (See Mac Póilin and Andrews's *BBC and the Irish Language* (1993) for an extended discussion of the BBC's limited commitment to the Irish language in Northern Ireland. This contrasts with the strong support of Welsh in Wales and Scots Gaelic in Scotland for which programming, money [1.5 million pounds in 1991], and institutional support are abundant.) The advent of Teilifís na Gaeilge (now known as TG4) in 1996 has changed the nature and quantity of the Irish-language offerings overall to some extent, particularly as RTÉ is now mandated to develop more Irish-language programming.

The most recent addition to the Irish media scene is Raidió na Life (RnaL), a Dublin-based community radio station that has been on the air since fall 1993. Before RnaL came along, the only broadcast outlet available to Irish speakers, especially ones from the Gaeltacht, was Raidió na Gaeltachta (RnaG). Both Irish radio stations' overt policies toward the Irish language represent a different point on the language preservation continuum: conservation and dialect integrity in the case of RnaG and linguistic innovation in the case of RnaL.

Raidió na Gaeltachta: "Scheduled Regionalism"

Raidió na Gaeltachta got its start in the early 1970s, after now-historic protests by language activists in the Western Connemara Gaeltacht. Unhappy with the tokenism on the national radio and television stations, the activists started an unauthorized "pirate" Irish-language station in Connemara, the most populous of the Gaeltachts. The government responded by officially establishing and funding an all-Irish radio station in 1972, the Raidió na Gaeltachta heard today. Kiberd recounts the events leading to the formation of RnaG:

> In 1969, inspired by the Civil Rights movement for black emancipation in the United States, a group of activists in the Connemara Gaeltacht launched their own campaign to revitalize the Irish-speaking areas. . . . The demand was for industrial development in the region, for proper schools and villages, for an autonomous local authority, and for a broadcasting service in the native language . . . the Cearta Sibhialta (Civil Rights) movement was in most respects remarkably successful . . . it managed to detach Irish from the purgatorial fires of the school classroom and to present it as part of a global counter-cultural movement constructed upon "small is beautiful" principles. (Kiberd 1996, 567–68)

Indeed, as the only station in the world broadcasting to ethnic minorities at the time, RnaG was a "trail-blazing service in '72," according to Pádraig Ó Duibhir, manager of broadcasting services at Raidió na Gaeltachta. Now, throughout Europe, there are some 30–40 radio stations broadcasting in minority languages and assisting the promotion of what are termed the "lesser-used" languages (cf. Helen Ó Murchú, 1999 personal communication).

From the start, RnaG was intended as an Irish-language media service for people in the geographically far-flung Gaeltachts. While headquartered in the Connemara Gaeltacht, the station in fact broadcasts daily from the country's three primary dialect regions, and its signal can be heard anywhere in the country. The term used at RnaG offices to describe this conscious media juxtaposition of the separate Gaeltachts is "scheduled regionalism" (Pádraig Ó Duibhir, 1994 inverview).

The station broadcasts for about 12 hours daily. RnaG programming includes regular news broadcasts from the three major dialect areas, national and international news, sports, traditional music, lengthy interviews, current affairs programming, community notices, obituaries, and Sunday Mass.

"The job of evolving the language has fallen on us by default," Ó Duibhir said in 1994, before the presence of RnaL was established. All work at the station is conducted through the medium of Irish, except for some technical contacts done through English where necessary, he said.

Besides its impact on the language itself, including reported greater mutual intelligibility among the dialects (although no reported dialect leveling) and introduction of modern terms into the lexicon through reporting the news, the station also serves to reinforce traditional cultural practices. Their strict no-English policy extends to song lyrics. The station, with its professional mix of news and current affairs programming, has become the standard-bearer of the language and a model for quality Irish-language radio broadcast practice. Surveys indicate that listenership is highest among middle-aged and older speakers in areas farthest from cities, a relevant point in language contraction discussion.

Of all media offerings in Ireland—some 40 local radio stations, 3 national radio stations, TG4, and 2 national television stations (plus BBC, CNN, and Skye TV)—RnaG is the only nationwide medium that broadcasts completely in Irish. The situation is considered even less auspicious in print, with Irish-language papers arising and folding and only a standing weekly half-page in Irish in the English-language *Irish Times*. In contrast, the World Wide Web is making its own impact these days with new Web sites in Irish and new forums for language development.

Explicitly, the station's mission is to provide radio service and to "support revival of the language." The station focuses on two aspects of the language: conservation, particularly through its library of tape recordings of interviews, stories, traditional music, and so on; and development of the language, which means expanding the vocabulary to accommo-

date contemporary topics and concerns, particularly employing words that one would find in the everyday news (AIDS, computers, etc.).

A result of RnaG's 30-year tenure on the airwaves is that speakers report a higher incidence of mutual intelligibility across dialects (H. Ó Murchú, Krauss, and Ó Duibhir, personal communication). Despite their geographical separation, the dialects are considered mutually intelligible. However, a generation ago certain phonological features made total comprehension difficult, especially by speakers from either end of the country (Krauss, personal communication). RnaG's presence has effectively foreshortened the dialect continuum as it extends from the south to the north (and into Scotland). Given the strong affiliation and solidarity of speakers with the local dialects, reinforced by jokes told about other dialect speakers, it is likely that the radio's influence has extended to making speakers aware of correspondences with other dialects.

The strong identification with one's own dialect dictates listening preferences. Early on, RnaG discovered that speakers would tune in for broadcasts in their own dialect, but turn off when a broadcast in another dialect aired (cf. Ó Duibhir 1994), something that is easily observed in Gaeltacht households. For this reason, the station continues to rotate the dialect broadcasts within the broadcast day. The news from Donegal is never at the same time, for instance (although it is found within the time period allotted to the news, so listeners have necessary consistency). Sunday Mass, broadcast live from the Gaeltachts, is rotated each week by region. As previously mentioned, Ó Duibhir calls this deliberate mixing of the dialects within the stream of radio talk "scheduled regionalism" (1994 interview).

While it is important to consider the strong affiliations speakers have with their dialects, it is also significant to keep in mind that the *Gaeilge na daoine* (Irish of the people, the local dialects) is considered one language, part of the country's unified linguistic heritage. This attitude (and the related superfluous position of Scottish Gaelic in the Irish mind) is vividly illustrated in the general introduction to Ó Siadhail's *Modern Irish: Grammatical Structure and Dialectal Variation:*

> It is hoped that by giving an overall picture of the system, this wide description will illustrate the variation between the dialects against the unified background of the language. In the end, despite all the variation, and given the fact that Scottish Gaelic must be regarded on sociological grounds as a separate language, one is inevitably left with the sense that Irish is a single language. (Ó Siadhail 1989, 11)

Inter-dialect unity is also achieved through the *content* of the local broadcasts by reinforcing knowledge of community patterns, practices, and values, which are held in common across the dialects since they all share a similar socioeconomic history. The result is a sense of the importance of one's own dialect, and of the language overall, something RnaG has aimed at establishing. As a consequence, the station is considered "an important feature of Irish life," according to Pádraig Ó hAoláin of the Gaeltacht Authority (Údaras na Gaeltachta) in Galway (personal communication).

Listenership figures seem to bear out the perceived relevance to Gaeltacht speakers. At least one linguistic survey (cited in Ó Riagáin 1992) of the 6,000 residents in the southwestern Dingle Peninsula has looked at television and radio listening patterns. In the area where the language is most heavily used, the western end of the peninsula, 79% of the respondents said they listened to Raidió na Gaeltachta daily (compared with 33% in the only town in the region and 59% in the eastern end of the peninsula). The ratios are similar to those of respondents who watch Irish-language television programs when they are aired on national television: 51% in the western end of the peninsula reported a high rate of watching, compared with high rates from 26% in the town and 40% in the eastern end (Ó Riagáin 1992, 72).

RnaG itself reports high listenership—39%—within the totality of the country's Gaeltachts. Its surveys also indicate—and this is sociolinguistically relevant with respect to language endangerment—that "listenership is strongest in the over 35 age groups, in households where Irish is the main home language, in . . . [the west,] and among the farming community" (Raidió na Gaeltachta Audience Research Department 1989, 2). These average-listener characteristics have wider linguistic implications, one of which has been to set the stage for the evolution of Raidió na Life, as will be described.

RnaG very strictly follows its all-Irish, no-English mandate, even in song lyrics. A program producer must get management permission in advance to use English lyrics, and then "only to establish a theme or the atmosphere of the program," according to Ó Duibhir, RnaG's manager of broadcasting services. An example would be a verse or two from the song "The Galway Races" to introduce a program, in Irish, about the annual Galway hooker (tall sailing ship) races. There have been one or two interviews in English in the history of the station, but those circumstances "have been exceptional," Ó Duibhir said. (A short interview in English with the first president of the European Economic Community, Lord Thompson, was deemed "of sufficient importance" to be aired, Ó Duibhir recalled.)

The Irish-only mandate does not reflect sociolinguistic reality in the world outside the broadcast studio. That stance was good-naturedly ridiculed as not reflecting "real life" several years ago in an Irish-language soap opera (*Ros na Rún* [Headland of the Secrets]) in which a Gaeltacht-reared radio reporter fed Irish lines to the new manager of a Gaeltacht-based factory, a non-fluent Dublin-born learner, as she taped her interview with him. Her intention was to edit him later and make his on-air Irish sound fluent. Subtextually, the joke was on both of them—and microcosmically reflective of a century's worth of language preservation work and education in Ireland.

Raidió na Life: Gaeltacht of the Air

Raidió na Life programmers aim to fill the gap they perceive to be left by RnaG and pitch their programming to the urban dweller, especially targeting young Irish speakers who do not have the benefit of a Gaeltacht to promote the linguistic solidarity and exposure that RnaG achieves.

RnaL broadcasts out of Dublin from late afternoon to late evening daily. Whereas RnaG is transmitted countrywide, RnaL's community license signal extends only 18 miles into the greater Dublin area. Its programming includes news broadcasts, traffic and weather during commuting hours, current affairs, business and tax advice, music and arts programs, community notices, and a continually updated entertainment listing of what is going on in Dublin. Agricultural references, typical of Gaeltacht radio, are noticeably absent.

"The local service, the lost sheep, ram . . . is not interesting to Dublin. It's very parochial, and not listened to by people in the city," said Éamonn Ó Dónaill, a language consultant and one of the station's founders.

As only the second all-Irish media outlet at its inception, RnaL has been much discussed, criticized, and listened to since its on-air debut in September 1993. A national listenership survey conducted in late 1994 reported 14,000 listeners in the 15-to-early-30s age group in the Dublin area. This figure includes the tiny Gaeltacht of Ráth Cairn north of Dublin and areas to the west, where there are no mountains to obstruct the signal (Seosamh Ó Murchú, personal communication, 1995).

The station is run by a steering committee of seven people; three full-time employees (the station manager, the ad manager, and a technician), and a rotating pool of volunteers, mostly young and college educated. The station sees itself as an opportunity for language practice. "There's a confidence gained from working at the station. . . . People who never thought they would speak Irish now speak Irish exclusively. We never turn anybody away," said Ó Dónaill (personal communication 1994), referring to the work philosophy that allows for a job of some sort for anyone who wants to participate.

The station's utilization on the air of speakers whose Irish varies greatly in fluency, as well as those who speak a low-prestige variety (Dublin Irish) nonetheless spoken extensively by the bilingual natives of the urban area, has two interesting results. First, the station staffers essentially disregard received assumptions about preservation practice in Ireland; and second, they can be seen as introducing new strategies to the language-development arsenal.

The station has three primary goals, not dissimilar to RnaG's and considered very carefully by the original organizers, but tailored to the urban environment:

• to provide a language service to Irish speakers living in Dublin, including those at the local all-Irish schools, who have no convenient contact with the language once they leave school;

• to enhance the status of the language via a modern discourse channel—the media—and in so doing show people that the language, generally associated with traditional activities, can be adjusted to modern life; and

• to appeal to a younger audience by using contemporary music.

This last point—music as a vehicle for promoting the language—is considered a key factor by many people involved in the station, who saw that traditional music values and language values were perceived to be inseparable (an attitude toward the language that RnaG consciously or inadvertently fosters with its programming goals). According to Ó Dónaill, writing in a 1995 issue of the Irish-language journal *Oghma* (translated from Irish):

> It is arrogant to say that young people ought to listen to the kind of music that interests us and that they are not properly Irish unless they do the same! This sort of thing puts people against the language. Irish isn't a package deal—a person should be able to be interested in the language but ignore other aspects of the culture if he or she is inclined to do that. (Ó Dónaill 1995)

By offering mainstream and world music *(ceolta na cruinne)* as well as traditional styles (such as *sean-nós*, or old-style singing), it is RnaL's intention to attract attention to the language via popular culture and discussion of contemporary concerns. This creates a new association with Irish, one which can form a basis for using Irish in other contemporary ways and foster its growth. "The change has to come from within the Irish language. I think it's important for Raidió na Gaeltachta and the media to talk about contemporary issues . . . so the language will evolve," Ó Dónaill said.

An early criticism of RnaL revolved around music: that it was failing in its mission as an Irish-language radio station because it presented a great deal of English through song lyrics (some 80% of the music programming is in English). But the philosophy was to get young people interested first, according to Rónan Ó Dubhthaigh,[4] RnaL's first station manager, who equates music policy with language policy.

> People would say there's more English on the station than Irish, if you took the lyrics into account. But people are going to listen to English music anyway. They're going to listen to music they like. That's something like a language policy—you can't tell people what they like. You give them what they like. You try to introduce them to (additional) things (in the process). (Ó Dubhthaigh, personal communication, 1995)

Ó Dubhthaigh also backgrounded the issue through one of the genres characteristic of broadcast media: the station promo (a short phrase or jingle accompanied by music that identifies the broadcast outlet and is taped and aired regularly). One station promo runs as follows:

> *Labhairtear dhá teanga ar an aer—an Ghaeilge agus an ceol.* (Two languages are spoken on the air—Irish and music.)

The station, articulating that two languages are spoken on RnaL—Irish and music—manages to alter existing linguistic power relations. Without denying the importance of English in the bilingual Irish culture, or even in RnaL programming, the slogan makes a strong statement by subverting expectations of what a language can be. In this instance, it gives music the status of a second language. Irish and music are equally paired, striking a deep connection in Irish heritage, and the cultural shaping force of English is diminished in importance.[5]

In the process of developing the station's language-related goals, its organizers have managed to emphasize language production over prescriptive constraints on speaking the language, mitigating generations of internalized linguistic insecurity. Since Gaeltacht speakers already have access to and identification with their own speech community, RnaL, using the urban arena and topics relevant to urban life in relation to its stated language-planning goals, could be seen as constructing a speech community over the airwaves in Dublin—a de facto Gaeltacht of the Air.

The station is also building an Irish language–speaking community of its own, as Irish is the language used by the staff as it goes about its business of producing radio. As previously mentioned, the station is staffed almost exclusively by volunteers, most of them in their early 20s, college educated, and natives of Dublin with limited or no connection to the Gaeltachts. No matter the level of proficiency, all who work at the station, whether on air or not, are expected to use the language as they go about their daily business. Some volunteers have produced weekly shows for over six years (Cotter 1999).

The station attracts volunteers who want experience either with media or with Irish in a workplace setting. The station sees itself as a training ground for careers at other media outlets in Ireland, both Irish and English. Several volunteers who were interviewed in 1995, 1997, and 1999 indicated they planned to find English-language media jobs following their stint at RnaL. One steering committee member said that the best volunteers at the station were those with a strong commitment to journalism first and the language second.

Underlying both the philosophy of RnaL and its resultant language-use practices is a conscious focus on *growth* of the language, rather than the more traditional emphasis on *preservation*. In this view, growth comes from a focus on use and not from a focus on retaining all the characteristic features of a language seen to be inevitably slipping from communicative importance. Given the history of the preservation movement in Ireland, this is a radical departure from previous approaches to "the language issue."

Ó Dónaill indicates that at "RnaL. . . . There is a desire to get away from the old worn-out rhetoric (e.g. 'It's part of what we are') and not make the fact that the station operates through Irish an issue. The station is striving to promote Irish in an indirect, non-didactic way. Most of the young people there aren't involved for ideological reasons" (personal communication, 1996).

Several of the people associated with RnaL emphasized that their own personal perspective on language work, as well as RnaL's, is attuned to language growth and not language preservation. This means that mistakes, disfluencies, and English-dependent loan translations—which are of interest to linguists considering language loss processes—are tolerated in an effort to produce language outside of the classroom and in a workplace environment. Seosamh Ó Murchú, an editor at the publishing house An Gúm and former RnaL consultant, remarked that one "can't put [a language] in a preservation container. Only in the last couple years have we moved to actively take the language out of the preservation jar and put it [out] so it will develop" (S. Ó Murchú, 1995 interview).

Taking the language out of amber is not merely a sentimental exercise. It forces the language to expand its domains of use, the contraction of which is a characteristic of a dying language (cf. Dorian 1981, 1991; Fishman 1972). Ó Dónaill (1995) writes (my translation from Irish): "We must do our best to look at ways to bring the language into new domains." (Despite RnaG's tendency to emphasize traditional Irish community practices, linguistic and cultural, it must be pointed out that the radio station in recent years has been attempting to gear some of its programming for younger, urban Irish speakers, with very popular results [James McCloskey, personal communication]).

To further establish its position as a language of use in a workplace domain, RnaL puts journalism and its governing principles in the foreground. The result is that language preservation issues—a favorite topic among activist users of the language—are discussed only if they are newsworthy, according to former RnaL station manager Rónan Ó Dubhthaigh (1995). Instead of being discussed as if it were a hospital patient, the language is being *used*. Performance is evaluated with reference to the norms expected of a media practitioner (can the presenter produce a story in a media genre, can a presenter work under deadline, can a presenter sound like he or she is speaking within a broadcast context, etc.).

At RnaL, with news coming first, language is backgrounded as a communicative tool and not foregrounded as a symbol. The following excerpt from an extended discussion with Ó Dubhthaigh illustrates the station staff's focus on the necessary principles of journalism (such as finding a good story, getting scoops, and asserting themselves as a credible media source). It also demonstrates the collegial feel of a group of like-minded volunteers working to accomplish a professional task involving language:

> The people help each other out . . . one of the programs is Um Thráthnóna which is a half-hour news program—very difficult to do in Irish. . . . And that was a program everyone helped out with: "Oh! Story! Person! Phone number! Yes, have it here, boom, off you go!" . . . We had some very, very good producers and some very, very good programs and some very, very good scoops.
>
> For instance, when Cathal Goan was announced as the head of Teilifís na Gaeilge his first interview was on Raidió na Life, even though he was working on RTÉ at the time. And that even gave him a kick. The Irish press that was still in existence at the time phoned us up and said, "you know, would you have the number for Cathal Goan?" "Well, actually we're going to be interviewing him at quarter past six." "Oh, are you! Will you get me a tape of that and send it over?"
>
> So little things like that. We were getting there first. We were doing things that were a little bit towards the cutting edge. We were getting our scoops.
>
> It also helped assert us as a station that wasn't just following. We were creating something, as well. (Ó Dubhthaigh, 1995)

ACCOMPLISHMENTS OF IRISH-LANGUAGE RADIO

What have the stations accomplished in terms of language revitalization? RnaG's stated goals are to establish Gaeltacht community links through language and to enhance the contemporary status of Irish. A logical third goal, which is not strictly part of RnaG's ideology, would be that of alleviating an historically ingrained linguistic insecurity, which RnaL more explicitly addresses. RnaL's goals are to evoke language change from within. Specifically, RnaL intends to give people an outlet for the language they learned in school and a reason to learn the language; to provide a service to urban Irish speakers who would otherwise be isolated from each other, particularly the ones attending all-Irish schools; and, with RnaG, to show people that the language can adjust to modern life—that one can talk about anything through the medium of Irish.

Unity of Speech Community

RnaG appears to have been successful in fulfilling its intentions to establish inter-Gaeltacht connections. As stated earlier, RnaG both differentiates the dialect areas with its explicit broadcasts from the three regions and unites the dialect areas through the common language and through the temporal and discourse structures of the medium. Unity among the Gaeltachts is also achieved through the content of the local broadcasts by reinforcing knowledge of community patterns, practices, and values, including artistic ones, which are held in common across the dialects since they all share a similar socioeconomic history. The result is a sense of the importance of one's own dialect and its connection to the language overall. Additionally, there is the reported higher incidence of mutual intelligibility among speakers of different dialects.

Raidió na Gaeltachta also serves an integrative function in the larger bilingual social context, mirroring existing language policies in industry and education. News broadcasts are modeled on the BBC and are characterized by Anglo-

American broadcast discourse structure and intonation patterns, which is particularly evident in non-dialectal news readers. Additionally, the admittedly cautious insertion of various loan-words into the Irish news texts and occasional evidence of on-air code-switching, especially in interview contexts, reflect what occurs in the language generally, not just in the media. Overall, the tendencies are conservative and not innovative, a feature of most Irish genres.

The structures of the broadcast genre, borrowed as they are from the English-language broadcast milieu, reinforce the dominant English-language status quo but for the purposes of furthering the continuity and vitality of the minority language. Much as speechwriters or editorial writers "borrow" status and position by citing an expert, minority-language radio tends to borrow its status and position by sounding like the dominant-language media of the larger culture. This can be viewed as a necessary maneuver for garnering credibility, particularly when the minority language has little inherent or historical status in the public or institutional sphere, as is the case with Irish. Simultaneously, the local content programming on RnaG reinforces a sense of Gaeltacht community. As previously mentioned, radio programs cover items of Gaeltacht interest and promote traditional verbal and musical art forms (which Watson [1989] has credited the English-language media for eroding), as well as hybrid musical forms that rely on an interplay of traditional and contemporary resources.

The combination of Anglo discourse structure and Irish-interest content makes the language seem both normal (using familiar structures of the dominant language community) and special (using the referents of a once-stigmatized politically powerless community in the public, legitimizing sphere). The nature of this blend, that is to say, the negotiation of dominant ideology with the "core values" (cf. Smolicz 1992) or linguistic attributes of the minority-language community as expressed through the language of the media, could be a most revealing area for future research. The activities of the "intertextual gap" (cf. Brody 1995 and her Maya radio data, which document the simultaneous use of traditional Maya speech genres and target-Spanish-language radio genres; as well as Jaffe 1994 and Corsican-French forms on radio; and Spitulnik 1994 and Town Bemba forms on radio) would appear to vary according to social and linguistic history, offering evidence to support various theoretical positions about language change (e.g., Thomason and Kaufman 1988) or answer questions of social meaning posed by language-obsolescence researchers such as Woolard (1989).

In some ways RnaG's language conservation goals exclude the possibility of spontaneous innovation or flexibility, which is where RnaL steps in. With two decades of RnaG paving the way, RnaL is able to take another direction, filling certain gaps, particularly with respect to repairing linguistic insecurity, rampant in speakers who are not from the Gaeltacht. On the local level—in the RnaL studio itself—volunteer staffers with only little school Irish are speaking Irish with confidence months later. Everyone is given a job and everyone made to feel that his or her contribution is important. This extends to the linguistic realm. In the small world of the RnaL studio, the community of speakers has managed to alleviate linguistic insecurity and make the use of Irish (and a disfavored Dublin form at that) a high-status endeavor.

Since RnaL is more interested in affording young speakers an opportunity for practice than in meeting traditional standards of usage, the language on the air is marked by forms that accomplish a speaker's communicative goals at the expense of idiomatic Irish. Often, the sentence and intonation patterns resemble English more than Irish. Even a short broadcast segment provides ready examples of loan translations of the English equivalents, such as *Cad tá difriúil* 'What is the difference' and *ar an aer* 'on the air'.

This attitude toward use brings together speakers for whom Irish would have remained an important but abstract relic of the school years, like some cherished but seldom opened yearbook. (Compulsory Irish in school has succeeded in making nearly every citizen familiar with the language, as Hindley 1990 describes in detail, but has not been able to expand domains for its use.) The needs of both audience and radio workers are considered in RnaL's approach, which is focused on building a speech community in the urban context, a context not historically sympathetic to the cultivation of an Irish-speaking speech community. The distinctive features of mass communication, the disjunction of place between community and audience, actually works in RnaL's favor. A nontraditional location—the airwaves—is used to create a nontraditional community. A comment by Bell (1991) is relevant here: "Radio is the most adaptable medium, and it is radio which has been most successful in overcoming the divide between communicator and audience" (85). For speakers lacking access to and cultural affinity for the traditional rural strongholds of the language, RnaL creates its own place, in essence its own Gaeltacht.

There are few venues—none significant—in which to practice Irish-language journalism, according to Ó Dónaill and others involved in the growth of RnaL and of Irish-language television, station TG4. They see Raidió na Gaeltachta, Raidió na Life, and TG4 as a place to foster this development. Should this plan succeed, one can imagine Irish radio and television journalists bringing into modern times the Irish legacy of the oral tradition, with broadcasters functioning as experts or "elders" on the various Gaeltachts of the Air.

Contemporary Relevance

One of the factors that has stood in the way of a reemergence of Irish is that it has been "deprived of contemporary status," according to the Gaeltacht Authority's Pádraig Ó hAoláin (personal communication). His view is shared by both RnaG and RnaL personnel. That the language can hold its own in the contemporary marketplace of ideas, via the channels of mass media, is considered a triumph by many in Ireland. That a language which can easily handle topics such as turf cutting or *poitín* making can also report on the war in Chechnya and Ireland's complex economic connections to the European Community is seen, especially via the radio, as a sign of its viability in contemporary society. Promoting the Irish language's contemporary status is part of both stations' overt linguistic philosophies, but their procedures differ. RnaL goes further by including more of the icons of urban life. TG4, the Irish-language television station, takes it yet further.

A slogan of the Gaeltacht Authority, which promotes the economic interests of the various Gaeltachts as well as the linguistic ones, is "normalise to popularise." If Irish citizens see and hear Irish being spoken on the radio and TV, its prestige rises, its former "rural" taint disappears. What is "normal" becomes popular, no longer stigmatized. TG4 broadcasts out of the Connemara Gaeltacht, not far from RnaG, providing typical programming, such as sports, news, features, and children's educational programs. It is a "contemporary venue for the transmission of Irish," according to Brían Mac Aongusa (1995 interview), who headed the startup of Teilifís na Gaeilge and is a longtime proponent of Irish-language broadcast media.

Besides providing a television outlet for people "who choose to speak Irish first in their homes," the station is also intended to encourage development of an Irish-language film and video industry.

CONCLUSION

Despite the reported differences that exist between the two radio stations in terms of approach to language maintenance, it is easy for an observer to see that each serves a vital, though different, purpose in enhancing the status of Irish. Their roles are complementary. RnaG adopts English-language discourse forms to give Irish-language media authority but maintains a strict policy of Irish-only content, preserving the language as it is spoken in the Gaeltachts, the traditional repositories of the language. RnaL innovates with a hybrid form[6] that challenges assumptions of the language's position in Irish life as well as the structural form of the language itself and meets the needs of urban speakers, creating a Gaeltacht of the Air.

Both facilitate Irish-language competence among interlocutors in their respective speech communities, reflecting the linguistic profiles of their target audiences. Together, they have the potential to expand the base of Irish speakers. RnaL and RnaG make a powerful statement about the social contexts of language use, their positions at either end of the preservation-growth spectrum affording a natural laboratory to consider sociolinguistic and discourse parameters that characterize language in flux.

The larger question, the extent to which the media can alter the effects of centuries of linguistic domination, is an open-ended one, and a wider comparative orientation will likely offer some answers.[7] Besides promoting language visibility, many minority-language media users, such as we find in Ireland and elsewhere, are attempting to publicly legitimize their language by using the recognized power of the mass media. I suggest that more linguists look at media in the same careful way they have observed the influence of religion and education on language change. Research of this nature can only present a fuller picture of the media's role in language obsolescence and revitalization.

Notes

1. Even calling the language "Irish" requires certain clarification. In Ireland, the term for the language is "Irish" (or "Modern Irish"). "Gaelic" has pejorative connotations (cf. M. Ó Murchú 1985) suggestive of its earlier history as peripheral to Irish life and marginal to the powerful institutions that wielded influence over citizens.

2. In some ways, the Irish situation over the past 150 years mirrors aspects of the decimation of American Indian languages, in that a level of usage necessary for maintaining fluency in the native language became nearly impossible to achieve. In both cases, there was government or political interference and a lack of overall educational resources; a devaluation of culturally identifiable discourse practices, especially in the oral tradition; educational practices that isolated children—physically and emotionally from the community of native speakers; and speakers' internalization of a belief in the inferiority of their native language. (See Hinton 1994 and Crawford 1992 for compelling examples from American Indian history.)

3. Geographical isolation from speakers of other dialects or languages is a key factor in preservation, as contact and its linguistic and cultural ramifications never even become an issue. Factors working against isolation, including broadcast media, which quite literally bring the outside world into the home, as well as improved roads and the privately owned automobile, have been discussed in relation to lesser-used languages generally by Dorian (1991) and in relation to Irish by Hindley (1990). Taniguchi (1955), in the decade before significant economic improvement of the standard of living also changed Irish social structures (cf. Kiberd 1996), cited how the "influence of education, wireless, films, and travel all militate against the survival" of unique varieties of language, including Irish English (Taniguchi 1955, vi).

4. Ó Dubhthaigh, a longtime Irish-language radio journalist, was RnaL's first station manager and now heads the country's first Irish-language radio and television certificate course at University College Galway.

5. This statement implies broad claims about the cultural echoes of the traditional past making an impact on present genre forms. This conceptualization is based on attitudes observed among Irish people, most vividly elucidated in an 8 January 1994 essay in the *New York Times Book Review*, "Why I Choose to Write in Irish, the Corpse That Sits Up and Talks Back," by the Irish poet Nuala Ní Dhomhnaill. She talks about her decision to write poetry in Irish and what its implications are. The issue is her identity and what she is capable of expressing in Irish. Since Irish cultural history includes stories of magic-and-human interaction, metaphysical permutations of being that are described in the old stories, she feels she can only speak of magic-human interaction in the modern world by using the vehicle of Irish. She would not—indeed, she says could not— talk about these concepts in English, because they are not part of the English linguistic or cultural heritage. In an indirect way, she supports Hale's (1992) claim that the loss of linguistic diversity means the loss of diverse ways of conceptualizing the world.

6. Similarly, Gal (1989) observes that narrow-users of Hungarian in the Hungarian-German bilingual community of Oberwart are more innovative than broad-users in certain kinds of word formation. While narrow-users exhibit the greatest lexical loss, they compensate through innovation. Lack of fellow speakers contributes to lexical loss, but the solidarity contributes to innovation.

7. See Martin 1996 for a discussion of radio production and its language-saving possibilities in North American tribes.

References

Bell, Allan. 1991. *The language of news media.* Oxford: Basil Blackwell.

Blom, Jan-Petter, and John J. Gumperz. 1972. Social meaning in linguistic structure: Code-switching in Norway. In *Directions in sociolinguistics: The ethnography of communication,* ed. John J. Gumperz and Dell Hymes, 407–434. New York: Holt, Rinehart and Winston.

Brody, Jill. 1995. Orality, radio, and literacy in the intertextual gap. Paper presented at Linguistic Society of America annual meeting. New Orleans. 7 January.

Cotter, Colleen. 1999. Raidió na Life: Innovations in the use of media for language revitalization. *International Journal of the Sociology of Language:* 135–47.

Coulmas, Florian. 1992. *Language and economy.* Oxford: Basil Blackwell.

Crawford, James. 1992. *Hold your tongue: Bilingualism and the politics of "English only."* Reading, Mass.: Addison-Wesley.

De Fréine, Seán. 1978. *The great silence: The study of a relationship between language and nationality.* Dublin: Mercier Press.

Dorian, Nancy. 1981. *Language death: The life cycle of a Scottish Gaelic dialect.* Philadelphia: University of Pennsylvania Press.

———. 1991. Surviving the broadcast media in small language communities. In *Educational Media International* 28: 134–137.

Edwards, John. 1994. *Multilingualism.* London: Routledge.

Fishman, Joshua. 1972. Societal bilingualism: Stable and transitional. In Fishman, *The Sociology of Language,* 91–106. Rowley, Mass.: Newbury House.

Gal, Susan. 1989. Lexical innovation and loss: The use and value of restricted Hungarian. In *Investigating obsolescence: Studies in language contraction and death,* ed. Nancy C. Dorian, 313–331. Cambridge: Cambridge University Press.

Hale, Ken. 1992. Language endangerment and the human value of linguistic diversity. In Hale et al., Endangered languages. *Language* 68, no. 1: 1–42.

Hindley, Reg. 1990. *The death of the Irish language: A qualified obituary.* Routledge: London and New York.

Hinton, Leanne. 1994. *Flutes of fire: Essays on California Indian languages.* Berkeley: Heyday Books.

Ihde, Thomas W., ed. 1994. *The Irish language in the United States: A historical, sociolinguistic, and applied linguistic survey.* Westport, Conn.: Bergin and Garvey.

Jaffe, Alexandra. 1994. Media, language, and identity on Corsica. American Anthropological Association annual meeting, Atlanta, Ga. 2 December.

Kiberd, Declan. 1996. *Inventing Ireland.* Cambridge, Mass.: Harvard University Press.

Mac Póilin, Aodán, and Liam Andrews. [1993]. *BBC and the Irish language.* Belfast: ULTACH Trust.

Maguire, Gabrielle. 1986. Language revival in an urban neo-Gaeltacht. In *Third International Conference on Minority Languages: Celtic papers,* ed. Gearóid Mac Eoin, Anders Ahlqvist, and Donncha Ó hAodha, 72–88. Clevedon, England: Multilingual Matters.

Martin, Kallen. 1996. Listen! Native radio can save languages. In *Native Americas: Akwe:kon's Journal of Indigenous Issues* 13, no. 1: 22–29.

Murphy, Judy. 1999. Numbers using Irish in Gaeltacht declining. *Irish Times,* 12 January.

Ní Dhomhnaill, Nuala. 1995. Why I choose to write in Irish, the corpse that sits up and talks back. *New York Times Book Review,* 8 January, 3⁺.

Ó Dónaill, Éamonn. 1995. Amharc Neamhléanta ar staid na Gaeilge faoi láthair [An unscholarly look at the current state of the Irish language]. In *Oghma* 7, 57–65, ed. Seosamh Ó Murchú, Mícheál Ó Cearúil, and Antain Mag Shamhráin. Dublin: Foilseacháin Oghma.

Ó Murchú, Máirtín. 1985. *The Irish language.* Dublin: Department of Foreign Affairs and Bord na Gaeilge.

Ó Riagáin, Pádraig. 1992. *Language maintenance and language shift as strategies of social reproduction: Irish in the Corca Dhuibhne Gaeltacht, 1926–1986.* Baile Átha Cliath: Institiúid Teangeolaíochta Éireann.

Ó Siadhail, Mícheál. 1989. *Modern Irish: Grammatical structure and dialectal variation.* Cambridge: Cambridge University Press.

Raidió na Gaeltachta Audience Research Department. February 1989. Gaeltacht Areas Listener Survey, February. Unpublished document.

Smolicz, Jerzy J. 1992. Minority languages as core values of ethnic cultures: A study of maintenance and erosion of Polish, Welsh, and Chinese languages in Australia. In *Maintenance and loss of minority languages,* ed. Willem Fase, Jaspaert Koen, and Sjaak Kroon, 277–306. Amsterdam and Philadelphia: John Benjamins.

Spitulnik, Debra. 1994. Code-mixing and ideologies of hybrid vs. "pure" language use. Paper presented at American Anthropological Association meeting, Atlanta, Ga. 2 December.

Taniguchi, Jiro. 1955. *A grammatical analysis of artistic representation of Irish English (with a brief discussion of sounds and spelling).* Tokyo: Shinozaki Shorin.

Thomason, Sarah Grey, and Terrence Kaufman. 1988. *Language contact, creolization, and genetic linguistics.* Berkeley: University of California Press.

Watson, Seosamh. 1989. Scottish and Irish Gaelic: The giant's bed-fellows. In *Investigating obsolescence: Studies in language contraction and death,* ed. Nancy C. Dorian, 41–61. Cambridge: Cambridge University Press.

Woolard, Kathryn. 1989. Language convergence and language death as social processes. In *Investigating obsolescence: Studies in language contraction and death,* ed. Nancy C. Dorian, 355–369. Cambridge: Cambridge University Press.

The Mono Language

KEN HALE

Department of Linguistics and Philosophy
Massachusetts Institute of Technology
Cambridge, Massachusetts

Mono belongs to the northernmost subgroup of Numic, which is in turn the northernmost branch of the Uto-Aztecan language family. Uto-Aztecan languages are spoken in an area extending from near the Canadian border southward to El Salvador in Central America, a respectable territorial range.

As a Western Numic language, Mono is most closely related to Northern Paiute, another member of that subgroup and the Uto-Aztecan language which is the farthest north. And as a Numic language, Mono is reasonably closely related to Southern Paiute (see Chapter 20), a member of Southern Numic (Steele 1979).

The North Fork (or Western) variety of Mono, which figures in this chapter, is the topic of a grammar written in the 1950s by Sydney Lamb (Lamb 1958). One of Lamb's supervisors was the late Mary Haas, the linguist who, through her own work and that of her students, not only brought the linguistic wealth of California to the attention of linguistic science but also trained an impressive number of the linguists who now work on the native languages of California and who are involved in language revitalization programs in that state and elsewhere.

Lamb's grammar is remarkable because it represents a relatively homogeneous linguistic tradition, being based largely on the speech of a single excellent speaker of the language, the late Lucy Kinsman, of North Fork. The grammar is also remarkable for the consistent manner in which its author both utilized and advanced the methodological principles of the structuralist linguistics of the period in which he did his fieldwork. It is one of the very best examples of that model applied to a Native American language.

The sound system of Mono is wonderfully representative of the phonological genius of the Numic languages. The language has a relatively small inventory of consonants and vowels, but it has a highly regular system of alternating stress placement, consonant spirantization and gemination, and voicing alternations which result in a pronunciation characterized by a rich variety of distinct sound segments, including fricatives matching each of the stop consonants, fortis and lenis variants of the stops, and voiceless vowels. The Numic languages have played an important role in the linguistic study of the sound systems of natural languages. Mono is a classic example of the rule-governed relation between an abstract and parsimonious phonological representation and the rich and diverse pronunciation which is heard in the spoken forms of actual words and sentences.

This chapter is about the development and use of an interactive multimedia CD-ROM entitled *Taitaduhaan ("Our Language")* for teaching aspects of Western Mono language and culture. The authors are forthright about the work that is involved in making an effective CD-ROM, and they are justifiably enthusiastic about the pedagogical promise of well-made CD-ROMs in language revitalization programs.

References

Lamb, Sydney M. 1958. Mono grammar. Ph.D. diss., University of California, Berkeley.

Steele, Susan. 1979. Uto-Aztecan: An assessment for historical and comparative linguistics. In *The languages of Native America: Historical and comparative assessment,* ed. Lyle Campbell and Marianne Mithun, 444–544. Austin: University of Texas Press.

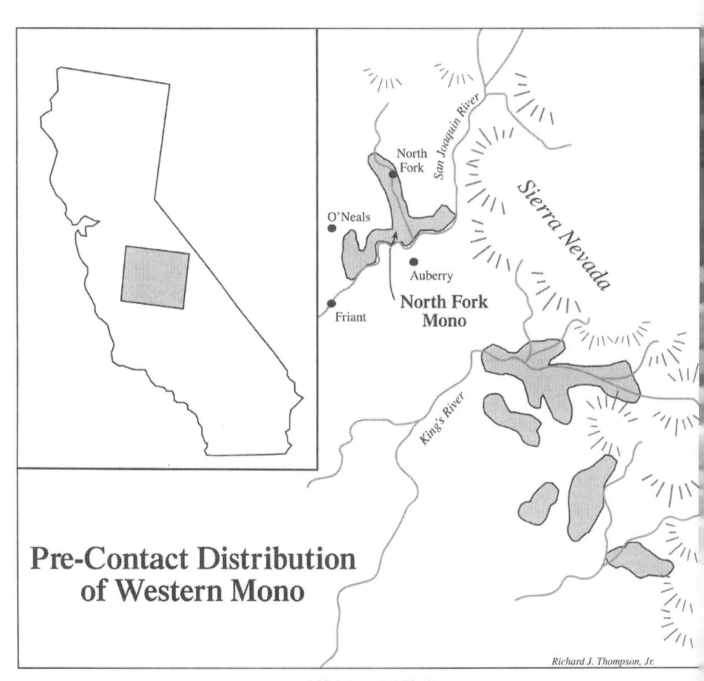

**Pre-Contact Distribution
of Western Mono**

North
Fork

O'Neals

Auberry

**North Fork
Mono**

Friant

San Joaquin River

Sierra Nevada

King's River

Richard J. Thompson, Jr.

MAP 25.1   Mono, in California

25

On Using Multimedia in Language Renewal
Observations from Making the CD-ROM *Taitaduhaan*

PAUL V. KROSKRITY

Department of Anthropology
University of California, Los Angeles
Los Angeles, California

JENNIFER F. REYNOLDS

Department of Anthropology
University of California, Los Angeles
Los Angeles, California

At a time when most of the remaining languages of Native North America are threatened with extinction and their associated communities are struggling for resources in order to engage in language renewal efforts (Krauss 1996; Leap 1988), linguists must necessarily confront what Nora England (1992) has termed "the obligation of linguistic research." One of these obligations, which is most relevant for the present discussion, is to make linguistic resources that are available to speakers of the language (England 1992, 35). While valuable, works aimed more at preservation and documentation of linguistic detail and targeted at professional elites can only seem insensitive to the unprecedented numbers of communities, at this historical moment, struggling to combat linguistic obsolescence. But if the 21st century poses a uniquely severe challenge to linguistic diversity, as global economic forces continue to bolster the "symbolic capital" (Bourdieu 1991) of "world" languages and diminish that of indigenous languages (Krauss 1996), it also provides new technologies for information manipulation and control. In addition to aiding in the production of conventional print media, computers, the wide array of relevant software programs, and other new technologies now make possible multimedia works which offer new and exciting possibilities for communities looking to create their own educational resources to promote ancestral languages, either by attempting to restore or strengthen fluency levels or by generally connecting people to their linguistic heritage through renewal programs of the "language and culture" type (Leap 1988; Brandt 1988; Palmer 1988). This chapter explores the development of a CD-ROM, *Taitaduhaan ("Our Language"): Western Mono Ways of Speaking,* by the present authors along with Rosalie Bethel, an elder from the North Fork Mono community. This ongoing project provides the basis

for reflecting on the possibility of extending the use of multimedia to other communities which confront language maintenance and renewal issues. In the present chapter, we describe how we designed and produced the CD-ROM and, on the basis of our experience, make some suggestions for those who consider using multimedia in language renewal efforts. Then, in the following sections, we introduce the Western Mono community, describe the structure of *Taitaduhaan,* and make general recommendations about the use of multimedia.

THE WESTERN MONO SPEECH COMMUNITY

Today Western Mono is an endangered language spoken by members of the Mono community in various central California towns. In communities like North Fork, Auberry, Dunlop, and Sycamore live about 1,500 Mono Indian people (Spier 1978). Within this dispersed community, there are approximately 41 highly fluent speakers and perhaps as many as 100–200 people with some knowledge of the language (Hinton 1994, 27–31).[1] Almost all the highly fluent speakers are 65 years of age or older. By "highly fluent" here we mean speakers who know their language well enough to spontaneously perform extended narratives of either the traditional or personal variety. Not many highly fluent speakers, apart from those few who are currently participating in the dyadic immersion programs associated with the Advocates for Indigenous California Language Survival (Hinton 1999, 10), use Western Mono with younger speakers. Children are more likely to hear their ancestral language spoken in an institution of formal education than in their homes. But many of the

317

programs which reach children have important but limited goals which emphasize vocabulary rather than grammar. There are also adult education programs involving Western Mono, but we do not have more than anecdotal knowledge of their educational objectives, pedagogical styles, and degree of success. But the rise in such efforts at language maintenance and renewal can only bode well for a community which 20 years ago appeared quite apathetic about the imminent death of its ancestral languages. In terms of its genetic-historical classification, Western Mono is a Uto-Aztecan language which is closely related to other neighboring languages of the Numic branch—Northern Paiute, Eastern Mono, and Panamint (Miller 1983).

But Western Mono's status as an endangered language is surely attributable not to its family tree but rather to the hegemonic influence of Spanish and Euro-American invasions. A full appreciation of the impact of these colonial influences in shaping "language ideologies" in contemporary Western Mono communities is beyond the scope of this chapter (see Kroskrity 1999 for a more elaborate treatment). Nevertheless, it is important to mention three interrelated precolonial language ideological patterns of use as well as the linguistic discrimination of the colonial period as preparatory background for understanding the relevant historical and cultural factors which informed the dictionary and multimedia efforts within the Mono Language Project. By "language ideology" I mean "the cultural system of ideas about social and linguistic relationships, together with their loading of moral and political interests" (Irvine 1989, 255). The three precolonial language ideologies that can be reconstructed as "dominant" (in the sense used in Kroskrity 1998) are syncretism, internal diversity, and utilitarianism. Syncretism is a value on linguistic borrowing from neighboring languages which characterized many California Indian groups (Silver and Miller 1998, 212–18). These intertribal relations often included intermarriage, trade, political alliances, and multilingualism. With intermarriage and multilingualism pervasive in Mono-speaking communities, it was an unlikely environment to produce a folk 1:1 correlation between specific languages and corresponding ethnic identities such as that which characterized Euro-American "Andersonian (Anderson 1983) linguistic-cultural nationalism" (Silverstein 1996, 127).[2]

In addition, members of the community also emphasized the utilitarian nature of language—language as a tool or a technology. When the Mono community experienced language shift from Mono to English earlier this century, many parents felt it was inappropriate to teach their native language to their children when it appeared that economic change was necessitating more and more use of English. Several of the oldest members of the community reported that their parents refused to teach them their ancestral languages and rationalized this choice by describing their children as *kumasa-tika* 'bread-eaters' who would no longer need a language associated with hunting and gathering and acorn-

processing activities (like Mono) but would instead require English as the language of the emerging cash economy.[3] This more traditional view of languages as tools as well as the linguistic discrimination faced by Mono people in the schools and promoted by the federal and state governments played a role in reducing the number of speakers who would pass their language of heritage on to younger generations.

Though the ethnocidal educational policies of Euro-Americans did much to link Mono and other indigenous languages to a "stigmatized ethnic identity"—often an important factor in cases of language shift as in Dorian's (1981) study of East Sutherland Gaelic, Gal's (1979) research on Hungarian speakers in the Austrian community of Oberwart, or Kulick's (1992) examination of Gapun language shift, such practices did not and could not dictate English as the language of the home. The utilitarian view of language which associates it with technoeconomic strategies prompted many multilingual parents to make English the language of the home because of its enhanced utility in a continually more encompassing cash economy.

Today the language shift is almost complete in that English now performs virtually all the functions once performed by Western Mono. The one domain in which Mono language and song persist is in native religious activities, where Mono is strongly preferred. But the lack of a vital ancestral language has not led to a collapse of the Western Mono community. In their own view, Mono people are such not by virtue of speaking an ancestral language but by participation in native activities—the festivals and the funerals—and by assisting their family and friends within the group. The language was viewed as significant, but not any more so as a cultural resource than a knowledge of basket making or plant use.

Three interrelated developments seem to signal a new day for Mono as a symbol of Mono cultural identity: its incorporation in "language and culture" programs in the schools, its symbolic role in the battle for federal recognition, and the Native American Languages Acts of 1990 and 1992 all promoted a rethinking of local linkages between a language of heritage and an ethnic identity. It is now fashionable for Mono people to call themselves "Nium," using the native self-designation as a loanword into local English.[4] Local schools have used a combination of federal funds and local monies to create Mono "language and culture" classes for students of all ages. These classes, as mentioned above, are not all designed to restore fluency to the community but rather for the purpose of familiarizing Mono and other children with important cultural vocabulary (kin terms, food names, place-names) and linguistic routines (such as greetings and closings). These terms are explicitly linked to Mono culture and identity and represent curriculum innovations on the basis of improving the self-image of Indian students. Students who receive these lessons certainly receive a very different message from their early classroom experience than the one experienced by elders like Rosalie Bethel and her generation.

These elders, like their peers in other Native Californian groups, were forbidden to use their native languages in school settings (Hinton 1994, 173–79).

On another front, Western Monos have been one of many California Indian tribes to seek federal recognition. The rigorous criteria that must be met by candidates for recognition do not explicitly mention languages, but they do mention the need to demonstrate maintenance of cultural continuity. Thus even a partial reversal of language shift—a kind of linguistic "tip" (Dorian 1989) in the direction of the indigenous language—even if it approximates the limited goals of so-called language-and-culture language renewal programs, does represent a development of great personal and political significance for many members of the Western Mono community.

Against this backdrop, members of the Mono community initiated what was to become a long-term project involving linguistic anthropology personnel, including me, from UCLA. Using her niece, Orie Sherman Medicine Bull, then a graduate student in film and television, as a contact person, Rosalie Bethel, a North Fork Mono elder with special expertise in the Western Mono language, inquired whether I had any interest in helping her systematically write and record her ancestral language. For approximately 10 years prior to the Mono Language Project in 1981, Bethel had dutifully recorded words from the Mono language on index cards. Using a folk orthography which did not consistently distinguish vowels and which represented the same consonant sound in several alternative ways, Bethel had nevertheless produced a rudimentary form of what was to become the first Western Mono dictionary. Though her transcriptions lacked phonological accuracy and systematicity, they nevertheless provided a key resource for the recollection of these forms through elicitation, recording, and the use of an orthography which was generally recognized by Americanists and utilized in the Smithsonian's multivolume reference work *Handbook of North American Indians*.

In its early stages, the Mono Language Project resembled a cultural exchange program. Bethel came to UCLA in 1981 for the winter quarter and became the key consultant for a field-methods class of students who were both training and contributing new materials for the descriptive goals of the project. That summer, several student researchers and the project director, Paul V. Kroskrity, went up to North Fork to conduct additional research and to engage a broader segment of the community in linguistic workshop meetings. These meetings were designed to convey the goals of the project, present preliminary results (such as sample pages of dictionaries, and standardized orthographies), gather new information, and get community feedback on our accomplishments and our problems.

Over the years, this project produced two editions of a practical dictionary of Western Mono, a pedagogical grammar, and, most recently, the aforementioned CD-ROM. We treat the subject of how the CD-ROM project relates to the important task of dictionary making in another article (Kroskrity, in press), and will concentrate here only on the connections between the CD-ROM and the phase of the Mono Language Project which occurred immediately prior to the actual startup of the multimedia phase. Several years before the authors of *Taitaduhaan* participated in the Iowa Multimedia Workshop for Endangered Languages, members of the Mono Language Project had begun to collect video recorded examples of native language interaction and storytelling. Over several years a small collection of Western Mono speech was collected, analyzed, and translated for the purpose of documenting Mono narratives and conversational storytelling.

In 1996 Brenda Farnell, the pathbreaking author of the only published CD-ROM of Native American storytelling—*Wiyuta: Assiniboine Storytelling with Signs* (Farnell 1993)—hosted and organized the aforementioned summer institute on developing multimedia projects for Native American communities where the ancestral language was threatened. Farnell, assisted by Joan Huntley and her staff at Second Look Computing, taught participants, including the authors of this chapter, how to make multimedia projects. After one month at the institute, we returned to UCLA, where we completed the project, made it completely cross-platform, and began the testing stage which precedes publication.

WHAT IS *TAITADUHAAN: WESTERN MONO WAYS OF SPEAKING?*

Taitaduhaan, meaning "our language" in the Western Mono language, is an interactive CD-ROM designed to be informative, useful, and entertaining to a wide range of users who have an interest in learning more about this California Indian people by seeing, hearing, and understanding four performances of traditional and contemporary verbal art in the native language (with translation). The CD-ROM is interactive because readers and users select—through simple clicking operations of a mouse or touchpad—the types and levels of information that they want or need to understand the performances. The fact that the CD-ROM can be navigated in a variety of ways means that it can better serve a variety of audiences. And since the performance features of oral traditions, such as tone of voice, facial expression, gesture, rhythm, and volume, are not effectively captured by print media, these authentic performances by a knowledgeable elder are most effectively represented in their fullness by this new medium. In sum, this new computer technology provides the best possible means of appreciating native oral traditions both for their own sake and for the purpose of learning more about these embattled but persistent native cultural communities.

Because the CD-ROM provides both a general appreciation of California Indian verbal art forms as well as a detailed analysis of the language of performance, it has a broad audience both within the Mono community and among students and scholars of American Indian Studies, anthropology, comparative literature, folklore, linguistics, and education. The CD-ROM is a valuable tool for both community groups and individuals to gain a closer familiarity with their indigenous languages and oral traditions. The CD-ROM allows individuals to hear and practice sounds by hearing and seeing examples of words and sentences in which all the sounds of the language can be identified. Readers and users need only have minimal computer literacy to run the CD-ROM since it is a self-contained product which always provides help menus and prompts to those who need guidance regarding either the correct use of buttons or the explanation of specialized vocabulary used in language analysis or cultural explanation. Educational institutions from junior high schools to university graduate programs could also use this resource as a way of combating the lack of pedagogical materials on the Western Mono and, more generally, on all Native Americans in California, especially the dearth of audiovisual materials which represent their oral traditions.

Organizationally, the CD-ROM begins with a title screen containing a photograph of Mono Indian baskets while a lively gaming song is sung. As this song continues, timers automatically open "credit" and "purpose" screens which identify the authors and the goal of introducing Mono Indian language and culture to audiences both within and outside of the Mono community. As the song ends, the main menu screen appears, offering four performance selections and two background selections (see Figure 25.1).

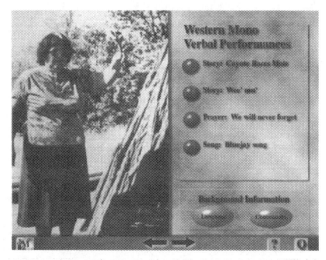

FIGURE 25.1.   Main Menu. This is the main menu screen. It offers the user the choice of four different performances as well as additional background on either the Western Mono Language or community. By rolling the cursor over these buttons, the user is sent to appropriate sub-menus to make additional choices. To the left of these buttons stands Rosalie Bethel, coauthor and native speaker and performer for *Taitaduhaan*. Notice the navigation bar on the bottom of the screen containing (from left to right) clickable icons for the Main Menu, Back, Forward, Help, and Quit buttons.

Two gray buttons marked "Community" and "Language" represent background choices. Pushing the first of these buttons reveals a menu of options to learn more about the community through an introductory text, photographs, maps, and a brief biographical sketch of Rosalie Bethel, the Mono elder who performs on the CD-ROM. Pushing the Language option reveals a menu of options that includes seeing and hearing examples of all the pronunciation units of the language as well as language maps and language-family trees which locate the Mono language in linguistic history and geography.

The main menu choices involve four performances. These include two stories—"Coyote Races Mole" and "Wee'mu'" (a Mono bogeyman figure)—a prayer, and a lyrical song for children. The user can choose to navigate each of these performances in two distinct ways. One choice is to play the selection from start to finish with synchronized English subtitles. The other is to examine each of these performances sentence by sentence (see Figure 25.2). In this mode each sentence appears in a text box containing the Mono-language sentence, a detailed morpheme-by-morpheme translation, and a free translation. In this mode many words and phrases appear in red, and when the user clicks these on they reveal additional linguistic and cultural explanation.

In many ways, Taitaduhaan resembles Farnell's *Wiyuta*. Both, for example, use narrative performances of highly fluent speakers as vehicles for learning more about both the narrative artistry of the performers and the linguistic structures of the languages they used. As such, they take a different approach from that used in other multimedia works, like those of the Arikara Language Project (Parks 1998), which use grammar lessons and pronunciation exercises to provide the basic structure of the CD-ROM. *Taitaduhaan* does differ from *Wiyuta*, which served as the pioneering prototype, in several ways. For one, *Taitaduhaan* has an elaborate pronunciation guide which permits users to see a movie of Rosalie Bethel pronouncing the letter on which they have clicked. Since orthographic matters have been a source of confusion for many members in the Mono community, this feature becomes a much-needed self-pronouncing guide to an orthography which is still not well established in the community because of the paucity of native language literacy materials. Since Farnell was more concerned with notating the signs of Plains Sign Language, which are simultaneously given as the Assiniboine is pronounced, *Wiyuta* needed to divide its analytical attention between the signed and the spoken versions of the narratives. Lacking this need, *Taitaduhaan* could instead provide more background on both the language, including the elaborate pronunciation guide, as well as the community.

Another difference is in the use of so-called hot text in *Taitaduhaan*. While both CD-ROMs have this interactive feature, it is deployed in somewhat different manners. In *Wiyuta*, for example, hot text is used to create a form of intertextuality, connecting, for example, a place-name used in a

FIGURE 25.2.   The Examine Movie Mode: An Example. This is screen 14 of the story "Coyote Races Mole" in the Examine Movie mode. In this mode each sentence of a performance is playable as a separate movie and presented with three types of text. The top line is in the practical orthography of the Western Mono community. The second line is a word-for-word translation which also includes grammatical glosses (like OBL and TNS) that are explained in a Help Menu. The bottom line is a free translation in English. Note that in the color-coded screen the suffix -na is printed in red, indicating that it is interactive hot text.

story with a map illustrating that place-name. In *Taitaduhaan,* the hot text provides more of an alternative path of navigation. Hot text offers the user an optional elaboration of a point of grammar or a cultural explanation by merely clicking on any word in the Examine Movie Mode which appeared in red (as opposed to the normal black). (See Fig. 25.3 for an example.) These hot texts were sometimes explanations by the authors in a text box, movies in which Rosalie Bethel would explain a discourse or other cultural practice, or illustrative photos with audio explanation. This interactive feature was considerably fortified and enhanced in *Taitaduhaan,* in part because it was designed for a broad range of users who might choose very different navigational paths depending upon their interests and knowledge base.

A final difference between these CD-ROMs is in the different ways the narratives are presented. Both *Wiyuta* and *Taitaduhaan* experiment with ways to convey the verbal artistry of the performed narratives. But in the former, when users choose to see a movie of the entire story, they are given only an unsubtitled version performed simultaneously in Assiniboine and Plains Sign Language. To see the text, in either Assiniboine or English translation, one selects a different mode in which texts in each language scroll in a coordinated manner as the user hears the narrative. In *Taitaduhaan,* the entire movie of each performance can be seen along with a synchronized text track which displays the English translation. This treatment permits a user who is unfamiliar with Mono to better understand the relationship between the narrative content and the prosodic and nonverbal behavior of Rosalie Bethel as she performs it.

MAKING A CD-ROM

There are at least three stages which must be planned ahead of time in order to program a CD-ROM using an authoring tool software package. These stages include (1) the collection of different media, (2) preparing and formatting the media, and (3) the overall program design. All of these stages can be quite labor intensive and require a considerable amount of time to complete. Our CD-ROM project *Taitaduhaan* was particularly labor intensive and time consuming because of the complicated program design. Since we were highlighting the importance of verbal performances, we chose to give our users two different modes through which to interact with the video media. This required designing submenus for each of the four verbal performances. Moreover, within each performance's sub-menu the user could choose to view the entire performance with English subtitles or examine the performance sentence by sentence. Our largest video file, Coyote Races Mole, contained 72 sentences, which required editing the video into 72 segments; creating 72 individual text files which included the sentence written in the Mono orthography, the linguistic gloss, and an English translation; and finally programming all of the screens so that they would be linked together in a linear fashion to ensure that the user would move through them in the order in which they had originally been performed. So, as made apparent by this example, these stages may overlap and impact one another. However, in the following sections they will be treated as discrete stages in order to provide the reader a detailed account of just how much work and planning are required to successfully produce an interactive CD-ROM using multimedia. Examples from our experiences making *Taitaduhaan* will be

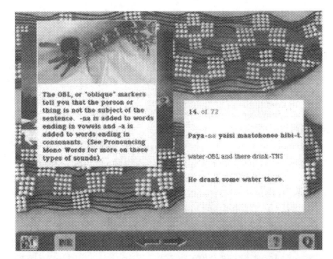

FIGURE 25.3.   Hot Text Revealed. This is the same screen as in Fig.25.2, but here the user has clicked on the interactive hot text -na, producing a pop-up screen (partially obscuring the movie box) that contains an explanation of oblique case marking in Western Mono and a cross-reference to the pronunciation guide for additional examples.

included to illustrate all of the stages that we went through during this process.

Choosing and Collecting Media

There are two steps that one must think about at the beginning of this stage. First, one must consider the different kinds of media that he or she may want to include in the multimedia project, and second, one must decide which ways are the most appropriate to collect the media. CD-ROM programs are a superior medium of representation when it comes to combining image, sound, and text. Since verbal art has played a central role in the language revitalization movement in the Western Mono community, we decided that the CD-ROM should also focus on verbal performances. In classes on the Mono language, curricular materials were often developed out of stories, so using verbal art in the CD-ROM seemed like an appropriate extension of practices which were already happening in Western Mono native literacy classes.

Video and audio recordings are generally better at representing verbal performances than written texts because they do not lose the prosodic and paralinguistic features which make performances dramatic and entertaining. Ethnopoetic scholarship on Native American verbal art has emphasized the importance of attending to volume, pitch, rhythm, parallelism, and gesture (Hymes 1981; Tedlock 1972; Wiget 1987), yet these are often ignored in most textual forms of presentation, including those of most curricular materials used in Mono classes. But multimedia CD-ROMs permit "real-time" movies of actual performances to be presented along with textual representations of various types (e.g., free translation, word-by-word analysis, and local orthography). This combination powerfully integrates the aesthetics of an oral tradition with the efficiency of various forms of literacy. By so doing, the "movies" convey not only linguistic knowledge but also an aesthetic sense of storytelling that is a valuable part of the cultural discourse associated with the ancestral language.

In addition to providing an outstanding means of "capturing" some of the most transcriptionally elusive qualities of an "oral tradition," multimedia CD-ROMs also offer a uniquely appropriate medium for introducing, or explaining by example, local orthographies. In the Western Mono community meetings in which orthographies were discussed, a frequent complaint was the difficulty of reading native language terms and sentences in an orthography which was so like that of English that it often invited mispronunciation in the direction of English. The Guide to Pronouncing Mono Words in *Taitaduhaan* illustrates every orthographic letter used in the final version of the orthography that developed during the Mono Language Project (Kroskrity, in press). This feature helps the user to understand, through the video and audio of brief, illustrative movies featuring Rosalie

Bethel pronouncing native terms, each orthographic symbol to be exemplified. The symbols that are exemplified include both those that are already familiar to Mono people because of their literacy in English and the few new symbols which must be created to accommodate Western Mono phonology. Perhaps the best example of the value of having a visual component comes in the form of the movie which is played when the user selects the vowel [i], one referred to by linguists as "barred *i*." This vowel is—in articulatory phonetic terms—a high, mid, unrounded vowel. In English, non-front vowels tend to be pronounced with lip rounding, and since most Monos know English better than they know Mono, this frequently occurring vowel is often pronounced as if it were an English [u]. But seeing Rosalie Bethel pronounce words with the barred *i*, such as the example *iya* 'sore', provides a visual corrective since it clearly demonstrates that this vowel, unlike "u," is pronounced without lip rounding (see Figure 25.4). Thus, different kinds of video and audio can be used in creative ways on a CD-ROM to more accurately represent and teach American Indian languages. From presenting the aesthetics of the oral tradition to representing the phonetics of ancestral language pronunciation, this medium has important educational implications for teachers and learners alike.

However, there are cautions and drawbacks to working with video and audio. First of all, the original recordings should be of the highest quality. Video- and sound-edit computer programs can make only minor improvements to

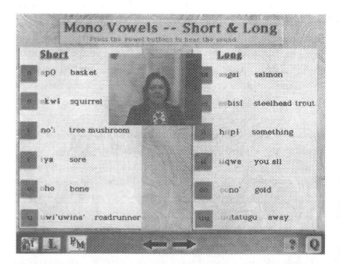

FIGURE 25.4. Pronunciation Guide: An Example. This screen is one of a set making up the pronunciation guide. In these screens, the user moves the cursor to the letter to be pronounced. When this is done, as in the illustration above, a movie appears in which Rosalie Bethel pronounces the selected word. The present screen is designed to both show the inventory of Mono vowels and to display the fact that vowel length is an important feature of the Mono sound system. Note that for this screen the icons on the left permit the user to return to either the Main Menu, the Language (background) Menu, or the Pronouncing Mono Words submenu.

poorly lit, out-of-focus, hard-to-hear original recordings. These problems can be avoided if care is taken when making the recordings. For the CD-ROM we recorded Rosalie Bethel in both live and elicited performances. In both types of settings it is important to plan ahead and create the best environment for recording. Make sure that there is just the right amount of light for filming and that it remains fairly consistent over the time video recording is taking place. The camera should be on a tripod (space permitting) and placed close enough to the performer to give the user the sensation of "being there." We have found that a Hi-8 video camera produces some of the best-quality footage because it has more visual detail than standard 8mm video. Better still is the new technology involving digital video cameras (DVDs). These new cameras, though more expensive, produce the highest quality images and—when used with appropriately powerful computers—can permit you to directly input video data without having to convert (i.e., digitize) your movies. This makes them both better and more efficient than either Hi-8 or standard 8mm.

But regardless of which type of video recorder is used, there are some general guidelines which should be followed. First, it is important to use the highest quality media available—the best videotape which is compatible with your camera. Second, video recording should be done with the best lighting, and it should be consistent. Once we recorded Rosalie Bethel in semishade, and the tree shadows partially covered her face off and on throughout the recording session. The video recordings produced under these circumstances were all right, but the constantly shifting light and shadow created havoc at the digitization stage, when all these irrelevant changes are captured as information and stored, and ultimately led to an unsatisfactory set of movies which could not be used in a multimedia project. Third, where possible, shoot with the least complex background, since any complexity will again be costly in digitization since it is read as relevant information even though backgrounds are, by definition, relatively unimportant. A simple background thus creates fewer distractions and less irrelevant detail that must be captured in the digitization process. Finally, all actual video footage should be shot using manual focus. Practice ahead of time with the focus so that you can control it. If you shoot the footage with an automatic focus, the video camera will blur the image for an instant as it adjusts to a performer's movements or to other changes in the environment. Avoid overuse of zooming in or out.

In sound recording we strongly recommend the use of an external professional microphone whenever you make audio or video recordings (with sound). The microphone should be placed as close as possible to the performer so that you record the best sound quality. Check the recording levels before recording so that the sound is not distorted. Omnidirectional microphones tend to record sound coming from all directions, which means that you will collect not only the sounds

you are trying to record but also many other sounds which could be distracting (cars driving by, a helicopter passing overhead, a dog barking, etc.). One way to avoid this is by using transmitter mics that can be worn by the person targeted for sound collection. These wireless, battery-operated mics send signals to the receiver, which can be directly plugged into the video camera. The pronunciation guide movies for *Taitaduhaan* were made using these mics, and they produced speech specimen quality sound. Remember that your video footage will be useless if the sound quality is terrible, and in linguistic projects there is nothing more important than good sound.

These are only a few tips to keep in mind when collecting video and audio recordings. Finally and most importantly, you should feel comfortable and confident working the camera, and you should work with people who agree to being recorded. The only way to gain confidence is to practice and experiment with the camera before going out and collecting the actual media for your CD-ROM. If the people who agree to work with you see that you are confident and know what you are doing, they feel more at ease and generally deliver better performances. We have also found that it is rarely a good idea to simply do a recording session involving only the speaker and the video recorder. Speakers need audiences who appreciate their performances, and they will feel more responsible as performers if they have an audience of their peers to monitor and support them. Certainly some accomplished storytellers can perform for the camera, but most people feel more relaxed when talking to their peers rather than talking "for the camera."

A second problem with using video or audio media on CD-ROM is that they take up a lot of memory. Digitized video files, either made from Hi-8 analog or directly input from digital video cameras, are enormous, and they will eventually need to be compressed so that they take up less space on a CD-ROM. Unfortunately, compressing video requires sacrificing some of the quality. There is not too much you can do to get around this problem except limit the number and size of your video files. We were able to include over half an hour of compressed video files on our CD-ROM, and in retrospect we still could have fit on at least 15 minutes more along with all the other media files in the program.

Of course, there are many other kinds of media that can also be collected for CD-ROM multimedia programs. Photographs, slides, maps, charts, drawings, cartoons, music, texts, clip art, and anything else that can be scanned and made into a digital image or sound are usable media for a CD-ROM. We were against using pre-prepared clip-art images of American Indians or their material culture. Most of these images are stereotypical and do not even remotely resemble images of Western Mono material culture or lifeways. Instead, we preferred to include actual images of the community, its members, and their artwork. For example, we were able to directly scan some of Rosalie Bethel's beadwork collars and belts.

The scanned three-dimensional images of her beadwork were beautiful and provided an impressive backdrop for screens of the different verbal performances. We also scanned into the computer maps of the Western Mono communities, linguistic and tribal maps of California which highlight the Western Mono territory, and we created a historical linguistic diagram illustrating Uto-Aztecan language families. Any other images included on the CD-ROM which we did not scan we were able to design using other software programs (e.g., Adobe PhotoShop).

Again, it cannot be emphasized enough that the CD-ROM is a valuable tool which can be used to connect sound, image, and text in new and creative ways. This is particularly useful to communities that are trying to promote standardized orthographies and create a population of readers who feel comfortable with new written representations in the ancestral language of the community. Pronunciation guides and language drill exercises on a CD-ROM program can make great inroads into demystifying graphemic representations of languages which previously had no tradition of writing.

Preparing and Formatting Media

Once all of the media for a CD-ROM project have been collected, the next stage is preparing the media to be inserted into a software program. The first thing that you should do is familiarize yourself with the requirements and limitations of the authoring tool software. What kinds of naming conventions should you use to name all of the media files? Are you planning to cross-platform your final CD-ROM project? The answer to this question will affect the naming system that you decide to adopt. For example, many of the authoring tools require that you follow MS-DOS naming conventions in order to create versions for both Mac and IBM platforms. If you begin to make a CD-ROM project and use incorrect naming conventions, you will have possibly doubled the amount of work ahead of you. Another question to consider is in which formats should media be saved. Should you keep duplicate files saved in different formats (one for editing media and another for saving a final version that the authoring tool can read)? How should you store the media (e.g., in different folders or all in the same folder)? The answers to these questions vary depending upon the multimedia program you select.

You should know the answers to all of these questions before you start working with your media.

The second thing to consider at this stage is that different kinds of media require different kinds of software, preparation, and formatting. Video footage, if it was not originally shot with a digital camera, must be digitized. Make sure, first, that you are using a computer capable of capturing video footage and storing it, and second, that you have the appropriate software programs to edit the footage. Some video-editing programs are more complicated to learn than others

are. We used a very simple video-editing program to edit the video footage. It also allowed us to insert text tracks at the bottom of each frame for subtitling. Some programs are more elaborate and allow you to add other sound tracks. For example, you can add ambient music or other special effects to the video footage. These programs may also allow you to make still photographic images into movies. The type of program you choose will depend on how you plan to edit your films. Next, you will need some sort of software to compress and flatten the video files so that they take up less space on the CD-ROM. Compressing movies is easy to do, but it consumes a lot of time. Computers can take hours to compress relatively short film clips. Finally, whatever software program you choose, make sure that the video footage is saved in the correct format. This is crucial if you plan on making the CD-ROM cross-platform.

Audio tracks and sound that you record must also be transformed into a format that a computer can understand. Sound-editing programs often make you "record" the sound into the computer. Make sure that you check all of the recording levels in the software program to see whether they input the sound so that it is at the correct volume and not distorted. These software programs also allow you to play around with the sound and add special effects. You will have to decide if this is appropriate for your particular project.

Photographic and other scanned images can and should be manipulated to improve image clarity and quality as well as to conserve memory. Images can be blown up, made smaller, darker, brighter, in different colors, in black-and-white, and so on. Some programs allow you to draw or write on top of images. You should explore the different tools available to you in the software program. Although digitized still images take up less space than sound or video files, they still can occupy lots of memory. So make sure that you take into consideration the following points: (1) color photographic images take up much more memory than black-and-white, and (2) the larger the photographic image is, the more memory it occupies. All of these variables can be manipulated to help you conserve memory.

Texts can be generated using either a word-processing program or the same software that you used for manipulating and creating graphic designs. Text files produced in Word can be read as "scrollable text" in a CD-ROM program. These texts can be as long as you want, and you can choose the color and type of font that they will be viewed in. PhotoShop text files are not scrollable, so you are not able to fit as much text on a single screen. One problem with computer fonts and American Indian orthographies is that oftentimes the fonts that you have on hand in your word-processing program do not have all of the necessary symbols to represent the different sounds. This may require that you find and purchase a font that does meet your needs, or it may require that you design your own font. This latter option can become an extremely labor-intensive task. We ran into problems representing only two sounds in Western Mono. The orthographic conventions required that these two sounds be represented with a strikethrough formatting in the word-processing program (*i* and *g*). This created two problems for us once we inserted them in the CD-ROM authoring tool program. First, the authoring tool that we used interpreted words with the strikethrough format to be read as "hot text," which made the text a site for interactivity. Second, the strikethrough format could not be seen once it was inserted in the program. So all *i*'s and *g*'s would have lost the strikethrough format and be read as "hot text." To get around this problem, we had all scrollable texts be in English, and any other texts in Western Mono were prepared in an Adobe PhotoShop program. We literally had to draw all the strikethrough lines in every occurrence of *i* and *g*.

We also had to design many other kinds of screens that were created using the graphic design capabilities offered in the Adobe PhotoShop program. These images were treated just like any other photographic or scanned image. The images that we downloaded from the Internet were also prepared using this type of software. One thing to remember is that you will need to reformat the dimensions of the image and change its .JPG or .GIF file format to a format that the authoring tool can recognize.

Design and Organization of the Program

There are at least two levels of organization and design that you must plan for when producing a CD-ROM. First, you must consider how to combine the media in creative and interesting ways; second, you must consider how the user will navigate through the program.

Combining Media

When we designed *Taitaduhaan* we gave considerable thought to how we should group and organize the different kinds of media. We envisioned an interactive program that provided information for different types of audiences. The English-subtitled verbal performances in Western Mono can be enjoyed in their entirety by both those who do and those who do not understand the ancestral language. They also may be viewed one discourse unit at a time. This second mode provides a more in-depth linguistic analysis, which also has interactive hot texts to raise awareness of specific grammatical forms in Western Mono. All of Rosalie Bethel's verbal performances were combined with the scanned images of her beadwork. So verbal art was linked with a different kind of Western Mono artistic tradition.

Aside from the three verbal genres (story, song, and prayer) presented, there are also two other sub-menus which provide background information on the Western Mono community and language. The community sub-menu includes a photo page with hidden pop-up texts, a screen which features a biographical sketch of Rosalie Bethel, two screens of maps, and a screen which offers bibliographic resources for those interested in reading more about the Western Mono community. The language sub-menu has a pronunciation guide of Western Mono words, a screen which provides information about the different verbal genres featured on the CD-ROM, screens on the American Indian language families present in California and related to Western Mono, and a different bibliographic resources screen which lists texts about the Western Mono language. Screens that featured scrollable texts had photographs from the community as the backdrop and that featured Mono sounds and words had computer-generated plain backgrounds so users would not get distracted when they were listening and watching Rosalie Bethel pronounce the different examples.

In designing your own CD-ROM program, the most important thing to keep in mind when thinking about the organization of the media is to create a structure which makes it easy for the user to figure out and be consistent throughout the entire program. For example, we never combined video with other photographic images. We wanted the video performances to take center stage, so to speak. Also, in order to make reading scrollable texts visually interesting, we used photographs of different types of Western Mono material culture. Finally, we even chose only those colors that are most commonly found in Western Mono artwork to color-code the different sub-menus of the CD-ROM. All of these touches help create a framework within which the different kinds of media can be made to interact together to make the user's experience interesting and visually stimulating.

Navigation

The second level of organization that you must consider when planning a CD-ROM project is how to make the program easy for all sorts of users to navigate. Not all users of your program will have a wealth of experience using computer technology. This must be kept in mind when planning the pathways between different screens in your CD-ROM program. Users will get frustrated quickly if they feel lost in the program or if they cannot figure out how to enter or exit from different screens. When we were planning our CD-ROM we wanted to make it very easy for the user to always return to the main menu or exit the program. So we created two different "spaces" on the screen to help a user navigate through the program. To illustrate this, we will explain the specifics of interactive button organization on *Taitaduhaan*.

Once the user starts the *Taitaduhaan* program, they have no control over the navigation for the first two minutes. We created a series of three timed screens which automatically appear and disappear as Rosalie Bethel sings a Western Mono gambling song. These screens include a title page, a credits page, and a page which profiles both Bethel and Kroskrity's understanding of what language is and what it means to the Western Mono community. When the song ends, the last screen disappears and the user sees the main menu page. It is from this page that a user may enter any of the sub-menus of the program.

From that point on, all screens are divided into two different spaces, a toolbar region and the main screen region. The toolbar includes "clickable buttons." The user may click on any of these buttons in order to make a navigational choice. These clickable buttons may be of several classes: menu buttons, arrows, help, and quit. The main menu button is located on every single screen of the program along with the help button and the quit button. Thus users may choose to return to main menu, enter the help menu, or quit the program from anywhere within the program. Arrow buttons and sub-menu buttons become interactive once a user has entered one of the sub-menus (i.e., once he or she has chosen to enter the sub-menu of a verbal performance or a background information sub-menu). Once the user is inside a performance screen, a community screen, or a language screen, he or she may click on the sub-menu button to see what other screens are available, or the user may use the arrow buttons to move forward and backward within the sub-menu. We decided to make these buttons clickable so that the user must make a conscious effort to choose and click in order to navigate through the program menus.

The main screen region includes many other different kinds of interactivity. In menu screens, the primary navigational buttons are "rollover" bead buttons. All a user has to do is roll the mouse over the button and he or she is automatically sent to a particular sub-menu page within the program. We decided to make these buttons roll over so that new users with little experience can learn how to gain control of the mouse. Only minimal effort is required to navigate the program. All users need to do is move the mouse and they are bound to be sent into one of the verbal performance sub-menus of the program. Once users have learned how to use a mouse, they can better control which rollover button they wish to enter. Again, all of these buttons help the user navigate between screens and regions of the program.

There is a second class of interactive spaces in the main screen region which allow the user to access different media within a screen. These interactive areas may be red regions, red buttons, or a red font and may be linked to hidden texts, photographic images, sound files, or video files that provide extra information about the particular screen in which the region was found. Other interactive areas which do not include hidden media, include a video control bar or a scroll bar. The video control bar allows the user to play, pause, rewind, or fast-forward through a movie or a performance. Scroll bars allow the user to scroll through texts or images.

Thus, when planning how a user should be able to navigate through a program, the designer must be consistent with how he or she indicates pathways. Designers should also make it easy for the user to access these pathways. We made

our program into a series of sub-menus. Toolbar buttons made it easy to enter any of the menus from practically anywhere in the program, and the rollover sub-menu buttons allowed a user to enter and navigate within a particular menu. Finally, we did not change the shape or the spatial location of these buttons in different locations of the program, so users can recognize the pattern and make better navigational choices as they move through the program.

Though we have provided practical guidelines and suggestions for making media and for considering design, we have not discussed what is actually entailed in the process of programming an interactive CD-ROM. We will not address the actual programming process here because it will be different for each project depending on the authoring-tool package of one's choice. There are many authoring tools available, and these change rapidly in terms of the basic programs, updated versions, new products, and old products falling out of commercial support. *Taitaduhaan* was created on Apple Media Tool 2.0, an icon-based program that allowed users to design multimedia projects without writing a line of programming (see Figure 25.5).

But although this program was well reviewed and highly successful in creating cross-platform projects when we first began the project in 1996, it was dropped shortly thereafter by Apple, which also discontinued its technical support to users. Though an unofficial Web site for Apple Media Tool users still exists, we feel that those who are in a position to select the authoring tool should do so only after a long period of deliberation and consultation to find a product which seems not only to be best suited to their representational needs but also enjoys support—ideally both from a commercial publisher and from technical advisors who are associated with the project.

In addition to knowing the documented strengths and weaknesses of available programs as well as measuring the availability of support for each of these options, we feel that project developers should never lose sight of their intended audiences. Will these be individual community members? Institutions such as museums, schools, and libraries? What types of computers do they currently have, and what are they likely to get in the future? Do they have the necessary 4× CD-ROM drives or not? Does it make sense to go cross-platform? Certainly if all intended users have similar equipment, say either IBM Windows PCs or Macs, then perhaps all the effort of trying to make projects cross-platform may be better directed to making more and better single-platform products.

FIGURE 25.5.   Behind the Screens. This illustrates a portion of different component screens of *Taitaduhaan* and how they are linked together to permit users to navigate between them. Note in the upper-left-hand corner the sequence of Title Screen to Credits to Goals to Main Menu—the cornerstone of the entire program. This view of how the program is composed is available only to the authors; users see only the individual screens and the media they contain.

Those seeking to make CD-ROMs for language renewal programs should not be deterred by the perpetual predictions of new technologies making the older instantly obsolete after only a few years of existence. While technological innovation is ongoing, the need for such multimedia resources exists *now*, at a point in time at which a lack of action can produce irreversible language attrition and even language obsolescence (Dorian 1989). Yes, somewhere down the road DVD will replace CD-ROM, but this is still many years away. Similarly one hears about the Web as if Web pages have now made multimedia CD-ROMs obsolete. But we suggest that rather than seeing this as an eclipsing technology that replaces CD-ROM, it is better viewed as a different product entirely. While both support multimedia projects and can make them available to many people, the CD-ROM still seems better suited to the interests of speech communities who want a bit more control of their linguistic resources and would like to limit access to serious users.

CONCLUSIONS

Without reiterating points made earlier in this chapter, we would like to close by highlighting four concerns that we offer both as motivations and as warnings for language-maintenance program developers and personnel. One, understand the limits and costs of CD-ROM technology. Though not prohibitive in cost, CD-ROM technology is expensive, especially in the need for hardware (computers, scanners, video cameras, CD-ROM "burners," etc.), software, consultants, and technical services (e.g., digitizing video and audio data). Multimedia projects are also costly in time, since many activities require much planning, cooperation between people with various kinds of expertise, and considerable effort to execute. Clearly the most important thing in language revitalization is to increase the opportunities for speakers to use and learn their ancestral language in interpersonal exchange. Multimedia technology will never replace this as the highest order priority in language revitalization. Though it can increase opportunities to see and hear the ancestral language—especially in those communities where there are very few speakers—this technology is clearly not a quick fix for language renewal programs but rather an additional resource which needs to be developed in addition to other strategies for language maintenance. It definitely requires a long-term commitment of funds, supplies, and personnel in order to yield results.

Two, multimedia projects offer a unique opportunity to create curriculum materials which are recipient-designed for the community. Because these projects can incorporate the aesthetic forms of Native American communities, they provide a means of creating curricular materials that are centered on the language and culture of a particular community. Even communities that number in the hundreds can create state-of-the-art curricular materials using multimedia technology which represent their languages and aesthetic forms. In *Taitaduhaan,* for example, all the images are direct representations of local cultural and linguistic forms from Western Mono people. This immediacy allows communities to have a greater hand in their own self-representation and permits them to create their own representation in response to what is usually a lack of culturally appropriate curricular materials.

Three, multimedia program developers need to have a clear idea of who their intended audience will be so that the program can be designed to address its needs. Developers must know who will use the program in order to assess appropriate fluency levels in the ancestral language and determine appropriate goals. They must also know what kind of computer equipment is available in the community (either through individual ownership or through tribally based educational programs institutionally housed in schools or museums). Making programs interactive should be viewed as a means of addressing multiple audiences with different needs and interests, or as a means of allowing the same audience to navigate the program in more challenging ways as it grows in relevant background knowledge.

Four, multimedia CD-ROM projects must be developed in close coordination with other aspects of the language renewal effort. It is critical that these projects use practical orthographies that are acceptable to the community so that there is consistency across all activities aimed toward language renewal. Conversely, communities in which there is not a tradition of native language literacy may find in multimedia an ideal means to introduce a new orthography and provide a more truly self-explanatory, self-pronouncing guide which will help to demystify the new orthography for users by bypassing the natural tendency to use the English pronunciation values as the implicit phonological model.

Notes

1. Some younger speakers have knowledge of their ancestral language's grammar and vocabulary, but they often know more than they can say, and this makes it unlikely that they will be able to transmit this passive knowledge of the language to the next generation. Two important reasons for the relatively high number of self-reported speakers in census and other survey data are the availability of courses both in and outside of schools, which greatly increases the number of people with some knowledge of the language, and the increased prestige of native languages for younger speakers, many of whom have adopted the language as an emblem of Mono identity. Western Mono is not alone in experiencing a rebirth of local interest in ancestral languages by native groups. Indeed, this is happening elsewhere in the state and all over the United States more generally.

2. This "Andersonian" model, which tends to equate linguistic unity and national identity, operates as both a folk and an academic model for understanding language and identity relationships. The folk model is clearly related to homologous European folk models. The academic model, as Michael Silverstein (1996) has argued, has provided many graphic examples of how the language ideology of Euro-American

scholars—here the Andersonian model, which represents an uncritical adoption of a folk model—has falsified the linguistic diversity of native North American speech communities. We share with Silverstein and other linguistic anthropological colleagues a great sense of ambivalence about the work of Benedict Anderson (1983). On the positive side, we applaud his acknowledgment of the role of language in the constructivist project of creating communities, national and otherwise, through linguistic products and practices. But on the negative side, we reject his claim that nations in the making must be monolingual communities which "naturally" share a common language. Indeed, this Andersonian precondition appears to be more a product of European and Euro-American language ideologies than of a substantiated finding.

3. Unless otherwise indicated, the Mono orthography used in this article is the revised version of Bethel et al. (1984) currently used by the Mono Language Project. It uses the Roman alphabet but adds three symbols: *i*, a high, central, unrounded vowel; *g*, a back-velar "g"; and *'*, a glottal stop. In addition, capital letters at the ends of words (e.g., *-A* or *-U*) indicate voiceless vowels.

4. This word is reproduced from a poster used to advertise the Annual Mono Indian Days celebration in the summer of 1997. It is not written in the Mono Language Project orthography (where it would be rendered Niiml).

References

Anderson, Benedict. 1983. *Imagined communities: Reflections on the origins and spread of nationalism.* London: Verso.

Bethel, Rosalie, Paul V. Kroskrity, Christopher Loether, and Gregory A. Reinhardt. 1984. *A practical dictionary of Western Mono.* North Fork, Calif.: Sierra Mono Museum.

Bourdieu, Pierre. 1991. *Language and symbolic power.* Cambridge, Mass.: Harvard University Press.

Brandt, Elizabeth A. 1988. Applied linguistic anthropology and American Indian language renewal. *Human Organization* 47: 322–29.

Dorian, Nancy C. 1981. *Language death: The life cycle of a Scottish Gaelic dialect.* Philadelphia: University of Pennsylvania Press.

———. 1989. *Investigating obsolescence: Studies in language contraction and death.* Cambridge: Cambridge University Press.

England, Nora C. 1992. Doing Mayan linguistics in Guatemala. *Language* 68: 29–35.

Farnell, Brenda. 1993. *Wiyuta: Assiniboine storytelling with signs* [CD-ROM]. Austin: University of Texas Press.

Gal, Susan. 1979. *Language shift: Social dimensions of linguistic change in bilingual Austria.* New York: Academic Press.

Hinton, Leanne. 1994. *Flutes of fire: Essays on California Indian languages.* Berkeley: Heyday Books.

Hinton, Leanne. 1999. The advocates. *News from Native California* 12, no. 3: 8–12.

Hymes, Dell. 1981. *"In vain I tried to tell you": Essays in Native American ethnopoetics.* Philadelphia: University of Pennsylvania Press.

Irvine, Judith. 1989. When talk isn't cheap: Language and political economy. *American Ethnologist* 16: 248–67.

Krauss, Michael. 1996. Status of Native American language endangerment. In *Stabilizing indigenous languages,* ed. Gina Cantoni, 16–21. Flagstaff: Northern Arizona University, Center for Excellence in Education.

Kroskrity, Paul V. 1998. Arizona Tewa Kiva Speech as a manifestation of a dominant language ideology. In *Language ideologies: Practice and theory,* ed. B. B. Schieffelin, K. A. Woolard, and P. V. Kroskrity, 103–23. New York: Oxford University Press.

———. 1999. Language ideologies, language shift, and the imagination of a Western Mono Community: The recontextualization of a Coyote story. In *Language and ideology,* ed. Jef Verschueren, 270–89. Antwerp: International Pragmatics Association.

———. In press. Language renewal and the technologies of literacy and postliteracy: Reflections from Western Mono. In *Dictionaries of indigenous languages of the Americas,* ed. William Frawley, Kenneth Hill, and Pamela Munro. Berkeley: University of California Press.

Kulick, Don. 1992. *Language shift and cultural reproduction.* Cambridge: Cambridge University Press.

Leap, William. 1988. Applied linguistics and American Indian language renewal: Introductory comments. *Human Organization* 47: 283–90.

Miller, Wick R. 1983. Uto-Aztecan languages. In *Handbook of North American Indians,* vol. 10, *Southwest,* ed. A. Ortiz, 113–24. Washington, D.C.: Smithsonian Institution.

Palmer, Gary B. 1988. The language and culture approach in the Coeur d'Alene Language Preservation Project. *Human Organization* 47: 307–17.

Parks, Douglas R. 1998. Language maintenance through multimedia technology: The Arikara Language Project. Paper presented at the 97th Annual Meeting of the American Anthropological Association, December 2–6, 1998, Philadelphia.

Silver, Shirley, and Wick R. Miller. 1998. *American Indian languages: cultural and social contexts.* Tucson: University of Arizona Press.

Silverstein, Michael. 1996. Encountering language and the languages of encounter in North American ethnohistory. *Journal of Linguistic Anthropology* 6: 126–44.

Spier, Robert F. G. 1978. Monache. In *Handbook of North American Indians,* vol. 8, *California,* ed. R. F. Heizer, 426–36. Washington, D.C.: Smithsonian Institution.

Tedlock, Dennis. 1972. *Finding the center.* New York: Dial.

Wiget, Andrew. 1987. Telling the tale: A performance analysis of a Hopi Coyote story. In *Recovering the word,* ed. B. Swann and A. Krupat, 297–336. Berkeley: University of California Press.

26

Can the Web Help Save My Language?

LAURA BUSZARD-WELCHER

Department of Linguistics
University of California at Berkeley
Berkeley, California

THE GROWING NUMBER OF ENDANGERED-LANGUAGE WEB SITES

The number of Web sites on endangered languages has risen dramatically in the past few years. While there are no published counts of these sites, even a casual observer would notice that the amount of information on endangered languages available on the Web is substantial, and growing. Five years ago there were only a few sites; now there are more than one could visit in the course of a week. By using a search engine, one can find references on the Web today to just about any endangered language.[1]

There are probably several factors contributing to this abundance of endangered-language Web sites. One is the overall exponential growth of the Web. According to Netcraft, an Internet consulting company, the number of sites on the World Wide Web has increased from approximately 80,000 in 1996 to over 11 million as of 2000. Another factor is a growing public awareness about endangered languages. In the last decade we have had the Native American Languages Act (1990), Michael Krauss's trailblazing article "The World's Languages in Crisis" (1992), and several conferences and symposia on endangered-language maintenance and revitalization.[2] Other factors include the development of new software programs that allow people to create Web sites without needing to know HTML,[3] Internet access through television, and the growth of technology, including faster and less expensive computers and Internet connections. In Native American communities, an increase in tribally funded programs, coupled with governmental programs such as the E-rate, have probably increased tribal members'

connectivity at home, school, and work to some extent, and consequently the number of sites developed by Native Americans for their heritage languages.

This proliferation of endangered-language Web sites raises the question of the role these sites and their developers will play in endangered-language maintenance and revitalization. This paper attempts to evaluate this role by surveying a representative sample of sites. An analysis of this information raises several issues about the Web itself as a technology in language maintenance and revitalization as well as the use we presently make of it.

A DATABASE OF ENDANGERED-LANGUAGE WEB SITES

The survey of endangered-language Web sites was conducted by following the links on two main index pages:[4] Karen Strom's links page and Lisa Mitten's native languages page. These indexes primarily link to sites on indigenous languages of the Americas. Both are widely known, used, and linked to in return by the community of native-language site developers.[5] For each site, the following information (where available) was collected and entered into a database:

1. Endangered language or languages addressed
2. Title of page
3. URL[6]
4. Date accessed
5. Date of last update

331

6. Description of language material available on the site
7. Information on the source of the material
8. Stated purpose of the site
9. Any special technology required to access and use the information on the site
10. Where the site was indexed
11. Who developed the site
12. The source of the language content (fluent speakers, documents, etc.)
13. Category type (individual or group) and affiliation (tribal, affiliated, or unaffiliated) of site developer

In total, 50 sites on Native American or Canadian Languages were included in the database, which provides a kind of snapshot of the current use of the Web in endangered-language maintenance and revitalization.[7] Of the sites listed on the links pages, only those on individual languages were considered; so, for example, a site that lists the numbers 1–10 in 14 Native American languages would not be included. Organizational sites were included if they represented an action group for a particular language or language family, but not sites for organizations that represent Native American languages overall, such as SSILA (the Society for the Study of Indigenous Languages of the Americas). These sites are very valuable to those working on endangered languages; however, they were not included in order to focus on smaller grassroots activities of individuals and tribal groups.

ANALYSIS OF SITE INFORMATION

In order to evaluate the Web as a tool in language maintenance and revitalization, it is important to have answers to a number of questions: Who creates endangered-language Web sites, and why? Who uses them? What kind of content do they have? The discussion in this section, which is based on an analysis of the database information, addresses these issues.

Who Creates Endangered-Language Web Sites?

It is fairly easy to tell who creates endangered-language Web sites, since the creator (known as the *site developer*) usually provides this information in the content of the site, or in a special credits section. Table 26.1 contains a summary of the database information on site developers, who were categorized by type and affiliation. The developer type could be either an individual or a group. The developer affiliation included three categories: "tribal" for sites created by a tribal member or for an official tribal Web site (usually one with organizational information, and links to many tribal departments and programs); "affiliated" for individuals or groups collaborating or consulting with a tribe, such as a linguist or university; and "unaffiliated" for individuals or groups working outside a tribe. For some sites, developer type and/or affiliation were unknown.

Looking at the data first by developer type, we find that 38% of the 50 Web sites are maintained by groups. Of these, only 4 are official tribal sites. Since many tribes have their own Web site, one might expect to find lots of official tribal sites with language pages, but this expectation was not borne out. In fact, over half of the sites in the sample (52%) are developed and maintained by individuals. This is surprising, since it takes a lot of time to develop and maintain any sizable Web site, and many of these people must be working on their site in their spare time, for free. While it is exciting to see such dedication, this can also pose problems for both the individual developer and site users, as will be discussed below.

Looking at the sites again based on developer affiliation, we find that less than half of the sample (48%) are developed by individuals or organizations that are either tribal or are affiliated with a tribe. This means that in many cases, tribes will have less say about the content of and access to language Web sites. While this leaves the door open to potential conflicts, for the most part, the content providers who post substantial amounts of previously unpublished language materials are usually either working closely with tribal mem-

TABLE 26.1 Site Developer Information

Type	Affiliation				Total	Percent
	Tribal	Affiliated	Unaffiliated	Unknown		
Group	4	8	5	2	19	38%
Individual	4	8	8	6	26	52%
Unknown	0	0	0	5	5	10%
Total	8	16	13	13	50	100%
Percent	16%	32%	26%	26%	100%	

bers or are tribal members themselves—that is, are in some way answerable to the tribal community.

Why Do People Create Endangered-Language Web Sites?

A few developers stated their goals in creating a Web site. These five statements are reproduced below:

"It's [sic] purpose has always remained the same for me. I created it to give people information that they might not be able to acquire, and educate people about Iroquois people. Over time it has evolved, taken on different forms and constantly has changed. Mostly I try to stick with the goal of giving people the chance to learn about Iroquois people."
—Iroquoian (d)

"This Site is Dedicated to the Preservation of ANISHINABEBI-MADISSIWIN [the Anishinaabe way of life]" —Ojibwa (c)

"These on line materials are provided mainly for the benefit of Potawatomi people who wish to learn the language, but who may have little or no access to the nakendumwajek who live on the reservation in Kansas. A secondary but still important audience is non-Potawatomis who are interested in Potawatomi or Indian culture. We share here a small slice of Potawatomi life, and ask that you please be careful in your study and with what you do with this information."
—Potawatomi (b)

"This site is dedicated to the preservation and revitalization of Unyæshæötká', the language of the West Virginia Mingo."
—West Virginia Mingo

"The Kualono World-Wide Web (WWW) service has been designed by the University of Hawai'i at Hilo—Hale Kuamo'o office primarily to service the Hawaiian language speaking communities worldwide. Although the majority of information is in the Hawaiian language, we have included some resources in English for those interested in learning the Hawaiian language or interested in learning more about Hawai'i's indigenous language, and the strides currently being made to ensure its perpetuation and continued growth."
—Hawaiian (b)

These statements show that endangered-language Web site developers see their sites as contributing to the goals of language maintenance and revitalization. Sites have the role of education as well as advocacy for the heritage language and culture. The last three statements also suggest that developers see the potential of their Web sites for use in language learning and teaching. As will be discussed below, although most sites in the database do not contain a statement of purpose, it is possible to form hypotheses about the intended purpose of endangered-language Web sites based on the kind of language content of the sites.

Who Uses Endangered-Language Web Sites?

In order to plan how to best use the Web for language revitalization, it would be useful to have some statistics about site users. Are they local tribal members? Widespread community members? People outside of the community? Of what age? However, it is much harder to determine these statistics, since on most noncommercial sites visitors remain anonymous. The Internet marketing industry is buzzing about new methods of quietly tracking site visitors to see who they are and where they go. This is not something most site users who relish their anonymity are particularly happy about. So even if the "little folks" on the Web had access to such tracking software, many would probably be very reluctant to use it. A means of overtly obtaining this information is to request it in a registration form that site visitors fill out online. This requires a short computer program (known as a CGI script) that takes the form information and sends it to a database maintained by the developer, or more simply, to the developer's e-mail address. Since this is somewhat complicated and therefore extra time to maintain the database is required, it is not surprising that none of the sites I visited had a registration form to fill out. More and more, however, these CGI scripts and forms are available from Internet service providers (ISPs) for free, and Web sites backed by databases are likely to be the norm in the future.[8]

While user information is unavailable from the Web sites themselves, one can make educated guesses about site use based on published statistics. According to the U.S. Census's most recent report on this subject, *Computer Use in the United States* (1997), one in five Americans uses the Internet. Most people who use the Internet do so from home, but the likelihood of having a computer at home is still heavily dependent on educational attainment and income. Age is also an important factor. Of people over 18, younger people are more likely to use the Internet than older people. That is, 32% of people aged 18–24 do, 27% of people aged 25–44, 25% of people aged 45–54, and only about 8% of people aged 55 and over. This last figure is very important for our discussion since in many cases elderly people are the only fluent speakers left in a community, and as a group they use the Internet the least.

Detailed figures on use of the Internet by tribal members are not available, but according to a government report on the digital divide, access to the Internet by Native Americans is much lower than the national average. One factor is the cost of computer equipment and monthly Internet access fees. Also, many tribal communities are located in rural areas where Internet access lags behind what is available in urban areas. While tribal members may not have access to the Internet at home, it is more likely that children will at school, since several programs have targeted schools for the purchase of computers and installation of Internet access. The "E-rate," a national program begun in 1998, provides schools with discounted Internet access and networking equipment.[9] The 4Directions project, underway since 1995, has been installing networks of computers that can access the Internet at high speeds in Bureau of Indian Affairs (BIA) schools. There are currently 185 BIA schools serving over

46,000 students. Of these, 19 have been targeted in the first stage of the program, with plans to increase this to 24 schools by 2001 (Aust, Newberry, and Resta 1996).

What's Out There?

There is quite a variety of content on the sites included in the database. The most popular types are listed in Table 26.2 in order of decreasing frequency (most sites have multiple kinds of content, so a single site may be listed under several content types). These include community information (organization information, Web rings, or a set of links); information on writing (font information, free font downloads, and discussions of writing systems); lists of vocabulary and phrases, or both; texts (stories, conversations, and liturgical texts); reference materials (online dictionaries or grammar notes); teaching materials (language lessons, pronunciation guides, and games); e-commerce; and audio. Each of these types will be discussed below, as well as less common kinds of content such as video, BBSs, and live chat.

Community Information: Organizations, Web Rings, and Links

Content with a community-building function is the type that occurs with the highest frequency on endangered-language Web sites (21 sites, or 42%; see Table 26.3). This includes information on the developer's organization, sets of links to other sites, and Web rings. Web rings are groups of linked Web sites; sites share a common thematic content and encourage visitation to sites that might not otherwise get linked. In addition, 10 sites (20%) had information on the organization sponsoring the site. For 4 of these sites (8% of the total sample), there was no additional language content. A total of 6 sites (12%) had a set of links, and 5 sites (10%) were included in Web rings, which were: the Native American Ring, The Tsalagi Ring (for Cherokee sites), Ring of Languages and Linguistics, and the Eastern North American Native Peoples Web Ring.

TABLE 26.3   Sites with Community Information

Organization information	Links	Web Rings
Algonquian and Iroquoian	Athapaskan	Iroquoian (c)
Ojibwa and Iroquoian	Chinook Jargon	Cheyenne
Comanche	Ioway-Otoe	Cherokee (c)
Hawaiian (a)	Navajo (a)	Cherokee (a)
Iroquoian (b)	Potawatomi (b)	Ojibwa (c)
Iroquoian (d)	Ojibwa (b)	
Navajo (a)		
Navajo (b)		
Potawatomi (b)		
Yukon Languages		

Writing: Fonts and Orthography Discussions

Of the sites in the sample, 28% had content on writing systems (see Table 26.4). This includes discussions of fonts (7 sites), offering fonts for free download (7 sites), and discussions of writing systems (7 sites). The latter are usually short descriptions of the development of particular writing systems accompanied by a chart of symbols. One site, Cherokee (b), has online lessons for learning to use the writing system.

Vocabulary and Phrases

Of all sites, 16 (32% of the total) have lists of vocabulary and/or phrases, accompanied by English translations (see Table 26.5). And of these, 10 had lists of vocabulary and/or phrases as the only form of language content (20% of the total sample). Two of these sites had accompanying sound files.

While some vocabulary lists are organized alphabetically or are unordered (this is frequently the case with shorter lists), the most common means of organization of vocabulary is a list by topic. This is a useful format for language

TABLE 26.2   Content of Sites

Content Type	n	%
Community information	21	42%
Writing	16	32%
Vocabulary, phrases	16	32%
Texts	11	22%
Reference materials	10	20%
Pedagogical materials	9	18%
E-commerce	7	14%
Audio	6	12%

TABLE 26.4   Sites with Information on Fonts/Orthographies

Fonts	Orthography discussions
Cherokee, Cree, Hawaiian, Inuit/Inuktitut, and Mayan	Cherokee (b)
Cherokee (f)	Cherokee (d)
Hawaiian (a)	Ojibwa (c)
Cherokee (e)	Hupa
Hawaiian (b)	Inuktitut
Navajo (a)	Potawatomi (b)
Inuktitut, Cree	Yukon Languages

TABLE 26.5 Sites with Vocabulary/Phrases

Organized by semantic topic	Organized alphabetically
Iroquoian (d)	Iroquoian (c)
Cheyenne	
Arapaho and Cheyenne	Unordered lists:
Ojibwa (c)	Oneida
Hupa	Lakota (a)
Potawatomi (a)	Iroquoian (a)—with sound
Abenaki	Secwepemc (British Columbia)
Algonquin—with sound	
Ojibwa (a)	
Natick	
Ojibwa (b)	

learners and teachers, since each topic could easily form the basis for a set of lessons. Common topics include:

- Animals: birds, horses
- Natural world: weather, earth, forests, sky
- Cultural artifacts: food, money, furniture, clothing
- Grammar and conversation: nouns, verbs, questions, commands, greetings
- Semantic categories: numbers, colors
- Calendar and seasons: days, months, seasons, holidays
- Cultural phenomena: songs, stories, personal names, tribal names, place-names
- Human body and relationships: words for body parts, terms for kin, emotions, sickness, tastes, human life stages, relationships
- Activities: school, play

Texts

The next most common kind of content is native language texts, usually with accompanying translations in English, occurring in 11 sites (22% of the total sample; see Table 26.6). Four of these sites (8%) had sound files, which allow the site visitor to hear the text. Texts include narratives by fluent eld-

TABLE 26.6 Sites with Texts

	With sound:
Cheyenne (c)	
Chinook Jargon	Inuktitut
Hawaiian (b)	Lushootseed
Hocak Wazijaci	Michif
Navajo	West Virginia Mingo
Potawatomi (b)	
Yukon Languages	

ers, some traditional stories, conversations, and sacred texts such as Bible translations.

Reference Materials: Dictionaries and Grammar Notes

Reference materials were found on 20 sites (40%), including notes on grammar and online dictionaries (see Table 26.7). Three sites in the sample had grammatical information in the form of short grammar notes. This kind of technical information is less common. In fact, 2 of these sites were created by linguists (Cheyenne and Potawatomi (a)). While the hypertext format of the Web is an ideal medium for writing and using grammars, there were no examples of extensive online reference grammars in the sample.

A total of seven sites (14% of the sample) have online searchable dictionaries (see Table 26.8). The size varies from a couple hundred words to thousands of entries. Some, such as the Cherokee and Chinook Jargon dictionaries, are compiled from published documents.[10] Others, such as the Potawatomi dictionary, are the result of original research. Some are indexed alphabetically, and most are searchable by the English or Native American language keyword.

Teaching Materials: Lessons, Pronunciation, and Games

Teaching materials were included in 9 sites (18% of the sample; see Table 26.9). These include short language lessons, guides to pronunciation (one with sound files), and

TABLE 26.7 Sites with Grammar Notes

Cheyenne
Lakota (a)
Potawatomi (a)

TABLE 26.8 Sites with Online Dictionaries

West Virginia Mingo: searchable in Mingo and English. 2823 entries. Entries sorted by semantic field.

Cheyenne: searchable in Cheyenne or English. Size not specified.

Lakhota (c): Lakhota-English dictionary. 4000 entries. This dictionary is only available by paid yearly subscription.

Alabama: Large Alabama-English dictionary. Not searchable, but indexed alphabetically by Alabama and English first letters. Size not specified.

Cherokee (d): White Dove's Cherokee Dictionary (about 100 words, with syllabic pronunciations)

Chinook Jargon: Shaw's dictionary of Chinook Jargon. About 250 words. Listed alphabetically with a supplemental English index.

Potawatomi (b): Listed alphabetically by English and Potawatomi, or can be searched by English or Potawatomi keyword. Many words have sound files. Large, although number of entries isn't specified.

TABLE 26.9   Sites with Teaching Materials

- *Language lessons*
  West Virginia Mingo (Iroquoian)
  Cherokee (c)
  Lakhota (c)
  Inuktitut
- *Games*
  West Virginia Mingo — hangman
  Cheyenne — crossword
- *Pronunciation guides*
  Cherokee (c)
  Dakota — with sound
  Arapaho and Cheyenne

TABLE 26.11   Sites with Audio

- *Pronunciation guides*
  Dakota
- *Vocabulary/phrases*
  Algonquin
  Iroquoian (a)
- *Texts*
  Inuktitut
  Lushootseed
  Michif
  West Virginia Mingo

games. While in many cases sites are used as repositories of language information, these materials indicate that site developers are exploring the possibilities of the Web as a language transmission and teaching tool.

E-Commerce

Seven sites in the sample (14%) had information on ordering language materials (see Table 26.10). For four of these sites (8% of the total sample) this was only language content. In the past, language materials developed by endangered-language community members have had very limited distribution. Now, however, true to the spirit of e-commerce, the Web offers a "24/7" opportunity to order hard-to-find publications.

Audio

One benefit of the Web is that it can transmit content using a variety of media. One of the most useful for language learners is audio. Seven sites in the sample have audio files (see Table 26.11). These files are usually linked to the text of vocabulary, phrases, or texts. One site (Dakota) uses sound files in its pronunciation guide.

Less Common Language Content

Some of the less common kinds of content on these sites are also the most innovative (see Table 26.12). These include presenting material without translations in such a way that the learner understands what the content means, technologies such as e-mail lists, e-mail archives, bulletin board system (BBS) discussions, live chat,[11] and in the case of a Hawaiian site, the option to use the site all in the native language.

TABLE 26.10   Sites with E-Commerce

Iroquoian (d)
Cheyenne
Cherokee (a)
Cherokee (b)
Lakota (b)
Lushootseed
Jicarilla Apache

TABLE 26.12   Sites with Less Common Language Content

- *Non-translated materials*
  Dakota — colors to teach sounds, writing
  Hupa — images to teach vocabulary
- *Bibliographies*
  Athapaskan
  Ioway-Otoe
- *E-mail list/archive/BBS*
  Siouan (Omaha-Ponca — e-mail list/archive)
  Ojibwe (BBS)
- *Chat*
  West Virginia Mingo (Iroquoian)
- *Video*
  Hawaiian
- *Bilingual sites*
  Hawaiian
- *Elicited sentences*
  Michif
- *Academic papers*
  Salish

What's Cool?

Believe it or not, "cool" drives a lot of development on Web sites. What use is it to have blinking text? Java applets that make icons spin around on a page? These gizmos do not provide any extra content, but they send a message: "I'm cool, I'm plugged in to what's happening, I know what's going on." For endangered languages, the commotion raised by a cool site can have the important function of increasing the language's prestige (especially among younger people) and its domains of use. Young people also take great pride in helping build a community language site (these make excellent school projects).

Cool Technology

On the Web, new technology is always cool. Fortunately, many of the new technologies can be adapted to Web sites for language teaching. For language learning, it is important to hear the language, better to see and hear it used in context, and best, of course, to be able to use it in context. The new multimedia technologies make it increasingly easier to hear, see, and use language and reduce the need for reliance on literacy for language transmission on the Web.

As discussed above, some of the sites in the sample have audio files. Incorporating sound into a Web site requires some technical knowledge. The most common formats for these files are .AU (called "audio") and .WAV (called "wave"). With audio, the developer usually transfers a recording to digital format (one can do this by plugging an external analog or digital tape recorder into a computer). These sound files are then posted to the Web site's server so that people can download the file and listen to it. While sound can take up a lot of space and can take a long time to download, most audio files are now compressed. MPEG3 is a popular compression format. There is usually some loss at the very high and low end of the sound spectrum, but this is not noticeable, particularly for speech. MPEG files are considered to be CD quality. To listen to MPEG files, users must download a "plug-in" for their browser and set the browser preferences to use a particular plug-in for certain kinds of files. Plug-ins are programs that run automatically when you open up a particular kind of file. Another audio format, known as RealAudio, allows the sound file to play as it is being downloaded. This means that users do not have to wait a long time for a file to download before listening to it.

Video is a much less common type of medium in the sample, being used only on the Hawaiian bilingual site.[12] However, it is becoming more common, and larger sites are now making use of it. In order to make original videos available on a Web site, several kinds of technology are required. For video clips that the user downloads from the site, the analog or digital video files are transferred to a personal computer (PC) and then sent to be stored on the server computer. When someone visits the site, they click on an icon and the video downloads onto his or her PC. Because video takes up a lot of bandwidth, you have to have a reasonably fast computer and connection to the Internet in order to easily download and view the files. With most new computers and the new DSL and cable modem connections, this is not a problem.

Another relatively new technology is live video broadcasting over the Internet. This requires a video camera, a PC, a fast connection to the Internet, and some free software. Video encoding software (such as Real Media) goes on the PC, and the video broadcast software (such as Real Media Server) goes on the server. Then, as you videotape, your PC encodes the data and sends it to the server, which then broadcasts it on your Web site. When users visit the site, they see a live broadcast. Since this requires much more equipment and some technological expertise, this is usually only done for special Web events. It is important to keep in mind that average video nowadays streams at three frames per second, which is noticeably choppy. This is probably fast enough to get linguistic information from gestures and large movements, but less helpful for using a speaker's mouth movements as speech cues.

Bulletin board systems (BBSs) and live chat are an easy and inexpensive way of providing interaction between site users. With a BBS, users post notices in a central location. Other users can then visit the location and comment on the postings. This way an extended archived discussion organized by topics can be maintained. For real-time communication, people can use chat. First, participants must download a free chat program. Then, at a specified time, everyone meets at the same chat location (usually called a chat room) and has a nearly real-time conversation by typing in a window on their PCs. Using chat therefore requires a writing system that people are comfortable with and that is easy to type.

Although this fact is less obvious, providing information for free is definitely cool. Many people do not have access to archived information, dictionaries, or recordings of texts. While a number of people still do not have access to the Internet, popular information is commonly distributed by somebody's accessing the information, printing it, and then sharing photocopies. In this way, communities become aware of the existence of language Web sites even if many of its members do not use the Internet.

While all of these technologies are very exciting, it is important to keep in mind that to make use of them, particularly audio and video, people need to have access to a newer computer with an up-to-date browser and a fast Internet connection. Most people today connect to the Internet by using a telephone dial-up number using a modem speed of 28.8 or 56K, both of which are slow in terms of taking advantage of new media formats. The good news is that cable modems are becoming more and more common and are much faster than standard dial-up modems.

Top 10 Cool Sites

Of the sites in the sample, 10 "must visits" are included here (in no particular order). People working on endangered languages should be aware of these sites both for their importance in the online community of endangered-language site builders and for their innovative content.

- **Karen Strom's Links Page and Lisa Mitten's Native Languages Page.** These are two of the most important link pages for people working on Native American languages.
- **4Directions.** 4Directions is a project that is intended to "create a virtual network of Native American schools and communities." Eight schools are currently part of the program, whose goal is "to assist Native American schools in forming a community of learners who would use technology to communicate, assist each other, share in the diversity of the various cultures, and, ensure that Native peoples' voices are heard in the emerging information age" (The 4Directions Challenge).
- **Hupa (Danny Ammon's Hupa language Web page).** This site is designed and maintained by Danny Ammon, who was an apprentice in the master-apprentice language program and is now a second-language speaker of Hupa.[13] He has an alphabet chart and a list of numbers and verb forms, but what is truly creative is his use of images on the Hupa Words page. There are no English translations—only pictures! This is important, because it frames language learning in Hupa. This is one of the central ideas behind the master-apprentice program, and he has carried it over to his Web site design.
- **Siouan (Omaha-Ponca) [Siouan languages].** This was the only site in the database that maintains an e-mail list with archives. The messages seem to be largely on academic linguistic subjects (the site is maintained by the linguist John Koontz). However, a list could be on any topic (for example, community concerns), and could be used by any special interest community.
- **Ojibwa (a).** Besides lots of other cool stuff, this site has an online forum and BBS. Time to practice your Anishinaabemowin! Most of the action seems to be taking place on the BBS.
- **Cheyenne [Cheyenne language Web site].** This site has lots of materials and lots of different kinds of language materials. There is general information on Cheyenne and its endangered status and a very good discussion on linguistics and the role of linguists. It has a searchable online dictionary, grammar notes, 17 glossed texts (with notes), a set of words and phrases listed by semantic category, and a

Cheyenne flash card program available for free download (other language materials are available by order). There is also an extensive set of links to other Native American language Web sites.

- **Potawatomi (b) [Potawatomi Web].** This site is widely linked to and admired for the vast amount of material on Potawatomi language and culture. The site developer, Smokey McKinney, is an innovator in language Web site design. His was one of the first sites to incorporate an extensive online wordlist, which he has added to over the years. The list also has sound files for many of the words on the list, spoken by his father, Jim McKinney. The dictionary is alphabetized and can be searched either in English or Potawatomi. The most recent addition is a set of liturgical texts (from missionary records) with translations.
- **West Virginia Mingo.** This is a site developed by an amazing team: Dr. Thomas McElwain, who is a faculty member of the University of Stockholm and a speaker of Mingo; Jordan Lachler, a graduate student in linguistics at the University of New Mexico; and Sean Burke, a computer programmer who also has an interest in language. Together they have created a site full of good humor and great language materials, including online chat, language lessons, Bible translations, 23 short texts, a reference grammar (in progress), and a searchable dictionary of nearly 3,000 entries. Most of the materials are text based, but there are a few sound files as well.
- **Hawaiian (b) [Kualono].** This site is so cool, it's bilingual! It is designed by the University of Hawai'i at Hilo for Hawaiian speakers worldwide. You can choose to visit the site in Hawaiian, English, or both. There are links to Hawaiian videos, but they did not seem to be working when I visited the site.

DISCUSSION

When evaluating any technology as a tool, one must consider the benefits or limitations of the technology itself as well as how people use it. The answer to the question "Can the Web help save my language?" therefore depends on the strengths or weaknesses of the Web as a technology as well as the effectiveness of our current use of it to achieve the goals of language maintenance and revitalization.

Technology Issues

The analysis of information on endangered-language Web sites in the previous section ("Analysis of Site Information") highlights two facets of Web technology that impact our ability to make use of it in language revitalization: Web access and the dominance of text as a means of communication on the Web.

Web Access

If Native American communities are to take full advantage of Web technology for language maintenance and revitalization, they will need better access to the Web, on modern computers, and at modern speeds (that is, at least 56K modems, but even this is considered slow by today's standards). This is gradually becoming a reality, thanks to tribal and federal programs and the efforts of groups like 4Directions. It is also likely that because of these programs, the best access (in terms of computers and connection speeds) will be in schools and tribal offices. In fact, these may be the only places where many people will have access to the Web, if they do not have a computer and Internet account at home. Since developing, maintaining, and contributing to a Web site requires computer time apart from other work and school projects, it is worth considering initiatives to provide computers and Web access to community members at home.

The second issue of Web access is the age gap in computer use. Very few older adults have access to computers or the Internet or use them if they do. There are many programs that target Internet access for children in order to help prepare them for higher education and their future jobs, but elders tend to get overlooked. This is a serious problem for language maintenance and revitalization efforts on the Web since elders are frequently the only fluent speakers. In my experience, older adults love to use computers once somebody takes the time to show them how to use it and how to connect to the Internet and helps them when they get stuck or frustrated. There are many benefits to having elders online. For example, a friend of mine, a fluent Potawatomi elder, recently got an e-mail account. Because we live nearly 2,000 miles apart, it is expensive to communicate by phone, and letters are slow. Now that he is online, we have been corresponding with each other in Potawatomi. He also responds to questions from learners of Potawatomi from around the country. There is something about e-mail and the way it is integrated into the routine of our daily lives that makes it easy and appealing to use. The messages we send are typed, which of course requires that both parties know and use the same writing system, but there are several inexpensive programs that allow you to send short voice messages instead (some programs also allow you to include a picture).[14] Just think how great it would be to get e-mail in your native language! In order to encourage elders to use e-mail, tribes might consider installing a computer with Internet access in a location where elders gather and showing them how to use it. By reserving use of the computer just for elders or by allowing elders to have first priority, they would not have to compete with younger people for computer time.

Writing Systems, Fonts, and Literacy on the Web

There is a considerable focus on writing systems on endangered-language Web sites. Many sites have discussions of writing systems, orthography charts, and pedagogical materials for learning writing systems. In part, this focus probably reflects the orthography debates taking place in many Native American communities. However, probably the most significant reason for addressing writing on Web sites is that Internet technology has developed around the written channel for communication. E-mail is the most obvious example of this, but even with the graphic capabilities of the Web, most sites rely heavily on writing for content as well as site navigation. Even chat and instant message sessions, which come close to approximating real-time communication, rely on text. Audio and video, which could be used to transmit spoken language, are much more difficult to incorporate into Web sites using current technology. Unlike audio and video, text does not require much memory and is quickly transferred over even the slowest of Internet connections. The dominance of text for communication on the Web makes it very difficult to create language Web sites that do not depend on writing and poses a particular problem for the development of Web sites for communities with unwritten languages.

In order to post language content on the Web, most site developers have therefore had to contend with orthography and font issues. In some cases, developers have to modify existing orthographies to make them Web friendly. Writing systems that use roman letters transfer most easily to the new media, although diacritics are often a problem.[15] Other writing systems, such as Cree syllabics or the Cherokee syllabary, do not use roman letters. For these languages, developers have to figure out a way to incorporate a language font onto their sites. Usually the site user must download a special font onto their computer in order to be able to see and use the site. Font downloads and installations can be difficult, and users may give up on the site rather than trying to tackle the technology required.

Usage Issues

While technology is an important factor in evaluating the Web as a tool in endangered-language maintenance and revitalization, Web technology is constantly being modified and improved. A technological problem today may therefore not be a problem tomorrow. Ultimately, we are probably less constrained by technology than by psychology; that is, how we think about and use the Web. The information collected on endangered-language Web sites suggests four focal issues relating to Web use: Web publishing, the relationship between developers and site users, the presentation of language content, and how we relate to the Web and interact on it.

Web Publishing

Many people working on endangered languages find it very difficult and expensive to get their materials published. Most large printing houses will not publish them, because they are unlikely to make a good profit with a small print run. Desktop publishing is an alternative, but the books still may be expensive, and one must then be a book distributor.[16] As indicated by the sites examined here, more and more people are turning to Web publishing because it is easy and inexpensive, and because the materials posted on the Web are then free for people to download, use, and print.

Yet Web publishing creates issues of its own. One issue is worldwide access. This was less of a problem with self-published language materials, which tend to have more local (community) distribution. Language materials have also been printed as anthropological and linguistic works, but these also tend to be of a limited distribution, either because they are very expensive books to acquire, or because they are written in academic terms, which limits their popular appeal. However, once a Web page is posted, anyone who can locate the URL can look at it. The World Wide Web, true to its name, allows worldwide access to that information. Many communities will have concerns about what kinds of materials should be posted and who should have access to the materials, as well as when such materials should be used. Some feel that the language itself must not be shared with outsiders. Such concerns may discourage people from publishing language materials on the Web at all. Communities must weigh the issues of access against potential benefits of sharing information. In some cases, there is the risk of the information's otherwise being lost.[17] Yet if a community wants to limit access to its materials on the Web, there are several possible solutions. The first is to keep sensitive material off the Web entirely. If some language should be accessed only at certain times of the year, one can remove access to it during restricted periods by removing links to it or by moving the information off the server altogether. In order to restrict access to community members, Web sites can be password protected. This solution is more labor intensive and less secure. A creative solution to the problem could be to create an internet (small "i"), a network of computers where access from the outside is restricted. Such an internet is being used in Hawaiian immersion programs, where children from different schools can carry on discussions with each other using a local internet bulletin board.[18]

A couple of other issues stand in the way of publishing materials on the Web. The first is posting document drafts or work in progress. This is an excellent collaborative approach that benefits both the community and developer. The community will have immediate access to materials, whereas they might otherwise have to wait years for a finished document to be published, and the developer can get very useful feedback from the community—people can point out mis-

takes, suggest alternative analyses, and provide new information. However, posting drafts on the Web can potentially cause problems with later attempts to publish the materials. The developer may have trouble finding a publisher or may have to remove or restrict the information available on the Web site. The second issue concerns the peer review process, a gatekeeping institution in traditional print publishing. Peer review is not common on the Web. This is often touted as a virtue of the Web, since everyone can have a voice by creating his or her own Web site. However, the price for this freedom is that it can be very difficult for site users to know if online information is accurate or in any way authoritative. This absence of information gatekeeping discourages professionals and academics (such as linguists) from Web publishing, since meeting peer review is essential to their reputation and livelihood.

The Relationship between Communities and Site Developers

In communities where there are few fluent speakers, as is the case with many Native American languages, people who are in the process of learning the language are often called on to share what they are learning with others.[19] This is the case with endangered-language Web site developers who are often language learners. As learners, their grammar is likely to contain errors and differences from the grammar of the language they are in the process of acquiring. Linguists have studied the process of second-language acquisition and have found that as with first-language acquisition, errors are a natural and unavoidable part of the learning process. However, because site users tend to think of these developers as information providers, they expect the information provided to be accurate and authoritative and may become angry if they discover errors. The occurrence of errors may be reduced by posting language material provided by fluent speakers. In general, this is the strategy taken by linguists when they elicit sentences and texts. Yet when the information is filtered through a nonfluent speaker, there is still the chance of misreporting speech and making misanalyses. It is important for site developers to keep this in mind and to consider cautioning site users about the possibilities of errors in language content.

There are additional problems with seeing site developers as information providers. Most endangered-language Web sites are developed by individuals, which means that a lot of the work of documenting, cataloging, and sharing language information falls on just a few people. As a language maintenance or revitalization technique, this does not spell success; rather, it probably spells burnout for the people doing all the work. What would improve the situation for both developer and language community is a shift from seeing the developer as an authority or information provider to seeing the developer as a community collaborator. This helps place the responsibility of language maintenance on the community as a whole, rather than just a few individuals.

The Presentation of Language Content

There are a number of parallels between the kind of language content on endangered-language Web sites and NSL (Native [American] language as a second language) classroom language content. Problems identified in NSL classrooms, even in some immersion programs, include presenting vocabulary and phrases out of context, overconcentrating on "grammar-translation" and writing, teaching by translating into English, and using English as the "frame" language of the classroom. We have noted that lists of vocabulary and phrases in isolation are one of the most common kinds of language content on these Web sites. Vocabulary building is important for any language learner, but this should be a part of a larger oral fluency program. Presenting vocabulary in isolation and as the only kind of language content runs counter to modern theories of second-language acquisition, which stress the importance of language learning in context.

Another popular content is native language texts with accompanying translations. These texts, which are often traditional stories, have great cultural value, and providing extended discourse allows learners to see language used in grammatical context. As a language teaching methodology, grammar-translation was commonly used in foreign-language classrooms in the earlier part of the century and is the traditional method for learning Latin and Ancient Greek. Of course, the goal in the latter case is not oral fluency (Latin and Ancient Greek are "extinct" languages), but literacy. Translating texts and studying translated texts is an excellent way to gain a rapid understanding of grammar, and listening to connected fluent speech can give one a good ear for the language. However, used alone as a language learning methodology, grammar-translation is unlikely to produce fluent speakers.

The focus on writing on endangered-language Web sites seems to parallel the focus on literacy over oral fluency that is present in many (even oral) language classrooms. According to Dauenhauer and Dauenhauer (1998):

> Confusion about the role of literacy is common in NSL (Native Second Language) instruction, and literacy is obviously a component of materials development, even where it is intended for teachers to present materials orally. Many teachers become enthusiastic about literacy after participating in teacher-training workshops and are eager to teach it, but forget that while they already know the language, their students do not. They tend to substitute literacy for building a base in oral fluency.

This dominance of text for communication on the Web impacts its potential for language teaching, since, if the goal is fluency, written communication is of secondary importance to oral communication.

Another parallel with NSL classroom content is the linguistic frame—the language that provides the structure and primary content. Native language content on these sites is introduced and discussed in English and is almost universally translated into English (the Hawaiian bilingual site is a noteworthy exception). English is used as the framing language partly because the Web constrains the kind of media available for language teaching. Without text translations it is difficult to provide enough context to facilitate understanding. This will probably change as video technology gains a stronger foothold on Web pages.

While it is possible that endangered-language Web site developers are using what happens in NSL classrooms as a model for teaching on the Web, it is not hard to find similar methodological problems in other kinds of formal language teaching contexts. Popular beliefs about language teaching probably derive from experiences people have had with language learning in the classroom and with other methods, such as commercial language-learning tapes. If the Web is to be used for language teaching (rather than primarily as a repository of information), developers will have to rethink the way they present language content. Developers might also look into current research in the fields of education and second-language acquisition, either by reading research reports or by consulting with field experts, in order to inform the kinds of decisions they make about how to structure language material on the Web.

Metaphors and Models of Web Interaction

A few years ago, I joined the ranks of endangered-language Web site developers by creating a Web site for primary use by the Potawatomi community, whose heritage language, at less than 50 fluent speakers around the United States and Canada, is critically endangered.[20] As a linguist involved with several Potawatomi language programs, I intended to use the site for the purpose of posting program information and notices. However, I soon saw the potential of the site as a way to share scarce language materials and as a place on the Internet where speakers, teachers, and language learners could meet and support each other's interests and efforts. In addition, the presence of the site on the Web would advocate and encourage the use of Potawatomi. The site included four kinds of content: program information and announcements, language materials (sections from a grammar in progress), a link to send me e-mail, and a bulletin board where site users could hold discussions by posting messages to each other. Note that even with this basic content, the site already has several functions: providing information, obtaining information and feedback from site users, and fostering communication among site users, all of which contribute to building and supporting a community. I offer this example to show that Web developers create sites and post the information they do for a particular reason, although these reasons are not usually consciously articulated. Information on a Web site is not just information; it is information with a function and a purpose. If we can determine what these unstated functions are, we will be in a better position to evaluate the role of the Web in endangered-language maintenance and revitalization.

Several sites have only one kind of language-related content, which I call "primary function content," listed in Table 26.13. This means that either the whole Web site or the site's language pages function solely (at least for the time being) to provide this kind of information. One kind of primary function is *establishing identity*. Language content used for this includes lists of vocabulary and phrases, which are the most accessible kind of authentic language. Another primary function is *community building*, with such content as organizational information, links, and Web rings. Site developers may work alone physically, but the Web itself is highly social and interactive. The fact that these sites are on Strom's and Mitten's link pages at all says something about the importance they place on networking, since one must either spend time talking to people who share a common interest or spend a significant amount of time navigating the Web before locating important link pages. The third primary function is *commerce*, the content in this case being e-commerce. In *Measuring the Growth of the Web*, Matthew Gray of the Massachusetts Institute of Technology reports that as of 1995, e-commerce sites represented at least half of all Web sites (this proportion is probably much higher today). Metaphorically, the Web is like any big convention or community gathering where you meet people (community building), introduce yourself (identity function), and sell stuff (e-commerce). This is true of the Web as a whole and of the community of endangered-language Web site builders.

The primary content functions identified on the Web sites here support the idea that this metaphor structures many of the interactions that take place over the Web. That is, when on the Web, we are primarily concerned with meeting people who share our interests, establishing our own identities, and engaging in commerce. This seems true for the Web in general, but it certainly is the case for the Web sites we have looked at here. This is not the only possible metaphor, however. We can also think of the Web as a repository of cultural information—a virtual library (you may have even noticed that I have done much of the research for this paper using materials found on the Web). For communities interested in documenting their language, the Web (or a local internet) can be a place to efficiently organize, store, and share lots of cultural information. Many sites in our sample are currently creating these virtual libraries. In fact, for some of the sites (such as the Mingo site), they are just about the only source for language information. However, neither the "gathering"

TABLE 26.13   Primary Function Content Type

Content Type	Multiple Content	%	Only Content	%
identification	16	32%	10	20%
community building	21	42%	4	8%
e-commerce	7	14%	4	8%

metaphor or the "virtual library" metaphor helps much if the goal is to create new speakers of the language. For this I believe we need to change the way we think about the Web and the way we interact on it.

I suggest that the Web can be a *virtual speech community*, a constructed immersion setting where members of the speech community meet, interact, and communicate in the native language. Probably for many people who have seen television bring English or Spanish into their homes, any new technology that "invades" the home may be seen as a threat to the home language's existence. However, the Internet is different from television. Television is a one-way information flow from the network to a passive home audience. The Internet is not one-way, nor is it passive. People receive information, but they create and send it too. The Web is a very social place that encourages participation and community building.

While real face-to-face interaction will always be the primary domain of language learning, many *real* speech communities would nevertheless benefit by having an added *virtual* community. A good example is the Potawatomi Language Scholars' College. The Potawatomis live in communities separated from each other by hundreds of miles. Several communities themselves are widespread, with members living all over the country. There are fewer than 50 fluent speakers, mostly elderly people. Many of these speakers do not have the opportunity to use their language. Moreover, there are many people who would love to learn Potawatomi but do not live anywhere near native speakers. The college helped bring fluent speakers from all different Potawatomi communities together as well as younger people interested in learning the language. But this college only meets for a few weeks a year. What a benefit a virtual community would be if all throughout the year, participants could meet each other online, learning new language and reinforcing their language use.

While we wait for video teleconferencing over the Web to become mainstream, there are lots of ways to improve community participation on Web sites, such as having online forums, bulletin boards, and e-mail lists. Try encouraging the use of these (or set up special forums) just for the purpose of using the native language. Encourage participation by fluent speakers. One fluent speaker will draw many learners. The next step is to try online chat (you might try participating in the Mingo chat to see how it is done). One way to make this less intimidating for second-language speakers would be to have language materials available on a particular subject that will be the topic of the chat.

CONCLUDING THOUGHTS

As a learner of an endangered language and as a site developer, I am excited by the possibilities of the Web for language learning, teaching, and community building. However, a skeptical observer might point out that few endangered-language Web sites have substantial amounts of language content, and what content there is seems to mostly consist of short lists of vocabulary, words and phrases presented out of context—hardly the ideal way to learn to speak a language. One might think that, for all the hype, the Web is just another technology craze—a diversion requiring great amounts of time and money which in the end will not help keep endangered languages alive. On the other hand, the Web is a technology we are only beginning to take advantage of. Considering how new most of these sites are, developers may be just starting to add language content. If so, these early indications, coupled with the rapid growth of Web technologies for audio and video, suggest that the Web is growing in its potential as a language revitalization tool. It is therefore probably best to take a balanced approach of experimenting with the new technology while maintaining a healthy skepticism toward it. For example, any new technology for language teaching ought to be evaluated for its potential effect on cultural dynamics: one must realize that the Web is no substitute for the complex face-to-face interaction that takes place among speakers in a real community.

My position in this discussion has been that we are only beginning to realize the potential of the Web for language maintenance and revitalization. As new technologies develop and more people access and use the Web to do more things, the importance of the Web in creating and maintaining community can only grow. As people working in endangered-language maintenance and revitalization, we currently limit ourselves by the way we think of the Web, what it is for, how we interact on it, and how it can be used. I encourage communities and site developers to think of the Web as being capable of functions such as providing the opportunity for community members to meet and use language interactively with each other.

Notes

1. This essay was originally developed for a seminar on endangered languages taught by Leanne Hinton at Berkeley in the fall of 1999, where it benefited from group discussion and suggestions. I would also like to thank Brian Beilenberg for his comments and suggestions on an earlier draft of this paper and James Buszard-Welcher for providing his expertise on Web technologies. The author can be contacted by sending correspondence to Laura Buszard-Welcher, University of California, Berkeley, Department of Linguistics, 1203 Dwinelle Hall, Berkeley, CA 94720, or by e-mail at webmaster@www.potawatomilang.org.

2. See, for example, the Web sites on Stabilizing, Teaching, and Revitalizing Indigenous Languages.
3. HTML, or HyperText Markup Language, allows text to be converted into Web pages.
4. A link is highlighted text on a Web page, which, if you click on it, will take you to another Web site. Web sites often have a separate page devoted to a collection of links.
5. There are several other link pages worth visiting, including one at Wayne Leman's Cheyenne site.
6. URL stands for Uniform Resource Locator and is the address of the Web page or site.
7. The Strom and Mitten index pages include links to sites outside of the Americas, as well as sites in Central and South America. These are important sites; however, they were not included in this sample in order to focus on a geographic and linguistic area that I was more familiar with.
8. For a discussion, see Greenspun 1999.
9. For the government announcement of the E-rate program, see the *President's Coalition Update Newsletter*. For an informational brochure (available using Adobe Acrobat Reader) see *A Parent's Guide to the E-Rate*.
10. For a discussion of how to do this with an example from Tohono O'odham, see Miyashita and Moll 1999.
11. Being on an e-mail list is like subscribing to a newsletter. You send your address to the person maintaining the list, and then you receive any e-mails that are addressed to the list. An e-mail archive is the set of these e-mails saved in a particular location for reference purposes. A BBS is like an e-mail archive, but instead of receiving e-mail posted to a list, you visit a Web location where the messages are posted and stored. Usually the messages are grouped in "threaded discussions" where users post messages in response to each other. Live chat is a kind of program that allows multiple users to type and receive messages immediately; the closest version on the Web to a live discussion group.
12. The links to video clips were not working when I visited the site.
13. See Hinton 1997 for details on the master-apprentice program.
14. These programs allow you to send short (approximately 60-second) voice messages over the Internet. With a modem, however, these messages can be very slow to send and receive, making voice e-mail (at least for the time being) more of a novelty than a useful technology.
15. For example, in writing Potawatomi we use an accented "e," like this: é. Although by using special software I can insert this character into the HTML text, when I send e-mail messages, the character is changed to a symbol from the ASCII set. One way to get around this problem is to assign special characters or sequences of characters for use on the Web. For example, in German text on the Web one frequently finds the letter "e" representing a vowel with umlaut, so ö would be written oe on the Web, ü would be written ue, etc.
16. For a discussion of what is involved, see St. Clair et al. 1999.
17. For a discussion of these issues in Alaskan native communities, see Dauenhauer and Dauenhauer 1998.
18. See Warchauer and Donaghy. 1997 for a discussion of the Hawaiian Leoki BBS.
19. For a discussion of issues on learners as teachers, see Hinton 1999.
20. There are several Web sites with information on Neshnabémwen. Most Potawatomi tribes have official Web sites with some language content. There are also a few sites with significant language content developed by tribal members. For links to these sites, visit <http://www.potawatomilang.org/References/links.html>

References

4Directions. Available at <http://www.4directions.org/>.

Aust, R., N. Newberry, and P. Resta. 1996. Internet strategies for empowering indigenous communities in teaching and learning. Available at <http://www.4directions.org/Resources/INET96.html>.

Dauenhauer, N., and R. Dauenhauer. 1998. Technical, emotional, and ideological issues in reversing language shift: Examples from southeast Alaska. In *Endangered languages: Language loss and community response*, ed. L. A. Grenoble and L. J. Whaley, 57–98. Cambridge and New York: Cambridge University Press.

Falling through the Net: Defining the digital divide. Available at <http://www.ntia.doc.gov/>.

Gray, M. 1995. Measuring the growth of the Web. Available at <http://www.mit.edu/people/mtgray/growth>.

Greenspun, P. 1999. *Philip and Alex's guide to Web publishing*. San Francisco: Morgan Kauffman.

Hinton, L. 1997. Small languages and small language communities. *International Journal of the Sociology of Language* 132, 83–93.

Hinton, L. 1999. Language revitalization and language change. Unpublished manuscript.

Krauss, M. 1992. The world's languages in crisis. *Language* 68: 4–10.

Miyashita, M., and L. Moll. 1999. Enhancing language material availability using computers. Available at <http://jan.ucc.nau.edu/~jar/RIL_9.html>.

A Parent's guide to the e-rate. Available at <http://www.stw.ed.gov/products/download/1573.pdf>.

Potawatomi Language Scholars' College. Available at <http://www.potawatomilang.org/PLSC/plscindex.html>.

President's Coalition Update Newsletter. Available at <http://www.ed.gov/inits/americareads/Newsletters/update981201.html>.

Revitalizing indigenous languages. Available at <http://jan.ucc.nau.edu/~jar/TIL.html>.

Society for the Study of the Indigenous Languages of the Americas. Available at <http://trc2.ucdavis.edu/ssila/>.

Stabilizing indigenous languages. Available at <http://jan.ucc.nau.edu/~jar/TIL.html>.

St. Clair, R., J. Busch, and B. J. Webb. 1999. Self-publishing indigenous language materials. Available at <http://jan.ucc.nau.edu/~jar/RIL_11.html>.

Teaching indigenous languages. Available at <http://jan.ucc.nau.edu/~jar/TIL.html>.

U.S. Census. 1997. Computer use in the United States. Available at <http://www.census.gov/>.

U.S. Public Law 101-477. 101st Cong., 2d sess., 30 October 1990. Title I, Native American Languages Act. Available at <http://www.ncbe.gwu.edu/miscpubs/stabilize/ii-policy/nala1990.htm>.

Warschauer, M. and K. Donaghy. 1997. Leoki: A powerful voice of Hawaiian language revitalization. *Computer Assisted Language Learning* 10: 349–362.

Web server survey. Available at <http://www.netcraft.com/>.

URLs

Language Sites Included in the Database

Abenaki. <http://hmt.com/abenaki/>.

Alabama (also Coeur d'Alene, Klallam, and Sanich). <http://www.ling.unt.edu/~montler/Alabama/>.

Algonquian and Iroquoian. Sweetgrass First Nations Language Council. <http://www.schoolnet.ca/aboriginal/sweetgra/index-e.html>.

Algonquin. Algonquins of Golden Lake. <http://fox.nstn.ca/~hila/nation/speak.html>.

Arapaho and Cheyenne. Arapaho language page. <http://www.cheyenneandarapaho.org/araplang.htm>.

Athabaskan (Cahto, Lassik, Nongatl, Sinkyone, Wailaki, Chilula-Whilkut, Hupa and Tsnungxwe, Bear River, and Mattole). California Athapascan home page. <http://www.geocities.com/Athens/Parthenon/6010/>.

Cherokee (a). The Cherokee companion. <http://intertribal.net/NAT/Cherokee/WebPgCC1/CC1home.htm>.

Cherokee (b). Cherokee language lessons. <http://www.powersource.com/cocinc/language/>.

Cherokee (c). Cherokee messenger. <http://www.powersource.com/cherokee/lang.html>.

Cherokee (d). Cherokee script projects. <http://www.geocities.com/SunsetStrip/Stadium/7075/cherokee/CherokeePages.html>.

Cherokee (e). Freeware Cherokee font information. <http://joyce.eng.yale.edu/~joant/Cherokee.html

Cherokee (f). Proposal for encoding the Cherokee script. <http://www.indigo.ie/egt/standards/jl/jalagi.html>.

Cherokee, Cree, Hawaiian, Inuit/Inuktitut, and Mayan. Yamada Language Center. <http://babel.uoregon.edu/yamada/fonts/cherokee.html>.

Cheyenne. Cheyenne language Web site. <http://www.mcn.net/~wleman/cheyenne.htm>.

Chinook Jargon. The Chinook jargon: Trading pidgin of Northwest Indians and pioneers. <http://www.geocities.com/Athens/Delphi/6460/jargintr.htm>.

Comanche. Numu Tekwapuha Nomneekatu. <http://www.skylands.net/users/tdeer/clcpc/index.htm>.

Dakota. The Dakota language homepage. <http://www.alliance2k.org/daklang/dakota9463.htm>.

Hupa. Danny Ammon's Hupa language Web page. <http://www.dcn.davis.ca.us/~ammon/danny/Hupa/HupaLanguage.html>.

Hawaiian (a). 'Aha Pūnana Leo. <http://www.ahapunanaleo.org/>.

Hawaiian (b). Kualono. <http://128.171.15.130/OP/>.

Hocak Wazijaci. Hocak Wazijaci Language and Culture Program. <http://www.mwt.net/~hocak/>.

Inuktitut. Inuktitut: The language of the Inuit people. <http://www.arctic.ca/LUS/Inuktitut.html>.

Inuktitut and Cree. Proposed pDAM for unified Canadian Aboriginal syllabics. <http://www.indigo.ie/egt/standards/sl/n1441-en.html>.

Ioway-Otoe. Ioway-Otoe. <http://spot.colorado.edu/~koontz/tracks/jgtiombib.htm>.

Iroquoian (a) (Cayuga and Mohawk). Six Nations Polytechnic. <http://www.snpolytechnic.com/language.htm>.

Iroquoian (b) (Mohawk, Onondaga, and Cayuga). Iroquois language and songs. <http://aboriginalcollections.ic.gc.ca/language/index.html>.

Iroquoian (c) (Mohawk, Onandaga, and Cayuga). <http://www.ohwejagehka.com/index.html>.

Iroquoian (d). Kanienkehaka language. <http://www.axess.com/mohawk/kanienkehaka.html>.

Jicarilla Apache. Jicarilla Apache audio materials. <http://www.hanksville.org/NAresources/indices/announce/jicarilla.html>.

Lakota (a). Grammar. <http://www.enter.net/~drutzler/pagee.htm>.

Lakota (b). Lakota Wowapi Oti Kin (Lakota language and book resources). <http://maple.lemoyne.edu/~bucko/language.html>.

Lakhota (c). Sioux heritage. <http://www.lakhota.com/default.htm>.

Lushootseed. Lushootseed facts. <http://www.kcts.org/product/lush/facts.htm>.

Michif. The Creolist archives speech. <http://www.ling.su.se/Creole/Archive/Michif-Speech.html>.

Natick. Welcome to Wequai. <http://www.geocities.com/TimesSquare/3199/natick.html>.

Navajo (a). Navajo language. <http://www.angelfire.com/nv/navaholang/language.html>.

Navajo (b). Navajo language, associate of arts. <http://www.ncc.cc.nm.us/degrees/NLang.html>.

Navajo (c). Sacred mountains. <http://hanksville.phast.umass.edu/poems/motherearth/sacredmtnsnav.html>.

Ojibwa (a). Anishinaabe. <http://www.ncs4.net/ojibwe/>.

Ojibwa (b). Ojibwe language and culture: Language. <http://www.citilink.com/~nancyv/ojibwe/>.

Ojibwa (c). (Anishinaabemowin/Chippewa). Chippewa [Ojibwe] [ojiipewa] Language Anishinabemowin~. <http://www.angelfire.com/wa/chippewalanguagebook/>.

Ojibwa and Iroquoian. Woodland Cultural Center, Native American Indian Center of Excellence. <http://www.woodland-centre.on.ca/languages .html>.

Oneida. Oneida Indian Language Project. <http://www.oneida-nation.net/ language/index.html>.

Potawatomi (a). A grammar of Potawatomi. <http://hpsg.stanford.edu/rob/ pot/grammar.html>.

Potawatomi (b). Potawatomi Web. <http://www.ukans.edu/· ·kansite/pbp/ talk/home.html>.

Salish. Linguistics papers and abstracts. <http://web.mit.edu/troberts/ www/ling/papers.html>.

Secwepemc (British Columbia). SCES language department. <http://www .secwepemc.org/monas.html>.

Siouan (Omaha-Ponca). Siouan languages. <http://spot.colorado.edu/ ·koontz/>.

West Virginia Mingo. Mingo-EGADS.<http://www.speech.cs.cmu.edu/ egads/mingo/index.html>.

Yukon languages (Gwich'in, Han, Kaska, N. Tutchone, S. Tutchone, Tagish, Tlingit, and Upper Tanana). Yukon Native Language Center. <http://www.yukoncollege.yk.ca/YNLC/>.

Web Rings

Ring of languages and linguistics. <http://www.webring.org/cgi-bin/ webring?home&ring· lang>.

The eastern North American Native peoples Web ring. <http://www .geocities.com/Heartland/Park/8030/webring.html>.

The Native American ring. <http://www.geocities.com/RainForest/Vines/ 2063/nativesring.html>.

The Tsalagi Ring. <http://www.geocities.com/BourbonStreet/8632/>.

Indexes

Leman, Wayne. Native American languages. <http://www.mcn.net/ ·wleman/langlinks.htm>.

Mitten, Lisa. Native languages page.
    <http://www.nativeculture.com/lisamitten/natlang.html>.

Strom, Karen.
    <http://www.hanksville.org/NAresources/indices/NAlanguage.html>.

PART VIII

TRAINING

27

Training People to Teach Their Language

LEANNE HINTON

Department of Linguistics
University of California at Berkeley
Berkeley, California

Perhaps the greatest cause of failure in the teaching of endangered languages is inadequate teacher training in language-teaching pedagogy owing not to a lack of diligence on anyone's part, but to lack of opportunity and training resources. People who actually know an endangered language may not be those with any background in teaching and may in fact be past retirement age anyway. For those young enough to teach and educated enough to have a background in teaching, this may or may not include any background in language teaching. Most teachers are not speakers of endangered languages, nor even members of the same community or ethnic group. Someone who does not know the language has no simple way of learning it—as we have seen, most endangered languages are not taught at the university. And even someone who knows the language and has a teaching background is unlikely to have training in language teaching. The university classes aimed at language pedagogy are either about teaching English as a second language or are aimed at foreign-language teaching. Furthermore, good language pedagogy is not taught everywhere. It is still often the case that a graduate student becomes a language teacher through being hired to actually teach the language of his department, with on-the-job training. This is potentially a good way to learn how to teach, if the on-the-job training is good (though it often is not), but it leaves out the person who is not a Spanish or French major but wants to learn how to teach a rare and endangered language. Even good professors of language pedagogy have spent their lives training people to teach world languages and may never have thought about the important differences between teaching a world language and teaching a language of a tiny population, with no writing system or literature. Since language pedagogists also are unlikely to know anything about a particular endangered lan-

guage, communities often turn to linguists to help them develop language-teaching programs. Linguists know a great deal about the linguistic structure of a given language but lack training in language pedagogy; thus a linguist can come up with a good book of grammar lessons, but rarely does he or she have the background to understand the methods needed to effectively teach that grammar to students. Linguists are prone to explaining the structure of a language rather than teaching the language in such a way that someone can actually end up using it—two very different tasks.

This is not to say that the acquisition of excellent pedagogical training is impossible. Indeed, there are a growing number of revitalization programs that have achieved good training for language teaching. (See, for example, Chapter 15, by Terry and Sarah Supahan.) Foreign-language teaching experts are beginning to develop an interest in endangered indigenous languages and turning their attention to the plight of these languages. Linguists specializing in endangered languages have begun to read and take classes in language pedagogy, thus improving their usefulness to language revitalization. Native educators, seeing the need for good training for teachers' aides and other community people being hired in the schools, have begun to develop classes and workshops in response to the need. Such organizations as SIL (Summer Institute of Linguistics), LINA (Linguistic Institute for Native Americans, run by Chris Sims in New Mexico), and the California Foreign Language Project have been of tremendous help in developing well-trained language teachers.

Bauman (1980), in his seminal work on Indian language retention, discusses the ways that people do get training. Those directly involved in the educational component of a revitalization program have acquired their training in several different ways. In bilingual education, there are relatively

349

few credentialed Indian teachers (though their numbers are increasing rapidly), so much responsibility falls on the teacher's aide, an uncredentialed person who knows the language. The teacher's aide is the most important staff person in the classroom but also frequently has the least background in education and language teaching. Much of the teacher's aide training is done on the job by the teacher or other staff people, and a lot of it is sink-or-swim and learning by experience. Consultants may also come to the school to give in-service training. More and more frequently, teacher's aides are asked to attend pre-service training workshops or courses, usually in the summer and outside the community. Ideally, these workshops or courses will give credit toward an eventual degree.

Bauman also points out that community members must also be trained in order for teachers and program administrators to gain their interest and support and to create a pool of potential staff people in the future. The staff of a revitalization program will find themselves training community members in linguistics, language learning methods, reading and writing the language, and so on.

The chapters that follow present descriptions of several training projects for teachers and native scholars of endangered languages that have been of key importance in helping community people get the training they need to work effectively in language revitalization.

Reference

Bauman, James J. 1980. *A guide to issues in Indian language retention.* Washington, D.C.: Center for Applied Linguistics.

Inuttut and Innu-aimun

KEN HALE

Department of Linguistics and Philosophy
Massachusetts Institute of Technology
Cambridge, Massachusetts

As the reader will learn in the first paragraph of this chapter, the coincidence of the similarity of the initial two syllables of the language names Inuttut and Innu-aimun is just that—a coincidence. The two languages belong to utterly distinct language families, there being no demonstrable genetic, or family tree, connection between them. Inuttut belongs to the Inuit language complex of Eskimo-Aleut, while Innu-aimun belongs to the Cree-Montagnais-Naskapi language complex of the Algonquian family. The principal historical connection between the languages of this chapter, also referred to simply as Inuit and Innu, is their coexistence in Labrador.

All Innu people are fluent in their traditional language. On the other hand, while Inuttut has many fluent speakers, the language has been in decline during the past four decades. These differences have an effect, of course, on the nature, design, and linguistic focus of training programs for teachers serving the two populations in Labrador. Thus, the teaching of the Innu language itself does not figure prominently in the discussion here, while the teaching of Inuttut is, by contrast, a prominent feature. Conversely, writing in Innu is something that requires special attention in training, being considered somewhat difficult to master. Literacy for fluent speakers of Inuttut is less of an issue given the nature of the traditional orthography.

This chapter is about language-related training and materials development for Inuttut and Innu students whose careers are destined to be involved in one way or another with those languages, for instance, as interpreters and translators or as teachers at various levels of schooling, including the university. The overall project is made difficult by virtue of the distances involved. St. John's, Newfoundland, where Memorial University is headquartered, is far from most of the Labrador communities which must be served, and the most practical and effective setting for carrying out training for the Labrador Innu and Inuttut communities is in those communities. Special effort must be made to bring together the essential ingredients—that is, the instructors from St. John's and students from scattered points in Labrador—at some practicable point, such as Nain.

A large number of important observations and ideas are made in this chapter, including the following practices in training teachers of Inuttut:

(1) The "cohort" approach to teacher training is adopted to ensure the existence of a corps of trainees with common expertise. This approach helps to overcome the limitations stemming from the inevitably small total number of Inuttut language teachers and the often short time a given individual can devote to this work. Moreover, a cohort of Inuttut-speaking linguistics students will result in a community of teachers capable of using the basic principles and technical vocabulary of linguistics in discussing language problems with each other.

(2) For teaching Inuttut as a second language at the university, a three-stage "mentoring" program is utilized in training native-speaking lecturers. According to this system, the native speaker first works as a teaching assistant with a linguist, who works as an instructor in the class. In the next phase, the roles are reversed, with the native speaker functioning as the lecturer and the linguist as teaching assistant. Finally, the native speaker works alone as a fully established lecturer.

The cohort and mentoring approaches described by Alana Johns and Irene Mazurkewich in this chapter are rational and promising responses to certain shortcomings inherent in local-language teaching programs. Among other things, they permit quick, if not immediate, involvement of native speakers in the teaching process, even in situations where supporting texts and ancillary teaching aids are lacking.

Inuttut and Innu-aimun in Labrador

Ungava Bay

Quebec

Atlantic Ocean

Hebron

Okak
Nutak

Nain
Davis
Inlet
Hopedale
Makkovik

Postville
Rigolet

Labrador

North West
River
Sheshatshiu
Happy Valley - Goose Bay

● Inuttut
□ Innu-aimun
▲ Both Languages Spoken

Richard J. Thompson, J

MAP 28.1   Inuttut and Innu-aimun in Labrador

28

The Role of the University in the Training of Native Language Teachers
Labrador

ALANA JOHNS
Department of Linguistics
University of Toronto
Toronto, Ontario, Canada

IRENE MAZURKEWICH
Department of Linguistics
Memorial University of Newfoundland
St. John's, Newfoundland, Canada

In Labrador there are two aboriginal languages which are still spoken as a first language.[1] These are Labrador Inuttut,[2] a member of the Inuit language family which stretches from Siberia to Greenland, and Innu-aimun,[3] a member of the Algonquian language family which stretches from Alberta to the east coast of Canada and down into the northern United States. As is often the case with minority languages, both these languages are politically separated (in this case through provincial boundaries) from neighboring communities which speak very closely similar dialects. These political boundaries tend to dissipate human energy and financial resources that could otherwise be harnessed for a common purpose.

In this article we will provide a brief outline of the history of these languages with respect to formal schooling and describe the history and current status of the academic programs at Memorial University of Newfoundland which are designed to provide training to Labradorians to teach the general provincial curriculum to northern public school students. These programs also aim to train teachers to teach cultural and language subjects particular to Labrador. It is this latter function which we will address in this chapter. Our discussion is intended not as a how-to, but instead as an overview of issues that confront academics at a university level who are involved in programs for training native language instructors. Our goal is to provide a useful frame of reference for other people, both inside and outside the university, to exchange ideas for making the best possible program the university can provide. Indeed, the first and most basic question is whether the university should be involved in training native language instructors. We think that the answer is yes: the university has a level of research expertise and resources that can be useful to communities that are struggling for the first time with the issue of language maintenance. However, this does not mean that the traditional structure of university courses should not be modified to take into account the background and culture of aboriginal students—clearly, we feel that modifications can and should be made.

BACKGROUND TO LANGUAGE EDUCATION IN LABRADOR

It is important to note the distance (approximately 750 air miles) of northern Labrador from the provincial capital of St. John's on the island.[4] In addition, travel to and within northern Labrador, where Inuttut and Innu-aimun are spoken, is mainly by air, which is expensive. No roads exist between the communities, and although water and land travel is possible, it is slow and dangerous. This distance has resulted in Labrador's having a different, more autonomous history than that of the island. On the island of Newfoundland, European settlers predominated to the extent that the original native peoples disappeared.[5] In Labrador, however, European settlers lived amongst, married, and shared culture with the Labrador Inuit. The descendants of these intermarriages are known as the Kablunângajuit (literally, "those resembling white people") or Settlers; they form a large and prominent part of modern northern Labrador society and live alongside the Labrador Inuit. The Labrador Inuit Association is made up of both groups. The Innu, on the other hand, have had relatively little contact with Europeans until recently. There has been very little intermarriage and they have consequently maintained their traditional lifestyle, language, and culture.

Naturally, before European contact, there was no need for language education in either Inuttut or Innu-aimun, as these

355

were monolingual communities. With the coming of Europeans, missionaries, and Western concepts of education, there were many changes. For the Inuit, the first of these educational initiatives was conducted entirely in Inuttut. The Moravian missionaries, who had started a mission in Greenland in 1733, came to Labrador in the late 1700s speaking the West Greenlandic dialect (now called Kalallit oqaasii), which was probably more similar to Labrador Inuttut then than it is now. Nevertheless, West Greenlandic still had some differences from the Labrador variety. The Moravian missionaries, having received formal training in West Greenlandic, would have been somewhat perplexed at differences found in the Labrador speech and in all probability would have considered the Labradorian dialect to be somewhat nonstandard. A reaction to the encounter of a new dialect is often negative. This would lead to a false notion of there being a standard language against which the Labrador dialect would not compare favorably.[6]

Under the Moravians, Labrador Inuttut was the main language of instruction for Inuit children, while at the same time settler children were learning English. All of this changed when the province of Newfoundland joined Canada in 1949. It became obligatory for instruction to be in one of the official languages, English or French, and English was chosen as it was the language of the rest of the new province (see Borlase 1993, 276–82). Watts (1996) states that the change in language took place "without prior preparation or input from the Inuit." As a result of Canadian and provincial educational policies, Labrador Inuttut was effectively removed from the system.

Another historical change that affected Labrador Inuttut was the social upheaval caused by the resettlement of two more northerly communities of Inuit (Nutak and Hebron) into the more southern Inuit communities. Government and health officials felt that the Inuit inhabiting small northern communities needed to be relocated to communities where they could be provided with more adequate health, welfare, and education services (cf. Brice-Bennett 1977). As Watts (1992) points out, "[T]hey were told that the government store would be pulling out within the year and that the (Moravian) church would follow. They were promised, like others, better things, including housing, which was very late, in the end, in coming." This move took entire groups of people, who traditionally lived in small family hunting camps and followed a more or less seasonal nomadic lifestyle, to communities which were unable to provide the same degree of subsistence or even to accommodate the influx of such a number of monolingual Inuttut-speaking people into the existing community patterns. This move increased the number of monolingual Inuttut-speaking people in the three coastal communities where they were resettled but introduced yet more dialects in those communities. Over the past 40 years, Inuttut has been undergoing a decline to the extent that it has dis-

appeared in some communities and is threatened in those in which it remains.

Because of the lack of contact between the Innu and Europeans, Innu-aimun was not affected until 1949. Innu-aimun has remained in a healthy state; it continues to be the first language, with English being learned as a second language.

We can see that the Inuit and Innu have very different language issues to contend with. The Inuit are facing language loss and are trying to both maintain and revitalize the language, while the Innu are wrestling with the question of what role English should play in the future of their communities (where English currently has a small but growing presence).

- The issue of standardization and the effect it has on related dialects is a common problem in languages around the world.[7] This problem becomes further compounded when the language in question is a minority language under duress.

PROGRAMS FOR LABRADOR TEACHERS AT MEMORIAL UNIVERSITY OF NEWFOUNDLAND

Early Years: The TEPL Diploma

The Labrador Inuit Association held an education conference in 1977 which motivated the introduction at Memorial University of Newfoundland of a new program to train Inuit and Innu language and culture specialists as teachers' aides in the classroom. As a result, the Teacher Education Program in Labrador (TEPL) was established in 1978 with the help of federal/provincial funding for post-secondary native education (see the section below called "Financing"). The program courses were offered primarily off campus in Labrador for Innu and Inuit who were often mature students whose family obligations required that they remain in the community. Aboriginal students who did choose to study on campus were quite isolated culturally and did not have much support within the university or the community of St. John's. The main problems with the program were twofold. One was that the courses were offered infrequently, leading to frustration on the part of the students. They felt that not only were they not completing the program in a timely fashion, but they could not be expected to remember the content of related courses over long stretches of time. The second problem was that the subjects offered within the TEPL program were not oriented to teaching aboriginal language and culture but instead to general educational practices and subjects. The only courses oriented toward Inuttut and Innu-aimun were two linguistics courses, whose focus was not pedagogical. Each student would take one such course. The only language-teaching instruction they received was from an education course on the topic of teaching English as a second language.

At the same time, there was general pressure from the northern Labrador communities to hire teachers from Labrador in the public schools. Because many teachers were from the island of Newfoundland or other parts of Canada, they often did not stay long in the northern communities, nor were they familiar with the unique aspects of the culture of Labrador. The people of Labrador felt that such employment should go to residents from Labrador who would provide continuity in the educational system and were familiar with the cultural heritage.

Critics of the TEPL program within the university at the time pointed out that the program was based on assimilationist policies and that not enough native input in the form of community and teachers consultation was involved. These criticisms still hold for the current programs discussed below.

- The goals of a program in teacher training should be reflected in the courses and the delivery schedule of the program.

The B.Ed. (Native and Northern) Degree

As mentioned above, Labrador communities were demanding that a greater proportion of teachers be of local origin, that is, Inuit, Settler, and Innu. With increased funding (see the section below called "Financing"), a new Bachelor in Education (Native and Northern) program was established in 1989 whose main purpose was to train teachers from and for Labrador. While the program is not restricted to students from any particular ethnic background, it was expected that the vast majority of students wishing to specialize in this area would be from Labrador and therefore from the three main groups mentioned above. The major change between the TEPL and the B.Ed. program is that the degree leads to a higher level of teacher status and salary. Once the degree program was in place, it attracted an increasing number of Settler students, of whom a lower proportion know Inuttut (see also the section below called "Financing"). The shift in goals between the two programs went from training teachers how to teach specialized aboriginal subjects (for which, as described above, there were few courses intrinsically designed to meet this need) to training teachers to meet the general educational needs of northern Labrador communities, which includes many common cultural components (see the section above called "Background to Language Education in Labrador"). The language component is not shared cross-culturally in Labrador, although in the past some Settlers were fluent in Inuttut. As a result the language courses went from being a small part of a small program to a small part of a big program, even though both the communities and the students themselves (speakers and nonspeakers alike) clearly saw language as a prominent issue.

As of 1997, the five-year program consisted of 50 courses ranging in topic from math and English to psychology. Within this program, two language-oriented courses are compulsory for all students. These courses (described below in the section called "Linguistics and Language Courses") give linguistic training to speakers of Inuttut or Innu-aimun and language training to nonspeakers of Inuttut. There is no demand for an Innu-aimun language course, as members of the Innu Nation all speak their language fluently.

Speakers who choose to specialize in native language teaching within this program can take four further courses in Inuttut or Innu-aimun literacy and language teaching; however, many of these courses are still in development (see the section below called "Manuals").

Divisions within the university, like political divisions within a language area, sometimes lead to artificial separation. It is not clear to those of us on the linguistic side of things (Faculty of Arts) what the content will be and how the instructors will be trained for the language-teaching courses (Faculty of Education). It is important that the students be taught by someone who has either a great deal of training in language pedagogy or a great deal of experience teaching Inuttut in the classroom, or preferably both.

- It is absolutely vital that there be courses on the pedagogical aspects of teaching a specific aboriginal language.

Linguistics and Language Courses

The following discussion will focus solely on the courses offered by the linguistics department. In the early stages of the TEPL program, there were two linguistics courses available for Inuit, and these were taught sporadically throughout the 1980s. The only faculty member specializing in Inuktitut left in the early 1980s, leaving no one in the Department of Linguistics to teach the courses. On occasion, individuals outside the university with full-time commitments of their own taught the linguistics courses. In the mid-1980s the university hired an applied linguist with a research interest in Inuit language acquisition, and in the late 1980s another linguist with a specialization in Inuktitut syntax was hired. With respect to courses for the Innu, a university linguist specializing and fairly fluent in Eastern Algonquian started teaching linguistics courses to the Innu of Labrador in the early 1990s.

Inuttut Linguistics Courses

At this stage, although there had been an increase in the number of Settler and Inuit students in the program who did not speak Inuttut, all students were required to take the same two linguistics courses. It was clear that those who were speakers of the language could best use a course which gives the student the confidence and knowledge to talk about and investigate their own language, that is, the skills of the language professional. At the same time, the nonspeakers needed to learn to speak the language. The two goals could not be accomplished in the same classroom. As a result, two streams were created of two courses each.[8]

- Teachers who speak a native language must be afforded special recognition and respect for this knowledge and provided with the linguistic and pedagogical training to teach the language.

Teacher Training Language Courses

The teaching of Labrador Inuttut in the public schools was and is one of the most challenging tasks for teachers in Labrador because course materials are so few and often must be created from scratch. Even though the Curriculum Centre in Happy Valley–Goose Bay is very busy keeping up with these needs, the teachers still have to make most of their own materials. One of the unfortunate and common problems in this sort of situation is that many materials are simply translated from English, producing less-than-natural native language style (see also Mercurio and Amery 1996).

Although Labrador students were very eager to take education courses, most of them would only take them if they were offered in Labrador. Students from the more isolated communities and instructors from St. John's and/or Happy Valley–Goose Bay were flown in to join the majority of the students in one of the larger communities such as Nain (also the most northerly community). Due to the expense of accommodations, as well as the fact that these individuals were away from their families and work commitments, the courses were sometimes taught in an accelerated format of 4 or 6 weeks rather than the usual 13 weeks that an on-campus course would take. The logic supporting the shortened format was that the students would be taking only one of these courses for the entire period, that is, eight hours every day.[9]

The first time that the linguist from Memorial University taught the linguistic courses, she co-taught them with Beatrice Watts,[10] who was curriculum director for Inuttut for the regional school board and had previously taught the courses. Team teaching proved to be invaluable, since all levels of expertise were covered. It has since served as the pattern of training for the university native instructors for the program. Co-teaching also provides continuity when the same course is taught by different people because a shared curriculum develops.[11] Nevertheless, each instructor develops the course content and delivery along his or her own lines.

- Expertise from a number of perspectives is crucial for the development of teacher training programs, and, especially in the early stages, this may require joint efforts.

Inuttut Language Courses

As mentioned above, a number of students in the program lacked courses in Inuttut as a second language. As a result, two language courses were developed. These courses crucially involved the aid of students who had completed Inuttut linguistics courses (i.e., speakers) and who became assistants, and later instructors, for the language courses. The language courses were a success from the outset. Close to 20 students enrolled in the first course (given on the main campus of Memorial University in St. John's). Some of these students were from the general student population, some were from the native community residing in St. John's, and others were from Labrador but not enrolled in the teacher education programs. Growing numbers of younger, university-age students from Labrador were coming to the St. John's main campus to study, in part due to the availability of funding for post-secondary education for native students. The main effect of this influx was that a critical mass of friends and relatives was now present on campus, making the university experience much more attractive. These students were excited at the chance to study Inuttut, especially alongside other Labradorian students.

One of the yet-unresolved issues having to do with these courses is how to ensure that the students acquire an adequate oral ability in the language. The main goal of studying Inuttut is to use it in an oral medium, and the usual language-teaching materials in the form of language labs and so on are not available. We have made efforts to highlight the oral elements of the course by spending more time in the classroom on spoken interaction and by making oral tests a significant component of the grade. In the future we hope to see computer-assisted language materials, as well as improvements in our ability to measure oral success.

- It is important in terms of status of a native language within its own region that it be taught at the university level.

Innu Linguistics Courses

The linguistics courses given to the Innu students in the program (who are all strongly fluent in Innu-aimun) are oriented around issues concerning literacy and grammatical analysis. While writing in Inuttut[12] is not a major issue, given that the orthography is sound-based and adaptable to the individual's dialect, Algonquian writing systems have been developed with a standard that does not always reflect the speaker's language and hence is more difficult to master. Innu in Labrador, who also use the Roman alphabet for writing, are not always enthusiastic about the standard system that has been proposed, and this has created difficulties.[13] The courses have been taught infrequently. This creates a problem of continuity, since sometimes the content of previous courses has been forgotten by the time the next course is given (see also the section above called "Early Years: The TEPL Diploma").

Apart from the linguistics courses, a major issue for the Innu students in the teacher education programs is that the Innu are generally less proficient in English. This causes great academic difficulties for them in taking university-level courses in the current framework. This issue—that they are actually not in full control of the language used to instruct them—has been completely ignored within the program. For example, English-literature instructors of Innu student teachers normally do not have training in English as a second language. This puts such instructors in quite a quandary, as they are unable to provide the appropriate assistance.

In general, the program for the Innu appears to be even less satisfactory than that for the Inuit. We will not have any further comment on the Innu portion of the program.[14]

- Language of instruction for native teachers is an important issue.

A COHORT APPROACH TO NATIVE-LANGUAGE TEACHER TRAINING

We use what we refer to here as a cohort approach to the training of teachers of Inuttut. By the cohort approach, we mean that individuals who are in language professions should receive training that allows them to develop a common expertise. The rationale behind this approach is that the number of Inuttut-speaking teachers in the program is small, their ability to devote time away from their families is limited, and neither the community nor the school system fully appreciates that schoolteachers with little training and support and few materials cannot maintain the language on their own (see the section above called "Early Years: The TEPL Diploma" and the section below called "Native Language Instruction: The Situation in the Public Schools"). In addition, one cannot assume that each individual will continue as a native language teacher. Thus, for a wide variety of personal reasons (career changes, etc.), it is important that a healthy number of speakers be trained as language teachers. A number of excellent language teachers have left the school system in Labrador, and it is difficult to say how much of this is due to the job conditions of being a native-language teacher as compared to the attractions of the new job. In any event, attrition is a real concern and must be taken into account.

The goal of the linguistics courses is to develop a cohort of Inuttut-speaking teachers who can discuss language issues with each other using a shared linguistic knowledge and terminology. Teachers, as language professionals, should feel confident discussing aspects of grammar and dialect difference both among themselves and with students and the inevitable outsiders who ask them questions about their language. We feel they should be able to have discussions on these matters both in English and especially in Inuttut. There is a correlation between the choice of the language of instruction for a particular topic and the language which will be used to discuss that topic in future discussions. Where the topic is the native language itself, care should be taken to avoid the situation where discussion of the language by native speakers is conducted only in English (see Burnaby, MacKenzie, and Salt 1997 for one solution to this problem).

As an example of the cohort approach, the linguistics courses for native language teachers were often combined with those for interpreters and translators (see the section below called "The Interpreter/Translator Training Program"). In addition, another small group of language teachers was being trained to teach at the university level, thereby increasing the overall number of language professionals. There are now three groups with linguistic training: public school language teachers, interpreters and translators, and university language teachers. A final factor in encouraging the development of a cohort is that the courses be taught as frequently as possible. Cohorts cannot develop when a course is taught, for example, every three years (see also the section above called "Early Years: The TEPL Diploma").

- It is crucial that a critical mass of language professionals exist to provide support for each other and input into language policy.

The Interpreter/Translator Training Program

The Torngâsok Cultural Centre in Nain has a community-based program for training interpreters and translators of Inuttut.[15] In the Interpreter/Trainer (I/T) program, students receive training in professional development, technical skills, and translating and interpreting. They also study a number of academic subjects, including two Memorial University courses: a course on the history of the Labrador Inuit and the linguistics of Inuttut course described above. For a number of years the linguistics course was delivered in Nain to a class containing both I/T students and students enrolled in Memorial University's teacher education program. Although students differ in educational background, the mix in the classroom generates stimulating discussion. Generally speaking, the students in the B.Ed. program have higher academic skills in the sense that they are used to studying, taking tests, and so on. In contrast, the interpreter/translator students generally are more mature and have stronger language and cultural skills. They are selected for the program based primarily on their language skills rather than their formal school background.

By the end of the course, some of the interpreter/translators have learned that academics is within their reach, while the teachers have learned that consultation and discussion of language issues is fruitful. The course evaluations consistently show that each of the two groups feels it has benefited from the presence of the other group in the class. In addition, it appears that certain professional bonds are possible between members of the groups.

When the linguistics course is taught with combined education and I/T students, the format is slightly different. More group work is done, especially the translation of linguistic concepts and definitions into Labrador Inuttut. This approach has been inspired by the work of Louis-Jacques Dorais, who provides grammatical terminology in Arctic Québec Inuktitut. We should mention that Dorais 1988 is the textbook for the linguistics courses, since the Québec and Labrador dialects are quite similar. Labrador students, following this model, proposed a term for syllables: *nipillât*, roughly translated as 'multiple (communicative) sounds'. A definition proposed by students for this term is *uKausini tusâtsauKattatuk atautsikadlugit uKakallâtaugamik*. Roughly translated again, this would be: 'It's heard in words as a single short spoken element'. One can easily see that students who are capable of making such definitions have grasped the concepts.

Delivering the course to combined student groups is an efficient use of limited time and resources. A final benefit is that such courses also provide an opportunity for crossover of students from one area to another. One of the best students in the I/T programs became one of the best speaker/students in the B.Ed. program and later taught some of the university courses.

- Where resources are limited, sharing is both necessary and fruitful.

Training Native Language Teachers for University-Level Language Instruction

As mentioned in the section above called "Inuttut Language Courses," we consider it appropriate and necessary that native languages be taught at universities of countries where those languages are spoken. Aside from this consideration, there is also a need for language courses for non-fluent students enrolled in the Native and Northern teacher education programs. This in turn created a need for language teachers at the university level (see also the section above called "Teacher Training Language Courses").

Where these university teachers are fluent speakers of the language and have some university education but lack the standard graduate level degree, mentoring was used to familiarize them with university teaching procedures, standards, and so on. The mentoring of university level language teachers proceeds ideally as follows:

Stage 1

A number of the most promising speakers within the program were employed individually as assistants for the courses in Inuttut as a second language given by the Department of Linguistics. As teaching assistants, they helped prepare the language teaching materials and worked in the classroom, aiding the students in their pronunciation. The linguist was in charge of the organization of the course, the preparation of materials, teaching, testing, and administrative duties.

The reason mentoring is so important is that although these students/teachers are speakers of the language, in fact virtually no materials exist for the teaching of Inuttut as a second language. It is impossible to overemphasize the importance of this fact. Almost every instructor of a language course at the university level uses published materials produced by other experts as the basis for their course. This option is simply unavailable to Inuttut teachers.[16] The mentoring process allowed the students/teachers to learn aspects of course materials preparation, to develop adult second-language teaching methodologies, and especially to deliver courses at a level appropriate to university education. This latter issue is important not only for university standards but to avoid the danger of the course being watered down. Finally, the stage of being a teaching assistant, rather than the lecturer, allowed the students/teachers to gain confidence in the classroom.

Stage 2

The next stage of the process was a reversal of the roles, so that the speaker (who had previously worked as the teaching assistant) took on the responsibility (and salary) of lecturer in subsequent deliveries of the course. The linguist worked as teaching assistant, helping to prepare course materials, aiding students in their pronunciation, and serving as a consultant for marking and evaluation.

Stage 3

The final stage of the process is intended to be that the speaker will be the lecturer on his or her own with support from the department. By this point the lecturer is familiar enough with the department to know where things are and who to ask for information.

One Labradorian speaker has gone through all three of these stages, while another taught at stage 1 twice and then taught two language courses at the university in January 1998 with some limited support from faculty (stages 2 and 3 combined). This same teacher taught on her own in the summer. Finally another speaker with a lot of high school teaching experience co-taught with a linguist (in place of stages 1 and 2) and then immediately went on to stage 3.

- University-level native language instructors require supplementary support in initial stages due to the innovative nature of their responsibilities.

Manuals

The Faculty of Education at Memorial University has been preparing for native instructors to teach many of the courses (in response to the communities' demands) within their teacher education program.

One of the ways used to lay the groundwork for this transition is through contracts to faculty for the creation of manuals to teach the courses.[17] Unfortunately, this sometimes results in the cart's being put before the horse, as it is difficult to write manuals for courses which have never been taught. As mentioned above in the section called "Training Native Language Teachers for University-Level Language Instruction," there have been very few teaching materials developed for Labrador Inuttut, so creating course manuals is a difficult task indeed.

Preparing a manual to train teachers to teach a language in their communities is not the same as preparing one to teach them to teach math. Since many textbooks exist on the topic of the teaching of math (or English, for that matter), these can be used as a basis for writing a math text customized for a particular culture or community. In contrast, the language knowledge of the speakers of the community is not already written up but must be painstakingly brought into written or formal form through the efforts of speakers or linguists. This makes the preparation of manuals based on linguistic properties labor intensive. Imagine if the writers of the math manuals had to discover the math themselves! While the teachers are certainly able to converse in the target language in the classroom, the question remains as to which teaching methods are effective for the teaching of the language. Note that some of the students in the public schools are learning Inuttut as a second language (see the section below called "Native Language Instruction: The Situation in the Public Schools").

Knowing that our first efforts at preparing manuals would be only drafts for the future, we prefer to teach the courses before preparing manuals. We want the future teachers of these courses to benefit from our experiences of the sorts of things that went well or went wrong in these courses. We provide as much in the way of course materials as we are able to within a short time: exercises, vocabulary lists, and such for the language courses, and an introduction to linguistics with Inuttut examples for the linguistics courses.

The manuals that have been produced under the contractual system have not been subject to any evaluation of their effectiveness. There are no guidelines to follow in the preparation of the manuals. There is no follow-up discussion with the authors. The only measure of success of this process seems to be the production of the manuals; in other words, quality is not a factor.

Although each manual is financed equivalent to the delivery of one course, the number of manuals under contract adds up to a considerable amount which otherwise could have gone into team-teaching the subject. This would have inevitably produced a bulk of materials which later could be made into a text. In addition, the manuals should be written in Inuttut (and not just translated from English).

Recently, two literacy courses for Innu-aimun were developed. In addition, two course manuals for Inuit have also been written (Johns and Tuglavina 1999). One concerns oral aspects of the language and is designed to focus students' attention on the issues and importance of oral literacy. In the course, students learn how to expand both their own oral skills through speeches on different topics and so on as well as how to enhance the oral skills of others. The second manual focuses on written literacy and reviews the orthography system and language-learning issues surrounding it. In the course, the students are required to create their own literary materials through transcription of elders' stories and through their own composition.[18] One innovation of these two courses is that they were designed to be taught predominantly, if not exclusively, in Inuttut.

- The teaching of an aboriginal language requires principled development of materials.

Native Language Instruction: The Situation in the Public Schools

The communities in Northern Labrador and the school boards are aware of the language loss which is occurring (Mazurkewich 1995). While the school boards have responded by creating an immersion program from K to grade 3 in the schools, there is a tremendous lack of materials for young children in Inuttut to support the teachers who are involved in the immersion program. Beyond grade 3, Inuttut is taught as a subject, and materials in the higher grades are even more scarce. Parents decide whether or not to put the children into the immersion program. When the first-language program was introduced in Nain in 1987, the community in fact responded positively and overwhelmingly to the immersion program. Since then, a number of problems have arisen. For example, children entering the immersion program vary in their knowledge of Inuttut, some coming from homes where Inuttut is the main language, others from homes where no Inuttut is spoken. Effectively, this means that the children for whom Labrador Inuttut is a first language are learning in the very same class with the same materials and tests as those for whom Inuttut is a second language. While egalitarianism is endemic to Labrador culture, it is likely that this situation is less than ideal for the first-language speakers and may even be detrimental to the maintenance of their language.

Most of the burden of language retention is perceived to be the responsibility of the public school teachers. Some Inuttut-speaking parents speak to their children in English all the time at home. Nevertheless, they often feel that their children's lack of ability to speak Inuttut reflects the abilities of their teachers and the school system. Linguists and teachers all know that this is an unrealistic view and that the level of success of a language program depends on factors beyond the boundaries of the classroom—for instance, the vital role of widespread community efforts in ensuring intergenerational maintenance of the native language. In any event, within the current context, the Inuttut teachers are under stress where they are thought to be responsible for a situation which is largely beyond their control. Such a situation surely cannot be encouraging for teachers.

There is also a feeling by some in the community that there are teachers teaching Inuttut whose language skills are not as strong as they should be. If such situations exist, this in all probability stems from the fact that those whose English skills are stronger are more likely to succeed in the Western educational system—that is, those whose English skills are weak and whose Inuttut is strong have less likelihood of becoming teachers since all measures of their academic worth are done via English.

- Language instruction in the school cannot substitute for community and family responsibility for language maintenance.

Dealing with the School System

Decisions on hiring and placement of teachers rest with the school board. While the school board has been quite supportive of the reintroduction of Inuttut into the school system, this is not always reflected in its hiring practices.

The center for Inuttut curriculum development is located in Happy Valley–Goose Bay, where the school board is, but the majority of the schools, teachers, and students who are learning Inuttut or already speak it live in the more northerly communities at considerable distance.

Teachers in Nain have asked for more direct control over curriculum development; in fact, they would prefer that the materials be developed locally.

The recent negotiations over land claims will in all probability solve this problem by placing education within the control of the Labrador Inuit Association. The Innu are negotiating concurrently their own settlement.[19]

- Native language education is more efficiently administered by local groups, especially when speakers of the language are in charge of major decisions.

PASSIVE BILINGUALS

In the language classes we have encountered students who know quite a bit of the language but are far from fluent and do not use the language at all or feel comfortable speaking it. Often these students have an extensive passive knowledge and even a wide vocabulary but lack the ability to make sentences in the language. As this problem is found not only within the B.Ed. program but within the communities of northern Labrador, it is interesting to speculate whether there are particular methodologies which would serve the needs of this type of student. Often where a language is nearly extinct in a community—for example, Rigolet in Labrador—the largest pool of potential speakers are the adult passive bilinguals who are the children of the few remaining speakers.

Within the context of the language courses we offer, we have observed that while a passively bilingual student often starts the course well ahead of the other students who know nothing of the language, he or she often falls behind in later stages of the course, usually when the sentence grammar is introduced. It appears as if having heard and used the language as a child disinclines these students to study it formally. In our classes we make special efforts to have passive bilinguals feel comfortable, for instance, having them tutor the beginners in early stages. We consider it a very important question as to whether and, if so, which improved language teaching methodologies can build upon these students' latent knowledge. For the present, we feel that their contributions are underutilized and their needs not met.

Bobaljik and Pensalfini (1996) describe language loss within a community as successive replacement of the language by the dominating language, for example, English, over a number of generations. From our observations in Labrador, this describes how a community loses language, but within any one family this takes place within only one generation. Once a particular generation of children is raised as passive bilinguals, the language is gone from that family, since children in future generations of that family are unlikely to be raised in Inuttut. For this reason, we view passive bilinguals as the last-chance generation. We may be mistaken.

A related issue is the role of oral language in the schools. Without careful planning and monitoring, it is possible that students will achieve a literate but not an oral competency in the language (see also the section above called "Inuttut Language Courses"), where they know a great deal but are too shy or inhibited to speak it with others or among themselves.

- A major question is whether and how the knowledge of passive bilinguals can be reactivated.

DIALECT DIFFERENCES

It is important that where the language teacher speaks a dialect differing somewhat from the dialect used in the teaching materials, this teacher be capable of modifying the materials to fit his or her own dialect. In the past, some teachers have felt that differences between their speech and that of the teaching materials indicated poor language skills on their part.[20] The impression that they spoke an inadequate or incorrect form of the language was unfortunate, not only because it is not true, but because it undermined their confidence and led to confusion on the part of the young children they taught. The appreciation of dialect differences and the appropriate measures to deal with them are also a concern of the Labrador East Integrated School Board, and Beatrice Watts has taken pains to straighten out misconceptions surrounding this topic.

Following the lead of Louis-Jacques Dorais of Université Laval, who has made great efforts to create materials designed to explain Inuit dialect differences to linguists and speakers of the language (see, e.g., Dorais 1990), we have made dialect differences one of the main topics of the linguistics courses. It is also discussed to some degree in the language courses. Another important reason for the focus on dialect differences is so that speakers of the language will not "tune out" speakers of other dialects (whether in person or on the radio or television), but instead will take an interest in the other dialect, perhaps even improving their comprehension of it.

Watson 1989 (46) describes speakers of different dialects of Scottish Gaelic switching to English rather than making "the effort of continuing to struggle with one another's comparatively unfamiliar native speech forms." We suggest that dialect differences potentially divide speakers of a language and that education can serve in small measure to counter this division.

The OkâlaKatiget Society, which is a Labrador Inuit radio and television broadcasting and training organization located in Nain, has played an instrumental role in establishing communication amongst Inuit communities, as well as throughout northern Canada. Their efforts to record and promote activities of the Inuit living in isolated communities also serve as an important conduit for enhancing dialect comprehension and maintenance.

We believe that lack of dialect comprehension contributes to the endangerment of a language as a whole. We note that the English language, which is widely spoken in many parts of the world, has many different dialects, and that any one speaker usually has the ability to understand (but not speak) numerous other dialects of English. It may be that one factor which contributes to this ability is simply exposure to variants. If our view is correct, then a language has a greater chance of maintaining or increasing its number of speakers where there is an increase in the number of speakers able to communicate with one another. In contrast, where the number of speakers able to communicate with one another (but not the total number of speakers) is less, there is a proportionate decrease in the chance of the language's maintaining

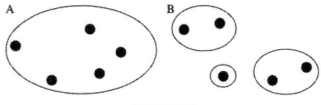

FIGURE 28.1

(or increasing) its number of speakers. We can illustrate these two scenarios as in Figure 28.1.

Assume that the language on the left has five dialects whose speakers are able to communicate with one another. The language on the right has five dialects, but speakers of only two pairs communicate with one another, and one dialect is effectively an isolate within the group. We argue that the situation on the left is a more healthy situation for language survival and that efforts of communities as well as simple linguistic exposure can produce the larger group from the smaller groups—that is, mutual intelligibility between dialects can be increased somewhat with education and practice.

• Each speaker should know that his or her own dialect is legitimate.
• Each speaker should be exposed to the value of other dialects.

FINANCING

Funding for the entire teacher program comes from monies allotted to post-secondary native education through a federal and provincial agreement.[21] Memorial University of Newfoundland has not provided any financial support, except possibly overhead. The flow of this funding is controlled to some extent by the respective native organizations, that is, there is a type of client relation with the Labrador Inuit Association and the Innu Nation in that funds can be withheld should the university not follow the educational agenda set by the native groups. Funding has been provided to the Faculty of Education at Memorial University, which has used the money to develop the TEPL and the B. Ed. Programs and to contract instructors to teach the courses (and write manuals).

This financial arrangement has provided for a certain degree of expediency in the developing and delivery of courses. This is undoubtedly a benefit not found everywhere. The size and flexibility of the budget allow the university to plan programs and courses and modify them as necessary. From a linguist's perspective, this means that one can put on a course quickly, even with a small enrollment, when the appropriate situation arises.

For example, the advantage of quick financing of courses became clear when a speaker of Siglit Inuvialuktun from the western Arctic came to study for a year at Memorial. Since dialects are a big focus within the linguistics course, we were able to put a course on that very semester—that is, without advance planning—for the Labrador speakers on campus as well as the Siglit speaker.

The federal government of Canada provides funding which covers the costs of tuition and living allowances for aboriginal students at the post-secondary level. Many of the Settlers receive this federal funding through the Labrador Inuit Association, as they are LIA members. This has entailed that a larger number of monolingual-English students have entered the teacher education program (see the section above called "The B.Ed. (Native and Northern) Degree"), resulting in the two streams (language for second-language learners and linguistics for speakers).

- It is important that native organizations have control over educational funding.
- Educational financing of native language programs should be structured in such a way that an efficient response to changing needs is possible.

THE FUTURE OF THE ROLE
OF THE UNIVERSITY

Although we are unable to speculate about the future of the education programs in Labrador, we suggest that the progress made so far—namely, the introduction of Inuttut courses in the schools and the training of Inuit teachers and university instructors who not only teach the language but act as role models for children in the communities—are positive steps for aboriginal language restoration and maintenance. As we have pointed out at length, this must be sustained by the continued development of appropriate materials and language manuals (see also Drapeau and Corbeil 1996). In the end, however, none of these efforts will succeed without the determination of the Inuit communities to play a proactive role in the maintenance of their language and culture.

It also seems to us at this point that only through having native control of the training of teachers, such as is in place in Québec, can communities plan and put into effect a comprehensive educational package where language takes center stage. The university does not at present provide enough teacher training within the native language. Assuming native control, it is an open question as to what the role of the university should be in the future with respect to these programs.[22] The role could be anything from simply a monitoring function to being a full partner in providing the best courses and knowledge that North American learning centers can offer, both in English or French and in the native language.

We also see that the number of language professionals in modern Labrador society is growing. We believe that it is the responsibility of the university to provide further support and expertise for these professionals so that they can meet the needs of their communities.[23] Memorial University, like other universities, exists to further the pursuit of higher knowledge and to serve society, in particular the society which immediately surrounds it. Clearly the aboriginal communities of northern Labrador are members of this constituency. For a university to work toward a community's goals is not a one-way process (from either side), but involves a rapprochement between the cultural and educational goals of the community and what the university is capable of offering in the way of programs and expertise, keeping in mind its general mandate. It is meet that many universities have finally changed their perspective on aboriginal communities from seeing them as objects of study to seeing them as partners.

There have recently been additional positive initiatives at Memorial University of Newfoundland. An aboriginal studies minor program which is open to both aboriginal and non aboriginal students was introduced in 1998. This is an interdisciplinary program involving the Departments of Linguistics, Anthropology, History, English, and Social Work. Some of the students from the Native and Northern B.Ed. program are taking the aboriginal studies program as their minor. In part this is because the aboriginal studies program has a strong focus on aboriginal languages (Inuttut, Innu-aimun, and Micmac), in many cases requiring the same courses as those in the B.Ed. program. Another initiative under discussion is the establishment of a Centre for Native Studies to be located in northern Labrador. In spite of these times, in which only short-term technical and economic achievements are measures of improvement, we believe that university programs are a long-term benefit to the societies with which they interact. We hope that Memorial University will further commit itself both in energy and in financing to support modern Labrador aboriginal groups in determining their future.

Notes

We would like to thank Hiromi Matsumura and Frank Riggs for discussion of some of the issues considered here.

1. Labrador is part of the Ungava Peninsula on the mainland portion of the province of Newfoundland. The majority of the population live on the island portion of the province. There is a small group of Micmac people who live on the island.
2. The term Inuttut has often been used to refer specifically to the dialect spoken in Labrador. The term Inuktitut is generally used to refer to the language throughout Canada, although in the western Arctic the people call their dialect Inuvialuktun.
3. In fact, there are two distinct language varieties spoken by the Innu people in Labrador: that spoken in Sheshatshiu and that spoken in Davis Inlet.
4. Borlase (1993) states that Labrador is 292,000 square miles with a population of 29,231. It is known for its beauty and for living conditions

made difficult by a severe climate (cold and wind), which makes it unsuitable for farming. This characteristic has protected it from large-scale European settlement. The recent discovery of a rich mineral deposit at Voisey's Bay has resulted in an influx of people from outside the area.

5. However, recently Ralph Pastore (personal communication), an anthropologist from Memorial University, has argued that the Beothuk and Innu were descended from the same parent population and in time became separate groups of the same continuum. In any event, the Beothuk did not survive on the island.

6. For a detailed discussion of some of the linguistic issues regarding early Moravian contact, see Novak 1999.

7. See also Rice and Saxon, in press.

8. Recent developments have run counter to this streaming. In an effort to develop a cohort of language teachers (see the section called "A Cohort Approach to Native Language Teacher Training"), the program has focussed on getting a group of speakers to take the courses together. Unfortunately, neither the university nor the community committee in charge of selecting these students has a rigorous means of identifying speakers from nonspeakers. As a result, the group of "speakers" consists of individuals with knowledge of only a few words or phrases of Inuttut, passive bilinguals, completely fluent Inuttut-English bilinguals, and older, nearly monolingual Inuttut speakers. Logically, some of these subgroups will not be getting the education and training they need in one classroom. This situation shows that there is a need for a standard means of testing language knowledge. The testing and identification of speakers should be done by fluent professionals.

9. In recent years, groups of Memorial courses have been put on in Happy Valley–Goose Bay during the summer in a four-week format with two-hour classes daily for each course, thereby creating a temporary campus of Inuit studies at the community college during the month of July. Since there are residences there, students' families can accompany them. With two-hour classes, students can take two courses at the same time, however, they get much less time for practice and tutoring by the instructor. Students who already have a lot of academic discipline are more likely to succeed in such classes.

10. Beatrice Watts, who speaks Inuttut, has been one of the main forces behind the reintroduction of Inuttut into Labrador schools. As a result of her contribution to the establishment of public school programs, courses, and materials, not to mention language policy, she was awarded an honorary doctorate by Memorial University of Newfoundland in 1992.

11. In recent years, co-teaching has taken place with a number of different combinations of linguists and speaker-teachers. In 2000, a different linguist was introduced into the mix.

12. It should also be mentioned that the Labradorian Inuit, because of their early contact with the Moravian missionaries, use a Roman alphabet for writing. The Inuit in Québec and the Arctic region (excluding those in the western Arctic who use another Roman system) primarily use a syllabic writing system.

13. For both Innu and Inuit literacy goals, a constant problem is the fact that there is as yet very little of interest to read in the language. Both are still very oral cultures, and the best literature is spoken.

14. For a description of a successful teacher training program, where the language of instruction is Cree, see Burnaby, MacKenzie, and Salt 1997.

15. The current status of this program is in question due to funding issues.

16. Indeed, many of the facts of the language have to be "discovered" by the teacher-speaker, as both grammars and dictionaries are often incomplete.

17. The faculty who have been making the manuals are largely nonnative, since there are no native faculty as yet. In some cases, native teachers or curriculum developers from the school boards are coauthors of the manuals. Each set of manuals is funded (through Memorial) in the amount which it would cost to teach one course for 13 weeks, and where coauthorship is the situation, this amount must be subdivided among the authors.

18. These two university courses were taught for the first time in the fall of 1999 by a new teacher-speaker with reported success.

19. In Québec, such agreements led to native control over native education (see Burnaby, MacKenzie, and Salt 1997).

20. This is a common problem. The first dialect to be written down assumes the mantle of the "standard."

21. We believe, since funding issues are so important to the structure and operation of native language programs, that funding should be included as a topic within courses of the native teacher-training programs. Knowing where the money comes from becomes crucial in securing continuing and additional funding. It is very often the students in the course who will be in charge of funding initiatives in the future, and the sooner they start thinking about them, the better.

22. We emphasize here that control of language issues should be in the hands of speakers of the language, not just members of the community.

23. Over the years, Labrador has produced a remarkable number of excellent language specialists: Beatrice Watts, Rose Jeddore (see Jeddore 1976, a dictionary of Labrador Inuttut written by a group of Labrador Inuit), the late Sam Metcalfe, the late Auggie Andersen, Rita Andersen, and many more. If this talent were ever harnessed together, the results would be formidable.

References

Bobaljik, Jonathan David, and Rob Pensalfini. 1996. Introduction. *Papers on language endangerment and the maintenance of linguistic diversity*, ed. Jonathan David Bobaljik, Rob Pensalfini, and Luciana Storto, 1–24. MIT Working Papers in Linguistics 28. Cambridge, Mass.: MITWPL.

Borlase, Tim. 1993. *The Labrador Inuit.* Labrador East Integrated School Board. Labrador: Happy Valley–Goose Bay.

———. 1994. *The Labrador Settlers, Métis, and Kablunângajuit.* Labrador East Integrated School Board. Labrador: Happy Valley–Goose Bay.

Brice-Bennett, Carol. 1977. Land use in the Nain and Hopedale regions. In *Our footprints are everywhere: Inuit land use and occupancy in Labrador,* ed. C. Brice-Bennett, 97–203. Nain Labrador Inuit Association.

Burnaby, Barbara, Marguerite MacKenzie, and Luci Salt. 1997. Factors in aboriginal mother tongue education: The Cree School Board case. In *Papers of the Twenty-Ninth Algonquian Conference,* ed. David H. Pentland, 62–73. Winnipeg: University of Manitoba.

Clarke, Sandra, and Marguerite MacKenzie. 1980. Indian teacher training programs: An overview and evaluation. In *Papers of the Eleventh Algonquian Conference,* ed. William Cowan, 19–32. Ottawa: Carleton University.

Dorais, Louis-Jacques. 1980. *The Inuit language in southern Labrador from 1694 to 1785.* Mercury Series 66. Ottawa: Museum of Civilization.

———. 1988. *Tukilik: An Inuktitut grammar for all.* Québec: Association Inuksiutiit Katimajiit and Group d'Études Inuit et Circumpolaires (GÉTIC).

———. 1990. *Inuit Uqausiqatigiit: Inuit languages and dialects.* Iqaluit: Nunavut Arctic College.

Drapeau, Lynn, and Jean-Claude Corbeil. 1996. The aboriginal languages in the perspective of language planning. In *Québec's aboriginal languages: History, planning, development,* ed. Jacques Maurais, 228–307. Philadelphia: Multilingual Matters.

Jeddore, Rose. 1976. *Labrador Inuit Uqausingit.* St. John's: The Labrador Inuit Committee on Literacy, Department of Education.

Johns, Alana, and Sybella Tuglavina. 1999. Oral Inuttut [manual developed for a course on oral literacy in Labrador]; Reading and writing in Inuttut [manual developed for a course on written literacy in Labrador]. Native and Northern Teacher Education Programs, Faculty of Education, Memorial University of Newfoundland.

Mazurkewich, Irene. 1995. The attrition of Inuttut as a first language. Paper presented at the Symposium on Language Loss and Public Policy, "Shift Happens," University of New Mexico, Albuquerque, June 30–July 2, 1995.

Mercurio, Antonio, and Rob Amery. 1996. Can senior secondary studies help to maintain and strengthen Australia's indigenous language? In *Papers on language endangerment and the maintenance of linguistic diversity*, ed. Jonathan David Bobaljik, Rob Pensalfini, and Luciana Storto, 25–57. MIT Working Papers in Linguistics 28. Cambridge, Mass.: MITWPL.

Novak, Elke. 1999. The "Eskimo language" of Labrador: Moravian missionaries and the description of Labrador Inuttut, 1733–1891. *Études Inuit Studies* 23: 173–97.

Rice, Keren, and Leslie Saxon. In press. Issues of standardization and community in aboriginal language lexicography. In *Dictionaries of indigenous languages of the Americas*, ed. William Frawley, Kenneth Hill, and Pamela Munro. Berkeley: University of California Press.

Watson, Seosamh. 1989. Scottish and Irish Gaelic: The giant's bed-fellow. In *Investigating obsolescence: Studies in language contraction and language death*, ed. Nancy Dorian, 41–59. New York: Cambridge University Press.

Watts, Beatrice. 1992. Honorary degree convocation address, Memorial University of Newfoundland, 29 May 1992.

———. 1996. Inuit of Newfoundland and Labrador: Past and present. Plenary presentation at the 10th Études/Inuit/Studies Conference. St. John's, Newfoundland, August 15–18, 1996.

Languages of Arizona,
Southern California, and Oklahoma

LEANNE HINTON
Department of Linguistics
University of California at Berkeley
Berkeley, California

As described in Chapter 3, with the advent of bilingual education Native Americans began to explore it a means toward maintaining their languages, although it was eventually obvious that they must go even further and work toward revitalization in the face of continuing language decline. For many Native American languages, bilingual education was an avenue to the development of writing systems and written native literature, and in many cases the actual teaching of the languages at school. Although the best language-teaching methods were rarely available to the staff, there was a great deal of teaching of vocabulary and grammar, as well as a strong emphasis on native literacy and the development of new native-language written genres such as poetry and essays. Perhaps most importantly, bilingual education resulted in a generation of children who were proud of their language, which helped to heal the wounds created by the older boarding-school policies where the previous generations had been taught that their language was a thing of shame.

It was clear from the beginning that the training of bilingual-education teachers was woefully inadequate for Native American programs. Most training in bilingual education was aimed at people who would teach Spanish, and to a lesser extent some of the other immigrant languages. Much of what was taught in training programs was irrelevant to Native American languages, and there were many issues important to Native American bilingual education that were not dealt with in university training centers. Furthermore, most of the native speakers who would teach in bilingual-education programs did not have an educational level that would allow them to attend graduate school, or else did not have bilingual-education training programs in nearby locations.

To deal with these problems, in San Diego in 1978 the Yuman Language Institute was founded, a summer course offering training in Yuman linguistics, writing systems, and curriculum development. The next year the institute moved to Arizona and broadened to include more languages. It is now known as the American Indian Language Development Institute (AILDI), and recently it celebrated its 20th anniversary.

Southern California and Arizona are home to Uto-Aztecan, Athabaskan, and Yuman languages, and in the early years, AILDI participants mainly came from these language groups. Now it has spread to groups from all over, but with a strong showing still from the local communities. Uto-Aztecan and Athabaskan have been described elsewhere in this volume; the Yuman languages will be described briefly here. Yuman is a language family that spans parts of southern California, western Arizona, and Baja California. The present reservations and rancherias for the Yuman groups are all within their original homeland, though their holdings are much reduced since the European invasion. The branches of Yuman are California-Delta, consisting of the Cocopa and Diegueño languages (some varieties of Diegueño are called Kumeyaay); the Pai branch, which includes the Northern Pai languages of Havasupai, Hualapai, and Yavapai in Arizona and the geographically distant Paipai of Baja California; the River branch, whose extant languages are Mojave, Quechan (Yuma), and Maricopa; and the Baja California language Kiliwa, the most divergent of the Yuman languages. Also closely related to the Yuman languages is the extinct language of Baja California, Cochimí, a name that is sometimes used by other Yuman people of Baja California to describe themselves.

In 1990 the Oklahoma Native American Language Development Institute was set up based on a three-year grant and modeled after AILDI. Oklahoma had a very different language situation. Before direct intervention of the United States in the affairs of the lands west of the Alleghenies, what is now Oklahoma was peopled by the Comanches, Kiowas, Kiowa Apaches, Osage, Wichita and Caddo. The Jicarilla Apache range also included a small part of western Oklahoma. In the early 1800s the United States was still an eastern seaboard nation. A growing white population was demanding ownership of the rich lands occupied by the Five Civilized Tribes, who had already given up large amounts of their traditional land holdings and were refusing to give up more. The solution finally agreed on by Congress was the Indian Removal Policy, signed into law in 1830 (Prucha 1988). Although the tribes and their supporters in Congress fought bitterly against the enactment of Indian Removal and the Supreme Court even declared it unconstitutional (*Cherokee Nation v. Georgia*), Indian Territory was established in the west and forcible removal took place at great cost of life and livelihood. The Cherokee removal was called the Trail of Tears, and an estimated 25% of that group died on the journey (Franks and Lambert 1994). It was through this terrible policy and the various treaties that followed forcibly with many tribes that the Five Tribes—Choctaw, Creek, Chickasaw, Seminole, and Cherokee—arrived in the land that is now Oklahoma. During the Civil War, the Five Tribes were split in their allegiance to North and South, but despite the split, after the war, the fact that some of the Indians had sympathized with the South provided an excuse to strip the Five Tribes of half of Oklahoma to create reservations for other tribes. In subsequent years the Arapaho, Cheyenne, Comanche, Iowa, Kaw, Osage, Potawatami, Pawnee, Ponca, Sauk and Fox, Yuchi, and many others were all deposited in Oklahoma. The Delaware, pushed westward from their original home on the East Coast over several centuries, also eventually settled in Oklahoma, as well as the Shawnee. Geronimo and his fellow Apache rebels were also brought to Oklahoma and confined at Fort Sill after their initial incarceration in Florida. One of the last tribes forcibly removed to Oklahoma was the Modoc of southern Oregon and northern California. As for the original Oklahoma tribes, most of them lost any of their territory outside of Oklahoma and were confined to the portion of their lands that was in Indian Territory. Approximately 150 separate tribes now live in Oklahoma as a result of this history.

Any notion that Indian Territory would remain such for long was destroyed by the Westward Movement. Increasing pressure to make added lands available for white settlement caused lawmakers to look again to Indian Territory and to define it as too big for the needs of the Indians there. By 1890 the Territory of Oklahoma was set up, and soon afterward the Indian Territory was broken up and allotted out. The end result of this history is that Oklahoma is one of the most linguistically complex parts of the United States, which has resulted in different kinds of language problems, policies, and issues that were addressed by the Oklahoma institute.

References

Franks, Kenny A., and Paul F. Lambert, 1994. *Oklahoma and Its People.* Helena, Montana: American and World Geographic Publishing.

Prucha, Francis Paul, 1988. United States Indian Policies, 1815–1860. In *History of Indian-White Relations,* ed. Wilcomb E. Washburn, pp. 40–50. Handbook of North American Indians, vol. 4. Washington, D.C.: Smithsonian Institution.

Indigenous Educators as Change Agents
Case Studies of Two Language Institutes

TERESA L. MCCARTY
Department of Language,
Reading and Culture
University of Arizona
Tucson, Arizona

LUCILLE J. WATAHOMIGIE
Peach Springs School District No. 8
Peach Springs, Arizona

AKIRA Y. YAMAMOTO
Department of Anthropology
University of Kansas
Lawrence, Kansas

OFELIA ZEPEDA
Department of Linguistics
and American Indian Studies Program
University of Arizona
Tucson, Arizona

In the summer of 1978, 18 parents and elders representing Diegueño, Havasupai, Hualapai, Mohave, and Yavapai language communities traveled to San Diego State University for the first Yuman Language Institute. There, they worked with academic linguists and bilingual educators who shared their interest in the written forms of Yuman languages, and who were committed to using linguistic knowledge to improve education for indigenous students. What has come to be known as the American Indian Language Development Institute (AILDI) began with this small group of people. The institute's influence would eventually reach far beyond the Yuman language family. In June of 1999, AILDI prepared to usher in the new millennium by celebrating its 20th anniversary with participants from around the world.

Conceived by Hualapai educator Lucille Watahomigie, academic linguist Leanne Hinton, and the late John Rouillard (Sioux) of San Diego State University, the first institute enrolled 18 native speakers of five Yuman languages. The only program requirement was that participants be native speakers interested in working with their respective languages (Hinton et al. 1982, 22).

The focus of that institute was "Historical/Comparative Linguistics: Syntax and Orthography of Yuman Languages." The following year, joined by the late Milo Kalecteca (Hopi), then director of the Bilingual Education Service Center at Arizona State University, and linguists Ofelia Zepeda (Tohono O'odham) and Akira Y. Yamamoto, the institute teamed academic linguists with 50 native speakers in an intensive four-week program. During this time institute participants examined their languages, developed practical writing systems, designed curriculum, and created native-

language teaching materials. The title of this second institute, which included Tohono O'odham (formerly called Papago) and Akimel O'odham (Pima), was "Orthography, Phonetics, Phonology, and Curriculum Development."

Since its inception in San Diego, the institute has been hosted by Northern Arizona University in Flagstaff, Southwest Polytechnic Institute in Albuquerque, Arizona State University in Tempe, and the University of Arizona in Tucson. Each year AILDI faculty had to renegotiate institute summer sites. Since 1990, however, AILDI has been permanently housed at the University of Arizona.

During a three-year period beginning in 1992, a sister organization held summer institutes in Oklahoma. This was the Oklahoma Native American Language Development Institute (ONALDI), whose education functions, like those of AILDI, were in principle continuous. Under its new name, Oklahoma Native Language Association Workshops (ONLA), the work of ONALDI did in fact continue beyond the original three years, using a new format and scheduling structure better suited to the needs of Oklahoma native communities.

In the first section below, certain essential features of AILDI are presented. In the next two sections, ONALDI and ONLA are discussed. The discussion of ONALDI includes the basic organizational and philosophical background of the organization and an example of course content in the form of a language research activity for participants. Although AILDI, ONALDI, and ONLA are unique in many ways, they also represent cases which can be examined for their implications and applicability to other linguistic and sociocultural contexts. We therefore include "lessons learned" from each case, and we conclude with more general recommendations for indigenous community–based language maintenance and revitalization.

THE AMERICAN INDIAN LANGUAGE DEVELOPMENT INSTITUTE

Since it began in 1978, AILDI has seen its participants grow in number and diversity. In recent years the institute has enrolled approximately 100 participants each year, representing language groups throughout the United States and Canada and from as far away as Venezuela, Brazil, and Taiwan. Altogether the institute has prepared over 1,000 parents and school-based educators to work as researchers, curriculum developers, and advocates for the conservation and development of indigenous languages and cultures. Most participants are native speakers of an indigenous language, but AILDI welcomes participants from all backgrounds who are concerned with the maintenance of indigenous languages and the application of linguistic and cultural knowledge to classroom practice.

AILDI Goals and Pedagogy

"I used to wonder why the students would just sit there when the teacher gave them all these verbal directions. I know now that it was because they did not understand. I used to wonder why, when the teacher would ask the student to write a story about a city or an unfamiliar place, they would only write one or two sentences. . . . They were only trying to tell us that there was not anything of meaning to them. This will give you an idea of what I've learned at the institute."

—*Bilingual teacher assistant and AILDI participant*

AILDI's overarching goal is to incorporate indigenous linguistic and cultural knowledge into school curricula in ways that affirm indigenous students' identities, support their academic achievement, and promote the retention of their languages and cultures. The statistics on Native American students' school performance are well documented: Indigenous students are significantly overrepresented in low-ability, skill-and-drill tracks, and they experience the highest school dropout rates in the nation (U.S. Department of Education 1991). Equally well documented are the school-based causes underlying these outcomes: curriculum "presented from a purely Western [European] perspective," low educator expectations, loss of "the wisdom of the older generations," and a "lack of opportunity for parents and communities to develop a real sense of participation" (U.S. Department of Education 1991, 7–8).

Our hope is that through their involvement in the institute, participants will return to their home communities with the knowledge, skills, and support necessary to challenge the English-only, deficit-driven pedagogies that have historically characterized American Indian education and debilitated in-

digenous students academically. Just as important, we seek to heighten awareness about the preciousness of indigenous languages and assist participants in maintaining their heritage languages and identities. Finally, we aim to prepare academic professionals such as ourselves to engage in mutually beneficial research and teaching activities in indigenous communities.

With these goals in mind, AILDI holds this basic view of language teaching:

> Language is not taught by mere word lists and grammatical drills. And native literature is not fully appreciated by pupils if it is presented in translation. Language and literature can be taught most effectively by teachers who are native speakers of the language and are trained to teach in elementary and secondary schools with language materials and literature produced by native speakers. (Watahomigie and Yamamoto 1992, 12)

AILDI emphasizes bilingual and bicultural education within a whole language paradigm (Goodman 1986; Fox 1992), experiential and interactive teaching strategies, alternative assessment such as literacy portfolios (Tierney et al. 1991), and what Jim Cummins (1989, 1992) has called "empowerment pedagogies." Over the course of four weeks, institute participants engage in collaborative research, dialogue, critique, and bilingual and bicultural materials development—the same types of learning processes in which they might engage their own learners at home. "My learning experiences at AILDI were very relevant to what is happening in *real* classrooms," one participant reports. "I learned skills that I can use in whatever I may do in the future."

Sharing and cooperative work are central to institute coursework. A recent participant recalls "sharing our creative writing in class, laughing and crying. . . . We had fun learning together." Frequently participants from the same school district or language group work on joint projects. When AILDI funds have permitted, elders have been invited to work with participants from their communities on language teaching projects. Participants also observe, practice, and coach each other in microteaching learning centers (discussed below), a forum for piloting the methods and materials developed over the course of four weeks.

In these ways, AILDI has adapted Cummins's (1989, 1992) framework of fourfold empowerment, as illustrated in Figure 29.1:

(1) *An additive/enrichment approach:* Schooling for indigenous children should add to and enrich—not replace—the cultural and linguistic resources children bring to school.

(2) *Local education control:* Indigenous communities have great knowledge of their language and culture which should be the foundation of children's learning in school. The community should have input into and control over the school curriculum.

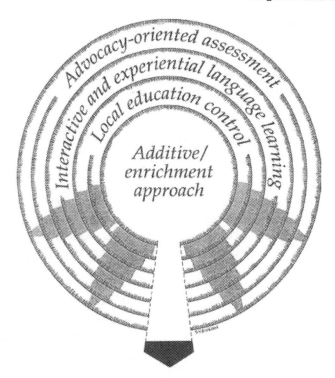

Advocacy-oriented assessment

Interactive and experiential language learning

Local education control

Additive/ enrichment approach

Identity affirmation
Language and culture maintenance

FIGURE 29.1   AILDI empowerment pedagogies

(3) *Interactive and experiential language learning:* The content and organization of instruction should encourage students to use language naturally and creatively in meaningful contexts, enabling children to inquire, critique, and generate their own knowledge.

(4) *Advocacy-oriented assessment:* Assessment should be holistic and authentic, allowing children to display their full array of linguistic, cognitive, and affective strengths; assessment should *not* be another means of gatekeeping or of justifying deficit labels and remedial treatments.

Organizing Institute Experiences

"I've learned that I have many skills, and it made me proud to be Indian."

—Bilingual teacher and AILDI participant

AILDI creates a learning-teaching environment in which participants can affirm their identities and power to act as change agents within their home communities. During this four-week summer residential experience, participants attend classes, work individually and in small groups on curriculum and linguistics projects, critique existing curricula, and develop new texts such as thematic units, autobiographical and biographical literature, poetry, dictionaries, and children's and adolescent's storybooks. All of these materials can be used in participants' classrooms and communities. Each year a theme is selected around which coursework and guest speaker sessions are organized. For example, the 1999 AILDI theme was "One Voice, Many Voices: Recreating Indigenous Language Communities," and in 2000 it was "Traditions and Innovations in Teaching Indigenous Languages."

Participants choose from a suite of interrelated linguistics and educational methods courses, enrolling for a total of six semester hours. Classes run from approximately 8 AM to 4 PM, Monday through Friday, and are complemented by special evening sessions featuring speakers and topics related to the theme of the year. As an example, the courses offered in 1999 included: (1) Recreating Indigenous Language Communities; (2) Native American Literatures and Writers; (3) Learning Language Structure through Activities and Games; (4) Bilingual Curriculum Development; (5) Linguistics for Native American Communities; (6) Educating the Culturally Diverse; (7) Computer Applications for Language Teachers; and (8) Strategies and Approaches for Reversing Language Shift.

One AILDI hallmark is microteaching or "lessons in miniature," which participants demonstrate at the end of the institute. Microteaching is an opportunity for participants to engage as both learners and teachers within a collegial environment of knowledge and support. Individually or in teams, participants present a language and culture learning activity based on their curriculum projects and conducted in their "favorite" (or heritage) language. Several microteaching centers operate concurrently, with participants demonstrating two consecutive times. This allows them to refine their practice following peer feedback from the first demonstration and enables all participants to observe a larger number of centers.

Microteaching is scheduled for one to two days. It is one of the most powerful learning experiences at the institute—a celebration of participants' work and a hands-on opportunity to exchange a multitude of language teaching materials and ideas. "I am a visual learner," one participant states in a reflection on the benefits of microteaching. Another says that microteaching enabled her "to pick up ideas from other teachers."

AILDI also facilitates the credentialing and endorsement of participating educators. All AILDI courses apply toward university degree programs and bilingual and English-as-a-second-language (ESL) endorsements. Degree advisement workshops and individual advisement are scheduled throughout the four weeks. "I like the one-on-one meeting," a participant remarked. "I was able to ask questions and state some concerns." In addition, post-institute advisement and periodic on-site courses taught by AILDI faculty enable AILDI participants to work toward their teaching and graduate degrees during the regular academic year.

AILDI is characterized by sharing and communal learning. Microteaching and other small- and large-group activities, including after-class gatherings, aim to create a community of co-learners and co-teachers. "The collaboration of other nations is tremendously resourceful," an AILDI participant writes, adding, "Bonding with other Indian educators is my greatest strength to advocate language and culture maintenance." The building of collegial relationships is enhanced by the fact that participants and guest faculty share housing in one of several apartment complexes or dormitories. When institute enrollment was still relatively low, faculty members conducted evening tutorials at the dormitories to assist participants in their linguistic and curriculum projects. Currently, such conferencing occurs directly after class at the university. Participants also are encouraged to bring their family members to the institute. Family-style housing near the campus and family activities during weekends and after class are arranged for this purpose.

Institutionalizing AILDI

"To implement a bilingual program, we first have to have funding and administrative support, then community support."
—*Bilingual teacher and AILDI participant*

As this participant suggests, the keys to institutionalizing any program are adequate funding and an acknowledged "place" for the program within the host institution and the larger community. AILDI has enjoyed strong support from tribes and indigenous communities, who have contributed to participants' attendance through tribal and school grants. However, paying for staff, faculty, guest speakers, promotional literature, teaching materials, and other basic operations requires a stable financial base and an institutional home. This has been a major challenge for AILDI and its faculty. A brief review of AILDI's history illustrates those challenges and how they have been addressed.

The original Yuman Language Institute was funded by a National Endowment for the Humanities grant to San Diego State University obtained by Watahomigie, Hinton, and Rouillard. As the institute evolved to include additional language groups, it became the centerpiece of a federal Title VII (Bilingual Education Act) grant for parent training administered through the Title VII–funded Bilingual Education Service Center (BESC) at Arizona State University in Tempe. Institute faculty included the service center staff as well as AILDI's original faculty. In 1982, the U.S. Congress reauthorized Title VII, transforming the BESC into the National Indian Bilingual Center (NIBC), which served American Indian bilingual programs nationwide. NIBC continued to support AILDI and 16 regional institutes until the NIBC contract was eliminated in 1986 by a subsequent Congressional reauthorization. For several years thereafter, AILDI

was administered by the Arizona Department of Education and funded by federal grants obtained by that agency. While this allowed the institute to continue to offer courses at Arizona State University, AILDI's administration by an external agency mitigated against the program's institutionalization within the university.

Throughout the years, continuity in AILDI's curriculum, pedagogy, and goals has been assured by the presence of a core faculty that includes the cofounders Watahomigie and Yamamoto, Ofelia Zepeda, and Teresa McCarty, who worked at NIBC and the Arizona Department of Education. In 1989, Zepeda and McCarty became colleagues at the University of Arizona. With their long-standing interest in institutionalizing the institute, they assumed responsibility for codirecting it, joining the resources of their respective departments and colleges to sponsor the 1990 AILDI. AILDI has since been housed in the Department of Language, Reading and Culture within the College of Education, receiving support from that department and college as well as from American Indian Studies, the Department of Linguistics, the Graduate College, Extended University, Summer Session Office, and the Office of Undergraduate Student Affairs.

Throughout the period of transition to the University of Arizona, AILDI enrollments continued to rise. University administrators voiced their approval of the institute, and the heads of the cosponsoring departments and vice president for research actively assisted Zepeda and McCarty in obtaining funds and graduate assistants to coordinate registration and housing. The Graduate College dean cited AILDI as one of the university's "showcase" programs, and in 1993 it was recognized in a national study commissioned by the U.S. Department of Education as one of 10 exemplary programs serving teachers of minority students (Leighton et al. 1995). Nonetheless, lacking office space, operational monies, and sustained clerical and administrative help, the program struggled to survive. These difficulties led to the cancellation of the 1992 institute.

The situation grew more desperate until pressure by AILDI's codirectors and their department heads secured $25,000 in university funds for a full-time program coordinator, and in 1993 Karen Francis-Begay (Navajo) was hired. This and the provision of an office and equipment within the Department of Language, Reading and Culture breathed new life into the program. In 1995 an opportunity arose to apply for permanent state funds. That year, 17 years after the institute began, AILDI was awarded a permanent annual budget of $75,000. This budget supports the coordinator, a part-time secretary, supplies and operations, some participant stipends, and year-round community outreach, recruitment, and retention activities. We continue to seek additional funds each year for participant scholarships and guest speakers. However, AILDI at last has secured a financial base and a place within its host university.

The Impacts of AILDI

*"Speaking two languages is better than one. . . . As I go back home,
I want to work with program directors, teachers, and my community
to let them know bilingual education works and how important it is."*
                                                    Teacher assistant and AILDI participant

AILDI's most immediate impacts can be readily observed in indigenous schools, classrooms, and communities. Previously unwritten languages have been committed to writing and in some cases standardized. As institute participants have returned to their home communities, they have refined and published their summer projects, creating a small but growing indigenous literature. "Writing in my own language to create lessons for classroom use" is a typical participant response to questions about the most useful aspects of their AILDI experience. The numerous materials developed in Hualapai, Havasupai, Tohono O'odham, Akimel O'odham, Western Apache, and Navajo are but a few examples of the ways in which institute coursework has been transformed into locally relevant curricula (see Figure 29.2). Just as important, AILDI has been an integral force in the credentialing and endorsement of native teachers, many of whom have assumed administrative and other leadership positions in their local schools.

All of this has the potential to bring indigenous students' experiences directly into the classroom, building on their linguistic and cultural resources instead of treating those as deficits, and engaging students in using their experiences to learn. While no comprehensive study has been undertaken to document the extent to which this has occurred, a 1988–89 Arizona Department of Education study of Arizona participants is worth noting. The study followed 25 Indian and non-Indian AILDI participants from four reservation schools for one year (McCarty 1993). Data included observational records and videotapes of classroom interactions, teachers' logs, student writing samples, achievement records, and participants' responses to written questionnaires. At the conclusion of the academic year, the study reported "dramatic improvements in students' oral and written language development" associated with cooperative learning strategies developed at the institute and follow-up workshops, greater involvement by parents and elders in classroom literacy experiences, and a willingness by teachers to relinquish English basal readers and workbooks for locally meaningful materials. In one teacher's words, "The training finally gave me the courage to throw out the workbooks and get students involved in *real* reading and writing" (McCarty 1993, 91).

These local-level changes occurred simultaneously with larger tribal and national policy developments. During institutes focused on language planning and policy, AILDI participants began to work on tribal language policies for their communities. Within a few years, formal policies had been adopted by the Tohono O'odham, Northern Ute, and Pascua Yaqui Tribes; the policies proclaimed those languages as official languages within their respective communities. These and other codes and policies for Navajo and Northern Cheyenne advocate bilingual-bicultural education and call upon schools to act "as a vehicle for the language, whether it is restoring, retaining, or maintaining it" (Zepeda 1990, 249).

At the national level, AILDI participants and attendees at the 1987 Native American Language Issues (NALI) Conference, held in conjunction with AILDI, drafted a resolution addressing the endangered state of indigenous languages and the need for federal support of their maintenance and perpetuation. The resolution was sent to key federal-level decision makers, including Senator Daniel Inouye, then head of the Senate Select Committee on Indian Affairs. In 1988, Inouye succeeded in introducing the Native American Languages Act based on this resolution. Signed into law in 1990 by President George Bush, the act declares the U.S. government's policy to "preserve, protect, and promote the rights and freedom of Native Americans to use, practice, and develop Native American languages" (Public Law 101-477, Sec. 104[1]). Although its funding has been meager, the Native American Languages Act has propelled some of the boldest new initiatives in indigenous language revitalization (see, e.g., Chapter 17 in this volume).

AILDI also has served as a model for the recruitment and retention of indigenous students into the university and for developing a new paradigm for teacher education. AILDI is

FIGURE 29.2 Examples of curriculum materials developed by AILDI participants

the only program of its kind on campus, and the only program in the state to offer an approved curriculum for bilingual and ESL endorsements in American Indian languages. It is the only American Indian language program to provide a multicultural, multilingual immersion experience. "I had a wonderful experience [at the institute]," an alumna writes, "largely because of the other participants." She continues: "I knew that the immersion with people of other cultures would enrich me and it truly did—even more than I could have guessed." These qualities and AILDI's direct relevance to tribal communities make it a natural vehicle for recruiting American Indian students to the university. In its first four summers at the University of Arizona, AILDI enrolled 162 undergraduates, most of whom were Native American teacher assistants. Of these, 12 (or 7%) have matriculated in education degree programs, and 4 have graduated. During the same period, the institute enrolled 181 graduate students; 35 have matriculated and 25 have graduated with master's degrees. Several of the latter have gone on to pursue education specialist and doctoral degrees.

It is perhaps for all of these reasons that AILDI has been adapted and replicated in Indian communities throughout the United States. Between 1983 and 1986, credit-bearing institutes based on the AILDI model were held for Northern Ute, Ojibwa, Navajo, Lakota, Cherokee, Osage, Kickapoo, Shawnee, Cree, Northern Plains, Western Apache, Arapaho, Shoshone, Tewa, Zuni, and Keresan language groups (Swisher and Ledlow 1986). More recently, Yamamoto and his colleagues initiated the Oklahoma Native American Language Institute to address Cherokee, Chickasaw, Choctaw, Creek, Kickapoo, Omaha, Potawatomi, Sauk-Fox, Shawana, and Euchee language education concerns. "The strength of the institute model," Swisher and Ledlow note, "is that it presents academically sophisticated concepts to educational practitioners who ordinarily might not have received such training. This is critical to American Indian bilingual projects, who necessarily develop their own curricula" (1986, 63).

AILDI and Indigenous Language Maintenance

"It's scary how important language is. . . . If I only had someone from my school to help me, this is what I would do: Make a curriculum to benefit the students from kindergarten to eighth grade, speak just in my native language to the kindergartners and repeat this system every year until the kindergarten children are in the eighth grade."

·*Bilingual teacher and AILDI participant*

Over the years, AILDI has increased the value of the linguistic and cultural capital brought to school by indigenous students through its facilitation of curricula, programs, and personnel able to make use of that capital. Just as important, AILDI has helped transform indigenous linguistic and cultural resources into political capital. Recognition of the im-

portance of indigenous languages and cultures does more than merely validate them; it increases their value and the power of those who speak and control those linguistic and cultural resources. By creating curricula and programs to articulate local resources with local schools and by simultaneously preparing and credentialing local educators, AILDI has empowered its alumni in their school systems. Moreover, AILDI has reinforced the collective power of its alumni by building a network of indigenous educators committed to a shared philosophy for indigenous language maintenance. These educators not only have strengthened threatened languages and built more effective school programs, they have influenced federal policy toward those goals, such as the Native American Languages Act.

The teacher's statement that introduces this section, however, suggests the limits of that power. Just as sustained funding and administrative support have been difficult for AILDI faculty to secure, such support and control over local curricula remain elusive for many AILDI participants. Hence, AILDI's influence on indigenous language maintenance is indirect and constrained by local circumstances. The key to language maintenance, Fishman (1991, 1996) insists, is intergenerational language transmission—the natural communicative processes in the home, family, and community through which succeeding generations replenish their speakers. Such processes are difficult for outside institutions such as schools and university programs to create.

Nevertheless, AILDI has been a catalyst for reinforcing these processes by placing an overt moral and academic value on heritage languages and by assisting practitioners in establishing new contexts and genres for native language use. "I would like to be an informed advocate for bilingual education," an alumnus states, "and convince fellow teachers, administrators, the school board, parents, and community members about the need for our language revitalization." Another says, "I will be an inspiration and educator of language maintenance for my students."

While AILDI cannot "save" endangered indigenous languages, it has mobilized significant efforts to stabilize them. "I'd like to have my grandchildren learn our tribal language," a Hualapai elder recently told us, "because if they don't, . . . nobody will ever speak Indian again." This elder presents an urgent charge. AILDI has played a critical role in addressing that responsibility, but it cannot act alone. Ultimately it is local stakeholders—AILDI alumni and their communities—who must identify and consciously shelter specific domains for speaking and privileging the heritage language. AILDI has helped to nurture these language planning efforts, but they have only begun.

Lessons Learned from AILDI

What have we learned from more than 20 years of involvement with the American Indian Language Development Institute? In this section, we reflect on what our experiences have taught us, in the hope that this will be useful to others engaged in similar work.

Lesson 1: The Need for Focus and Commitment

AILDI began not with the ambition to be all things to all language groups, but with community-specific goals for indigenous language and literacy development and a shared commitment to reform local education practices. Although the institute now serves a much larger constituency, it remains anchored to the needs of indigenous communities and education personnel. This focus guides the development and delivery of AILDI's curriculum and contributes to the successful integration of linguistics and methods courses and their consistency over time. We have added new courses and workshops as participants' interests in particular topics have evolved; courses on parent involvement, creative writing in indigenous languages, and media and computers are examples of this. However, core courses in linguistics and bilingual-bicultural curriculum development are offered each year, and all AILDI participants are assured of a learning experience that enables them to apply linguistic and cultural knowledge from their home communities directly to educational practice.

The opportunity to engage with and understand the experiences and struggles of fellow participants is essential to AILDI. At the same time, participants and faculty recognize the need to concentrate on specific issues and problems within individual language communities. AILDI seeks to strike a balance between this concentration on local language issues and the opportunity to learn from the successes and problems experienced by others. The unique advantage of AILDI derives from the diversity of languages, communities, participants, and faculty it represents.

AILDI also has been characterized by a high degree of staff commitment. This is the virtue of its community-based focus. Because AILDI faculty and staff are either members of indigenous communities or nonnatives with a long history of involvement in those communities, they have high expectations for the communities' children and a vested interest in helping them succeed. A great part of children's school and life success, we believe, is a strong foundation in their heritage language and identity. We recognize that the institutional reforms necessary to build this foundation do not occur overnight; they must be cultivated over time from the community's human and material resources. AILDI and its faculty and staff are dedicated to that long-term process.

Lesson 2: The Need for Outreach and Local Follow-Up

AILDI is more than a summer program, although that is its central activity. Languages have been written and high-quality materials developed because AILDI faculty and staff have continued to collaborate with institute participants throughout the school year. Collaboration has entailed site visits by faculty, designing and implementing local research projects, telephone and e-mail consultations, and co-involvement on materials development. Many participants return to the institute year after year. The personal relationships developed through this extended contact have not only promoted local curriculum reform, but helped establish lasting ties between indigenous educators and AILDI faculty and staff, and by extension, between indigenous communities and the university. The overall effect has been to generate widespread tribal support for the program and make the university more approachable and "user friendly." This mutually beneficial process has facilitated the certification and endorsement of indigenous educators and helped institutionalize the program within the university.

Lesson 3: The Need for Permanent Funding and a Home Base

As is typical of Indian education programs, AILDI has depended for its livelihood on external grants. Such short-term funding forced AILDI faculty to knit together a program each year from disparate financial resources. Instability in funding mitigated against institutionalizing the program and created a vicious cycle of uncertainty and impermanency.

After years of work, AILDI at last secured a permanent budget and home. While no recipes exist for achieving such an outcome, we offer this advice: Begin early in communicating the program's goals and organization to individuals who are in a position to help. We met frequently with deans and department heads to familiarize them with the program, being careful to relate AILDI's goals to the larger university mission. Brief but informative narratives were helpful, as were detailed budgets showing actual and anticipated expenditures, and contributions from various departments and university offices. Most university administrators recognized the academic and public relations benefits of the program; when apprised of offers to help by other departments, they usually found funds with which to assist AILDI. We followed every contribution with an invitation to the institute and with letters showing whom and how particular administrative funds had helped. In the meantime, we sought and received funds from external sources, including the National Endowment for the Humanities and the Arizona Humanities Council.

These measures served two purposes. They enabled AILDI to survive during its first years at the University of Arizona, and they made key administrators aware of the program and the extent and urgency of its financial needs. Along the way we were allocated official space within an established department. This enhanced the program's visibility and credibility both within and outside the university. When the Arizona legislature made it possible to apply for permanent funds, AILDI already had a visible university presence, strong tribal support, and advocates within the system to shepherd and promote our funding request.

The keys to institutionalizing AILDI, then, were perseverance, communication, a vision of where the program fit within the larger institution's mission, and a firm commitment to program goals.

Lesson 4: The Need for Administration from the Inside Out

Institutionalization would not have occurred without the presence of tenure-eligible faculty within the host institution. For years AILDI remained institutionally marginalized because its faculty were guests from other institutions, or were university staff of short-term, federally funded Indian education programs. Guest faculty continue to serve the institute and provide much of its direction, depth, and breadth. At the same time, administration by two local university faculty members and, since 1993, a permanent full-time coordinator, has been instrumental to AILDI's success. This has made it possible to work on a year-round basis from the inside out and to permanently seat the program within the host institution.

THE OKLAHOMA NATIVE AMERICAN LANGUAGE DEVELOPMENT INSTITUTE AND THE OKLAHOMA NATIVE LANGUAGE ASSOCIATION WORKSHOPS

Over 11% of all Native Americans in the United States reside in the state of Oklahoma, making up 5.6% of the Oklahoma population. Two-thirds of Oklahoma's Native Americans live in rural areas, primarily in the most easterly 47 counties. One of the characteristics of Oklahoma Native Americans is that they have never had reservations, although certain land allocations were provided to tribal groups. The U.S. census and Oklahoma Indian Affairs Commission identify 34 major tribal groups with more than 400 members.

According to the Oklahoma Department of Education, in 1992, when the Oklahoma Native American Language Development Institute (ONALDI) was first held, there were 66,151 Native American students enrolled in Oklahoma public schools. Of these, 25,138 (38%) were identified as "limited English proficient" (LEP). Several programs had been created to serve Native American and other LEP students. Yet the state of Oklahoma had only two teachers who were trained to address these students' needs, neither of whom worked directly with students in the classroom. There were 44 Title VII bilingual projects in Oklahoma, 36 of which were Native American language programs. Of the 36, eight were newly funded, and the urgent need for bilingual-bicultural teachers was evident.

Based on an assessment conducted among Native Americans in Oklahoma, some professional development needs were identified: (1) instructional methods and techniques; (2) knowledge and skills for curriculum and materials development; (3) development of assessment instruments; (4) strategies for recruiting parents and language resource persons into instructional processes; (5) development of linguistic knowledge and skills for researching indigenous languages; and (6) meeting the state mandates for bilingual and/or ESL endorsement and certification. ONALDI was established to address these needs and funded by a three-year Title VII Short-Term Teacher Training grant, which provided specialized professional development activities during summer institutes, workshops, and follow-up activities.

ONALDI's goals were to (1) develop the capacity of teachers and paraprofessionals to work effectively with Native American students; (2) build on the strengths of indigenous parents and language resource persons by engaging them in school-based instruction; (3) provide specialized training toward bilingual and/or ESL endorsement and certification; and (4) develop the capacity of school administrators to better support programs for Native American students. These goals were to be achieved by providing participants with opportunities to study principles of bilingual-bicultural education, the nature of language and its relationship to culture and society, theories of first- and second-language acquisition, and ways to develop academically sound, culturally relevant curricula.

Like AILDI, the ONALDI model consisted of two major components: curriculum development and linguistics. A healthy language and cultural education cannot be carried out without a solid understanding of the interrelationship between language and culture. At the same time, in-depth knowledge of language and culture alone will not guarantee appropriate instruction. Thus, ONALDI provided two complementary emphases simultaneously. As in AILDI, morning sessions in the summer workshop focused on linguistic activities, in which the curriculum teaching staff also participated. Afternoon sessions covered the philosophies, principles, and methods of curriculum and materials development, using the morning linguistic activities as input for further development. The morning linguistic staff also participated in afternoon sessions. In this way, the two components were integrated; the institute products and outcomes were the result of this cooperative teaching and learning arrangement.

The ONALDI Model

ONALDI was formulated in response to the content and urgency of the Oklahoma Department of Education requirements for bilingual and ESL endorsements and the expressed needs of indigenous communities, educators, and parents. The model is set out as follows, with each aspect feeding into the next:

(1) General discussions on the nature and structure of human languages as a means of studying specific languages.
Results: Courses fulfilled some endorsement requirements; participants gained general knowledge of how languages are structured and acquired by children.

(2) Examination of our "favorite" languages (Cherokee, Chickasaw, Choctaw, Creek, Kickapoo, Omaha, Potawatomi, Sauk-Fox, Shawana, Euchee, Spanish, English), using the knowledge and skills acquired in (1), above.
Results: Participants wrote a grammatical sketch of each of their favorite languages.

(3) Curriculum development: theories and practice.
Results: The courses here provided necessary knowledge and skills to design curriculum. They also fulfilled endorsement requirements.

(4) Designing language- and culture-specific curriculum using the language materials developed and the linguistic knowledge acquired in (1)–(3) above.
Results: Participants developed "master plans" for a bilingual-bicultural curriculum, as well as unit and lesson plans.

(5) Development of language- and culture-specific teaching materials based on the unit and lesson plans developed in (4), above.
Results: Participants produced age- and context-appropriate language teaching materials such as alphabet stories, other stories, pop-up books, poems, and games ready to be used in participants' language programs.

(6) Synthesis: Learning from each of the language groups to strengthen the sense of shared humanness and respect for the uniqueness of each language community.
Results: A balanced, nonethnocentric approach to education (i.e., multicultural education).

Like AILDI, each year of ONALDI was marked by a theme. Developing a theme each year and a sequence of themes for multiple years were important planning activities that helped the coordinators and participants clarify goals as well as logistics, such as who should be involved in what capacity, what physical facilities were needed, and what kind of budget would meet these needs. ONALDI themes included "Multilingual/Multicultural Education and Native American Children," "Assessment of Linguistic and Cultural Competence of Native American Children," and "Oral and Written Traditions in Native American Communities."

Academic Courses

Courses were designed to provide participants with an opportunity to learn both theories and practice in language teaching and to develop student-centered culturally and linguistically relevant curricula and materials. The courses were sequenced so that by the time they had completed three summer institutes, participants would have the basic requirements for the bilingual and/or ESL endorsement. The second institute, for example, included these courses:

(1) *Language Acquisition and Development,* a three-credit linguistics course designed for students who had taken introductory linguistics, bilingual education, and/or ESL courses. Participants reviewed research on first- and second-language acquisition and applied principles to teaching in indigenous classrooms. They also developed native language and ESL materials.

(2) *Theories and Methods for Educating Indian Children,* a three-credit curriculum course designed to address two major questions: "Why do some children, as groups, experience greater success in school than others?" and "How can educators and parents promote the academic and life success of Indian children?" Topics covered included theory, research, and practice in bilingual education and related fields such as anthropology and sociolinguistics, with an emphasis on applying principles to teaching using cooperative, holistic, and interactive strategies.

(3) *Testing and Evaluation in ESL and Bilingual Education,* a one-credit curriculum course that examined language assessment in bilingual and ESL programs, including a review of standardized tests and teacher-developed assessments. This course continued as part of the follow-up seminars throughout the year, and participants earned an additional two credit hours toward their endorsements.

Language Research Activities and Projects

Throughout the courses and follow-up activities, ONALDI participants continued to explore aspects of their respective heritage languages, especially in relation to processes of language development in children. In curriculum courses, they were asked to develop a long-range language curriculum, units and lessons based on an overall plan that dealt with the issues they had examined in their linguistics course.

Developing unit and lesson plans necessarily led to developing language teaching materials. Some of the work in this area required participants to conduct basic original research on their languages. These activities engaged participants in formulating linguistic theories or hypotheses and testing them with new language data. Figure 29.3 shows an example of a language research activity from the second ONALDI.

Oklahoma Native Language Association and Workshops

Intensive summer institutes or workshops that last for a few weeks can cover a wide range of topics while simultaneously providing meaningful and durable learning experiences

I. **Review the morphology and syntax by examining the following in your language:**
   A. Possessive expressions
      1. Kinship terms
      2. Body parts
      3. Abstract ideas (e.g., my thought, my feeling, etc.)
      4. Animals
      5. Objects
   B. Using the nouns you have examined in (A), above, add number words.
      1. Where does the number word come from in relation to the noun?
      2. Does the use of the number word reveal anything interesting about the form of the noun? (Does the form of the noun change?)
   C. Select several verbs and examine how forms may change when you say:
      1. I am,...you are,...s/he is...
      2. We are,...you all are,...they are...
   D. Now try with questions and answers such as, *Who* cooked the beans?
      1. *I* cooked the beans (or, *I* did).
      2. *You* cooked the beans (or, *You* did).
      3. *S/he* cooked the beans (or, *S/he* did).
   E. Try with the plural forms: we, you all, and they.
   F. Examine the differences between the statement (or descriptive) sentences and command sentences:
      1. You are running around the building.
      2. Run around the building!
      3. Please run around the building!
   G. Experiment with other forms:
      1. We are running around the building.
      2. Let's run around the building.
      3. Shall we run around the building?
      4. Why don't we run around the building?
      5. You are running around the building.
      6. Why don't you run around the building?
      7. Won't you run around the building?
      8. I wish you would run around the building.
   H. Using the verbs you have used in (C), examine the differences between:
      1. [What do you do on Saturday? (habitual)]
         I do my homework for Akira.
      2. [What are you doing? (right now)]
         I am doing my homework for Pat.
      3. [What did you do last Saturday? (immediate past)]
         I went to the farmers' market (instead of doing homework).
      4. [What did you do last summer? (distant past)]
         I attended the 1992 ONALDI.
      5. [Where did your people come from? (far distant past)]
         Our people came from the Great Lakes area.
      6. [What are you going to do for lunch? (immediate future)]
         I am going to our favorite restaurant in Choctaw.
      7. [What will you do when the institute is over? (distant future)]
         I will go home and do nothing for a month.
      8. [What will you do when you retire? (far distant future)]
         I will start a language program in our community.

II. **Summarize the results and prepare reports. You can organize your report as follows:**
   A. Topic (when you finish (B) and (C) below, the topic will "jump out" for you)
   B. Language data: Present language data
   C. Observation and generalization: What patterns do you detect in your language data? You will be formulating your own theory or hypothesis on the language phenomenon from a limited amount of the data. Any hypothesis must tested against more data, and either confirmed, modified, eliminated, or reformulated.
   D. Add more examples whenever you can. Are they exceptions to what you have said in (C)? Accumulate more examples. You may find they are not really exceptions.

III. **Based on the level of your language learners:**
   A. Develop unit plans.
   B. Develop at least one lesson plan for a selected unit.
   C. Prepare materials you need for that lesson.

FIGURE 29.3   Example of a language research activity at ONALDI

for participants. The reality for teachers and parents in Oklahoma Native American communities, however, is that they cannot afford to take time off from their family and community responsibilities to be away at an institute for sustained periods of time. ONALDI arranged family-type housing for participants, but even so, being away from home for several weeks posed a hardship for elders and families with children.

Some way was needed to provide similar learning opportunities in a series of shorter institutes held in closer proximity to participants' home communities. After much thinking, Euchee language activist Greg Bigler, Carol Young of the Tribal Studies Program at Northeastern Oklahoma State University, and Akira Yamamoto established an organization of Native American language teachers and community people, the Oklahoma Native Language Association (ONLA), in 1996. Linguistic and educational workshops for teachers, parents, and community language resource people became one of the association's important activities. Through her university, Young arranged college credit for workshop participants at a modest fee. Yamamoto provided instruction, forming a team with Bigler and Young for ONLA and its workshops. Yamamoto also recruited several of his graduate students to the linguistic workshop team.

Another major activity of ONLA is its annual Native Language Use Conference, at which teachers, parents, and elders share successes, issues, and problems faced by their language programs. They discuss possible ways to make their programs more effective and participate in at least one workshop that focuses on a particular language-teaching approach such as immersion. ONLA held its first conference in Preston, Oklahoma, in October 1996, and it continues to organize the conference each year.

ONLA workshops use the ONALDI model as a guide; the workshop organizing team plans at least five workshops as a single series. Issues to be addressed in organizing the workshop include the following:

(1) *Participants.* There is no knowing in advance who will participate in a particular workshop. Thus, workshop presenters must be prepared to review what was covered in previous workshops, yet provide something new for continuing participants.

(2) *Workshop sites.* The selection of workshop sites is based on convenience; the organizing team seeks to encourage participants from as many language groups as possible. This reflects the team's basic philosophy that sharing among different language programs is more important than focusing on a single program. To date, workshops have been held in Tulsa and Oklahoma City, where Young has been able to coordinate course credit and sites with other institutions of higher education.

(3) *Facility.* Oklahoma is fortunate to have a higher education center in Tulsa that consists of a number of different colleges and universities—a beautiful building complex with modern educational technologies. Young's university is part of this consortium, and she has been able to arrange the use of the facility without difficulty. Classrooms have large tables, an overhead projector, and a computer cable, and they are clean and comfortable—ideal for learning and producing language materials in groups.

(3) *Instructional staff.* With no major funding to cover expenses, it is difficult for the organizing team to find linguists, educators, and computer specialists who can provide services at the workshops. With a small fund set aside for ONLA workshops, Yamamoto has been able to support his graduate students' travel, lodging, and other expenses. These students' contributions have been essential to the workshops.

Since 1996, ONLA workshops have attracted participants from the communities of Absentee Shawnee, Cheyenne, Choctaw, Comanche, Cherokee, Euchee, Kickapoo, Kiowa, Lenape, Loyal Shawnee, and Muskogee. Several cycles of linguistic instruction have been completed, covering a range of subject matter from pragmatics to phonology. At each workshop, the major goal has been to produce language teaching materials based on the knowledge gained at that workshop, thus effecting its immediate application. Both ONALDI and ONLA have succeeded in preparing language teachers, helping them refine their curricula, and producing new teaching materials. The majority of ONALDI participants, for example, have applied their experiences at the workshop to establish new programs, enrich existing ones, and shift focus from language preservation to language maintenance. An evaluation of the institute shows that continued learning opportunities for teachers, language resource persons, community members, and academic linguists is vital to the revitalization, maintenance, and development of Oklahoma Native American languages.

Lessons Learned from ONALDI and ONLA: Steps for Starting an Institute or Workshop Series

The transformation from ONALDI to ONLA involved adapting the institute model to that of a workshop series. The questions that must be addressed are, by and large, the same as those that must be addressed in building an institute of the type organized by AILDI or ONALDI. Those questions, and the lessons they suggest, are outlined below.

Question 1: What is the population for whom the institute or workshop series is intended? For example, will participants represent Native American and tribal communities? Public schools? Elementary or secondary education personnel? Colleges? Answers to these questions will help determine what strategies should be employed in recruiting participants. Especially important are the desires of indigenous communities: Who should be contacted? Should the selection of participants be left to the tribal council?

Question 2: What language group(s) and proficiencies will be represented? For example, will participants be speakers of a single language or many? Will they all be native speakers of their heritage languages, or will nonspeakers also be included? Answers to these questions will help determine the content of the institute or workshops. If only one language is involved, the curriculum may be fairly straightforward; when diverse languages are involved, a more complex plan may be required. Similarly, if all participants are fluent speakers of an indigenous language, activities will be very different from a situation in which fluent speakers and partially fluent speakers or nonspeakers are involved. These considerations lead to additional questions:

Question 3: What are the training needs? If all participants are native speakers, they may still represent a range of backgrounds and skills: those with no experience teaching their heritage languages and those who have extensive teaching experience; those who have worked on language materials development and those with little or no experience in such work; those who have done some linguistic work and those who are novices. More likely, there will be a mixture of these and other, unanticipated categories as well. Once the training needs are identified, the goals and objectives of the institute or workshop can be formulated.

Question 4: What are the goals of the institute or workshop series? Thought must be given to both long- and short-range goals. Should the institute or workshop train native speakers to be language researchers in their communities? Curriculum or materials developers? Language teachers? When the goals are identified, specific objectives for reaching each of them can be developed.

Question 5: What are the most effective strategies for achieving those goals? What form should the institute or workshop series take? What are the possible models? Should the activity be community based or affiliated with a nearby university? What are the advantages and disadvantages of one model over others?

Question 6: What will help ensure that the selected model achieves its goals? Are the necessary physical facilities and equipment available? Are rooms with tables available? What size rooms are needed, and how many? What materials are needed? Consider whether video or tape recorders, computers, printers, software, a chalkboard, butcher and construction paper, and other materials development supplies are needed and available. These may seem small matters, but space, equipment, and supplies will determine the quality and quantity of the language teaching materials produced.

Question 7: What type of specialists are needed and how many? Should there be a linguist for each language group represented? Are bilingual education and computer special-

ists needed? Who should be contacted? How will the staff be selected?

Question 8: What is to be expected from each member of the instructional team? It will be necessary to clearly identify staff in relation to the goals of the institute or workshop; the match must be the best possible.

Question 9: How much money will be required to meet material and staffing requirements? Who can be contacted to find out where and how funding can be obtained? A partial answer to this last, very important question may be obtained from resources listed in the *Native Language Revitalization Resource Directory,* compiled by the Institute for the Preservation of the Original Languages of the Americas (IPOLA), and available at <ipola.org>. While this publication deals primarily with the Americas, it also includes an international section. Also helpful is the Clearinghouse for Information on Endangered Languages, under the directorship of the Japanese linguist Tasaku Tsunoda (<tsunoda@tooyoo.l.u-tokyo.ac.jp>). These institutions have been established to assist scholars and community-based project personnel in locating information on endangered languages and programs relating to them; the institutions are not sources of funding themselves. For funding of Native American language programs in the United States, indigenous communities and allied organizations may seek assistance under the Native American Languages Act, the Endangered Language Fund (contact Douglas Whalen at <whalen@haskins.yale.edu>), and the Foundation for Endangered Languages (contact Nicholas Ostler at <nostler@chibcha.demon.co.uk>).

CONCLUDING THOUGHTS

The foregoing sections on AILDI, ONALDI, and ONLA highlight the logistical challenges of these initiatives. Their greatest challenge, however, is more substantive and essential: the life-and-death struggle for the survival of indigenous North American languages. Uniquely positioned by their community foundations, AILDI, ONALDI, and ONLA have been prominent among the forces for strengthening indigenous languages and the cultural-ethnic identities they represent. Yet in the final analysis, the survival of indigenous languages is dependent on choices about language enacted within native speakers' homes and communities. AILDI, ONALDI, and ONLA can light the path, but their participants must lead the way. Still, when we consider the path without the light, we are reassured of the purpose and value of these institutes and workshops.

In conclusion, we share these suggestions for community-based language restoration:

(1) Talking *about* what to do to rescue endangered languages is important, but it will not in itself reverse the shift toward English. Begin using the language *now*—at

home, in the community and school, and in other domains reserved exclusively for the heritage language.

(2) Do not criticize or ridicule errors; use them as learning and teaching points.

(3) Be a risk taker; look at your children and learn from them.

(4) Learning is fun; don't stifle it by making it overly difficult or boring.

(5) Through children, involve the parents; through parents, involve the grandparents. Start small and expand the circle.

(6) Set aside internal community/school/tribal politics for the benefit of the language renewal work at hand.

(7) Recognize that your language is a gift. In this sense, it is the speakers' responsibility to ensure that the language is used and given life in succeeding generations. "Our Creator has created the world for us through language," AILDI participants have observed, "If we don't speak it, there is no world."

(8) This is the time for each person to do her or his part. Each must assume responsibility. The stakes are high. Begin now—don't wait for someone else to do your part.

(9) Finally, remember that others share your mission and are part of your network of support. Together, educators, parents, elders, academics, and other allies can create a powerful team for securing the future of indigenous languages—and the indigenous communities and identities these languages represent.

References

Cummins, Jim. 1989. *Empowering minority students*. Sacramento: California Association for Bilingual Education.

———. 1992. The empowerment of Indian students. In *Teaching American Indian students*, ed. Jon Reyhner, 3–12. Norman: University of Oklahoma Press.

Fishman, Joshua A. 1991. *Reversing language shift: Theoretical and empirical foundations of assistance to threatened languages*. Clevedon, England: Multilingual Matters.

———. 1996. Maintaining languages: What works and what doesn't. In *Stabilizing indigenous languages*, ed. G. Cantoni, 186–98. Flagstaff: Northern Arizona University, Center for Excellence in Education.

Fox, Sandra. 1992. The whole language approach. In *Teaching American Indian students*, ed. Jon Reyhner, 168–77. Norman: University of Oklahoma Press.

Goodman, Ken. 1986. *What's whole in whole language?* Portsmouth, N.H.: Heinemann.

Hinton, Leanne, Margaret Langdon, Linda Munson, John Rouillard, Akira Yamamoto, Lucille Watahomigie, and Ofelia Zepeda. 1982. A manual for the development of American Indian and Alaska native language workshops. Unpublished report prepared under the auspices of National Endowment for the Humanities grant #ES-0013- 79–50.

Leighton, Mary S., Amy M. Hightower, and Pamela G. Wrigley. 1995. *Model strategies in bilingual education: Professional development*. Washington, D.C.: Policy Study Associates and U.S. Department of Education, Office of Bilingual Education and Minority Languages Affairs.

McCarty, T. L. 1993. Creating conditions for positive change: Case studies in American Indian education. In *NABE Annual Conference Journal*, ed. L. Malavé, 89–97. Washington, D.C.: National Association for Bilingual Education.

Swisher, Karen, and Susan Ledlow. 1986. *National Indian Bilingual Center annual report of fiscal year 1985–1986*. Tempe: Arizona State University, National Indian Bilingual Center.

Tierney, Robert J., Mark A. Carter, and Laura E. Desai. 1991. *Portfolio assessment in the reading-writing classroom*. Norwood, Mass.: Christopher-Gordon.

U.S. Department of Education. 1991. *Indian nations at risk: An educational strategy for action*. Final report of the Indian Nations at Risk Task Force. Washington, D.C.: U.S. Department of Education.

Watahomigie, Lucille J., and Akira Y. Yamamoto. 1992. Local reactions to perceived language decline. *Language* 68: 10–17.

Zepeda, Ofelia. 1990. American Indian language policy. In *Perspectives on official English: The campaign for English as the official language of the USA*, ed. Karen L. Adams and Daniel T. Brink, 247–56. Berlin and New York: Mouton de Gruyter.

The Navajo Language: III

KEN HALE

Department of Linguistics and Philosophy
Massachusetts Institute of Technology
Cambridge, Massachusetts

Navajo has been a college and university subject for many years now. It is taught regularly at, among other places, the University of New Mexico (Albuquerque and Gallup campuses), Northern Arizona University (Flagstaff), the University of Arizona (Tucson), and, of course, Diné College (formerly Navajo Community College, with campuses at Tsaile, Arizona, and Shiprock, New Mexico).

The community of college- and university-level students interested in some aspect of the process of "learning Navajo" includes at least three quite different populations. On the one hand, there are those who already speak the language and wish to learn how to write it, and possibly to gain some conscious understanding of its grammar as well. And, on the other hand, there are those who do not know the language at all and seek to learn to speak it, as well as to write it and understand its grammar to some extent. In addition, as Clay Slate points out in the following essay, there is a third and important group of potential learners of Navajo. These are people who have knowledge of the language in the manner commonly referred to as "passive." Typically, a person in this group is said to understand the language, without being able to speak it. But this third group is, in reality, more complex than this, as it includes individuals, sometimes called "semispeakers" (including the "latent speakers" of Slate's essay), who have some speaking ability but in their own judgment and that of others fail to achieve the level of "full fluency." Such assessments are highly subjective, of course, and they are often a source of tension among the speakers of a language. But the existence of less-than-fully-fluent speakers is a reality, and many people readily place

385

themselves in this category—an important one, because for some languages speakers in this category are the majority (see, for example, Chapter 2 on the Australian language Lardil).

These considerations make it quite clear that the audience for courses on Navajo is complex, even at a single institution. In fact, each of the three groups of potential learners briefly sketched in the previous paragraph is substantially represented in the population of students taking Navajo courses at Diné College. And each group has its own measure of internal diversity, a diversity which is also well represented at Diné College. If we add to these the many non-Navajo students taking Navajo language courses at various universities, the complexity of the audience becomes formidable, placing an enormous burden on language teachers, curriculum designers, and teaching materials.

Ready availability of textbooks on Navajo is a relatively recent phenomenon, though Father Berard Haile's excellent four-volume *Learning Navaho* was published by St. Michael's Press during the years from 1941 to 1948 (and reprinted in 1971–72). This is an extremely interesting work, consisting of easily digestible dialogues and much discussion of Navajo grammar and many aspects of Navajo culture. It was never fully available, however, since it was not easy to obtain, few people knew about it, and the Navajo was written in the technical Athabaskan (and general Americanist) phonetic orthography of the time. Nonetheless, for those who did manage to acquire these volumes and study them from beginning to end, they were nothing less than a treasure, truly a linguistic gold mine. Many important observations about Navajo syntax and semantics were first written down in those volumes. In a similar format to Haile's work, Irvy Goossen's smaller and very popular *Navajo Made Easier* (1973) has for many years been a favorite Navajo language textbook. It is written in the standard Navajo orthography used in Young and Morgan's 1943 *Navaho Language* and in most later publications.

The two-volume text entitled *Diné Bizaad Bóhoo'aah: A Conversational Navajo Text for Secondary Schools, Colleges, and Adults,* and the literacy text *Diné Bizaad Bee Na'adzo: A Navajo Language Literacy and Grammar Text,* first published in 1986 by the Navajo Language Institute, are explicitly structured to serve a wide and diverse range of students, from absolute beginners to fluent speakers seeking to become literate in Navajo. These are among the texts used at Diné College, and they are the first texts whose production was a joint effort by both Navajos and non-Navajos, including the Navajo linguist Paul Platero. They amount to more than a simple language text, as they introduce the student to many useful concepts of linguistics and language pedagogy, as well the spoken and written language. Quite apart from the textbooks now available, college-level Navajo language teachers and students of Navajo are especially fortunate in having access to Robert Young and William Morgan's *The Navajo Language* (1987), the supreme repository of Navajo linguistic knowledge. To use this work requires instruction, and Diné College wisely devotes an entire course to that purpose.

Material resources are just a part of the teaching situation, of course. Teaching always takes place in a sociopolitical and cultural context. Its success depends very much upon an acceptable apportionment of the responsibilities. This aspect of language teaching and learning is discussed at some length.

References

Goossen, Irvy. 1973. *Navajo made easier.* Flagstaff, Ariz.: Northland Press.

Haile, Berard. 1941–48. *Learning Navaho.* St. Michaels, Ariz.: St. Michael's Press.

Witherspoon, Gary, et al. 1986a. *Diné Bizaad Bóhoo'aah I and II: A Conversational Navajo text for secondary schools, colleges, and adults.* Farmington, N.M.: Navajo Language Academy.

———. 1986b. *Diné Bizaad Bee Na'adzo: A Navajo language literacy and grammar text.* Farmington, N.M.: Navajo Language Academy.

Young, Robert, and William Morgan. 1987. *The Navajo language.* Albuquerque: University of New Mexico Press.

30

Promoting Advanced
Navajo Language Scholarship

CLAY SLATE

Center for Diné Teacher Education
Diné College
Navajo Nation
(Tsaile, Arizona)

There is a pervasive tension that shapes this piece. By request, and for important purposes, it is being written for a non-Navajo audience. Though the non-Navajo audience is certainly not homogenous, it is the incongruities in interests, needs, and knowledge that distinguish that non-Navajo audience from a Navajo audience that concern me. The ambiguity and manipulation in Navajo-Anglo relations promote misunderstanding and mistrust, of motive and message. A major claim of this piece is that the vitality of an intellectual forum for advanced work on Navajo (and perhaps any indigenous language) must recognize the absolute primacy of the speakers of Navajo as audience. In adherence to this, I am here writing through a Navajo audience first.

INTRODUCTION

The Navajo Language Program (NLP) at Diné College was expanded over a 10-year period between 1986 and 1996. Several dozen collaborators have achieved gains throughout the NLP. This has allowed Diné College to more fully exercise its role in promoting the language. Of course, the work is built on a century-old foundation of scholarship about Navajo. Constant work has been done on Navajo at Diné College since its beginning, as Navajo Community College, in 1968, including the time that William Morgan taught here. However, I will focus on the ten years from 1986 to 1996.

The guiding principle of this recent development is both simple and profound. At the core of the best work to be done on Navajo there must lie a forum of scholars. This group must develop a synergy of critical interplay that values all community voices and concerns, and it must follow a well-circumscribed path: the seminal work is done by Navajos, in Navajo, for a Navajo audience, and for Navajo purposes. Hereafter, I will refer to this formula as that of the Core Forum. At Diné College we have promoted this Core Forum, and maintenance and promotion of the Core Forum will be pursued. Only with the goal of maintaining the primacy of this type of work are we striving for the best, as academics.

The number of issues anyone may study about Navajo is, as with any language, practically inexhaustible. To delimit these issues, it has been crucial at Diné College to concentrate on the distinction between the fields of Navajo language and Navajo linguistics, and also to clarify the significant areas of overlap and cross-fertilization. There is room in these fields for everyone. Of course, the work is difficult, and novices must undergo extensive preparation before producing work not undermined by serious errors. This is most markedly true for those who do not speak Navajo or who are unfamiliar with its structure or with Navajo life and talk. The academic careers of Navajo language and linguistics scholars follow one of three paths: (1) they do inaccurate work and pawn it off on the large and ignorant audience that wants to be told about the Indians; (2) they limit their field of inquiry to arcane matters, maintaining an etic accuracy by studying minutiae; or, best (3) they define their study focus in collaboration with a Navajo-local forum and thoroughly expose their work, at minimum, to this forum. Diné College's task in the Navajo Language Program has been, and is, to build and nurture this Core Forum, (1) by Navajos, (2) in Navajo, (3) for a Navajo audience, and (4) for Navajo purposes.

(1) Work done by Navajo-speaking Navajos is informed by a richness of resource and an access to intuition about grammaticality and acceptability unmatched elsewhere. Both for synthesizing and analyzing Navajo, those who

389

speak Navajo fluently and articulately have tremendously valuable tools available. Any forum that does not include informed, collaborative, critical input from Navajo-speaking Navajos is unacceptably vulnerable to inaccuracy. This is true of all Navajo language forums, without exception, and is probably true of all but the most radically delimited Navajo linguistics work.

Navajo-speaking Navajos also have an understanding of the Navajo community and an appreciation of its openness to and need for certain foci in research, curriculum writing, and composition. Decisions about what work to do that are made with this knowledge are more likely to produce work that will be used, that will draw response, that has permanence. This permanence is one of ongoing impact, and also one of ongoing presence of authors, since non-Navajos come and go on the Navajo Nation, but Navajos stay, or at least always return. Thus work done by Navajos nurtures a Core Forum.

(2) The second aspect of nurturance of the Core Forum is that primacy be given to work conducted in Navajo. This is difficult and has been realized only partially (though in increasingly more settings). Of course, symbolically this is important. Those who work on Navajo are often the most visible champions of the language, promoting its perpetuation. Promoting Navajo while conducting one's professional life in spoken or written English is inherently contradictory. A related benefit of doing Navajo language work in Navajo is that it forces constant coinage and circumlocution in the language. This growing edge of the language is, in and of itself, a vital part of the organism.

Of greater importance is the fact that when talk and writing are in Navajo a social solidarity and synergy arise from the specificity of audience identification that speakers and writers make. Navajo language professionals on the Navajo Nation are struggling with the ongoing demise of the language while working at perhaps its most significant growing edge. In general they cannot waste time on marginal matters or be distracted by topics possibly more taxonomic than physiological. Theirs is a forum that needs, most of all, ideas, energy, and creative problem-solving talk. When the talk is in English, this same group (including non-Navajos, who often dominate talk) immediately becomes more disjointed. Some of the reasons are social: a Navajo speaking Navajo presents a different social self to other Navajos than does the same person when speaking English. Other reasons have to do with the structure of discourse: when talk or writing is conducted in English the presupposition pools, remarkability set, and general background knowledge of English speakers tend to constrain or propose what is said.

(3) The third feature of the Core Forum is that the most seminal work to be done on Navajo must be addressed primarily to a Navajo audience. Frankly, this is the hardest audience to address, the one most willing to withhold approval until its standards are met, the one with the most to gain or lose, and the one most consistently patient and interested. This audience has a permanence, not of a year or two, but of a lifetime and across generations. These people have time to reflect (even years) before responding (compared to the five minutes given at professional conferences). Of course, the Navajo audience is itself heterogeneous—in what it will read or listen to and in what it knows and cares about—so finding it a circumscribed audience is a problem that each writer and researcher must solve.

Giving this audience primacy has radical results. First, it shapes what is said. In some matters of a more technical or arcane nature, an academic must make more preparatory remarks than would be made to a graduate linguistics seminar at most universities. Concurrently, authors must take greater care, especially with the accuracy of data and glosses, but also with claims about processes. It is always a rigorous exercise to face an audience that, when kept in the talk, can rapidly generate counterexamples.

To the extent that work on Navajo is for purposes of the academy, such focusing will also be beneficial. When small slices of a language are carried away to be presented as data to naive audiences, relatively untested work may outlive its usefulness. When a large community of native speakers, with sophisticated analytical knowledge about the language, are a sine qua non of critical audiences, the forum will have a rigor of an entirely different nature. Even small slices of data, discussed by this audience, may well be critically examined for decades. Further, as discussed next, the topics considered to be reasonable ones for research will come to be of a different nature, a radical departure from present practice, and maybe the most needed one.

It will be argued that focusing all work on a Navajo audience might prevent important advances from being made, advances that can only be made by addressing a narrow, expert audience. First, no claim is being made that the Core Forum should be the only forum. In contrast, the claim is that if the work does not eventually impact that forum it will be ephemeral. Further, although our attention in scholarship (indeed, the only thing that some will consider scholarship) is often on the most intellectually complicated and groundbreaking work, such work requires that one have a broad and deep foundation of perhaps more mundane but equally valuable scholarship.

A further contention, of racism or reverse discrimination, must also be addressed. In positing the primacy of Navajo authorship, there is no intent of exclusiveness or an exercise of blind racial politics (though the perception is not infrequent). Certainly there are non-Navajos who have access to resources and expertise that many Navajos do not. Even where there are Navajos with specialized expertise, often they are spread too thin. If, for example, it is important to provide instruction or research in articulatory phonetics for teachers of English as a second language (ESL) or Navajo as a second language (NSL), the key issues are of quality work and accessible results, whoever does it.

(4) The fourth element of the Core Forum is that the work be for Navajo purposes. One compelling reason for this is the circumstance of "brain drain" that often pulls the most capable Navajo scholars away from crucially important work. There is no intent here to delegitimize any particular area of Navajo language work, but it is necessary to prioritize. For example, projects working to reverse the decline of Navajo deserve more attention and resources than those which investigate Navajo as data for other concerns. A second rationale for making Navajo purposes primary is that these purposes are often relatively more applied in nature, and it is in the application (or re-explanation) of findings that deficiencies are discovered and improvements made.

The ideas of a Core Forum have guided the development of the Navajo Language Program for years. However, the reality of day-to-day problem solving has often demanded that other agendas and perspectives be addressed. This is good, since the practical task of institutionalizing quality Navajo language work at Diné College should never be threatened by rigid ideology. The extent to which the principles of the Core Forum have been adhered to or set aside can be examined by reference to the more concrete details of the NLP.

CONTEXT

Navajo is spoken by about 80,000 people in New Mexico, Arizona, and Utah. A few older people are monolingual in Navajo. Though over one-half of the Navajo children do not speak Navajo, thousands are still fluent. Navajo is an Athabaskan language, and its closest sisters are the Apache languages.

Of the lexical categories of Navajo, the verb is by far the most complex, morphologically. A single Navajo verb can have more than 10 morphemes. Syntactically, Navajo is SOV in word order, and about two-thirds of its phonemes differ from English. The incongruity of the Navajo and English languages and cultures make Navajo hard for English speakers to learn, and vice versa.

The Navajo Nation is about the size of West Virginia. Navajos have been here for at least 800 years; in many cases one family has been in one place for several hundred years. In general, life is extremely rural. Of Navajo homes 30%

have no electricity, 50% no running water. Subsistence stock raising, farming, traditional arts, and herbal and traditional medicine are still important economic and cultural features of Navajo life, though the wage economy dominates economic life more and more. Navajo people are close to the land, and there is constant reference in many Navajo sacred and ordinary discourses to the fact that the Navajo world is bounded by the four sacred mountains. Though wage and salaried labor are now ubiquitous, unemployment is at minimum 40%. For educators, economic factors are crucial in two ways: to the community, the role of schools as a source of jobs sometimes takes priority over anything else, and those Navajos with the best school jobs tend to be the most anglicized.

Perhaps because the reservation is large (and many Navajos are therefore isolated from anglophone society), perhaps because of the large number of Navajos, and certainly through Navajo commitment to the perpetuation of culture and language, Navajos have maintained the day-to-day viability of their language better than other U.S. tribes, and Navajo has a real chance at long-term survival. A prominent portion of the mission statement of Diné College calls upon it to "promote, nurture, and enrich the language and culture of the Navajo people."

Navajo faces powerful and effective language oppression, de jure and de facto. It still is proscribed from or held in low esteem in institutional settings such as schools, churches, hospitals, and the workplace. Even advances made for Navajo in schools over the last 15 years have only been possible in coalition with those promoting Spanish, other indigenous languages, and "foreign" languages (Navajo is used by some college students to fulfill the foreign-language requirement, but many schools give no credit to a speaker of Navajo; he or she is required to study a third language in college or high school).

Few of the 240 schools that educate large numbers of Navajo youth do much with the language. The Navajo child who comes to school dominant in Navajo is often never given any opportunity at school to grow intellectually in Navajo; the Navajo child who comes speaking little or no Navajo will learn none in most school settings. Here, the "standard curriculum" of schools that recognize only the cultural capital of anglophone society has succeeded in delegitimizing and crowding out a well-exercised and locally validated body of knowledge. A market-oriented press has never found sufficient profit in publishing materials in Navajo, and Navajos have not had the clout to get Navajo language materials on any state-approved textbook list.

The workplace often uses the language skills of Navajos: to sell to the Navajo consumer or buy from the Navajo producer, to deliver health care, or to aid the anthropologist. In fact, all other things being equal, all jobs done on or near the Navajo Nation are better done by someone who speaks Navajo, and it is astounding that some jobs (e.g., police work) do not require it. Even recently established positions that do recognize the need for Navajo language skills, such as that of certified court interpreters (now required in the New Mexico and federal courts), do not officially require that its practitioners use the advantages of Navajo literacy (e.g., for accessing glossaries). Further, seldom are Navajo language skills compensated adequately. For example, schools that want "bilingual money" from the states employ Navajo bilingual aides but pay them close to minimum wage and give them little meaningful support, planning, or authority. We still lack ballots in Navajo (though certification of Navajo poll interpreters is underway).

A few public and Bureau of Indian Affairs (BIA) schools have pioneered quality Navajo language work. Diné College has been able to build upon this critical foundation. Programs at the Rock Point School, the Rough Rock School, and the Fort Defiance Elementary School are the best known. Many other schools are making an effort now to advance locally developed quality work, and as more Navajos move into certified and administrative positions, this trend should continue. Advances have concomitantly been made at the state and federal levels, with increasingly active Navajo involvement. Navajo language teachers are being endorsed by New Mexico, and now Arizona. A new Arizona mandate requires public schools to teach a second language, which may be Navajo.

The role of the Navajo Nation government in this struggle is central but deeply conflicted. Set up in the 1930s to rubber-stamp mineral extraction agreements, the Navajo Tribal Council was initially a tool of the BIA. More recently, the shape and texture of limited Navajo sovereignty has brought more critical examination and control to Navajos. Yet the Navajo Nation government still struggles to escape the neo-colonial mold. Navajos who speak English, but not Navajo, have success at almost every level, but monolingual Navajo speakers have had severely limited access, as either clients or employees. As a macrocosm, the government honestly reflects the ambivalence—nay, multivalence—many Navajos feel toward Navajo, and even Navajo-speaking politicians at higher levels, from school superintendent to tribal official, are often reluctant to take vanguard positions promoting the language.

There have been some recent advances. Official tribal education policy states that Navajo will be taught "to every child, at every grade level, in every school on the Navajo Nation." However, the tribe does not control funding for the 240 schools, which have largely ignored this 1982 mandate. Collaboration between state Departments of Education and tribal officials concerned with language matters is limited, but ongoing. For instance, the Arizona and New Mexico Departments of Education depend upon the tribal department to conduct testing and certify fluency of Navajo speakers seeking bilingual and Navajo language state endorsements. (Diné College acts as the agent for the Navajo Nation for this test-

ing.) Yet collaboration between states and the Navajo Nation is uneven. Though tribal government (wisely) is unwilling to take over responsibility for funding and supervising all Navajo schools or of trying to certify teachers, it is at the same time (again wisely) loath to fully accept the authority of the states and the BIA. A similar relationship exists between the Navajo Nation and Diné College, keeping them often at a lamentable arm's length. Thus, although verbal, heartfelt support for Navajo language efforts from tribal leaders is the rule, smooth cooperation is not.

Ambivalence, grounded in a tribal sovereignty always under negotiation, is both institutional and personal. On one hand, affirmative-action programs now effectively promote Navajo expertise and Navajo voices. Yet at Diné College it is those instructors who are Navajo who are most vehemently vilified by students when they are "too hard." Likewise, the chairman of the Navajo Nation issued a proclamation that all Head Start centers on the Navajo Nation would use immersion programs, in Navajo. Yet this was done in an absence of curriculum or teacher training programs, though well-conceived work on these is underway, using partly nontribal resources. Finally, though most tribal council delegates speak Navajo well, almost all paperwork is in English, and the Navajo Nation has never acted to make Navajo the official language of the nation or even require that road signs be in Navajo.

Some clarity has been cast upon the issue of limits on sovereignty or authority at the governmental, school, or even personal level by Benjamin Barney, in an analysis of what he calls "administrative prostitution." At the dyad level, an Anglo and a Navajo work together closely in Janus fashion, coordinating their messages and purposes to keep them unified, each depending on the other to reveal the Anglo face or the Navajo face to the public, as each situation dictates. Typically, the Anglo will be the writer and the Navajo the spokesperson. The "prostitution" portion of the relationship comes about when either gives up his or her principles to maintain the unified front that makes the relationship more powerful than the simple addition of two. Though this double-faced relationship is common, it is also dangerous, and difficult to keep on solid footing. Of course, collaboration is important—no one person can do everything. An unfortunate side effect, however, is that the growth of each person can be stunted by dependence upon the complementary resources of the other. For example, Navajo-English bilinguals are almost exclusively Navajos, or those of mixed parentage. Anglos rarely learn Navajo, which does not bode well for the future, since part of an effort to reverse the loss of Navajo lies in successful NSL. Though the circumstance of a Navajo-Anglo partnership should be an excellent opportunity for an Anglo to learn Navajo, the codependence discourages it.

At the governmental level, an analogous love-hate relationship exists between the tribe and the BIA, each of which is dependent on the other, often in dysfunctional ways. Whenever the tribe publicly shows itself capable of providing for itself in ways that the BIA has traditionally done, ongoing federal or BIA support (and the BIA's reason for existence) is threatened. The result of this situation is sometimes a buck-passing phenomenon, such as the one in which Diné College is badly underfunded by the federal government but cannot get hard money commitments from the Navajo Nation.

At times the same relationship exists with state and county governments. Within this political dynamic, Navajo impact on southwestern political matters is predictably marginalized. During the struggle to establish the Arizona Foreign Language mandate, which has opened the door for Navajo to be taught in many schools, the tribe could send only infrequent, mixed messages, while the opposition nearly won the day arguing against "unfunded mandates." In the struggle over the official-English amendment to the Arizona constitution, the Navajo Nation did not effectively oppose it.

Thus progress in the Navajo Nation context is uneven, drawing on available commitment, energy, and organization. A blend of opportunity and courage brings advances. When the tribe put together a coalition of southwestern colleges to get Navajos certified as teachers, the director of the tribe's education department, Anita Pfeiffer, decreed that scholarships for this program would go only to Navajo speakers. Furthermore, she decreed that students would be required to take five courses in Navajo language from Diné College. This single decision significantly expanded the community of Navajo-literate teachers prepared to teach Navajo. Yet Pfeiffer absorbed a great deal of criticism by those who called these requirements overly restrictive, as she did later when she took the responsible position that teachers who seek bilingual certification must be not only speakers, but also Navajo literate. Of the other Navajos or Anglos in positions of authority, for example as school superintendents, only a few have openly supported Navajo. With ambiguous messages coming from tribal government, strong local leadership becomes indispensable, since many districts, and especially the border districts centered in Page, Arizona; Gallup, New Mexico; Farmington, New Mexico; and Blanding, Utah, have been hostile, persistently obstructionist, or at best indifferent toward bringing quality Navajo work into their schools, despite large populations of Navajo students.

In addition to issues of the local neocolonial structures which Navajo language work must struggle to transform, one must add the context of institutional activities that study and report on Navajo, and Navajos. Some of these activities are anthropological or linguistic, and the academic careers of its practitioners are dependent upon their addressing audiences that are naive about Navajos. These researchers can be more sure of themselves when addressing naive audiences than they can be on the Navajo Nation, and by working on Navajo for non-Navajo purposes they can also reside in more comfortable urban settings. There are even now a half-dozen

Navajos with doctorates in linguistics or language-related fields. Yet, if they work for universities, they too can become institutionally constrained to meet the expectations of either the academic community or the Navajo community, with neither time nor resources to do both. If they choose to become garden-variety linguists, their work has minimal application on the Navajo Nation, and even when expertise is needed in applied phonology or syntax, they have even been passed over in favor of non-Navajo scholars. If they choose to make their work more useful to communities, their "applied" orientation renders their careers more vulnerable. It is even uncomfortable for such scholars to work for or speak to both audiences. Once a college in Pennsylvania approached Diné College's Center for Diné Studies to collaborate to produce materials usable by both colleges. Though there were energetic and committed people on both sides, ultimately the needs of the two audiences could not be intertwined.

The same forces apply to those writing stories about Navajos, fiction or nonfiction, such as Tony Hillerman or Rodney Barker. The pattern holds also for publishers, even those generally considered accurate and authoritative. For example, *Smithsonian* magazine recently published an article on the Navajo Code Talkers in which a number of Navajo words were printed. Yet *Smithsonian* resisted transcribing older work into the accurate standard Navajo orthography, choosing instead to stylistically pander to a larger audience. A laudable counterexample is the U.S. Board on Geographic Names, which recently has opened its official recognition processes to non-English orthographies.

There are hopeful signs, in this time of enhanced telecommunication and easier travel, that the broad field of Navajo studies, pursued for so many valid reasons, can begin to have a critical unity of structure that will render it at once more accurate and more responsible to the community under investigation. For instance, there have now been nine annual Navajo studies conferences, usually attracting around 500 participants, held on or near the Navajo Nation. They attract many Navajos and blend practitioners, academics, people with extensive traditional knowledge (though not nearly enough of these), educators, and students.

Other institutional influences on Navajo include some radio stations which allow Navajo broadcasts—most, however, only briefly and at odd hours (an exception, the Farmington, New Mexico station KNDN is entirely in Navajo, except the country music). One consistent supporter of the language is KTNN, the tribally owned 50,000-watt station. KTNN uses much Navajo, though sometimes it is criticized when its announcers are not as fluent as some listeners. Since 1989 many Diné College students have read their compositions over KTNN. Navajo language work has also been influenced by churches. Some have promulgated virulent anti-Navajo attitudes; others have hymnals in Navajo. The strong presence of the Native American Church, welcoming Navajo language, and of healing ceremonies by the traditional medicine men (over 1,000 of whom are practicing) are also pervasive influences.

A final key sociolinguistic factor is the diglossia of the Navajo community. An ever-increasing portion of Navajos are monolingual in English, the power language for most settings and functions (seldom is a memo, a resolution, or a sign written in Navajo), and there are few communities where Navajo is spoken everywhere. Of course, certain functions cannot be done in English, from the establishing of *k'é* (the stitching together of family and clan) to the conduct of traditional healing ceremonies. Yet many settings where Navajo dominance might be considered crucial have already become almost exclusively English. For example, the children of many Navajo language teachers do not speak Navajo; it is not spoken to them in the home.

DINÉ COLLEGE'S NAVAJO LANGUAGE PROGRAM

In this context the Navajo Language Program seeks to thrive at Diné College. Diné College was the first tribally controlled community college, federally established in 1968 by the Navajo Community College Act and chartered by the Navajo Nation. The Board of Regents is entirely Navajo. As mentioned before, the Diné College mission statement strongly charges it to focus on Navajo studies, and much has happened in 28 years. Diné College is notoriously poor, and the salaries it pays professors lag badly behind those of public school teachers. Further, the campuses are in rural, insular locations, sometimes creating social tension. Recent funding cuts have made intracollegiate politics rigorous. Thus, the issue of support for the Center for Diné Studies (housing the NLP) is a concrete issue of allocation of limited monies. There is no faculty tenure and little fat anywhere in the budget. Expanding one program often means shrinking (or abolishing) others, and factors of student load, transferability of courses, number and employability of graduates, and the college mission are carefully examined. Ambivalence about the worth of Navajo language study is quickly revealed in bold relief.

Many Navajos and others at Diné College have played roles developing the NLP. At one point (in November 1989) the college president hired three new full-time professors at once, creating positions others felt were more needed elsewhere. There have been recurring attempts to reduce the size of the NLP faculty, to use materials funds for other purposes, and to restrict course offerings. During the advising and scheduling process, some have acted upon sincere feelings that Navajo language classes are unimportant. Attempts by the NLP to put Navajo on an equal footing with English for the satisfaction of the communications portion of the college general requirements have been resisted fiercely. Attempts to install a stipend on Diné College salaries for those literate in

Navajo were rejected. Until the onset of Diné College's Diné Teacher Education Program (which began in the fall of 1996), no course outside the NLP had employed written Navajo much.

Yet dozens of people have promoted the NLP in meaningful ways. The Center for Diné Studies has had strong leadership from David Begay, Harry Walters, Herbert Benally, and Bernice Casaus. Personnel in Diné College community campus programs have often committed scarce resources. Poorly paid adjunct instructors and overworked bureaucrats have driven great distances to deliver instruction and support. Other parts of the college have contributed hardware and technical support, sharing of training opportunities, and supportive recruitment, scholarships, and advisement.

Clarification of program goals has been founded on several major precepts. First, the NLP is a language program, not a linguistics program. For limited purposes, a good analogy is that of English programs at universities. Those programs would never be headed by linguists, nor would they accept linguists' research and instructional goals. The highest goals of a language program are promotion of fluency, articulateness, literacy, and quality composition; the brightest and most energetic scholars and teachers and the most time must be focused here. In contrast to a linguistics program, a language program concerns itself more with poetry than phonology, more with culture than information science.

Of course the NLP has benefited from the insights of linguistics, especially Navajo linguistics. For example, in lexicology, morphology, and syntax, the Young and Morgan dictionaries provide Diné College with an entire course, our NAV 401, on dictionary use and on descriptive grammar. Here we have developed effective pedagogical grammar materials (a 20-page set of pedagogical grammar charts is available upon request) and homegrown methods. We cover the concept of paradigms, the elements of Athabaskan lexicography, parts of speech, some morphological analysis, and some morphophonemics. We have extracted from the detail of the Young and Morgan work usable and comprehensible classroom materials and then written materials and exercises to supplement Young and Morgan.

In phonology, phonemics, phonetics, and orthography, we use the work of Young (1968), Kari (1976), and others in our Navajo Linguistics (NAV 289) course to provide insights into the Navajo sound system and orthography. For ESL or NSL teachers, an understanding of articulatory phonetics and Navajo-English comparative phonemics is important. NAV 289 uses work by Yule (1985), Sapir (1975), Crystal (1980), and others both to introduce language majors and teachers to linguistics and to indicate applications. We also draw upon students' unique skills to point them toward groundbreaking work. For instance, our unit on discourse analysis (providing schoolteachers with tools for teaching effective oral and written composition) uses as its material for exercises the *Historical Selections* (1954) that Young and Morgan collected. Our present professors and students bring unique tools and knowledge to analysis of these texts, which should result in broadly applicable discoveries. The work in sociolinguistics, irreplaceable for budding Navajo language activists, is equally exciting.

One thrust of pedagogy that has lent us guidance, creativity, and rigor for our courses in writing (for native speakers), and in teacher training, is the whole-language movement. Its focus is on communicative pedagogies that integrate speaking, listening, reading, writing, and thinking into collaborative and individual projects that address real (as opposed to school-only) audiences. Many a class has read and discussed Goodman's *What's Whole in Whole Language* (1986), translating it into Navajo, analyzing concepts, and projecting applications. Goodman's work and that of colleagues such as Altwerger, Edelsky, and Flores (1987) has provided useful grounding for our course in how to teach Navajo to the native speaker (NAV 350). In this upper-level course students and teacher work, Freire-style, on rich, collaborative compositions. Initial products are often done on butcher paper. Follow-up products are word processed, and then desktop published, electronically published, or printed in local newspapers or journals. Our students at this level, mostly Navajo women, are mature and committed, and the whole-language concept allows the flow of a Navajo collaboration with a momentum not forced by normal school constraints.

Of course, no teaching ideology can be allowed to supersede the expertise and judgment of experienced teachers. Once Tony Goldtooth and I team-taught our eight Navajo Language Teaching endorsement classes throughout two summers, taking a cadre of 15 teachers (the first to get state endorsements for teaching Navajo) through these core courses. I insisted that from the first, in the reading and writing courses (NAV 211 and 212), we use entirely whole-language activities, eschewing Goldtooth's tried-and-true phonics coverage (and related practices such as dictation) for beginners. Thereafter, throughout their program, some students had difficulty with vowel tones, glottalized consonants, and other features of writing Navajo. I had been caught up in the controversy of whole language versus phonics. This type of foolishness we cannot afford. The work of Altwerger et al. (1987) provides guidance on how to see beyond such false oppositions.

The issue of publishing Navajo writing, that is, bringing forth Navajo literature, has been informed from many sources—on encouraging authorship, structuring collaboration such as peer editing (e.g., Kagan [see Brandt 1990]), and carrying out the mechanics of production. Especially useful has been Eliot Wigginton's work (1989). Wigginton's attention to detail shows in his descriptions of how to prepare students to become published authors. Much is directly transferable to the Navajo language classroom. An understanding of what was necessary for Wigginton's *Foxfire* books has enhanced our outlook on Navajo language teaching.

As a Navajo literature emerges, we concentrate on the interface between the oral and the literate. We turn to the treasure-house of mostly monolingual older speakers. It is not a simple matter to make the expertise of these people available. Though the college is owned and operated by Navajos, in the eyes of many, and in its ways of operating (both good and bad), it is still an anglicized institution, not sufficiently welcoming to the elders. Yet we have had some written materials available to us for years, such as the *Historical Selections, Áłchíní Bá hane'*, published by NAMDC; *Echo*, published by the Rock Point School; and audio materials recorded in the 1960s, known as the ONEO (Office of Navajo Economic Opportunity) tapes. We recently finished the Navajo Place Names Project, and the resulting multimedia and printed product, *Saadlátah Hózhóón*, has 53 lengthy narratives (edited audio and transcription) being used in our classes (more fully described below). The wealth of material in history, culture, herbology, animal care, traditional technology, ethics, and humor makes these texts central for us. We are investigating the interface between the audiences, structures, functions, and genres of advanced oral composition and those of the emerging literature. Years ago, clarifying the distinction between teaching transcription and teaching composition brought us forward. Now we must better conceptualize the guidance we can receive from the elders' language.

It is critical to orient ourselves to the elders. We hire storytellers and use elders as consultants throughout the Center for Diné Studies and in Diné College's Diné Educational Philosophy office. The elders are also an important audience to us. For example, the pieces that our students read over radio and publish in newspapers are often geared primarily to elders, as with one piece that explained to them what the Fourth of July was about. Someday perhaps the Navajo Nation will have soap operas (like those of the Yoruba of Nigeria) written in their native language.

Similar to whole-language in impact has been the concept of proficiency. We have especially benefited from work with foreign-language teachers. For them, the processes established by the American Council of Teachers of Foreign Languages (ACTFL) have provided a programmatic conceptual rigor, bringing the entire profession forward, in providing clear standards for placement, prescription, and achievement (cf. Omaggio 1986, 2–27, 444–49). In properly focusing Navajo language classes at Diné College, where almost all students are Navajos, the first hurdle is effective grouping of students. Students coming to us to "study Navajo" fall into at least four distinct groups. Group 1, the "rank beginners," is made of those Anglos who speak no Navajo, have never heard the language, and know nothing of Navajos. For them, foreign-language curriculum and pedagogy are appropriate (beginning with NAV 101). Here we take the high level of difficulty of Navajo fully into account in setting performance goals. Group 2 is those "Navajo beginners" who do not understand Navajo, yet have been raised hearing Navajo around them and are familiar with Navajo concerns, topics, and speech manners. We place this group in with the rank beginners starting with NAV 101, though often groups 1 and 2 are not congruent in needs. Group 3, the "latent speakers," is made up of those Navajos who understand much Navajo but do not speak. Many of these go into advanced nonspeaker courses at first, such as NAV 102 or 201. However, this large group (perhaps 20% of the total) really falls through the cracks of our system, since appropriate pedagogy and curriculum for them would be a language arts approach, not a foreign-language approach. Some of these students immediately enter our speaker track courses, jumping in at NAV 211. Group 4, the "fluent speakers," take courses taught entirely in Navajo, focusing (in NAV 211, 212, and 301) on learning to read and write with accuracy and fluency (for speakers, accurate and fluent literacy is a prerequisite to all higher courses).

Placement is not an exact science, nor is it a one-shot evaluation, and we get students with characteristics in more than one group. This is owing partly to the emotional climate in which students are learning. Some rank beginners are immediately frustrated. Navajo beginners have normally suffered an approbation, when among Navajos, equal to that suffered by those with nonstandard English. Those latent speakers who have lived mainly among whites may have unconsciously masked their Navajoness for so long that they cannot reclaim it easily. For latent speakers and Navajo beginners, effective learning requires a shift in active procedures of self-identification. Even fluent speakers, for whom satisfying progress is perhaps most quickly available, find themselves in a new social role, wherein they are prized as students for speaking Navajo. Each group has a unique set of affective filters to work through, and each student has a personal background and personal resources that may affect this strongly. Some Navajo beginners have been often criticized, others not. Some Anglos are from the west and have extensive experience with Navajos and other Native Americans. Other rank beginners and Navajo beginners will not learn to comprehend much but will readily learn accurate transcription and phoneme/grapheme word-calling. Occasionally we get a speaker of an Apache or other Athabaskan language, which is a tremendous head start. Some fluent speakers have already had literacy work elsewhere and are placed forward in the speaker-track program. Some fluent speakers are not particularly articulate or talkative; others are glib, and others eloquent. Appropriate pedagogy takes all of these factors into account; evaluation must be ongoing. Sometimes we jump a student from one track to another, set a student back, or even suggest that a student repeat a course that he or she has already passed. One thing our professors never lose sight of is that a strongly motivated student must be given every opportunity. Several young people whom we would have labeled Navajo beginners turned out to be latent speakers and have become fluent, articulate, and literate in Navajo, to everyone's satisfaction.

One factor that has continually upgraded our efforts in proficiency evaluation, standards, and placement has been that we constantly train Navajo language teachers (mainly in our NAV 350 and NAV 351 classes), preparing them to make their own multifaceted proficiency assessment. Here the students design and try out instruments for proficiency assessment. We have benefited from supervising and evaluating dozens of excellent projects of this type.

THE COURSES

The Navajo Language Program has 13 active courses (the syllabi themselves, for all courses, are available on request) arranged in a two-track system, separating speakers from nonspeakers. Of the 600 students (99% Navajo) taking courses in any one semester, three-quarters speak Navajo or at least understand. We have taught these courses now many dozens of times.

The four courses for nonnative speakers of Navajo are NAV 101, 102, 201, and 202. Here we are teaching Navajo as a second (or foreign) language, using second-language pedagogy and curriculum. We have interacted with other foreign-language teachers and have studied and applied their methodology. Our NSL instruction is also strengthened by the fact that our professors teach NAV 351, the methods course for aspiring NSL teachers.

The development of NSL curriculum is a bootstrap phenomenon, and though there are now published materials, and many individual teachers with their own cache of constructed and collected curriculum, much remains to be done. Recently Martha Austin, Tony Goldtooth, and I have worked with Andrew Becenti, Lorraine Manavi, and others on new revisions of *Diné Bizaad Bóhoo'aah* (1995), published by Navajo Preparatory School. The inter-institutional collaboration that has upgraded these NSL materials is the kind of work by a Core Forum that should continue. Our NSL curriculum principles are eclectic. The curriculum is functionally based; students learn to accomplish greetings and introductions (using the kinship system), give descriptions and directions, express time and quantity, buy and sell, navigate circumstances of eating and cooking, name common objects and places, work in concrete collaborative and common "survival" situations, inquire of others about the language, and discuss common subjects. Some grammar is taught—students learn to use structures such as negativizers, plurals, the simpler neuter verbs, the question makers, many types of pronouns, the time and space enclitics, and paradigms of the common active verbs in their most common inflectional realizations. Much remains to be done for construction of effective NSL curriculum, however. Work currently underway by Wayne Holm, Laura Wallace, and Irene Silentman, on immersion curriculum for Head Start centers, should provide insights even for a college program, as will work recently finished by Robert Young detailing the paradigmatic regularities of verb derivation.

Construction of Diné College's syllabi has taken years of group input to discover what is doable and well sequenced. The collaborative process by which the faculty has composed, criticized, and constantly revised syllabi has nurtured the Core Forum. Our professors must travel great distances to collaborate, and all are individuals with unique backgrounds and motivations (e.g., some are Christians, some traditionalists). Focused activities such as the revision of curriculum help us set aside differences. Issues of sequencing and prerequisites, scheduling, staffing, standards, and input from public school teachers are dealt with here.

Navajo is a language so radically different from the Indo-European languages that much of the curriculum and some of the principles used for teaching the other languages are not applicable here without significant alteration. No true nonspeaker learns Navajo well by taking only these courses, but students who take all four courses can advance into the lower intermediate levels (where one can accomplish limited functions though still not converse at any length).

We have also added what we refer to as a community language practicum, created mainly by Martha Austin and Lorene Legah. For NAV 102, 201, and 202 (the last three nonspeaker-track courses), all students negotiate with the instructor a field-based portion. Depending on the course, each student spends from 15 to 45 hours acquiring Navajo by using it in the community. Credit for these courses is 4 semester hours; the practicum time is considered lab credit. At the semester's beginning, the student works with the professor negotiating an individual practicum contract. For example, our NAV 201 students spend 30 hours in practicums. One-third of this time is spent attending public functions that are in Navajo, such as chapter-house meetings, traditional ceremonies, or church services. One-third is spent in cooperative work activities carried out in Navajo, such as working with college kitchen staff or helping at monolinguals' homes. The final third is spent in one-on-one conversation with a fluent speaker. Here, our first priority, since our students are Navajos, is to hook them up with an older relative willing to "invite them into the club of Navajo speakers" and begin the nurturing process that a new speaker must go through. Where this is not available, a tutor is assigned. For all parts of the community practicum, evaluation is done by having students compose and deliver oral reports to the class.

We are using these contracts in this way because of a couple of noticeable characteristics of how Diné College's second-language teaching must work. As a field, the teaching of foreign languages has within its name a problematic element: the word "foreign." To maximize language acquisition, good second-language teachers match classroom content and method with "real-world" factors for which they are preparing students. In classrooms, the communicative activities used for instruction and evaluation are similar to or identical with one another and are informed in detailed and creative ways by the communicative activities of the real world. Yet for foreign-language teachers the real world is, by definition, far away and therefore not available for teacher or student to examine and experience. The real world where the foreign language is used is dynamic, multifaceted, and difficult to model effectively in a classroom. Thus, for a teacher to fit curriculum to the real world, and for a language learner to come to be able to deal with it, much focused and energetic attention to detail is exercised. Yet the object is simply not there for examination—it is far away.

For some foreign-language teachers, and for Diné College, a solution is at hand. For teachers working with a language that is not truly foreign, a language for which there is a local group of speakers, the tools are available. This is the situation for many Spanish teachers, and sometimes for teachers of other languages. It is often true for teachers of U.S. indigenous languages, languages that are not at all foreign, and even less foreign than English. In the case of Navajo, people are on their traditional land, and the language has been here far longer than English. The design of language acquisition processes must directly take these resources into account. Thus, although in teaching nonspeakers we take a foreign-language approach, we keep in mind that Navajo is not a foreign language for our students. It is a local language, available not only right outside the classroom door (office workers and maintenance personnel at Diné College speak Navajo fluently), but even in students' homes and extended families. Thus there are resources available for teaching Navajo that teachers of truly foreign languages have to send students abroad to get access to. This factor points out concretely what our task in NSL for Navajo students is. These students do not speak Navajo because its use was not required of them in the home or extended family, even though there were always Navajo speakers present. When these children did not acquire Navajo, a rift developed in Navajo society, mainly a generational rift (though a town-and-country rift as well).

In conversing, people perform their most social function, and when they stop conversing, social distance increases. The social process of language exists not so much within heads as in the negotiated social space between mouths and ears. Language is both the glue and the content of social networks. Each person has an idiosyncratic way of being "raised into" each new social network he or she encounters, a way that becomes this person's idiolect. This idiolect comes into being only in the real world where language is exercised. For our students, the learning of Navajo is a mending of the rift in Navajo society. More often than not, when our students exercise the community language practicum contracts, they find themselves working with their own elders, learning from them. Having students work with these people can and should be more important than classwork, with implications both for Navajo society and for the student's long-term language learning. Further, this activity brings something from the college to the community of speakers, since it often involves students' reading stories and other texts to elders (thereby expanding the audience for literature) and bringing the elders' ideas into the Core Forum.

A final issue of importance for addressing the strengths and weaknesses of our nonspeaker track is its use by latent speakers. We often get students who understand much Navajo, but, for reasons of either reluctance to risk ridicule or lack of use of Navajo in their most common environment (perhaps they have lived off-reservation for years), lack the confidence or competence for the introductory speaker-track course (NAV 211). These students often go to our NAV 102 or 201 classes to enhance fluency before concentrating on literacy. However, their needs are not the same as those of second- and third-semester rank beginners, and we should develop courses in Navajo language arts that are better designed for them.

Now we will examine our speaker-track courses. Our courses for Navajo speakers start with the literacy and composition courses, NAV 211, 212, and 301. We teach them to about 300 students per semester. NAV 211 covers phonics instruction with some writing in simple genres, group work on a language experience model, structured oral interactions, and reading. NAV 212 is more functionally oriented, mainly with whole-language activities, and students also get some grammar. In NAV 301 students advance to write compositions in Navajo, mainly narrative and description. Each student reads his or her most advanced work over KTNN or has it published in the *Navajo Times*. In these courses, which are centered on writing, we often have taught our students to word process in Navajo, an instructional task that should be borne by our word-processing teachers (in Diné College's business department). It is an indispensable skill, in this era of desktop publishing, for optimizing the impact of each Navajo language teacher.

Much effort has gone into selecting reading material for these three literacy courses so that it is readable, accurate, and on-target. These popular courses are most important for the eventual emergence of a Navajo literature. In the future, we will move away from teaching basic literacy as the elementary and secondary schools improve, but for now most students coming to us have no Navajo literacy. Students finishing NAV 301 must write a well-organized 300-word descriptive composition in Navajo in a two-hour period, with more than 70% of their words spelled perfectly.

Next, students in our AA degree program in Navajo language take our Navajo Linguistics course, NAV 289 (described above), our Navajo Grammar course, NAV 401 (also see above), and an upper-level Navajo culture course, NIS 371 (Navajo Philosophy), in which they must write their papers in Navajo. Then students who wish to get Arizona and New Mexico state endorsements for teaching Navajo must take two 4-semester-hour courses: NAV 350 (Teaching Navajo to the Native Speaker) and NAV 351 (Teaching Navajo as a Second Language). These two courses include teaching practicums. In both courses we have some students who will teach in high schools and others who will teach kindergarten, or even Head Start. Frankly, this is problematic, but we have not yet had the resources for more than one track.

In NAV 350 we help prospective Navajo language teachers enhance the growing literacy movement in Navajo. Here they learn to teach children who already speak Navajo (or at least understand it) to read and write. Those thousands of children in the schools who are learning to read and write Navajo will create the Navajo literature.

In NAV 350 and NAV 351 we have often overreached, not having enough coordinated support from education classes being taught at Diné College or other institutions. Yet it will continue to be necessary to show students the road from theory to application in Navajo. For example, we cover concepts of curriculum construction, making our students conversant with each major facet of a successful Navajo language curriculum. Here students get experience constructing scope and sequence curriculum from the points of view of functions (see Omaggio 1986, 444–49), topics, settings, genres, interlocutors, grammar, and vocabulary. As mentioned above, students also do extensive work in units on proficiency, whole language, the interface between literacy and orality, the use of existing Navajo language materials (each student here produces two pieces of children's literature), the sociolinguistics of the Navajo Nation (also covered in our Navajo Linguistics course), and, most importantly, teaching methodology.

Any one of these areas, particularly pedagogy, could easily constitute its own course. We introduce teachers to varied teaching methods, some of which they exercise in practicums: videotaping, oral skills activities such as storytelling or giving directions, phonics, journals and diaries, book publishing, literature study, thematic units, interviews, peer tutoring and peer editing, response writing, drama, letters and notes within classroom functions, autobiography, and use of literacy skills in nonschool settings such as clinics, courts, chapter houses, the home, and radio. With selected areas, students are required to carry out lesson plans in practicums.

In NAV 351 we prepare teachers to deal with students who speak and understand little or no Navajo. Here teachers are helping children to regain their birthright, access to the treasure-house of the language. Though most Diné College students speak Navajo, a majority of today's Navajo children do not. In preparing teachers for this clientele, we have a major task.

Some NAV 350 material is useful in 351, for example, concepts of proficiency and information on sociolinguistics, and we cover complementary ground. Other units cover principles of second-language learning (including work on the nature of the learner), NSL curriculum development principles (including exposure to FLES [Foreign Language in the Elementary School], FLEM [Foreign Language Elementary Immersion], and FLEX [Foreign Language Elementary Exposure] programs), and NSL methods and materials. Again, the methods unit is our focus, with work on total physical response, community language learning, the Silent Way, the Lozanov method, teaching through music, role playing, games, the Natural Approach, and language immersion. Students again produce literature (for nonnative speakers) and construct lesson plans for practicums.

The practicum elements of these two courses are still inadequate. We do not have fully adequate student teacher setups. At present we require, for each course (350 and 351), 22½ hours of practice. Often in the summers local school districts have collaborated with us to conduct exemplary schools on teaching Navajo. Here our student teachers have usually organized curriculum around the concept of settings, with individual classrooms using the Navajo appropriate to hogans (or houses), stock care settings, stores, farms (or gardens), recreation, and the like. We have rotated groups of children through these settings, the organization of groups being based on whether the children are rank beginners, latent speakers, or fluent speakers. Student teachers have been rotated through settings and required to use lesson plans in various topic areas and with all types of students. Other practicum situations have been more ad hoc, and less effective.

NAV 350 and NAV 351 are taught in Navajo, and the students write only in Navajo. Here Diné College students begin to exercise their literacy for many purposes and to write for real purposes to real audiences associated with work in schools. These prospective teachers compose literature for children, lesson plans for practicums, and Navajo summaries of articles read in English. This is done both with individual assignments and with group writing.

The amount of group writing done in these courses is central to the development of Navajo literature and to the nurturing of the Core Forum. In group writing activities students exercise a critical appraisal of written Navajo, as authors, as editors, as audiences, and from other perspectives. Here we are initially using a language experience model, with the felt-tip marker in the hand of the professor, and then graduating to group writing activities, where students rotate through various Kagan (see Brandt 1990) roles such as recorder, editor, spokesperson, devil's advocate, taskmaster, and gopher. We also graduate in activities from transcription to composition. The overriding concept here derives from Freire's work, where the tools of literacy are used by a community to remap the world, to reconceive the dynamics of the community. Most students who advance to our upper-level courses (we normally have about 200 students per semester in nonintroductory speaker-track courses) are mature adults,

mainly women, many in mid-career. Thus, the level of discourse and the projected functions and audiences for the products are always well thought out and valuable. For many, participation in a college forum of all Navajos, only in Navajo, is a new and liberating experience, one that powerfully nurtures our Core Forum.

CERTIFICATION, TRANSFERABILITY, EMPLOYABILITY, AND ACCREDITATION

These eight teacher endorsement courses (including NIS 371, Navajo Philosophy) are our program centerpiece. (Two other courses, NAV 231, Navajo Medical Terminology, and NAV 478, The Athabaskan Roots of Navajo, are at the developing edges of new program thrusts in translating and interpreting and comparative linguistics.) Much administrative work went into convincing state Departments of Education to accept the eight endorsement courses to satisfy state competency requirements. For Diné College to offer courses at the junior and senior levels (300- and 400-level courses), it was also necessary and ultimately useful to alter Diné College's accreditation status with the North Central Association. Finally, the development effort has required that we spend years constructing, improving, and maintaining the courses, including ongoing cycles of review, rewrite, and distribution to distant sites. Each instructor and site has had to learn to teach them well and to find materials, standards, and appropriate pedagogy. The acquisition of books and machines, the recruiting and funding of students (often with significant tribal support), and myriad other issues were part of this effort.

The application of these courses to official teacher certification, with the Arizona and New Mexico Departments of Education (the state of Utah has trailed in this area), has had political, technical, and bureaucratic elements. The establishment of new endorsements, in our heavily "certified" society, is appropriately the object of careful scrutiny, and bowing to the authority of state Departments of Education for the certification of Navajo language teachers is not a small matter. Yet it is state certification that constrains the hiring practices of public schools on the Navajo Nation, not a tribal imprimatur, and access to jobs is a priority issue for prospective Navajo language teachers. For establishing endorsements in New Mexico and Arizona, two different routes were followed. For New Mexico, the argument was made that Navajo language teachers should be certified just as are foreign-language teachers. Thus, within the "Modern Language Teaching" endorsements, a route was established for Navajo. The problem with this approach is that Navajo is not a foreign language. Allowing it to be grouped with the foreign languages can be a concession to leaving it permanently as a secondary or ignored part of public school curriculum. Yet the Navajo endorsement retains its own character, with the competencies list that must be demonstrated for it being unique to Navajo—for example, in its emphasis on the fact that many of a Navajo language teacher's students will be speakers of Navajo.

The route followed for Arizona was to first establish a "Bilingual Endorsement" for the entire state, the argument being that many Arizona schoolchildren are bilingual and bicultural, and that teachers must be well prepared to work effectively with them. Later, we worked through the state Department of Education to have them accept our Navajo language teacher training courses to qualify a teacher for the Arizona bilingual endorsement. (This designation for Navajo language teachers is flawed and may prove to be dangerously inaccurate. The situation in New Mexico, in which a bilingual endorsement is distinct from a language teaching endorsement, is better.) In Arizona, as in New Mexico, the process of argumentation was to cross-index the syllabi of Diné College's courses to the skills lists of state school board regulations. The promotion of Navajo will always be partly political, and an understanding of the legislative and regulatory framework must be kept up to date. Care must be taken, however, that the states' lists do not become a driving element in syllabus construction, since the lists reflect little or no expertise in indigenous languages.

Another central player in certification issues is tribal government. Navajo tribal government has had limited final authority over teacher certification. Just as with school curriculum, standardized testing, and other mechanisms of centralized control and supervision, power comes with holding the purse strings, and most taxing and spending authority is with the state governments. Yet the Navajo government has exercised authority in several ways. Three have impacted Navajo language matters: (1) the tribe administers an extensive scholarship program, and has targeted monies well on Navajo language teacher certification; (2) cooperating with the states, the tribe conducts language proficiency testing, certifying the oral and literacy proficiency of aspiring Navajo language teachers. This is important and provides the tribe with the opportunity to reject those who would call themselves bilingual or native language teachers but who cannot speak, read, and write the language; (3) the Navajo Nation Tribal Council has passed official tribal policy stating, "The Navajo language is an essential element of the life, culture, and identity of the Navajo people. The Navajo Nation recognizes the importance of preserving and perpetuating that language to the survival of the Nation. Instruction in the Navajo language shall be made available for all grade levels in all schools serving the Navajo Nation. Navajo language instruction shall include to the greatest extent practicable: thinking, speaking, comprehension, reading and writing skills and study of the formal grammar of the language." Although the tribe has limited purse-string power to enforce this policy, it has provided support for the language in many venues.

Certification is important: it leads to jobs. We would be doing students, and the Navajo Nation, a great disservice if we were to lure students into courses providing no job skills. We have retained a well-organized database of students and have used it to help school administrators find good teachers. Further, we work with language activists in school administrations and boards so that those with advanced skills are rewarded on pay scales, per course, per endorsement, or in some other way. This work requires that we assertively call, write, and travel to meetings with school officials, promoting Navajo in their systems.

Schools do not provide the only jobs for Navajos with demonstrable language skills. In the tribal, federal, and state courts there has been progress recently toward assuring that interpreters are qualified. In media work, whether with television, radio, or newspapers, people with skills are often overwhelmed with demands that they exercise them broadly. Other fields in which Navajo language skills are useful include medical interpreting, entertainment, police work, and any business that has Navajo bilingual or monolingual clients. Our program has not directly addressed these community and job needs, but there is opportunity for growth.

A further concern in stabilizing the program has been transferability of courses. Students at Diné College often expect to finish a degree elsewhere, without wasting precious time and funding. It would be irresponsible to not articulate our program well with other colleges. Many Navajos have hundreds of hours of college credit, but no degree. To avoid this, we have entered into extensive transferability agreements with colleges across the southwest. This is an ongoing bureaucratic, technical, and political task. Transferability of courses must be established and then protected. Arizona has a well-organized state process. In the other states it must be done on an institution-by-institution basis. Some colleges have a few courses similar to ours and can evaluate some syllabi or grant credit for satisfying their foreign-language requirement. Others have degree programs such as speech and hearing science, linguistics, or anthropology where advanced Navajo language skills can be used. Often it is easier to get another college to agree to accept courses if they get something. For example, four other colleges who participate in the Navajo Nation effort to certify Navajo teachers were willing to accept five required Diné College Navajo language classes for their tribally funded students, since scholarships and other funding were in place. Yet making this agreement permanent, beyond the scholarship funding period for the project, was difficult with three of them. In another case, a university was willing to grant useful credit, but only if Diné College would help with the testing of those who wanted to get credit by examination at the university site.

The transferability issue is central to the overall question of authority and legitimacy in Navajo language work. In terms of power and voice, a disparate relationship exists. It is of little consequence to a large university if a tribal college does not accept their courses, but to the tribal college, especially if it does not grant the bachelor's degree, transferability is crucial. Thus, even in a field where the preponderance of knowledge and interest in a language is at the tribal college, the universities to which students will be transferring hold an unearned amount of relative power to grant academic credit. Often at Diné College we have waited, sometimes for years and often in vain, for insufficiently knowledgeable professors and bureaucrats at distant colleges to come to decisions that affect the academic careers of Navajo students and the viability of the NLP.

Accreditation is similar. Diné College's accrediting agency is the North Central Association (NCA), which examines and accredits most postsecondary institutions in the Southwest. Only with difficulty can colleges can operate without their imprimatur. In 1987, all of Diné College's courses were freshman (100-level) and sophomore (200-level) courses. As the NLP expanded, it became necessary to offer courses at the 300 (junior) and 400 (senior) levels. For this we had to have NCA approval, requiring documentation of qualifications of instructors, rigor of syllabi, centrality of the program to the college mission, availability of resources, transferability of courses, employability of graduates, and the like. These requests were generally reasonable, and the process was useful in its structuring of our self-examination. It compelled the institution to focus its resources appropriately. The result was that Diné College's letter of affiliation with the NCA was altered to show the Navajo Language Program as accredited to offer courses at the junior and senior levels. We still could not offer a bachelor's degree—nor did we want to, since there were as yet no clear employment opportunities for graduates of such a program.

Though our experience with the NCA did prove to be positive, this supervisory structure could be perilous for work with Native American languages. The authority lies with people not knowledgeable about native languages, or the needs and desires of native communities. Their decisions can be momentous for language programs and their beneficiaries. Though theirs is a role that probably must be filled, it should be exercised by individuals who know about indigenous people and languages.

RESEARCH AND MATERIALS

Community colleges have seldom considered research to be primary. Professors teach five courses per semester (as opposed to three in most universities) and normally have no release time for research or writing. With exceptions, tribal colleges have followed this model. Yet, in the native studies departments this is problematic. The voluminous material about Navajos has mostly been produced by non-Navajos, in English, for non-Navajo purposes (such as the drive for tenure or self-promotion in the marketplace of "Indian experts"), and for a wealthier non-Navajo audience. Though Native Americans are the world's most-studied people, the materi-

als produced by the anthropology and linguistics industries are often only marginally useful here, where both professor and students are members of the group being studied. Thus, ongoing research and curriculum development have been necessary and are crucial for nurturing the Core Forum.

Within the NLP, there have been dozens of research and curriculum development projects. They have produced classroom materials, books, and electronic materials for Diné College or wider audiences and have investigated community needs and recorded traditional knowledge. Though it is a struggle to get research funded and authorized (even with soft money) in an impoverished tribal college, research and curriculum development (along with teaching) are the lifeblood of the Core Forum.

Much is needed for the schools. All Navajo language teachers struggle with immense demands put upon them for unusual and often unappreciated expertise and persistence. Many schools with administrators who know little of Navajo expect Navajo language teachers to write their entire curriculum, from scratch. Thus, where Navajos have constructed quality, well-targeted curricular materials, literature, and other compositions of Navajo knowledge, something of lasting value has been created. Some of this research is ethnographic, some analytical. A good example is a project now being run (by Wayne Holm, Irene Silentman, and Laura Wallace) within the Navajo Nation government that combines analytic and ethnographic work. This project is working to establish the pragmatics, vocabulary, and use of the inflectional and derivational system of Navajo for constructing an immersion curriculum for Navajo Head Start centers. The data being analyzed come from real Navajo language use in Head Start centers. The analysis will be used for the construction of an effective language-acquisition curriculum for immersion programs in the centers.

Many other projects combining research, technical advances, and curriculum development are pursued. Several issues must be addressed. For effective production of written materials, and for teaching of and through Navajo in schools (an activity that should, in short order, create a community of scholars that can excel at investigating the language), there are many ongoing needs for effective computer tools. For example:

(1) A good Navajo spell-checker would give a boost to the emergence of Navajo literature.
(2) We need a Navajo speech synthesis application through which students could type in a word and listen to its pronunciation. Perhaps the same project could have speech recognition applications.
(3) An online Navajo-English dictionary would be useful for a number of tasks and settings. This work was begun at Diné College in the summer of 1996. The Young, Morgan, and Midgette *Analytical Lexicon of Navajo* was experimentally made available, with search tools, on a Web page. It performed some functions ideal in a com-

puterized lexicon tool for Navajo but suffered from the lack of an HTML Navajo font.

(4) In general, the font problem has haunted Navajo typing and publishing. For example, though there are, thanks to Garth Wilson and Lennox Morey, almost two dozen critiqued and polished Navajo fonts for Macintoshes, of the two or three present Navajo fonts on IBM-PC compatible computers all have drawbacks and lack compatibility. Over the years, people at Diné College and elsewhere have produced Navajo font solutions for Digital Rainbow computers, Apple IIe computers, IBM-compatibles, and others. All have been useful, though various Macintosh solutions have been most used. Issues such as standardization of keyboard layout and ASCII assignment are crucial to cross-platform use of materials and development of fluent and accurate word-processing skills in students. Diné College has promoted collaboration on these issues, but with insufficient headway.

Another future direction is that of organizing collaboration between Apaches and Navajos on Southern Athabaskan. At present, the annual Athabaskan Language Conference attracts mainly linguists who are not Athabaskans and thus addresses mainly their goals. When pan-Athabaskan collaboration, and specifically work on Apache, is carried out by well-qualified Athabaskans, for Athabaskan purposes, in Athabaskan languages, and for Athabaskan audiences, the quality, depth, and permanence of the work will exceed that of other paradigms. Across the southwest, Apache peoples have relatively good access to one another, the languages are relatively co-intelligible, and many tasks that communities of speakers will want to undertake may be similar. If academic and economic resources were available, skilled people would commit their careers to this advanced intellectual work. Such analytical and creative work, pursued within a Core Forum of Athabaskans whose work overlaps into other projects such as coinage, grammatical work, or cultural studies, would make the entire field of Athabaskan studies more energetic and rigorous.

There is other badly needed work that might be considered too technical, pedagogical, "applied," or politically aggressive for academia to undertake. For instance, there is a need for coinage and elaboration work in election terminology, medical interpreting, courtroom interpreting, and other professional areas. Such direct work on the Navajo lexicon must be collaborative and thus based in extensive oral critical interplay. It can only be done within, and to the benefit of, the Core Forum. Other areas are less technical and more conceptual, or even political. For example, it is time that we lay to rest, permanently, the misconceptions that plague the development of quality Navajo language and bilingual education programs. One is that of the "alingual" or "semilingual" child, an idea that perpetuates the use of the deficit models for content and pedagogy that are so deadly for Navajo chil-

dren. A related difficulty is the confusion that surrounds efforts to both maintain and re-establish English submersion programs, disguised as "sheltered English" programs. As elsewhere, it unclear whether the work to be done is more the discovery of new knowledge or simply political and persuasive work; however, in part this issue relates to that of who the audience for research will be.

The most important challenge is that of the demise of Navajo. Though there is as yet not a well-organized Navajo language movement working to reverse language shift, momentum is building; but as Fishman shows, even massive resources can be wasted. Success depends upon a mature understanding of the social and grammatical processes to be addressed. In *Reversing Language Shift* (1991), Fishman posits that the minimal nexus for retention of a language is home-family-neighborhood-community. Each of these four terms, and especially the latter two, has a unique character in Navajo that must be well described prior to any active social engineering. This work can only be effectively done by Navajos, at a Navajo college, over years. This is not to say that a Navajo language preservation movement would have nothing to learn from other movements, such as those of Yoruba, Hausa, Igbo, Vietnamese, and Māori. Relatively successful movements, such as those involving Catalan or Hebrew, should be investigated, as well as those which have spent resources to limited avail, such as Irish. Each endangered language is unique; each struggle, whether it results in loss or victory, is essentially local. Yet Navajo will learn much from Guarani, Hawaii, and Quechua, and contribute to Aymara, Jicarilla, Otomí, and Basque.

Important language perpetuation work must be done in data gathering about present status and structure. (The work recently done by Platero [1992] is useful, but it must be expanded and deepened.) Data must measure fluency and articulateness across ages, locations, topics and functions, and so on, and be reported in a useful way to those who can impact the health of the language at Fishman's home-family-neighborhood-community nexus, and at other sites as well (e.g., schools). Criteria have been identified for measuring language death; we must apply these to accurate Navajo data, both for descriptive and prescriptive reasons. Such work will have the integrated rhetorical, research, planning, and praxis goals of overcoming denial about the present state of Navajo.

Schools (including Diné College) play a role in the reversal of language shift by producing Navajo literature. In part, this should involve the retranscription (into standard orthography) and republishing of materials such as Washington Matthews's *Navajo Legends*, Sapir's *Navajo Texts*, the texts of Berard Haile, and the varied materials at the Wheelwright Museum at Berkeley and in the Doris Duke Collection at the University of New Mexico Library. A similar task will be transcription of the hundreds of ONEO tapes and the ethnomedical work done by Martha Austin-Garrison and Oswald Werner. A different, and finally larger, role will be that of publisher of all sorts of Navajo literature being written. These tasks may at first appear to be pedestrian, even mechanical, and unworthy of the label "research." In fact, the skills and knowledge required for this work, and the impact on the Core Forum, will be substantial.

The process of gathering, organizing, and using effective materials is ongoing. The issues of (1) security of materials and (2) making appropriate materials accessible imbue this work with a certain tension. To repeat, the appropriate materials for a post-secondary indigenous-language program at a tribal college address an audience that is Navajo, and that has well-grounded knowledge and opinions about and interest in these subjects. Quality materials for an audience that is Navajo and is addressing a Navajo audience in Navajo, though they exist, are scarce, and the outside marketplace will not bring a volume of products here. Some few things are available, produced by the now-defunct Navajo Reading Study, the Rough Rock Press, Rock Point School, the Native American Materials Development Center, the Navajo Academy, the *Journal of Navajo Education,* and others.

Scarcity of materials is problematic for Navajo language programs in all schools. One difficult problem is that of copyright. Of course, market forces will not provide materials produced for profit without copyright protection. Yet often advances in Navajo language school program development are slowed when materials go out of print. However, when there are Navajo students hungry to use materials that in many cases were elicited from elders no longer living, it can be galling to encounter a legal morass denying access. Perhaps someday the Navajo Nation government will alleviate this difficulty legislatively. Sharing must become the rule, not the exception.

Many other issues exist: fitting materials into syllabi and prescribed student activities, avoiding over-legitimizing published materials while ignoring oral and local knowledge, setting up and using difficult lending and filing procedures, wrestling with what level of resources to commit to your own publishing efforts, and drawing the distinction between instructional and archive materials. Orienting a post-secondary indigenous-language program toward a dependence upon and permanence in written and recorded materials is a task fraught with difficulty. Many fine instructors turn effectively to oral and local resources, and appropriately so (though the NLP at Diné College has not yet effectively integrated the language and narrative expertise of our Navajo culture instructors into Navajo language classes). Yet program permanence must transcend the knowledge and social networks of single individuals, and courses of study will be maximally effective only if they can be distributed for use to other sites and instructors and used as templates for related work.

The sharing and distributing of materials present ongoing problems. Those with usable materials locally are often wary about sharing them generally. Their reasons are understandable: materials may be misused or mistreated, credit for authorship may be stolen, and one's job security can be threatened if one's skills are matched by others'. However, the processes of creation, polishing, and distribution of local expertise are at the heart of nurturing the Core Forum. At Diné College we have worked, with some success, on providing resources and building the trust and critical interplay necessary for effective sharing.

A recent curriculum and literature development project was the Navajo Place Names Project, Saadlátah Hózhóón. We interviewed elders about the names of 53 places, the etymologies of those names, and personal and historical events that occurred there. We then integrated audio, transcribed text, maps, photos, and composed analytical text (all in Navajo) into a multimedia computer product, now being used with Navajo speakers on the Navajo Nation.

This advanced our overall goals. Through it we tied language to land, illuminating and enhancing their relationship. Further, we interfaced oral and written compositions, using texts of an authentically Navajo nature elicited from the most articulate speakers of Navajo, bringing these texts to a knowledgeable, critical audience. These texts, in Navajo, by Navajos, for a Navajo audience, now provide indispensable ground for continuing to form the first well-established Native American literature, in Navajo. Integral to this process has been the legitimization of Navajo names and Navajo stories as they live in this land, which has been a creative exercise in Navajo sovereignty. Finally, the project has helped to lower the walls (and fences) between school and community that plague the Navajo educational circumstance, by opening our doors to expert community voices. The maintenance and enhancement of Navajo are central elements of nurturing the intergenerational and horizontal Navajo social fabric. With this project, Navajo children and adults continue to hear from elders.

In the project, school activities have been added, through which students most often conduct community research. The narratives provide our students the inspiration to write about and discuss issues, events, opinions, and values of the interviewees. The curricular result is broad in terms of student products, such as poems, essays, stories, and scripts reflecting the lives and heritage of our students. The narratives reflect the social reality of the Navajo world which, when expressed in Navajo, has important elements that have been excluded historically from schools, such as the K'é system, through which one carries out social responsibilities and expresses respect and intimacy.

The 5- to 20-minute texts we elicited were of many types. In some, the interviewees' main intention was storytelling. Others spoke to younger Navajos directly, extolling them to follow their traditional teachings. Some interviewees spoke against a background of concern for their own property use interests, detailing the litany of their existence on the land. All used the land as a mnemonic device, revealing a topography of the mind. Interwoven in the texts is a history of the last 150 years in the northeast corner of the Navajo Nation. Only recently have Navajos fully entered the industrial age, with concomitant changes in the economy, family, values, and community. This project strengthens a continuity that is hard to come by.

Gathering and using machines in the NLP has been its own developmental effort, impacting the language, the teachers, the students, and even the culture substantially; there are opportunities, but also dangers of abuse and waste. We have wrestled with funding, placing, and scheduling video cameras, audio and video recorders of various qualities, transcribers, cameras, photocopiers, bookbinding machines, VCRs and televisions, high-speed tape copiers, and all sorts of lower-level tools from paper punches and paper cutters to reel-to-reel recorders and 16mm projectors. Some decisions have been driven by function, some by availability of funds, some by fascination with the next toy.

There has been a similar eclectic mix to using computer tools. For functions, word processing (of everything) and databases (of medicine men, students, archive materials, and even a Hypercard stack of phonemes, sounds, and culture) have led the way. However, fax machines and modem-fax, scanners, computer projectors for classroom use, and a multitude of software applications, from sound editing to Web pages, graphics manipulation, optical character recognition, and multimedia construction have all stumbled, glided, or roared through our program. They have sometimes enabled us, often frustrated us to distraction, and occasionally mesmerized us, keeping us from more important tasks.

PROFESSIONAL DEVELOPMENT

Central to the internal quality of the Core Forum is our commitment to our own professional development. To carry out innovative projects and processes, we have sometimes made ourselves into unique instruments of those processes. Though there was no outside institution that could train us, we received some support from Goddard College in Vermont (through its offering of a master's program to our instructors) and the University of New Mexico (especially through the LSA's Summer Institute in 1995). The most useful activities for us have been on-site courses and workshops, using local expertise or invited scholars. Professional development projects have extended from two days to five months, on topics as varied as pedagogy, phonology, phonetics, comparative Athabaskan work, lexicology, desktop publishing, word processing, and reversing language shift. On-site activities have resulted in rooted and permanently useful growth in our courses, growth that comes from theory challenged by practice, with authority from elsewhere being required to meet standards dictated by local needs. The process is not without problems. The transition from coworker, professor, or supervisor to costudent or teacher can create unexpected tensions or threats. Evaluation that should be entirely formative can be viewed as summative, and being asked to share can feel like a rip-off. Nevertheless, it is exciting to find unforeseen paths into more effective and extensive Navajo language work.

All colleges have temporary and adjunct professors. Diné College is very spread out, with seven major instructional sites, the most distant being spread 400 miles. Even at the two main campuses (with a total of five full-time NLP professors), there is turnover. Elsewhere, most instruction is by adjuncts, underpaid and usually supervised by relatively uninformed administrators. Yet the adjunct professors' work is indispensable to our work and to their communities. Many have been energetic, well organized, and effective; some have not. With demand for courses high, local administrators have sometimes settled for personnel who slip into teaching Navajo culture in English, or whose teaching competence is not like that of the full-time professors. To support all adjuncts, we have concentrated on cyclical upgrading of standard syllabi, provision of materials and tools (such as computers), face-to-face work sessions, and cycles of team teaching. Finally of course, new teachers arrive and come to prove themselves. Each brings new material, works well with his or her own unique subset of students, and contributes to the Core Forum.

Formative evaluation and preparation is complemented by summative evaluation, such as the backtracking by transcript of students who have difficulty in our upper-level courses on the main campuses. Frankly, summative evaluation (by which continued employment is decided) is inherently uncomfortable. Sometimes Diné College has had long-term relationships with instructors who were not accurate spellers or articulate speakers (even Anglos who knew some Navajo were used). Some have charged that negative evaluation of adjuncts was due to dialect variation, or that adherence to standards was authoritarian. Working with this problem constructively is a sensitive ongoing administrative task, fraught with the danger of creating fractiousness. Yet, though Diné College must clearly favor most Navajo language and literacy teaching, its defense of standards is critical as a model to show that quality Navajo language work can be done. For decades, Arizona, New Mexico, and Utah have allowed schools to pretend that they were carrying on Navajo-English bilingual education programs when in fact they did not even employ any personnel who could read and write Navajo. Thus standards were held low, with insufficient materials, resources, and commitment from the institution. With others, we are still changing the concept of the possible, and we must provide accurate recognition of expertise.

Not all teaching of Navajo language and literacy must be according to Diné College's standards. A new elitism should not replace colonial structures. The popular literacy movement that swept black Southern communities in the 1950s and 1960s, described by Horton (1988), provides an excellent model for what could occur. Even the teaching of Navajo literacy for limited purposes, as in Navajo churches, gives the language greater functional breadth.

One constant problem was having an Anglo (the author) in a central NLP position. His limited speaking and comprehension of Navajo were often a burden, for several reasons: (1) because of his deficits in understanding language and culture, he usually could not contribute critically to content decisions about instructional materials or make accurate judgments about student placement; (2) he did not have useful intuitions about grammaticality; and (3) the situation of an Anglo having even limited authority about Navajo language matters has colonial overtones undermining Navajo sovereignty. Yet he had useful knowledge in linguistics and pedagogy. Thus, his professional development program too became important. He needed to study to boost comprehension and speaking, carry out related study of Navajo culture and history, and develop culturally appropriate interpersonal skills. These sorts of professional development activities of course come at a cost. To the extent that they are not accomplished, the person is ineffective; accomplishing them takes time, energy, resources.

DIRECT SERVICES TO
THE NAVAJO NATION

Tribal college language programs receive constant community requests for language services. Assistance with spellings is given most days. Translations (simple and difficult) are needed by hospitals and clinics, the courts, government, other academic enterprises, retailers, manufacturers, police, legislative bodies, and many other entities. There is consistent demand for development of materials (e.g., bilingual glossaries), either collaboratively with the requester or alone. Often the program becomes a distribution center for materials such as software (e.g., fonts, which have been provided to requesters as diverse as individual schoolteachers and the Presidential Inauguration Committee of 1992) or paper (one cannot deny the request of a Navajo parent living in California or North Carolina who wants to teach her child Navajo, or a Navajo federal prisoner facing many years of incarceration). We often conduct testing of Navajo fluency or literacy, or review or edit tools for others. Many requests result in reference to other resources. This role of cultural broker or bridge is dangerously seductive—seductive because a gatekeeper gets power and knowledge, dangerous because it can pull the program away from more concrete achievements or logjam the work of others.

Usually the time required for an individual request is minor (though the cumulative time is considerable), and one proceeds. Finally, each request must be measured as to how it draws the resources of the program away from its central tasks. Each request must be treated with gravity; it is finally only if the program becomes useful and meets the needs of the Navajo community, as felt and expressed by that community, that it will receive the wholehearted support and collaboration (e.g., in recruiting and local fund-raising) needed.

APPROPRIATE STRUCTURES
FOR NAVAJO LANGUAGE WORK

In its growth, the NLP has become part of a web of people and processes that accomplish multiple functions. These actors are not yet well enough orchestrated to agree very much, avoid internecine strife, or escape from duplication of efforts. Achieving better organization (democratic, not monolithic) is our task. The actors and implications of this web reach beyond Diné College, but will draw upon tools, processes, experiences, and dreams being used at Diné College for nurturing the Core Forum.

The Core Forum should bring aggressive, informed criticism to each issue, in a tone and with a distribution that people will hear and use. Navajo language scholars and teachers everywhere are often not aware of each other's work and have never met, owing in part to great distances and insufficient travel and communication resources. Sometimes this results in insufficient appreciation, one for another, of the difficulties and richness of each person's work, and in poorly informed critical interplay. One set of solutions to this problem is well-organized communication. Our databases, with addresses, academic records, and related information, are a key tool for disseminating information (e.g., address labels), helping employers find qualified teachers and translators, organizing special gatherings such as summer seminars and language rejuvenation meetings, and conducting program evaluations. Similar tools (perhaps expanded as a directory) will be used to establish an Internet mailing list. Our students, as a subset of the Core Forum, should eventually be linked for dialogue and support, such as is done by the Breadnet system used by the Breadloaf School of English.

Finally, the most important and effective networks are geographically local, with members having daily and weekly contact. The NLP has promoted locally supportive networks of Navajo language teachers throughout the reservation, with limited success. We need local organizations, leadership, funding sources, missions and functions, and so on. Though activities that the NLP has sponsored at Diné College campuses are important for face-to-face contact, they do not create permanent collaboration. This will come only through intentional organization building.

Here we must concentrate on Navajos as the critical audience for Navajo language work. This is not simple; for example, there is only an emerging audience for Navajo language writing. For instance, since 1994 the *Navajo Times*, which belongs to the Navajo Nation, has sporadically printed one page per week in Navajo. This small production of Navajo literature (submitted mainly from the Chinle school district, Diné College's classes, and the Rock Point school) is widely used. Yet lengthier materials, such as those published in the *Journal of Navajo Education* or in books, reach a very small audience. A number of tactics are employed to build audience: posters in schoolrooms, public signs in businesses and schools, bumper stickers and T-shirts, the use of Navajo for common greetings and closings in letters, the reading of Navajo compositions over the radio, and school programs.

A thorny problem involves production of Navajo materials for both Navajos and non-Navajos. Though it might seem doubly beneficial to produce materials for both, this seldom proves workable. Much that Navajos know cannot be comfortably revealed elsewhere. Aware of the dangers and possible abuses inherent in the nurturing of imperialist nostalgia or the objectification of Navajos that resides in much anthropological writing, Navajos are often unwilling to put Navajo texts into Anglo hands. Often, although materials are composed in Navajo and translated into English, publishers are unwilling to include the Navajo text (this was even true recently in a painful instance for an academic publishing house putting out a volume on indigenous language survival).

When there is an audience ready to read advanced Navajo literature, writers will write it. The inverse—that when important Navajo literature has been written, an audience will learn to read it—may or may not be true. For decades there has been a significant amount of ceremonial, oral history, and historical material recorded and transcribed by anthropologists. This material is in a variety of orthographies and often out of print or missing from library collections. Yet though the texts are dense in the knowledge of articulate elders, there has as yet been no consistent, vocal demand for it in the standard orthography. (Of course, this sort of knowledge is traditionally and presently transmitted orally, and there is no broad awareness of the existence of these transcribed texts.)

Community orientation is also important. The key sector of the community is the elders. The collaboration of schools with elders has been largely insufficient, and not fundamentally transformational of the school or community. For historical and even architectural reasons, the school is a forbidding place for Navajo elders, usually no more welcoming than a border town. The community is ambivalent about many of the school's functions, including Westernized social discipline and employment training that sends students elsewhere. The language of power, and often the only language heard aloud in the school, is English. The elevated social position that does give Navajo elders respect and voice in other settings (home, chapter house, religious activities, and social gatherings) does not operate at school. This usually continues even when school personnel come to students' homes; from the first confrontations about compulsory schooling up to the present, traditional voices have been muted or silenced.

This is systematically damaging for school-based Navajo language study. To understand the impact, imagine an English program trying to operate effectively within an institution unwelcoming to the best English literature or the most articulate speakers and dramatists. Transforming this situation at Diné College, "putting out the welcome mat" to articulate speakers, must become a high priority. This forum, which is *of* the college, will not necessarily have to be *at* the college. Having school activities at venues where Navajo elders are comfortable has been sporadic, but its potential is unfathomably rich. Literary events such as storytelling present the most obvious ground, but even the most sophisticated research or composition activities, from the creation of specialized glossaries to filmmaking, attain their richest realization with the elders' contribution. We must also involve elders in providing support for language learning, thereby matching the noninstitutional method of sending children off into the mountains to herd sheep with grandma for the summers.

Schools must also, in multifaceted ways, be useful to their communities. Though parents and elders will see the school as useful in promoting the learning of Navajo, the product of this work is generally very dispersed. Well-focused activities which produce concrete and immediate benefits, such as those carried out in the cooperative work activities that our nonspeaker-track students accomplish in their community language practicum, are easily institutionalized (and probably provide our most effective acquisition settings). Navajo elders are often short on physical and financial resources and energy, and design of all community-based activities should take into account their concrete usefulness.

Community involvement comes through the network of committed people working for years inside and with the institution who have come to know and trust each other, the Core Forum. A student who drives 250 miles a week at night to class shows a persistence that others notice. Some struggle through sickness, even terminal illness, and family crises without quitting. Programs treasure adjunct instructors who, working at low salaries with little support at isolated sites, effectively teach literacy to students. Others who intermittently but substantially contribute are professors, educators, and linguists at cooperating and competing post-secondary institutions based off-reservation, particularly when these people are Navajo (and thereby part of Navajo social structure). Bureaucrats and administrators in schools or tribal government also play key roles in securing scholarships, recruiting and registering students, finding classrooms, and arranging compensation for acquired skills. Whenever funds are involved, for scholarships, positions, or materials, there are reports to be made to school boards and tribal committees. Navajos on these groups are heard by the Core Forum and do legitimately represent many community interests. Principals are also key people, for hiring those trained in Navajo language work. Thus we must indicate to principals what skills prospective Navajo language teachers have, inquire as to what skills the principals think the teachers should have, and assist with recruiting for open positions. Just as a committed person in a distant institution is a treasure to be nurtured, a recalcitrant administrator or bureaucrat in various parts of a system (e.g., personnel departments) can damage access to Navajo language to an entire system.

Assisting principals of schools with recruiting has been an interesting and sensitive issue where jobs are scarce. We have had an understandable tendency to urge principals to lure the most qualified people, even from a distance. Though this is sometimes successful, it often cannot be done, or is only a short-term solution, since housing and transportation quickly become problems. The alternative is often to hire a local person, a fluent speaker but untrained, and then require that person to take classes. Though this often means that a new program starts with frustrations, or even with long-lasting negative results, the use of a local person is generally advisable.

Inclusion and participation in the Core Forum is of course vague and fluid. Not everyone likes, trusts, or even respects everyone else. The skills or resources of one or another will come to the forefront in any single issue or coalition. Factions form, and jealousies arise. People have defended their programs against the world, and often become defensive toward one another, to protect jobs or to compete for limited resources. Sometimes people who have secure positions resist working with newcomers; after years of being referred to as language experts, and as others arrive with different or greater expertise, they find safety in retreat. However, if we can retain a focus on Navajo language work being done in Navajo, by Navajos, for Navajo purposes, and for a Navajo audience, these barriers are not insurmountable; a cooperative solidarity does arise.

As gains are made in expanding and deepening Navajo language work, we are finding ourselves teaching new Navajo courses and accomplishing innovative projects in institutions that have had little exposure to academic Navajo. The permanent and deep rooting of Navajo there depends upon the delivery of rigor. When high-quality students and products come from a certain program, it is more likely to attract students and resources. A central, measurable element we have concentrated upon has been the fluency and spelling accuracy of our student writers. The skills of such people are in steady demand, and it has been necessary that we certify with precision what the minimum level of skills is for passing our courses. There has been considerable pressure from students who claim to speak differently or who use their own writing "system" that is "just as good," or who will assail instructors who have failed them (it can be particularly painful for a Navajo speaker to fail in a Navajo language class). Each of these situations is handled sensitively, but without retreat from the standard orthographic conventions (which have been largely in place, in the case of Navajo, for

50 years). The decision that we made as to the level of spelling accuracy and fluency that a student had to show at the end of the NAV 301 class has been a very helpful standard. Though it has caused plenty of friction, and many students have had to retake courses, attaining this standard has put us in a position that other institutions now strive to match. For our instructors, there has been increased pressure to check volumes of papers in very detailed ways, which can take many hours. The result, however, has been a breaking of the logjam in other areas of Navajo language work that depend upon literacy skills.

A language program run by indigenous peoples should strive to become the leader in every phase of study about the language. This is a necessary part of fully regaining ownership of intellectual resources and products. Yet for this to happen, the depth and the quality of this work must exceed that of external, instrumental work. At this stage, standards come from the outside, sometimes because work from there is of higher quality and sometimes because it is from more authoritative institutions or journals. For example, as mentioned above, the ACTFL proficiency standards, developed elsewhere, have proven useful for bringing concrete standards to Diné College's nonspeaker courses and speaker-track literacy courses. However, local proficiency standards are being refined, appropriate to local circumstances; it is these that will inform Navajo language curriculum.

A different order of authority was evident in discussions, to which Diné College contributed, at the U.S. Board on Geographic Names, when, again as mentioned previously, the board recently made the responsible decision to officially begin allowing diacritical markings for map labeling. Among others, Diné College submitted testimony, arguing for accuracy. When such a commitment to rigor is combined with the natural authority that a tribal college brings to issues related to its language, the possibilities for appropriate academic progress are doubly enhanced. This issue of phoneme-grapheme correspondence is one with which Navajo literacy instructors wrestle daily. A portion of the testimony that was submitted is included here:

> A broad range of arguments can be brought to bear upon this question, but the central issue, and the one that should carry the day, is that of accuracy. Each of the world's languages has its own unique set of phonemes. Each phoneme is represented by a set of allophones (realized sounds), one of which is used in any particular sound environment, the selection having been made in a rule-bound way (the set of rules also is unique to each language). The boundary between sets of allophones is the phonemic distinction, the sound difference that makes a difference in meaning.
>
> As orthographies are developed for any one language, they are designed to accurately reflect these phonemic distinctions. Usable, practical orthographies that will gain popularity among those literate in a language are often based on the Roman alphabet, but alterations (diacritical markings) are often necessary for the sake of accuracy. Ignoring any of the alterations of an established orthography can result, at best, in the sudden creation of thousands of homographs (words that are spelled the same, though they have different

pronunciations). At worst it results in words that are unreadable by anyone. The loss is measurable and heavy—etymological analysis is degraded or destroyed, and mispronunciations and misconceptions, even by native speakers, multiply.

This issue of map labeling is an important one for Native Americans, since the misspelling or elision of Native American names from maps has been one factor in the historical land grab. This is but one of hundreds of areas where language use has practical consequences, and in many areas of emerging work at Diné College there are potentially important gains to be made.

To reiterate, there is no more important project for a language program than the struggle to perpetuate the language. Effectiveness is the foremost consideration to take into account. Any successful RLS effort must be designed from the minds, mouths, and hands of the native speakers of Navajo and must be completely contextualized within the action schemes of these speakers.

The reinvigoration of Navajo is not only an opening-up to the words of Navajo, but also an opening-up to the voices of those who do and will speak in that language. If college activities are designed in a way that treats local community talk as irrelevant to the college program, that very fact, of not acknowledging the importance of local knowledge and local will, is of itself oppressive and has the effect of further supplementing the cultural hegemony that is crushing Navajo (though Diné College is a tribal college, it still often slips back into a BIA role). Thus, the effectiveness of all efforts to perpetuate Navajo must be judged not only by their internal rigor, but also by their contextual attachments to community discourse. Key indicators as to whether those activities are truly designed to feed a local transformative discourse through which Navajo can be reinvigorated are the factors of author and audience. The primary work must be designed and carried out by people who speak Navajo, and the primary audience must be made up of speakers. Successful RLS requires an expert focusing of limited resources. We cannot expect Diné College to be a permanent player in every community, but we can expect Diné College to be importantly circumspect.

To promote the future of a language, one works at its growing edge. The Navajo Language Program at Diné College has worked to be that growing edge by nurturing the establishment of new genres and functions in Navajo, opening up settings for Navajo language work, enabling a range of interlocutor roles, and urging the elasticity of Navajo to respond to broad demands. Our syllabi, our workshops, and the methods of our teachers and colleagues have resulted in writing in many genres, among them news reporting, résumés, autobiographies, memorandums, resolutions (even by the Navajo Nation Council), lists of all sorts, recipes (by the thousands), diaries and journals, personal letters, mission statements, advertisements, religious texts, stories, jokes, directions, descriptions, persuasive pieces, argumentation, charts and graphs, time lines, indices, interviews, drama, note taking, poems, songs, movies and documentaries, and short stories. In many cases there has not yet been sufficient exercise of a genre, or enough feedback, for the genre to take on recognizably standard characteristics. It has been important to not charge ahead too rapidly. One danger is that an emerging genre of Navajo writing might be built entirely on an English model, only overlapping or even undermining an existing oral Navajo genre. It is these existing Navajo oral genres we are trying to use as templates for emerging types of Navajo writing, new genres that can fulfill the needs of a Navajo audience.

The NLP also works to broaden and strengthen the settings in which Navajo has a voice. One major thrust has been to engender and assist efforts to bring the language into all of the 240 schools that have a large number of Navajo students. Another has been to promote Navajo in newspapers (such as the *Navajo Times*), magazines (such as *Inter-Tribal America*), and journals. There is also an ongoing effort to get Navajo out of its departmental ghetto at Diné College into other programs, courses, and spaces at the school. Thus, the struggle even for Diné College to put Navajo on an equal footing with English proceeds. The investigation and promotion of the sociolinguistic factor of setting is a task that will continue at Diné College.

The analysis of topics which are discussed in Navajo has been a richly rewarding facet of discovering and nurturing the growing edge of Navajo. Those topics that stand out clearly, in relief against English, are "traditional" in nature—conversation and composition about rural, land-based lives and the parts of Navajo culture that are least anglicized. Here there is talk of family and clan, ethics and values, history and beliefs, animals, plants, medicines, the earth, and a multitude of other topics. The content and structure of composition in these topics is often quite dissimilar to that of how English is used to discuss them. The compositions can thus seem quaint and arouse a romantic nostalgia for non-Navajos. A nostalgia for a (possibly) disappearing way of life also affects Navajos at times, and of course it is the elders (and most articulate speakers) who live out on the land who can speak most eloquently about these things. In one of our place-names stories an elderly Navajo woman recalls, when she was a little girl, running gaily alongside her father's wagon and having her long skirt become twisted into the axle, nearly pulling her under the huge wheels. Such stories bring with them a wealth of context. From the seed of these topics, a rich web of Navajo thought can be accessed. Thus the topics are naturally considered the centerpiece of curriculum construction projects and the font of much creative thinking.

For the NLP, however, a tension exists here, a tension to be tapped for its fullest fruit. Navajo is a modern language, a language spoken today by people who travel the world; even the elders buy cars, wire their houses, travel great distances, and speak of current events. New terms are created, and existing ones are applied to new concepts (as in English). Problems are solved in Navajo, and dreams are dreamed. For the NLP to both use its existing resources and realize their potential in the struggle to perpetuate the language, our faces must turn both ways. As we select topics to write about or to assign to students, it is the creative discovery of how to find our audiences and how to accomplish our goals with language that will find or form our literary genres. It is uncertain whether this writing will include fiction to match that of a Garcia Márquez, poetry that brings in the wealth of traditional chants, or history that can compete with the one-sided stories of this land that dominate mainstream thought. Yet there is a flow of creativity to come, and the NLP is working to unleash it, sponsoring workshops, bringing publishers and writers together, transcribing the oral compositions of the elderly and wise, and bringing public attention to Navajo language composition in various other ways.

Though we have learned much in our 28 years of teaching Navajo at Diné College, there remain major strides to be taken for scholarship in Navajo to be exercised at the highest level. Some will come about through further integration of language and teacher training, some by development of history and culture courses that use Navajo oral language and literacy to fuller advantage, some by a concentration on further analytical work in linguistics, some by providing more extensive job-oriented Navajo language skills, and some through the aforementioned effort to further Navajo literature and literacy. Along each of these strands, there will be curriculum and professional development, and issues of funding and authority and rigor.

There are resources to support this effort. There are now many dozens of highly skilled Navajo language professionals who have dedicated their careers to this work, people who have much to offer at the college level. There are also institutions that will provide funding for well-designed projects—the national and state humanities councils, other federal and state funding agencies, various private foundations, tribal government entities, and generous individuals. Securing such financial resources is, frankly, a process that can pull one's eyes from the prize, requiring substantial time and energy and possibly compromising program priorities. The process of proposal writing can be a frustrating waste of time, where a multitude of groups are given false hope and suckered into competing for severely limited resources. Even the process of kowtowing to the needs of outside agencies so as to undertake projects is problematic—it acknowledges and reinforces the legitimacy of outside authority in making important decisions about indigenous language matters. Decisions about which funding to seek or accept must be made on a case-by-case basis; no such decision lacks ethical or short-term and long-term tensions. Yet ongoing relationships between the NLP and these agencies have often been two-way streets, where the voice of local concerns is listened to with interest and concern, finally lending it clout. For the present, such fund-raising is part of our ongoing duty.

With these efforts and research projects, Diné College has developed a forum of teachers, students, and scholars who rigorously investigate and create with Navajo on the Navajo Nation, Navajos addressing Navajos. The academic processes at Diné College directly access the resources of the community, building the Core Forum of increasingly expert and active intellectuals. The rigor of the work is enforced externally (through constant examination of all work done on Navajo) and internally (as all must put their work before a highly critical audience motivated by an intent to immediately use knowledge). Authority increasingly resides with Navajos, and the functions of promoting and perpetuating Navajo come to the forefront. As the NLP looks to the future, promoting the growth of a new literature, securing permanent venues for the language, and growing toward bachelor's and master's programs, human and institutional resources are here, and the potential is unprecedented.

References

Altwerger, B., C. Edelsky, and V. M. Flores. 1987. Whole language: What's new? *The Reading Teacher,* November.

Austin-Garrison, M. 1991. Bee Ákohwiinidzinígíí Binahjj' Ak'e'alchí Bíhoo'aah. *Journal of Navajo Education* 9, no. 1: 43–50.

Bobo, K., J. Kendall, and S. Max. 1996. *Organizing for social change: A manual for activists in the 1990s.* Santa Ana, Calif.: Seven Locks Press.

Brandt, R. 1989–90. On cooperative learning: A conversation with Spencer Kagan. *Educational Leadership.* December–January: 277–80.

Crystal, David. 1980. *A first dictionary of linguistics and phonetics.* Boulder, Colo.: Westview Press.

Fishman, Joshua A. 1991. *Reversing language shift: Theoretical and empirical foundations of assistance to threatened languages.* Clevedon, England: Multilingual Matters.

Freeman, D. 1996. "To take them at their word": Language data in the study of teachers' knowledge. *Harvard Educational Review* 66, no. 4.

Freire, P. 1970. *Pedagogy of the oppressed.* New York: Continuum.

Gee, J. 1987. Orality and literacy: From the savage mind to ways with words. *TESOL Quarterly,* December: 719–46.

Goodman, K. 1986. *What's whole in whole language.* Ontario: Scholastic.

Horton, Myles. 1988. *The Long Haul.* New Market, Tenn.: Highlander Center.

Horton, Myles, and Paulo Freire. 1990. *We make the road by walking.* Philadelphia: Temple University Press.

Illich, I. 1971. *Deschooling society.* New York: Harper and Row.

Jackson, M. 1993. Bee Nidí'nóotjjlígíí. *Journal of Navajo Education* 10, no. 1: 21–25.

Kagan, S. 1989–90. The structural approach to cooperative learning. *Educational Leadership,* December–January: 273–76.

Kari, J. M. 1976. *Navajo verb prefix phonology.* New York: Garland.

Lather, P. 1986. Research as praxis. *Harvard Educational Review* 56, no. 3: 257–77.

Lopez, B. 1988. Narrative and landscape. In *Crossing open ground.* New York: Vintage Books.

Marr, D. G. 1981. *Vietnamese tradition on trial, 1920–1945.* Berkeley: University of California Press.

McCray, K. (1992). Diné Binahagha' Yee Da'dókeed. In *Ninaagóó Ádahooníiligíí Ba Ákonínízin* 9, no. 2. Rock Point, Ariz.: Rock Point Community School.

McLaughlin, D. 1992. Power and the politics of knowledge. In *Diversity as resource,* ed. D. Murray. Alexandria, Va.: TESOL Press.

Native American Materials Development Center. 1984. *Álchíní Bá Hane',* book 1, *Navajo children's literature.* Pine Hill, N.M.: Ramah Navajo School Board.

Navajo Nation Education Policies. 1984. Window Rock, Navajo Nation, Ariz.: Navajo Division of Education.

Omaggio, A. C. 1986. *Teaching language in context: Proficiency-oriented instruction.* Boston: Heinle and Heinle.

Platero, Paul. 1992. *Navajo Head Start Language Study.* Window Rock, Ariz.: Navajo Division of Education.

Richard-Amato, P. A. 1998. *Making it happen: Interaction in the second language classroom.* White Plains, N.Y.: Longman.

Sapir, E. 1975. *Navaho texts,* ed. H. Hoijer. New York: AMS Press.

Slate, C. 1990. Validity, perspective, and purpose of on-site research, professional development, and literacy instruction. Paper presented at the Annual Meeting of the American Anthropological Association, New Orleans.

Slate, C. 1992. Civil rights and the Navajo language. In *Living the dream in Arizona: The legacy of Martin Luther King, Jr.* Tempe, Ariz.: Arizona State University Foundation.

————. 1993. Finding a place for Navajo. *Tribal College: Journal of American Indian Higher Education* 6, no. 4.

————. 1994. Navajo linguistics on the Navajo Nation. Paper presented at the Annual Meeting of the American Anthropological Association, Atlanta.

Slate, C., M. Austin-Garrison, B. Casaus, and D. McLaughlin. 1996. Diné Bizaad Yissohígíí: The past, present, and future of Navajo literacy. In *Athabaskan Language Studies,* ed. E. Jelinek, S. Midgette, K. Rice, and L. Saxon, 349–90. Albuquerque: University of New Mexico Press.

Slate, C., T. Goldtooth, and M. Jackson. 1989. Navajo literacy in a postsecondary setting: Work in progress at Navajo Community College. *Journal of Navajo Education* 7, no. 1.

Slate, C., et al. 1986–96. *Diné Bizaad Bóhoo'aah,* books 1 and 2, *High school texts for the learning of Navajo.* Farmington, N.M.: Navajo Preparatory School.

Slate, C., ed. 1995. *The Young and Morgan pocket dictionary of the Navajo language.* Tsaile, Ariz.: Center for Diné Studies.

U.S. Public Law 101-477. 101st Cong., 2d. sess., 30 October 1990. Title I, *Native American Languages Act.*

White, Richard. 1983. *The roots of dependency: Subsistence, environment, and social change among the Choctaws, Pawnees, and Navajos.* Lincoln: University of Nebraska Press.

Wigginton, E. 1989. Foxfire grows up. *Harvard Educational Review* 51, no. 1: 24–50.

Young, R. 1968. *English as a second language for Navajos: An overview of certain cultural and linguistic factors.* Albuquerque, N.M.: Bureau of Indian Affairs.

Young, R., and W. Morgan. 1987. *The Navajo language: A grammar and colloquial dictionary.* Albuquerque: University of New Mexico Press.

Young, R., and W. Morgan, with S. Midgette. 1992. *Analytic lexicon of Navajo.* Albuquerque: University of New Mexico Press.

Young, R., and W. Morgan, eds. 1954. *Historical selections.* Phoenix, Ariz.: BIA.

Yule, G. 1985. *The study of language: An introduction.* New York: Cambridge University Press.

PART IX

SLEEPING LANGUAGES

31

Sleeping Languages
Can They Be Awakened?

LEANNE HINTON

Department of Linguistics
University of California at Berkeley
Berkeley, California

There are at present many languages in the world that have fallen silent. A language is silent either because there is no one left who knows it, or because those who know it no longer have any domain left in which to use it. In some of the literature, such languages have been called "moribund" if there are people who retain knowledge but have no way to use it, or "dead" or "extinct" when there are no living speakers. I prefer the less final metaphor of "silence," or L. Frank Manriquez's "sleep."

Michael Krauss points out that out of close to 200 languages in North America, only about 20 are actually learned by children from their parents now. Thus, most of the languages are falling asleep. The same process is happening on all the continents of the world, perhaps to a lesser degree in some cases, but with the same end result in view. Ever more rapidly the processes of communications, globalization, displacement, and environmental destruction are resulting in abandonment (whether voluntary or involuntary) of their language by the affected communities. The question is, can the languages ever be awakened, if those who see them as part of their heritage wish to do so? We see many people trying, and there is always some kind of successful result, whether just a few vocabulary items are inserted into daily speech or the language becomes the mode of daily communication again.

DOCUMENTATION

Perhaps the most important thing to do when a language is down to a few speakers is to document the knowledge of those speakers as thoroughly as possible. This can be done either by linguists and ethnographers or by the communities themselves. Sadly, communities in the grip of language shift are often unaware that it is taking place, or are unconcerned about it, or for various reasons are unable to do anything about it, until the shift is almost complete. But scholars have been documenting languages for hundreds of years (for some languages, thousands of years), so that some languages that have no speakers left still have enough documentation that it is possible for a motivated person to learn them.

I pointed out in Chapter 1 that linguists who have been documenting languages in the 20th century have usually focused on grammar and vocabulary and have often failed to document the most important aspects of a language for users: the pragmatics of language use. People trying to revitalize a language want to know how to greet each other, what the rules of conversation are, how the language is used to express anger, love, gratitude, and politeness. How people *interact* through the language. And what about the gestural components of language, and facial expressions? Are these not also important parts of communication? The development of language revitalization efforts around the world is thus educating linguists about what is important in documentation.

Community members themselves are beginning to take on the task of documenting their own last speakers. People are developing audiotape and videotape documentation practices, and in some communities, archives of such documentation are being developed for the sake of good preservation practices and general access.

To begin the process of reclaiming an unspoken language, the first step is to find and acquire copies of whatever documentation of the language exists. Besides publications, there may be a rich store of unpublished documentation, such as linguistic field notes, field recordings, and old manuscripts. There may be other documents as well, such as letters, old

413

newspapers, and so on. Most of the documentation will be in university or museum archives and libraries (see Chapter 1). Someone first starting out to reclaim a language that has been lost will need to do a lot of research on what documentation exists, where it is, and how to access it. Sometimes getting copies of the documentation is difficult and expensive. The Acjachemem people of southern California, for example, found that there was a large collection of recordings of their language at the Smithsonian Institution that had been collected decades before on aluminum disks by J. P. Harrington and his assistants. These disks had never been transferred to a modern sound medium, and so the Acjachemem found a grant to pay for the transfer and copying of the disks onto audiotape so that they could have copies.

RECONSTITUTION AND MODERNIZATION

Sometimes documentation itself is inadequate, and "reconstitution" is necessary if a community wishes for language revitalization. Reconstitution is extrapolation from whatever information exists to guess what the language might have been like. Related languages may also be used to help with reconstitution. To give a simple example, let us suppose that extinct language A is related to better-documented language B, and we find a sound correspondence between the two languages such that wherever A has a "t" sound, B has a "ch" sound (e.g. the word for "dog" might be *tati* in A and *chachi* in B). Now let us suppose the word for "birch tree" has been lost in A, but we find that it is *chikol* in B; thus we could adopt the word *tikol* in A as our best guess of what it might have been. One example is the Esselen of central coastal California, who have only a small amount of documentation of their language, from the mission days. The linguist David Shaul worked with one Esselen organization to reconstitute aspects of that language. Another example is the Acjachemem (Juaneño), mentioned above, who have several groups working on their sleeping language, including one active group called the Children of Temayuwut. The Acjachemem language, a member of the Uto-Aztecan language family, does not have a great deal of documentation; this is partly because the anthropologist A. L. Kroeber, early in the 20th century, examined it in comparison with Luiseño, which had a fair amount of documentation already, and declared that Acjachemem was "a dialect of Luiseño" and therefore did not need separate study. There are in fact some important sound distinctions at least between the two varieties, but it is true that they were mutually intelligible. Given the lack of documentation on Acjachemem, Kelina Lobo (a graduate student at Berkeley and a member of the tribe who is conducting classes in the language as a project of the Children of Temayuwut) has come to the conclusion that the best way to start the process of reclaiming the language is through the study of the well-documented Luiseño. Ultimately, she hopes to learn enough about the sound differences between the two languages to be able to give her language back the sound system it once had.

We have already discussed in several chapters the inevitability of language change, in order for people to talk about the objects, actions, and concerns that form their present-day environment. This holds true for the awakening of sleeping languages as much as for the languages that are recovering from a less severe state of decline. For example, Quirina Luna is making a strong effort to revive the Mutsun language to whatever extent she can, and one of her many projects is to bring some vocabulary items into usage at home. Common words that can relatively easily be inserted into consciousness for frequent usage are "hello," "goodbye," "please," and "thank you." However, these are words that are components of Western practices, not necessarily of Mutsun practices, and no such words were ever recorded for Mutsun. Undeterred, Quirina has created words to fill these new functions, using traditional word-construction rules that she and linguist Natasha Warner recovered from the documentation that exists.

"Hello"	*misYmin tRuhis* 'good day'
"Welcome"	*akkuy misYmin* 'enter well'
"Thank you"	*tRumsanak kannis* 'it pleases me'
"Please"	*tRumsamiy kannise* 'please me'
"Goodbye"	*wattiniy misYmin* 'go well'
"sincerely" (in a letter)	*kan-sireesum* 'with my heart' [1]

It is funny, poignant, and thought-provoking to realize that the most commonly used words in Mutsun right now are words that never existed when the Mutsun language was still alive.

BEGINNING THE PROCESS

A language with no speakers at all cannot be taught using the immersion methods that have been touted so strongly in this book—at least not until someone has learned the language fluently enough as a second language to be able to teach it himself or herself. But if there are no speakers at all, then the first learners (who might later become teachers) must depend on whatever records have been made of the language as the basis from which they will learn. If there is a large literature, such as is the case with Cornish (see below), then there is a good basis for highly motivated people to learn the language. Because there is no one to teach the language, the first learners of a sleeping language will have to learn on their own. In many cases, especially for some of the small-community indigenous languages, there will be no available learning materials, and the pioneers in language reclamation will have to make such materials themselves. If the language has never had a standardized writing system, the pioneers may need to develop one themselves. Language revitalization may start slowly, with a few words at a time; for instance, the former Wiyot chairman Cheryl Seidner decided that she would begin revitalization with the introduction of two words—"yes" and "no"—to the tribal council, insisting that they use those Wiyot words instead of English when voting. A person may even find that he or she has no community support for revitalization but will nevertheless create valuable learning materials that will someday be much appreciated by another generation.

DEVELOPING DOMAINS OF USE

For revival of a "silent" language, the written form is almost definitely going to take on a far greater importance than the spoken form, because in most cases the written form is the primary means from which someone might have a hope of learning it and using it. It is very often the case that the descendants of those who once spoke a now-sleeping language live far away from each other and are a small minority within an ocean of speakers of the dominant language. The written word may be the only form of expression for those people who have learned their language of heritage as a second language, and the easiest form of communication with other people. Thus written genres will be very important—the communicative genres of letters, e-mail, and the like; the pedagogical and scholarly genres of grammars, dictionaries, and learning materials; and the artistic genres of poetry, novels, and plays.

It will of course also be the goal of the proponents of revitalization to encourage the revival of spoken domains of use. Spoken art forms may develop from the written, such as oral poetry readings or productions of plays. Language proponents may use the telephone to communicate with each other. Pot-luck dinners, public speeches, and informal gatherings can be used to encourage the use of the language, as can special weekend retreats or summer camps.

We have seen that for an endangered language, the family is the last bastion against language loss, once the language of schools, public affairs, the marketplace, and the workplace has shifted to the dominant language of the region. But, interestingly, the family household may also be the last to regain use of the language when it is being revitalized. Once the family loses the language, the children and later descendants become dependent on second-language learning programs outside the family, and this may remain the case for a long time. One of the three cases described below is Cornish, whose last native speaker died 100 years ago. It is being actively revived as a literary language and used orally in occasional gatherings by its enthusiasts, but it is not a language of the home anywhere. Another success story described below is Hebrew, which had no native speakers for 2,000 years but was maintained in religious literature and worship and learned primarily at religious institutions. At last, in this century, it became a language of home, through a series of historical events that made its role as a first language useful again. Perhaps the lesson here is in the word "useful." Families may have strong ideological reasons for wishing their minority language to stay alive, but at the same time they have even a stronger sense of responsibility toward their children to make sure they learn a language at home that will help them make their way in the world. Only when a minority language has a measure of strength outside the home will families who have gone through a generation or more of speaking some other language feel sufficiently secure about the language to bring it home again. There are to be sure heroic exceptions to this rule, as we will see in our discussion of Hebrew, and as we have seen for Hawaiian (Chapters 12 and 13); but the exceptions are usually among forward-thinking families who are leaders in the development of the usefulness of their language of heritage within the community. The third case I describe here is about one such forward-thinking family—Daryl Baldwin and his wife and children, who have made the Native American language Miami the language of their home.

SUCCESS STORIES AND BEGINNINGS

Hebrew

Certainly it would never have been correct to call Hebrew "extinct," since it never ceased being used as a language of religion, even though it ceased being a language of the home for two millennia. The land of Palestine is the ancestral homeland of the Jews. There Hebrew was spoken and written for many centuries, until political events resulted in the shift of their daily language to Aramaic, which had become the dominant language of the Middle East about the second century BC. Starting with the Romans, various ruling powers scattered the Jews across Europe and even farther over the centuries by expulsions, prejudice, and, in the last century, out-and-out attempts at genocide. Throughout the millennia the Jews shifted to the languages of the countries they found themselves part of. For two millennia Hebrew was gone from the home, the marketplace, and daily affairs. Always, however, the Jews kept their ancestral language, Hebrew, alive as a language of religion.

The father of modern Hebrew was a Lithuanian Jew named Eliezer Ben-Yehuda who became interested in the revival of the Hebrew language and devoted his life to its revitalization and modernization. Jews by then spoke many different languages. The only language that they held in common was ancient Hebrew, which was a sacred language, limited to religious purposes, and possessed no vocabulary for the everyday subjects of modern life. Ben-Yehuda saw Hebrew as the language that could reunify the Jews coming to Palestine from all over the world, but much work would be needed to make Hebrew practical for everyday usage. Ben-Yehuda coined nearly 4,000 new Hebrew words based on ancient Hebrew roots and completed 10 volumes of a monumental Hebrew thesaurus. His work provoked much controversy: many felt that it was sacrilegious to secularize this sacred language and were highly critical of Ben-Yehuda's work. Perhaps most controversial of all, Ben-Yehuda made Hebrew the language of his home and taught his children Hebrew as their first language.

In the late 19th century, Zionists began a wave of new settlement in Palestine. Hebrew was the only language the settlers, who came from many different linguistic backgrounds, had in common, and Ben-Yehuda's work allowed it to be adopted by the Zionists. It was thus inevitable that modern Hebrew would become the official language of Israel when the state was established in 1948. Today Hebrew is spoken by about 5 million Israelis and is still the language of prayer for Jews throughout the world. Modern Hebrew is quite changed from ancient Hebrew, but some liken the relationship between biblical and modern Hebrew to be something like the relationship between modern English and the plays of Shakespeare.

This revitalization of a language that had not been spoken in daily life for 2,000 years is an inspirational model for others whose languages are no longer spoken.

Cornish

Cornish is a Celtic language that was once spoken in part of the United Kingdom. It thrived until sometime in the 17th century, when the encroachment of English began to stimulate language shift. Factors involved in its decline included "the introduction of the English prayer book, the rapid introduction of English as a language of commerce and most particularly the negative stigma associated with what was considered by Cornish people themselves as the language of the poor" (quote from Agan Tavas, Cornish language advisory service Web site, <http://www.clas.demon.co.uk/>).

The last native speaker of Cornish died in the late 19th century. But even before then, a man named Henry Jenner was beginning to revive it. Jenner's documentation of Cornish was followed by the work of a team headed by Morton Nance, resulting in the standardization of Cornish and a full set of grammars, dictionaries, and periodicals. As the Cornish language advisory says, "Cornish is not dead and has not been for very many years (if it ever was)."

Today, Cornish is spoken by many people as a second language, though it has not been revived (yet) as a language of the home. Most people learn the language as adults, since most schools have not yet begun to offer it. Agan Tavas and other organizations have extensive publishing activities for the publication of fiction and nonfiction works, reprints of Cornish classics, and even current magazines. There are classes and correspondence courses, and organizations lobby for the support of the Cornish language in the schools and for recognition by the government. Cornish-language broadcasting is heard on Radio Cornwall. People with an interest in Cornish write to pen pals in Cornish and can go to meetings, dinners, plays, and other social events where they are able to speak and listen to the language.

Miami

Both Hebrew and to a lesser extent Cornish have large populations that are in a position to have ambitious programs to reactivate their languages. Not all communities are that large or have the resources to do what those two languages have done. And yet a single individual can produce miracles for even the tiniest of language communities. The Miami Nation has branches in the states of Indiana and Oklahoma. The last speaker of Miami died in 1962. Luckily, however, there is a very large body of documentation of the Miami language, spanning more than 200 years. A few years ago, the linguist David Costa worked with the materials to write a brilliant dissertation on Miami morphology, creating the first coherent analytical account of the language (Costa 1994). Daryl Baldwin, a member of the Indiana group, is a gifted individual dedicated to the revitalization of his ancestral language, and has done wonders with it. He got a master's degree in linguistics at the University of Montana specializing in Miami syntax, and then, using Costa's work and his own, he taught himself how to speak the language. As he learned, he taught his wife and children as well, to the point that Miami is the first language of his youngest children. He and his wife have chosen to home-school the children, which allows them to immerse their children more thoroughly in the Miami language than would otherwise be possible. Along with two other families who have also become dedicated to the revitalization of Miami, they are in the beginning stages of recreating a speech community.

LANGUAGE AWAKENING FOR SMALL COMMUNITIES

Not every community has the human resources that helped in the revitalization of Hebrew, nor the degree of documentation that Miami is lucky enough to have. But a language revitalization program need not be extremely ambitious. It may not have as its goal the reintroduction of the language as the primary language of interaction, but rather may simply want to give the language a small place in ceremonial life or have a few phrases to use in community interaction. That might be as far as it goes, or it may be the beginning of something larger—sometimes it is hard to tell which until it happens.

A number of languages of California, lacking any speakers, are now being studied by the descendants of speakers in hopes of some measure of revitalization. Descendants of over a dozen languages are attending yearly workshops at the University of California, Berkeley, to find and study documentation on their languages (see Chapter 32). Tribal organizations and tribal nonprofits are seeking funding and using it to develop writing systems, transliterate existing literature, and use the literature to create dictionaries, phrase books, grammars, and pedagogical materials. People are bringing the languages back in small steps, such as a recent Salinan funeral for an elder, where the prayers were said in the Salinan language, or at a storytelling conference where Linda Yamane told a story in Rumsien, or at a centennial celebration of a mission where Quirina Luna read the Mutsun names of the people buried there. When Quirina Luna got married recently, she asked Linda Yamane to perform the wedding ceremony in Rumsien.

These efforts are small and young, and at this point the main thrust is to learn enough vocabulary and grammar to be able to insert a few phrases into what must otherwise be communication in English, and to be able to create, rehearse, and perform certain important speech acts such as prayers and other kinds of ceremonial speech in specialized contexts. Perhaps such limited use of these languages will be the maxi-

mum extent of these particular revitalization programs; but even these results are extremely meaningful to the descendants. Perhaps the most important lesson to learn from both the small and large efforts to date is that it may be just a few people, or even a single person—a Henry Jenner, an Eliezer Ben-Yehuda, or a Daryl Baldwin—who begins the process. This might be done with community support or without it, at the beginning. But even without the initial support of the community, a single person can begin something that other people might join in later, and that can eventually grow like a snowball rolling downhill.

Note

1. In the Mutsun writing system developed by Quirina Luna and Natasha Warner, "sY" stands for a palatal *s* and "tR" for a backed *t*.

References

Costa, David. 1994. The Miami-Illinois language. Ph.D., diss., University of California, Berkeley.

Hinton, Leanne. 1996. Breath of life—silent no more: The Native California Language Restoration Workshop. *News from Native California* 10, no. 1: 13–16.

32

The Use of Linguistic Archives in Language Revitalization

The Native California Language Restoration Workshop

LEANNE HINTON

Department of Linguistics
University of California at Berkeley
Berkeley, California

Universities and colleges can and should play an important role in assisting indigenous peoples in their quest for language revitalization. Besides their functions in research and teaching, these institutions also often maintain large archives of linguistic materials on indigenous languages, which can be of key importance to language revitalization. The most obvious situation in which these archives are critical is in the case when a language is no longer spoken natively by anyone. Then any written, audio, or video documentation is the only remnant of the language, and their use the only path to revitalization.

This is a report on a workshop held for four years so far at the University of California, Berkeley, for Native American languages with no speakers. Each year, a group of 20–30 California Indians, representing close to 30 different languages over the years, have met together with linguists for a week to learn how to find linguistic materials and make use of them for language learning purposes. The workshop is primarily for the benefit of people whose ancestral languages have no speakers left at all, although some people attended whose languages do still have a few speakers. The event was sponsored by Berkeley and the Advocates for Indigenous California Language Survival, organized by Leanne Hinton and L. Frank Manriquez, and has been funded by various organizations, among them the Graduate and Social Sciences Divisions of the University of California, Berkeley, the Townsend Center for the Humanities, the California Council for the Humanities, the LEF Foundation, the Native California Network, and the Advocates for Indigenous California Language Survival. When we first began the workshop, I named it "The Lonely Hearts Language Club." However, my co-organizer thought this title less humorous than hopeless and so renamed it "The Breath of Life—Silent No More

Native California Language Restoration Workshop." It has been known by various shortened versions of this title ever since.

Table 32.1 shows a list of the languages represented by the native scholars over the years it has taken place. Patwin, Central and Northern Pomo, Hupa, Yowlumni, and Wukchumni each have anywhere from one to a dozen living fluent or semifluent native speakers, and Bishop Paiute has many; the rest have none.

WORKSHOP GOALS

The goals of the week-long workshop are:

(1) to introduce the participants to the resources the university has available on their languages—publications, dissertations, field notes, and sound recordings—and show them how they can have access to these now and in the future;

(2) to give the participants some fundamental linguistic concepts that would allow them to utilize these materials, in particular,

    (a) learn how to read the phonetic alphabets linguists used to transcribe the languages,

    (b) learn some of the basic linguistic vocabulary they find in publications about their languages, and

    (c) learn some of the fundamentals of morphological and syntactic analysis and important ways their languages are organized differently from English;

(3) to help participants learn to use organizational and analytical tools such as database programs to help with their research on their language;

419

TABLE 32.1 Languages Represented at One or More
of the Breath of Life Workshops

Family
   Branch (or language if there is only one in the branch)
      Language

Penutian
   Costanoan
      Rumsien
      Mutsun
      Awaswas
   Miwokan
      Coast Miwok
      Sierra Miwok
   Wintun
      Patwin
      Nomlaki
      Wintu
   Maidun
      Nissenan
      Konkow
      Northeastern Maidu
   Yokuts
      Wukchumni
      Yowlumni
Hokan
   Pomoan
      Central Pomo
      Northern Pomo
      Eastern Pomo
      Southern Pomo
   Chimariko
   Salinan
   Chumash
      Ventureño
      Barbareño
Uto-Aztecan
   Tongva (Gabrielino)
   Acjachemem (Juaneño)
   Bishop Paiute
   Mono
Algic
   Wiyot
Athabascan
   Mattole
   Hupa
   Wailaki

(4) to show the participants some ways that they can extract useful language out of these materials (we ask for oral or written products at the end of the week—such as the beginnings of phrase books of communicatively useful phrases, or a reading aloud of a story in their language, or a language lesson based on their work); and

(5) to familiarize the participants with language teaching and revitalization literature and methodology.

AGENDA

Besides several teaching staff that run lectures and discussions with the whole group, each language or group of related languages has a linguistic assistant/mentor working with them closely—graduate students and faculty at the university or visiting from elsewhere. Also extremely important to the workshop is the generous assistance of the various archivists at the libraries, museums, and archives on campus, where materials on California languages are kept.

Mornings of each day are spent in a conference room teaching linguistics; in the early afternoons are tours of the archives and libraries; and late afternoons the participants are free to work in whichever archive or library they prefer, with their student/faculty mentors if they want them. In the evenings the participants work together on homework assignments in the dorm.

After the first workshop, in subsequent years we attempted to have about half the participants be returning people and half new. Each of the annual workshops has had a different focus. The first was centered primarily around finding the materials and becoming familiarized with phonetic writing (in order to read the field notes and publications). When native scholars must depend on linguistic materials in their efforts at language revitalization, being able to read those materials is of course essential. Participants were asked to find passages in their language which they would study and read out loud to the group. As a result of these exercises, participants were later able to memorize and recite texts of importance to them, such as prayers, or stories, a skill which now is frequently put to use in their communities for special events.

While phonetics has also played an important role in subsequent workshops, the second workshop concentrated on developing materials and lesson plans and on the use of storytelling (utilizing linguistic texts) in language teaching. The third workshop added a more sophisticated grammar component for several groups, who learned how to construct novel grammatical sentences in their languages.

In 2000, the workshop had a strong orientation toward how to turn written materials into spoken language—that is, how to work with the materials in order to learn to speak the language oneself. A special guest instructor was Daryl Baldwin, a member of the Miami Nation of Indiana and Oklahoma. The last native speaker of Miami died in 1962, so his language is in the same condition as the ones in California that this workshop serves. What is so exciting and special about Daryl is that by utilizing written materials on Miami, he has learned his language proficiently and made it the language of his home. His wife and all four of his children speak it; and for his youngest two children, it is the first language. Daryl showed us the analytical, language-learning, and teaching methods that he used to accomplish this tremendous language feat and helped the participants understand the hard work and sacrifice that was needed in the process.

PHONETIC READING

Reading phonetic writing is considerably easier than writing it. To read phonetic writing, one only has to recognize the symbols and know how each phonetic symbol is pronounced. In writing, one has to be able to recall the symbols themselves and also to interpret which sound is being uttered. One may not be able to hear clearly whether a sound is glottalized or not, or whether it is a "front *t*" or a "back *t*." In reading a transcript, on the other hand, someone else has had to make all those decisions (we hope correctly). On the other side of the scale, if you want to write a language you can choose a single writing system to do so; but if you want to read a language, you may well have to learn more than one writing system. There may be several writing systems in which the materials for a given language are found, so participants learn to make equivalency tables where a given sound is shown in all the various orthographies it is written in. An example of such an equivalency table was created by one of the participants, Danny Ammon, for the Hupa language, which had no fewer than 10 different writing systems, including those developed for practical use by the tribe over the years and those by linguists of different eras. The participants are given homework assignments to practice reading passages out loud in their languages. Besides this, instruction is given on the more common writing systems such as J. P. Harrington's (one of the most productive documenters of California languages in history). Phoneticians give extra instruction on the exact pronunciation of sounds different from English.

GRAMMATICAL ANALYSIS

Instruction is given on how to do morphological and syntactic analysis on a language, and also how to read the analyses that have been written about one's language. Basic linguistic terminology is taught, such as what a morpheme is and what the components of a word are (e.g., root, prefix, suffix) and what the parts of speech are and how they behave differently in different languages. The participants are given exercises in morphological analysis and taught to expect that their language may have a different word order than English, as well as different parts of speech; different ways of expressing such grammatical features as tense, aspect, person, and number; and different ways of constructing sentence types. The student mentors are especially important here, as they assist the participants in the reading and interpretation of technical material and in the analysis of data in their language.

THE DEVELOPMENT OF REFERENCE AND LEARNING MATERIALS

The participants are taught ways of organizing the materials they are using (such as on file slips or in notebooks or computer database programs) to suit their goals. If they want to make a dictionary, they can use the week to gather words and sample sentences, to understand what a citation form is, to make decisions about ordering, and so on. They may prefer to work on a phrase book instead, which will focus more on useful phrases and present vocabulary in semantic groups rather than alphabetically. If they are focusing on stories that are in the literature, they may wish to look at the presentation of that story in book form, with illustrations. As for grammar, we look at how aspects of grammar can be presented in the form of a reference grammar, with no arcane linguistic jargon, so that members of the community will be able to understand it. We also go over teaching methodology and how the material the participants have in front of them might be used to teach the language to others. We look at the goals of a given language lesson, what activities might be used to help teach the lesson, and so on.

WHAT HAPPENS AFTER THE WORKSHOP?

Some of the participants in the workshop are working on their languages year round, having in some cases developed a partnership with their student or faculty mentors to do various projects. Some participants are writing dictionaries and language lessons based on the linguistic materials found in the archives and occasionally making tapes to go with them. Some have obtained funding and begun community language programs. One participant has now entered graduate school to increase her expertise in linguistics for the ultimate purpose of language teaching and revitalization for her community.

Many people do not realize that the resources of a university are open to anyone, not just students and professors. Perhaps one of the key lessons taught in these workshops is that any person wanting to do research in the archives of a university has a right to do so. Over the last century, while linguists were collecting language data for posterity, I do not know if they fully realized who "posterity" would be. Native people are now seeking access to materials on their languages as often as or in many cases more often than professional scholars. The university can thus play an important role in community-based language revitalization, simply by caring for the archives of linguistic data and making those data readily available to people who wish to access it. As native people themselves become the documenters of the languages that still have speakers, the university can be of added assistance to language survival by serving as a safe repository for the new documentation produced by native researchers. This can only happen in an atmosphere of mutual trust. Such trust can be built by workshops such as these.

I will end this chapter with an extended excerpt from Hinton (1996), written after the first workshop, trying to describe the depth of emotion that this workshop carried with it. Perhaps more than anything else, the importance of language revitalization is illustrated through the feelings engendered in people who find their language again after it had been wrested away from them.

This workshop was a tremendous success, thanks in part to all the people on campus who worked so hard to prepare for it and implement it. But it was the participants themselves who created the atmosphere that made this such a memorable event. I think not a one of us realized how emotionally intense this workshop would be. The participants immediately bonded with each other and with the staff (especially the grad students) into a completely focused working group. The participants brought to the workshop a spirit and depth of feeling about the materials that powered it with the strength of jet fuel. They arrived each morning filled with enthusiasm, and bubbling over with questions about their materials. At the archives they awed the archivists with an avalanche of questions, and just dove into the materials brought out for them to examine. The joy of discovery was palpable, as they found some new piece of their ancestral language, often uttered by their own grandmothers. The archives came alive with laughter; and almost every one of the archivists said to me afterwards, "they brought life to the collections that has never been there before."

Each day was filled with a myriad of small but exciting discoveries. Some of the discoveries, just to name a few:

Cynthia Daniels, the Central Pomo speaker, who never knew how to count above 20 has now learned the numbers up into the hundreds, thanks to a publication by anthropologist Barrett.

Rick Adams, whose family has a story about the sudden and permanent disappearance of their infirm great-great uncle early in the century, found in the publications by A. L. Kroeber a note that he had brought the man to the Bay Area and put him in a rest-home here. Rick had also been bothered by the fact that all the Nissenan publications he saw were not like the words his elders knew from their past; and finally in the C. Hart Merriam collection at the Bancroft Library, he found the word-lists that fit his own dialect.

Norma Yaeger, Patwin, found ethnographic field notes on Patwin names that will be extremely helpful in their on-going naming ceremonies, where the names of ancestors are given. She also pored with deep emotion over materials Ken Whistler collected from her own grandparents and great-aunts and uncles.

Frank Ross, Coast Miwok, said one morning he had long wanted to know the word for "the Creator" in his language, and that afternoon he found it on one of the Harrington microfilms, along with another 400 pages or so of linguistic notes on his language that will keep him occupied for years.

Each participant had several or even many epiphanies of this sort during the week. The participants were also remarkably quick to learn the linguistic lessons. Most of them had been gazing at linguistic materials for years, and because of this they only need a brief instruction to fully grasp the meaning of what they were looking at. The week abounded with utterances like "Oh, so THAT'S what 'irrealis' means"; or "Oh, so THAT'S how to pronounce that strange mark in Harrington's materials." By the end of the week, not only were the more advanced participants able to read out loud fluidly in

their own language, but they were also able to read their fellow-participants' languages out loud too.

Besides finding materials and learning how to organize and work with the linguistic information coming from them, we asked them to settle into specific projects in order to have a focus for the week. Since it is the ultimate dream of all the participants for their language to be spoken in the community again one day, the theme for the projects was "usable language." A number of options were suggested to them—for example, they could find words and phrases that could be utilized in their daily lives as a first step toward language revitalization, and put them into a phrase book. Or read us a story out loud, or give us a lesson on a construction of some sort such as command forms.

Like the entire week, these projects were presented with heartfelt emotion. The two Salinan participants constructed a conversation together and demonstrated it for us, introducing it by describing how they feel about the fact that this is the first time in fifty years or so that two Salinans have held a conversation together in their language.

Linda Yamane, story-teller, expressed the same feeling. She has long been telling Rumsien stories in English that she has found in Harrington notes. Now she plans to begin telling them in Rumsien, and for her project she read one of them to us out loud. She said it is just in the preliminary stages—as she analyzes the story further, she will be adding affective intonation of various sorts, and memorizing it, and turning it into a real performance.

There were four tribal chairs in the group, and some of them have an interest in bringing language into council proceedings. Cheryl Seidner, Wiyot chairwoman, has made a phrase list that includes the words "yes" and "no" that she has since directed her council to use during votes, and other such useful phrases. Her favorite, that she plans to use as a kind of mantra, is the phrase found in one of Kroeber's publications (and verified and slightly corrected by Karl Teeter during the week via email), "I shall not become angry."

I want to make an aside here about what is no doubt the most controversial aspect of 2nd-language learning to linguists—and that is the issue of imperfect learning. The materials are imperfect (Merriam, Barrett and Kroeber, for example, had well-known phonetic gaps in their transcription), and often very incomplete. With this workshop and other language learning programs, during language use, learners switch to English often, and even when talking their language, use a great deal of simplified or English-influenced grammar. This simplification and influence from the dominant language is sometimes called "pidginization." We discussed this at length in the workshop, and the participants had some excellent thoughts about the issue. I think the most interesting statement about this was made by Cody Pata, Nomlaki. Cody, who had just turned 21, has some Hawaiian ancestry, and went to Hawaii at age 15, where he was taken on by the elders, taught Hawaiian language, song, and dance, and then given a job teaching in the Pūnana Leo schools, the Hawaiian immersion preschools. Now a fluent speaker of Hawaiian, he decided to apply his experience to Nomlaki, which he considers to be his real identity. But he came home in March to find not a single Nomlaki speaker. Unwilling to give in to discouragement, he has been working with Nomlaki materials, and became the star student of our workshop. He introduced his presentation at the end of the workshop by telling us about the nature of Hawaiian Pidgin English, which he described as a mixture of Hawaiian, Japanese, Filipino, and other languages mixed in with English. He said that his secret goal for the workshop had been to learn how to pray in Nomlaki; but since he didn't know enough of the language to do so yet, he constructed a "Pidgin Nomlaki" prayer, which consisted of mostly Nomlaki words in an English grammatical frame. As he learns more about Nomlaki words and grammar, he says, he will keep on refining this prayer until it is pure and authentic Nomlaki.

His presentation was a great gift of permission to the other participants. It provides a way for people to use their heritage language for communication even when they don't know it very well.

From the first moment of each workshop, when we used L. Frank's idea of introducing phonetics to the participants by having their nametags written phonetically (Cody was one of the early arrivals and caught on so quickly that he became the main name-tag writer for the later arrivals), the week was marked by high spirits. The participants stayed in the dorms together, and reported that they never got any sleep because they couldn't bear to be apart. They would keep on talking until 2 or 3 each morning, dream about their languages for a few hours, and then arrive at the conference room before the coffee was made, ready for more. There were also periods of intense griefwork during the week, especially one evening when we had cultural sharing around a fire pit near the dorms, where after some fine singing and story-telling (some of which were learned from linguistic field notes and archival tapes), people began to give testimonials about what language loss and language learning means to their lives, and their feelings about the terrible history of California that language loss is a result of. (Lest we forget—Cheryl reminded us, for example, that most of the present Wiyot population can trace their ancestry to a lone survivor of the massacre of the Wiyots, a baby who was found cradled in his dead mother's arms.)

But after the grief, more joy and more jokes. My own most vivid memory of the week is listening from my office where I was preparing the next day's presentation, listening to people working on materials in the Survey Room next door, where eight or nine people would gather each afternoon to work on the linguistic treasures they had found there. People would be calling out to each other "Ooh, aah! look at this!" "Listen to what I just found!" and peals of laughter would burst out every few minutes from those dry and dusty archives. The dust just FLEW all week.

All of us have been changed in some way during these workshops, both the participants and the staff, as the human side of linguistics was so poignantly expressed. It was the kind of linguistic work that inspires poetic expression. Some participants dreamed songs about it during the week and sang them to us. Linda Yamane wrote a long epic poem about it. We certainly succeeded in our goal of letting the California Indians get to know the university and realize that it is here for them to use. But we faculty and students also had displayed in front of us a great lesson about who the most appreciative audience of our work is. There is no-one in the world who has more at stake and is ultimately more concerned with the quality of our work than the members of the speech communities themselves. The work of Harrington, Merriam, Kroeber, Barrett and others has never been respected as thoroughly by linguists or treated with such passionate gratitude by them as it is today by the Native Californians. The workshop was a powerful enough experience that I believe it will affect the way our students who were lucky enough to be part of it will do their own research. I think they will never forget their present or future audience of the community, who will, as our workshop participants did with the previous generations' researchers, someday cradle and care for our linguistic materials like their own babies.

Reference

Hinton, Leanne. 1996. Breath of life—silent no more: The Native California Language Restoration Workshop. *News from Native California* 10, no. 1: 13–16.

The Ohlone Languages

LEANNE HINTON

Department of Linguistics
University of California at Berkeley
Berkeley, California

The Ohlone or Costanoan languages were spoken around and to the south of the San Francisco Bay in California. The term "Costanoan" derives from the Spanish word *costanos* 'Coast people'. They are of the debated Penutian stock, definitely related to Miwok languages; Miwok and Costanoan together have been labeled the "Utian" branch of Penutian by the linguist Catherine Callaghan (Callaghan 1962, 1982). There was no unified "Ohlone tribe"; instead, there were about 50 independent communities, each with its own set of village sites that people would inhabit at different times of year, and each, no doubt, with its own speech variety. These various dialects fit together into eight different languages: Karkin (spoken on the Carquinez Strait); Chochenyo (spoken in the East Bay); Tamyen (sometimes called Santa Clara), spoken around the south end of San Francisco Bay and lower Santa Clara Valley; Ramaytush (also known as Doloreño), spoken on the San Francisco Peninsula; Awaswas (also called Santa Cruz), spoken in Santa Cruz County; Mutsun, spoken along the Monterey Bay and inland from there; Rumsen (or Rumsien), spoken in Carmel and the Big Sur region; and Chalon (or Soledad), spoken along the Salinas River (Hinton 1988).

Starting in 1770, seven missions were established in Ohlone territory: San Carlos, Soledad, San Juan Bautista, Santa Cruz, Santa Clara, San José, and Dolores (San Francisco). Ohlones became bilingual in Spanish during that era, but the influence was not just one way: a few of the Hispanic people at the missions learned to speak Ohlone as well. One of these, a priest named Felipe Arroyo de la Cuesta, wrote a grammar and phrase book of Mutsun ([1861] 1970).

425

When the Mexican government closed the missions in 1835, most of the land in the area had been turned into ranches, and the Ohlone people were disinherited from their original land as well as from their mission communities. The Gold Rush and the takeover of California by the United States completed the dispersion of the Ohlones. By 1935, there were no fluent speakers left, although even now there some are Ohlone descendants who know a few words of their ancestral tongue by word of mouth through the generations, and a number of Ohlone native scholars are relearning their languages through field notes compiled by linguists.

One of the linguistically interesting things about the Ohlone languages is the verb stem alternations that take place under certain morphological conditions. Ohlone languages have the rare characteristic of requiring inversion of the final vowel and consonant under certain conditions. This pattern of metathesis in verb stems has fascinated linguists for generations (Okrand 1979; Andrew Garrett, personal communication).

References

Arroyo de la Cuesta, Felipe. [1861] 1970. Extracto de la gramatica mutsun, o de la lengua de los naturales de la mision de San Juan Bautista, compuesta por el rev. padre fray Felipe de la Cuesta. . . . Nueva-York, 1861. Reprint, New York: AMS Press.

Callaghan, Catherine A. 1962. Comparative Miwok-Mutsun, with notes on Rumsen. *International Journal of American Linguistics* 28: 97–107.

————. 1982. Proto-Utian derivational noun morphology. In 1982a (ed.) *Proceedings of the 1981 Hokan languages workshop and Penutian languages conference,* ed. James E. Redden, 71–77. Occasional Papers on Linguistics 10. Carbondale: Department of Linguistics, Southern Illinois University.

Hinton, Leanne. 1988. The Ohlone languages of the San Francisco Bay area. *News from Native California,* May–June: 23–24.

Okrand, Marc. 1979. Metathesis in Costanoan grammar. *International Journal of American Linguistics* 45: 123–30.

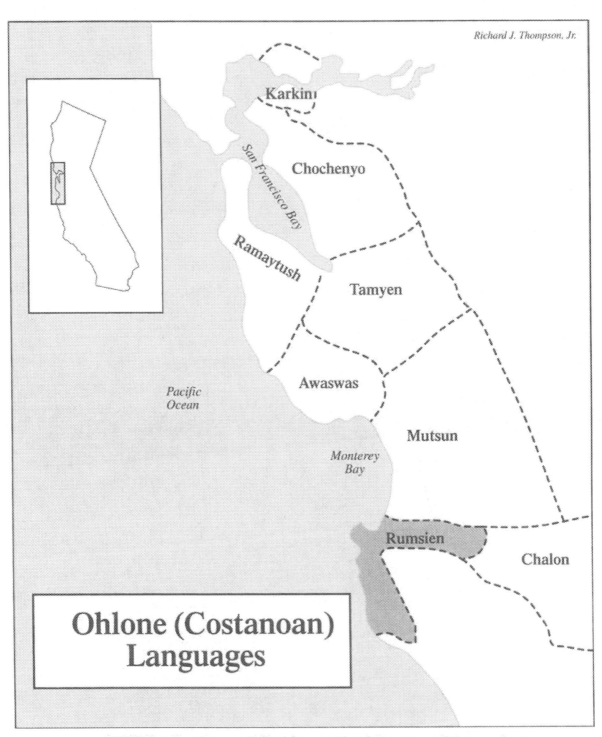

Richard J. Thompson, Jr.

Karkin

San Francisco Bay

Chochenyo

Ramaytush

Tamyen

Pacific
Ocean

Awaswas

Mutsun

Monterey
Bay

Rumsien

Chalon

Ohlone (Costanoan) Languages

MAP 33.1   Ohlone languages, California (names and boundaries reconstructed after contact)

33

New Life for a Lost Language

LINDA YAMANE

Independent Scholar
Seaside, California

I did not grow up with the language, stories, or songs of my Rumsien Ohlone ancestors. Luckier than some, I at least knew the names of those who had come before me, leading back to the time when Spanish missionaries and soldiers first settled in the Monterey area.

> The
> beginning
> of the end
> of a way of life.
> Disruption
> displacement
> subjugation
> disease
> ——
> these
> took their toll.
> Speak your language?
> No.
> Spanish
> is what you must
> emulate,
> the "gente de razon"
> the "people of reason."
> Freedom?
> No.
> We decide
> when you come
> and when you go.
> We know what is best,
> after all.
> And nothing about you
> is much good
> except that you have a
> soul
> which we can
> save.
> And we need you
> to do our work, so
> you can be our slaves.

The mission system was short-lived, but its effects lived on. As more and different peoples came into California, native peoples began to scatter and intermarry. Finding themselves at the bottom of the social structure, with little future but to do other peoples' dirty work, it was not easy to feel proud of who they were. Alcoholism and poverty were rampant. It is no wonder that they felt little incentive to teach their children and grandchildren the language.

> Wine and whiskey
> cut down
> these Carmel Indians
> *como guardaña*
> otherwise
> there would be some alive
> to help this work
> on the language.
>
> *La unica vieja*
> *que hablaba el idioma*
> the only old lady
> who would speak the language
> in our hearing was
> *la Omecia.*
> All the others
> did not like us young people
> to listen.
> —Isabel Meadows,
> 1932, age 86

Traditions went underground——so deeply that most (or at least many) were lost. Our families learned to blend in so well that we eventually "disappeared" to the outside world, and the anthropologists declared us extinct.

We were not extinct, but our languages and many other traditions were gone or nearly gone. That is why I grew up know-

429

ing of my Indian heritage, but little of our traditional culture. My grandmother and I were very close and she told me the stories of her family and her growing-up years. It was through her stories, more than anything else, that my sense of extended family and view of our family's history formed. She had learned about plant uses, but not our language or other cultural traditions. As a young adult, I began to wonder about the language, songs, and stories of our ancestors.

> No elder to learn from
> so
> I looked to books
> not knowing where else to go.
> The books I found
> didn't say much
> though,
> except that we didn't exist.
> I went to the mission—
> would I find something there?
> What I found was
> emptiness
> sadness
> and despair.
> Where,
> I wondered
> (and still do)
> is the story of the people
> who
> built this place
> filled this place
> labored
> and
> died
> in this place?

This modern tourist attraction—the mission—did not have what I was looking for, but little by little the questions I had about our language and basketry, stories, and songs began to lead me in many directions. Eventually, I connected with people familiar with out-of-the-way resources. And one day, someone told me about the John P. Harrington field notes and where I might find them on microfilm.

This was the real beginning for me. John Peabody Harrington, a linguist working for the American Bureau of Ethnology, spent several years in the 1930s working with older Rumsien people in the Monterey area. He worked primarily with Isabel Meadows, sitting with her for hours, writing down her recollections of language, history, stories, songs—anything she remembered and shared.

My first visit to the San Jose State University library to look at these field notes was an adventure in itself—and a lesson in perseverance. I had called in advance and talked to an assistant who offered to have some microfilm waiting for me at the desk. I was on the verge of finding something I had been seeking for so long.

I arrived at the appointed time, introduced myself, explained the reason for my visit, and waited excitedly for the microfilm. But, to my surprise, they could not find it at the desk. Surely it must be there, I thought. The person had been

so kind, and had promised. They looked again, but there were none to be found.

This was a setback, but not a problem, I thought. I asked them to point me in the direction of the Harrington microfilms, and I would simply pull my own reels. To my surprise, not one of them knew where the microfilms were located. Another setback, but not a problem, I thought. I then asked them to show me to the card catalog so we could locate the materials that way. Not in the card catalog, they replied. This was a problem! I found it impossible to believe that something in a library was not cataloged.

They were all very kind, but unable to help me. "Come back another day," was their advice. There was a certain librarian who would know where the microfilms were located. But I stood there, incredulous—and I could not make myself walk away. Clues to my culture were in this room, perhaps just feet or inches away. How could I leave when I was this close? I began walking the aisles, hoping that I would stumble upon the right shelf or cabinet.

I walked down row after row of shelves, scanning desperately for that name—John P. Harrington. I did not find it, but my persistence paid off, for soon one of the assistants came looking for me with good news. They had located someone on another floor of the library who knew where the Harrington materials were stored.

Miraculously, she led me to a set of vertical storage drawers. They were identical to so many others, with one exception—these were labeled "John Peabody Harrington." A guide to the Harrington microfilms helped me decide which reels to begin exploring.

My first choice was a reel containing Rumsien vocabulary, collected by Alphonse Pinart in 1878 and reviewed by Harrington with his primary Rumsien informant, Isabel Meadows, in the early 1930s. I was near disbelief as I rolled my way through frame after frame. I had to remind myself this was not a dream—and I began making copy after copy after copy. No matter that each would cost a quarter. How could I leave any of it behind?

> What I thought lost
> was now before my very eyes
> held within
> my very hands
> —
> the words of my ancestors!

Several years later, I learned I could have bought the same vocabulary listing for less than $10. But that was not important. It was the beginning that was important—no matter what the cost. Now I know that there were several vocabularies collected from Rumsien speakers in the late 19th and early 20th centuries by Pinart, Henshaw, Kroeber, Taylor, Merriam, and others. They are obscure publications not readily available to the average person in the average library, but these are what made the beginning of my Rumsien language learning possible.

I started by learning words that I could relate to—words that had significance for me.

ana 'mother'
apa 'father'
iswin 'son'
tarakta 'sky'
ummun 'hummingbird'

I began like a baby, taking on a few things at first and building from there. I remember sitting awake in bed, late into the night, when the world was dark and quiet and my family sleeping. Because I had a young child, it was the only time I had to myself, and I would sit with these ancient words on my lap, going over them again and again in my mind. At first, I felt shy about saying them aloud—even though I was the only one who would hear.

ieiexem 'pelican'
siirx 'golden eagle'
kallen 'ocean'

Giving voice to these words gave me a new challenge—pronunciation. It was sometimes confusing because different linguists or collectors of these vocabularies had used different orthographies to transliterate what they had heard. Some were trained linguists, others were not. I took the time to sort these out, so I could be as accurate as possible.

It was also not always clear where to place the accent. When I finally learned to understand Harrington's way of indicating accent, a whole new world of understanding opened up for pronunciation. I still find it valuable to compare words from different vocabulary sources for consistency. I sometimes get a clue from one that sheds light on another. And over time, I have come to realize that more often than not, the accent in Rumsien words is on the first syllable. Seeing this pattern has given me a basis for making my own informed decisions in cases where the accent is not provided.

From vocabulary and pronunciation I graduated to phrases.

ka rukk 'my house'
ka wattin 'I go/I am going'

The natural progression from here, of course, is to combine phrases into simple sentences.

Ka wattin rukk.
'I'm going home.'

After several years of being limited to sentences in the present tense, I developed a burning need to learn other tenses. This was made difficult by the fact that there is very little documentation for Rumsien in the way of organized grammar. I initially thought there was none, but discovered that Alfred Kroeber had published a small amount of grammatical information. It was, however, a mixed blessing, because I was overwhelmed by his linguistic terminology.

It is known
that in many American languages the pronominal elements
exist only in composition.
The verb is conjugated subjectively
and often objectively
by the affixion of these elements.
In the noun
possession is expressed by the affixion
of pronominal elements which may or may not be identical
with those used with the verb.
These pronominal affixes
are one of the chief means by which
the language has structure.

—Alfred Kroeber, 1904

Tackling this grammar was one of my goals for a week-long language restoration workshop at Berkeley in the summer of 1997. I needed to translate Kroeber's technical terminology into language that I could understand. It was with dread that I sat down and struggled through it page by page. Actually, it was sentence by sentence, and sometimes word by word. When completely stymied, I cried "Help!" and one of the graduate linguistic students assisting us that week came to the rescue. She would explain a term, and I would translate it into language that a nonlinguist would understand and then plod my way through another paragraph. I am still attempting to absorb the grammar, and I am slowly beginning to incorporate and understand how to put this information to use.

There is a wealth of language information within the Harrington field notes, but it has not been compiled and organized. This is my next step—and a daunting one it is. I have already explored thousands of pages on microfilm, and moving from one frame to another, I never know what I will find next. I have been extracting cultural information and filing it by category. There is history, song, mythology, genealogy, basketry, language, customs, and more—all intertwined. I have begun organizing vocabulary into an informal dictionary format, in hopes of making it easier to locate a specific word. Of course, the biggest job ahead will be reviewing the remaining field notes to glean the raw data. Then the hundreds of phrases and sentences will need to be organized into some kind of coherent and usable assemblage. These will be the key to clarifying, with certainty, the grammatical structure of our language. Kroeber's brief grammatical analysis of Rumsien was based on a very limited language sample provided by people with a limited recollection of the language, and even I have found omissions in his work. Corroboration from other sources is essential.

Another challenge will be to decide upon an orthography that can be easily interpreted by the average person. I would like to avoid using specialized symbols to write our language and hope to find a way to use the alphabet available on any home computer. This is an important step in preparation for teaching the language to others.

Working with our language has taught me much about the culture of the past, introducing me to things I could not have learned from any book, and verifying the existence of things we have assumed were part of the Ohlone world. Language is a key to our culture, with the power to connect us through time and open the world of the past.

rechum 'rabbit-skin cape'
ilup 'a handkerchief made of fine grass, longer than broad, and worn in the hot sun'
lupak 'white face paint'
hotoi 'tobacco bag'
mahsh 'nettle thread'
oxhanun 'seed paddle for gathering oats'
teperin 'small mush or soup-bowl basket'

Some Rumsien words are for things that are not part of our modern world. Likewise, I wonder how we will create words for things that did not exist in our ancestors' time. Isabel Meadows told Harrington a story that has given me some ideas, and also revealed that we are not the first Rumsien people to face this dilemma.

> Viviana came into Sparalino's store early in the morning
> to see if Sparalino wanted to buy soyosos [huckleberries].
> She asked him, "'Ann-root kakk siiy?'"
> (Where's the whiskey?)
> Rather than asking him to give her some,
> she said it this way.
> Amado Mendez answered, "Kuuwe rottey."
> (There isn't any.)
> And how Viviana laughed,
> that Amado could talk some Carmeleño.

Reading this, I wondered what *kakk siiy* meant. *Siiy* means water, but I did not know what *kakk* meant. Then I learned that *kakk* means "bitter." They needed to create a word for something that was not in their vocabulary, and so they called whiskey "bitter water." We will obviously need to create many words for this modern world, and *kakk siiy* serves as a great example.

> Isabel Meadows said:
> What pretty talking "la gente de antes"
> [the people of the past] had,
> when they were all together
> speaking the language.
> But the strangers that came weren't able
> to understand it,

and for this reason they didn't understand
how to appreciate the language.
But the tone of it—the sound of it—
was so pretty.

Our language, stories, baskets, and songs connect us to our past. They connect us to the people we have come from and to our land. These things empower us with the truth, defy the stereotypes. They bring us pride and dignity. People used to say that Indian people did not have language, they just talked with grunts. Now we can teach ourselves and others about the beauty and complexity of our languages. Our children and grandchildren can grow up with the same stories told generations ago. When I weave a basket, people can look at it and hold it and know that our ancestors were resourceful, intelligent, artful people. When we sing our songs, speak our language, tell our stories, and weave our baskets, we bring their beauty out into the world again and we bring honor and respect to our ancestors.

It is not easy, and it is never, never straightforward. You work at it and you take time to absorb it. Then you start to see pictures and patterns, and little by little the pieces begin coming together. I thought I would never know the sound of our language or songs, the intricacy of our baskets, or the richness of our stories. But now, incredibly, I not only know what our language sounds like, I can speak it. I sing our songs, have compiled two books of our stories, and am weaving our baskets. It has been a lot of work and excitement, mixed with frustration and, occasionally, an overwhelming feeling that I will never get through it all.

I did not make an academic decision to learn our language. It evolved into something I could not ignore or stop. Sometimes I have wondered why I am doing this. I have wondered if it really matters. Who will do anything with it? Who will benefit? Who really cares? Then, from time to time, a little thing will happen—someone, young or old, will light up to learn the words or ways of our ancestors. A seed is planted. Maybe it will be during my lifetime, or maybe it will be later that the reason is revealed. But for now, it is something that must be done on faith. It is simply work that must be done.

Uttitha 'that is all.'

About the Editors

LEANNE HINTON obtained her Ph.D. in linguistics from the University of California at Berkeley, with a thesis on Havasupai language and music. She is now a professor of linguistics at the University of California, the director of the Survey of California and Other Indian Languages, and a consulting member of the Advocates for Indigenous California Language Survival. She has been involved in language maintenance and revitalization for 25 years, consulting for Native Americans in bilingual education, development of writing systems, and language revitalization programs in California, Arizona, New Mexico, Oklahoma, and Alaska. She is a cofounder of the American Indian Language Development Institute, and one of the designers and trainers of the Master-Apprentice Language learning program. Among her books is *Flutes of Fire: Essays on California Indian Languages* (Heyday Books, 1994), which focuses in part on language loss and revitalization in California.

KEN HALE obtained his master's and his doctorate at Indiana University in the 1950s, with theses on Navajo and O'odham (Papago). He has taught linguistics in the anthropology departments at the University of Illinois and Arizona, and since 1967 he has been teaching and doing research in the Department of Linguistics and Philosophy at the Massachusetts Institute of Technology. His primary research has been on the syntax, morphology, and lexical structures of the Pama-Nyungan languages of Australia, the Uto-Aztecan and Athabaskan languages of the Southwest, and the Misumalpan languages of Nicaragua and Honduras. He has been interested since 1964 in working in support of the principle that the study of Native American languages will mature best and grow as a science when native speakers of the languages involved are enabled to assume career positions in the discipline of linguistics. He has participated in the educational programs of the American Indian Languages Development Institute (AILDI) and the Navajo Language Academy (NLA).

About the Authors

ROBERT ARNOLD was first engaged with native languages issues in 1970 when he prepared a plan for major expansion of bilingual education in southwestern Alaska. Over the next few years he guided the establishment of public radio and television stations in rural Alaska (at which both Yupik and Inupiaq were employed), served as principal author of a book on the Alaska Native land claims, and founded the Center for Equality of Opportunity in Schooling at the Alaska Native Foundation. Following the Lau decision, he sponsored mediation meetings between the Office of Civil Rights and the Alaska Department of Education as well as the preparation (by Gary Holthaus) of a handbook of bilingual education for teachers and administrators. In 1989 he authored a report and recommendations for the improvement of rural education for the Alaska legislature. Now largely retired, he has described his more recent work on language matters in his report on the enactment of national Native language legislation.

MARIE ARVISO, a Navajo, comes from the Mariano Lake community in New Mexico. She attended Calvin College and the University of New Mexico; both her B.S. and M.A. degrees are from the University of New Mexico. She has worked in Christian, public, and bureau schools, both on and off the Navajo Reservation, for a total of 37 years. She came to the Window Rock school district in 1964 and worked there for 25 years. She conducted an exemplary bilingual program there and developed the most widely used test of oral Navajo language proficiency. She became principal of the Fort Defiance Elementary School in 1979. The Navajo Immersion program was set up at FDES under her leadership. She retired from the District in 1990. She worked until relatively recently at the Crownpoint Community School and is now on the school board of that school.

ANNA ASH has been working in the area of Australian Aboriginal language maintenance for several years. She worked with Ngakulmungan Kangka Leman (the Language Committee of Mornington Island) on the production of the *Lardil Dictionary* and *A Learners' Guide to Lardil.* Anna is cur-

rently developing a Yuwaalaraay–Yuwaaliyaay–Gamilaraay dictionary database, and has begun a Ph.D. on Aboriginal language reclamation in northern New South Wales, with the School of Languages, Cultures, and Linguistics at the University of New England, Armidale.

REBECCA BLUM-MARTINEZ is an associate professor in the College of Education at the University of New Mexico. She has worked as a consultant to the Cochiti Keres language maintenance efforts since 1992.

PAMELA BUNTE is a professor of anthropology and linguistics at California State University, Long Beach. She has worked with Southern Paiute tribes on various linguistic and applied anthropology projects since the 1970s. Presently, the main focus of her research is Southern Paiute language and culture with an emphasis on San Juan Paiute narrative and song performances and Paiute language socialization. She is completing transcription and analyses of Southern Paiute performances as part of an NEH/NSF grant on the Numic languages. She also has been involved in doing applied anthropology projects for the San Juan Paiutes; for example, she and Robert Franklin did the research leading to the 1990 Federal acknowledgment of the San Juan Paiute. Land claims, the formation of a tribal court system, and the development of a constitution (the project discussed in Chapter 20), are additional San Juan Paiute projects in which she has participated. Other projects she currently is involved in include federal acknowledgment research for the Little Shell Chippewa Tribe of Montana and language performance and language socialization research among the Cambodian community in Long Beach, California. Professor Bunte has been involved in Paiute language support since 1975, when she and Kaibab Paiute Lucille Jake prepared an orthography for Kaibab Paiute. This orthography was used by the Kaibab people and by the Utah Paiutes in materials they developed. The San Juan Paiute tribe also has adopted this orthography. Professor Bunte presently is preparing a dictionary and a bilingual set of Paiute texts. She also is working with the San Juan tribe on revisions to their plan for language renewal.

She spent her sabbatical (1999/2000) with the San Juan working on Paiute language projects.

LAURA BUSZARD-WELCHER is a graduate student in linguistics at the University of California, Berkeley. Over the past ten years, she has worked with Potawatomi tribes to develop community language programs and language materials. From 1995 to 1998 she helped develop and coordinate a multitribal ANA grant project which brought together fluent Potawatomi elders from different communities with younger adults to participate in a summer language revitalization program. One of her current research activities is a linguistic analysis of the Potawatomi language, including a grammar, dictionary, and set of texts. Her doctoral research is a study of a set of syntactic constructions in Potawatomi discourse. She also developed and maintains a website devoted to promoting the use of the Potawatomi Language.

COLLEEN COTTER is an assistant professor at Georgetown University, teaching in both the linguistics department and the communication, culture, and technology master's program. She investigates linguistic and cultural dimensions of language, media, and community. Her work on the use of Irish-language media to support minority-language revitalization is one component of her research. She divides her time between fieldwork in Ireland and fieldwork in American newsrooms. She is currently writing a book on ethnographic approaches to the study of news media language in the United States. Her interest in Irish started in 1991 during a year-long field methods course at UC-Berkeley. A seminar on endangered languages taught by Leanne Hinton, subsequent summers in language schools in the Irish Gaeltacht, her own professional background as a former reporter and editor, and field discussions about language and the use of Irish in "normalizing" public discourse domains such as media and advertising led to her dissertation on the case of Irish-language media in Ireland's revitalization context.

JESSIE LITTLE DOE FERMINO is a Mashpee Wampanoag. She was recently a graduate student of linguistics at the Massachusetts Institute of Technology, and she received her master's degree in June 2000. Her focus is on Algonquian languages with major emphasis on the Wampanoag language. She is currently the co-chairperson for the Wôpanâak Language Reclamation Project. Jessie is currently teaching the Wôpanâak language to the Wampanoag community with the goal of reclamation. Her master's thesis was a grammar of the Wôpanâak language.

ROBERT FRANKLIN was professor of anthropology and chair of the anthropology department at California State University, Dominguez Hills, at the time of his death from cancer in August 1997. Pamela Bunte's co-researcher and husband, he had been an equal partner in their research on Southern Paiute verbal art and had been completely committed to the San Juan Paiute people, working on numerous applied projects for them. He completed his part of the NEH/NSF research, analyzing a number of Paiute stories and creating a database for Paiute lexical items. He was especially active in federal acknowledgment research. In addition to working on the San Juan Paiute acknowledgment, he headed the research teams for the Little Shell Chippewa and the Gabrielino tribes' federal acknowledgment efforts.

STEPHEN GREYMORNING received his Ph.D. in political anthropology from the University of Oklahoma in 1992. His dissertation topic, *Indigenous North Americans and the Ethnocentrism of the Courts,* focused on a cross-analysis of several United States and Canadian Supreme Court cases that were responsible for changing the political status of Indians in North America. From 1988 to 1992 he taught courses on linguistics, comparative Indian legislation, and aboriginal self-government at the University of Alberta in Canada. In December 1992, Dr. Greymorning accepted a two-year contract to serve as director of the Arapaho Language and Culture Project for the Wyoming Indian Schools (K–12) on the Wind River reservation at Ethete, Wyoming. While his academic interests have focused on aboriginal sovereignty issues, he continues to develop programs and strategies toward revitalizing American Indian languages. Dr. Greymorning has served as the executive director for the Arapaho Cultural and Language Immersion program on the Wind River reservation in Wyoming since 1996. His most noted project was negotiating the production and distribution of the Walt Disney movie classic *Bambi* translated into the Arapaho language. Dr. Greymorning is currently an assistant professor at the University of Montana in the departments of anthropology and Native American studies.

WAYNE HOLM, an Anglo, has worked in Navajo education for over 40 years. His wife and children are Navajo. His B.S. is from Northern Arizona University, and his Ph.D. is from the University of New Mexico. He worked with the Rock Point Community School—one of the few K–12 Navajo-English bilingual schools—for about 25 years. In 1981 he and his wife Agnes Dodge Holm had Fulbright fellowships in New Zealand, where they had a chance to work with Māori-language bilingual programs. He worked with Marie Arviso in setting up the Navajo Immersion program at Fort Defiance in 1986. He has worked for the Navajo Nation's Division of Diné Education for the last eight years.

ALANA JOHNS is an associate professor in the Department of Linguistics at the University of Toronto and formerly taught at Memorial University of Newfoundland, where she helped set up Inuktitut language courses at the university level. She continues to balance her research on morphosyntactic theory with teaching linguistic courses in Labrador for language teachers and interpreter/translators.

KAUANOE KAMANĀ is director of the Hawaiian medium laboratory school program of Ka Haka 'Ula O Ke'elikōlani College at the University of Hawai'i at Hilo. She also is a founder of the 'Aha Pūnana Leo and its current president. Kauanoe was born and raised on O'ahu and spent summers on her parents' home island of Moloka'i. Hawaiian was spoken by her grandparents and to a lesser extent her parents. Kauanoe obtained a B.A. in Hawaiian Studies and an M.A. in linguistics at the University of Hawai'i at Mānoa while also pursuing traditional training in hula in the hālau Nā Pualei O Likolehua. She has taught Hawaiian and courses in Hawaiian from preschool through university levels. With her husband, William H. Wilson, Kauanoe moved to Hilo in the late 1970s to develop a Hawaiian Studies B.A. program, which has since become its own college. They have raised their two children as first-language speakers of Hawaiian, and as a family the four have been at the forefront of developing Hawaiian medium education.

JEANETTE KING is a Pāakehāa (non-Māori) lecturer in the Māori Department of the University of Canterbury, New Zealand, where she teaches Māori language. Her research focuses on the revitalization of the Māori language, particularly among adults, the majority of whom are second-language learners. In addition she has researched and written on Māori English—the variety of New Zealand English spoken by many Māori. She has been involved in Kōhanga Reo (Māori language preschools), bilingual schooling, and Wānanga Reo (Māori language camps for adults). She also has had Māori stories for children published by the New Zealand Government publications unit for schools.

PAUL V. KROSKRITY is professor of anthropology at the University of California, Los Angeles, where he has served as the chair of the Interdepartmental Program in American Indian Studies since 1985. He received his Ph.D. in anthropology from Indiana University in 1978. He has conducted long-term research in two Native American speech communities—the Arizona Tewa of First Mesa (Hopi Reservation) and the Western Mono of central California. His research interests include language contact, language and identity, verbal art, indigenous language renewal and the use of multimedia technology, and language ideology. His publications include *Language, History, and Identity: Ethnolinguistic Studies of the Arizona Tewa* (1993) and the edited volume, *Regimes of Language: Ideologies, Polities, and Identities* (2000). With Bambi B. Schieffelin and Kathryn A. Woolard, he is coeditor of and contributor to *Language Ideologies, Practice and Theory* (1998). His current projects include the completion of the CD-ROM, *Taitaduhaan: Western Mono Ways of Speaking,* with coauthors Rosalie Bethel (North Fork Mono) and Jennifer F. Reynolds, and a book project on traditional narratives, *Growing With Stories: The Narrative Reproduction of Arizona Tewa Cultural Identity.*

IRENE MAZURKEWICH is associate professor and was formerly head of the Department of Linguistics at Memorial University of Newfoundland. Her research has focused on issues of language acquisition and bilingualism, as well as minority language maintenance, in particular with the Inuit of Labrador.

TERESA L. MCCARTY is professor of language, reading, and culture at the University of Arizona, where she also codirects the American Indian Language Development Institute. For the past 20 years she has worked closely with the Navajo Community School at Rough Rock, Arizona, and with indigenous bilingual education programs throughout the United States. Her research focuses on indigenous language education and language planning and policy. With Ofelia Zepeda she has coedited special issues on these topics for the *Bilingual Research Journal* and the *International Journal of the Sociology of Language.* Her most recent book is an ethnographic and oral history study of Rough Rock entitled *A Place To Be Navajo.*

GERALD MORGAN acquired all his education in England (including learning Welsh), but has spent his whole career in Welsh education. A year's teaching in a newly established Welsh-medium secondary (high) school convinced him of secondary schools' value in language maintenance and enhancement. After several other posts, including six years as principal of an Anglesey secondary school, in 1973 he achieved his ambition to be the first principal of a new Welsh-medium secondary school at Aberystwyth. In 1989 he moved into adult education, teaching Welsh and local history at the University of Wales; his English volumes include *The Dragon's Tongue* (the first popular history of the Welsh language), *This World of Wales,* and *A Welsh House and Its Family.* He has a lively interest in Native American culture and language, and has visited a number of tribal lands. He and his Welsh wife Enid, an Episcopalian priest, have three Welsh-speaking sons.

SAM L. NO'EAU WARNER is an assistant professor of Hawaiian in the Department of Hawaiian and Indo-Pacific Languages and Literatures at the University of Hawai'i at Mānoa. A native Hawaiian, he was one of the founders of the 'Aha Pūnana Leo, Inc., in 1983, but is no longer associated with the organization.

REGIS PECOS is the executive director for the New Mexico Office of Indian Affairs. He has served twice as lieutenant governor for the Pueblo of Cochiti and is one of the councilmen appointed to the Cochiti Indian Education Task Force. He presently serves as a regent for Princeton University.

PAUL PLATERO is tribal administrator for the Cañoncito Navajo community near Albuquerque, New Mexico. Prior to assuming his present position, he served as director of the Office of Research and Planning of the Division of Education of the Navajo Nation. He has worked in Navajo language scholarship and education for many years. In the 1960s and 1970s, among other things, he taught at Rough Rock Demonstration School and Navajo Community College, and he served for a period as assistant director of research and curriculum development for the Native American Materials Development Center in Albuquerque. He also developed language proficiency instruments for Navajo and Apache, and he prepared a Navajo grammar and literacy text book for Navajo Mission Academy, Farmington, New Mexico. He received his master's degree in linguistics at MIT in 1974, with a thesis entitled "A Study of the Relative Clause in Navajo," and he received his doctorate at the same institution in 1978 with a dissertation entitled "Missing Noun Phrases in Navajo." He has taught at Brigham Young University, MIT, and Swarthmore College, as well as at Rough Rock and Navajo Community College. He is to a great extent responsible for giving impetus to the continuing tradition of summer Navajo linguistics workshops in which Navajo teachers are given training in linguistics, curriculum development, and language pedagogy.

JENNIFER F. REYNOLDS is a graduate student of anthropology at the University of California, Los Angeles. She has been conducting long-term ethnographic and linguistic research in highland Kaqchikel Maya towns in Guatemala. Her research interests include language and identity, language ideologies, language socialization, narrative, political economy, and indigenous language renewal and the use of multimedia technology. Her current projects include the completion of the CD-ROM, *Taitaduhaan: Western Mono Ways of Speaking,* with co-authors Rosalie Bethel (North Fork Mono) and Paul V. Kroskrity, and her Ph.D. dissertation on the influence of linguistic ideologies in caregiving strategies in a Kaqchikel Maya community in Guatemala.

CHRISTINE P. SIMS is an assistant professor at the University of New Mexico. She is finishing up her dissertation for a Ph.D. from the University of California at Berkeley. She is chairman of the Linguistic Institute for Native Americans, Inc. (LINA, Inc.) and a member of the Acoma tribe. For many years she has organized summer training institutes in Albuquerque for Native American language educators of the Southwest. She has also consulted for many groups, including the Pueblos of Zia, Cochiti, Laguna, Taos, the Ute Mountain tribe, and her own community, Acoma. She continues to work with these and other Native communities in language planning, training native speakers to teach language, and developing community-based language maintenance and revitalization programs.

CLAY SLATE has worked for the Navajo Nation for many years, first as a teacher at the Mexican Hat School, later as director of the Literacy Program at Navajo Mission Academy, curriculum writer for the Navajo Language Institute, director of the Navajo Language Program at Navajo Community College, and most recently has been at Diné College to investigate the development of an early childhood education program. He received his Ph.D. in the Educational Linguistics Program at the University of New Mexico in 1989. He also has consulted in the design and implementation of Navajo bilingual education programs, and consulted for the Jicarilla Apache Department of Education to help in the planning of language revitalization programs. He also has worked in Mexico and the Philippines.

TERRY and SARAH SUPAHAN teach the Karuk language at the local elementary school where they live on the Klamath River in Northern California. They have taught Karuk language courses through Humboldt State University and the College of the Siskiyous. Sarah is the director of the Indian Education Project for the Klamath-Trinity School District as well as the Native Languages Coordinator. Terry and Sarah are also consultants in private practice specializing in language curriculum development, instructional methodology, and Tribal and Community Development.

LUCILLE J. WATAHOMIGIE is director of state and federal programs at Peach Springs Unified School District No. 8, in northern Arizona. Earning her master's degree in education at the University of Arizona, she also directed the Teacher Education Program for American Indian students there. In 1975 she returned to Peach Springs to direct the Hualapai Bilingual Program, helping it to become a national Academic Excellence Program under Title VII of the Bilingual Education Act. During this time she also cofounded the American Indian Language Development Institute. She has authored numerous bilingual children's books and, with Leanne Hinton, coauthored *Spirit Mountain: An Anthology of Yuman Story and Song.*

WILLIAM H. WILSON is married to Kauanoe Kamanā and joined with her upon their engagement in 1975 in a commitment to work toward the revitalization of Hawaiian. Like Kauanoe, Bill is a teacher and administrator at the University of Hawai'i at Hilo. Bill was born in Honolulu and spent a number of his teenage years in Europe, Mexico, and his parents' home area of the Midwest. During this period he began to teach himself Hawaiian, which he continued to pursue at the University of Hawai'i at Mānoa. While working on his doctorate in linguistics, Bill served as the Hawaiian translator in the Hawai'i State Archives, developing an interest in Hawaiian language legislation there. Bill and Kauanoe moved to Hilo in the late 1970s to develop a Hawaiian Studies B.A., which has since become its own college. They have raised their two children as first-language speakers of Hawaiian, and as a family the four have been at the forefront of developing Hawaiian medium education.

AKIRA Y. YAMAMOTO, professor of anthropology and linguistics at the University of Kansas, has worked with the Hualapai Indian community for the past two decades, and with various language projects in Arizona and Oklahoma. He chaired the Linguistic Society of America's Committee on Endangered Languages and Their Preservation. His recent publications include a coedited special issue of *Practicing*

Anthropology called "Reversing Language Shift in Indigenous America," an article called "Training for Fieldwork in Endangered-Language Communities" in the same issue, and a coauthored article called "Creating Language Teams in Oklahoma Native American Communities" in the *International Journal of Sociology of Language.*

LINDA YAMANE, Ohlone basketweaver, singer, and storyteller, traces her ancestry to the Rumsien Ohlone, the native people of California's Monterey area. She has been active in researching and retrieving Rumsien language, song, folklore, and basketry—traditions that were once thought lost. Linda is an independent scholar, writer, illustrator, and graphic designer. She also is the newsletter editor for the California Indian Basketweavers Association.

OFELIA ZEPEDA is professor of linguistics at the University of Arizona, where she codirects the American Indian Language Development Institute. Her research focuses on the Tohono O'odham language, indigenous literacies, and endangered languages. She is the series editor of *Sun Tracks,* an American Indian literary publication, and the author of *A Papago Grammar, Ocean Power: Poems from the Desert,* and numerous scholarly articles and book chapters. In 1999 she received a five-year MacArthur Foundation Fellowship Award in recognition of her unique lifetime contributions to the protection and cultivation of the indigenous languages of the Americas.

Index

Printed in the United States
By Bookmasters